German Social Democracy and the Rise of Nazism

German
Social Democracy
and the Rise of
Nazism

D O N N A   H A R S C H

The University of North Carolina Press   Chapel Hill & London

© 1993 The University of North Carolina Press

All rights reserved

Manufactured in the United States of America

Library of Congress Cataloging-in-Publication Data

Harsch, Donna.

German social democracy and the rise of Nazism / by Donna Harsch.

p. cm.

Includes bibliographical references and index.

ISBN 0-8078-2098-9 (alk. paper)

1. Sozialdemokratische Partei Deutschlands—History—20th century. 2. Socialism—Germany—History—20th century. 3. National socialism—History. I. Title.

JN3970.S6H37 1993

943.085—dc20 93-6869

CIP

97 96 95 94 93 5 4 3 2 1

TO MY PARENTS,

Jean and Henry Harsch

Contents

Preface, ix

Abbreviations, xi

Introduction, 1

1 Social Democracy in 1928, 17
The SPD's Fraternal Organizations, 19
Political Tendencies in the SPD, 23
Organization of the SPD, 25
The Social Composition of the SPD and Its Electorate, 28
The SPD's Ideology, 32

2 Indian Summer, 38
The 1928 Election Campaign, 38
Analyzing the Election Results, 41
The Panzerkreuzer Affair, 46
The Controversy over Unemployment Insurance, 51
Opposition, March–August 1930, 59

3 Where Stands the Enemy?, 63
Assessing the Republic's Situation, 64
The 1930 Campaign, 79

4 The Struggle Begins, 86
Origins of the Toleration Policy, 87
Mobilizing the SPD, 99
Who Voted for Hitler?, 105

5 Living with Toleration, 127
Prussia, 127
Growing Doubts about Toleration, 131
What Is to Be Done?, 138
Demoralization, Autumn 1931, 145

6   The Debate over a Crisis Program, 152
        Down with Reparations?, 153
        Confronting the Economic Crisis, 155

7   The Iron Front, 169
        The Impact of the Iron Front, 173
        The SA Ban and Brüning's Fall, 184
        The July Reichstag Campaign, 187
        The Destruction of the Prussian Bulwark, 190

8   Into the Abyss, 203
        Pragmatism versus Principle, 204
        The Schleicher Interlude, 220
        In the Grip of the Enemy: Principle versus Opportunism, 224

        Conclusion, 239

        Notes, 247

        Bibliography, 353

        Index, 385

A section of illustrations showing political posters of the 1920s and 1930s can be found beginning on page 111.

Preface

I began work on this project almost ten years ago and have incurred many debts to those who spurred me to focus hazy thoughts, facilitated the research, sharpened my prose, or just lent a friendly ear. This book started out as a dissertation at Yale University, under the able direction of Henry A. Turner, Jr. Initially in two excellent seminars and, later, in his comments on my work, he challenged me to think more clearly and express myself more precisely. His views on Weimar Social Democracy and on the Weimar republic in general have influenced me probably even more than I myself realize. He was a careful and sensitive reader of the dissertation from whom I learned much about writing as well as about history. From Peter Gay, a second member of my committee, I learned much about German culture in several seminars as well as profited from his insightful criticisms of the dissertation. I did not have the pleasure of taking classes with Paul Kennedy, the final member of my committee, but found his comments on the thesis most valuable. While in Germany in 1983–84 I benefited from stimulating discussions with the historians Detlef Lehnert and Peter Lösche. I would especially like to thank Hans Mommsen, who shared with me some of his vast knowledge about the Weimar republic and the SPD. His perceptive questions helped me to define the project. Here in the United States, Steve Grosby, Sarah Maza, Brian Ladd, Cathy Potter, and David Kaiser read and commented on all or parts of the manuscript. Two anonymous readers for the University of North Carolina Press made important suggestions that tremendously expedited the process of turning what was still a dissertation (though already revised) into a book. Lewis Bateman, executive editor at the press, is to be credited with selecting such conscientious, insightful readers. I am most grateful to him, however, for believing in the manuscript from the beginning. Ron Maner did a wonderful job of guiding the book, and me, through the editing process. Stephanie Wenzel was a sensitive and careful copyeditor.

I am most grateful to the Deutscher Akademischer Austauschdienst for supporting a year of research in Bonn. I would also like to thank the archivists at the Archiv der sozialen Demokratie of the Friedrich-Ebert Stiftung for being patient and helpful with an often bewildered American graduate student. In particular, I want to express my warm gratitude and affection for two women on staff at the Ebert-Stiftung, Ursula Clauditz and Hilde Holtkamp. They introduced me to scholars they knew, challenged my ideas about the Weimar SPD, and became friends. I would also like to thank the archivists and their assistants at the International Institute of Social History, the Bundesarchiv, the Hessisches Staatsarchiv, the Niedersächsisches Hauptstaatsarchiv Hannover, the Nordrhein-Westfälisches Staatsarchiv Münster, and the Archiv des Deutschen Gewerkschaftsbundes.

My greatest thanks go to my husband, George Loewenstein, my first reader and most candid critic. He, a nonhistorian, often understood better than I what I wanted to say. Above all, he has been there through it all in a thousand ways.

Abbreviations

The following abbreviations are used in the text. For source abbreviations used in the notes, see pages 247–48.

ADB   Allgemeiner Deutscher Beamtenbund (General Federation of German Civil Servants)

ADGB   Allgemeiner Deutscher Gewerkschaftsbund (General German Trade Union Federation; Free Trade Unions)

AfA-Bund   Allgemeiner freier Angestellten-Bund (General Free Employees' Federation)

BVP   Bayerische Volkspartei (Bavarian People's Party)

DBB   Deutscher Beamtenbund (German Civil Servants Federation)

DDP   Deutsche Demokratische Partei (German Democratic Party)

DMV   Deutscher Metallverband (German Metalworkers' Union)

DNVP   Deutschnationale Volkspartei (German National People's Party)

DVP   Deutsche Volkspartei (German People's Party)

KPD   Kommunistische Partei Deutschlands (Communist Party of Germany)

NSBO   Nationalsozialistische Betriebszellen-Organisation (National Socialist Factory Cells Organization)

NSDAP   Nationalsozialistische Deutsche Arbeiterpartei (National Socialist German Workers Party)

RDI   Reichsverband Deutscher Industrie (National Association of German Industry)

RGO   Rote Gewerkschaftsopposition (Red Trade Union Opposition)

SA   Sturmabteilung (Stormtroopers)

SAJ   Sozialistische Arbeiterjugend Deutschlands (Socialist Workers Youth of Germany)

SAPD   Sozialistische Arbeiterpartei Deutschlands (Socialist Workers Party of Germany)

SPD   Sozialdemokratische Partei Deutschlands (Social Democratic Party of Germany)

USPD   Unabhängige Sozialistische Partei Deutschlands (Independent Socialist Party of Germany)

WTB   Woytinsky-Tarnow-Baade economic plan

German Social Democracy and the Rise of Nazism

Introduction

This book explores how and why Germany's largest, best organized, and most disciplined party, the SPD, was outmaneuvered at every
level by the NSDAP between 1928 and 1933. Because Social Democracy
constituted the most important popular pillar of the Weimar republic, its
inability to confront effectively the Nazi assault on the republic is central
to the story of Weimar's dissolution. I examine the SPD's response to the
rise of Nazism within the context of a wider Social Democratic struggle to
secure the foundations of the Weimar republic. Because the contours of
that effort were shaped by the complex and ambivalent relationship of Social Democrats to the society in which they lived and to the traditions of
their own movement, these too are discussed. The narrative opens in
1928 when, with the SPD at a peak of political and organizational accomplishment and the NSDAP at its nadir, Social Democrats saw their movement and, therefore, the republic as strong and healthy. In the Reichstag
elections of May 1928, the SPD emerged victorious with 29.8 percent of
the electorate supporting it, while the NSDAP garnered a measly 2.6
percent. The SPD not only maintained its position as the largest party in
the Reichstag, but a Social Democrat became chancellor in a cabinet that
included three other SPD ministers. The SPD's cabinet role was the
pinnacle of Social Democratic participation in the Weimar political system: 889 German mayors were Social Democrats along with 7,662 city
councilors and 31,348 communal representatives. The SPD formed the
largest delegation in several state legislatures. Most important, a Social
Democrat headed the regime in Prussia, the state with two-thirds of
Germany's population and land. To recruit the voters who stood behind
this phalanx of representatives, the SPD published 202 daily newspapers
and numerous periodicals, pamphlets, and books. Over 937,000 party
members, more than in any other German party, distributed this literature and agitated for the SPD.[1]

The SPD formed the core of German Social Democracy, which also
encompassed the ADGB, which had 4.9 million members—by far the
largest German union federation.[2] The 3-million-member Reichsbanner
Schwarz-Rot-Gold, the country's largest defense league, formed a third
element of Social Democracy. The movement also included an impressive
array of cultural organizations such as the Workers' Sports Federation

(770,000 members), the Proletarian Freethinkers (581,000), the Proletarian Bicyclists (220,000), the Friends of Nature (79,000), the Workers' Samaritan League (40,000), the Workers' Radio League (314,000), and the Workers' Choirs (440,000). Social Democratic consumer cooperatives served 2.8 million members.[3] The trade unions, the Reichsbanner, the cultural organizations, and the cooperatives published their own newspapers and owned office buildings, schools, libraries, and camps. This multispoked movement turned around the hub of the SPD, the political representative of social and cultural interests, the collective memory of the past struggles of the German workers' movement, and the programmatic embodiment of the democratic socialism that inspired this sprawling network.

In 1928, Social Democracy was not just large but expanding; this upsurge followed sharp losses in members and voters during the hyperinflation and political turmoil of the early 1920s. That contraction had come, in turn, on the heels of an earlier blossoming of Social Democratic influence, popularity, and organization in the first months of peace and democracy in 1918–19. The second swell of the mid-1920s saw the SPD's vote increase by 3.8 percent between the Reichstag elections of December 1924 and May 1928; SPD membership grew by 17.4 percent from 1925 to 1929; ADGB membership, by 17.7 percent in the same period. The Reichsbanner, founded in 1924, rapidly attained massive proportions. Social Democratic cultural and women's organizations also experienced a second spurt of growth.[4] In 1928, among working-class movements in the capitalist world, only the Socialist Workers Party of Austria surpassed German Social Democracy in political clout, relative size, and variety of cultural, social, and defense leagues.[5]

Despite its extraordinary organization, impressive size, and upward trend in 1928, over the next four years the SPD successively lost control of the national government, "tolerated" a conservative regime, and was shunned by a reactionary cabinet. The determination of conservative forces to strip the SPD of power culminated in the forceful overthrow of the SPD-led government of Prussia by the Franz von Papen regime in July 1932. In its rise to power, parallel to the SPD's loss of authority, the NSDAP increasingly set the terms of political discourse, outstripping the SPD in the electoral arena and brutalizing its supporters in street battles. In power, the Nazi regime acted decisively to break up Social Democracy. By mid-1933 it had disrupted and forbidden SPD meetings; beaten up, arrested, and murdered Social Democrats; banned the Reichsbanner; enticed the Free Trade Unions to abandon the impotent SPD, only to "coordinate" them and imprison their leaders; smashed or confiscated Social Democratic libraries, printing presses, buildings, and financial assets; and banned the party. This speedy destruction met no organized resistance, although the membership of the SPD and many of its fraternal associations had remained intact throughout the erosion of its political influence.

Observing the course of the SPD's demise, some historians have assumed that the party made little effort to stave off the Nazi threat and the republic's dissolution. During Weimar's last years, they argue, the party stood immobilized, even paralyzed—a giant with feet of mud. The SPD's passivity, it has been suggested, demonstrated a deficient sense of urgency about the NSDAP.[6] From this viewpoint the story of Weimar Social Democracy is part of the chronicle of National Socialism, that is, as Karl Dietrich Bracher put it, the "history of [the NSDAP's] underestimation."[7] As Helga Grebing has argued, however, to judge Social Democracy guilty on this count is unfair. For one thing, the SPD's intent and motives cannot be faulted.[8] Social Democrats tried to prevent the triumph of Nazism in order to save the republic and democracy, a claim that cannot be made without qualification for any other party or major political actor in the complex and unsavory maneuvers of the late Weimar years. The SPD had more than good intentions, however. Social Democrats, as a rule, did not underestimate Nazism but misunderstood it. The magnitude of the danger was appreciated; its nature and sources, less so. After September 1930, cognizance of the Nazi threat was great, and the very passivity of the SPD's politics corresponded to the party leadership's understanding of how best to ward off this danger. The genesis and character of this awareness and of its strategic expression need to be examined to discover how and why Social Democracy acted in an ineffectual manner.

The case of Social Democracy is, in fact, even more complicated than this justification suggests. Because Social Democrats took the Nazi threat seriously, they engaged in an intense dialogue about the character, roots, and social basis of National Socialism and subjected their own party to critical analysis. From this discussion arose diverse challenges to official SPD interpretations of Nazism and the SPD's predicament, and to the strategy and tactics that flowed from them. Weimar Social Democrats offered explanations of the NSDAP's rise and the SPD's crisis that foreshadowed those put forward by historians; they suggested reforms of their party and solutions to the Weimar republic's crises that still fuel debates over how and whether the republic could have been saved.[9] Understanding this discussion and its feeble results is as important as analyzing the SPD's actual strategy and tactics, for not only in the rigidities of party practice but in the dialectic between that practice and resistance to it lies the explanation of why no effective strategy emerged.

Although this book does not condemn the SPD, it presents a critique of it and so stands in the tradition of historical scholarship that has focused on characteristics of the Social Democratic movement rather than on external obstacles that hobbled the SPD in its struggle against Nazism. Works in this "internal" tradition can be divided into two categories: one perspective has concentrated on the SPD's structure and sociology as causes of its immobility; the other, on problematic characteristics of its ideology. While many internally focused historians concede that the SPD's behavior was determined by many factors, they assign primacy either to structure or to ideology. Only a few scholars have interwoven these in a balanced interpretation that sees the SPD as victim of its ideological and structural "traditionalism."[10] I too offer a synthetic explanation, but one that draws in a third factor to account for the deep commitment Social Democrats felt toward the ideology and structure of their party: political culture. The SPD's politics emerged from internal conflicts and compromises over how to interpret its ideology, deploy its organization, and preserve its culture. Social Democratic practice was a dance composed of traditional patterns and rhythms interspersed with newer variations and interrupted by a perpetual argument among its choreographers about what new steps to incorporate while guarding purity of form and original content. The dynamism of Social Democracy's internal life led, paradoxically, to its external immobility.

Authors who emphasize structural causes of the SPD's immobility have focused on three features of the Weimar party: bureaucratization, aging, and "bourgeoisification." They point out that the Weimar SPD had lost its "movement" character, had trouble attracting young supporters, and had become diluted by nonproletarian elements.[11] I have three objections to this traditional structural explanation. Along with several recent studies, I think that it overemphasizes the bureaucratization of the SPD and misses the movement enthusiasms that continued to motivate many Social Democrats.[12] Sociological explanations have focused too exclusively on the SPD and not on Social Democracy as a whole. In particular, the cultural organizations and the Reichsbanner were still imbued with the spirit of a movement, not the routines of a bureaucratic machine. A narrow focus on the SPD also neglects the structural complexity of Social Democracy and in particular the significance of the ADGB leadership as a second locus of power within it. Finally, the SPD's alleged bourgeoisification only has explanatory force in the context of its ideology and political culture as there is no a priori reason why a nonproletarian party should suffer political immobilization.

The structure of Social Democracy was not only bureaucratic, hierarchical, and rigid, but also protean, multicentered, and evolving. Horizontal fissures ran between the levels of the SPD, and vertical splits developed between the SPD and the other organizations within Social Democracy. These fractures worked against a unified response to the rise of Nazism or to the crises that the NSDAP exploited. Within the SPD, apparently monolithic decision making hid competing priorities among the organization's different levels and geographic regions. Party bureaucrats tended to deny or ignore organizational dissonances rather than respond to them. Yet some functionaries promoted reforms only to find their efforts blocked from either above or below. Depending on the issue, Social Democrats at all levels both demanded reform and resisted change. Reforms that were enacted at one level often counteracted those implemented at another and so had the effect of further immobilizing the SPD rather than revitalizing it.

Even more than in the party alone, organizational diversity was both boon and bane of the broader Social Democratic movement. Most significant were the divergent priorities of ADGB officials and SPD leaders. Differences also strained relations between the SPD and the Reichsbanner, between the SPD and the cultural organizations, and between these and the ADGB. The resulting tensions, conflicts, and distrust absorbed energy and time needed to solve the external crises that exacerbated internal discord. Beneath the appearance of unified decision making and action, fragmented policymaking and halfhearted implementation increasingly plagued Social Democratic behavior and dulled its impact. Compared with its archrival, the NSDAP, Social Democratic activity suffered from insufficient central coordination. The lack of unity of purpose was a consequence of the different tasks and interests of each pillar of Social Democracy—party, unions, Reichsbanner, and cultural organizations. Because only the core membership of each ancillary organization consisted of organized Social Democrats, their leaders represented overlapping, but not equivalent, constituencies. Diversity of perspective also rested on subtle variations in the political outlook of these leaders. Nuance acquired substance under the peculiar and compounded pressures of the early 1930s—when Social Democracy faced not only a terrible depression and ever less cooperative bourgeois parties and businessmen, but a bitterly antagonistic mass Communist party to its left and a ballooning populist party to its right, the NSDAP. Issues such as the relative importance of the social and political gains of the republic, how to overcome the depression, and how to handle the reparations problem evoked discordant responses from leaders of the party, the trade unions, and the Reichsbanner. Aggravated by the economic crisis, these differences drove wedges between Social Democracy's various associations. Yet they also led to temporary alliances and unity of purpose between circles traditionally at odds with each other such as the SPD's left-wing and trade union leaders, or the Left and the Reichsbanner. This process of ideological differentiation and splintering, punctuated by shifting regroupments and single-issue combinations, also occurred inside the SPD. The antagonism between its left-wing and centrist leaders grew, but so too did subtle differences within the Left itself and among centrist leaders. A "new Right" separated from the party's traditional right wing, but these neorevisionists shared certain concerns and aims of the party's Left.

Historians who focus on the SPD's ideology have generally identified the fundamental fault in the Social Democratic worldview as that between its commitment to Marxism and its commitment to parliamentary democracy. Liberal and conservative historians of the SPD have emphasized that this contradiction conditioned the ambivalent attitude toward coalitions with bourgeois parties, reluctance to accept national political responsibility, and Marxist reservations against broadening its social base or adopting pragmatic economic measures.[13] Critics from the Left, on the other hand, have found the Weimar SPD too willing to compromise with bourgeois forces, overly focused on parliamentary politics, too reluctant to mobilize the masses, unjustifiably hostile to the Communist Party, and not Marxist enough.[14] That the SPD can be criticized from opposite directions indicates its inner contradictions. I do not think, however, that the SPD can be criticized coherently from either perspective because internal dissonance led to inconsistent behavior. Moreover, while I agree that the centrist leaders of the SPD straddled a fault between Marxism and parliamentary liberalism, I think this was only one version of a more profound contradiction between Social Democratic social understanding, which was based on class, and the Social Democratic political worldview, which was based on the individual. This contradiction was compounded by a less prominent opposition between voluntaristic and deterministic tendencies.[15] Determinism had roots in German Social Democrats' interpretation of Marx's theory of the demise of capitalism and in the enforced impotence of the prewar SPD.[16] Voluntarism was fed by reforming and improving impulses that had long motivated German Social Democrats.[17] Under the impact of the crises that rocked late Weimar, one could not predict from the outset what kinds of combinations of inclination and belief would occur inside the SPD.

Weimar Social Democrats identified the basic divisions in society as those between social classes and saw the motivating force behind political action as class interest. Social Democrats expressed many variations of a class-based explanation of social identification—from classic class-struggle ideology, to a commitment to the working-class composition of the SPD, to a pragmatic emphasis on the immediate concerns of organized workers. Diverse formulations of the meaning of class were united by a tendency to underestimate the influence on human behavior of political interest or other kinds of social identification.[18] As will be seen, the reigning class-based worldview faced internal challenges that were central to debates about how to confront the Nazis and the depression.

Social Democracy's political worldview was democratic. Social Democrats spanned the spectrum of democratic republican thought—from "counsel" socialism, to direct democracy, to parliamentary liberalism. They ran the gamut from civil libertarians, to pluralists, to majoritarians; from communalists, to federalists, to centralists. Lassallean tendencies competed with attachments to local autonomy. Social Democrats were united in their commitment to popular rule based on social equality and to a republican form of state. Republicanism had not been a prominent feature of prewar socialist ideology in Germany, in part because of the need to protect Social Democracy from monarchist repression.[19] However, in reaction to the violence of antirepublicans and the chilliness of "republicans of reason" after 1918, the SPD became ever more committed not only to a republic, but to the *Weimar* republic and its constitution.[20] The subtle shadings within the democratic republicanism of Social Democrats also took on significance in the struggle to save the Weimar republic from the Nazi onslaught.

As this discussion of ideology suggests, the line between Right and Left inside Social Democracy was not straight. This dichotomy is not without significance (if only because Weimar Social Democrats themselves employed it), but it obscures the multiplicity of viewpoints inside the SPD.[21] In particular, the radical versus reformist scheme applied to explain the schism in Imperial Social Democracy only badly illuminates Weimar Social Democracy. For one thing, the term *radical* is fraught with ambiguity. As Mary Nolan's study of the radical Düsseldorf SPD reveals, in the 1918–19 revolution, *radical* meant different things for different workers. Düsseldorf workers, active in the council movement and committed to democratization, exhibited scant interest in socialization of that city's scattered industry, while Ruhr miners played a trivial part in the council movement but took militant action to socialize the mines.[22] In the 1920s, some left-wing Social Democrats were committed cultural socialists eager to forge a "new person" from all-too-human workers, while others believed that people would only be transformed after the socialist revolution.[23] The political work of radicals assumed disparate forms as well; in Saxony, the historic center of left-wing Social Democracy, the SPD was deeply engaged in communal politics, while leftists in Frankfurt scorned such exertions and concentrated on the big national issues.[24]

Reformist is just as misleading. In practice, virtually every Weimar Social Democrat was a reformist, willing to take part in government under certain conditions. More important, this term veils differences between revisionists and those who might be termed ameliorators, or classic reformists.[25] Eduard Bernstein, the father of revisionism, did not develop a theory of reformism; rather, he tried to transform Social Democracy into the radical democratic party he believed it was at heart.[26] Weimar neorevisionists continued this struggle, while before and after 1918 ameliorators focused on the improvement of workers' daily lives. Thus, just as diverse leftists weighted the significance of politics, culture, or economics differently, so were rightists divided on these issues. A simple radical/reformist dichotomy also obscures wide areas of consensus among Weimar Social Democrats. Besides the broad swath of theoretical agreement described above, unanimity existed on practical issues. Social Democrats active in city government, from radicals in Berlin and Leipzig to reformists in Frankfurt to revisionists in Munich, were, for example, uniformly enthralled by "Red Vienna," although they disagreed about the reasons behind the accomplishments of their Austrian comrades.[27]

These ideologies drew on currents in the political culture or "collective mentality" of Social Democracy that also defy an easy radical/reformist classification. The historian Dick Geary is right that a "Social Democratic consciousness at the base of the party . . . transcended the ideological divisions at the level of the leadership" and, I might add, caused leaders and followers to respond similarly to certain signs and phrases used by political opponents.[28] As shown below, this consciousness was also a source of contention and confusion. To define Social Democratic consciousness, the historian has to analyze Social Democratic symbols and (oral and written) language. Based on my reading of the evidence, I characterize this consciousness as associationism.[29] This political culture revolved around a self-conscious and highly organized sociability that centered on clubs and leagues (*Vereine*) whose forms and norms profoundly shaped Social Democratic rituals and beliefs.[30] On a practical level, these *Vereine*—cultural, economic, and political—worked for reforms to make contemporary society more equitable and democratic. At the same time, they represented ideals that would be implemented only under socialism. On an experien-

tial level, these (not so) small societies were the prototypes of the society of
the future. The primacy of the association underlay the infamous "organizational fetishism" of Social Democrats as much as did the need to bring
cohesiveness and stability into the unsettled and hostile environment in
which workers lived.[31] Extensions of the Social Democratic associational
network into new areas, such as the blossoming of cultural organizations
in the 1890s or of paramilitary formations in the early 1920s, often
occurred from the bottom up and even against initial skepticism from
SPD and trade union leaders.[32]

The politics of this culture were republican and democratic; its social
world was that of the skilled working class.[33] The roots of Social Democracy's political culture ran deeper than Lassallean or Marxist influence.[34]
Social Democracy coalesced in the 1850s and 1860s from the rejection by
workers' associations of bourgeois tutelage and participation.[35] Unity and
solidarity were at the heart of Social Democracy and were defined in social
terms.[36] Thus, the working-class social composition of Social Democracy
was integral to its associationism. As forms of sociability, however, these
associations shared the same roots as the voluntary associations of the
bourgeoisie. Like them, workers' associations were freely constituted societies that rejected the *Stand* (estate) divisions of the aristocratic world,
and like the bourgeois voluntary societies, they were defined not only by
how one came to be associated but by how one associated, that is, democratically and equally. The politics of the workers' association, shaped by
the form of association and by older popular traditions, were essentially
radical democratic: egalitarian, social, rational, anticlerical, republican,
and suspicious of representation.[37] Democratic republicanism was built
into Social Democratic associationism and remained its substratum despite theoretical adulteration by Marxism and practical diversion toward
liberal parliamentarism.

Social Democratic consciousness did and did not adjust to changed
conditions after 1918. Ideally, the republic was the association writ large,
and in fact the Weimar republic allowed the Social Democratic association
to flourish.[38] The real and potential advantages of the Weimar republic
were registered by Social Democrats and elicited vigilance against its
enemies. The far-from-reluctant republicanism of rank and file Socialists
was evident in the massive general strike against the Kapp putsch in 1920
and, later, in the popularity of militant republican organizations such as
the Reichsbanner and the Iron Front.[39] The Weimar republic did not
meet the Social Democratic ideal, however, because Social Democrats'
republicanism rested on Jacobin rather than liberal assumptions, because
postwar society remained capitalist, and because basic institutions such as

the army and the justice system were not politically transformed.[40] Social
Democratic associations had to continue to represent the future in a
twofold sense, working to realize their aspirations in the larger society
while living the future within the movement. The efforts of active Social
Democrats to purify the association from corruption turned their political
culture inward. Democratic ideals and class sociability were focused on
the association itself: was it democratic? was it egalitarian? was it proletarian? was it . . . Social Democracy?

Party activists tried to impose their understanding of "Social Democrat-
icness" on the policy of the party and the behavior of its leaders, especially
at the local level. As a result, they directly and indirectly affected party
politics. As SPD leaders with political responsibility grew distant from the
movement's traditional culture and impatient with its mores, they were
reproached by activists at the base. The diverse beliefs and impulses of
Social Democratic consciousness pulled even those most attuned to it in
divergent directions politically, although its most steadfast sentries tended
to lean toward the left.[41] The social attachments and democratic concerns
of this culture grounded the SPD's official ideology, making revision and
adjustment to new circumstances difficult; its introversion fed passive
tendencies, while its extroversion reinforced active currents in the ideology and practice of the SPD.

This interpretation of Social Democratic culture shares much with that
of Peter Lösche, Michael Scholing, and Franz Walter, who have used the
appellation *Solidargemeinschaft* (community of solidarity) to characterize
Social Democracy's cohesiveness, the intense loyalty of its active members,
and its introversion.[42] To Ferdinand Toennies's term *community* they appended *solidarity* to emphasize the mutual support that braced Social
Democratic comradeship and to highlight its origins in the proletarian
milieu of early industrialization. As they do, I focus on certain ideal
typical features of Social Democratic culture. In practice, these were more
or less prominent, depending on when Social Democracy had put down
roots in a city and on the level of development of its local *Vereine*. Historically, its vitality was correlated with the percentage of skilled workers in
the local economy. Once rooted, however, this culture found vociferous
defenders among Social Democrats from varied social backgrounds.[43]
Active commitment to Social Democratic culture atrophied as the SPD
evolved into a complex organization run by a bureaucracy and, after
1918, intertwined with the state. Throughout the 1920s, however, its
spirit animated many Social Democratic cultural organizations and the
party's left wing.[44] Moreover, as I argue below, the intense political struggles of the republic's final years reinvigorated Social Democratic con-

sciousness at the base of the SPD, the Socialist trade unions, and the Reichsbanner.

Although I have benefited immensely from the work of Lösche and his collaborators, I am not completely satisfied with their representation of Social Democratic culture. First, the word *community* is misleading. The origins of this community lay in the bourgeois association (or society), and these roots continued to nourish Social Democracy in the Weimar years. Social Democratic sociability was not just about communal solidarity but about free, equal, and democratic association. Second, not only the group sociology of Social Democracy needs to be explicated, but also its political culture, which was, as I have suggested, radical democracy. Finally, the complicated relationship of the group to the external world needs to be elucidated. In my view, ambivalence lay at its source. Social Democracy was at once isolated from and tied to a bourgeois society whose early precepts and ideals it had internalized and re-formed. The dissonances of Social Democracy's political culture allowed for the possibility of different evolutions, depending on circumstance and leadership. Its reforming instincts could be turned outward, and its republicanism could serve as the basis for an assertive democratic movement. However, its social exclusiveness, *Lagermentalität* (fortress mentality), and urge to improve the association could obstruct efforts to break out of impotence and isolation.[45]

A second school of interpretation of the SPD's role in the dissolution of the Weimar republic repudiates the type of explanation offered here as overly focused on endogenous causes of the party's predicament. Scholars in this tradition have pointed to barriers that would have stumped even a structurally reformed and politically unified party: the antidemocratic tendencies of Germany's bourgeois and aristocratic elites,[46] the antagonism of the urban *Mittelstand* and of farmers toward the SPD,[47] Germany's confessional split between Catholics and Protestants,[48] the ravages of the depression that destroyed the terrain of social compromise and augmented a crisis of political legitimacy,[49] the "social fascist" theory of the KPD that targeted the SPD as its main enemy,[50] and the perfidy of the Free Trade Unions in 1932 and 1933.[51] Several historians have defended the SPD against charges made by its critics, arguing, for example, that Social Democrats recognized the Nazi threat and developed an analysis of fascism.[52] It has also been suggested that the SPD was less bureaucratic than the structural critics have maintained and that the party leadership did begin the process of turning the SPD into a *Volkspartei* (people's party).[53] I agree with these particular defenses but incorporate them into a critical assessment. I also concur that external obstacles severely limited the SPD's maneuvering room. Nonetheless, I think that the SPD had some freedom of movement and that its ability to exploit the possibilities for action depended on developments inside the party. Neither its structure, its ideology, nor external conditions predetermined the party's failure to do so.

Clearly, any interpretation of the Weimar SPD's struggle against Nazism is associated with an explanation of Weimar's demise. In assuming that the SPD could have possibly succeeded, I join those who do not think the Weimar republic was fated to fail in general or to destruction by the Nazis in particular. In the recent historiography of the Weimar republic the assumption of contingency is gaining ground, but the battle remains an uphill one.[54] The Nazi seizure of power magnifies the "hindsight bias" against which every historian must work: the Third Reich is an outcome of momentous significance that mesmerizes the historical eye.[55] Only with effort can one think of the Nazi dictatorship as one of several possible consequences of the crisis of the Weimar republic and, thus, as undetermined. Given the republic's Imperial prehistory, even greater effort is required not to see the Weimar republic as doomed to succumb to some authoritarian opponent. It is especially difficult to keep a sense of open-endedness when studying the last crisis-ridden years of the republic.

In the 1960s and 1970s, interpretations of modern German history were dominated by a theoretical perspective that made no attempt to resist this hindsight bias. This viewpoint saw the roots of National Socialism's extreme authoritarianism and racism in Germany's divergence from Western Europe's democratic evolution after 1848, its national unification from above in 1871, and the "illiberalism" of its state and bourgeois cultures before 1918. Its *Sonderweg* (peculiar path) carved an ever deeper rut from 1870 to 1933.[56] In this scheme, the First Republic is reduced to an interlude between the Second and Third Reichs—its failure proof of continuity and peculiarity. Over the last fifteen years, a series of frontal attacks by historians of Wilhelmine Germany have thrown into question this view of Imperial society.[57] The critical avalanche has spilled over into post-1918 studies with the effect of giving the Weimar republic a history of its own.[58] Freed from the lockstep of continuity and determination, the Weimar republic can be seen not only as a precursor to failure but as evidence of the possibility that democratic parliamentarism and pluralistic culture could have succeeded in Germany after 1918.[59] I subscribe as well to the explanation of the republic's dissolution that assigns preeminence to politics. This *Primat der Politik* accounts for the unpredictable course of the republic's last years.[60] It also suggests that the actions of political leaders, while far from the sole content of politics, made a difference. Although I argue that the dynamic of the SPD's interrelationships shaped the course of events, I agree with Wolfgang Mommsen that the SPD suffered a crisis of leadership or, better, a crisis of vision that creative leaders could have addressed.[61]

However, just as the Weimar SPD did not begin as a tabula rasa whose story its leaders could write, neither did the Weimar republic. A mix of the modern and the premodern characterized its society, its economy, and its political culture—and affected the political choices made.[62] If, as Detlef Peukert recently argued, the Weimar republic succumbed to a crisis of the "klassischen Moderne," this crisis acquired a particular shape and valence in Germany because the modern discontents of broad circles were ideologically formulated and politically mobilized as rejection of modernity, rather than as demands for fulfillment of its promise.[63] The theorists of continuity who insist on the persistence of the traditional, then, have a point. Sustained by memory and its distortions, political culture resonates with images, symbols, and myths from the past, only gradually coming to reflect new conditions.[64] How does the historian effect a synthesis that allows for contingency *and* continuity?[65] On one side stands a historical perspective that sees Weimar's modern social and economic reality as the key to its history; on the other, a theory that sees as determinant a political culture and ideologies that abhorred modernity.[66] Thomas Childers has recently suggested that attention to the language of political discourse can break the impasse. Language mediates between reality and thought, defining the first in the process of expressing the second. By endowing social experience with meaning, the language of political discourse constitutes as much as it reflects that experience. As Childers has shown in the case of the corporatist imagery used by Weimar's bourgeois parties, in Germany this language drew on traditional idioms and metaphors that "had remained in the mainstream of German social and political life" despite modernization of the economy and the society.[67]

Childers has also pointed out that the "multiple identities" of all human beings are a source of contradictory impulses in the same person and in a political culture.[68] The heterogeneous composition of social consciousness helps explain how the new and the old could coexist in Weimar politics. I have touched on some of the contradictory elements in Social Democratic culture. Bourgeois culture in Germany was just as complex, a mix of modern and premodern notions.[69] Just as Social Democracy had been shaped by the bourgeois association, so the SPD had indelibly imprinted bourgeois political culture in the late nineteenth century by introducing the politics of mass mobilization and participation. Whether used to express progressive or reactionary demands, modern politics supplanted the older elitist politics of notables.[70] In the space between contradictions in the political culture lay the opportunity to forge a new amalgam between the traditional and the modern. The NSDAP did just that—by glorifying mass politics while attacking democracy; by enshrining archaic occupational divisions while mythologizing the *Volksgemeinschaft* (people's community); by praising professional privileges while excoriating those of the rich, powerful, and well-connected; by appealing to socialism while demonizing Marxism; and by extolling national unity while dehumanizing Jews.[71] This combination of contradictory attitudes and desires was particularly repugnant and, as it turned out, virulent; but neither its constellation nor its popular success was determined by a peculiarly German authoritarian past, nor was a different constellation impossible.

Rather than *a* continuity, one must insist on continuities. Weimar culture not only encompassed multiple identities but, in fact, several bourgeois cultures (e.g., Catholic, Protestant, and Jewish) and several working-class cultures (e.g., Social Democratic, Catholic, and Communist).[72] The *Sonderweg* thesis ignores those lines of continuity that got severed in 1933, presenting a picture of an intolerant, but harmonious, culture.[73] In fact, Weimar's political culture was strikingly cacophonous. Diversity did not mellow into pluralism because, as Peter Lösche and Michael Scholing have pointed out, it did not rest on a consensus about political fundamentals and human rights, the common ground in which a profusion of viewpoints can grow into a civic culture. Instead, cultural values became the banners of political armies engaged in battles over the very nature of state.[74] These battles simmered throughout the Weimar republic, which was not only a new state but a state associated (by its enemies) with military defeat. The struggle gave signs of petering out in the mid-1920s, only to be rekindled by a crisis of political legitimacy that was, in turn, spurred by the economic misery of the early 1930s.

The undeniable impact of the worldwide depression on Weimar's fate raises questions about the role played by economic interest and structure.[75] Here, too, the interaction between circumstance (the depression) and constant (social structure) had unpredictable consequences that reinforced the primacy of politics. On one hand, as many authors have suggested, the polarization between employers and workers in the depression narrowed the parliamentary maneuvering room for the parties that represented these interests.[76] As Reinhard Neebe has argued, however, social polarization enhanced the autonomy of executive authority rather than the clout of social interest groups. The executive, in the form of a chancellor backed by the president of the republic and emergency powers, implemented a crisis strategy motivated by considerations more political than economic.[77]

No monocausal explanation of the Weimar republic's dissolution will suffice, and the multitude of factors that contributed to its demise should not be forgotten in a study of the SPD's struggle to save the republic. Yet the reverse is also true—an understanding of the SPD's dilemmas is crucial to an interpretation of the republic's dissolution. Even when, as after March 1930, the SPD did not play a direct role in policymaking, Social Democracy was an "absent presence" that influenced the behavior of political rivals, the executive, and social interest groups. The SPD was the party most identified with the republic and the party with the largest and most loyal membership; it was, moreover, a party connected with a powerful social interest group, the Free Trade Unions, and a party with an ideology of proven appeal and a record of practical accomplishment. Most of all, the SPD was the party the NSDAP had to surpass electorally if Adolf Hitler was to attain his end of destroying democracy with its own means. The contempt he and other Nazis expressed for the SPD only disguised the preoccupation of the Nazi movement with Social Democracy. More than any other mass movement in Weimar Germany, Social Democracy was the antithesis of National Socialism: the former was a movement centered on interests and ideas; the latter, on politics and power. As a social movement, the SPD's class base and hostility to privilege of all kinds stood opposed to the estatist populism of the NSDAP. As a cultural movement, Social Democratic pluralism and humanism were an affront to Nazi racism and radical intolerance. As an organization, both the democratic and the bureaucratic features of Social Democracy were antithetical to the charismatic *Führerprinzip* of Nazism. As a political machine, the SPD's rational discourse contrasted with the emotionalism and violence of the NSDAP. As a parliamentary party, its commitment to negotiation and compromise was alien to the absolute hegemony demanded by Hitler. Yet while the Nazis despised Social Democracy, they recognized the power of its worldview and envied its success as a movement that penetrated all aspects of its adherents' lives. To emulate its success and to destroy it, they raided its arsenal of methods, tactics, and even ideals, twisting and reforging the weapons that they stole. The NSDAP became, in a sense, the SPD's mirror opposite. For this reason, to examine the scruples, principles, and responsibilities with which Social Democrats wrestled is to see in reverse how a profoundly unscrupulous, unprincipled, and irresponsible political movement could become the republic's heir.

The structure of this book reflects the interpretation sketched above. Chapter 1 provides a snapshot of Social Democracy's associations and their political culture, and of the SPD's social composition and ideological tendencies in 1928. The following chapters are chronologically arranged and discuss the cardinal issues that arose in the SPD's struggle to save the republic as it unfolded between 1928 and 1933. Critical political choices made by Social Democrats are treated as case studies whose course reveals much about the why and how of the SPD's ultimate failure. I examine SPD decisions that aroused controversy at the time and that have been the stuff of historical debate ever since: the Panzerkreuzer affair in August 1928, the fall of the Social Democratic regime in March 1930, the decision to tolerate Brüning in October 1930, the formation of the Iron Front in early 1932, and the choice not to resist the Reich coup against Prussia in July 1932 or the appointment of Hitler as chancellor in January 1933. I cover the electoral campaigns of 1928, 1930, and 1932, discussing the SPD's propaganda, agitation, and electoral sociology and Social Democrats' own analyses of these. The extraparliamentary activities of the SPD are also appraised.

Social Democrats expressed their ideas about politics and society not only during debates about political decisions but also in a series of theoretical arguments that directly affected the SPD's struggle against Nazism. These focused on the nature of fascism (chapter 3), the class basis of Social Democracy (chapter 5), ways to overcome the economic crisis (chapter 6), and mobilization of the Social Democratic ranks (chapters 5 and 7). Debate took place in many different forums—party congresses, the local press, and local assemblies—and in the closed meetings of Social Democracy's ruling bodies, in the SPD's internal journal, and in private correspondence. I draw on evidence from all these sources as well as from police records and internal reports of the KPD and the NSDAP.

Certain relationships form the axes of the story: between SPD leaders and their critics, between left-wing and right-wing critics, between party authorities and active members, between the SPD and the Free Trade Unions, and between the SPD and the Reichsbanner. Because the sequence and pace of events influenced the evolution of these relationships, their ebb and flow are traced over the course of the narrative. The process by which the SPD came to be immobilized was dynamic, if only because the memory of earlier decisions and reactions to them modified subsequent choices and responses. The process was not, however, linear. The SPD did not simply become ever more paralyzed but experienced fluctuations in activity: remission and reinvigoration came in the wake of demoralization. Nor did awareness of the Nazi threat constantly heighten: relapse and retreat to old verities followed periods characterized by intense concern and impressive insight.

Social Democracy in 1928

Judging from its portrayal in popular novels, the SPD played a very different role on the Weimar stage than it did on the Imperial stage. *Der Untertan*, Heinrich Mann's satire of Wilhelmine Germany, characterizes the Social Democratic machinist Napoleon Fischer as a devious and double-dealing, but dangerous and effective, spokesman of the oppressed. In contrast, Hans Fallada's late Weimar novel, *Bauern, Bonzen, und Bomben*, depicts a party of lead feet, bound by the special interests of organized labor although represented by a clever man with a broader perspective than his constituents. A bureaucrat, not a rabble-rouser, Bürgermeister Gareis is enmeshed in his town's political relationships, unable to exploit them from without. Mann's Fischer is an outsider; Fallada's Gareis, an insider. Did this fictional transformation correspond to reality? In fact, scholars dispute the degree of cultural isolation of prewar Social Democracy, variously seeing its realm as a "negatively integrated" subculture,[1] an "alternative" culture,[2] or a culture at once integrative and emancipatory.[3] It has been argued, for example, that nationalism infected Social Democratic workers more than contemporaries recognized.[4] Nonetheless, virtually all studies concur that, politically and socially, prewar Social Democrats were shunned outsiders. In comparison, Weimar Social Democrats seemed significantly more integrated. Most dramatic was the transformation in the relationship of the SPD and ADGB to the state. Identification with the republic was not just ideological, but practical: at the provincial, state, and, especially, communal levels, Social Democrats participated in government.[5] Like Bürgermeister Gareis, they no longer stood outside the system.

Economically, the position of Social Democrats was not transformed. Workers' wages remained low, their housing inadequate.[6] In an ongoing controversy over the relative gains of labor to capital in the 1920s, some scholars argue that these were substantial, while others insist that even in Weimar's "golden years" workers barely recouped the drastic losses of 1914–24. They agree, though, that the Free Trade Unions did win significant wage gains for the majority of workers from 1924 to 1928 and that the gap between the wages of skilled and unskilled workers decreased to some extent.[7] Indirect evidence, such as advertisements for auto repair shops, appliance stores, savings banks, and restaurants in SPD pamphlets and newspapers, suggests that workers took some modest part in Germany's (underdeveloped) consumer economy.[8] In 1927, a national unemployment insurance bill increased the security of workers in Weimar's high-unemployment economy. Notable too was state intervention in the bargaining process through binding arbitration, a change perceived by both employers and unions as more in the interest of labor than of capital. About 100,000 delegates sat on factory councils (mandated by law in 1920) where they deliberated shop floor issues.[9] Off the shop floor, Social Democratic workers took advantage of the low-income apartments, schools, swimming pools, libraries, and adult education halls built by municipalities.[10] More difficult to quantify but not insignificant, the gulf between the cultural lives of the urban worker and the urban bourgeois shrank as city dwellers from diverse backgrounds participated in the new mass culture of fashion, hits, heartthrobs, and slang via radio and film.[11]

Some historians contend that political integration, greater prosperity for at least some workers, and mass culture corroded the walls around the socialist fortress and that the decay of proletarian culture sapped the vitality of the SPD.[12] Others note that, in fact, only *after* 1918 did Social Democracy reach its peak of organizational differentiation and penetrate all aspects of its members' lives; however, they add, expansion spread the movement too thinly, while participation in government breached the boundary between the SPD and the bourgeois world, so that inner atrophy set in.[13] Historians also point out that as the gap between Social Democracy and bourgeois society narrowed, the breach between it and other proletarian cultures widened, in part because the skilled workers who formed its nucleus benefited more than unskilled workers from housing and other social programs.[14] In addition, mass culture exerted a stronger pull on less-skilled, younger, and female workers who had not cut their teeth on the male-centered, craftworker associationism of prewar Social Democracy.[15] Above all, Social Democracy no longer encompassed the socialist working-class world but faced competition from German Communism.

A second group of scholars claims that despite these developments the integration of Social Democratic into bourgeois culture did not occur. In the warmer climate of the republic, they say, Social Democracy's separate culture blossomed, not withered.[16] Adalheid von Saldern has suggested that diverse external influences, in fact, produced paradoxical results: Social Democratic culture both did and did not erode. No longer in sharp opposition to the state, it grew less political yet remained committed to its autonomy and forms of solidarity.[17] Saldern's point that isolation and integration were not mutually exclusive is well taken. Weimar Social Democrats demonstrated marked ambivalence in their attitudes toward the larger polity. The beloved slogans and songs of ritual occasions expressed related, but divided, loyalties. In celebration of the reunification of the majority SPD and Independent Socialists in 1922, for example, an SPD assembly in Munich shouted a triple "Long live the republic!" and then sang the *Workers' Marseillaise*. Socialist festivals commemorated the working class and the republic.[18] The intensity of Social Democrats' affection for the republic waxed and waned inversely to that of the middle class. In rocky periods, they professed, at once defiant and bitter, "[The republic's] only protector is the organized working class."[19] Ambivalence toward the larger society even permeated the Reichsbanner, the only SPD fraternal organization that, on paper at least, embraced bourgeois republican groups. At the founding meeting of the Munich Reichsbanner in 1924, its chairman beseeched a skeptical (Social Democratic) crowd to accept the Reichsbanner as a "compound of associations (*Vereinszusammensetzung*)." Social Democrats distrusted not only bourgeois who might join their associations but workers who strayed beyond the pale. Reichsbanner activists continually entreated less dedicated members to forsake "bourgeois sport leagues," although these were proletarian in composition.[20]

The dilemma of integration versus isolation produced tensions inside Social Democracy's cultural organizations, within the SPD, and between the SPD and its fraternal associations. Stripped of the appeals to principle that adorned them, most major political fights in the SPD boiled down to disagreements over whether to retain or to tear down the walls between Social Democracy and the rest of German society. When the SPD entered the national cabinet in 1928 for the first time in five years, this old conflict flared anew, fed by discomfiture over participation in a coalition with bourgeois parties. This issue also plagued the SPD's effort to stave off the Nazi threat—should it counter the assault on democracy and republic by going after the same social groups the NSDAP attracted or by securing a proletarian fortress? To understand the complex evolution of this quandary after 1928, an overview of the composition and ideology of Social Democracy in 1928 is necessary.

The SPD's Fraternal Organizations

The largest organization within Social Democracy was the ADGB. The Free Trade Unions were administered by a formidable bureaucracy, paid and volunteer, estimated by a staff member in 1927 at 200,000 (of whom about half were factory council delegates). Union membership, almost five times greater than the SPD's in 1928, comprised the party's main reservoir of votes. About two-thirds of all Social Democrats belonged to the ADGB or to the AfA-Bund, while only 10 to 15 percent of Free Trade unionists were in the SPD.[21] As representatives of 85 percent of all organized workers in Germany, the Free Trade Unions were a weighty interest group, an ally not to be taken lightly. Since the 1890s, when union membership first outpaced the SPD's, union autonomy had grown apace. In the Mannheim Agreement of 1905, the Free Trade Unions had won parity with the SPD: on issues of joint concern the two leaderships were "to seek a mutual understanding in order to achieve unified procedure."[22] In the Nuremberg Resolution of 1919, the ADGB declared its political neutrality and rejected intervention in its internal affairs by any party, including the SPD. Union leaders tended to present themselves as the true representatives of the working class in public affairs, a role the SPD could not fulfill, they intimated, because it had to compromise with bourgeois forces.[23] Nonetheless, informal and formal ties were abundant, and power and influence in the relationship did not flow in only one direction. Union officials represented the SPD in parliamentary bodies at all levels of the republic. Of its 152-member Reichstag delegation of 1928, more than one-fourth were trade union officials.[24] The unions also provided financial support in electoral campaigns.[25] Cooperation existed at the highest levels: Otto Wels, cochairman of the SPD, and Peter Grassmann, vice-chairman of the ADGB, attended each other's executive committee meetings.[26]

Trade union leaders strongly supported the Weimar republic. In 1928, Theodor Leipart, chairman of the ADGB, wrote, "The trade unions are so closely and beneficially connected to the state that in practice the question of approval or disapproval of the state no longer has meaning."[27] Yet this support, crucial to the republic's survival between 1918 and 1923, grew passive as the ADGB retreated from the political stage in the mid-1920s and tended to intervene in politics only on issues of wages and *Sozialpolitik* (social welfare policies).[28] As union political involvement declined, state intervention in labor-management disputes escalated so that the Free Trade Unions relied ever less on the independent strength of organized workers to resolve conflicts. As favorable settlements won with state help piled up, ADGB admiration for the Weimar "system" grew, but this regard rested on union officials' high estimation of its social and welfare policies more than on deep attachment to its democratic foundations.[29]

The second most significant fraternal organization was the Reichsbanner. In 1924, as the republic reeled out of a year of intense crisis, Social Democrats formed the republican defense league. The impulse came from rank and file defense formations that had sprung up in Saxony and Bavaria, the two states most threatened by antirepublican forces in 1923.[30] SPD leaders, hostile to the idea of a military-style bund and to the cooperation of the Saxon Proletarian Hundreds with the KPD, at first looked askance at these groups. In the end, the executive bowed to pressure to establish a defense league but, against leftists, insisted that it become an all-republican, rather than a proletarian, organization.[31] Members of the Center and Democratic parties sat on the Reichsbanner's executive committee. In practice, the Reichsbanner remained heavily Social Democratic in composition and became ever more closely identified with the SPD. Its 3 million members were not all party members, but an estimated 90 percent voted for the SPD. The Reichsbanner was larger than the SA or the German Nationalist Stahlhelm but, unlike these right-wing paramilitary groups, did not engage in serious military training until 1932.[32] In its first years, with its aggressively republican and antiaristocratic songs and rhetoric, it acted as a propaganda machine for the republic and as a watchdog against antirepublicanism.[33]

In contrast to the official posture of the Reichsbanner, most Social Democratic leisure organizations vociferously defended proletarian, socialist sociability. Ironically, at their origins in the 1890s, many Social Democratic cultural organizations were imprinted with such bourgeois ideals as humanism and the universalism of "high" culture, imparted by literati and Social Democrats eager to realize for the masses the humanitarian aims abandoned by the bourgeoisie.[34] A new infusion of bourgeois cultural reformism came in the early 1920s and was especially noticeable in the enthusiasm for nature and health among the Young Socialists.[35] The cultural avant garde also impinged on the tastes of Weimar Socialists, at least at the local level. In Kassel, the tenth anniversary of the 1918 revolution was celebrated with pacifist poems by Kurt Tucholsky, Ernst Toller, and Franz Werfel on a program with republican verses by Freiligrath and Herwegh, heroes of 1848.[36] Simultaneously, in their very *Vereinsfreudigkeit* (enthusiasm for clubs), Social Democrats resembled the philistine middle class. In Frankfurt in 1929, 11,678 Social Democrats participated in 160 clubs—100 athletic groups, 37 choirs, 11 chess clubs, 9 "columns" of the Workers' Red Cross, and 2 ramblers' branches.[37] These activities were also beloved by Germans of other political persuasions and social backgrounds.[38]

Social Democrats' humanist ideals, catholic tastes, and comparable leisure pursuits did not induce bourgeois society to open its arms to their culture. Prominent bourgeois moderates such as Gertrud Bäumer, co-chairwoman of the Federation of German Women's Associations and a

Reichstag delegate of the DDP, actually branded SPD cultural politics for its "radical rationalistic liberalism."[39] Not only was bourgeois associational life suffused with militarism and nationalism antithetical to Social Democratic culture, but its parallel activities, such as singing and card playing, took place in segregated middle-class clubs and pubs.[40] In the few instances when bourgeois groups did make overtures, Social Democratic associations guarded their autonomy. The Workers' Sports Federation, the largest single Social Democratic cultural organization and an intensely prorepublican one, repeatedly rejected offers of cooperation by the German Athletic Club, a bourgeois association that was, in fact, 80 percent proletarian.[41]

Social Democratic associations were not necessarily distinguished by their class makeup, but by their class outlook. Even organizations formed after 1918 that openly embraced republican virtues or bourgeois self-help notions directed their message at untapped working-class constituencies, not at the middle class. A grassroots effort spawned the Kinderfreunde, an association for proletarian children that was a raging success: by 1930, 120,000 children, 10,000 adult helpers, and 70,000 parents enjoyed it programs. Its director, the left-wing Social Democrat Kurt Löwenstein, hoped to instill workers' children with class pride and democratic, egalitarian ideals by having them participate in minirepublics at camps and meetings. Workers' Welfare, also new and thriving, was the only Social Democratic league that was majority female and run by a woman, Maria Juchacz. She and other SPD leaders conceived of it as an adjunct to state agencies, but it blossomed into a full-fledged self-help organization that engaged in tasks similar to those of bourgeois women's charitable groups.[42]

Resistance to integration stemmed in part from loyalty to class sociability. To Social Democratic sports enthusiasts, workers were morally compelled to participate in self-consciously proletarian events.[43] They complained when SPD newspapers reported on "bourgeois sport." Rank and file Social Democrats were appalled to discover that Erhard Auer, chairman of the Bavarian SPD, had joined "every possible bourgeois association." Periodically, his disloyalty to socialist sociability embroiled the Munich SPD in bitter internal battles that distracted it from outside work.[44] Isolationist tendencies also stemmed from the determination to live by Socialist principles. Under pressure from younger players, Socialist athletic leagues grudgingly introduced competition and citation but continued to prohibit spectator sports.[45] Vigilant Social Democrats also insisted that internal sociability be nondiscriminatory and open, in contrast to the elitism and secrecy of bourgeois social relations. The ranks erupted in anger in 1927 when they got wind of the existence of a

Masonlike lodge that tapped functionaries in the SPD, ADGB, and consumer cooperatives. Impressed by the furor over this "secret association" and fearful of bad press, the SPD executive committee denied prior knowledge of the Weltbundloge (League of Nations Lodge) and ordered its dissolution.[46]

Clearly, Social Democrats did not always agree among themselves about what constituted Social Democratic culture or how isolated it should be. Particularly hotly debated were activities imbued with militarist connotations, such as rifle practice. Social Democratic shooting clubs existed but encountered opposition from some party members as an "aping of bourgeois methods."[47] At times, two cherished ideals clashed with each other. When Berlin's district executive committee submitted a resolution to the party congress of 1929 to bar SPD officials from religious affiliation, the national executive, supported by a majority of delegates, rejected this as a violation of freedom of conscience. At the local level, nonetheless, members repeatedly insisted that Social Democrats, especially functionaries, cut all ties with organized religion and send their children to schools without religious instruction (which were introduced in 1918).[48] Historically, both anticlericalism and freedom of belief have democratic, not socialist, roots. Yet leftists, in particular, saw anticlericalism as part of the Social Democratic covenant. In their eyes, the failure to live in consonance with this precept connoted the tainting of Social Democracy by bourgeois hypocrisy.

Political Tendencies in the SPD

At first glance, the political spectrum inside the Weimar SPD resembled that of the prewar party, with a leadership that held a centrist position between the poles. The executive committee, the top body in the party, was composed largely of centrists. Three members, Arthur Crispien, Wilhelm Dittmann, and Rudolf Hilferding, had been leaders of the left-wing USPD that had split from the SPD in 1917 in opposition to its continued support of the war. Back in the mother party, Hilferding became editor of the SPD's new theoretical journal, *Die Gesellschaft*, and emerged as the theorist of the party mainstream.[49] The party's left wing KPD consisted substantially of ex-Independents who retained their earlier convictions. Paul Levi, the most gifted and eloquent left-wing strategist in the SPD until his untimely death in 1930, had been Rosa Luxemburg's lawyer and close friend. He briefly led the fledgling Communist Party and then a splinter group before joining the USPD not long before it reunited with the SPD. In 1928 he combined his monthly *Sozialistische Politik und*

Wirtschaft with the new journal, *Der Klassenkampf*, edited by Max Seydewitz. Seydewitz was the pivotal figure in a far leftist tendency with which
Levi cooperated, somewhat uneasily. Both Levi and Seydewitz represented Saxon districts in the Reichstag.[50] Less insistently opposed to
the leadership than the *Klassenkampf* group was an amorphous tendency
that included well-known Social Democrats such as Siegfried Aufhäuser,
Reichstag member from Berlin and chairman of the AfA-Bund, and Toni
Sender, Reichstag member from Dresden and editor of *Frauenwelt*, the
SPD women's magazine. A sizable block of leftists sat in the Reichstag.[51]
They operated from a popular base in Thuringia and Saxony, which
together comprised 17 percent of total SPD membership. Other left-wing
strongholds were Berlin, Breslau, Frankfurt, and Stettin.[52] As a rule,
leftists found greatest support in urban and industrialized districts. They
were also influential in Socialist cultural organizations and youth groups.

On the SPD's right flank, reformists shaded into centrists but placed
more emphasis on nuts-and-bolts work and less on theory, Marxist or
parliamentarian. Trade union officials, who had sustained reformism
since the 1890s, often fit this bill, rarely speaking in Reichstag on issues
other than those directly affecting organized labor.[53] Many older *Staatspolitiker*, who had championed patriotism and cooperation with bourgeois
forces even before 1914, could be classified as reformists. Of the various
political tendencies in the SPD, neorevisionism fits least comfortably into
a model of the party's ideological spectrum based on a prewar scheme. Its
adherents followed Bernstein in their desire for the SPD to jettison ob-
solescent Marxist assumptions, acknowledge the centrality of ethical concerns, and become a people's party. Unlike Bernstein, however, they
viewed patriotism as a potentially positive, integrative political force.
Younger neorevisionists were also impressed by the antimaterialist socialism outlined by the Belgian Hendrik de Man in *Psychology of Socialism*
(1926), a book condemned by orthodox Marxists.[54] Revisionists shared
with younger leftists the conviction that socialism was a "matter of the
heart" as much as the pocketbook, and with the entire left wing, they
called for more democracy in the SPD.[55] Most of all, though, neorevisionists were militant republicans who passionately argued the political significance of such symbolic issues as the colors of the flag.[56] They described
themselves as Lassalleans and often invoked the French Revolution as
their ideal.[57]

Historically, SPD rightist intellectuals published in *Sozialistische Monatshefte*, which advocated coalition with bourgeois parties at home and cooperation with France abroad. In 1930, a neorevisionist journal, *Neue Blätter
für den Sozialismus*, appeared, the product of cooperation among Social

Democrats from two different backgrounds: religious socialists such as Paul Tillich, Eduard Heimann, and Wilhelm Sollmann came together with the remnants of the Hofgeismar circle in the Young Socialists in 1923, whose core—August Rathmann, Theo Haubach, Franz Osterroth, Carlo Mierendorff, and Gustav Dahrendorf—remained in the SPD.[58] These men became heavily involved in the Reichsbanner, whose second-in-command, Karl Höltermann, agreed with their viewpoint.[59] Julius Leber, editor of Lübeck's *Volksbote* and a Reichstag delegate, and Kurt Schumacher, after 1930 a Reichstag member from Stuttgart, were also young militant republicans (although not connected with the *Neue Blätter* circle).[60] Unusual in the SPD, almost every prominent figure in this loose tendency came from a bourgeois family and had earned a university degree. Many were war veterans who presented themselves as spokesmen for the generation of 1914.[61]

A third group of rightists in the SPD was neither strictly reformist nor revisionist. *Staatspolitiker* put down roots in Prussia, where the comparative frailty of right-wing parties and the vigor of the Weimar parties (Catholic Center, DDP, and SPD) facilitated compromise among the republican parties. Otto Braun, Carl Severing (twice Prussian interior minister), Albert Grzesinski (interior minister and later Berlin police president), and Ernst Heilmann (leader of the Landtag delegation) steered a steady reformist course in Prussia. Social ties and ideological affinities existed between these politicians and the militant republicans, although they did not join in their younger comrades' antibureaucratic campaigns or publicly endorse their calls to revise Marxism.[62]

Organization of the SPD

In 1928 the SPD's 937,381 members were divided into 33 districts that corresponded to the electoral districts of the Weimar republic. Four hundred subdistricts and, in 1929, 9,544 local clubs (*Ortsvereine*) formed the base of the organizational pyramid.[63] At its apex sat the executive committee, which administered the party between congresses. As the executive gained new prerogatives over the years, the SPD had become ever more centralized. By the Weimar period, the executive appointed paid secretaries to the districts, owned all SPD property, and had the power to expel anyone who "worked against the party." It chose 6 to 9 Reichstag candidates for the national election list (elected with the "leftover" ballots that were part of Weimar's system of proportional representation). One Weimar Social Democrat recalled that the executive committee made all major decisions without consulting the rank and file.[64] The executive committee was notably stable. About 19 people sat on it at any one time, but between 1918 and 1933 only 31 served altogether. Their average age was 54. Little competition existed for these highest posts in the SPD. Even oppositionists generally voted for the official slate, evidently seeing constancy as a valuable quality of political leadership. The majority of executive members stemmed from skilled worker backgrounds. Of 27 for whom information exists, only 6 had attended university. Led by Otto Wels and Hermann Müller, the executive constituted a powerful, stable, and predictable force in the SPD. Müller acted as the political-parliamentary leader, while Wels, characterized by the historian Richard Hunt as the "perfect stereotype of a party boss," managed the organization.[65]

The larger party council convened quarterly to weigh executive decisions and vent the concerns of provincial Social Democrats. Composed of the districts' appointed secretaries and elected chairmen, it generally deferred to the executive's expertise on national affairs.[66] Each subdistrict also had an elected chairman. Altogether 20,000 to 30,000 paid apparatchiks, elected and appointed, worked for the SPD. The party also called on the services of an army of volunteers, including the chairmen and treasurers of local clubs.[67] These "little people" distributed leaflets and drummed up subscribers for the party press, routine activity that, according to left-wing critics, numbed political thinking and shrank horizons.[68] These activists chose the delegates to the party congress, where, in theory, they pronounced on the issues of the day, pondered the pros and cons of a new course, and elected the executive. In fact, even before 1914, the congress had become, in Peter Nettl's words, a "ritual celebration of political ideology" instead of a "supreme legislative assembly."[69] In the Weimar era, about 25 percent of the delegates had some organizational claim to a voice and/or vote as members of the executive, party council, or Reichstag delegation. Moreover, not local clubs but district congresses (dominated by functionaries) elected delegates (mainly functionaries).[70] Chaired by Otto Wels and with an agenda proposed by the executive, a majority nearly always approved the leadership course. Superficially at least, the party functioned like a well-oiled machine. As Theo Haubach, a neorevisionist critic of *Verbonzung* (bureaucratization or bossism), remarked, "The SPD is excellently administered, but in no way led."[71]

The SPD's Reichstag deputation stood outside the regular party structure, but its leadership was intertwined with the party leadership. In 1928, fourteen of the nineteen executive committee members sat in parliament. Except when chancellor of Germany, Hermann Müller was cochairman of both the executive committee and the Reichstag delegation. Nonetheless, the candidate selection process remained quite democratic. Sub-district organizations made the initial selection, district leaders arranged the candidates on priority lists, and regional congresses confirmed the choices. The executive committee could, but rarely did, intervene to replace unpalatable candidates.[72] It did not need to interfere: the SPD delegation had accumulated more seniority than any other.[73] As a result, its members were aging; in 1928, 52 percent were over fifty years old. Its social makeup had changed little since 1912, with about 65 percent having once been workers (very few still were). Almost all working-class deputies had been skilled workers, while middle-class representatives stemmed in large part from the intelligentsia, not from white-collar positions. The second largest SPD delegation sat in the Prussian Landtag and in 1928 was composed of 3.6 percent workers, 10.9 percent white-collar employees, 9.6 percent civil servants, 21.2 percent ADGB officials, and 14.6 percent party functionaries.[74]

The party press became less independent in the Weimar years as the executive acquired new powers, such as the right to decide the "ideological position" of (locally chosen) editorial boards (a prerogative it never exercised).[75] The Social Democratic Press Service provided news and editorials to local papers, making their voices more uniform. On the good side, this service allowed Social Democrats to publish more newspapers in the Weimar years than ever before (or since). The number peaked at 203 with 1.3 million subscribers in 1929. Squeezed by the economic downturn, Social Democrats published 196 newspapers in 1930, 176 in 1931, and only 135 in 1932. In 1925 and 1926, much to the chagrin of the SPD's left wing, Wilhelm Sollmann, editor of Cologne's SPD daily, wanted to depoliticize the party press in order to attract the large proletarian readership of bourgeois dailies.[76] Despite Sollmann's efforts, the SPD press remained not only partisan but very polemical by modern journalistic standards.

Confronted with the power of the party hierarchy, increasing centralization, and an aging leadership, left-wing and neorevisionist Socialists charged that the SPD was bureaucratized and ossified. Certainly it had spawned an octopuslike bureaucracy. However, older customs countered bureaucratic hegemony. When it came to free speech, the SPD continued to contain not just vestiges, but whole veins of internal democracy. In part this virtue was the child of necessity since dissidents controlled important subdistricts. In part it reflected the style of leadership in the SPD. Centrist leaders tried to isolate critics or shame them into silence, but rarely gagged them. The bureaucratization thesis also overstates the depoliticization of the functionary corps. Even left wingers conceded that district membership meetings (attended by delegates rewarded with a mandate for dogged day-to-day work) rarely criticized party policy, while gatherings of the functionary corps were quite outspoken.[77] The executive committee itself was neither monolithic nor all powerful.[78] Significant policy disagreements erupted within the leadership, especially in times of crisis. In particular, relations between the party's top leaders and the Reichstag delegation were often inharmonious.[79] Social Democrats in the Prussian government formed a third power center. Minister-President Otto Braun did not sit on the party executive, yet he (and the Landtag delegation) exerted palpable influence that at times rubbed against the grain of both the party executive and the Reichstag delegation.[80]

The Social Composition of the SPD and Its Electorate

The social provenance of Weimar Social Democrats was less likely to be proletarian than it had been before the war. In 1930 roughly 75 percent lived in working-class households, compared with over 90 percent in 1914; 60 percent were workers, compared with 73 percent in 1926. By 1930 about 17 percent of members were working-class housewives, 10 percent were white-collar employees, and 3 percent were civil servants, above all, secondary school teachers. In some cities, deindustrialization of the SPD was more dramatic. By 1922 only 43 percent of members in Berlin were industrial workers; 25 percent were employees in public service, and 13 percent were civil servants.[81] A national survey of 117,247 members in 1930 showed the percentage of employees and workers in the public sector at 13 percent, suggesting that SPD workers were shifting from factories to public jobs as railway workers, mail carriers, and the like.[82] A contemporary described the Hamburg organization in 1932 as an amalgam of three subgroups: harbor workers and shipbuilders; white-collar workers in industry, government, and (Social Democratic) consumer coops; and housewives.[83]

The majority of industrial workers in the Weimar SPD, as before the war, were skilled or semiskilled. A sample of members in Lower Franconia revealed 51.67 percent to be artisans or skilled workers and only 17.66 percent unskilled. Party functionaries were even more skilled (62.4 percent) than the membership. In Bavaria at least, the SPD was a party of "little" people, but not the oppressed. Because Bavaria was less industrialized than Germany as a whole and certainly less than those regions where the SPD was strong, its artisanal quota there was higher than elsewhere; however, the ratio of skilled workers was not. Unskilled workers turned increasingly to the KPD rather than to the SPD.[84]

The SPD was also aging, especially in contrast to the KPD. In 1930, 18.1 percent of Social Democrats were under 30, compared with 31.8 percent of the KPD; 55.4 percent had passed 40, compared with 35.5 percent of Communists. The aging of the SPD signified that people joined and stayed. In 1930, 38 percent of party members had joined at least ten years earlier, while 47 percent had joined less than five years before.[85] The party's aging also signaled difficulty in attracting youth. Its youth groups were virtually the only fraternal associations that languished in the mid-1920s. The SAJ declined from 110,000 members in 1924 to half that size in 1927, while the Young Socialists stagnated at a tiny 4,000. Young people who did join the SPD were often the children of Social Democrats. The social provenance of younger members reflected the limited but real social mobility of Social Democratic working-class families. After skilled metalworkers, the largest occupational group in the SAJ was white-collar employees.[86]

This evidence poses a classic "half-empty, half-full" problem. Some historians believe that the Weimar SPD was "on the road to a people's party."[87] Others see these changes as relatively insignificant.[88] The SPD's sociological base was shifting in the Weimar years, yet it remained, by a large majority, a working-class party skewed in the direction of older male skilled workers and their wives. Placed in the context of the stagnation of industrial labor as a percentage of the work force (43 percent in 1907, 42.1 percent in 1925) and the growth of the service sector (21.5 percent in 1907, 27.4 percent in 1925), the deproletarianization of the SPD is even less striking. Compared to the population as a whole, it was still lopsidedly proletarian.[89]

The SPD could not hope to introduce socialism democratically if it relied on urban working-class votes, given the burgeoning army of white-collar employees, the large population of rural laborers, and the stubborn refusal of small businesses and farmers to wither away as Marx had predicted. This predicament disturbed party leaders such as Rudolf Hilferding. In his speech at the SPD's Heidelberg congress in 1925, he acknowledged that the SPD must attract employees and farmers.[90] Yet Erhard Auer, the chairman of the Bavarian SPD, faulted the Heidelberg program, which Hilferding helped draft, for having no "general appeal and popularity (*Gemeinverständlichkeit und Volkstümlichkeit*)" and for skirting the "central question" facing the SPD: to remain a workers' party or to become a people's party.[91] In fact, by 1928 between a quarter and a third of SPD voters were nonproletarians, of whom by far the greatest number were white-collar workers, mostly public employees and technicians.[92] This shift seemed appropriate to some Socialists who saw salaried workers as the SPD's natural "political reserve."[93] Still, the SPD made little sustained effort to attract them.[94] Although the head of the Free Employees' Federation, Siegfried Aufhäuser, defended the special prerogatives of employees against the imprecations of his comrades in the ADGB, the AfA-Bund continually lost members after a propitious beginning, representing only 8 percent of employees by 1926, compared with 15 percent in 1920. Its slide exemplified the SPD's lack of allure for employees. Jürgen Winkler has shown that the percentage of employees voting SPD actually declined between 1912 and 1924.[95] Party propaganda continued to insist that employees were proletarians blinded to reality by false consciousness. Though Hilferding and others recognized the futility of such arguments, they rang true to Social Democratic workers who harbored a not always concealed animosity toward "haughty" employees and their privileges.[96]

Civil servants comprised the second largest group of nonproletarian SPD voters. The SPD's strategy for luring *Beamten* vacillated between flattery and harangues on their duty to accept proletarian status. In its parliamentary capacity, the SPD never infringed upon their occupational privileges, though in this case too, the Free Trade Unions publicly censured these entitlements.[97] Those civil servants who did join the SPD were often maligned as "November socialists"—opportunists who signed on only after the SPD became *salonfähig* (socially acceptable).[98] Eager to prove their socialist mettle, many Social Democratic civil servants succumbed to the "last through the door" syndrome and tried to erect obstacles to deter less intrepid colleagues from following them. In league with working-class comrades, they demanded that all civil servants in the SPD abandon the politically neutral DBB (whose 1 million members made up 80 percent of all civil servants) and enroll in the (Socialist) ADB, with 170,000 members.[99]

The SPD made few inroads into the old *Mittelstand*—the urban and rural self-employed. Most Social Democrats disdained the urban self-employed, and its members responded in kind. Rather than fight restrictive credit policies that hurt independent producers, Social Democrats accepted the demise of artisans and small retailers as inevitable. An effective appeal to these sections of the *Mittelstand* seemed, at any rate, hopeless because they loathed Socialist consumer cooperatives.[100] In contrast, at least programmatically, the SPD made more economic concessions to small farmers than to any other non-working-class group. Hilferding, Karl Kautsky, and others realized that small agricultural producers were not "sinking," although they were in trouble. The SPD adopted a new agrarian program in 1927 that called for the breakup of large estates, rather than nationalization, and for a *Sozialpolitik* for farmers. From 1928 on, the SPD pushed for measures that would decrease subsidies for big landowners, while protecting small producers and consumers. Farmers, however, continued to see Social Democrats as *"agrarfeindlich* (hostile to agriculture)." In part, overtures came too late; the new policy had no chance to seep into public consciousness.[101] The SPD, moreover, did not treat the issue as politically urgent or publicize its initiatives in rural regions, though these areas were seething with unrest by the late 1920s.[102] Such negligence reflected not just lack of will but a dearth of agitators who spoke the language of farmers.[103] At bottom, again, lay the ambivalent attitude of the ranks. At a Munich public meeting in the awful autumn of 1923, a locally prominent Social Democrat decreed, "Cooperation with farmers, large or small, is impossible." Nonetheless, a year later the Munich SPD sent agitators into the surrounding countryside to rally support for the Reichsbanner. Not surprisingly, they found few takers.[104]

After 1918 the SPD was also afflicted by a "gender gap" in its electorate. Unlike any other Imperial party, the SPD had consistently pressed for female suffrage. Once enfranchised, however, women voted disproportionately for moderate to conservative bourgeois parties, especially the Center Party, and against the SPD (and the KPD and, at least initially, the NSDAP).[105] The SPD worked to win women in general and to persuade working-class women in particular to exercise their franchise right. Besides directing propaganda at women, it nominated women as Reichstag candidates; they made up 13 percent of the delegation in 1930.[106] The gap between female and male voters shrank but did not close. Contemporaries estimated that in 1919 the proportion of men voting for the SPD was 14 percent greater than the proportion of women, while in 1928 it was 7 percent higher and in 1930 about 3 percent larger.[107]

While the centrist leadership wished the SPD could attract nonproletarians, it did not carry out aggressive campaigns to this end.[108] Revisionists pressed for an active effort to transform the SPD into a *Volkspartei*, while the left wing goaded the SPD to go after proletarians lost to the KPD, claiming that once it had again proven itself as a *Klassenpartei* (class party), employees and civil servants would naturally turn to it for leadership.[109] On the Right, the Free Trade Unions also resisted efforts to broaden the SPD's social appeal, or at least such was the practical effect of its invective against the privileges of employees and civil servants. Privately, union officials wondered if the SPD adequately represented the interests of the working class; some wanted to turn the SPD into a "party of labor," and a few even dreamed of a separate trade union party.[110]

Though ever less a purely proletarian party in its composition or electorate, Social Democrats talked as if the SPD were one and so undermined its ability to become a bona fide people's party. In his opening address to the party congress that adopted the new agrarian program, Otto Wels proclaimed, "The fight is for the political soul of the German working class." Presenting the results of a sociological study of party membership, another speaker claimed the figures rebutted the charge that the SPD had become "*kleinbürgerlich* (petit bourgeois)."[111] The Hamburg SPD, though a center of neorevisionism, asserted that "despite having made inroads into the entire population . . . , the [Hamburg] SPD can still claim the right to be called a workers' party in the broadest sense of the word." Social Democratic festivals and pageants catered to the movement's self-image as the once and future haven of only and all workers.[112] The ranks shunned language that blurred class distinctions. When, in the strife-torn Bavaria of December 1923, SPD Reichstag deputy Toni Pfülf contended, "The German people must again become a people's community (*Volksgemeinschaft*)," she provoked an outcry from her audience of twelve hundred Social Democrats. One man lectured her, "'People's community' is the worst kind of slogan! There can be no people's community for the worker because of his class position."[113]

The SPD's Ideology

In the 1920s Social Democrats struggled to clarify their views about three interrelated issues. The first was economic: How could German society be made both more equitable and prosperous? The second was national: How could Germany maintain its national integrity without succumbing to the militarism of the past? The third was political: How were democracy and the republic to become rooted in Germany? Social Democrats of all political complexions shared the conviction that these issues were connected by the need to "democratize" the economy, the army, the educational system, and government administration, and to make these institutions more "social"—focused on social welfare rather than on individual profit. However, they disagreed about how to democratize and socialize and about which of these had the higher priority.

Social Democrats quarreled less among themselves about their economic program than about national and political questions. In the mid-1920s, Rudolf Hilferding won most of them to his theory of organized capitalism, developed during the 1924–28 period of economic stabilization. He assumed an era of more or less crisis-free development under the domination of giant corporate producers. In his view, monopoly limits on market forces marked progress toward socialization, since the erosion of competition would culminate in a state takeover of the economy. Thus, once Social Democracy won majority rule, it could make the transition to socialism peacefully. Although Hilferding rejected revolution, his analytical tools were Marxist, and he did not abandon Marxist precepts about class relations.[114] Leftists in the SPD did not challenge his economic reasoning, though Siegfried Aufhäuser pointed out that the expansion of capitalist power was dangerous for the working class and warned that the SPD dare not abandon its representation of proletarian interests.[115] The Social Democratic right wing, in contrast, liked the political implications of Hilferding's economic analysis but had little use for its Marxist foundations.

Despite agreement that the socialization of the economy was desirable, the idea receded ever more into the background as a practical matter, dusted off for ritual proclamations at SPD and ADGB congresses. Instead, the SPD followed the trade unions in advocating "economic democracy." Hilferding's friend Fritz Naphtali, director of the Free Trade Unions' Economic Policy Research Institute, developed this program, inspired by ideas of codetermination and workplace democracy fought for by workers in 1918–19.[116] At the ADGB congress in 1928, Naphtali argued that a genuinely democratic economy could not be constructed under capitalism but important steps in that direction could be taken. In fact, as Naphtali pointed out, public economic activity had already made inroads against capitalist anarchy and production for profit. Moreover, the market economy's increasing centralization incited public demands for supervision of production that would culminate in state organs of control on which the trade unions should sit as representatives of the general interest.[117] In adopting Naphtali's program, the ADGB acknowledged that the road to socialism lay in the incremental growth of public intervention in the economy. The majority of Social Democrats agreed.[118] This broad, rather vague goal linked economic and political reform but did not inspire the day-to-day practice of the SPD or the ADGB. Their actual social-economic program was *Sozialpolitik*—above all, an eight-hour day and unemployment insurance. Such policies made the Weimar republic an advanced welfare state for its time and constituted the most significant social-economic gains won by Social Democrats since the revolution. All wings of the party accepted the place of honor accorded *Sozialpolitik* in propaganda and in the concrete work of SPD Reichstag, state, and municipal deputies.

On the issue of nationalism, rightists wanted to adopt patriotic rhetoric as a corollary to acceptance of the new state. They hoped to stamp out socialist hatred of the military, believing that a reformed Reichswehr could only come about with a reformed Socialist attitude toward the army, though they did insist, of course, that the Reichswehr be democratized and "republicanized." They did not repudiate socialist internationalism but saw it as a cause that was unlikely to rally support for the republic.[119] Some left wingers accepted the principle of national defense but insisted the Reichswehr must be transformed before Social Democrats could seriously discuss the need for an army.[120] Others opposed any bourgeois military force and called for "proletarian defense" (a working-class militia that would defend Germany if the nation were attacked).[121] National defense confused political lines more than any other issue because Social Democrats of many stripes deeply distrusted the German military. Thus, a confirmed *Staatspolitiker* such as Otto Braun was an antimilitarist who had rocky relations with the Reichswehr, while centrist executive committee members such as Hermann Müller and Friedrich Stampfer basically accepted the revisionist position but shied away from using patriotism to forge attachment to the new state.[122] All Socialists supported "fulfillment" of the Versailles peace treaty, though they found its terms unfair.[123]

The most fundamental question facing the SPD was its stance on parliamentary democracy and the republic. The basic division on this issue has often been characterized as one between leftists, for whom the democratic republic was a phase in the struggle for socialism rather than an end in itself, and centrists and rightists, who embraced the new state. Leftists insisted on the distinction between social and formal (political) democracy, arguing that in a capitalist society the bourgeoisie controlled the state by definition.[124] Along with many in the party ranks, they protested the tendency of centrists, much less rightists, to slight class struggle as a motor force of history. Several SPD districts took umbrage at the failure to refer to this basic Marxist concept in the draft proposal for the 1921 (Görlitz) program. The final draft reincorporated class struggle but presented it as the historic justification of the socialist effort rather than as a mandate for social war. In consequence, Independent Socialists, who returned to the fold in 1922, insisted on a new program, which Hilferding, one of their number, helped write. Rightists faulted this Heidelberg program as equivocal in its endorsement of the new state, while Paul Levi felt it bent too far in this direction.[125]

By 1927 Hilferding not only had become an eloquent voice for democracy "for its own sake" but had diverged from the Marxist view of the state as the instrument of the dominant social class. In his keynote address at the Kiel congress in 1927, he argued for unqualified support of the Weimar republic and democracy. First, he maintained that the political hegemony of capital had been broken because German workers could potentially win state power and set aside private property. Second, he spurned the notion that "bourgeois" or formal democracy could be separated from social or proletarian democracy. Democracy, plain and simple, was the "cause" of the proletariat; thus, "support of democracy and the republic is the party's most important interest." Those who did not see this had "not grasped the ABC of political thinking."[126] The majority of delegates endorsed his position against that of the Left Opposition.

In fact, the breach between the Left, on one side, and centrists, *Staatspolitiker*, and neorevisionists, on the other, over the republic and democracy was less clean than at first appears. The Left construed the leadership's outright endorsement of the Weimar republic as an encomium to the status quo and repudiated it as such. Many leftists were, in fact, staunch defenders of the republic as it *should* be. Paul Levi, for example, focused relentlessly on what was yet awry, exhorting Social Democratic politicians to purge the republic of its many enemies in its administration, courts, and army.[127] SPD leaders tended to react irritably to the criticisms of Levi and his associates, detecting in them a disguised assault on the constitution and the state's foundations (and a reproach for mistakes made by the SPD in the 1918–19 revolution). Though they recognized that the republic needed to be republicanized, party leaders handled the matter gingerly, convinced that democratization would progress slowly through compromise with and cajolery of the bourgeois parties.[128]

Moderate leftists came quite close to Hilferding's viewpoint, endorsing, in particular, the pluralism on which his defense of parliamentary democracy rested. Ernst Fraenkel argued that the pressure of organized interest groups on the state bureaucracy and their participation in government decision making would eventually democratize the administration. He also believed that powerful voluntary organizations (both labor and employer) acted as integrative forces in the republic.[129] For their part, neorevisionists welcomed Hilferding's rejection of the Marxist theory of the state but felt he did not adequately address the problem of forging mass support for the republic. In contrast to both Fraenkel and Hilferding, Hermann Heller, a legal scholar who inspired many neorevisionists, maintained that only "national feeling" could integrate the working class into the new state and so give it a stable foundation.[130]

To complicate matters further, delegates to the party congress who sanctioned Hilferding's ringing endorsement of democracy may not, in fact, have grasped the ABC's of political thinking in the sense that he intended. Much evidence suggests that Social Democrats—from the ranks to the Reichstag delegation—remained attached to direct democracy and were still suspicious of representation. Social Democrats in the National

Assembly of 1919 insisted that the Weimar constitution provide for plebiscites and referendums. Throughout the Weimar years the rank and file attempted to regulate the presence of SPD deputies at Reichstag sessions, expressing fury over slack attendance. Only comparatively few Socialists (such as those who served as ministers in the national and Prussian cabinets, and Prussian Landtag delegates) broke decisively with this allegiance to direct democracy.[131] This extensive yearning for direct democracy lay behind the Left's critique of parliamentary government, a fact that did not mollify centrists piqued by left-wing sniping at formal democracy.[132]

The practical question that roiled relations between the Left and centrists and neorevisionists was whether to join coalitions with bourgeois parties. At the Kiel congress, this tactic won majority support, but leftist holdouts argued that as long as the SPD could not form a majority government, it should remain in opposition.[133] In real life, even many centrists were uncomfortable with institutionalized compromise at the national level. On the other hand, left-wing rejection of coalition was not principled. They accepted cooperation if necessary to uphold democratic rights or, conversely, when the party could hope to win concrete gains for the proletariat. As a rule, they did not inveigh against the Weimar Coalition in Prussia.[134]

Despite much unacknowledged agreement on principles, the strategic and tactical differences between the majority and the opposition were significant. Often the leadership seemed only to affirm, Pollyanna-style, what had already been won, while the opposition denied, ostrichlike, that any basic changes had taken place. Neither attitude was particularly fruitful. Left-wing denial was risky in a state with such powerful right-wing enemies. Yet mere defensiveness ignored the many faults of the republic that, if addressed, could win popular support for democracy and the new state. As Hans Mommsen has argued, the leadership did not plan how to extend democracy, only how to defend it.[135] Exactly because he was an eloquent defender of democracy "for its own sake," Hilferding offers the most fascinating example of this failure. He recognized that the Weimar republic suffered from a crisis of political legitimacy yet did not develop a program to address this crisis.[136] The majority now had a reformist theory but no reforming practice—partial, but broad, goals for change within the existing system. The opposition, on the other hand, had goals but no plan for how to become a majority party. For different reasons, neither group viewed Social Democracy as the arbiter of the general issues facing their society. One faction saw it as the defender of the principles of the existing state; the other camp saw it as the embryo of the future society within that state.

The Weimar experiment was an overlay of advanced democracy, urban cultural pluralism, and progressive welfare programs on a social pattern inherited from Imperial times. Weimar society was divided along traditional and corporate, not just capitalist and class, lines. Germany was still backward in many ways; major reforms remained to be carried out. Socialists made piecemeal attempts to address the problem. They advocated judicial reform and appointed republican officials. After 1927, on paper they stood for breaking up landed estates in East Prussia. In 1929, "defense guidelines" reaffirmed their intent to reform the Reichswehr. Yet they did not make deep-seated inequities their cause, even to the extent that before the war they had taken the lead in the struggle for equal franchise rights in Prussia and Saxony.[137] Weimar Socialists advocated either political or social, but not popular, democracy. The SPD's lack of goals and its inability to project itself as a party that could lead the nation, as opposed to a part of it, will be important themes in the chapters that follow.

Indian Summer

From June 1928 to March 1930 the SPD had the leading role in the national government, led regimes in Prussia and Braunschweig, and had a significant presence in the governments of Hamburg and Baden. These months constituted the second heyday of Social Democratic political influence during the Weimar republic, and yet the party was unable to use its power productively. During this same period, the NSDAP prepared the ground for its stunning electoral gains in September 1930. Many factors beyond the SPD's control contributed to the Social Democratic stalemate and the Nazi rise, including the reluctance of the bourgeois parties to pass social reform measures and the onset of the depression. The decisions, activity, and program of the SPD, however, also contributed to its inability to address the economic and political concerns of most Germans, much less solve these problems in a manner that would have enhanced the popularity of the party and the republic at a time when democracy stood under mounting attack.

The 1928 Election Campaign

In February 1928, Wilhelm Marx's government, a conservative coalition of the DVP, the Center Party, the BVP, and the DNVP, fell apart over the issue of educational reform. Reichstag elections were set for May 20 to coincide with Prussian Landtag elections. The SPD had been in opposition in the Reich since late 1923, although in December 1925 and again a year later, Social Democrats were approached about the possibility of taking part in a Great Coalition (SPD, DDP, Center Party, BVP, and DVP). SPD leaders opposed such participation, reluctant to share power again with the DVP after the experience of 1923 when Social Democrats felt they had first been betrayed by Gustav Stresemann's party and then had suffered for its policies at the polls in 1924. High unemployment in 1925 and 1926 also reduced the appeal of government responsibility.[1] On the other hand, SPD opposition was not always intransigent. Social Democrats voted with the first Marx government against DNVP no-confidence motions in the summer of 1924 and, in January 1926, abstained in a confidence vote in order to allow the formation of Hans Luther's new cabinet. Throughout these years, the SPD supported Stresemann's foreign policy, at times more loyally than his own party. Nonetheless, the SPD did find an oppositional voice. Most spectacularly, in December 1926 Philipp Scheidemann exposed secret Reichswehr activities such as the maintenance of a Schwarze Reichswehr and cooperation with rightist paramilitary organizations and with the Red Army, all of which violated the terms of the Versailles treaty.[2] Social Democratic deputies also pressed for reforms in the administration of justice.[3] In 1927, for the first time since 1918, they voted against the budget. Yet, also in 1927, the SPD, encouraged by the Free Trade Unions, cooperated with the *Bürgerblock* (ruling coalition of mainstream bourgeois parties) to enact an unemployment insurance law that for Social Democrats became the linchpin of the republic's social welfare policies.[4]

As did the dilemmas of Social Democracy's cultural organizations and the Reichsbanner about whether to mingle with bourgeois associations, this erratic course revealed the ambivalence of Social Democrats about their relationship with the political representatives of bourgeois society. The SPD's extraparliamentary activity showed a similar pattern of insecurity about its political identity. In 1926, it initially opposed the Communists' call for a referendum on the expropriation without compensation of the former royal houses' property. Urged by its left wing, however, the SPD decided to join and, in fact, assumed leadership of the campaign for the referendum. The effort failed but rallied much popular support, garnering 36 percent of the vote. It also greatly boosted the morale of Social Democrats in the provinces by restoring confidence in the party's role as the defender of the oppressed against the rich and privileged.[5]

Based on recent regional returns, Social Democrats predicted that they would emerge victorious on May 20.[6] In 1927, the SPD booked impressive gains in Braunschweig and, with 46 percent of the vote, now presided over a minority Socialist government in that state. In February 1928 the Hamburg SPD won 35.9 percent of the vote, compared to 32.4 percent in 1924.[7] The SPD's electoral advances rested on the relative economic prosperity of the mid-1920s that enhanced political stability and undermined support for antirepublicanism. It also benefited from its oppositional role at the federal level. At the same time, its leading position in Prussia worked to its advantage. Minister-President Otto Braun, who had headed a Weimar coalition since 1921, stood at the peak of his popularity. Friend and foe saw the "Prussian dictator" as a socialist strongman in control of his cabinet, adroit not only in making political compromises but also in extracting concessions from his partners. Republicans also respected Prussian Interior Minister Albert Grzesinski for his stubborn efforts to fill important administrative offices with Weimar's supporters.[8] Under these happy signs, the party electoral machine rolled into action in April 1928. Speakers at campaign rallies and meetings denounced the *Bürgerblock*. A campaign film, *Your Destiny*, played to audiences all over the country.[9] The SPD was still the party that held the most parades and rallies in the greatest number of cities and towns across Germany. Cars equipped with loudspeakers and plastered with banners cruised streets, broadcasting the SPD's demand for *Kinderspeisung statt Panzerkreuzer*— food for children instead of money for the *Bürgerblock*'s "pocket battle-ship" program.[10]

In contrast to its efficient methods, the party's message was confused. Social Democratic newspapers announced a gamut of diverse intentions. *Vorwärts* promised to fight tariff profiteers, expose reactionary magistrates, inspect workplaces, and protect the "people's assets," while Cologne's *Rheinische Zeitung* called for housing construction, stable agricultural prices, and an end to educational privilege. The *Hamburger Echo* pledged democratization and administrative reform, a new economic policy, and fair taxes. The *Leipziger Volkszeitung*, a leftist SPD organ, advocated "full democratization to effect socialism," while the centrist Hanover *Volkswacht* proclaimed, "Forward to the Social Republic."[11] Only antimilitarist slogans were common to all Social Democratic papers. In contrast with the NSDAP's later skillful manipulation of specific regional grievances, the heterogeneous Social Democratic slogans were not attuned to local concerns. Neither strategic regionalism nor an overarching national theme characterized the campaign. A left-wing detractor faulted the absence of a clear and concrete focus, suggesting as such a focus either a social issue such as housing construction or one with moral appeal such as judicial reform.[12] Other leftists, calling for a "class struggle campaign," suspected that the vagueness of party slogans reflected leadership reluctance to tie the SPD to a specific program that might shut it out of a coalition.[13] The SPD relied on the negative, but appealing, promise to get rid of the *Bürgerblock*.[14] The *Nicht Panzerkreuzer, Kinderspeisung* slogan was a favorite at the local level, no doubt because it gave spice to otherwise bland propaganda and because antimilitarism was a potent ingredient in the Social Democratic worldview.[15]

Special election newspapers for factory workers, women, employees, and potential Communist voters targeted those whom the SPD hoped to galvanize. Given the gains in party membership among white-collar workers and women between 1924 and 1928, such a focus promised electoral benefits.[16] At the same time, with its call for stable agricultural prices, Social Democracy nodded in the direction of people who had shown little interest in the SPD—small farmers suffering acute economic distress, from Schleswig-Holstein to Thuringia to Bavaria. In Schleswig-Holstein, where huge farmers' demonstrations rocked market towns in early 1928, Socialist journalists and agitators emphasized their new agrarian program's advocacy of small farmers.[17] Such all-purpose slogans can hardly have convinced rural producers of the seriousness of Socialist concern. Neither conviction nor opportunism spurred the SPD to make a major issue of small farmers' grievances. No doubt the antirepublican and antisocialist sentiment of angry farmers discouraged such an effort. In this case, however, farmers' disgust with their traditional parties, liberal or rightist, ran just as high. Prorepublican organizations such as the Bavarian Peasants' League, roused by a populist fervor, were on the prowl for new political allies.[18] The turmoil in the agrarian camp gave impetus to the creation of narrow-interest-based parties and so contributed to parliamentary instability. With energy, determination, and imagination, Social Democrats could have possibly retarded this process, while beginning to carve out a rural base of support. Rather than chart such a risky course, even revisionist and centrist SPD dailies painted the campaign in the dramatic colors of the class struggle, describing it as a phase in the proletariat's struggle to transform society in its image, and so devoted their energies to mobilizing their core constituency.[19]

Analyzing the Election Results

The results greatly pleased Social Democrats.[20] They won twenty-two new seats in the Reichstag, gaining votes in virtually every region in the Reich. In Prussia the Landtag delegation picked up twenty-three seats. The size of SPD delegations also swelled in Württemberg, Bavaria, Oldenburg, and Anhalt. Various district and regional party organizations that had earlier suffered from demoralization and even disarray, such as Munich, Stuttgart, and Saxony, rebounded internally and recovered their voting bases.[21] Social Democrats eagerly set out to sketch the profile of the new SPD voter. They believed the SPD had cut into the working-class electorate of the bourgeois parties rather than of the KPD, since the Communist vote also increased substantially, though less evenly. Impressive gains in Cologne-Aachen, Düsseldorf, and Munich were judged to have come from disgruntled Catholic workers. The SPD had even managed to pick up votes in certain rural districts.[22] Historical scholarship has largely confirmed the contemporary analyses of the SPD's vote, pointing out that it rested above all on the mobilization of organized workers (who in 1928 voted in higher percentages than other social groups) and, to a much lesser extent, on the SPD's ability to reattract voters from other social groups, such as East Elbian rural laborers, who had voted Socialist in 1919 before turning away in disappointment.[23]

With pleasure, Social Democrats analyzed the defeat of their bourgeois opponents, especially the DNVP's slide from 20.5 percent to 14.2 percent. The bourgeois parties lost not only to the SPD but also to the KPD and right-wing splinter parties. Georg Decker, a Menshevik émigré who wrote for *Die Gesellschaft*, detected a "striking similarity" between the May 1924 and May 1928 elections: the high percentage of votes taken by splinter parties. In May 1924, proletarian voters scattered their votes among a variety of candidates or stayed home. Now, in May 1928, middle-class voters registered displeasure with their traditional parties, particularly the German Nationalists. Decker attributed low voter turnout (74.5 percent compared with 77.7 percent in December 1924) to the "confusion and signs of disintegration" in the bourgeois camp. In his eyes, this disarray made a coalition "relatively harmless" for the SPD. Noting the intense pressure for unity among the bourgeois parties in the aftermath of the elections, Decker did not see such efforts as menacing because the petite bourgeoisie would not submit to the political leadership of "big capital." As long as *Kleinbürger* continued in their "temporary" rejection of the SPD, the republic would rest on a balance of class power.[24] Decker combined insights with a peculiar blindness to the implications of his analysis. He found heartening the very trend that scholars have pinpointed as a sign of a "deepening legitimacy crisis" of the party system—the proliferation of small parties that championed the special economic interests of subsections of the *Mittelstand*.[25] Decker recognized that millions of nonvoters were waiting to be mobilized by some party and even remarked on NSDAP increases in a few pockets of the country. Yet he did not address the problem of how the SPD, from the position of power it enjoyed after the election, might win disheartened citizens. This awareness of political trouble spots mixed with complacence about how the SPD should address these areas came to characterize much Socialist commentary in the months to come.

For Social Democrats, the one real dark spot in the election returns was the rise of the Communist vote. The KPD did especially well in heavily industrialized areas, such as Berlin, the Ruhr, Cologne-Aachen, Düsseldorf, Hamburg, and Saxony. The SPD vote rose only slightly in Leipzig and Dresden and not at all in the Chemnitz-Zwickau-Plauen triangle, in contrast to hefty Communist gains.[26] In Berlin, the KPD's surge also gave grounds for alarm: the SPD received 34 percent of the vote, up from 32.5

percent in December 1924; the KPD, 29.6 percent, up from 19.2 percent. An SPD functionary in Berlin charged that his comrades had made no effort to reach beyond secure circles and, most disturbing, had left campaigning at factory gates to the KPD. Still, analysts found the same silver lining to KPD gains that would later cushion the pain of Nazi electoral progress. The Communists had siphoned working-class votes from the DNVP, the strongest party in the capital in May 1924. Having abandoned their reactionary proclivities, these voters, it was argued, could be easily brought under Social Democratic influence.[27]

Social Democrats also discussed whether, and under what conditions, the SPD should join a coalition. More broadly, debate centered on how the party should exploit its electoral victory to gain maximum influence. Most Socialist newspaper editors agreed with the executive committee that a coalition with bourgeois partners was preferable to opposition or a united front with the KPD.[28] Leftist dailies cautioned against joining a coalition but did not dismiss the idea.[29] They campaigned for preconditions on Social Democratic participation in a coalition, while pointing out that the election results showed the benefits of opposition.[30] When it became clear that the Reichstag delegation would not make entry into a cabinet contingent on concessions, leftist districts and journals came out against participation, arguing that the SPD had a better chance of effecting change from the opposition, where the threat of growing Socialist popularity could be used to wrest concessions from a bourgeois executive.[31] If the party did enter the government, the only way to remain true to its proletarian nature lay in holding to a set of demands to guide its representatives over rough political terrain. Socialist ministers, in the leftists' view, should speak for the party ranks in a very immediate sense. Such a strategy certainly offered one solution to the difficulties faced by Social Democratic ministers in a regime with parties that objected to their social, political, and cultural aims.

Centrists were also not unqualified fans of a coalition. The private correspondence of the editor of *Vorwärts* as well as discussions at the base of the party revealed anxiety about the chances of exacting significant gains for workers and the poor in a coalition with an extremely unfriendly DVP,[32] and, the Hanover *Volkswacht* cautioned, a coalition was only worthwhile if SPD ministers could wrangle concessions for the masses.[33] In contrast to leftists, centrists focused on the control of important ministries by reliable Social Democrats, a strategy followed in Prussia with notable success.[34] This plan assumed that Social Democratic ministers would not only understand what was essential and what was dispensable in Socialist aims, but that they would have the force of character to stand up to stubborn opponents. As a rule, however, the SPD had not chosen its candidates on the basis of such traits. In fact, party leaders greeted independent, self-reliant politicians in their ranks suspiciously.[35]

The personnel paradox arose even before the coalition was formed. The executive committee had to decide who would be the Social Democratic candidate for chancellor. Otto Braun hoped to become chancellor while remaining Prussian minister-president. He did not push his candidacy after he realized that the executive committee, especially Otto Wels, had settled on Hermann Müller as its choice. Müller, cochairman of the SPD since 1919, was popular inside the SPD. Because he spoke several languages, for years he had been seen as the SPD's "foreign minister" and in 1919 he had served as the republic's foreign minister. Though neither a gifted speaker nor a forceful personality, Müller had integrity and a general competence about affairs of state that had earned him the respect of people outside the SPD, including Reich President Paul von Hindenburg.[36] Both the ranks and Socialists in the Prussian administration recognized Braun as the more forceful politician and, after the Müller government fell, wondered wistfully whether the fate of the SPD-led government would have been happier under Braun.[37] Nonetheless, the top leadership did not seriously consider him as its choice for chancellor.

Braun himself only wanted to be chancellor if he could also remain head of the Prussian government. Concentration of power in the hands of one Social Democrat was, however, sure to raise objections from coalition partners, especially the DVP. Braun had worked assiduously to keep the People's Party out of the Prussian cabinet. In exchange for accepting Braun's chancellorship, the DVP would certainly have insisted on entry.[38] In all probability, the Center Party would have demanded the Prussian minister-presidency as its price. Under no conditions did the party leadership want to give up control of Prussia, recognizing the power of Prussian policymakers to guard the republic and, on a more prosaic level, prizing their ability to dispense patronage jobs.[39] Social Democratic decision making on this issue rested on a defensive conception of the SPD's role in the republic. Prussia carried much weight but in the end was dependent on the Reich. From such a bastion, one could only hope to hold what had already been won.

In the national coalition, the SPD assumed a defensive posture of protecting existing measures and ensuring the continuity of the republic, not of further democratizing it. According to Hilferding, the party had to join the government to maintain democracy, stabilize the parliamentary system, and exert influence on foreign policy. Statements by the party council and the Reichstag delegation stressed the SPD's willingness to take responsibility for government affairs.[40] *Responsibility* played a much bigger role in the Social Democratic vocabulary about government than *power*.

In a series of frustrating meetings in June, representatives of the SPD, the BVP, the Center Party, the DDP, and the DVP groped for a common ground on which to form a cabinet. When it proved impossible to form a party-based Great Coalition, Müller and Stresemann worked out a "cabinet of personalities" that included ministers from each of the parties as individuals, not as representatives of their party delegations.[41] Writing during this wearying process, Paul Levi criticized the SPD's method of forming a regime, first for its lack of vision. When the Center Party and the DVP queried, "Where is this government headed?," the reply, "to the republic," was less than enlightening. Second, Levi faulted the timidity that kept the SPD from using the authority conferred by its electoral victory. Levi warned, "If [power] is left lying in the street, any *Hanswurst* can grab it. Let us be warned by Stalin's example: the road to the dissolution of the state leads not only over barricades; the crippling indifference of those who govern can be just as dangerous." After two weeks of tedious negotiations, Levi concluded, the public had lost interest in the fate of the government.[42]

Not only leftists despaired of their leaders' disinclination to exploit their power and project goals. Wilhelm Hoegner, after 1930 an SPD Reichstag deputy from Munich, cited "lack of goals" as the most serious ailment afflicting his party in the 1920s. He recalled the excited comment of a Munich Reichstag delegate about the 1926 campaign against princely compensation: "At last we have a tangible political goal again."[43] Julius Leber, a neorevisionist who also sat in parliament, felt that Müller squandered the initial enthusiasm for his regime by not introducing a "republican-parliamentary period of reform" to douse the "flickering light of feudal conservatism." He blamed this dereliction on "the dead weight of Marxism" as well as on Müller personally and on the Reichstag delegation; yet with the Marxist Levi he agreed that "those first weeks and months prepared the beginning of the end. The malicious word 'Müllerism' was coined then."[44] Levi, Hoegner, and Leber touched on the crux of the Social Democratic dilemma in the Great Coalition. Over the next two years aimlessness and lack of initiative repeatedly tripped up the Social Democratic ministers. These weaknesses also gave rise to the first important crisis of the provisional cabinet.

The Panzerkreuzer Affair

The Müller cabinet's first significant decision unleashed a storm of protest in the SPD more intense than any since the revolution. On August 10, just before adjourning for summer recess, the cabinet decided unanimously to approve funding for the Panzerkreuzer A, the first ship of the pocket battleship program proposed under the Marx government. General Wilhelm Groener, the minister of defense, pushed hard to have this thorny issue tackled by the shaky cabinet at an early date. Fearful that the coalition would founder on this stumbling block and convinced that the current budget had enough surplus to allow this expenditure, the four Social Democratic ministers succumbed to his pressure. Müller and Severing, the Social Democratic minister of the interior, balked only briefly before approving the funds for the first ship.[45] Thus, on the eve of Germany's Constitution Day, which only Social Democrats celebrated with enthusiasm, and while leading Socialists were attending a peace conference of the Socialist International in Brussels, the cabinet cleared the way for the production of this controversial cruiser. The timing was not felicitous.

The overwhelming majority of Social Democrats, including Otto Braun, strongly objected to the four battleships projected by the Panzerkreuzer program.[46] They associated any naval expansion with Admiral Alfred von Tirpitz's prewar imperialistic *Flottenpolitik*.[47] They also considered it financially wasteful, preferring butter to guns on principle and convinced of the futility of these particular ships for national defense.[48] As a result, the Panzerkreuzer program had stirred up political dust in the last weeks of the Marx regime. After a Reichstag majority voted to include it in the annual budget, Otto Braun convinced several states to join Prussia in a maneuver to quash it in the Reichsrat. By raising an objection to the budget, the Reichsrat returned it to the Reichstag, where a two-thirds majority was required for approval. Since the budget needed to be passed quickly, a compromise was reached whereby the construction of the Panzerkreuzer could not begin until the budget situation was reviewed in the fall.[49] Subsequently, Social Democracy had made the Panzerkreuzer the focus of its campaign. As policymakers and politicians, Social Democrats had taken a stand against a naval buildup.

Contemporaries were struck by the fact that in the August controversy, Social Democrats across the spectrum of party opinion reacted angrily to the decision of Ministers Müller, Hilferding, Rudolf Wissell, and Severing to approve the Panzerkreuzer. The hostile response of the left-wing party press came swiftly, a magnified version of what became its stock response to decisions made by the cabinet. In contrast, the initial stance of many centrist and right-wing SPD papers was cautiously negative; a few editors even defended the decision. The "tumult among factory workers" provoked by the decision, however, quickly propelled the provincial press to register disapproval. Not only the rank and file was upset. State legislators, city councilors, and district secretaries generated much of the heat in the "Panzerkreuzer scandal."[50]

District and local organizations all over Germany convened special meetings that condemned the ministers' decision. In Württemberg, Kurt Schumacher, just then emerging as a figure with popular appeal, assailed the decision in meetings all over the state.[51] Resolutions demanding that the ministers resign poured out of Saxony, Braunschweig, Aachen, Berlin, and various small localities. In Dresden, the moderate leftist Siegfried Aufhäuser suggested that a party assembly dispatch a protest to Berlin, but he was successfully countered by the Young Socialist Walter Fabian, who presented a resolution demanding the SPD leave the coalition, hold a special congress, and organize a referendum against the Panzerkreuzer program.[52] Police observers reported membership meetings as "extraordinarily well attended." In Munich, Severing had to defend himself before a crowd of eight hundred people whose very vocal irritation prompted local leaders to close debate prematurely.[53] For all the excitement, most districts did not call for the Social Democratic ministers to leave the government, a trend *Vorwärts* noted with relief.[54] Speakers such as Wilhelm Sollmann in Cologne and Schumacher in Stuttgart, unabashed supporters of coalition, formulated resolutions that condemned the decision but not the coalition. After the Reichstag delegation and the party council formally expressed their regret over the decision, most provincial resolutions simply endorsed this statement. When the KPD began a campaign for a referendum on armaments, centrist SPD papers criticized internal demands of the same ilk.[55]

Moderates felt that the decision violated an important Social Democratic principle. Both Paul Levi and Julius Leber remarked that antimilitarism (despite August 1914) was one of the few sacred traditions of the German working class, especially when militarism took the form of "fleet imperialism."[56] Of course, the exigencies of realpolitik had caused many principles to be violated over the years without provoking such vehement disgust. In this case, however, antimilitarism had found expression as a specific political slogan in a campaign only lately ended. It had fired up the ranks and helped win the SPD greater electoral support than it had enjoyed since the first years of the republic. It was one thing to compromise, another to break campaign promises.[57] The outrage indicated a widespread belief in the strict accountability of representatives, indicative of attachment to direct democracy. According to Julius Leber, a "middling functionary" on the party council chided Müller for not heeding the "people's will." Müller retorted that he was a minister, not a "mail carrier." Rank and file Social Democrats endorsed the functionary's argument rather than Müller's rejoinder.[58]

Right wingers as well as leftists feared that this decision indicated Müller's inability to steer a course free of domination by his bourgeois partners. Otto Braun saw it as a blatant disavowal of his efforts in the Reichsrat in the spring and one that embarrassed him in front of other state governments.[59] Albert Grzesinski confided to Braun that he feared Müller lacked the strength of character to stand up to the military experts. Wilhelm Sollmann, editor of the *Rheinische Zeitung*, publicly questioned the justification of the Panzerkreuzer decision as necessary to keep the Center Party from bolting the coalition.[60] Kurt Schumacher urged the SPD to display not just responsibility but its "will to power," admonishing, "Social Democracy, get tough!"[61] Hugo Sinzheimer, another neorevisionist, feared that the Panzerkreuzer affair revealed Social Democrats' lack of appreciation of the importance of "personal political will" in a parliamentary democracy.[62]

The ministers did not effectively defend themselves inside the SPD and so compounded the damage caused by the original decision. They met jointly with the party council and Reichstag and Prussian Landtag delegations on August 18.[63] Braun, though sympathetic to the outrage in the party, feared such a meeting would fan the flames of discontent.[64] It occurred nonetheless and was a rancorous gathering indeed. The lack of trust between the Reichstag delegation and its own ministers shocked Toni Jensen, a Prussian Landtag deputy. She found Rudolf Breitscheid, cochairman of the Reichstag delegation, "unpleasantly demagogic." Müller and Hilferding sat "totally passive" under the barrage of criticism. Only Severing justified himself in a "lively" manner.[65]

Otto Wels, in the hospital in August, did not help draft the council's reprimand of the Socialist ministers, but upon his return to Berlin he accepted its wording. In November, when the issue arose in the Reichstag, he presented a Social Democratic motion against the Panzerkreuzer with a stridently antimilitaristic speech that incensed the SPD's coalition partners.[66] A majority of the Reichstag rejected the motion. Müller, Hilferding, Wissell, and Severing voted for it, maintaining party discipline and contradicting their earlier decision as cabinet members.[67] Arnold Brecht, who as Braun's ministerial director had devised Prussia's preelection disposal of Panzerkreuzer A, wrote later that the Social Democratic motion made sense only if party authorities wanted to leave the coalition. Since they did not, it was a "major mistake . . . to push the matter to the limit and thus deal a blow to the authority of the Social Democratic chancellor at the very beginning of his government."[68]

The denouement of the Panzerkreuzer drama highlights certain persistent conflicts between Social Democratic ministers and the Reichstag delegation. Concomitant with the popular belief in the direct ties between the ranks and Social Democratic ministers was the conviction that they must remain in constant and close communication with the Reichstag delegation, the body directly accountable to voters. Not only leftists, but leaders such as Rudolf Breitscheid and districts such as Hamburg and Dortmund complained that the ministers did not consult with the delegation before voting on the Panzerkreuzer.[69] Once the uproar began, the delegation asserted its latent power. In collusion with the party council, the delegation demanded closer cooperation between the ministers and "central party bodies."[70] In November the deputies succeeded in forcing the ministers to participate in a humiliating parliamentary vote that damaged the authority of the SPD government. The Panzerkreuzer affair provides a caution against a simplistic analysis of the bureaucratization of the SPD that assumes that the executive committee, and ministers who sat on it, dictatorially controlled policymaking.

Contemporaries, including Social Democrats, lamented the domination of party caucuses, and not only Social Democratic caucuses, over cabinet members from their ranks.[71] Some Social Democrats, however, claimed that their case was special: their ministers were leaders of a great movement and were representatives of the idea of socialism, so the tradition of ministerial deference to the parliamentarians had a unique legitimacy.[72] SPD ministers found highly irritating the delegation's presentation of itself as the fount of socialist wisdom. Hilferding, SPD finance minister, complained about this to Gustav Noske (who, as the much-hated SPD defense minister of 1919, knew what it meant to cross swords with the party). Hilferding found it almost "unbearable" to have the delegation constantly on his back. Because Hilferding and Müller could no longer exert direct influence, the delegation floundered in "complete confusion . . . without leadership or direction."[73] Yet neither Hilferding nor Müller acted to gain control over party deputies or to steer the cabinet in such a way as to win their trust. Instead, the tug-of-war between ministers and Reichstag members, influenced by party opinion, flared intermittently until the final cabinet crisis of the Great Coalition in March 1930.

Even while the Panzerkreuzer controversy raged, various Social Democrats recognized that it could have the salutary effect of democratizing the SPD. While revealing the inadequacy of democratic practice inside the SPD, it had awakened broad critical forces that had slumbered too long, they said. From the crisis could emerge a party that encouraged debate and discussion in its press and meetings.[74] One right-wing Socialist warned against returning to the "graveyard peace and quiet" that had reigned before May 20. Others saw a chance to break out of the endless cycle of fruitless coalition/anticoalition debates and have discussions about, as Carlo Mierendorff put it, politics and tactics.[75] For its part, the executive committee announced that the crisis revealed the need to discuss the party's defense policy and to choose new defense guidelines at the next congress in June 1929.[76] It did not engage the organization in a debate about the appropriate strategy and tactics in a coalition with bourgeois parties, so the SPD drifted without a conception of its role in the government. Not surprisingly, leftists criticized the leadership's sudden insistence on the need for a new defense policy as a maneuver to replace a discussion of the coalition's failures with an exchange about general principles. Less expectedly, young neorevisionists agreed that a rehashed military policy would not solve the problems which led to the Panzerkreuzer mess. Mierendorff found it an "illusion" to think a correct defense program would guard against tactical mistakes or get the party out of the "dead end of August 10."[77] Schumacher spoke in the same vein at the Magdeburg party congress in 1929. Also at Magdeburg, Theo Haubach regretted that the same mistake was being made in the defense discussion as in the continuing dialogue about coalition policy: the party disputed the foundations of its policies instead of the policies themselves.[78]

Tedious replays of debates on principles arose from the mutual suspicion with which the leadership and the Left Opposition regarded each other. The Left insisted on raising the coalition issue, but the leadership directed discussion into the well-worn groove of "defense policy in the republic." Wels, Hilferding, Müller, and other leaders ignored criticisms of how the coalition functioned, fearful that any debate about specific policies would quickly become one about whether the party should participate in a government with bourgeois partners. Insecure themselves about the coalition policy, they assumed a shallow reservoir of support for it in the party's ranks. They might have been correct in general, but in this debate and during the months to come, many critics were Social Democrats who did not question the policy but its execution.[79] Rightists such as Leber and Schumacher shared with leftists such as Levi the suspicion that SPD leaders did not know how to wield political power.

During the Panzerkreuzer affair there emerged a group of nonleftist critics of the leadership who would play an important role in the struggle against Nazism. This episode also sounded the depths of the reservoir of political idealism inside the SPD. The outcry indicated a yearning for goals broader than *Sozialpolitik* but more concrete than socialism, for which the SPD would stand firm. The incident and its consequences revealed that the Social Democratic ministers neither dominated the coalition nor controlled their own delegation. Already in 1928 we see the SPD's difficulty in fashioning for itself a role in the Great Coalition commensurate with its increased parliamentary strength and robust extra-parliamentary organization.

The Controversy over Unemployment Insurance

No subsequent action of the Socialist ministers stirred up the party as had the Panzerkreuzer decision, but in the ensuing months SPD dissatisfaction with the coalition government intensified as the regime's difficulties in tackling major issues accelerated. Over the next eighteen months the cabinet's energy was invested in negotiations to alter the reparations schedule set up by the Dawes Plan and in attempts to place Germany's internal finances on a stable basis—interconnected preoccupations because a significant decrease in reparations or a favorable payment plan would have given the government more money to spend on domestic programs and eased its revenue difficulties. Unfortunately, the deteriorating economy made both problems less tractable.

The Great Coalition eventually foundered on the financial quandary. In particular, disagreements about how to reform the unemployment insurance system occasioned big battles inside the coalition: how should the contributions of employers and employees be calibrated? should benefits be reduced? The SPD and the Free Trade Unions fastened onto this component of *Sozialpolitik* as the key to the maintenance of the Weimar system. In the end, the SPD Reichstag delegation voted against a compromise on the issue, thus bringing down the SPD-led government. Ever since the coalition's demise, scholars have argued about where to place the blame, criticizing either the SPD for giving up power over a "second rate issue" or reproving the uncompromising position of the DVP, which, like President Hindenburg, was eager to force the SPD out of the government.[80] I would agree with those who argue that the greater moral responsibility lies with the DVP and industrial circles for whom the attack on unemployment insurance funding was the opening foray in a war against Weimar's social programs. The SPD made a grave tactical mistake, however, in bringing down the coalition when it did and in abdicating power over this issue.[81] Many who hold the SPD culpable have impugned its parliamentary leaders for succumbing to the pressure of Free Trade unionists in the Reichstag delegation. As will be seen, by the spring of 1930 pressure emanated just as forcefully from the lower levels of the party itself.[82]

As the Panzerkreuzer furor subsided, so did criticism of the Great Coalition. Even in Saxony vociferous attacks on the coalition abated until Severing's compromise arbitration settlement of the Ruhr "Iron Conflict" in December 1928 elicited another volley of invective.[83] Outside Saxony, public disparagement of the coalition and discontent with leadership policies resurfaced in late May 1929. The *Hessischer Volksfreund* editorialized against continued participation in the regime and for a return to a "working-class point of view."[84] At the SPD congress in Magdeburg in June, growing discontent became evident to all observers. Thirty percent of the delegates rejected the executive's proposal to table motions critical of the coalition, the defense budget, or the Panzerkreuzer decision. Thirty-seven percent voted against the defense policy guidelines approved by the executive committee, and 42 percent supported an effort to return these to committee for revision. At Kiel in 1927, 24.5 percent of delegates had opposed a resolution that supported the principle of coalition, while two years later 30 percent recorded their displeasure with an actual coalition. Besides the usual centers of opposition in Saxony, Thuringia, Berlin, and Breslau, diverse districts in Pomerania, Hesse-Darmstadt, the Rhine-Ruhr area, and Baden voiced discontent. Düsseldorf, Hamburg, Stuttgart, and Frankfurt registered more than one vote of dissatisfaction.[85]

Majority speakers at the congress presented a rather tepid defense of the coalition. Hans Vogel, Breitscheid, Stampfer, Sollmann, and Müller all argued for remaining in the cabinet but conceded the paucity of its accomplishments. Sollmann and Stampfer admitted that few party members enthusiastically endorsed the coalition, while Vogel defended it as a "lesser evil." Stampfer insisted that once the reparations issue was cleared, the party would fight for "a farsighted financial policy with a social viewpoint." Oddly, the Left Opposition also toned down its message, not attacking the principle of coalition but asserting that this alliance should be abandoned because it had not yielded gains for the working class.[86]

The executive committee accepted a truncated version of a resolution submitted by Toni Sender and Siegfried Aufhäuser that listed demands to guide the ministers in their decision making. Besides statements against tax cuts and for an eight-hour day and regulation of cartels, it called for the stabilization of the unemployment compensation system.[87] Concern about this issue had bubbled up a month earlier, when the DVP made clear its determination to reform unemployment insurance funding in favor of employers.[88] In early May, Hilferding remarked sarcastically to Noske that many in the SPD deputation "would allow, if not the party, then at least democracy and the republic to go to the devil over the issue of thirty pennies more or less to the unemployed."[89] Along the same lines, at Magdeburg, Müller chided a leftist for claiming that the SPD was beholden only to the working class and not to the state; yet Müller and Hilferding sat back at the congress while top party leaders proposed making unemployment compensation the proof stone of the SPD's performance in the regime. Otto Wels told cheering congressional delegates, "No doubt can exist. The SPD will not be budged on unemployment insurance." Breitscheid averred that the unemployment fund would provide a better "basis for struggle" in the cabinet than did the Panzerkreuzer program. Stampfer reassured his comrades that should there be a showdown on this issue, "There can be no doubt about our decision. We would have to act according to the principle: the party and the government are two, but the party and trade unions are one." This avowal of solidarity in the ranks of Social Democracy brought the audience to its feet.[90] Thus, party leaders began the process of directing onto one issue the frustration of Social Democrats over the scarcity of accomplishments and scant popular resonance of their government.

Wels's assurance came as a great relief to ADGB officials for whom the DVP's fight against unemployment insurance represented "the struggle of the reactionaries against all *Sozialpolitik.*" Theodor Thomas, chairman of the roofers' union, interpreted Wels's words to mean that rather than accept reform of the unemployment insurance system, the SPD would leave the regime. His colleagues on the ADGB council vehemently agreed that resignation would be mandatory if the bourgeois parties insisted on reform.[91] Unionists were all the more encouraged by Wels's avowal because in recent months the regime had snubbed them. In May 1928, the ADGB had been as pleased as the SPD by the election results and looked forward to an era of close cooperation between an SPD-led regime and the social representatives of the working class. Theodor Leipart, ADGB chairman, deliberated with top Social Democrats about the SPD's conditions for participation in a coalition.[92] Six months later, union officials swallowed their disappointment over the terms of Severing's settlement of the Ruhr iron lockout. In the spring of 1929 they became alarmed by reports in the bourgeois press that during negotiations to build a genuine Great Coalition (as opposed to a cabinet of personalities), Social Democrats had agreed to cuts in social spending. In a tight-lipped communication to the Reichstag delegation, the ADGB executive committee asked the delegation not to discuss such matters without consulting the ADGB first.[93] At Magdeburg, Wels, Breitscheid, and Stampfer in effect promised to do just that.

As the economy deteriorated and the government's financial straits tightened in the summer of 1929, an acute crisis over funding the unemployment compensation system erupted, and union anxiety resurged.[94] Theodor Thomas warned Wels that if the SPD made concessions on this issue, "a mass flight of members from the party" was to be expected.[95] Taking the hint, Wels wrote Müller that this issue was a "vital question" for the party.[96] Müller, meanwhile, urged *Vorwärts'* editor Friedrich Stampfer not to offer public advice on how to solve the crisis because such interference riled relations in the cabinet.[97] In the end, the impasse among the regime parties was broken only when Foreign Minister Stresemann used virtually his last words to convince the DVP deputation to accept a compromise that temporarily shored up the program.[98]

As did many Social Democrats, union officials felt that a compromise on unemployment compensation would be the "straw that breaks the camel's back" because "coalition policy has produced so little that is positive" for workers.[99] The actions, and the inaction, of Finance Minister Hilferding drew the most fire. Breitscheid and Stampfer criticized him mildly at Magdeburg for how he handled budget deliberations that ended in cuts in expenditures and for approving a "tax-free loan" that released German industry and banks from taxes on earnings lent to the government. During the summer and fall, disapproval centered on his failure to present a plan to reform government finances.[100] The fragile settlement of unemployment insurance funding in September highlighted the need for Hilferding to tackle the budget problem and work out a stable basis for the fund. Instead, he allowed the fund to be burdened by greater claims without developing new cash sources to cover them.[101] Clearly, Hilferding did not relish grasping the prickly pear of finance reform. Marxist or not, he inclined to the classical economic solutions called for by German capitalists, including reductions in government expenditures and in burdens on business rather than increases in taxes.[102]

Hilferding's procrastination rankled all the more because under his urging Social Democratic ministers had shelved plans to expand social programs. This decision reflected concern over the financial health of the government but also fear that the coalition would crumble if social issues came to the fore. Ministerial inaction was in part conditioned by the SPD's lack of a comprehensive macroeconomic policy, a hole filled by neither "economic democracy" nor specific measures to extend public ownership.

Without such a policy, Social Democrats could only react defensively to the economic plans of employer organizations and the bourgeois parties.[103] For example, only after the RDI, as well as the DDP, published plans to cut direct taxes as a stimulant to business activity did the SPD delegation, frustrated by Hilferding's dawdling, present a finance package that proposed luxury taxes and reductions in the defense budget.[104] In agrarian policy, SPD ministers, breaking a long and revered tradition, caved in to pressure for higher tariffs as a way to bail out Germany's ailing agriculture, although these measures benefited large landowners and even hurt some small farmers.[105]

Encouraged by evidence of industrialists' disgust with the regime's drifting, Hjalmar Schacht, president of the Reichsbank, decided to join in the fray. On December 6 he dropped a political bombshell by publicly criticizing the government for not having balanced the budget. He demanded that no new outlays be approved and that national, state, and municipal budgets be put in order before adoption of the Young Plan.[106] Under this humiliating pressure, Hilferding had to produce a finance plan quickly. Three days later, he presented a proposal that the cabinet, in a fit of corporate solidarity, approved unanimously. The Reichstag delegations of the DVP and the SPD, less obliging than their ministerial counterparts, attacked this plan.[107] SPD deputies were upset by proposed income tax cuts balanced by higher (regressive) beer and tobacco taxes. They argued that these measures canceled the value of proposed increases in employer contributions to the unemployment fund. Initially, the delegation rejected the plan as unanimously as the cabinet had accepted it. The Free Trade Unions also spoke out against it.[108] Nonetheless, the government maintained its newfound unity. On December 12, after a forceful speech on the need for cooperation and compromise in the financial predicament, Müller called for a confidence vote. Center Party leaders worked out a formula for a confidence motion acceptable to all the delegation leaders of the regime parties.[109] The full SPD delegation approved the motion only after a stormy debate in which leftists insisted that acceptance implied endorsement of the finance program, while others argued that it merely registered support for the cabinet. In the Reichstag, twenty-eight Social Democrats abstained on the vote, thus registering their disapproval without violating party discipline.[110]

Just as the regime completed this painful defensive maneuver, Schacht fired a new salvo. When asked by an American bank if the Reichsbank would back a projected loan to the German government, he replied that he could not do so without an overhaul of the entire financial system, which, he regretted to say, was in even greater disorder than he had suspected. Picking up on this cue, the DVP clamored for Hilferding's resignation.[111] Although the Center Party and the DDP asked only for the resignation of his undersecretary, Johannes Popitz (who had devised the finance plan), Hilferding refused to desert Popitz, and on December 20 they both resigned. Müller, supported by Interior Minister Severing, decided to let them go rather than brave a possible no-confidence vote.[112]

By the end of 1929 the Social Democratic delegation simmered in anger over the government's domestic program. Smoldering mistrust of their ministers' ability to represent Social Democratic interests, which flared in the aftermath of the Panzerkreuzer decision, had been re-kindled. Although furious with Schacht, Wilhelm Keil conceded, "Our opponents have every right to exploit our weaknesses."[113] Müller recog-nized the failure of his government to provide leadership and feared the public did as well. During a delegation meeting in which many challenged Hilferding's resignation, Müller warned that if new elections were called, the SPD might lose fifty Reichstag seats.[114]

Certainly among rank and file Socialists these events fed coalition wea-riness and intensified nervousness about the future of the unemployment compensation fund. In early 1930, employer associations returned to the offensive on this issue. In response, Social Democratic preoccupation with the fate of the fund became obsessive, accompanied by growing accep-tance of the inevitable and imminent demise of the coalition. The *Klassen-kampf* circle called outright for the SPD to pull out.[115] Moderate leftists such as Aufhäuser and centrists such as Decker also questioned the value of putting up with "coalition cramps," especially on the unemployment insurance issue.[116] The *Hamburger Echo*, a procoalition organ, pointed out the pivotal importance of the unemployment fund to finance reform and emphasized that the limits of SPD patience lay there. Karl Meitmann, Hamburg's recently elected neorevisionist chairman, had to defend the coalition against a spirited verbal assault from the ranks at his district's annual citywide meeting. In Frankfurt, the annual conference narrowly rejected a left-wing Reichstag delegate's motion to leave the coalition. Speakers at district congresses in Cologne and Düsseldorf also denounced the coalition.[117] At trade union meetings, ADGB functionaries had to field ceaseless complaints about the SPD's role in the regime. Evidently unaware of the cantankerous mood inside the SPD, they charged that insulated party leaders did not appreciate the position of unionists who had to pacify disgruntled workers and parry Communist attacks.[118] They saw themselves as shock troops forced to rescue a beleaguered army from the tactical mistakes of incompetent generals.

Already frazzled by difficult budget negotiations, the cabinet reached yet another impasse over the unemployment compensation issue in early March 1930 when the DVP delegation rejected a compromise proposal, devised by its own finance minister, Paul Moldenhauer, for funding the insurance agency. Under the terms of Moldenhauer's plan, the agency could have raised the premiums paid by workers and employers up to 4 percent. Only several weeks later did Heinrich Brüning, the Center Party delegation leader, come up with an alternative: premiums would remain the same and the government would loan the fund up to 150 million marks. If the insurance agency continued to take in less than it paid out, the government could then either propose means for further savings, raise premiums up to 3.75 percent, or balance the insurance agency's budget—a polite way of saying benefits would be reduced. Except for Rudolf Wissell, the Socialist labor minister, who suspected a ploy to postpone cuts until later in the year, cabinet members accepted Brüning's proposal. Wissell's opposition threw the decision back to party delegations.[119]

Before the impasse became a deadlock, Carl Severing suggested at a cabinet meeting on March 3 that Müller ask Hindenburg for an order to dissolve the Reichstag. Backed by the president, the chancellor could then use Article 48 to pass decrees during the subsequent Reichstag campaign. Müller personally opposed this solution and doubted that Hindenburg would sanction it.[120] Meanwhile, Hindenburg was surrounded by individuals and groups outside the cabinet who pressed not for the dissolution of the Reichstag but for an end to the Müller cabinet.[121] East Elbian landowners, the right wing of the DVP, influential employers' circles, and General Kurt von Schleicher intrigued against the regime and schemed about Müller's replacement. Hindenburg settled on Heinrich Brüning as his choice. Neither Hindenburg nor his kibitzers had the power to topple the government, but their maneuvers gave resolve to hard-liners in the DVP delegation and made Brüning less willing to resist DVP demands.[122]

On March 26 and 27, in deliberations with other delegation leaders of the coalition parties, the SPD's representatives rejected the compromise.[123] Later on the twenty-seventh, the entire SPD delegation met to consider the agreement. Wissell strongly advised against acceptance. Chancellor Müller "made members aware of the consequences of rejecting the deal." Hermann Müller-Lichtenberg, a trade union leader, gave an impassioned speech against the proposal that, he claimed, amounted to a cutback in unemployment benefits because it assumed retrenchment in the fall. According to Stampfer, Müller-Lichtenberg "dictatorially" threatened trade union hostility to the government in and outside parliament if the party agreed to the compromise.[124] Otto Wels moved to adhere to Moldenhauer's proposal of March 5; all except five deputies approved this motion as the SPD's counteroffer, although it had already been rejected by the DVP.[125] At this point, "silent and serious," the chancellor left the room.[126]

All fifty-seven trade unionists in the delegation rejected the Brüning compromise. Though many of them normally stood on the delegation's right wing, in this case they formed a solid block with the roughly twenty-five delegation members who identified themselves with the Left Opposition. Not only this alliance but the vote's near unanimity is striking.[127] Müller-Lichtenberg's forceful defense of working-class interests no doubt influenced the vote of hesitant delegation members, but the Social Democratic focus on the insurance fund in the months preceding this session set the stage for this drama. Julius Leber recalled that no discussion of the wider political consequences of Müller's fall took place at the meeting. According to Max Seydewitz, the chancellor did predict that a crisis of state would ensue, but evidently the implications of such a development were not explored.[128] A month later, Paul Bergmann, a moderately left-wing Reichstag representative from Hamburg, told comrades there (who were distressed by the outcome) that the delegation had not intended to topple the government.[129] It seems that deputies believed the decision would be thrown into the Reichstag, where the government would have fallen in an open fight.[130] They wanted the SPD out of the government but did not want the onus of having caused its downfall. Indeed, the liberal press criticized the SPD for bringing down Müller.[131]

In Saxony, SPD editors and functionaries were ecstatic about the vote. Social Democratic papers in Düsseldorf, Breslau, Darmstadt, and Frankfurt also hailed the coalition's demise. Berlin's regional conference passed a resolution approving the delegation's vote. Contributors to *Das Freie Wort*, an internal party organ, also praised the decision.[132] Given the mood in Social Democracy in early 1930, expressions of pride at Socialist "toughness" were to be expected. More surprising were signs of opposition to the vote. In an unusual move, the Prussian Landtag delegation voted to condemn the decision.[133] Regionally prominent Social Democrats such as Karl Meitmann, Wilhelm Hoegner, and Julius Leber felt a serious mistake had been made.[134] Otto Braun blamed trade unionists less than SPD leaders, especially Wels, for failing to comprehend the consequences of the government's fall.[135] Hilferding warned that "one should not commit suicide due to fear of death," implying that the SPD had cut its political jugular because of anxiety over losing popular support.[136]

The *Hamburger Echo* chastised the delegation for bringing down the regime when it knew the "bourgeoisie is itching to use Article 48." In the *Echo*'s view, the initial mistake lay in passing the Young Plan (for which

the DVP needed SPD support) without having first negotiated the budget; second, Müller had allowed the parties' delegations to determine
policy; third, the SPD delegation forgot that the "survival of democracy is
more important than the economic, financial, or social policy of a government."[137] Not just in Hamburg, but around the country, Reichstag delegates encountered surprisingly little enthusiasm for their vote.[138] Deroga-
tory letters to Das Freie Wort competed with laudatory missives. One
functionary pointed out that in the coalition the party had only debated
whether it should get out; "Now out, the question discussed is: should we
take part again?" Without a national economic program and a "positive
plan for government," the writer found the debate idle.[139]

In retrospect, several factors emerge as determinant of the SPD delegation vote on March 27. The widespread belief that the fate of unemployment compensation symbolized that of Sozialpolitik combined with disgust
over the paucity of new gains for the working class to spread coalition
blues far beyond the ranks of the Left Opposition. Trade union anxiety
did not create this mood, though, to be sure, the shift to an anticoalition
position by reformist union leaders was especially significant. The memory of the Panzerkreuzer disaster certainly weighed on party leaders, who
feared a replay of that furor, and alerted critics to a pattern in the timidity
of Social Democratic ministers. Finally, inadequate understanding of the
extent and nature of the republic's burgeoning political crisis contributed
to a certain nonchalance about the fate of the regime. As will be seen in
the next chapter, by early 1930, Social Democratic concern about the
growth of radical antirepublicanism was on the rise. In the conflict over
unemployment compensation, however, social, not political, considerations determined the attitudes and behavior of SPD deputies.

Opposition, March–August 1930

Initially, the SPD adopted a sharp oppositional stance toward the
Brüning cabinet with its several decidedly conservative ministers. On
April 1 the SPD presented a no-confidence motion in reaction to Agricultural Minister Martin Schiele's proposed eastern aid package, which favored East Prussian estate owners at the expense of small rural producers
in other parts of the country. Brüning's barely veiled threat to enact his
economic plan against a Reichstag majority also alarmed the delegation.
Breitscheid declared that the SPD did not shrink before new elections and
cautioned Brüning against relying on Article 48. Throughout April, the
SPD voted against specific economic proposals of the government and
against Brüning's request for plenary financial powers.[140] The combative

public posture reflected the genuine relief of many SPD leaders at being freed of responsibility for unpopular economic measures; yet this opposition was in reality shot through with an ambivalence revealed in small but telling gestures. Breitscheid met with Brüning on the day before his cabinet convened. Both evidently spoke as if a return to a Great Coalition was the best way to solve the problems of governing the country. Breitscheid's sincerity in this conversation is less to be doubted than Brüning's. Even as it blasted Schiele's agrarian program, *Vorwärts* distinguished between "reactionary elements" and moderates in the cabinet who realized that no majority government could be formed without SPD participation.[141] Braun restrained Social Democratic representatives in the Prussian Landtag from overly vociferous attacks on the national government. Karl Höltermann, second in command of the Reichsbanner, stressed that the republican defense organization stood above party concerns and refused to pass judgment on the government.[142]

More significant, and certainly more surprising, than the SPD's overtures to Brüning was the desire to "decontaminate the atmosphere" on the part of the RDI, the powerful employers' association whose insistence on cuts in social spending had stiffened DVP intransigence in the conflict over unemployment compensation.[143] ADGB leaders agreed to meet with RDI representatives to hammer out a joint worker-employer declaration on economic and social policy. Meetings in May produced the basis for a statement, but the agreement fell apart at the last minute. Scholars disagree about the motivation behind the RDI's initiative. Udo Wengst has argued that industrialists, backed by Brüning, hoped to circumvent the SPD and work directly with trade unionists who seemed "relatively reasonable." Reinhard Neebe, on the other hand, has contended that moderate industrialists wanted to recreate the Great Coalition, if only to "burden [the SPD] with responsibility for things that must come." In this, the RDI diverged from the anti-SPD stance of President Hindenburg and Brüning.[144] Even if the urge for political cooperation did not play a role, these negotiations were of political and social significance. Because the Weimar republic rested on the social collaboration of big capital with organized labor, efforts to overcome growing alienation between employers and workers were crucial to the stability of the state. The talks revealed that in these early months of the depression and rising unemployment the ADGB and RDI were part of a "deflationary consensus" that saw decreases in wages, prices, and government expenditures as necessary to economic recovery. Consensus broke down over the practical, and important, question of whether wage or price cuts must come first.[145]

For their part, Social Democrats signaled readiness to deal directly with

Brüning, but he did not respond to their tentative advances. In late June, the SPD delegation published a set of "guidelines for overcoming unemployment," accompanied by the explanation that the SPD wanted to offer positive suggestions, not just negative criticisms of the government's program. The guidelines showed what the SPD would do "if it were in the government today or could decisively influence it."[146] Not the least bit radical, these policies called for modest public works measures, a lower discount rate, ratification of the Geneva treaty on customs policy, and reduction of military spending. An appended statement maintained that the way to fight unemployment was to increase mass buying power. The moderation of these guidelines was motivated by the delegation's desire to rebuild bridges to the bourgeois middle.[147] Wilhelm Keil, their author, hoped, above all, that Finance Minister Hermann Dietrich would drop his "poll tax" (an emergency flat-rate assessment on all taxpayers) in favor of a progressive special tax.[148]

As a parliamentary deadlock developed over Dietrich's finance program, the SPD delegation repeatedly displayed willingness to compromise. On July 1, Social Democrats abstained in votes on no-confidence motions presented by the KPD and DNVP. Keil practically pleaded with the regime to withdraw the poll tax, making it clear that the SPD would accept the rest of Dietrich's plan.[149] Breitscheid apprised Center Party deputy Thomas Esser of SPD willingness to strike a deal, but his note to the Catholic politician went unanswered. Nonetheless, the SPD abstained in the vote on the finance bill's first article. When the section with a special tax on civil servants' salaries was presented, however, the Social Democratic delegation voted against it, and the measure failed. Breitscheid defended this vote, explaining that the SPD had made clear its readiness to negotiate.[150] Given this background, it is clear that Brüning and Hindenburg bore greater responsibility than the SPD for the deadlock that gave Brüning an excuse to use Article 48 to implement the finance program on an emergency basis.[151] This step in turn provoked the SPD to respond with a motion for the Reichstag to nullify these decrees. Otto Landsberg, the delegation's legal expert, argued against the constitutionality of using Article 48 under conditions in which neither public order nor peace was endangered. When the SPD motion passed with the support of Nationalists loyal to Hugenberg, Brüning dissolved the Reichstag and a week later enacted the financial decrees under presidential authority.[152]

The circumstances of the SPD's Reichstag vote in July were very different from the delegation vote in March. This time the SPD stood firm in an open parliamentary fight and on an issue involving constitutional principles. While the March vote smacked of narrow, interest-group contrariness, the July vote was a stand for the general political welfare. Unlike in March, the party had shown itself willing to compromise on specific economic issues but resisted when Brüning refused to budge and tried to implement his financial package behind parliament's back. Beneath these differences, however, lay an ongoing lack of strategy that reflected the SPD's deeper puzzlement about how to proceed. Once again, backed into a corner, it used its power as the largest parliamentary block and had a decisive impact on the course of German political affairs; but again, it used its power in a negative manner. Rather than formulate and fight for a new policy, the SPD temporarily prevented others from implementing their plans. To a public that craved action on pressing economic issues, it only displayed its inability to develop and maintain a positive political strategy. Both issues lacked broad popular resonance—a social program that did not attack unemployment but protected some of the unemployed from its most serious consequences, and a political principle that defended the rights and prerogatives of a parliament that increasing numbers of Germans saw as ineffective and even obstructive.

Years later, Friedrich Stampfer cited the lack of an economic program as central to Social Democratic failure to win more popular support. Here, he wrote, the party lacked the self-confidence it had about "constitutional, social, and foreign policies." Julius Leber, ruminating in a Nazi prison cell in 1933, faulted instead the lack of a bold program for democratization.[153] Either an economic program or a plan for democratization would have bolstered the party and the republic. Instead, the SPD tended to swing between a much-criticized interest group mentality and a less-noted loyalty to abstract democratic principles. Blindness to the urgent need of a positive reform program was in part due to failure to recognize either the seriousness of the economic crisis or the peculiar features of the political dilemma.

Where Stands the Enemy?

In its middle years the Weimar republic enjoyed a respite from strident, violent antirepublicanism, and republicans worried less about the stability of parliamentary democracy. By early 1929, the rancor of parliamentary wrangling and the resurgence of antirepublican groups had again brought the phrase "crisis of parliamentarism" to the lips of sympathetic commentators on the republic's condition. Social Democrats were late to join this chorus, preoccupied as they were with the problems of the Great Coalition as well as sensitive to the talk about a crisis, which seemed to impugn the competence of the SPD-led regime. Signs of heightened Social Democratic concern about the state of the republic appeared only in late 1929. Even then, despite Nazi gains in regional elections, Social Democrats did not target the NSDAP as a major threat to the republic but subsumed it under a broadly defined German fascism. Impressive Nazi electoral gains in Saxony in June 1930 alerted Social Democrats to the marked vitality of the NSDAP, yet contempt for the Nazis as serious political opponents lingered. In the summer of 1930, Social Democrats saw the social gains of the working class as more threatened than the republic and identified the source of this threat as the rightward lurch of the bourgeois parties, especially the DVP but also the Center Party. For these reasons, despite circumstances that were dissimilar to those that had existed in 1928, Social Democrats again built their 1930 Reichstag campaign around an attack on the revived *Bürgerblock* rather than around an offensive against the revitalized NSDAP.

The level of concern about the NSDAP did not accelerate evenly among Social Democrats. Most noticeable was the contrast between the slow reaction at the top of the SPD and the relatively precocious response of provincial activists and lower functionaries who witnessed Nazi extraparliamentary activity at close hand and compared its quantity and innovations with SPD sluggishness and routine. Social Democratic interpretations of Nazism also varied. Assessments made in public speeches and the daily press diverged from those prepared privately for Social Democratic politicians or for publication in small-circulation journals. As will be seen, the latter contained insights gleaned from empirical observation of the Nazi movement. When addressing the masses, in contrast, Social Democrats trotted out stock characterizations based on ideological presuppositions. Before

September 1930, two estimations were most prevalent: Nazism as "new anti-Semitism" and Nazism as "capitalist tool." The first judgment was not based on careful study of *Mein Kampf* but on historical analogy; its proponents reasoned that the NSDAP, like anti-Semitic parties of the 1890s, would wither on the vine when the economy revived. The second interpretation cropped up more often (sometimes in tandem with the first): the Nazis were capitalist henchmen hired to smash working-class rights and prepare the road to naked dictatorship. The bourgeoisie would cast aside these pawns after they had seduced petit bourgeois voters disillusioned with the reactionary, elitist Right and had lured those workers who were susceptible to inflammatory rhetoric.

When not relegating the resurgent NSDAP to a supporting role in a reactionary script, Social Democrats classed it with the KPD as part of the radical camp. Both the Left Opposition and the SPD leadership employed this category, but for different reasons. SPD ministers in the Reich and Prussia, seeing a common radical threat to state security, highlighted the need for legal and police measures to defend the republic from possible putschist attempts. Leftists, on the other hand, focused on the techniques used by the radicals to snare proletarians. They pointed out repeatedly that both the KPD and the NSDAP exploited the political gap between Social Democratic principle and practice as well as the social gulf between Social Democratic leaders and followers. In leftists' eyes, the radicals could only be outmaneuvered if the SPD thoroughly reformed its ways. In particular, it must act ruthlessly against even the shadow of corruption among Social Democratic politicians, redistribute the salaries of honest ones, expunge bureaucratic deformities, and again become a proletarian party. These issues touched on the attenuation of Social Democratic culture and violations of its precepts since 1918. SPD leaders did not redress real abuses that tarnished the party's image among those individuals radicalized by the mushrooming economic crisis, in part out of self-interest, but also because of reluctance to admit to benign internal changes that belied the SPD's self-identity as the party of the class-conscious proletariat.

Assessing the Republic's Situation

After their ministers took office in 1928, Social Democrats tended to bridle at allegations of a crisis of parliamentarism. In a Reichstag session in November 1928, Breitscheid denied that such a crisis was developing. In June 1929, both Wilhelm Sollmann and Carl Severing took exception to a comment by the left-wing Center Party politician Joseph Wirth about a burgeoning parliamentary crisis.[1] In *Die Gesellschaft*,

Georg Decker referred disparagingly to "dictator talk," assuring Germans that they need not be frightened by the specter of fascism, for "there are enough forces at hand to implement democracy's formal political meaning as well as its social content."[2] At Socialist rallies in mid-1929, Breitscheid weighed the prospects for democracy in Germany. In Cologne, he observed that "in recent weeks rumors of dictatorship have finally been put to rest," because antirepublicans disagreed about what kind of government they wanted and lacked a leader with the "requisite personal authority" to carry out their antidemocratic wishes; even leaders of "big business . . . had no interest in unsettling the economy with political experiments." A second talk bore the blunt title "Is There a Crisis of Parliamentarism?" An audience of fourteen hundred heard Breitscheid conclude that while the republic was still "threatened and endangered," the fascist threat, the danger of naked dictatorship, had ebbed.[3]

At least in part, Social Democrats disavowed the existence of a crisis of political legitimacy because such a crisis assumed not just the enmity of inveterate republic haters but popular disillusionment with parliamentary government. In power, the SPD could be accused of partial responsibility for the growth of such a mood. Nonetheless, majority Socialists never maintained that the republic was safe and secure, if only because they hoped to remind republicans of the bourgeois center (DDP, Center Party, and DVP) that without the support of Social Democracy, the new state's life might be short indeed. Simultaneously, the "threat to the republic" was used to justify participation in coalition governments against the Left Opposition's call to shift to social radicalism. The ambivalent assessment of Weimar's health explains Julius Leber's retrospective charge that, at the time of the vote on the Brüning compromise in March 1930, awareness of the precarious political situation was minimal, even as party speakers ritually harped on "dangers to the republic."[4] Many Socialists wanted to believe in the republic's security even as they habitually reminded Germans of its enemies.

At the 1929 Magdeburg congress, Hans Vogel stressed that Social Democrats had to compromise in the coalition in order to avoid a crisis that would "foment the call for a dictator." Reporting on the work of the Reichstag delegation, Breitscheid insisted that parliamentary government in Germany could function if all the parties were as conscious of their responsibility to secure the republic as was the SPD. He rejected left-wing criticism of such responsibility, admonishing, "Think about it for once! If this regime falls, what will follow? Dissolution! Good! But do you believe democracy can function, if every few years people scream for dissolution? What other regime is possible? Only some kind of caretaker cabinet (*Beamtenkabinett*)."[5] Left critics of the Müller cabinet also discerned the rising tide of antirepublicanism but offered a different prescription to counter it. In May 1929 the *Hessischer Volksfreund* counseled leaving the coalition because the crisis of parliamentarism undermined liberal elements even in the Center Party and made a progressive policy impossible.[6] At Magdeburg, Toni Sender admitted that German democracy could not survive continual parliamentary crises that discredited the system in the electorate's eyes. She insisted, however, that a greater danger lay in trying Germans' patience with compromises: "The masses, after all, need to know why they should defend democracy, and we have the duty to make that clear through our deeds."[7] Rank and file Socialists, too, expressed both complacency and concern about popular attitudes toward the republic. Following the celebration of the tenth anniversary of the Weimar constitution, antithetical interpretations of Berlin's festivities emerged at a Reichsbanner meeting in Munich. An older comrade saw huge crowds in the streets as a sign of popular republicanism. A *Jungkamerad*, however, had sensed a "powerful countercurrent to the rally." Not only had Berlin policemen cautioned uniformed Reichsbanner members to steer clear of certain districts, but the young observer had personally detected an "anticonstitutional" mood in working-class pubs.[8]

To understand the evolution of Social Democratic perceptions of the republic's situation, one must distinguish between grassroots antirepublicanism and the antidemocratic attitudes of old-line reactionaries or, put differently, between the danger of a populist authoritarian majority and the threat of violent putschist bands. This distinction influenced how the SPD judged the Nazi party, the movement that lashed together these branches of antirepublicanism. Although Socialists realized that fascism fused populist and putschist authoritarianism, their understanding of this phenomenon was, naturally enough, shaped by Italian fascism's road to power. As a result, they focused more on the putschist than on the populist element in right-wing extremism. Social Democratic cognizance of the danger represented by German fascism only gradually and unevenly became synonymous with its awareness of a more profound and extensive crisis of democracy. Not until after the Reichstag elections of September 1930 did even the SPD's centrist leaders, much less the Left Opposition, define German fascism as the NSDAP.

In the heady aftermath of the 1928 Reichstag elections, Georg Decker had noted that, despite its overall rout, the Nazi party did well in a few isolated districts. In general, though, Social Democrats were struck by KPD gains that were more impressive and that had occurred among voters who should have voted for the SPD. The level of interest in the

NSDAP in the first year of the Müller regime can be gauged from party propaganda during the Saxon Landtag campaign in the spring of 1929. Provincial headquarters provided speakers with material against the KPD, the DNVP, the DDP, the DVP, and the Old Socialist Party, the Saxon SPD's bete noire, without a word against the NSDAP.[9] The *Leipziger Volkszeitung* emphasized the class nature of the coming election, pitting the SPD against the KPD and "bourgeois forces." Only upon analyzing the returns was the paper obliged to admit that the NSDAP had won a real electoral presence. The Nazis had almost doubled their share of the Saxon vote from the Reichstag elections a year before, from 2.7 percent to 5.3 percent. While the editor conceded that the *Bürgertum* had won the election, he believed that the Nazi contribution to this victory would increase the instability of the *Bürgerblock*.[10]

SPD concern about the NSDAP as a dangerous street foe and electoral rival only began to revive in the fall of 1929, spurred by the NSDAP's vigorous campaigns for local and state elections and against the Young Plan, all of which increased its urban visibility. Stormtroopers flooded into opponents' meetings, especially those of the SPD, reversing the pre-1928 situation in which Nazi rallies had been swamped by Communists and Roter Frontkämpfer-Bund members and, to a lesser extent, Socialists and Reichsbanner men.[11] In Baden the NSDAP began to campaign for the state elections of October 1929 a year beforehand. The campaign climaxed with a staggering 120 meetings between September 28 and October 6, addressed by rural experts and national figures. The NSDAP's vote rose dramatically in Baden's urban areas, although it remained low relative to the Socialist vote.[12] The Social Democratic reaction was typical for this early period of National Socialist electoral advances. On the one hand, the Baden *Volksfreund* confessed that in certain towns the SPD had lost working-class votes to the NSDAP. On the other hand, Theo Haubach, soon to emerge as a perceptive observer of the Nazis, denied that Baden's results gave cause for alarm, since the underlying trend was "Hitler gobbles up Hugenberg."[13]

Ernst Heilmann, the editor of *Das Freie Wort*, downplayed Nazi gains in municipal elections in Berlin and elsewhere in Prussia as well as in Chemnitz, Plauen, and other Saxon communities over the next several weeks. The NSDAP, he maintained, was the latest incarnation of German anti-Semitism, which, as before 1914, attracted the petite bourgeoisie and "unenlightened workers." After the NSDAP increased its vote in Thuringia to 90,159 (from 27,946 in the 1928 Landtag election), Heilmann found it more worthy of attention but saw no cause for alarm as "a few years of practical experience with these revolutionary heroes will suffice to cure the voters."[14] The *Leipziger Volkszeitung*, rarely in agreement with the rightist Heilmann on anything more specific than socialism, shared his Olympian calm in this matter.[15] Social Democrats at the local level demonstrated more foresight. In the fall of 1929, the Würzburg SPD, recently all but moribund, planned to carry out intensive work to counter the proselytizing activity of right-wing groups, especially the NSDAP. Members discussed the need for a defense plan and front, including possibly the KPD, to foil physical attacks by Nazis.[16]

Renegotiation of the reparations schedule, culminating in the Young Plan, provided the excuse for a great surge of Nationalist propaganda in the fall of 1929. In the petition drive to get signatures for a referendum against the Young Plan, the NSDAP was for the first time associated with the Stahlhelm and the DNVP and, according to many historians, rode the propaganda wave to nationwide prominence.[17] Simultaneously, this on-slaught helped discredit the republic. Alarmed, Social Democrats held rallies against the referendum but undermined their value in various ways.[18] Rather than analyze the political import of the campaign's popu-larity, the party press gleefully trumpeted its humiliations—the disap-pointing number of petition signatures, the defeat of the "Freedom Law" in the Reichstag, and its poor showing in the referendum.[19] The union press denounced the anti-Young campaign, and the executive committee of the ADGB even proposed to the non–Social Democratic union federa-tions a joint declaration censuring the referendum. When these unions balked at the idea, however, the ADGB decided not to proceed with its fellow Socialist unions (AfA-Bund, DBB, and ADB) for the rather lame reason that a delayed statement was worse than none at all.[20]

The Müller regime threw its prestige (and Hindenburg's) against the referendum but, according to Wilhelm Hoegner, it too adopted the wrong approach. By restricting itself to "factual corrections" of misinfor-mation and admonishing voters to choose between "reason" and "non-sense," the government portrayed the men behind the campaign as "fools" when they were, in fact, clever liars.[21] The Prussian government, in contrast, took the referendum effort very seriously. In a radio speech Minister-President Braun warned Prussian civil servants not to sign the petitions. State Secretary Hermann Pünder described the efforts of the Prussian regime to discourage the participation of government employ-ees and citizens—from enlisting the aid of "prominent personalities" to printing leaflets against the referendum.[22] Stampfer and Keil later regret-ted the SPD's general neglect of the issue of wounded national sensibility, manipulated so well not only by the anti–Young Plan effort but by the whole mountain of nationalist propaganda. According to Keil, the Socialist press simply ignored Chancellor Müller's speech at the League of Nations in September 1928, when he sharply condemned the political and economic "absurdity" of allied reparations policies.[23] This neglect reflected reluctance to use patriotism as a means of bolstering support for the republic.

Leading Social Democrats also discounted the power of two favored Nazi and Communist slurs against the SPD, both connected with the charge that Social Democracy stood for bureaucracy and hypocrisy. First, the extremist parties pilloried the high salaries and pensions of SPD politicians and government officials.[24] Prodded by left oppositionists for whom equality was fundamental to the Social Democratic association, rank and file Social Democrats took up this complaint, demanding prosperous SPD officeholders share their wealth with unemployed comrades. Provincial leaders tried to bury a demand that proved highly popular among the ranks. In the resulting internal battles, the advocates of equality went unsatisfied, and energy was diverted from outside activity.[25] To even greater effect, the KPD and the NSDAP exploited cases of corruption involving Social Democrats. Most notoriously, during Berlin's municipal election campaign in the fall of 1929 they regaled the nation with the juicy details of the Sklarek scandal.[26] The Sklarek brothers, owners of a clothing supply company in Berlin, had won a monopoly contract to supply municipal clothing and linen needs. Under cover of this agreement, they had devised a scheme to receive payments from the city treasury for faked deliveries. When they were arrested in September 1929, the brothers admitted that they had offered presents and low-priced furs to city officials and councilors, including several Social Democrats. Even more damning was the revelation that two of the three brothers had joined the SPD in 1928.[27] Vorwärts's coverage of the story was extremely cagey. Only after the capital had been abuzz with the affair for several weeks did the Berlin daily even mention the party membership of the Sklareks. At times its tone verged on the apologetic. The SPD was also slow to expel Social Democrats who had socialized inordinately with the Sklareks.[28] In contrast, the KPD instantly kicked out two implicated Communist city councilors, then proceeded to trumpet this action as proof of Communist vigilance against "bourgeois–Social Democratic corruption."[29] The scandal heightened tensions between the SPD and the KPD and certainly contributed to SPD losses, and to KPD and NSDAP gains, in the municipal election in November.[30]

SPD leftists, dominant in the Berlin party and frustrated by their lack of control over Vorwärts, were appalled by the muted, slow, and defensive reaction of the national leadership to the Sklarek scandal.[31] Julius Leber too criticized leaders for whom "solidarity with the party hierarchy" took precedence over their "sense of republican virtue."[32] The scandal stirred up this and other quandaries that militated against an effective response by the SPD. The paradigmatic character of these dilemmas gives the Sklarek case significance beyond its impact on the Berlin election. For one thing, it raised the problem of how to respond to anti-Semitic propaganda that tied the SPD to the Jewish community. Because the Sklareks were so-called *Ostjuden*, the *Völkischer Beobachter* and the German Nationalist papers paraded the scandal as more evidence of a nefarious Marxist-Jewish-republican conspiracy to rape and ruin the German taxpayer. Determined not to lend credence to racist slurs, *Vorwärts* never mentioned this aspect of the rightist attack; yet its silence may have also been motivated by the desire not to stoke the rightist charge that the SPD was the party of Jews.[33] Moreover, certain accusations in *Rote Fahne* probably reinforced the reluctance of the party leadership to acknowledge links to the Jewish community. In a scurrilous anti-Semitic story on Social Democratic dealings with the Sklareks, *Rote Fahne* "revealed," with stunning irrelevance, that Hugo Heimann, a Socialist Reichstag deputy, was "a very rich houseowner . . . and pious member of [Berlin's] Jewish Community," warning that anticlerical proletarians would "dispatch candidates [like him] to the devil" in the municipal election. *Vorwärts* retorted that Heimann bravely refused to repudiate his ties to a persecuted religious minority, implying that he acted out of political, not confessional, motives.[34] As the KPD knew, the Berlin SPD had recently resolved that party officials and candidates must sever all ties with organized religion, only to see this proposal quashed by the national leadership. *Rote Fahne* clearly wanted to exploit anger in the Berlin SPD over this breach of Social Democratic mores. Despite the liberal arguments used by party leaders in favor of religious toleration, and the consistent advocacy of the civil rights of German and East European Jews by all Social Democrats, the SPD never made minority or religious rights a major theme in its struggle to save the republic. In part, doubts about the seriousness of Nazi anti-Semitism explain this omission.[35] In addition, however, political cultural impediments prevented the SPD from making freedom of belief central to its attack on Nazi intolerance.

Most discomfiting of all, the Sklarek scandal threw a lurid light on the self-image of Social Democrats as the movement of the class-conscious working class. Not only *Rote Fahne* but also the *Völkischer Beobachter* trumpeted that the SPD had been exposed as a haven for moguls and racketeers, indeed as a "capitalist party."[36] When the SPD expelled the Sklareks, the majority of Berlin Social Democrats reacted with "pained incredulity" to the revelation that the brothers had membership cards.[37] After the scandal had simmered for several weeks, *Vorwärts* published a mild critique of SPD city officials who cavorted with "private business interests." This editorial, however, underscored repeatedly that the SPD must conform to a higher moral standard precisely because it was "the party of the working class," thus implicitly disclaiming substantial changes in the Berlin SPD's social composition (where only 43 percent were industrial workers in 1922) and insinuating that only workers, not the general public, demanded political probity.[38]

The NSDAP's success in Berlin as well as the prominent role of Wilhelm Frick in the cabinet of Thuringia after January 1930 prompted concern on the SPD's left flank. Noting the expansion of the Communist and Nazi voting bases, Paul Levi pointed out that their deputies' speeches in the Reichstag relied on essentially the same language to attack the SPD. Both parties also heaped scorn on the social as well as the political order, but the NSDAP reaped the greater harvest. He warned that the SPD must criticize not just capitalism but the republic if it were to compete with its radical rivals.[39] Social Democrats in Saxony, sooner than their counterparts elsewhere, concentrated on the Nazi problem as one of practical politics. In January 1930, public meetings focused on the "crisis in Saxony," that is, the inability of its parties to form a majority government. Hermann Liebmann, a leader of the Leipzig SPD, feared a replay of events in Thuringia. He suggested, ever so mildly, that the Saxon SPD might have to consider joining a coalition with the moderate bourgeois parties to prevent the "legalization of fascism" in Saxony. His talk provoked a lively debate in which most speakers spurned a coalition inspired by "Nazi-anxiety . . . which is entirely out of place." One comrade found the DNVP more dangerous. According to another, Liebmann was deluded in assuming the NSDAP, an "instrument of the big bourgeoisie," could be divided from the bourgeois parties. Others, though, endorsed Liebmann's viewpoint. One speaker even charged that the SPD must share blame for fascism's revitalization because "parliamentarism has not been made use of as its principles require."[40] A week later, Engelbert Graf, a prominent and colorful Saxon Socialist whose brilliant oratory and Bohemian style made him a favorite among Young Socialists, spoke in Leipzig on "the fascist danger and the working class." Graf took fascism's "nonreactionary" appeal to youth seriously. He characterized Nazism as a "political youth movement" that manipulated disillusionment with German democracy's defects, in particular, bureaucratic tendencies and corruption. However, he too described Nazism as "the tool of the bourgeoisie" and diluted the force of his message by asserting that not the republic but the SPD's social and economic goals were endangered.[41]

Saxon concern about the growth of the Nazi party is noteworthy in light of the resistance by left-wing Reichstag deputies to Interior Minister Severing's effort to pass a new version of the Law for the Protection of the Republic in early 1930. Promulgated in the wake of Walter Rathenau's assassination in 1922, this law allowed the Reich government to ban assemblies and demonstrations that endangered public order, advocated violence, or expressed contempt for republican institutions. In 1922, the SPD and Independent Socialists had been its strongest supporters.[42] Now, leftists in the SPD argued against renewing the law because they feared it would be used mainly against the KPD, not right-wing transgressors.[43] To document his case for a new law, Severing published a memorandum that outlined the daily "shooting, fighting, and stabbing of political opponents" engaged in by a minority of Germans. In the Reichstag, he infuriated the Left Opposition by referring to the potential social danger of high unemployment and warning of the KPD's putschist schemes.[44] Not only leftists found galling the state's imbalanced treatment of right-wing extremists and Communists. Karl Meitmann demanded the government act as "sharply and energetically" against the NSDAP as it did against the KPD.[45]

Government Socialists such as Severing, Grzesinski, and Braun concentrated on the need for laws that would allow the state to crack down on the antisocial activity of the radicals. In Prussia, Grzesinski barred mayors, local deputies, and civil servants from membership in the NSDAP or the KPD. Under a second Prussian order, civil servants could not be active in either of these "extremist" parties. Similar decrees were adopted by Social Democratic ministers in Hesse and Baden, although these applied only to a subset of public officials such as the police or teachers. In the province of Hanover, Noske prohibited high school students from membership in the NSDAP or Hitler Youth. Wolfram Pyta has argued that such efforts, although difficult to enforce, did hamper the activity of Nazis and were not used unfairly against Communists.[46]

Provincial leaders, such as Meitmann or even leftists, did not oppose state repression to protect the republic.[47] Their experiences with the radical Right on the streets, though, spurred them to see mobilization of the SPD as the more effective tactic for challenging the NSDAP. Such sentiment was even stronger at the base of the party, where growing dismay over the vitality of Nazism and the pale response of the SPD became evident in early 1930. Correspondence to *Das Freie Wort* exhorted local chapters to take the Nazis more seriously, pointing out that the NSDAP, the "most successful wing of the surging reaction," exercised a notable attraction on young workers and employees; writers compared the "tireless, nonstop" propaganda work of the Nazis with the lackadaisical efforts of Social Democrats, wondering, "Is there nothing left of our old Storm and Stress?"[48] Particularly lively was a debate in its columns about the pros and cons of swamping Nazi meetings as the Nazis did Socialist gatherings. Those opposed to imitating the Nazi practice, including editor Heilmann, downplayed the danger of Nazism, attributing its growth to deteriorating economic conditions. In contrast, a proponent of "meeting crashing" charged that his comrades, mistaking Marxism for fatalism, justified inaction with the excuse that "civic courage" could not alter the path of development.[49]

Unser Weg, the organ of Berlin functionaries, devoted a long article to the "Nazisturm auf Berlin" that had turned the NSDAP into "one of the most active parties," with meetings, rallies, and "intensive factory agitation carried out with great energy." The author criticized the Social Democratic tendency to dismiss Nazi crowds as the "scum of humanity." True, "sensation seekers," "driftwood," and "petit bourgeois" were drawn to Nazism, but, he averred, large numbers of employees and workers also attended their gatherings. He contended that the "economic conjuncture" only in part explained the Nazi renaissance; "good organization" must be accorded equal weight. His prescription for fighting this trend resembled that of others eager to combat the Nazi fever: increase Social Democratic public activity after educating functionaries about the content and style of Nazi agitation.[50] In Hanover, too, speakers at local SPD events urged greater party activity to confront the Nazi challenge.[51] In Munich, the youth wing of the Reichsbanner took on new vitality by devoting its meetings to discussions of fascism, especially the Nazi movement.[52]

Concern about the resurgence of the Right surfaced in the ADGB around the same time but was not focused on the NSDAP and had no practical consequences. Warned that the Stahlhelm and the NSDAP were recruiting members within the trade unions, ADGB officials circulated a questionnaire about this activity to member unions in January 1930. The eleven responding unions reported almost exclusively on Stahlhelm activity which, it turned out, was minimal, if only because unions such as those representing the printers and the machinists kicked out known members of the reactionary paramilitary league. The ADGB national committee discussed the results of the survey and debated whether right-wing activists should be excluded as a general rule, but it too focused on the Stahlhelm, barely mentioning the Nazis. In the end, the council did not change the policy of permitting each union to handle the problem as it preferred.[53]

Social Democratic intellectuals, like activists in the ranks and unlike union and party leaders, devoted new attention to the threat posed by the Nazi party in particular. In a pamphlet commemorating the tenth anniversary of the defeat of the Kapp putsch of March 1920, Carlo Mierendorff took the republic's pulse. While emphasizing that the constitution and the democratic state had survived despite violent opposition, he warned that in the revitalized NSDAP, Germany now had "a movement with programmatically fascist tendencies whose resonance in petit bourgeois and even proletarian circles dare not be underestimated." To the question "Is the democratic system secure or seriously threatened by fascism?" he replied, "Unless all signs deceive, a hard struggle lies ahead."[54] Georg Decker compared the current situation in Weimar Germany to the Jacobins' position in pre-Napoleonic France and to the period of Mussolini's rise to power. After these ominous analogies, he quickly pointed out that republicans of his day were less naive than their predecessors. Any putsch attempt would encounter the resistance of a broad, united defense. Thus, Berlin was not Rome. But perhaps it was Paris, for if a fascist dictatorship came to power without a coup, many "apparent" democrats and republicans might, like Napoleon's soldiers, greet it as a "completion" of democracy. Decker suspected that the "majority of the financiers of the Hitlerites" wanted not a coup but for the Nazi party to confuse the masses about democracy. He implied that parliamentary democracy was more likely to be toppled by an authoritarian dictatorship than by a "popular" one. Yet Decker saw the Nazi movement as of primary importance in the electoral arena. In response to this rigorously run organization with considerable sums of money at its disposal, he urged the socialist movement (i.e., the SPD and the KPD) to present a united defense and overcome its preoccupation with "petty special interests." The SPD, especially, needed to engage in more extraparliamentary activity in order to direct the "inner impulse of the movement towards the outside world."[55] More sanguine than Decker or Mierendorff was the editor of the *Frankfurter Volksstimme* who assured his readers that any sort of fascist coup would be smashed by a general strike. German workers, who were "no Italian illiterates," would battle the bourgeoisie until it "capitulated to the democratic will of the proletariat."[56]

Two memorandums, apparently written in early to mid-1930 for Prussian Interior Minister Albert Grzesinski, offer evidence that Socialist politicians, at least in Prussia, kept themselves informed about the Nazi upsurge. The "memorandum on the financial sources of the NSDAP" disavowed the contention "often made in the press" (including the SPD's) that the NSDAP got its money from big industrialists, asserting that this accounted for only a modest part of its overall income. "In the main," the pockets of party members and profits from public meetings and press sales supplied Hitler's financial assets.[57] The other memorandum discussed the NSDAP's history, organization, and goals, stressing the "high treasonous" nature of the party. It also assessed Nazism's rapid growth since 1925–26, comparing its Reichstag vote in 1928 to its communal votes in 1929. Among "endangered areas," the author counted Berlin-Brandenburg, Schleswig-Holstein, Silesia, and East Prussia; among social groups, the old *Mittelstand*, lower and middle government officials, teachers, and youth, especially students, were considered susceptible. He discussed the careful targeting of Nazi propaganda, which broadcast antiurban slogans in the countryside and leftist mottoes in the city; he also described the NSDAP's intense meeting schedule and its rotation of "systematically trained" speakers. He gave little credence to the NSDAP's "temporary alliance" with other right-wing groups, since it incessantly attacked them out of the other side of its mouth. After predicting that the NSDAP would make ever greater inroads into the voting pools of the heretofore impervious Center and Social Democratic parties, the memorandum concluded that the movement was a "very dangerous threat to the democratic state, despite different tendencies within it—the Strassers' left wing, Hitler's centrists, and Goebbels's 'fanatical fascists'."[58] One can only speculate about who besides Grzesinski read these perceptive analyses of the ways and means of National Socialism in mid-1930.

Whether stimulated by such sobering assessments or not, anxiety at the top levels of the SPD about the health of the republic and the growth of the NSDAP suddenly took concrete forms in the wake of Müller's fall. The Social Democratic delegation's decision not to engage in unfettered oppositional activity in the Reichstag was conditioned in part by concern about political instability.[59] In June 1930 the SPD's Central Recruitment Department published speakers' material, compiled by Otto Buchwitz, a left-leaning trade unionist, directed against the NSDAP. The pamphlet covered Nazi ideology and policies and included short biographies of prominent Nazis. Buchwitz outlined the "nonsense" of the NSDAP twenty-five-point program and exposed Hitler's capitalist backers (the Plauen textile industry, Robert Bosch, Emil Kirdorf, and Henry Ford). Buchwitz also wrote that Hitler was a closet monarchist.[60] The contrast between this material for public speakers and the private memorandums for Grzesinski is striking. One wonders about the effectiveness of speeches by Social Democrats that relayed Buchwitz's view of the NSDAP. Working-class audiences could, after all, compare his claims with those made in Nazi leaflets that ridiculed Severing's arbitration settlement of the Ruhr lockout as proemployer, attacked the *Bürgerblock*, denounced the Panzerkreuzer construction program, and called for taxes on the rich.[61]

The returns of the Saxon election of June 1930 delivered the first real shock at Nazism's advance. During the campaign, the *Leipziger Volkszeitung* devoted considerably more copy than it had a year earlier to the danger of a "National Socialist dictatorship".[62] Still the results came as a surprise. The SPD lost 50,818 of the 922,932 votes cast for it in 1929 and one of its 33 Landtag seats. The KPD gained moderately and added one seat to its delegation of 12. The NSDAP climbed abruptly, however, almost tripling its vote total and jumping from 5 to 14 seats in the Landtag, thus surpassing the KPD. Certain peculiarities of the Saxon situation dulled the impact of even this blow. The leftist-dominated Saxon Social Democrats had been in opposition for seven years. Moreover, the economic situation there had deteriorated even more than in the Reich as a whole. Majority supporters charged that the Saxon SPD's anticoalitionism had contributed to Saxony's rapid succession of elections that fed disgust with parliamentary politics.[63] Leftists retorted that the national party would have fared much worse. They refused to see Nazi gains as terribly alarming since these came at the expense of the bourgeois parties, to the ire of capitalists who, it was claimed, had spent much money on Nazi demagoguery against the SPD. *Vorwärts*, in contrast, acknowledged that the Nazis had attracted middle-class voters who should vote SPD, but, it concluded, these masses would in the future be more susceptible to socialist appeals, though "for the moment" their flirtation with National Socialism fortified the fascists.[64] Provincial activists, on the other hand, confronted Social Democratic failures and Nazi successes honestly. They contrasted the lethargy of SPD grassroots activity with the frantic efforts of Nazis and Communists and complained that their party lacked the élan displayed by the radicals in even the most obscure villages. One writer charged that, unlike the NSDAP, the Saxon SPD had been ill-prepared to wage a campaign.[65]

Who was attracted to National Socialism, and why? Social Democrats offered different, or at least differently weighted, interpretations of the causes and sources of Nazi growth, depending on their ideological viewpoint and the immediacy of their experience with the Nazi movement. Many recognized that the NSDAP exerted a pull on some workers.[66] While leftists insisted that this appeal was narrow, they were more likely to see the SPD as responsible for class defections.[67] Despite recognition that the NSDAP attracted "unenlightened workers," Social Democrats be-

lieved that the vast majority of Nazi adherents came from the small
and, especially, rural *Mittelstand*.[68] Lower functionaries in the SPD and
Reichsbanner urged fellow Socialists to engage in rural recruitment work
and to emulate the techniques of Nazi opponents.[69] An activist offered as
a model his experience in the backlands of the Vogtland, a corner of Red
Saxony where the Brown presence was overwhelming and the SPD was
"insignificant." A concerted effort during the Landtag campaign of 1930
produced SPD gains there, while in the Chemnitz district as a whole the
party lost badly. Social Democrats also carried out an intense recruitment
effort in Breslau's hinterland in early 1930. A participant reported that
blanket leafletting and lots of "ballyhoo" at the meetings had won followers in seven villages.[70]

Before September, the population group most widely recognized by
Social Democrats as highly susceptible to Hitler's appeal was youth who,
they argued, were "confused and seduced" by the Nazi emphasis on
action.[71] Concern about this trend was accompanied by a growing awareness of the SPD's failure to attract the postrevolution generation. Younger
Social Democrats expressed themselves bluntly on the reasons for this
failure. At a youth conference of the Lower Rhine district, speakers
pleaded with the district executive to coopt younger members. Describing
the makeup of the executive committee, one young man remarked bitterly that this body had earned the sobriquet "gallery of ancestors."[72]
Older Social Democrats often reacted defensively to the charge of *Verkal-
kung* (ossification). At Magdeburg, the executive committee's report conceded the need to win the votes of youth but contended that the party was
not as "aged and calcified" as some comrades were wont to complain.[73]
Judging by the frequency of this topic in correspondence to *Das Freie Wort*,
it was of great concern to lower functionaries and Social Democrats at the
base of the party who compared their own failures with the successful
techniques of the Nazis. One activist pointed out that the NSDAP had
taken the simple step of selecting talented youth, training them, and
"exploiting" them as speakers for young audiences. He could not understand why the SPD did not imitate such practices.[74]

In a pathbreaking article in *Die Gesellschaft*, Carlo Mierendorff offered
an analysis of the organizational, sociological, and ideological roots of the
"new Nazism" that was more comprehensive and perceptive than any
other assessment before the September elections.[75] Mierendorff argued
that the Nazi movement had a completely different character in 1930
than in 1924. Its current successes rested on a national organizational
foundation, not merely a Bavarian one, and an urban political machine,
not just a rural one. The secret of its electoral gains lay in the "unity and

preparedness" of this machine. "What until now no other party has achieved," he pointed out, "the NSDAP has doubtless succeeded in creating: an organizational apparatus to rival that of the SPD." Although the Nazi apparatus was still "embryonic," its immaturity was balanced by the vigor of the movement. Mierendorff rejected a simple comparison of the movement with anti-Semitic parties of the 1890s because the Nazi version "consciously anchors its racist theory in the economy," and combined nationalist sentiment with a focus on the "social problem."[76] As a result, Hitler's party possessed a strong appeal for the *Mittelstand*, white-collar employees, small and middle farmers, and students, all of whom felt threatened by "proletarianization." Noting the Nazis' ability to mobilize nonvoters, he guessed that the very "haziness" of the NSDAP's program helped it with the "politically least developed" part of the electorate who responded to the Nazi appeal to "feeling." In contrast, the SPD tried to enlighten and educate voters. As a vote stealer the NSDAP threatened the bourgeois parties more than it threatened the SPD, but, he argued, the SPD was not invulnerable as many of its "fringe" supporters voted out of feeling, not rational considerations. Though he predicted that the Nazi movement would eventually founder on its "inner contradictions," Mierendorff warned that this might not occur before it "made its decisive move (*zum Zuge gekommen ist*)." The SPD could not rely on the ravages of time but must act to thwart the National Socialist challenge.[77]

This empirically based inquiry into the nature of National Socialism shared both specific points and the interpretation of the memorandums written for Grzesinski. It provides more evidence that some Social Democrats early identified important factors behind Nazi success and their relevance and danger to the SPD. Mierendorff's distinction between the emotionalism of the Nazi appeal and the rationalism of the SPD, for example, became a major issue in the postelection debate about how the SPD could best counter the NSDAP. Although he mentioned that the fall of Brüning would increase the danger of Nazism, Mierendorff did not elaborate and in general did not draw out either the organizational or political implications of his analysis. The Reichstag campaign opened without a comprehensive assessment of the Nazi hydra or deliberation on a strategy to counter it by SPD policymaking bodies. Certainly, the SPD was not alone in its negligence. The bourgeois parties were even less attuned to the electoral threat presented by the NSDAP.[78] Nonetheless, the SPD's interpretation of Nazism as a fundamentally antiproletarian movement might have spurred the Socialist leadership in particular to develop a strategy to counter this threat.

The 1930 Campaign

The NSDAP was the party most prepared for an election campaign upon the dissolution of the Reichstag in July 1930. On July 25, Goebbels's Propaganda Department sent out directives on how to conduct the campaign. District propaganda offices distributed detailed reports on the course of the campaign to all local branches. They also received a brochure titled "Modern Political Propaganda." In Baden the Nazis transferred the groundwork for a state election to the Reichstag campaign, ending up with a mass saturation effort considered very effective by the police. Elsewhere, such as Hanover–South Braunschweig, the NSDAP held 300 to 400 meetings per week in the last month of the campaign. Despite many different (and contradictory) slogans, the Nazi campaign revolved around a central, unifying theme: the disintegration of German political life into a "heap of special interests."[79] In the 30,000 rallies the NSDAP held in the four weeks preceding September 14, its speakers lambasted the bourgeois parties and the SPD. Significantly, one of its favorite attacks on the bourgeois parties focused on their alleged friendliness to Marxist Social Democracy.[80]

The SPD's campaign paled by comparison.[81] Certainly, the party possessed an effective electoral machine, its hallmark among German political parties, and had prepared material specifically for this contest. Despite an impressive number of rallies and scores of leaflets and pamphlets, however, at core the party entered the campaign unprepared. For one thing, the SPD failed to adjust its propaganda style and methods to compete more effectively with the Nazis and the KPD. Social Democrats and their supporters remarked that the party had become too "moderate" and "dry," with little idea of how to draw in the masses so effectively seduced by the Nazis.[82] The party leadership did not perceive the urgency of rethinking the SPD's propaganda style, in part because it underestimated its radical rivals and reserved the party's biggest blasts for the *Bürgerblock*. More fundamentally, the SPD's campaign lacked a theme that could draw voters from outside its large, but restricted, electorate. This omission is especially noteworthy because SPD analysts recognized that nonvoters and those who normally voted for the non-Catholic bourgeois parties were the wild cards in the election. In a widely reprinted article, Kurt Heinig estimated that 25 percent of the electorate was composed of nonvoters and newly enfranchised voters. He divided the other 75 percent into three groups: "worldview" voters loyal to the SPD, the Center Party, or the BVP; voters influenced by the economic and political "conjuncture" who were likely to vote Communist, Nazi, or for the Economic Party; and a second unpredictable block of voters in the process of "structural regroupment" who traditionally voted for the DNVP, the DVP, or the DDP. He did not hazard a prediction about how the "20 to 25 million" undecided voters might divide their allegiances but urged the SPD to go after them.[83]

On the basis of regional returns, commentators realized that the Nazi vote would increase significantly, even dramatically. The SPD, therefore, devoted an appreciable amount of its campaign rhetoric to Hitler and his ideology and organization.[84] On a national level, this effort included material for SPD public speakers, leaflets, and reports in *Vorwärts* that focused on SA violence, Hitler's racism, and Nazi attempts to infiltrate the army.[85] *Anti-Faschist*, a biweekly supplement to local Social Democratic newspapers, contained cruder, popular attacks on the "Swastika pest," with jokes and cartoons. Prominent Socialists, such as Arthur Crispien and Philipp Scheidemann as well as Prussian cabinet members, focused campaign speeches on National Socialism.[86] Nonetheless, provincial Social Democrats still directed more of their energy against the NSDAP than did the organizers of the national campaign. Local agitators were confronted with the brute force of the Nazi onslaught as thugs broke up meetings and beat up Socialists. In Stuttgart, Social Democrats were all the more shocked by this wave of terror because, according to Wilhelm Keil, they had underestimated the NSDAP since 1928.[87] Editorials and rally descriptions from Frankfurt, Hanover, Düsseldorf, Darmstadt, Hamburg, Leipzig, and Stuttgart present a collage of cross-national concern about the growth and vitality of the NSDAP.[88] In Darmstadt, Carlo Mierendorff, a first-time candidate for the Reichstag, made the struggle against the NSDAP the heart of his campaign effort.[89]

Social Democratic alarm about the NSDAP was clearly on the rise. However, the quantity of propaganda directed against the Nazis is not as significant as its message or its place within a broader campaign strategy. Socialist propaganda portrayed the Nazis in two principal, and seemingly contradictory, ways. On one hand, Social Democrats branded the NSDAP as the "handmaiden" of capital whose "role [is] the maintenance of capitalist society."[90] As Rudolf Breitscheid put it, National Socialism was "at least for a section of the bourgeoisie . . . a battering ram to be used against the SPD and the trade unions."[91] On the other hand, the SPD castigated the Nazis as radical rabble, street rowdies, and hoodlums who appealed to bourgeois youth and the unemployed.[92] In this guise, the NSDAP was often lumped with the KPD.[93] During the campaign, as during the fight around the Protection of the Republic law, Social Democrats in political

office were most likely to see the KPD and the NSDAP as equally deserv-
ing targets of punitive legal measures to protect the state. By Prussian
decrees passed in January and July 1930, Nazis and Communists elected
as mayors in Prussian towns were denied government confirmation. In
June, Prussian civil servants were forbidden to hold membership in either
party, and Nazi uniforms were banned in public. In Hamburg, using a
local police law of 1879, authorities arrested a number of National Socialists and Communists shortly before the Reichstag election. Social Democrats in Hamburg's senate approved of this procedure, even though,
predictably, conservative judges imposed heavier sentences on the Communists.[94]

Most Social Democrats saw no contradiction in portraying the Nazis as
radical rowdies and the battering ram of the bourgeoisie. They believed
that National Socialism's true face was currently masked, even to many
capitalists. In an in-depth analysis of the NSDAP, Max Westphal, a member of the SPD executive committee, acknowledged that the "well-known
capitalist, Herr Klönne" had vilified the NSDAP as "half-Marxist," but,
Westphal assured Herr Klönne, had he heard Hitler's speech at a recent employers' meeting, he would modify his view. Westphal admitted
that the Nazis "appear very revolutionary, so that [in competition] even
the Communists have to remain at the peak of their radicalism." They
wrapped themselves in a socialist mantle to lure bourgeois youth in search
of the genuine article. Nazi attacks on the bourgeois parties were an
"agitational maneuver" that allowed the NSDAP to depict itself as an
absolutely new party, untarnished by association with the old, worn-out
organizations, and enabled it to exploit "party weariness" in the bourgeois
camp. Consequently, the bourgeois parties were draining into the Nazi
swamp. After siphoning these votes, according to Westphal, the Nazis
would turn around and safeguard the reactionary interests of the decimated parties. Evidence of the real nature of National Socialism lay in its
support of conservative regimes in Mecklenburg and Thuringia. Westphal concluded that the SPD had nothing to fear from this sham movement for a "deeper socialism."[95] In its campaign propaganda, meanwhile,
the bourgeois DVP insisted that the NSDAP kept its socialist principles
and hatred of private property hidden from the middle class and peasants, who should "beware of wolves in sheep's clothing."[96]

Local Social Democratic papers often carried a cruder version of Westphal's view of Nazism, exposing "princes and big agrarians" as members
of this self-proclaimed " 'workers' party' " and trumpeting "heavy industry" as the source of Nazi gold. In articles for the popular press, even
Carlo Mierendorff described the NSDAP as a "yellow" movement, though

he emphasized that it was autonomous rather than the kept creature of capitalists.[97] Social Democrats believed the identification of National Socialism as a capitalist tool would discredit it with the masses. This explanation also braced Social Democrats' sense of their own party as the embodiment of the class interests of capitalism's opponents. Besides discounting Nazism as a genuine social movement, they ridiculed Nazis and their followers as unworthy of serious concern. Wilhelm Sollmann, editor of Cologne's *Rheinische Zeitung*, lampooned Communists who took so "seriously and tragically" those "tens of thousands" who heard Hitler speak in Cologne; even a "semi-political person" could only laugh at such "stupid youths and petit bourgeois." In Braunschweig, the SPD district chairman informed an election rally, "You can't argue seriously with the NSDAP."[98]

One could, however, quarrel in dead earnest with the *Bürgerblock*. If anything, the SPD's attack on the regime parties in 1930 was more hostile than in 1928, not less so. To Berlin functionaries, Otto Wels described the dissolution of the Reichstag as a manifestation of the "social struggle between capital and labor." He mentioned the National Socialists but aimed his barbs at Brüning and his cabinet. He disputed the claim of liberals such as Joseph Wirth that the republic was afflicted by a crisis of parliamentarism, averring that the real crisis afflicted the bourgeois parties. Only the SPD, he said, defended democracy and the interests of the entire people. In this campaign, the party would fight "under our old red flags" because for "us it is a question of the victory of the social democratic republic." Berlin functionaries, many of them leftists, enthusiastically applauded this militant speech.[99] Similar in tenor was an editorial by Siegfried Aufhäuser. The class struggle in Germany, he avowed, had entered a new phase as the "bourgeois parties close ranks in ruthless struggle against Social Democracy, the defender of workers' rights." A union circular reminded members that "the thoughtful, class-conscious trade unionist knows that only the SPD represents the political interests of the working class."[100]

The campaign's tenor was shrill; its rhetoric, menacing. The minister for occupied areas, Gottfried Treviranus, ominously threatened the repeated dissolution of the Reichstag until it approved the cabinet's finance program. At a huge Reichsbanner rally in celebration of the eleventh anniversary of the Weimar constitution, Paul Löbe lambasted such intimidation from the regime.[101] When the Center Party charged that Social Democratic attacks on Brüning were "hateful," Breitscheid countered with a spirited defense of their vehemence.[102] The conservative bourgeois parties, for their part, not only excoriated Social Democracy directly but condemned the new German State Party (the former DDP) for its willingness to consider a coalition with the SPD.[103]

In the provinces, too, speakers fired their biggest salvos against Brüning and the government parties. In Frankfurt an orator characterized Brüning's cabinet as the "most reactionary since the revolution." At the campaign kickoff meeting in Düsseldorf, the district chairman focused his anger on the *Bürgerblock*. He at least mentioned the need to take a strong stand against the NSDAP; in the discussion, the Nazis did not come up.[104] In a speech in Hanover, Reichstag deputy Marie Juchacz did not once allude to the NSDAP.[105] Even Kurt Schumacher, extremely active against Nazism later, did not level his guns steadily against the NSDAP in his many campaign speeches in Württemberg.[106] The Free Trade Unions also underestimated the Nazi threat. Lothar Erdmann, editor of *Die Arbeit*, explained to his readers that the DVP and the DNVP were more dangerous than the NSDAP "with its small following."[107]

Social Democrats recognized quite clearly that the election results could potentially imperil democracy and the social gains of the republic. They saw their party as more isolated than it had been in years, arrayed against a reactionary front of "the employer associations and entire *Bürgertum* . . . along with the National Socialists and Communists." Seeing the election as part of the "struggle to stop the dismantling of *Sozialpolitik*," the ADGB shared the SPD's alarm and provided greater financial and agitational support to the party's effort than it had in many years.[108] Theodor Leipart characterized the central issue in the campaign as the "preservation of the democratic state form," including its role "as the regulator of economic life."[109] The Socialist press depicted the menace to workers and the republic as "fascist" and "dictatorial."[110] Berlin's party chairman warned that, standing before the possible "establishment of dictatorship in Germany," the proletariat must make September 14 a day of victory for Social Democracy against "German fascism."[111] The leader of Düsseldorf's Reichsbanner feared the outbreak of "civil war" should the SPD do especially well in the elections.[112] For all these commentators, however, *fascism* remained a broad, vague term, more or less synonymous with the reactionary, even conservative, Right. In the ADGB's *Gewerkschafts-Zeitung*, Brüning's emergency decree was castigated as "fascistic."[113] Breitscheid characterized the cabinet's program as the "German species of fascism."[114] In fact, different writers and speakers meant different things when they referred to fascism, but before September 14 few Social Democrats had in mind only or even especially the NSDAP when they warned of the fascist danger. The NSDAP was the handmaiden of the capitalists and, in fact, only one servant in the reactionary entourage.

Despite militant evocations of the class-against-class nature of the campaign, the party's positive slogans were neither radical, concrete, nor very evident. Social Democrats attributed Communist and Nazi growth to the economic crisis, but they offered no program to overcome rapidly rising unemployment. In June 1930, 2,638,000 Germans were unemployed, up from 1,360,000 in June 1929. In some branches of the economy, the rate of increase was even more dramatic; over the same year, the building trades went from 55,000 unemployed to 219,000; mining, from 11,000 to 67,000. Free Trade unionists, the main reservoir of SPD votes, comprised 900,000 of those without work; 18.8 percent of union membership was on the dole, and another 17.5 percent was on short time.[115] The serious nature of the crisis could also be seen in the increase in long-term unemployment, measured by the percentage of unemployed receiving municipal welfare support (18 percent in 1928, 23.6 percent in 1930). The drag on public funds was especially onerous in the many cities that had financed municipal construction with short-term loans in the 1920s.[116] Such developments did not bode well for the SPD because so much of its strength rested on its representation in municipal government.

Social Democrats particularly deplored employers' attacks on the wages of those still working but, again, proposed no specific measures to counter it. To help the unemployed and to reduce the "reserve army of labor," they called for public works, especially on a communal level, but rarely provided details.[117] Vorwärts advocated an "active policy for the economy." The state, according to this editorial, should intervene to reduce prices, make capital productive, and restrict its flight abroad.[118] How these things were to be accomplished was not explained. Indeed, Fritz Naphtali denied that a "general recipe" for overcoming the depression in Germany existed. Those who promised otherwise were engaged in an "election swindle." He outlined conditions that would decrease unemployment, such as greater "mass buying power," more exports, lower customs, and fewer hindrances on foreign investment.[119] While honest, this prescription was unlikely to fire the imagination of citizens who were out of work or fearful of going bankrupt.

To whom did the SPD address itself in this campaign? It directed appeals to youth, employees, civil servants, women, and farmers in the form of exhortations to "struggle under the red flag" or simply to "vote List Number One." The admonition "The class is all—professional status is nothing" may not have reassured skeptical white-collar workers and civil servants about the SPD's concern for their welfare.[120] Nonetheless, a speaker tried to convince a largely middle-class audience in a little town near Hanover that talk of Socialist hostility to the rural Mittelstand was a "slanderous fairy tale."[121] As in 1928, SPD slogans were mainly negative. In 1930, however, unlike in 1928, it faced competition from high-profile opponents on the left and the right whose rhetoric far outstripped its attacks on the social system and current regime, not to mention their repudiation of the republic and political system. The bourgeois parties might be falling apart of their own accord, but their deserters and those shopping for a first political home had to be convinced to choose the SPD over other alternatives. The SPD had no strategy to attract these millions of voters. Instead, it relied on catchwords that had traditionally rallied its core supporters without offering them, much less nonworkers, a way out of their economic misery.

The campaign's incoherence was rooted in confusion about the party's political options. Despite antagonism to the moderate bourgeois parties and to Brüning personally, occasionally a Socialist insisted that the SPD should be brought into a postelection government that all knew would most likely be headed by Brüning.[122] Suddenly, at the end of the campaign, Otto Braun, speaking from his relatively neutral position as head of Prussia's Weimar Coalition, called on the chancellor to distance himself from Treviranus's announcement that Social Democratic cooperation would be eschewed after the election. Brüning answered by questioning whether the SPD could work with a chancellor it had so vigorously attacked during the campaign. Braun responded that it could, but Brüning refused to commit himself one way or the other.[123] At a Hamburg rally on September 8, Braun again held out the olive branch, saying the SPD was willing to take on responsibility if given influence on financial, economic, and social issues commensurate with its political strength. Brüning did not reply. *Vorwärts* prominently reported this nonexchange on its front page.[124] Clearly, the executive committee stood behind Braun's forays into national politics. The ambiguity and confusion of the Social Democratic campaign stand in sharp relief in this final, poignant appeal to Brüning in the last week before September 14. It is doubtful whether such apparent waffling made a favorable impression on voters other than committed Social Democratic supporters.

The Struggle Begins

"The Reichstag elections of September 14, 1930, struck like a bomb," Julius Leber wrote in 1933. "In the Social Democratic camp depression and helplessness reigned for days." Critics complained at the time about the party leadership's "indecisiveness." Richard Kleineibst, a left-wing Social Democrat, regretted that the electoral outcome crippled the "responsible men with fear and paralysis" so they "hesitate, when they should act, and wait on events instead of taking hold and directing the course of development."[1] Lore Agnes, a Reichstag deputy from Düsseldorf, protested to her district organization that the party council was convened only after several days and then gave the word, "Wait!"[2] The consternation of the SPD's leaders is understandable. The NSDAP had skyrocketed from 810,127 to 6,409,610 ballots and from 12 to 107 seats in the Reichstag. The KPD vote had increased from 10.6 percent to 13.1 percent and from 54 to 77 delegates. The bourgeois middle parties seemed to be in the process of dissolution. Only the Center Party had held its own and had even won a few seats (from 62 to 68). The SPD lost just 575,000 votes but contracted to 24.5 percent from 29.8 percent of the electorate because voter participation increased from 75.6 to 82 percent. Its delegation shrank from 154 to 143.[3]

The SPD had correctly gauged the unpopularity of Brüning's economic program, but it had misjudged the breadth of the rejection of mainstream parliamentarism and the extent to which extremist nationalist propaganda had mobilized normally nonpolitical citizens.[4] Columns in *Vorwärts* revealed the party leaders' stupefaction about how to respond to this agitated temperament or, rather, which of its components to tackle—the anticapitalist or the antidemocratic. Public statements eloquently manifested the indecision about whether to interpret the elections as a mandate for economic revolution or for political counterrevolution. On September 19 the executive committee proclaimed the Reichstag's primary task to be the overcoming of the economic crisis with its mass unemployment, but on October 4 the Social Democratic deputation announced that the threat posed to democracy directly by the fascists and indirectly by the Communists required that the SPD's first concern be to secure democracy, constitutional government, and parliament. In this statement, the fight against unemployment received second billing.[5]

Higher-priority concerns influenced the political strategy and parliamentary tactic to be pursued. In weighing their options, SPD policymakers had to consider a dismaying array of unfavorable factors. The economic crisis was severe and worsening, both cause and effect of the sinister political developments. In immediate reaction to the election results, foreign creditors withdrew 500 million Reichsmark.[6] Of course the phenomenal growth of the NSDAP overshadowed all else. Its putschist past, revanchist nationalism, virulent antirepublicanism, contempt for democracy, and frightening insistence on being handed the reins of power made its popular appeal foreboding. For the SPD the only reassuring features of the political landscape lay in its own relatively good showing at the polls, the imperviousness of the Catholic electorate to radical seduction, and the existence of the Prussian bulwark under Otto Braun.[7]

Reckoning the debits and credits of the political balance sheet, the party leadership had to arrive at a strategy to overcome the threats to the republic without overly straining its reliable pillars of support. After the leaders' initial bewilderment, their necessary sense of emergency turned into a hypervigilant alertness to the immediate political situation.[8] Political panic and remorse over past parliamentary behavior seem to have influenced the leadership's decision making at this critical moment. Curiously, Socialist policymakers continued to view longer-term political development and the economic situation with equanimity. These contradictory perspectives grew from underlying assumptions about the lessons of history and an intense preoccupation with politics in the parliamentary arena. Rather than develop an overall strategy to confront the Nazi threat, the party elite worked out a parliamentary tactic through which it hoped to protect the Prussian fortress while keeping Hitler at bay. Party dissidents and provincial Socialists criticized this tactic without successfully challenging it. Instead, they initiated an extraparliamentary mobilization of the SPD. From this haphazard beginning, a hybrid strategy—defensive in parliament, offensive in Prussia and outside parliament—began to emerge, a strategy many Socialists felt had produced positive results for the republic and for Social Democracy by March 1931.

Origins of the Toleration Policy

Otto Braun was the first leading Social Democrat to take a clear stand on the formation of a new regime. On September 15 he gave an interview to United Press at which he appeared not depressed but energetic. He insisted that the worrisome electoral results posed no threat to Germany's constitution, public security, or foreign policy. The radical parties would not get a chance to execute their plans because "a big coalition of all sensible groups" would be formed that "will concentrate their entire force on fighting unemployment and improving living conditions among the masses."[9] Privately Braun had an intermediary inform Brüning that he was willing to become Reich vice-chancellor while remaining Prussian minister-president.[10] He hoped to bridge the gap between the SPD and the bourgeois middle parties, especially the Center Party, by informally linking the Reich and the Prussian governments. Braun also thought Hindenburg's resistance to SPD participation in a coalition could be overcome in this way and that the SPD Reichstag delegation would accept cabinet participation if one of its ministers were not only vice-chancellor but also Braun, with his reputation for toughness and with the power of the Prussian government behind him.[11]

Other movers and shakers also preferred a Great Coalition as a solution to the new parliamentary impasse. On the same day that Braun voiced his opinion, Ludwig Kastl, director of the professional staff of the RDI, called the chancellery and visited State Secretary Hermann Pünder. Speaking for the RDI, he pressed for a return to the Great Coalition. Individual industrialists let it be known that they too favored this route to avert a political and, thus, economic crisis. Although important businessmen vehemently disagreed, enough support for a Great Coalition was voiced by prominent capitalists to suggest that the election results had reduced the hostility of a section of big business toward Social Democracy.[12] Yet Braun and Kastl's proposed solution did not prevail. Brüning did not respond to Braun's public or confidential suggestions, just as he had left Braun hanging in their exchange during the campaign.[13] Brüning remembered that "many individuals" had advocated a return to a Great Coalition but explained that he had preferred to govern without Social Democracy, fearing that "solid cooperation" with the SPD would make the BVP, the Center Party, and center-right parties vulnerable to attack by the German Nationalists and the NSDAP.[14]

On the Social Democratic side, only Braun, who did not sit on the executive committee, put his cards on the table. Although at the end of the campaign Social Democrats had indicated they would join a cabinet with Brüning, their postelection attitude may have reverted to a less conciliatory stance, given the tremendous electoral tallies of two parties that could be expected to exploit Social Democratic participation in a coalition. We do not know how party leaders reacted to Braun's call for a Great Coalition. The historian Karl Dietrich Bracher has suggested that Braun's "trial balloon" originated with Hermann Müller.[15] Braun's biographer, Hagen Schulze, has argued that after his interview Braun retreated to his hunting lodge, hurt and embarrassed, not only because Brüning did not respond but because leading Social Democrats let him know they were not considering his vice-chancellorship or a Great Coalition.[16] *Vorwärts*, edited by Friedrich Stampfer, who *was* a member of the executive, appealed to Brüning to cooperate with Social Democracy but did not call for a coalition or say the SPD would support Brüning.[17] Whatever its attitude, the executive committee obviously believed the first gesture must come from the chancellor.

The outward process by which the Social Democratic leaders came to tolerate Brüning's cabinet can be traced. Hilferding invited Brüning and Hermann Müller to a private meeting over a cup of tea on September 23, more than a week after the elections. All three appear to have been less than crystal clear about what they wanted, but no one suggested a coalition.[18] A week later Brüning had another unofficial conversation with the Social Democratic leaders, including Otto Wels, at Pünder's home. During this "historic" discussion, Pünder excitedly confided to his diary, the idea of toleration was settled upon, although not ironed out: "unfortunately" the Social Democrats could not be included in a cabinet "as that would not be accepted on the right and is not offered by the left," but "what might be possible is Social Democratic support of the cabinet and our work."[19] Hilferding, Wels, and Müller presented a set of demands that did not include being taken into the government, not necessarily a sign that they would not have joined a cabinet. They asked for modest economic and political concessions, including abolition of the poll tax, restoration of cuts in sickness and unemployment insurance, and division of the July emergency decree into individual laws that could be passed through the Reichstag. Although Brüning neither asked them into the government nor accepted their conditions, the Socialist leaders decided to give his government passive support.[20]

Historians have argued that anxiety about Communist competition kept the SPD leaders from seriously considering participation in the government.[21] It would be hard to imagine that Social Democrats did not look over their left shoulder at the dread specter of Communism gathering up the votes of disaffected workers. But just how, and how much, concern about KPD gains influenced leadership decision making is difficult to estimate. Writing retrospectively, Ernest Hamburger, a Prussian Landtag deputy, named concern about losing votes as a reason the party did not join the government.[22] Prelate Ludwig Kaas, chairman of the Center Party, recalled that later in the fall Wels, Breitscheid, and Müller told him they considered the KPD more dangerous than the NSDAP.[23] A memorandum written for the chancellor's office in the weeks after the

elections, however, suggested that anxiety about the KPD contributed to
the decision not to oppose Brüning. The anonymous author believed the
SPD feared the KPD's ability to take better advantage of unrest that would
accompany an "executive shakeup."[24] At earlier points in the republic's
history, the existence of the KPD had reinforced Social Democratic accommodationism, so such reasoning is certainly conceivable. Anxiety
about the KPD played a part in the decision to tolerate but does not seem
to have determined it. On one hand, Social Democrats did not find a
Communist putsch likely.[25] On the other hand, they took seriously the
Communist challenge to the SPD as a party and attributed their losses
almost exclusively to KPD competition: unemployed, especially young,
workers had cast votes for the "Bolsheviks." Yet mainstream party papers
expected these voters to return to the SPD when the economic situation
improved; then the KPD would shrink back to the sect it really was.[26]

Historians have cited the SPD elite's wish to avoid resistance within its
own ranks and, especially, within the Reichstag delegation as another
reason the leadership did not enter Brüning's government.[27] No doubt
the leadership hoped to avoid a second Panzerkreuzer affair. Again,
however, it is difficult to estimate the degree of influence inner-party
opinion exercised on the decision to tolerate Brüning. By the time the
first meeting with Brüning occurred, Hilferding and Müller had more
than an inkling about internal views on what parliamentary tactic was
preferred. Müller urged Braun to return to Berlin from his cabin retreat
for the first Reichstag delegation meeting. At the party council meeting,
he explained, more widespread than "should be expected" was the opinion that the Right, including the Nazis, should be allowed to form a
government in order to expose its bankruptcy. Müller believed Braun
could argue persuasively against this viewpoint, which he predicted many
SPD deputies would share.[28] Braun would be effective because he was
"seen as the strongest unconsumed force on the Socialist side. . . . [At
party] gatherings and in the press, when government participation is
discussed, your name always comes up."[29] On one hand, council members
wanted to let the Right expose itself; on the other, they hoped Braun
would join the cabinet. If the leaders took their cues about party opinion
from council attitudes, they had to decipher a scrambled message.

In the daily press and at numerous functionary and membership meetings, provincial editors, party bureaucrats, and the rank and file aired a
variety of opinions about the political tactic to follow on the heels of
September 14. Although an observer in Berlin told the journalist Ernst
Feder, "Strong currents in the SPD would gladly see the Nazis join the
government," in fact, no consensus crystallized that could be character-

ized as favoring opposition or coalition, much less toleration.[30] As in the reaction to the Panzerkreuzer decision, sentiment for an offensive strategy emerged. Dissidents did not agree on the tactics of such a course but concurred, first, that the Great Coalition had hurt, not benefited, the SPD and, second, that the party possessed enough political leverage to undertake an active strategy.[31] This optimistic assessment of the party's strength was proffered, oddly enough, by the very people who also admitted to significant electoral losses by the SPD.[32] The leadership, in contrast, while making much of the SPD's good performance in the elections, doubted the working class's ability to carry out extraparliamentary action in defense of the republic.[33]

Local editors advocated coalition with conditions more often than they encouraged automatic opposition.[34] Surveying the situation with uncharacteristic caution, the editor of the *Leipziger Volkszeitung* concluded that the SPD would either have to join a coalition with the ultraconservative Economic Party or accept Nazi participation "which would give the Hakenkreuzler the chance to erect a fascist dictatorship with democratic means."[35] Several editors voiced a third alternative soon after the elections. Thus, Kurt Schumacher, newly elected to the Reichstag and presumably aware of the alternatives under discussion in Berlin, insisted that an "eventual toleration" dare not overburden the social sector and so improve fascism's chances.[36] In Hamburg, a center of neorevisionism, SPD district delegates and shop stewards weighed the political situation. Karl Meitmann called for an "active struggle for democracy." To "great applause," he insisted that "toleration of Brüning can and dare not be considered" because it would mean "renunciation of direct influence, yet full sharing of responsibility." The SPD "must fight for a government role," he demanded, reminding his listeners that "not only responsibility but power is the demand of the hour." Speakers in the discussion did not disagree with Meitmann, but the thrust of their comments differed. Whereas he wanted to press for government power, they stressed that certain basic demands must be fulfilled before the SPD could enter a government, insisting in particular on the withdrawal of the July emergency decree. The majority favored participation under this condition but did not shy from the alternative of opposition. Meitmann, on the other hand, saw Nazi inclusion in a regime as unthinkable.[37]

Siegfried Aufhäuser, addressing Berlin's functionaries on September 30, leaned toward opposition. While he agreed that the SPD should not "shy from responsibility," he stipulated that social policies "friendly to the working class" must be the price paid for Social Democratic cooperation. He disparaged as "unsocialist" the tendency to "place all hopes on one man, Otto Braun," and attacked Hilferding's defense of toleration that had just appeared in *Die Gesellschaft*. "Like a coquette," he protested, "we offer the bourgeoisie the charms of Social Democracy, instead of showing our fist. . . . We need the highest activity, true workers' politics!" The critics of coalition, he insisted, "don't underestimate the National Socialists, but believe it an illusion to think a profound people's movement can be overcome by [our] mechanical, formal participation in state power." Responsibility, he concluded, must be combined with "political energy."[38]

In the discussion afterward, district officials expressed intense bitterness at a party leadership that they held responsible for the KPD's startling victory in Berlin on "Black Sunday." Communists had polled the vote of every third Berliner, while the SPD had fallen to 28 percent from 34 percent. One functionary argued that the SPD dare not dally with the Brüning parties, which embodied the real fascist danger (a viewpoint shared by the top ranks of the SPD and the ADGB during the campaign). In a more reflective vein, another comrade described the quandary of the moderate Left and, ultimately, the party as a whole: "pure responsibility" would "batter" it at the polls, while "pure activity" meant a fight to the bitter end. He concluded that the only solution was a coalition that allowed for agitational freedom.[39]

Several days later a Special Berlin District Conference convened to hear Hilferding defend the Reichstag delegation's decision to make parliamentary government the SPD's highest priority. The exact form toleration would take remained unclear, but it was obvious Brüning would not be allowed to fall. Hilferding spoke against the "expose the Right" solution, challenging its advocates to explain how they would get the Nazis out once they were in. In his view, the elections had dealt a mighty blow to parliamentarism and democracy but did not constitute a defeat of the SPD. He questioned the feasibility of a general strike to resist dictatorship, given high unemployment and the unreliability of Communist workers. Antagonistic shouts from the floor punctuated Hilferding's speech. In the discussion one speaker ridiculed the leadership's *"Faschistenangst"*; the Nazis' greatest asset, he claimed, was the SPD's "cowardice." Another lamented the inconsistency of having attacked Brüning in the campaign but now supporting him. In contrast to Hilferding, these Berliners wanted to give first priority to social demands and openly advocated the "expose the Right" solution. By tolerating Brüning, they argued, the party would allow fascism time to develop until it could exercise power effectively. The meeting passed a resolution that called on the SPD to carry out a policy consistent with its posture during the campaign and proclaimed the SPD's determination to secure democracy, if need be with extraparliamentary means.[40]

In early October, functionary and membership meetings took place in Chemnitz-Zwickau, Bochum, Breslau, and Leipzig—all left-wing districts that opposed the still-undefined policy of support. At these meetings, as well as at gatherings in Munich, party members criticized the SPD's political vacillation.[41] In Leipzig, one thousand functionaries heard Engelbert Graf condemn the decision to support Brüning without concessions and then passed a resolution condemning it themselves.[42] Hilferding chose Breslau as the next leftist stronghold in which to peddle the leadership policy. In these early speeches of Hilferding's one sees the leadership's justification of toleration take form. In Breslau, unlike Berlin, he not only admitted that the party's strategy was defensive but emphasized this point. He refuted arguments in favor of Socialist opposition to a rightist cabinet. First, he believed the Nazis were already strong enough to consolidate a hold on power. Second, such an experiment would cause foreign credit to dry up and thus would sharpen the economic crisis. Finally, it would threaten the Prussian government. Having learned his lesson in Berlin, he refrained from disparaging "extraparliamentary possibilities." Speakers during the discussion all rejected toleration, but no consensus emerged in favor of either opposition or a coalition based on a "change of course."[43]

In the debate about what tactic to follow after September 14, the moderate Left, represented by Aufhäuser, Toni Sender, and others, charged that the party had turned from working-class politics toward collaborationism. With the far Left, represented by Ernst Eckstein and Seydewitz, they believed the party's losses stemmed from its participation in unpopular decisions during the Müller regime. They constantly reiterated that the party's strength lay in its mass support; its bargaining power in parliament was directly proportional to its popular base.[44] Unlike Seydewitz, though, and like the leadership, the moderate Left took the immediate Nazi threat seriously and emphasized the importance of democratic rights and the gains of the republic. Its adherents were genuinely torn about what parliamentary tactic to adopt. The far Left, in contrast, downplayed the Nazi threat to the republic. Its disciples sometimes argued that the time for protecting democratic rights was past and class struggle was now on the agenda.[45]

Neorevisionists, such as Karl Meitmann and Paul Gerlach, a Reichstag deputy from Düsseldorf, agreed with the Left that Social Democratic mistakes, not just economic problems and Brüning's policies, had contributed to SPD losses and the radicals' gains. They too were upset by the party's "zig-zag" course, but they did not see abandonment of class politics as the mistake.[46] Blaming instead Hermann Müller's lack of charisma and the seeming inability of most party leaders to understand the hard task of wielding power, Gerlach and Meitmann pointed to Otto Braun as the model to follow.[47] As did moderate leftists, neorevisionists eventually accepted toleration as an interim policy to parry the Nazi threat. Neither left-wing nor right-wing dissenters, however, believed that over the long haul a purely defensive policy and earnest lectures on the importance of democracy would excite disgruntled Germans.[48] Party leaders recognized this deficiency of the toleration policy but felt it also allowed for "the greatest freedom of movement."[49] The executive committee chose toleration rather than pushing to get into the government or going into opposition because forbearance conformed to their analysis of the political and economic situation and to their sense of what the party ought to do. It was not simply a compromise tactic that evaded the criticisms of Right and Left.

Social Democrats bandied different conceptions of responsibility in the debate about the SPD's parliamentary tactic. Neorevisionists linked responsibility to government power, while leftists refused to divorce it from extraparliamentary activity. The leaders stressed responsibility pure and simple. Braun, in *Vorwärts*'s full-fledged defense of toleration, explained that the SPD was saving the republic from its enemies by carrying out a policy that was "unpopular" but "responsible."[50] Remorse over Müller's fall, and desire to avoid a replay of the circumstances that occasioned it, contributed to the determination not to act rashly.[51] Party authorities, swayed by concern for workers' welfare and a sense of duty, consciously chose a self-sacrificing path at this fork.[52] In his memoirs, Severing wrote, "[The toleration policy] demanded a high measure of sacrifice. But these sacrifices erected walls which were supposed to protect the republic against the fascist onslaught. If they did not hold, the SPD could not be held responsible. So reasoned the majority of the [Reichstag] delegation, which was thoroughly aware of the great self-denial that this attitude entailed."[53] While Severing, Braun, and Hilferding underlined the SPD's duty to the republic, ADGB leaders emphasized the unions' duty to the SPD. When the national committee met on September 19, union leaders did not discuss their political preferences or the party's options. Instead, ADGB cochairman Peter Grassmann expressed satisfaction that the Free Trade Unions had "stepped out so openly for the SPD . . . considering how the elections turned out." He praised the unions for having "fought this campaign over the security and continuation of *Sozialpolitik*. With [this effort] we protected ourselves from the reproach that, given the outcome, the unions had not done their duty (*Schuldigkeit*)."[54]

Published defenses of toleration during its first months clearly show that the SPD leadership saw it, first and foremost, as a tactic to save political democracy.[55] Party leaders predicated protection of the general welfare on a retreat by the SPD from direct influence over the nation's fate. Union leaders evidently accepted this linkage. The notion that the SPD could best serve the republic from a defensive stance rested on several assumptions. First, Social Democrats wanted to reduce the Socialist irritant to bourgeois parties such as the DVP and the Economic Party that, if irked by the SPD, might turn to the NSDAP as a coalition partner or even resort to civil war. Second, many party and union leaders saw the SPD as an aggressive representative of workers' interests but a passive bulwark of the republic. The third assumption was that Brüning, if not the parties in his cabinet, could be trusted to secure the republic. Finally, the leadership planned to distinguish negative support from endorsement of Brüning's social policies and to challenge measures that harmed the working class. In defending toleration, Braun and SPD editors emphasized that support of Brüning did not equal approval of his government—Social Democracy took responsibility for the republic, not for his regime.[56]

Those who proposed toleration and those who grudgingly accepted it did so, above all, because they believed the NSDAP posed an acute threat to the republic. According to Hilferding, the dynamite in the situation lay in the combination of a mass movement from below with social reaction from above.[57] SPD leaders wanted most of all to prevent this combination from cohering in a political alliance. Their panic arose from the suddenness and unexpectedness of the NSDAP surge.[58] After having underestimated the NSDAP as an electoral opponent, many Social Democrats now feared a Nazi putsch.[59] As the days slid by and Hitler made no grab for power, fears of a coup subsided, but the conviction remained that violence would erupt if the SPD "took one foot off the democratic floor."[60] In early October, Braun told Prussian State Secretary Robert Weismann, "Prepare for civil war."[61] Crispien warned Berlin functionaries, "We must create tactical means to prevent civil war." Years later, Stampfer maintained that the only alternative to toleration was an armed struggle pitting the National Socialists, the president, the Reichswehr, and the bourgeois parties against the SPD and the unreliable KPD.[62]

The executive committee obviously did not agree with a government memorandum that argued that the election results made a compromise between capital and labor more possible, not less so. Because the business community felt more threatened by National Socialists than by Social Democrats, the author surmised, industrialists would now consent to efforts to reduce unemployment in exchange for reductions in wages and salaries.[63] According to Peter Grassmann, those "few" industrialists who had supported the Nazis "due to fear of Marxism" regretted this inclination after September 14.[64] Most Social Democrats, however, believed capitalism had nothing to fear from the Nazis since Hitler's "real intention" was "to repress the socialist workers' movement."[65] They made no effort to manipulate the doubts of German bankers and industrialists about National Socialism to their advantage. Though they knew that German business depended on the largesse of international banks, they did not exploit the open hostility of French and American financiers to cabinet participation by the NSDAP.[66] Paul Löbe complained that in return for the maintenance of a skeletal democracy, the SPD agreed to protect capitalism from the NSDAP's "revolutionary side."[67] Hilferding suggested, however, that the SPD could not demand more from "employers and agrarians" who were itching to unleash the NSDAP against the SPD and parliament.[68]

Not only did Social Democrats exact no social concessions in return for tolerating Brüning, they also sanctioned a political arrangement that saved parliamentary government by circumventing it. By propping up a minority regime, they took the power to bring down the government from the legislature and gave it to Hindenburg, allowing Brüning to rule through the emergency powers vested in the president by Article 48 of the constitution. Forty years later Ernest Hamburger testified to the trust Socialist leaders had placed in Brüning, admitting that if they had known of the antidemocratic, monarchist plans (and willingness to bring the Nazis into his cabinet) revealed in Brüning's memoirs, they would not have held to the toleration policy.[69] SPD policymakers, according to Wilhelm Hoegner, also counted on Hindenburg and the Reichswehr to remain loyal to Brüning and not to hand Hitler the reigns of power "under any circumstances."[70] If we assume Hoegner to be right, such sudden faith in Hindenburg and the Reichswehr command is difficult to fathom.[71] Julius Leber suggested that the reflexive turn to the Reichswehr in the aftershock of the election arose from a tendency to see the armed forces as an instrument of a feudal lord. In normal times, Socialists distrusted the military, but now, as society threatened to rend itself and the executive alone stood strong, they believed the army would stick by the president, unaffected by oscillations in the popular mood.[72] Is it possible to reconcile such a naive view of the executive and the army command with the fear of civil war? On one hand, SPD leaders feared that open social conflict would induce disparate bourgeois forces to cohere; but, on the other hand, they seem to have reasoned that the president and the Reichswehr, less pressed by economic concerns than politicians or social interest groups, would prefer the status quo, as long as a confrontation could be avoided. Thus, the leadership desperately maneuvered to avert the moment of crisis when class lines would be drawn and, in so doing, sanctioned the executive's growing autonomy from parliament and social interest groups.[73]

An alarmist perspective, then, dovetailed with certain routinist notions. Together, they fed hopes that the threat to the republic could be overcome with a vigilant but defensive parliamentary tactic. Drawing on Weimar's electoral history, Social Democratic leaders expected that Nazi voters, in search of fast redress of sundry grievances, would turn from Hitler in disappointment if his political plans were frustrated and the Nazi Reichstag delegation were forced to thrash about in impotent opposition.[74] The relevant analogy appeared to be the May 1924 Reichstag elections, held in the wake of the hyperinflation of 1923, when the KPD had benefited from Socialist losses and the rabidly antirepublican DNVP had made big gains. The SPD lost more drastically in 1924 than in 1930, its deputation shriveling to 100 from 171, but it had recovered 31 seats in December 1924 after passively supporting a minority regime during the summer.[75] From a weaker position than it had in 1930, the SPD had bounced back quickly, if not completely. This precedent suggested the advantages of sitting out a crisis while tolerating a conservative regime.[76]

Social Democratic leaders knew that the economic crisis was fueling the radical surge and that an upswing would sap the radical movements.[77] While they made a political about-face after the election shock, however, SPD economists produced no emergency plan to attack the crisis. Though impressed with its force, they believed this "typical crisis of the capitalist system" would run its course in one or two years.[78] In the fall of 1930, party leaders felt that the political crisis was both more acute and more tractable than the economic dilemma.[79] They assumed that Brüning's "sacrifice and save" policies would be of limited duration.[80] Meanwhile, "negative support" provided the freedom to criticize cuts in social outlays.[81] Social Democrats argued that government measures should cushion the impact of the crisis on the livelihood of the populace. They also condemned Brüning's program because it cut wages more severely than prices and protected large agriculture at the expense of urban consumers and small farmers. Instead, Social Democrats pointed out, buying power must be bolstered to provide the demand needed to encourage production.[82] *Vorwärts* also advocated moderate job creation programs and a shorter work week.[83] But without a fundamentally different plan to get out of the crisis, the SPD restricted itself to pressing for piecemeal changes in Brüning's draconian measures. This tactic and the economic analysis behind it were only seriously challenged after mid-1931 when the crisis suddenly and drastically worsened.[84]

The leaders' defensive strategy did have an offensive side. They calculated that they could save the republic by shoring up the Weimar Coalition in Prussia, where Braun could use his power to come down hard on Nazi street violence and a potential putsch. The SPD's sacrifices seemed a bearable price for protecting Braun's ability to act more offensively.[85] Therefore, Braun's position, strengthened relative to Brüning's after September 14, was not used as a bargaining chip in their negotiations with Brüning.[86] As Hilferding made clear in his speech in Breslau, pressure on the Center Party in the Reich or in Prussia might jeopardize the Prussian fortress.[87]

In the end, the leadership convinced its critics to give negative support a chance. At Müller's bidding, Braun attended the crucial Reichstag delegation meeting and convinced deputies of the necessity of tolerating Brüning. Only fifteen members voted against a resolution that made democracy and parliamentary government the SPD's first order of business.[88] According to Toni Sender, moderate leftists accepted a temporary defensive policy in the face of the threat to the republic posed by the election shock. Speaking in Hamburg, Aufhäuser appealed to the party base to stand behind its leadership.[89] The membership and apparatus, even in districts that initially condemned support of Brüning, responded to Aufhäuser's plea. An SA rampage against Berlin's Jewish shops on the day the Reichstag convened no doubt brought home to skeptical deputies and their constituencies the immediacy of the Nazi threat.[90]

On October 4 in Hamburg, the rightist Karl Meitmann spoke very differently than he had ten days earlier. After presenting the only two alternatives as Nazi participation in a regime or Social Democratic support of Brüning, he rejected the first out of hand. In Munich, an ex-Communist defended toleration to a sympathetic audience.[91] At its general membership meeting in November, the SPD in Düsseldorf passed Paul Gerlach's resolution in support of the delegation's course. Lore Agnes and others at the meeting criticized the policy but proposed no alternative tactic.[92] Arnold Kranold, a moderate leftist, lectured far leftists on the need for "closed ranks" in a treacherous period, reminding them that the "October 18 route" (when the SPD delegation abstained on no-confidence motions to oust Brüning) must be adhered to when the new emergency decree came out in December.[93] Whereas functionaries in

Leipzig had condemned toleration in early October, later in the month rank and file members endorsed the position of the Reichstag deputation.[94] Seydewitz, Kurt Rosenfeld, Eckstein, and others in the Left Opposition inveighed against toleration in *Der Klassenkampf* but did not break ranks in the Reichstag. Instead, nine deputies did not participate in the December vote on the emergency decree.[95]

Most Social Democrats adjusted with some difficulty to their role as the democratic pillar of a semiparliamentary regime.[96] Only as they realized the incapacity of the new Reichstag to make the difficult decisions required of it did rule by emergency decree take on an "inner justification."[97] In fact, new Nazi successes, Socialist losses, and the further "collapse of the bourgeois parties" in local elections in Baden, Mecklenburg, and Bremen bolstered the determination to keep Hitler from power, rather than causing the SPD to question the premises of its parliamentary tactic, as· *Der Klassenkampf* argued it should.[98] Aufhäuser, intensely involved in negotiations over the December decree, prepared party opinion for the vote to uphold it by highlighting the partial restoration of cuts in sickness and unemployment insurance won in negotiations.[99]

The December abstention behind them, Social Democrats settled into their new role more comfortably. A boost to morale came with the National Opposition's withdrawal from the Reichstag on February 10, 1931, after a majority voted to change parliamentary rules. The wording of no-confidence motions was set to prevent the rightist opposition from using them to force delegates to vote *for* Brüning's government; a second rule-change struck at Nazi and Communist deputies who abused parliamentary immunity.[100] Influential Social Democrats interpreted this endeavor as evidence of parliament's will to defend its integrity, a step toward closer cooperation with the Brüning parties, and a defeat of the Right.[101] Fritz Tarnow, a leading trade unionist and Reichstag deputy, believed the NSDAP's parliamentary fumbling had damaged its image; sooner or later the public would find laughable Nazi parliamentary incompetence. In Tarnow's view, Brüning's sudden majority also eased the political situation, but the SPD delegation must continue with its "so successfully begun action against fascism" since a crisis could arise at any time.[102] At the end of February 1931 the Social Democratic leadership believed its parliamentary tactic had produced tangible political results.

Mobilizing the SPD

Speaking in Breslau in October 1930, Hilferding argued that a peaceful parliamentary course would create an interim during which the

SPD could make itself "readier to fight (*schlagkräftiger*)."[103] The reasoning, one suspects, was ex post facto and was designed to persuade the skeptical; signs of a nationally coordinated effort to mobilize the SPD on an extraparliamentary basis did not appear until early January 1931. Among party intellectuals and provincial activists, on the other hand, the September elections sparked a lively and many-sided discussion about the extraparliamentary arena. Within a few months internal ferment led to a noticeable surge in SPD activity. The impetus came from below and from the Reichsbanner rather than from the party's national leadership. During this initial anti-Nazi mobilization, which continued into the spring of 1931, Social Democrats emphasized quantity—numbers of meetings and marches, extension of recruitment into new areas—rather than a different kind of agitation and propaganda or a revised program. Lower functionaries and grassroots activists were convinced that intense mobilization and good organization explained the NSDAP's success, while the business as usual attitude of the SPD had thwarted the Socialist party. Gradually it became clear that quantity alone could not sustain the enthusiasm of the already converted or, even less likely, lure the uncommitted. Only late in 1931, however, did fractious questions about the content, style, and audience of propaganda dominate debates about how to revitalize the SPD. As more Social Democrats argued that an effective extraparliamentary strategy required deep reforms in the SPD, the issue of mobilization from below became politically charged. In 1930, a few isolated voices on the far left and right of the SPD criticized the structure and politics of the party, but most activists and intellectuals concentrated on the tactic of more, and more visible, activity to stimulate the ranks and recruit fellow travelers.

Neorevisionist intellectuals, especially writers for *Neue Blätter für den Sozialismus*, spearheaded the effort to come to terms with Nazi growth and SPD stagnation. The election results spurred *Neue Blätter*'s editors to devote more space to political commentary and less to cultural critiques. At private conferences in November 1930 and January 1931, neorevisionists close to the journal met to discuss bureaucracy, age, and high salaries in the SPD, the characteristics of its left and right wings, and the need to rethink Marxism.[104] Two close friends in the *Neue Blätter* circle, Theo Haubach and Carlo Mierendorff, articulated most explicitly the peculiarities of the neorevisionist viewpoint: right-wing concern with personal leadership, as opposed to "principled class politics," combined with a left-wing critique of bureaucracy, emphasis on grassroots revitalization, and focus on extraparliamentary activity. According to the far Left, the party's defensive stance in parliament threatened to cancel the benefits of mobilizing the SPD in the streets.[105] In contrast, neorevisionists did not initially oppose toleration, at least in public.[106] Instead, they worked to transform the SPD's methods and style outside parliament. In early 1931 Mierendorff and several collaborators privately circulated "suggestions for the reform of party propaganda," which called for the SPD to retool itself to fight for an "aggressive democracy" and to attract the support of "social revolutionary elements" around Otto Strasser's wing of the NSDAP.[107] In published articles, however, Mierendorff and Haubach still restricted themselves to calls for more activity and for better directed and energetic agitation rather than for a shift in content and audience.

In "Password: Attack," published in the *Hamburger Echo*, Haubach described the election results as a "slap" for the SPD. Good slogans and hard work had not prevented its defeat. Alert observers, he asserted, could sense during the campaign that "our agitation barely broke through our own ranks to reach a wider audience." The SPD had entered an election field already plowed for months by the "feverish activity" of Communists and fascists. Moreover, the party aimed its propaganda at its own organization, not the broader electorate. The SPD's "agitation management" was "bureaucratically ossified"; it ran by a rigid "calendar schedule," not the "living needs of the moment." Now the party must retool for a major agitational offensive because not only its future but the fate of the democratic state hung in the balance.[108] In *Neue Blätter* Mierendorff elaborated on Haubach's argument: the SPD had failed to block the advances of the KPD and the NSDAP because the party leadership had directed the campaign at Brüning rather than at National Socialism, even though by June 1930 the Nazis had emerged as a formidable opponent that demanded an entirely new set of tactics and techniques. Mierendorff faulted a leadership that relied on a strong organization to rally its own troops instead of developing a strategy that encompassed the entire battlefront. The SPD entered slapdash into the fray with a faulty focus and tired methods. He concluded, "The main mistake . . . lies in the underestimation of extra-parliamentary activity. As if mesmerized, Social Democracy has faced toward parliament for years."[109]

Haubach, Mierendorff, and other revisionists were not alone in their conviction that much could be set right by mobilizing the SPD at its grassroots.[110] Calls for activity, mixed with a healthy dose of self-criticism, rang from the lower ranks of the party. *Das Freie Wort* was inundated by "dozens upon dozens" of letters that showed the determination of provincial Socialists to match the energy of the Nazis by transforming the SPD into a permanent agitation machine.[111] They noted that in districts with poor SPD returns, even the smallest villages had been flooded with Nazi meetings, rallies, and speakers. Many contributors argued (as had a few in the spring) that Socialists must take their opponents seriously, swarm into Nazi meetings, and argue with those present, not just insult them.[112]

Local activists made criticisms similar to those of neorevisionists. The party, they asserted, had not conquered new political territory and had focused too much on the big cities. Others complained, however, that higher functionaries were especially out of touch with the urban masses. To reforge ties, they should hand out leaflets and get out among the people, not just deliver dull speeches that inundated listeners with facts rather than filling them with enthusiasm.[113] Political criticisms cropped up less frequently. One writer argued that dusting off the red flags would not impress the *Mittelstand*. Several correspondents said the emphasis on unemployment insurance had backfired since people wanted jobs, not compensation. A few harked back to the stupidity of having left the coalition in March, while others wanted to go into opposition now.[114]

Lower functionaries did as they preached and took the lead in pushing the SPD into the streets and meeting halls in the winter of 1930–31. In Frankfurt, for example, an "action committee" of party, trade union, shop floor, and Reichsbanner representatives had the task of "prepar[ing] comrades for the extra-parliamentary struggle." This committee organized numerous meetings and marches throughout the fall.[115] The national leadership approved of this effort but did not initiate it. Not until late October did the party council even consider the "agitation issue." In November, *Vorwärts* featured scattered calls for increased activity, but only on January 1, 1931, did the recruitment campaign *Wo bleibt der zweite Mann?* begin.[116]

Nazi electoral successes in the fall fueled the conviction that more activity could make a difference. The leftist *Leipziger Volkszeitung* chided Baden Socialists for a lackluster campaign, contrasting the exemplary bustle of Leipzig's forty-five thousand Socialists who had shored up an "island in the midst of the yellow flood of fascist waves." The SPD, the paper cried, must "increase the number of active fighters!"[117] The Munich police noted increased activity by the SPD, which "turned itself almost exclusively toward the struggle against the NSDAP." Bavarian Social Democrats held meetings with antifascist themes not only in cities but in rural areas (although observers described the latter as only "moderately well attended").[118] Across Germany, in towns of all sizes, the number of public meetings, marches, and rallies organized by Social Democrats multiplied dramatically, especially after January 1, when the national executive added its imprimatur to mobilization of the SPD.[119]

Within this spate of activity, impulses toward cooperation with the KPD surfaced at the local level. Relations between the KPD and the SPD, never warm, had turned frigid in 1929. After several years of a course of realpolitik, the KPD had adopted an ultraleftist stance. Its press spewed insults at "class traitors," alternating denunciations of all Social Democrats with scathing attacks on the leaders of the SPD and the Free Trade Unions.[120] The SPD, on its side, did nothing to end the cold war between the working-class parties. The bloody outcome of fights between Berlin police and Communist demonstrators on May 1, 1929, in particular, embittered the KPD. As part of a ban on all demonstrations imposed in December 1928, the Social Democratic chief of police in Berlin had refused a permit to the KPD for the traditional May Day celebration in 1929. When the KPD marched anyway, the police moved forcefully against participants, who responded in kind and constructed barricades. In three days of fighting in Berlin's working-class neighborhoods, thirty-three people were killed. Rather than chastise the police, the Social Democratic minister of the interior in Prussia, Albert Grzesinski, banned the Roter Frontkämpfer-Bund, the KPD's defense league.[121]

Despite the *Feindschaft* between the two parties, a hostility that did not just emanate from their respective central committees, many workers on each side yearned for unity, especially in face of the new threat from the NSDAP.[122] The election results prompted a few Social Democratic and Communist functionaries to organize joint activities. In Altona, the SPD's local chairman spoke at a Communist rally of several thousand, including many Social Democrats. In Augsburg, a Social Democratic city councilor addressed a KPD rally. In Munich SPD leftists called for a joint anti-Nazi effort by the Marxist parties.[123] The police remarked on new cooperation between Communists and Social Democrats in Palatinate towns that lay far from district headquarters.[124] There were also instances of cooperation between Reichsbanner chapters and the KPD on the local level.[125] In Braunschweig, surrounded by a state where the NSDAP entered the government in September 1930, the only case of political cooperation between the SPD and the KPD occurred. After municipal elections on March 1, 1931, the SPD no longer enjoyed a majority on the city council, but Socialists and Communists together controlled eighteen of thirty-five seats.[126] Social Democrats proposed that the parties hammer out a joint plan of work. This proved impossible, but KPD and SPD councilors did band together to elect the council's chairman (a Social Democrat) and his first deputy (a Communist). The two delegations never cooperated after this initial vote that, nonetheless, stands as the high point of KPD/SPD relations after 1929.[127]

Much more pronounced than an urge toward working-class unity was a new determination to defend the SPD and the republic against attack. In the Reichsbanner the Nazi surge occasioned not resignation but a "will to defense" so intense that the organization was "reborn" with a renewed sense of mission.[128] In this case, too, much of the impetus came from middle functionaries who "pointedly criticized the Reichsbanner executive" for preelection languor. Appeals for republicans and Socialists to join the Reichsbanner proliferated.[129] In September it created defense formations (*Schutzformationen* or *Schufo*), which the Prussian police (*Schutzpolizei* or *Schupo*) were to train. Young, fit Reichsbanner men enrolled in this new suborganization that protected republican and party meetings. By the spring of 1931, 250,000 had joined.[130] The drive for active defense came not just from the neorevisionist Reichsbanner leadership but from two groups in Social Democracy that had earlier looked askance at the defense organization, although for different reasons. In December 1930, ADGB leaders praised the Reichsbanner for its post-September services to Social Democracy. Not only did the ADGB council promise greater financial support, but it chided the (comparatively left-wing) DMV for reneging on past commitments.[131] Even more significant was a new respect for the all-republican association on the part of leftists. In Leipzig, Dresden, and Chemnitz, ailing Reichsbanner chapters sprang to life. Saxons also founded purely Socialist "fighting squadrons (*Kampfstaffeln*)" which, in the main, peacefully coexisted with the Saxon Reichsbanner.[132] The *Leipziger Volkszeitung* called on Socialists to fortify the entire left front, including the Reichsbanner, and finally began to cover Reichsbanner rallies.[133] Otto Hörsing, the rightist national chairman of the Reichsbanner who had alienated the Saxon Left by supporting the Old Socialist Party, gave prorepublican speeches at demonstrations in Saxony.[134] The Reichsbanner also became noticeably more active in the left-dominated Breslau district.[135] *Der Klassenkampf* applauded the "spontaneous formation of Social Democratic defense groups . . . which do not compete with the Reichsbanner, but complement its defense work."[136]

Within the trend toward greater latitude on both sides, however, ran a thread of tension between Reichsbanner regulars and, in particular, special youth formations. In Breslau, Young Socialists formed the Young Proletarian Marshals (*Jungordnerdienst*), which advocated an independent working-class defense organization. Not only Young Socialists around the country but youth in the SAJ, the Reichsbanner, and the sports organization signed up. In Berlin a brawl broke out between *Jungordner* and resentful Reichsbanner activists after which the marshals, and later the Young Socialists, were dissolved in the capital.[137] Differences in the levels of militancy between young and old Socialists did not always place *youth* in opposition to party policy. In Munich a plan to institute an "alarm organization" (which aimed at amassing fifteen to twenty thousand men within two hours) was opposed by older comrades in the party and the Reichsbanner who did not want to fight armed Nazis and Communists. By December the emergency plan had been implemented in Prussia, where the idea originated, but the Munich leadership had to conduct negotiations with the city's clubs to convince members of the plan's safety.[138] Such incidents provide a corrective to the notion that the base was always more militant than its leadership.

Despite the strains surrounding the practical implementation and ideological content of defense, the Reichsbanner, like the SPD, succeeded in mobilizing itself in late 1930 and early 1931. It marched more often, in more cities, and in larger numbers than it had earlier.[139] Reichsbanner men crashed Nazi meetings, often swamping them. According to the Munich police, efforts to build the organization, especially in rural areas, had not yet won higher attendance at meetings or new members by January 1931, but by mid-March the campaign was yielding results.[140] In their extraparliamentary campaign, as in their parliamentary blocking effort, Social Democrats believed they were making significant progress by late February 1931. Erik Nölting, glowing after a radio debate with Gottfried Feder, which the bourgeois press judged a rout of the Nazi economist, told a Hanover audience that "the signs are multiplying that the Nazi wave is ebbing." Fritz Tarnow wrote that Social Democratic activity was on an upswing as big or better than any in the past, while the Nazi movement had "visibly abated."[141] Others believed that the Nazis had been thrown on the defensive, as shown by their recent ban on attendance of opponents' meetings and on opponents' attendance of theirs.[142] In tandem with the perceived success of their parliamentary tactic, Socialists felt extraparliamentary mobilization was paying off. Optimism about the anti-Nazi effort peaked in the spring of 1931.

Who Voted for Hitler?

The electoral returns of the fall of 1930 also occasioned a lively debate on issues crucial to the SPD's success on the electoral stage: the composition and motivation of the Nazi constituency as well as the social provenance of the Social Democratic electorate. This discussion tackled questions that have intrigued scholars ever since. From the 1930s to the 1970s the dominant paradigm in the electoral sociology of the NSDAP assumed it to be a movement that disproportionately attracted the lower

middle class.[143] Over the last decade this interpretation has been effectively challenged. By subjecting electoral data to sophisticated statistical
techniques, researchers have shown, first, that the lower middle class did
not vote as a block. Although independent shopkeepers and artisans did
vote lopsidedly for the NSDAP, white-collar employees did not.[144] Second, new studies indicate that the NSDAP enjoyed wider social support
than previously assumed and that, indeed, it emerged as Germany's first
(Protestant) *Volkspartei*.[145] Within these widely accepted revisions of the
lower-middle-class thesis, researchers disagree about which other social
groups contributed most to the Nazi rise, and how much. Richard Hamilton, in particular, has found that the upper middle class (higher civil
servants and professionals) voted disproportionately for the NSDAP.[146]
More controversial is the claim of Jürgen Falter and Dirk Hänisch that the
employed working class, although not the unemployed, contributed significantly to the NSDAP's growth. Against them, Thomas Childers has
maintained that workers voted at a relatively low rate for the NSDAP,
while admitting that the absolute number was large.[147] Childers and
Falter and Hänisch agree, however, that the majority of workers who
voted Nazi were not typical industrial or urban proletarians but were
those who lived in small towns, worked in handicrafts and small manufac-
turing shops, and were unorganized. In the university town of Göttingen,
for example, the percentage of lower-class voters choosing the SPD declined from almost 70 percent in 1928 to 40 percent in 1930, while the
percentage of poorer voters who chose the NSDAP stood almost exactly at
its national average (18.6 percent). Rural laborers were the most susceptible of all workers to Nazi appeal.[148] In considering the political background of the Nazi electorate of 1930, Thomas Schnabel has estimated
that 23 percent had not voted in 1928, 31 percent came from the bourgeois middle, and 21 percent were from the DNVP. Previous SPD voters
comprised 9 percent of the NSDAP vote.[149] Falter and Hänisch and
Conan Fischer have argued that especially *after* September 1930 the SPD
lost many votes to the NSDAP.[150]

Based on the crude statistical techniques available to them, most Weimar Social Democrats believed the Nazi vote to be heavily lower middle
class. Indeed, the long-standing view of National Socialism as a lower-
middle-class movement was originally presented in Theodor Geiger's
famous article, "Panik im Mittelstand."[151] Geiger, a leading member of the
ADGB and an economist, divided the "intermediate social layer" into an
"old" part (farmers, artisans, small retailers) and a "new" part (employees,
civil servants, the professions, some skilled workers). In contrast to recent
findings, he maintained that on September 14 the new *Mittelstand*, includ-

ing employees and civil servants of all ranks, had particularly favored the NSDAP, while artisans remained quite loyal to the interest-group-based Economic Party.[152] Other Social Democrats who agreed with Geiger examined particular aspects of the middle-class vote. Georg Decker noted that in Berlin, where the Nazis fared least well in the nation, they polled most heavily in neighborhoods where civil servants lived, although he did not distinguish between lower and higher civil servants. He did underline the striking Nazi success in Protestant rural areas, a correlation that has been confirmed by recent studies. Hans Neisser estimated the contribution of the *Mittelstand* to the total NSDAP vote: farmers, 20–25 percent; small retailers, craftsmen, employees, public servants, and pensioners, 55–60 percent.[153]

Despite their conviction that the middle classes voted disproportionately for the NSDAP, a number of Social Democrats recognized, as had some before the elections, that the NSDAP had support among diverse social groups and that the working-class contribution was not minuscule. According to Neisser, 15 to 20 percent of the Nazi vote came from industrial workers, an estimate Geiger found too high.[154] Decker admitted that even in Red Berlin some proletarians voted Brown, and he noted its especially high proletarian vote in the Palatinate, the Ruhr, and Chemnitz-Zwickau. Like many analysts today, Ernst Fraenkel argued that the Nazis attracted votes largely from "pre-capitalist working-class circles." The uniform national distribution of the Nazi vote, in contrast to wild variations in percentages of Communist ballots, also impressed Socialists. While Geiger took this as more evidence that the Nazi vote came from intermediate strata who lived in all voting districts, Decker saw it as proof that the urban appeal of the NSDAP should not be underestimated.[155] Hilferding went even further, dubbing the NSDAP a "catch-all party" that encompassed all social groups—from capitalists, generals, princes, and large landowners to the *Mittelstand*, farmers, civil servants, workers, and the déclassé. He conceded, "In Germany, with its keen class distinctions, to have breached these barriers is no mean accomplishment."[156]

Why had these various groups voted Nazi? Social Democrats most often ascribed the Nazi vote to anticapitalism.[157] According to August Rathmann, a founder of *Neue Blätter*, the NSDAP had tapped anticapitalist sentiment by maligning "mobile" capital.[158] Geiger agreed that economic conditions explained the Nazi vote, but he did not see it as anticapitalist or otherwise rationally motivated. He distinguished between two viewpoints prevalent in the *Mittelstand*. The old *Mittelstand*, especially artisans and small retailers, held to an outdated (*zeit-inadequät*) ideology, yearning for a simpler precapitalist society of small producers and sellers. Employees,

⸺rvants, and professionals, in contrast, tended toward a socially inappropriate (*standort-inadequät*) ideology, psychologically denying their objective affinities with the proletariat. Neither group had found a political home in the republic and floated from party to party. Now, sensing the futility of vote splintering, the *Mittelstand* had flocked to the Nazi banner because they were unable to function within the rational bargaining that was the modus operandi of interest-group politics. The lack of a positive program allowed the NSDAP to attract *Mittelstand* Germans despite their divergent economic concerns. They had voted in a crisis-induced fever laced with caste prejudice. They would again be on the prowl when the party could not deliver on its myriad promises.[159] Geiger and Hilferding assumed that women's "emotionality" made them vote disproportionately for the radical, irrational parties, while the "coolly reflecting manly sort" inclined toward the moderate parties. An anonymous article in *Vorwärts*, however, showed that, at least in Berlin, women voted less heavily for the radical parties than for the SPD; most of all, they voted Center Party and DNVP. Falter's analysis substantiates that in 1930 the NSDAP had noticeably less appeal for women throughout the country but that the gender gap was essentially closed by 1932.[160]

Of all the Social Democratic commentators, only Alexander Schifrin, like Decker a Menshevik émigré, completely forswore an economic interpretation in favor of a political one. He described the NSDAP as the "caricature of a worldview party" with a purely ideological appeal. Hitler's party, the "real, classic fascism," had succeeded in making itself the "axle" of the entire German Right. Social Democrats had focused on the "cold fascism" of the parliamentary stage, dismissed the Nazi movement as rehashed anti-Semitism, and so missed the "dynamite" in German politics, the "storm of true fascism, this violent counterrevolutionary sansculotte movement." Indeed, German fascism surpassed its Italian counterpart in its systematic use of terror, incessant activity, and will to power via the electoral route. More centralized than any other German party and with a highly articulated apparatus, the NSDAP was not burdened by the need to represent particular economic interests, in contrast to Social Democracy.[161] Thus, Schifrin identified as a boon the very characteristic Geiger saw as dooming the Nazis to ephemeral popularity. Schifrin also objected to Geiger's optimistic appraisal of the *Mittelstand*'s turn to Nazism: high voter participation and recourse "to the streets" constituted signs of democracy's vitality and "subjective proletarianization."[162] This faulty evaluation, Schifrin maintained, flowed from a sociological perspective. From a political perspective, one could see that the *Mittelstand* was using democratic and proletarian methods for its own antithetical goals.[163]

Schifrin addressed anew the question of National Socialism's ties to capitalist interests. Charges that "princes and capitalists" financed the Nazis continued to appear in the Socialist press.[164] Schifrin too found a connection but cautioned, "One must stress . . . fascism's independent existence . . . [for] not the mission of big capital in itself, but fascism's own being[,] . . . its will to power, brutality, and means of action make it the enemy of the socialist working class. These special characteristics do not lie in the economic sphere." Not monopoly capitalism or imperialism but democracy was the precondition of "true" fascism, and Nazism's raison d'etre was the destruction of democracy.[165]

Social Democrats also analyzed their own electoral performance. Neisser estimated that employees organized in the AfA-Bund and their wives, lower civil servants, farmers, and artisans represented over a third and up to two-fifths of Socialist ballots. Decker commented on the not insubstantial proportion of votes cast for the SPD in eastern districts with large estates, a turnout he attributed to the political network created by agrarian laborers' associations.[166] Commentators agreed unanimously that the party had lost the majority of its votes among industrial workers and that the KPD had picked them up.[167] They disagreed, however, about how to reverse the SPD's losses. Socialists such as Neisser wanted to parry the Nazi rise indirectly by going after young proletarian voters lost to the KPD; others such as Julius Kaliski wanted to counter Nazi popularity directly by trying to win rural voters with a new agrarian program.[168] Both Kaliski and Neisser were right-wing Socialists, but, significantly, Kaliski wrote for the revisionist *Sozialistische Monatshefte*, while Neisser worked for the ADGB. Their differences reflected similar divisions among party activists and functionaries, although after the election *Das Freie Wort* printed more letters that beseeched comrades to learn the language of the rural masses than urged them to polish up their proletarian mother tongue.[169] Indecision about which part of the electorate to target existed inside particular district committees. At a local conference, Hamburg Socialists were exhorted to agitate in rural areas, while an internal report planned to aim "limited resources" at unemployed workers and bolster the SPD's industrial network.[170]

Analysts focused in particular on the need to go after the urban *Mittelstand*, but again they were at odds about how to accomplish this task.[171] Holding to the traditional Socialist viewpoint, the trade unionist Geiger and the moderate leftist Ernst Fraenkel maintained that in a capitalist society no third front could survive outside the two great class camps. The temporarily cohered *Mittelstand* "zone" must eventually disintegrate as class divisions penetrated it. According to Geiger, Social Democracy could speed this process by appealing to the new *Mittelstand* with a successful social policy and an attack on unemployment. The party, though, could only hope to "neutralize" the old *Mittelstand* with various protective economic measures. Fraenkel was convinced that the SPD could break through the "false consciousness" of the "uprooted" *Mittelstand* by presenting "hard and clear" proof of its inevitable fate under capitalism.[172] Against Geiger and Fraenkel, Decker, like Schifrin, noted a "political transformation" characterized by the decline of the liberal parties and the shift of farmers to the right. He concluded that this sea change "places Social Democracy before the very difficult task of basically revising some of our old notions; namely, the general conception . . . that in class society . . . all forces gather at the two poles in ever greater mass, that all intermediate social strata disappear; instead we see these groups trying to establish their political independence against democracy." Walther Pahl drew the lessons of such a viewpoint: the party should neither wait for members of the *Mittelstand* to become proletarianized nor appeal to them as "proletarianizing layers." Rather, the SPD should recognize them as "special social strata," accept the "independent worth" of their middle position, and defend their particular "life interests." The *Mittelstand* should not be portrayed as "an appendage of the proletariat." To win the rural population, the SPD had to develop an agrarian production policy and break from an exclusively consumerist orientation.[173]

The debate about the sociological bases of the NSDAP and the SPD and about where to aim Socialist propaganda began auspiciously. The left centrists Schifrin and Decker, the neorevisionist Pahl, and others appreciated that the NSDAP was reshaping the terms of German politics. The trade unionist Geiger, the leftist Fraenkel, and the neorevisionist Rathmann did not. Clearly, at this point the division followed no distinct ideological fault. In these first months the debate occupied trade union, party, and Reichsbanner intellectuals as well as a few functionaries and grassroots activists; the national executive did not participate in this important discussion.

Reichstag campaign, 1924: The SPD proudly associated itself with republican emblems (the flag) and symbols of parliamentary power (the Reichstag building). The SPD's List 1 is declared to be "the ticket of working people." *Schaffendes Volk* can also be translated "the productive nation" and was a favorite phrase of far rightists, who wanted to distinguish "productive labor" from the Marxist conception of labor and from rapacious (*raffendem*; i.e., finance) capitalism. (Bundesarchiv Koblenz)

Reichstag campaign, July 1932: Now the SPD claimed, "The people are dying from this system," thus adopting the language of the NSDAP and the KPD. Yet the visual allusions show that the system under attack was not the republic but the monarchist restorationism of Papen (whose face is blue in the original) and his alleged Nazi allies. (Bundesarchiv Koblenz)

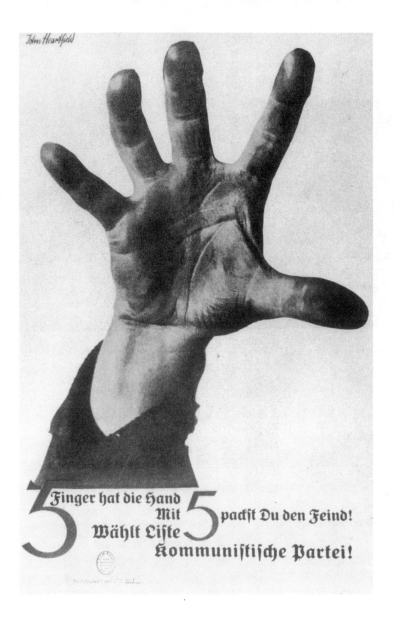

Reichstag campaign, 1928: John Heartfield designed this innovative poster for the KPD. Its slogan, witty but militant, proclaims, "5 fingers has the hand, with 5 you [can] grab the foe. Vote List 5, Communist Party!" Its image of a proletarian hand is simple, striking, and emotionally charged. (Bundesarchiv Koblenz)

Reichstag campaign, 1928: This SPD poster is visually complex, even confusing, although cleverly symmetrical upon closer inspection. Asking "Who will rescue Germany?," it contrasts the deeds of the *Bürgerblock* with those of the SPD. Militarism is attacked in general and in the specific form of the Panzerkreuzer. The *Bürgerblock* is associated with a longer working day, prisons, and weapons, while the SPD is represented by a father and child who have benefited from athletic fields, housing projects, and children's homes. (Bundesarchiv Koblenz)

Reichstag campaign, 1930: This was the kind of anti-Nazi propaganda that Chakhotin ridiculed as demoralizing rather than inspirational to Social Democratic workers. (Bundesarchiv Koblenz)

Reichstag campaign, 1933: Chakhotin's ideas are evident in this poster that conveys the strength of anti-Nazism (even though Hitler was in power) with an arresting abstract image and terse language ("Down with it"). The wedge (red in the original) evokes both the SPD's *Drei Pfeile* and the famous Bolshevik poster designed by El Lissitsky in the Russian Civil War ("Smash the Whites with the Red Wedge"). (Bundesarchiv Koblenz)

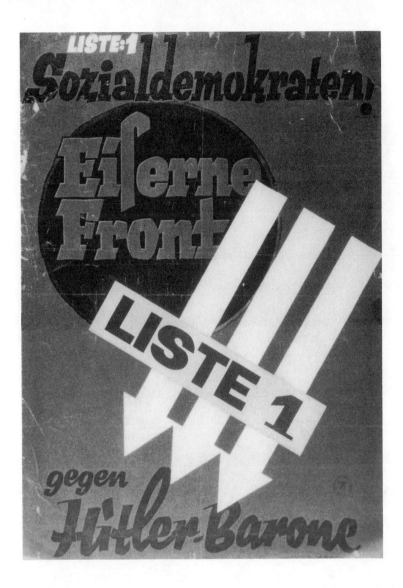

Reichstag campaign, July 1932: "Iron Front against Hitler Barons" features the Iron Front as prominently as "Social Democrats." The *Drei Pfeile* are portrayed as the weapons that will defeat the Hitler barons and are used visually to direct attention to this slogan. (Bundesarchiv Koblenz)

Drei Pfeile, 1932: These sketches were circulated as examples of how the three arrows could be wielded in graffiti. (Bundesarchiv Koblenz)

Prussian Landtag campaign, April 1932: The NSDAP borrowed the "work, freedom, and bread" slogan first used by the KPD (see below) and evocative of the Bolshevik cry of 1917, "peace, land, bread." The SPD also adopted "work, freedom, and bread" as a slogan in July 1932. (Bundesarchiv Koblenz)

Reichstag campaign, July 1932: In its effort to attract workers, the NSDAP copied the left-wing image of the Promethean worker. On one hand, this poster relied on standard Nazi caricatures that instantly identified Communist, Social Democratic, and Jewish enemies. On the other hand, it used the foes' own language (including the SPD's "Hitler barons" slogan) to lampoon them. (Bundesarchiv Koblenz)

Prussian Landtag campaign, 1924. (Bundesarchiv Koblenz)

1930: An example of National Socialist propaganda against republican corruption and, in particular, a representation of the Nazi focus on the so-called Sklarek affair in Berlin. In one volley, shots are fired at Social Democrats, Communists, Democrats, and Jews. (Bundesarchiv Koblenz)

1930: This call for "free" (i.e., Socialist or republican) civil servants to join the SPD is an example of the rare poster directed at this social group. The hats signify that all branches of the civil service from railroad and postal employees to the police and office bureaucrats would be at home in the SPD. (Bundesarchiv Koblenz)

Reichstag campaign, July 1932: This appeal to farmers shows the NSDAP's facility at using colloquial language ("We farmers are cleaning out the government"—literally, "pitching out the dung") and at targeting a social group within National Socialism. The Communist incendiary, the "tax and spend" Social Democrat, and the corrupt Jewish intellectual are puny foes but nonetheless dangerous. (Bundesarchiv Koblenz)

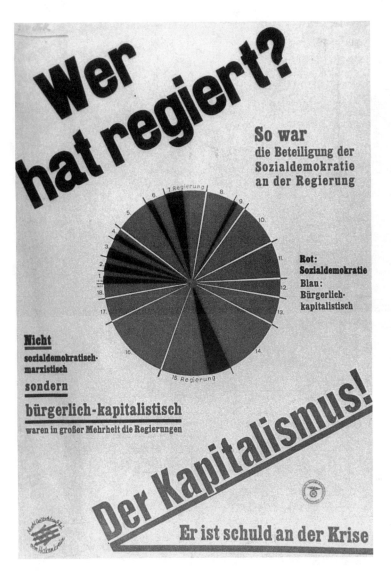

1932 (SPD): This poster answered the charge that, as the governmental party, the SPD was responsible for the crisis. Asking "Who governed?," its circle graph demonstrated that the SPD was numerically in the minority, concluding, "Not SPD Marxists but Bourgeois-Capitalists had the large majority in [various] regimes. Capitalism! It is at fault for the crisis." Its style shows that the SPD had not completely broken with its conception of propaganda as part of a rational political discourse that would win voters through enlightenment. (Bundesarchiv Koblenz)

Reichstag campaign, 1933: "Marxism is the guardian angel of capitalism." The NSDAP in power, in contrast, still used simple language and emotionally laden imagery to attack capitalism and to tie the SPD and the KPD to Jews and to capitalism. (Bundesarchiv Koblenz)

Living with Toleration

The hopes of Social Democrats in early 1931 did not prove well-founded. The year was grueling. Unemployment reached extraordinary levels. In January 1931, 4,886,925 people, about a quarter of the work force, were unemployed; by February 1932, 6,041,910, over one-third, had no job. In 1931, 92 percent of those out of work were blue-collar workers.[1] Government policies did nothing to cushion the population from the dire effects of the collapse of the private economy. Indeed, Brüning's emergency decrees severely reduced social welfare outlays, federal support to local and state governments, and civil service salaries. Also, high agrarian tariffs hurt urban consumers. Wages fell by 12 to 13 percent in 1931, while prices declined by only 4 to 5 percent. Both the economic crisis and Brüning's policies unfairly burdened the urban working class.[2] Not only workers but virtually all social groups viewed the ascetic "Hunger Chancellor" with bitterness. On the political front, the Reich government resisted Prussian pressure for a tougher stance against Nazi street violence. In addition, the results of local and state elections were uniformly unfavorable to the SPD. Nevertheless, the increasing hostility of big business toward Brüning as well as the unrelenting growth of the NSDAP cast the chancellor ever more as the lesser evil. Caught in a spiral of escalating commitment, the SPD executive committee hardened in its conviction that toleration of Brüning was the only feasible political course to follow. In the ranks, meanwhile, disillusionment with toleration spread. Discontent led to a break between the Left Opposition and the majority. Even leaders of the Reichstag delegation and the Free Trade Unions privately expressed doubts about the policy. More frequent than calls to alter the SPD's parliamentary tactic, however, were demands for reform of the SPD's propaganda and organization; yet significant change did not occur. By the late fall of 1931 the mobilization of the previous winter had petered out, and demoralization engulfed Social Democracy.

Prussia

Otto Braun acted swiftly to implement his plan to use Prussian state power against radical rowdyism. Appalled by the passive response of the Berlin police to the violence and vandalism of the SA on October 13,

1930, Braun spoke with Albert Grzesinski about the need for a "stronger hand" to guide the Prussian Interior Ministry.[3] He wanted to reappoint Grzesinski, but the Center Party's Landtag delegation continued to object because Grzesinski had divorced his wife. Braun chose Severing and appointed Grzesinski Berlin police commissioner. The bourgeois press interpreted these personnel shifts correctly: Braun planned to confront street violence vigorously. As Braun recognized, however, Prussian efforts against right-wing extremism required the cooperation of the Reich and other states. Without a nationally coordinated campaign, the Prussian government had to proceed on a case by case basis, which made its actions stopgap and fruitless.[4] In December 1930, the affair over the American film *All Quiet on the Western Front* revealed the Reich's ability to sabotage Prussia's efforts. Goebbels organized youth demonstrations outside Berlin theaters showing the film; the Nazis caused pandemonium at a crowded screening by releasing white mice and setting off stink bombs. The Prussian government moved swiftly against these provocations, and Grzesinski banned all parades in the city.[5] When Hindenburg pressed Braun to ban the film instead, the minister-president refused. Braun could not, however, defy the national film review board's decision, made under Reich pressure, to withdraw the film from circulation.[6] The Berlin public, who turned out for the antiwar film in droves, witnessed Prussia's humiliation, while Hitler's hand was strengthened by the Reich's overruling of Prussia's position.

Meanwhile the Prussian Justice Ministry pressured the Reich to take legal action against the NSDAP as a subversive organization. In August 1930 a memorandum documenting the party's criminal character had been given to Reich prosecutor Karl Werner in the hope that he would bring charges against Hitler and other leading Nazis. Despite repeated requests to respond, Werner did not even weigh the evidence until July 1931 and still did not act upon it. His laxity in the judiciary paralleled that of the executive branch. In December 1930, at the request of the Reichswehr, a cabinet meeting discussed the legal status of the NSDAP. The army command considered the party subversive and approved the dismissal of Nazi workers on these grounds. However, General Kurt von Schleicher, the army's liaison in the government, pointed out that recent labor court decisions against such dismissals had muddied the legal view of the NSDAP. The Reichswehr wanted clarification. Instead, Brüning wrapped up an inconclusive meeting with a remark that, according to Robert Kempner, "torpedoed Prussian steps towards energetic opposition" to the NSDAP. The chancellor argued that the regime could not yet take a position on the legality of the party and warned against employing "the same false methods" used against Social Democracy in the prewar era. The Prussians, disgusted as they were, could not pressure the national government into enforcing even mild measures against the Nazis until late 1931.[7]

As police commissioner, Grzesinski fulfilled Braun's expectations. Severing tended to be less interventionist. Before appointing Severing, Braun privately expressed concern that he lacked the requisite "energy."[8] As in the past, Severing did not match Grzesinski's zealousness in replacing civil servants of questionable republican loyalties.[9] Nonetheless, he did try to protect government bureaucrats, especially the police, from Nazi infiltration. All political activities by NSDAP sympathizers among the police, teachers, and other public officials were prohibited in Prussia (and among particular government occupations in Hamburg, Hesse, and Baden). Severing also worked to produce a law for the protection of the public order that the Reich government would endorse. In March 1931, after much haggling in Berlin, a Prussian emergency decree was instituted. It necessitated prior registration of all public political activities, required that any leaflet or poster be reviewed by the police, and made it more difficult for uniformed riders to pass out leaflets. Severing's strategy managed to circumscribe, if far from eliminate, antirepublican agitation among civil servants and in public spaces. Implementation of his tactics, however, depended on the political and personal proclivities of regional governors and, above all, local police chiefs. In addition, many successful interventions against actions that "created a climate of violence" were undermined by judges who gave offenders trifling sentences.[10] More fundamentally, Severing was handicapped by his reluctance to defy the Reich. When Arnold Brecht suggested that Prussia ban the SA, Severing rebuffed him, anticipating that the supreme court would strike down a ban and so allow the SA to reemerge in triumph. Instead he wanted the Reich to use Article 48 to prohibit the paramilitary organization.[11]

The Prussian minister of the interior had to deal not only with chronic antirepublican agitation by the NSDAP and the KPD but with a concerted effort to bring down his government. As did Social Democrats, Franz Seldte, leader of the Stahlhelm, believed, "Who rules Prussia, controls Germany." In October 1930 the antirepublican veterans' organization began a campaign for a referendum to dissolve the Prussian Landtag. In early April 1931 the NSDAP joined the propaganda onslaught against Braun and his regime, although it only endorsed the referendum per se in July. The KPD shocked its own cadres in July by joining the attempt to topple Prussia's Weimar Coalition.[12] Severing adopted a twofold strategy to counter this three-sided threat. First, he made it difficult to fulfill requirements for the referendum's petition drive. Still, by late April the promoters had collected 6 million signatures, far more than required. Second, he framed the March emergency decree so it appeared to be directed at radical—especially Communist—street agitation and propaganda, so winning the endorsement of Brüning and Hindenburg for measures that could also be used against the Stahlhelm campaign. In July, a new press law allowed the government to shut down temporarily newspapers whose content endangered public order or security.[13]

Prussia's efforts to defeat the Stahlhelm referendum raised vexed issues about the nature and extent of an active state policy to defend the republic. The central question touched the foundations of a democratic constitution: To what degree could a parliamentary state restrict the civil liberties of an abusive minority in order to protect the rights of the majority? In theory, many Social Democrats supported lawful measures that allowed the state to repress violent opposition.[14] Severing and policymakers in Hesse, Baden, and Hamburg curbed antirepublican activity in the hope that such efforts would break the "suggestive power" of the Nazis by demonstrating to fence sitters the state's ability to assert its authority.[15] Beyond the fact that they rarely managed to implement their plan to repress only rightists lay another impediment: Social Democratic attachment to civil liberties.[16] Prussia's efforts were viewed with ambivalence, justified on an ad hoc basis, and carried out with a guilty conscience. Leftists in the SPD were particularly averse to handing the police so much power to intervene in civic life.[17] A secondary issue concerned the extent to which the state should use the media to promote its interests against hostile viewpoints. Grzesinski advocated extreme state intervention. In May 1931 he urged Braun to play an active role in the propaganda war, using leaflets, posters, and radio to defend his government's record in an openly partisan manner, rather than publishing only explanatory statements, because "it would be disastrous to let things drift fatalistically, and, after the calamity, to rescue what can still be salvaged."[18]

In general, Grzesinski's prescription was not followed, but in one instance the Prussian government did energetically defend itself. The Interior Ministry used the powers allotted it by the July press law to force Prussia's daily papers, twenty-five hundred in all, to publish a front-page proclamation on the Stahlhelm referendum two days before it took place on August 9. This statement explained the significance of the referendum and urged citizens to stay away from the polls or to vote "no" if they felt pressure (in rural areas) to show up. Not mincing words, it ended, "Whoever wants a Soviet Prussia or a fascist Prussia will go to the polls and vote 'yes'."[19] Obviously, one cannot measure the impact of this announcement, but the referendum did fail, attaining only 9.8 million of the 13.2 million yes votes needed to pass. The high turnout for a referendum revealed an extraordinary level of political mobilization and dissatisfaction; yet the defeat of the measure prompted Social Democrats and the Prussian government to interpret the results as a victory for the republic. They were especially pleased that the number of yes votes fell far short of the combined tallies of the sponsoring parties in the Reichstag election of 1930.[20] Whatever its effect on the results, the Prussian proclamation definitely did not enhance Reich/Prussian relations. Hindenburg was furious at this application of the new press law, which he had seen as a way to clamp down on Communist calls for a Soviet Germany. He was, after all, an honorary member of the Stahlhelm. Brüning was persuaded to include in the next emergency decree a provision that Prussian officials must gain approval from the Reich interior minister for such declarations.[21] Thus, a definite act in defense of democratic government only provoked new limits on Prussia's room to maneuver around the obstacle of the national government. The "Prussian strategy," the offensive side of the overall SPD defensive effort, was proving difficult to implement.

Growing Doubts about Toleration

After their initial sense of triumph over the National Opposition's withdrawal from the Reichstag in February 1931, Social Democrats came to see it as a mixed blessing. With the Right absent, the SPD and the KPD had the requisite number of seats to form a majority. Hitler and Alfred Hugenberg, recalling the hot August of 1928, hoped SPD and KPD votes would torpedo Panzerkreuzer B, funds for which were included in Brüning's budget.[22] Soon after the rightist pullout, the Socialist press began to justify continuing cooperation with the middle parties despite an "apparent" leftist majority. If the SPD collaborated with the KPD, it was explained, either the Right would return to form a block with the middle or the Reichstag would be dissolved.[23] Publicists also prepared party opinion for acceptance of Panzerkreuzer B, arguing that, first, the ship would be built in any event and, second, the task was to keep Brüning and, above all, Braun in power.[24] In private negotiations with the SPD, Brüning claimed that the battleship was central to his disarmament policy and threatened to resign if it were defeated. Reluctantly, the SPD leadership agreed to persuade the Reichstag delegation not to oppose the ship.[25] Intense opposition to the Panzerkreuzer, and to toleration, erupted in a delegation meeting on March 18. Breitscheid read aloud letters from the rank and file demanding rejection of the ship. He, with Berlin's chairman,

Franz Künstler, and other leftists, pleaded with the majority to allow each deputy to vote his or her conscience. Hermann Müller, who was deathly ill, argued as vehemently as he could for a solid abstention. Braun, using Brüning's tactic, in effect threatened to resign if a "free vote" occurred.[26] Sixty members supported a unanimous abstention; forty opposed it. In the Reichstag on March 20, nine Social Democrats ("the Nine") broke discipline and, with the KPD, registered their opposition to the ship; nineteen others missed the roll call.[27]

Again, the pocket battleship program had stirred up acrimony in the SPD Reichstag delegation. Again, however, discord over political strategy, not military policy, lay at the root of the dispute.[28] In voting "no," deputies on the far left of the SPD registered intensifying discontent with toleration by opposing a program that they believed the rank and file found insupportable. As it turned out, the breach of discipline did not earn unanimous approval in the provinces. Important urban districts, including Chemnitz, Breslau, Düsseldorf, Frankfurt, and Bochum, endorsed the Nine's "no." In the flagship city of the Social Democratic *Solidargemeinschaft*, Leipzig, however, not only the *Volkszeitung* but the executive committee and a majority of the membership condemned the discipline break.[29] The Panzerkreuzer vote divided the *Klassenkampf* group from moderate leftists rather than widening support for the opposition.

In the midst of the Panzerkreuzer controversy, the Saxon leftist Engelbert Graf queried, "What are the limits to toleration?" If the SPD did not mark a line over which it would not step, it risked pursuing Brüning down the slippery slope. Graf prophesied that in the Landtag elections scheduled for early 1932, Prussia would be lost because of the very policy designed to secure Braun's tenure.[30] The *Klassenkampf* group took election returns in Oldenburg in May as an omen that corroborated Graf's warning. Until 1928, villages in this northwestern state had been bailiwicks of the DDP. By 1931, however, two-thirds of these voters had deserted the State Party (as the DDP was called after it fused with the more conservative Order of Young Germans in the summer of 1930). In the Reichstag election of 1930, the NSDAP had garnered 77,000 votes, an astounding gain over the 17,000 it had received in the Landtag elections of 1928. After mobilizing nationwide resources for the Oldenburg campaign of 1931, it emerged with 97,802 votes (37.2 percent).[31] The SPD slipped from 65,847 votes (in 1930) to 54,893; the KPD increased from 13,965 to 18,942. Although *Vorwärts* admitted that the results confirmed a continuing "trend toward radicalization," it attributed them in part to a "peculiar" social structure overloaded with small farmers disgusted by federal subsidies to large eastern landholders. *Der Klassenkampf* found

Oldenburg's very particularity cause for alarm, asking why a "liberal population of democratically inclined small farmers" had succumbed to the Nazi allure. It blamed not only Brüning's agrarian program but also toleration. Snubbed by the SPD, the people had opted for an alternative socialist solution.[32]

Increasingly, leftists denied that toleration was necessary to contain the Nazi threat. Some argued that the fascist menace had never been of the magnitude claimed by the leadership.[33] Others agreed with the party leadership that the danger had diminished since September 1930 but saw this improvement as reason to go into opposition.[34] In the weeks preceding the SPD congress at Leipzig in late May, *Der Klassenkampf* became ever bolder in its offensive against majority policy. Its editors urged the Reichstag delegation to demand parliament be convened, after SPD representatives in the Reichstag's senior council had voted against such a request. The Left Opposition believed that the party congress would endorse its critique of leadership policy.[35]

The Left Opposition sensed correctly that doubts about toleration were on the rise among the SPD's rank and file. In Hamburg, at a membership assembly that condemned the Nine's breach of discipline, speakers also questioned the seeming aimlessness of toleration and wanted an "active national policy or [to] oppose the Brüning regime." At their district congress, Berliners loudly voiced discontent. Darmstadt's *Hessischer Volksfreund* called for well-defined limits to SPD support to prevent Brüning from continuing to impose sacrifices on the working class without addressing the crisis.[36] Motions submitted by provincial organizations to the party congress demanded greater "activity" by the Reichstag delegation.[37] In party journals, intellectuals on the left and the right who had accepted toleration now suggested a partial redirection of SPD politics. While proud of the "historic achievement" that had robbed the Nazi movement of its "dangerous momentum," Georg Decker advised his party to develop a positive democratic policy to complement its negative antifascist course. Mierendorff could discern no benefits for the SPD from toleration except several inconclusive setbacks to the NSDAP. Only measures to alleviate the economic situation, he wrote, would reverberate to the advantage of Social Democracy.[38]

SPD leaders could read the signs of discontent; yet protocols of their meetings with the chancellor reveal reluctance to set limits on toleration despite scant success at squeezing concessions from Brüning. On March 17, Hilferding, Wels, Rudolf Breitscheid, and Paul Hertz protested Brüning's decision to adjourn parliament until November.[39] Brüning insisted the Reichstag must be silenced if his grand scheme was to work and again implied a political crisis would ensue if he did not get his way. Hilferding, Breitscheid, and Wels tried to impress on him their party's awkward position vis-à-vis its electorate as well as their difficulties inside the SPD Reichstag delegation and at the upcoming party congress.[40] Faced with Brüning's obdurateness, however, they finally agreed to adjournment through mid-October.

Because the burden of toleration weighed unevenly on Social Democratic leaders in the national legislature and in the Prussian executive, it produced fissures in the post-September consensus. In mid-May when the Reichstag delegation executive met with Severing to discuss how to tackle the issue of the soon-to-be announced second emergency decree, Wels argued for a separate program to underscore Social Democratic distance from the cabinet. Hertz, Hilferding, and Breitscheid suggested instead discreet pressure on Brüning to reveal his plans to them before the public unveiling of the decree. Severing rejected both tactics. He lectured his colleagues on the "Prussian connection," laying out the familiar logic: SPD power in Prussia rested on its support of Brüning; its defense against fascism depended in turn on the Prussian bulwark; its cardinal responsibility was to defeat fascism. Breitscheid responded plaintively, "When will that be?"[41] In letters to absent delegation members, Hertz admitted his own doubts about toleration and said many deputies wanted to serve Brüning a warning that cuts in wages and welfare would come at the cost of SPD support.[42]

Delegation leaders and Prussian ministers also disagreed about how long to muzzle a recalcitrant parliament. When the draconian cutbacks of the second emergency decree were announced on June 6, calls to convene the Reichstag rang on all sides. The decree slashed the salaries of public employees, especially at the local and state levels, and terminated unemployment benefits to youths living with their families. It not only heightened the misery of thousands of Germans, but it impinged on the autonomy of the states and municipalities while adding to their welfare outlays.[43] Nonetheless, Braun and Severing resisted pressure to convene the Reichstag. In a meeting of ministers and friendly party leaders, Severing warned that the KPD would foment ugly demonstrations if the Reichstag met. Breitscheid, who had just left a delegation meeting racked by a "passionate fight" over the new decree, objected that the SPD could not continue to mollify its supporters if Brüning persisted on his current course. Backed by Hilferding and Hertz, Breitscheid demanded the budget committee meet to "open a vent to air discontent." In fact, this motion was introduced, but it was suddenly withdrawn under renewed threat from Brüning to dissolve the Prussian coalition.[44] In a stormy session, the Reichstag delegation voted seventy to fifty-seven to oppose any motion to convene the budget committee or the Reichstag. Three (unidentified) members of the delegation's executive voted with the minority. *Vorwärts* claimed as a victory the circumvention of a crisis and Brüning's promise to negotiate with Social Democrats over social provisions of the decree.[45] To a party executive anxious to change the emergency decree without jeopardizing relations with the government, no doubt this did seem a victory, but at the cost of intensifying internal tensions.[46]

The battles in the Reichstag delegation were foreshadowed by conflicts at the party congress that met in Leipzig immediately before the unveiling of the emergency decree. The leadership, confident that it could win a majority of the delegation for its course, wanted the congress to grant the delegation complete freedom in its response to the emergency decree. Dissidents beseeched congressional delegates to retain the power to reject the decree and, thus, toleration. According to defenders of toleration, the main goal of the policy was to preserve parliamentary democracy by preventing an alliance of the Middle and the Right. Toleration was not predicated on rapidly overcoming the economic crisis or even on the imminent discrediting of fascism—extraparliamentary enlightenment of the NSDAP's supporters must accomplish that. Its secondary goal—to block the dismantling of *Sozialpolitik*—had been achieved. Majority speakers made much of the Left Opposition's lack of a clear alternative. In his report on parliamentary work, Wilhelm Sollmann dwelled inordinately on the disciplinary breach of the Nine, aware that many comrades abhorred any affront to unity in hard times.[47]

Moderate leftists, such as Aufhäuser, Toni Sender, and Franz Künstler, expressed anxiety about the future course of toleration but in the end supported majority policy. Far leftists argued fiercely against continued toleration. In a reversal of customary roles, the Left highlighted the atrophy of parliamentary prerogatives, while Wilhelm Dittmann ridiculed preoccupation with the Reichstag. Striking antiparliamentary chords traditionally played by the Left, he insisted that the extraparliamentary arena was now the main field of struggle. For the majority, the post-September mobilization of the party was proof of rank and file support for toleration, while the opposition interpreted it as an index of bitterness against the Nazis and economic misery.[48] Debate at the congress waxed stormy. Majority speakers were particularly aggressive.[49] Although the daily press and even *Der Klassenkampf* described the differences as tactical, anyone could see that these were tactical disagreements of a very heated kind.[50] In the roll-call votes the Left Opposition was badly defeated. A resounding majority rapped the Nine for breach of discipline and de-

manded conformity in future Reichstag votes. The congress also dissolved the Young Socialists, allegedly because they had failed to recruit
the nation's youth and overlapped with the SAJ, but actually because the
group was a hotbed of leftist radicalism.[51] A resolution on toleration,
proposed by the Berlin SPD, defined its limits as that imprecise point at
which the living standards of the working class came under unacceptable
assault.[52] Candid observers noted that widespread disgruntlement with
toleration was veiled by the SPD's tradition of inner loyalty proportional
to outer isolation. The *Hessischer Volksfreund* wondered why the leadership
did not encourage functionaries to air their unhappiness and use this to
exert pressure on Brüning, rather than devoting itself to clever maneuvers to humiliate a hapless opposition. Carlo Mierendorff regretted that
an internal imbroglio, not Brüning's decrees, preoccupied the SPD's highest policymaking body.[53]

The leadership could not savor its victory for long. As did the Reichstag
delegation, the SPD and the Free Trade Unions erupted in outrage
against the cutbacks in the June 6 emergency decree. Aufhäuser admitted
to Berlin functionaries that the decree had provoked "a passionate protest
from the working class."[54] This protest was echoed by Berlin Social Democrats, who roundly denounced SPD acceptance of the decree. In Munich,
"at almost every assembly of the party, Reichsbanner, or trade unions [in
June and July], opposition speakers" maligned the proceedings of the
Leipzig congress and attacked the decree. Not only did the ranks in
Bavaria's capital "condemn" cooperation with Brüning, but numerous
members threatened to "turn in their party books" if the SPD did not
change course.[55] After Gustav Dahrendorf censured the decree in a passionate speech, Social Democrats in the Hamburg Bürgerschaft (legislature) proposed that the senate ("cabinet") call for basic revisions. Hamburg legislators, however, obediently dropped their motion when the
Reichstag delegation decided not to oppose the decree.[56]

Free Trade unionists expressed even greater disgust. Not only the
decree's contents but the fact that Brüning met often with representatives
of industry and agriculture, while ignoring the ADGB, galled union
leaders.[57] The ADGB produced remonstrance after remonstrance against
the decree.[58] Privately, Theodor Leipart and others on the ADGB executive told SPD leaders that the unions "absolutely" rejected the decree and
warned that the edict would "foster radicalization . . . to the advantage of
the NSDAP and KPD." Nonetheless, they acknowledged that the SPD and
the trade unions must go "hand in hand" and rejected the tactic of "last
resort"—that is, a general strike.[59] At a meeting with the SPD, attended by

ADGB representatives, Brüning promised to consider revisions of the decree at a later date. Afterward, the ADGB board impressed upon its national committee the political necessity of swallowing the bitter pill.[60]

Union members were less reluctant to take to the streets or to link attacks on the decree with assaults on toleration. In Cologne thousands of public employees marched in protest.[61] At a delegates' assembly of Cologne's gas, water, and electricity workers, unionists, dismissing the keynote speaker's prediction that Brüning's fall would lead to dictatorship, insisted that the ADGB leadership change its course.[62] Numerous resolutions to the ADGB congress in late summer censured the decree as well as ADGB compliance with SPD policy. Metalworkers' locals, decimated by unemployment and under pressure from Communist members, produced many of these resolutions; at the congress DMV delegates repeatedly demanded "militancy."[63] To placate such sentiment, the ADGB executive submitted a resolution that called for revisions of the decree's "unbearable severity and restrictions on rights."[64]

Confronted with this fury against the emergency decree and a surge of sympathy for the Left Opposition's viewpoint, the SPD elite muted its claims for a parliamentary tactic so recently touted. Propaganda material for provincial speakers reiterated that the SPD took no responsibility for the policies of the regime.[65] In a radio talk, Hans Vogel, cochairman of the SPD, criticized the emergency decree and blamed capitalism for the crisis.[66] In *Die Gesellschaft* Hilferding attacked Brüning for alienating France and unbalancing the economy, for unfair and misguided attempts to balance the budget, and for his tendency to drive political bargaining to the crisis point. Yet he insisted that the SPD had no alternative to supporting the chancellor. If the party brought him down, not only would the economic and political situation drastically worsen, but the masses would blame Social Democracy. In *Vorwärts*, Stampfer emphasized the narrow limits of Social Democracy's influence on Brüning but claimed the SPD had prevented big capital and big agriculture from making good their bid for total power. Despite a common desire to shore up an unloved policy, these two members of the SPD executive assessed differently the popular movement that had occasioned toleration. They agreed that the NSDAP had swerved toward the traditional Right; but Hilferding feared it had become more dangerous as a result, while Stampfer perceived a "political advantage" in having torn off the Nazis' socialist masks.[67] They did not stand alone in their confusion about how to weigh the political prospects of the NSDAP, much less about how to respond to its continued electoral successes.

What Is to Be Done?

At Leipzig, Breitscheid summed up leadership thinking on the historical roots, ideology, and significance of European fascism. He argued that fascism originated in a "bourgeois-capitalist aversion to democracy." The term should not be diluted by calling governments such as Brüning's fascist, though he admitted that a fascist state did not necessarily discard all democratic vestiges. Indeed, fascism was an odd form of dictatorship because it attacked democratic practice, but not precepts, and did not challenge egalitarianism. Majority speakers made much of the parallel between Italy and Germany, hoping to justify cooperation with moderate bourgeois parties with allusions to the infelicitous consequences of the uncompromising stance taken by Italian socialists in 1922.[68] Breitscheid acknowledged that the promise of an anti-Marxist "classless society" had drawn people from all social strata to the prophets of the Third Reich. While Breitscheid only implied that workers were among these supporters, speakers' material put out by the executive committee conceded that "every party has workers' votes," giving this as a reason for the political "weakness" of the working class.[69] According to Breitscheid, NSDAP propaganda exploited SPD support of a bourgeois regime and trumpeted its own anticapitalism. In opposition to Stampfer and Hilferding, then, he suggested that the Nazis had not yet been exposed as part of the traditional Right. He believed that the NSDAP tie to business was only indirect, a "tendency."[70] Similarly, he argued that neither the bourgeois parties nor the capitalists had a monolithic perspective on the NSDAP. SPD policy was calculated to deter just such bourgeois unity. Majority supporters saw the NSDAP as a semiautonomous force.[71]

Der Klassenkampf writers, in contrast, defined it, now as before, as an adjunct of the bourgeoisie, while acknowledging that its popular backbone and its economic program were "purely petit bourgeois (*mittelständlerisch*)".[72] Leftists rejected the Italian parallel. They believed German fascism's economic foundation was monopoly capitalism, not latifundia as in the Italian case. Moreover, they argued, an intransigent stance against the bourgeois front could succeed because of the real clout of the German working class as opposed to the ostensible power of the Italian proletariat in 1920–21.[73] Leftists denied that capitalists actually intended to surrender power to the Nazis. In sum, they found Brüning's government worse and predicted less dire results from its demise than did the majority.[74]

A few leftists even rejected the notion that the SPD should try to win Nazism's followers among the petite bourgeoisie, maintaining that the working class could defeat the fascist threat without allies. Most leftists,

though, predicted that economic decline would erode the "false consciousness" of the middle strata.[75] Revisionists, meanwhile, grew increasingly impatient with the SPD's traditional approach to the *Mittelstand*.
Trenchant critiques of the isolation of Social Democracy from nonproletarians appeared, above all, in the Free Trade Union journal, *Die Arbeit*,
whose writers blamed the SPD's predicament on its acceptance of Marxist
immiseration theory.[76] Especially striking was a self-critical article by
Geiger in which he chastised himself for having ascribed petit bourgeois
antisocialism to false consciousness. In stark contrast to his *Panik im
Mittelstand*, in this piece Geiger confessed that the SPD had alienated the
new *Mittelstand* by insisting that proletarianization would drive it to an
alliance with workers. He accused, especially, "middle-level functionaries"
and the provincial press of ideological rigidity and the sin of "vulgar
Marxism (*Volksmarxismus*)."[77]

Insofar as it aimed any appeals at all at the middle classes, the daily
press's propaganda was certainly crude, repeatedly asking the *Bürgertum*
if it would join the "worker-millions who alone combat the privileges of
the powerful" or be led astray by Hitler, "whom the powerful subsidize."[78]
In 1931, however, lower functionaries across the country exhorted their
comrades to end neglect of the *Mittelschichten*.[79] Such calls fell on deaf ears
at least in part because party authorities and opinion makers were themselves captives of *Volksmarxismus*. In *Neue Blätter*, Günter Keiser described
the contradictory evaluations of the NSDAP found in nationally produced propaganda. One view presented National Socialism as an anticapitalist movement that ripened the "proletarianizing" *Mittelstand* for
socialism; the other perspective saw it as the "stirrup holder of capitalism."[80] Even revisionists had great difficulty relinquishing a two-class
analysis. Erik Nölting, for example, wrote (in *Vorwärts*, not some provincial daily) that under National Socialism's banner a "petit bourgeois
block" had emerged as a political "great power." He believed, though, that
this situation would prove to be ephemeral; as the middle strata succumbed to proletarianization, their consciousness would adjust to their
sociological position.[81] At Leipzig, Breitscheid too relied on the concept
of proletarianization, but he saw it as the precondition of National Socialism's success with the *Mittelstand*. Neither he nor other leaders urged the
SPD to concentrate on this allegedly declining social group. Instead,
toleration's supporters stressed that the SPD's parliamentary course was
intended to protect the "social interests of the working class."[82] In his
address to the AfA-Bund's congress of 1931, which was published as a
pamphlet, Aufhäuser warned that the economic tendencies of "advanced
capitalism" left no space for "people between the classes." He urged all

employees to give up bourgeois pretensions that divided them from the working class.[83]

Above all, the ADGB got off too easily in Geiger's analysis of Social Democratic difficulties in luring the new *Mittelstand*. While *Die Arbeit* encouraged the SPD to overcome its theoretical disdain for the new *Mittelstand*, the ADGB's pragmatic dislike of employee privileges impaired the SPD's ability to attract the middle strata. Aufhäuser had long wrestled with this dilemma. In his speech to the AfA-Bund congress, he promised yet again that "Socialism is no absolute leveler (*Gleichmacherei*)."[84] As early as 1930, Social Democrats had recognized the strong sympathies for the NSDAP of certain sectors of the civil service (such as railway, custom, and forestry officials). In an effort to counter this appeal, a pamphlet in 1931 reminded civil servants that "Social Democracy never impugned the status of the professional civil service."[85] Yet such a minor effort to reach out has to be compared with a "fiery speech" against white-collar *Sonderrechte* (special privileges), delivered at the ADGB congress in September 1931 by Clemens Nörpel, a labor law expert.[86] Political opponents no doubt made sure that more employees and civil servants heard about Nörpel's speech than read soothing pamphlets.

The issue of whether to make a concerted bid for the goodwill of farmers continued to plague the SPD. It is unclear whether such a campaign would have paid off. On one hand, recent scholarship has shown that agrarian areas became NSDAP strongholds later than previously assumed. According to Jürgen Falter, only after the September 1930 elections did the NSDAP make its decisive breakthrough among rural voters;[87] yet the later date also suggests that the cultivation of rural voters was an arduous undertaking. The NSDAP not only had plowed this territory assiduously since 1928, but it did not labor under the burden of a negative image. Whatever the chances of success, Social Democrats from rural districts wanted to go after farmers aggressively. The districts of Magdeburg and little Trupermoor submitted motions to the Leipzig congress for an SPD farmers' newspaper. Referred to the executive for consideration, this proposal was only acted upon in late 1932.[88] Propaganda did not completely neglect farmers between 1930 and 1933. Pamphlets employed language that blurred the line between urban workers and farmers, for example, by describing the SPD as the "representative of all producers in the city and countryside."[89] More concrete were reminders to farmers that the SPD no longer protected only consumer interests nor planned to expropriate middle-sized farms.[90] Unversed in current rural grievances, however, the SPD was reduced to plagiarizing from publications of the Reichslandbund, Germany's major, and increasingly Nazi-dominated, agrarian league. In one case, such "borrowing" consisted of invectives against imported eggs allegedly dumped on Germany by Jewish businessmen. Rather than address the concerns of rural producers, such as the high level of agrarian debt, SPD pamphlets asserted that shared interests set workers and farmers against antidemocratic capitalists and big landowners. Such avowals smacked of class struggle and were too abstract to foster much rural support. Moreover, Social Democratic resistance to taking up the call for tariff protection for small, as opposed to large, agrarian producers hurt the party among farmers.[91]

Geiger and others identified nationalism as a major barrier separating their party from the middle classes. Immediately after September 14, public and private intimations that the SPD should become more openly patriotic were voiced by Social Democratic right wingers. Julius Leber reported that at the first delegation meeting after the elections the venerable Eduard David warned against slighting widespread frustration over the Versailles treaty that was swelling the nationalist wave. At Leipzig, Wilhelm Hoegner argued for going beyond routine criticism of the treaty to open attacks on anti-German foreign policy in general. Hermann Heller, a legal theorist who was the beacon of many neorevisionists, attested that the SPD could call itself national without betraying its principles.[92] Severing, known to favor a more positive attitude toward national defense, nonetheless obliquely criticized such views in an article in *Sozialistische Monatshefte*, the Francophile voice among party journals. He cautioned against warmed-over National Socialist recipes and said instead the SPD should stress "our love for peace" and cooperation with France. Mierendorff, cautioning against bending too far in the nationalist direction, put forward the slogan "Overcome Versailles through Europe."[93] While officially the ADGB toed the party line, Geiger expressed the growing impatience of the Free Trade Union leadership with the SPD's reluctance to adopt a more national point of view.[94] In a practical sense, disagreement centered on whether the SPD should call for revision of the Young Plan or even cessation of reparations (discussed in chapter 6).

Social Democrats also blamed the party's propaganda style and psychological approach for its inability to attract nonproletarian or new working-class supporters. The initial effort to mobilize the SPD had succeeded in activating the party corps; but by late spring 1931 more activity had not enabled the SPD to break into new circles, and the campaign was losing steam. Many fewer notices of rallies appeared in the press, and a sense of frustration became evident.[95] Neorevisionists began to argue openly that the character and even the aims of SPD activity had to change. Theo Haubach wanted to turn the SPD into a "militant party" to confront the fascist "military party." The SPD must drop the "language of 1914," learn the ways of 1931, and carry out a "profound transformation of the workers' movement."[96] Neorevisionists and some lower functionaries also challenged the psychological assumptions behind party propaganda. A Munich Socialist stirred up a wrenching debate in *Das Freie Wort* by suggesting the SPD cultivate the "emotional side" of politics and whip up passion.[97] His opponents questioned the legitimacy of emotional agitation and claimed that the slow work of "enlightenment" would eventually pay off.[98] This division did not neatly straddle the Left/Right divide. Both the rightist Ernst Heilmann and left-wing commentators endorsed the "rational" approach. For many Social Democrats, adoption of the emotion-laden language and techniques used to such effect by the Nazis equaled adaptation to Nazi ideas. In their eyes, reason and rationality were as deeply imprinted on the Socialist ideal as its political and social goals.[99]

Critics of the party's anti-Nazi effort also argued that the attempt to reach new social groups must be nationally coordinated. According to Schifrin, the "Achilles' heel of German reformism" lay in its lack of a "unified strategic plan for the struggle to win the majority." In *Der Klassenkampf*, Comrade Z complained that party authorities did not target the Oldenburg elections as a national priority.[100] Compared to the highly orchestrated Nazi effort in Oldenburg and elsewhere, Socialist campaigns were decentralized.[101] Despite its claims to the contrary at Leipzig, the leadership did not grasp the urgency of confronting Nazi agitation in every electoral situation. The root cause of the Social Democratic dispersion of energy, argued a party member from Gelsenkirchen, lay in the lack of coordination among the Reichsbanner, Workers' Sports, the trade unions, and the SPD. He called for a "proletarian general staff" that would channel the impressive resources of Social Democracy's associations—from the "marching power of the Reichsbanner to the financial clout of the consumer cooperatives."[102]

Bureaucratic torpor contributed to the SPD's inability to break its routine and enter new territory. Organizational inertia was reinforced by a twofold psychological reaction: paralysis in the face of a multitude of problems and denial of the need for change. The defensiveness with which some bureaucrats responded to demands for change only exacerbated internal tensions, squandering energy and goodwill.[103] This dynamic characterized discussions of the SPD's aging, for example. The volume of letters to *Das Freie Wort* on the need to recruit youth showed that Social Democrats recognized the despair of German youth who suffered disproportionately from unemployment and received less protection from unemployment insurance or welfare measures. Marginalized and alienated, they succumbed to radical blandishments, especially those of the KPD.[104] The SPD's obvious lack of allure for youth touched a raw nerve among some functionaries, however, who denied the problem or extolled the hard-earned "experience" of older cadres.[105] Even Karl Meitmann, elected in Hamburg as a Young Turk, scolded SAJ members for mocking seasoned functionaries. Older rank and filers, in contrast, defended youth's need to criticize authority freely.[106] The dissolution of the Young Socialists by the Leipzig congress neither enhanced the SPD's ability to recruit among young Germans nor engendered better rapport between old and young Social Democrats.

The neorevisionist Julius Leber recalled angrily that September 14 in no way shocked the Reichstag delegation into "leaping over [its own] stagnating bureaucracy." It reelected its old executive, of which not one member was of the 1914, much less postwar, generation. The leadership ignored the acute *Bonzen* fatigue" that beset the ranks, induced by the antiboss harangues of the NSDAP and the KPD. Kurt Laumann, a leftist, remarked on the ever louder clamor against the "apparatus."[107] In the daily press, in *Das Freie Wort,* and at meetings, rancor burst forth against well-heeled Social Democrats who seemed insensitive to the misery of working-class members.[108] A functionary in Hamburg noted that factory workers cared less about the riches of Frick or Hugenberg than whether Socialist X or Y had his hand in the till or lived beyond working-class means. Echoing motions to the Leipzig congress from various districts, he called for reducing the salaries and pensions of party leaders.[109] A Berliner was applauded by fellow functionaries when he castigated Social Democratic "high earners" for not lifting a finger for the organization.[110] In Munich, a rebellion against the bourgeois style of life of Erhard Auer (editor of the *Münchner Post,* chairman of the Munich SPD, and member of both the Landtag and the Reichstag) turned into a revolt against all prosperous Socialists. Through mid-1931, inner strife in the city's clubs often eclipsed the anti-Nazi struggle.[111] Criticism of high salaries and pensions, including those of Social Democrats, also preoccupied the Hesse state congress in September 1931.[112] The desire to purify the association and restore its original egalitarianism was rekindled by the depression and the struggle against radical opponents. Paradoxically, this impulse distracted some Social Democrats from the external troubles that stimulated the concern.

Protests against the stultifying effects of bureaucracy rather than the embourgeoisement of particular bureaucrats emanated more often from intellectuals than from grassroots activists.[113] In the summer of 1931, the

Klassenkampf group published a pamphlet, *Die Organisation im Klassen-kampf*, that pilloried the SPD's undemocratic deformations. Fritz Bieligk complained about the inordinate power of the Reichstag delegation, dependent only on the approval of the SPD executive committee, not the congress. Leftists wanted all congressional delegates to be elected, not ap-pointed.[114] Neorevisionists defined the "crisis of party democracy" some-what differently. They regretted most the tenuous connection between leaders and members. In their view, a faulty conception of leadership and a bureaucratic promotion process had produced old, indecisive lead-ers who lacked charisma.[115] August Rathmann, Wilhelm Sollmann, Karl Meitmann, Walther Pahl, and Hans Müller all rued that for Social Demo-crats, "program" counted for more than their leaders' achievements, while election returns suggested that the wider public had reversed pri-orities. The republic, Meitmann claimed, had contributed to the leader-ship crisis in the SPD by drawing the best leaders from union and party bureaus and sending them into municipal and state offices. No one was left to train a new generation of popular tribunes, while older leaders had grown distant from the masses.[116]

Of course, the toleration policy itself blunted the SPD's appeal for broader support. Besides inhibiting Social Democratic reactions to Brü-ning's anti-working-class economic measures, toleration encouraged a seemingly contrary trend in party propaganda. Despite the pleas of func-tionaries and intellectuals to broaden its appeal, as a rule party propa-ganda spoke the traditional language of class not less but more than it had in the years just preceding. Not only did propaganda stress with a new vehemence that Social Democracy was a working-class movement, but it claimed that "Social Democratic workers alone are carrying the burden of the struggle against fascism. . . . They are the only true republi-cans."[117] SPD dailies in small towns touted the virtues of "class conscious-ness" and proudly proclaimed theirs a workers' party. Members were urged ever more insistently to abandon bourgeois associations.[118] This tendency spread throughout the Social Democratic movement. The ac-tivities and press of the Workers' Sports Federation were increasingly saturated with politics and devoted to the struggle against the NSDAP, while the Workers' Choirs, the most assimilationist cultural organization, reaffirmed its ties to the SPD. For the first time, this association followed others in luring workers *as workers* from bourgeois choral societies, en-treating them to join the "proletarian community" of "class-conscious workers."[119] This trend was doubly determined. Despite its support for Brüning, the SPD was increasingly isolated within national politics as the moderate bourgeois parties turned ever more rightward. As it had during

Imperial times the SPD responded by accenting its distinct social character, taking pride in its isolation. At the same time, toleration was unpopular not only among workers in general but within Social Democracy's
ranks. Again, as in the past, the SPD cranked up its class language in
proportion to the moderation of its reformist practice in order to infuse
its adherents with a sense of purpose and militancy that could allay
discomfort about the party's parliamentary course. In a crisis it retreated
to old lines of defense; yet, as will be shown in the next chapter, the
renewed emphasis on class allegiance was not accompanied by an effort to
win new working-class support by trying to overcome the ever deepening
depression.

What explains the party leadership's apparent nonchalance about find-
ing paths to new social strata or strayed members of the working class?
Breitscheid provided a hint at Leipzig when he insisted that toleration was
bearable so long as it did not weaken the central core of the SPD. A supporter of toleration pointed to the influx of members across the country
as proof that the policy had not hurt the SPD. He scorned those who were
overly concerned by electoral losses.[120] Stampfer later confirmed this
attitude: the party could deceive itself about its "invincibility" in 1931
because membership remained high. At the end of 1930 there were
1,037,384 Social Democrats; at the end of 1931 there were 1,008,953—an
attrition rate of less than 3 percent, despite an inhospitable political
climate and an internal split.[121] In part, this achievement can be attributed
to a lag that characterized the ratio of voters to members throughout the
Weimar years. It also attests, however, to the loyalty of all Social Democrats and, especially, to the determined efforts of concerned activists to
fight attrition. Ironically, the dedication and solidarity that enriched and
secured the Social Democratic association masked the corrosive effects of
practical and theoretical immobilization on the SPD's vitality. Despite an
avalanche of internal pleas for reform of SPD methods and ideas, the
leadership could deceive itself that these were not really necessary.

Demoralization, Autumn 1931

Passive opposition to the toleration policy had spread throughout
the SPD by late 1931. Complaints to local functionaries about the politics
of party and union leaders proliferated.[122] In Württemberg, Wilhelm
Keil's stubborn defense of toleration contributed to his eclipse, while Kurt
Schumacher's ever livelier offense against it augmented his popularity.[123]
Demoralization lay behind the abatement of activity in Dortmund after
the August referendum on the Prussian government. Munich and Nort-

heim also experienced fatigue. Even Reichsbanner chapters, plagued by a shortage of funds and uniforms, held fewer public meetings.[124] At Hesse's party convention, Mierendorff moved to instruct the Reichstag delegation "to distance itself sharply from Brüning and express its intention to end toleration if the regime does not change course." All delegates except one endorsed this motion, ignoring counterarguments by Dittmann, the representative of the national executive.[125] Discontent in Hamburg escalated after state elections dealt the SPD a distressing defeat on September 27. The SPD, led by revisionists, had constituted by far the largest party in Hamburg since 1918, sharing power in the senate with the DDP and the DVP. Now it barely held first place. From September 1930 it lost 10 percent (240,984 to 214,553) while the NSDAP gained 40 percent (144,684 to 202,506) and the KPD added 25 percent (135,279 to 168,674). Its Bürgerschaft delegation shrank from 60 to 46.[126] The results shocked the Hamburg party. The *Echo* confessed that Social Democrats had thought the "fascist wave" spent. It blamed losses not only on the economic crisis but on the SPD's "lesser evil politics," which the "masses do not understand."[127] A flood of letters to *Das Freie Wort* also held toleration responsible.[128] Certainly, lack of effort did not explain the results in Hamburg. The SPD held 100 indoor rallies, parades, and demonstrations in September. The regional organization also reformed its candidate selection process. Prodded by Karl Meitmann, the delegates' assembly restricted candidacy to comrades under 65 years of age, hardly a revolutionary innovation, although it did open electable positions on the list for several candidates under 40. The party's slogans and propaganda style, though, did not change. Leaflets and speakers carefully explained the roots of the political and economic crisis, recalled the SPD's record in Hamburg, and cautioned voters to exercise "reason."[129]

In Berlin, disgust with the fruits of cooperation with bourgeois parties was evident in the massive turnout for an SPD rally addressed by Heinz Neumann of the KPD and Franz Künstler, chairman of the Berlin SPD. Each ridiculed the other's politics, and the experiment yielded no nonaggression pact; yet even this joint appearance was astounding, given Social Democratic bitterness over the KPD's endorsement of the Stahlhelm referendum.[130] Desire among Berlin workers for unity on the Left must have been intense. Indeed, around the same time Socialists and Communists cooperated in a brief strike that protested the murder of a young worker by the SA in an industrial town outside Berlin.[131]

Intensifying dissatisfaction with the Reichstag delegation's tactic fueled tensions between the Left Opposition and the SPD leadership. The *Klassenkampf* group felt emboldened by signs of widespread disaffection, while the party leadership decided that an organized Left Opposition had become intolerable. New clashes culminated in the first major split in German Social Democracy since the war. On July 7, a number of *Klassenkampf* writers had secretly established a publishing house to print a weekly paper. The party executive found out about *Die Fackel* only when the first issue appeared in early September. Although the paper's editors moderated the tone of its articles, the leadership reacted angrily against this publishing venture. On September 22 a special meeting of the party council demanded that Seydewitz and coeditor Kurt Rosenfeld cease publication of the weekly. When they refused, the council expelled them on September 29. Within a few days others were shut out of the SPD, including a third Reichstag deputy, Walter Oettinghaus, who joined the KPD. Four other deputies voluntarily left the SPD. Joined by the entire district executive in Breslau, Ernst Eckstein, chairman of the SPD there, declared his solidarity with the expellees. In reaction, the regional party secretary stripped Eckstein and like-minded functionaries of their offices. On October 3 a rally of three thousand people in Breslau founded a new party, the SAPD.[132]

The split destroyed chapters of the SAJ, such as Dresden's and Lübeck's (where Julius Leber could not convince his protégé Herbert Frahm, also known as Willy Brandt, to remain in the SPD). Almost everywhere the most active youth left the party.[133] Despite disgruntlement with toleration, few older Social Democrats crossed over to the SAPD. Party loyalty, compounded by the memory of the USPD's failure, helped prevent a major split. Breslau, Zwickau-Plauen, Leipzig, Dresden, Thuringia and Hesse-Nassau lost notable numbers of members, but even these organizations survived.[134] Many committed leftists, including prominent oppositionists, did not desert the mother party. Several proclaimed their determination to stay "where the masses are."[135] A new left-wing journal, *Marxistische Tribüne für Politik und Wirtschaft*, soon appeared.[136] Nevertheless, the leadership had removed the thorn in its left side. Pressure to refurbish its traditional political culture was actually on the rise among Social Democrats (especially functionaries who had once been in the USPD), but no coherent opposition reemerged.[137] Despite the reverberations of the split and under the difficult external circumstances of the next year, Social Democrats tried to present a unified front to the world.

Expulsion of its most strident critics did not extricate the SPD from its uncomfortable political situation. In an effort to rebuild his cabinet with a more pronounced rightist slant, Brüning conducted negotiations with prominent industrialists, hoping to convince one to become his economic minister. Social Democrats feared the chancellor would succumb to business demands for reform of the unemployment insurance system and for the right to tamper with negotiated wage contracts. Breitscheid warned that Brüning's "risky game" would drive the SPD into opposition if his projected personnel changes indicated a new political orientation. According to Decker, aversion to toleration grew so intense "in broad circles of the membership as well as in leading circles of the party" that a vote against Brüning seemed "unavoidable" when the Reichstag finally reconvened on October 14, 1931.[138] The "leading circles" included Breitscheid, Hertz, Aufhäuser, and even Wels.[139] Yet no crisis erupted. Several developments convinced leading Social Democrats that powerful industrialists were deserting Brüning for the National Opposition. Two candidates whom the SPD bitterly opposed as ministerial choices—Albert Vögler, chairman of United Steel, and Otto Gessler, a former defense minister—refused to join the cabinet. Simultaneously, business associations launched a series of attacks on Brüning.[140] In the end, Hermann Warmbold of I. G. Farben accepted the post of minister of economics, while General Groener took over the Interior Ministry in addition to defense. With obvious relief, *Vorwärts* declared the political profile of Brüning's new cabinet "essentially unchanged."[141] More significantly, the convention of the National Opposition at Harzburg took place. The participants—the DNVP, the NSDAP, the Stahlhelm, and sundry individuals—formed the Harzburg Front. As have numerous historians ever since, Social Democrats discovered here concrete evidence of collusion between heavy industry and Hitler.[142] *Vorwärts* found particularly revealing the presence of Hjalmar Schacht at the meeting. The paper had announced many a "final exposé" of Nazi-capitalist complicity; but Social Democrats found this instance especially galling, and the lesson to be drawn was obvious: "social reaction" had cohered and "clear class fronts" had been revealed; the enemy stood to the right and Brüning did not stand with it.[143] On one hand, the formation of the Harzburg Front brought an even clearer shift to more class-oriented and militant language.[144] On the other hand, it reinforced the SPD's determination to continue its risk-averse policy; in the Reichstag's opening session, Breitscheid announced, "Harzburg has made us decide not to vote against Brüning's new cabinet."[145]

After this moment of solidarity with a beleaguered Brüning, Social Democratic frustration with his regime grew apace. In the late fall it centered on Groener's refusal to respond firmly to escalating SA street terror.[146] At a campaign rally in Darmstadt, Breitscheid declared that the Interior Ministry's hesitancy endangered toleration. He demanded that the government declare immediately whether it was prepared to struggle against fascism "with all means."[147] Breitscheid's sudden offer of limited cooperation with the KPD indicated perplexity at the top of the SPD about how to gain a handle of influence on Brüning. At a rally in Darmstadt, after demanding the government come down hard on fascism, Breitscheid proclaimed that the recent Communist decision to renounce terror tactics removed a major obstacle to common defense.[148] After the KPD brusquely rejected this tentative peace offering, *Vorwärts*, which normally ignored the Communists, responded in kind.[149] That door of possible escape was not tried again for many months.

In November a disaffected Nazi state representative gave the Frankfurt police documents that spelled out Nazi intentions "in the case of a seizure of power."[150] According to these Boxheim Papers (the plans were drawn up at the Boxheimer Hof), the SA's commands would become law on the spot; all arms would be confiscated, and resistance would be punished by death.[151] The Social Democratic interior minister of Hesse, Wilhelm Leuschner, pressed for an indictment of Werner Best, the state NSDAP leader, on the grounds of criminal subversion.[152] Instead, the national government shrugged its shoulders and wondered what all the fuss was about. Groener instructed Reich Prosecutor Karl Werner to proceed cautiously. The prosecutor did not find the subversive nature of the plans self-evident: an investigation was necessary. General Schleicher, eager for closer cooperation with the National Opposition, was responsible for Groener's policy of discounting even blatant evidence of Nazi putschist plans.[153] Brüning too, however, opposed a firm response. He did not want to disrupt secret negotiations between Best and the Center Party about a coalition in Hesse.[154] Hermann Göring reassured Groener of the legality of his party's aims, the NSDAP temporarily suspended Best, and the matter was dropped, although Social Democrats urgently pressed for state action.[155] Because of Groener's unwillingness to repress antirepublican terror, Prussian relations with the Reich Interior Ministry deteriorated. Severing argued in vain for measures against the ardent agitation of the NSDAP and the SA among civil servants. His obstinate belief that the Reich must act first made him reluctant to step into the breach, a stance that occasioned a tactical disagreement with Berlin police chief Grzesinski. Aware that the Prussian government possessed sufficient evidence to deport Hitler as an alien, Grzesinski wanted to arrest him at his press conference with American reporters in Berlin on December 11.[156] Severing agreed to this plan but changed his mind, not to be budged by Grzesinski or Braun, after Brüning vetoed the arrest. Grzesinski recalled the "disgust" of Prussian officials over the failure to exploit this opportunity to humiliate Hitler.[157]

Precipitous electoral losses in the late fall further narrowed the space in which Social Democrats had to maneuver. In communal elections in the small state of Anhalt, the SPD slid from 84,979 votes in September 1930 to 67,474. It was now trumped by the Nazis with their 76,430 votes. A week later the SPD lost in Mecklenburg. Most disappointing, after a feisty campaign in Darmstadt during which Wels, Breitscheid, and Severing stumped for the SPD, it lost badly in Hesse, and the NSDAP emerged as the largest party there as well.[158] Georg Decker conceded that a "second fascist wave" was washing over the country. In contrast to September 1930, dozens of eager analysts did not wrestle with the meaning of these results. At the end of the year, disharmony and confusion ran rampant in the SPD. When justifying toleration before mass audiences, SPD national leaders adopted a defensive tone.[159] From local leaders and editors came the plaintive cry, "Tolerate or not?"[160] Anton Erkelenz, a leading Democrat who defected to the SPD in 1930 because he saw it as the republic's only bulwark, now "feared we are annihilating ourselves without otherwise benefiting us or the republic."[161]

Other provincial Socialists, however, felt, as did the party leadership, that toleration remained the lesser evil,[162] and they did so for the same reasons that they had a year earlier, despite shifts in political alliances, massive deterioration of the economy, continued growth of the NSDAP, and Nazi infiltration of institutions such as the civil service and the army. The editor of the *Düsseldorf Volkszeitung*, for example, reassured Erkelenz that at membership and trade union meetings he had observed at first hand that the "working class understands the delegation's position." He reminded Erkelenz that "if Social Democracy creates difficulties for Brüning, it runs the risk of driving the entire bourgeoisie over to the fascist side." He offered another reason for measured optimism: the Reichswehr viewed Hitler not only with "skepticism" but with an "open scorn" that would "probably prevent [it] . . . from crossing over to Hitler's camp."[163]

In letters to the venerable Kautskys, leading Social Democrats too reflected on the prospects for democracy and the SPD. This correspondence revealed that the differences that divided Erkelenz from the editor in Düsseldorf had penetrated the party's ruling chambers. Paul Hertz told Luise Kautsky that he, Aufhäuser, and Breitscheid had pleaded in the Reichstag delegation's executive for a new course. They would have muted their objections "if our doubts about the final success of our policy were not becoming ever greater and we did not fear that despite everything the Nazis will sooner or later come to power." Stampfer wrote, in contrast, that although he found the situation "ghastly," he was confident the "flood" would recede sooner or later. German Social Democracy, he mused, had ever been "hesitant on the offensive but excellent on the defensive, which obviously corresponds to the character of the German worker."[164] For his part, Hilferding admitted to Karl Kautsky that Hitler's chances of gaining power depended "above all" on whether Brüning and the Center Party lost their nerve, as had the Protestant middle class. He lamented, "It is really horribly depressing what kind of crowd one must now go around with in politics," and in economic affairs the crowd was no less "grotesque." Still, Hilferding insisted to the leftist Arkadij Gurland, Brüning was the "only pillar against the fascist danger" because the working class was too weak and, besides, had failed to secure rural allies.[165] Hilferding's honest and despairing justification of endless support to the Hunger Chancellor compares favorably to Stampfer's glib vindication of passivity, but it was not the stuff of popular politics. Hilferding himself realized that lofty phrases about the workers' mission to save democracy "don't satisfy the psychological needs of the broad masses."[166]

More immediately worrisome than the psychic state of the masses was the angry reaction of the ADGB to extensive wage reductions in December's emergency decree. The ADGB national committee pressured the SPD to make "a thorough critique of social and economic conditions and especially of the emergency decree" and to demand the Reichstag be convened.[167] Union chiefs lamented the decimation of their ranks by unemployment; in private sessions several called for an end to toleration. The chairman of the hatmakers' union warned of a "strong desire [among the ranks] for a more independent trade union policy . . . that would free the unions from the politics of the party." Fritz Tarnow of the woodworkers defended toleration but admitted that in the fall elections "for the first time our people obviously deserted us." In the end the ADGB again submitted to the SPD's acceptance of the emergency decree, but at all levels of the Free Trade Unions the mood was bleak.[168] Clearly something had to be done.

The Debate over a Crisis Program

The ever worsening economic crisis strained union/party relations, driving a wedge between their priorities, highlighting subtle discrepancies in political outlook, and fomenting disputes over economic
issues. To a majority on the SPD executive and to many party functionaries, toleration of Brüning remained the only viable means for keeping
the NSDAP out of the cabinet and for maintaining Braun's power in
Prussia. Upset by electoral losses in state elections, they nonetheless took
heart from the loyalty of the SPD membership; pained by the party's
weakness on the national level, they found comfort in the fact that the
SPD controlled the most important state. These positive marks on the
balance sheet of toleration looked less impressive to the ADGB, whose
base was directly eroded by the depression and toleration's negative effects. The nationwide unemployment rate of trade union members in
1931 was 33.7 percent. Even grimmer was the fate of highly industrialized
work forces in Berlin, Hamburg, Saxony, Silesia, and the Ruhr who
labored in the most devastated economic branches—metal, mining, tim-
ber, textiles, and construction. While the SPD's membership was stable,
the ADGB fell from 4.7 million members in 1930 to 4.1 million in 1931.[1]
Pivotal industrial unions such as the metalworkers shrank at an accelerat-
ing rate: 941,000 in 1930; 827,000 in 1931; 690,000 in 1932.[2] Under conditions so unfavorable to labor, strikes became ever less effective weapons.[3] The ADGB's helplessness in the face of massive layoffs redounded
to the advantage of the Communist RGO. In factory council elections in
1931, the ADGB still captured 87 percent of all seats, compared with a
paltry 3.5 percent for the RGO. In the *Ruhrgebiet*, however, the RGO
garnered 29 percent of the vote, uncomfortably close to the ADGB's 36.4
percent. At a general meeting of the metalworkers in Munich in July
1931, 500 (of 12,000) members crossed over to the RGO in one fell
swoop.[4] Union functionaries had to heed the laments of workers such as
that of a raftsman who cried, "Work is what we want, damn it, honest,
decent work. . . . We only want work, nothing but work."[5]

Of course SPD politicians worried that the "ghost of unemployment"
made Germans vote Communist or Nazi, but their concern was less
immediate than union leaders' because the state of the economy only
indirectly impinged on the SPD's power.[6] As a result, trade union leaders

showed more interest than did party strategists in forging a program to overcome the scourge of unemployment. This interest generated tensions inside Social Democracy for several reasons. First, the solution that gained credence in the ADGB contradicted the SPD's reigning economic analysis; in fact, in party eyes the ADGB plan bore a disconcerting resemblance to Nazi "inflation schemes." Second, because the ADGB's crisis program called for deficit financing of public works projects, party leaders feared its propagation would alienate Brüning, committed as he was to slashing the budget. Hilferding, the SPD's major economic theorist and the most tireless champion of continued toleration, led the opposition to the ADGB in the debate over a crisis program. He was joined by Otto Wels, who discerned in the ADGB's campaign a challenge to the party's political hegemony inside Social Democracy. Surprisingly, SPD leaders received the tacit support of intellectuals and activists who questioned toleration but promoted their own solutions to Social Democracy's woes. A parallel effort by the ADGB to convince the SPD to renounce reparations fueled party suspicions that a hidden agenda lay behind its crisis program. Some leaders bristled at a second menace to cooperation with Brüning, an objection that dovetailed with a widely held perception that the ADGB was succumbing to the National Opposition's jingoism, autarkic fantasies, and Francophobia. This worry shaped SPD reactions to both of the ADGB's sallies into political economy, occupying the foreground of the discussion on reparations and poisoning the theoretical disputes that dominated the debate over a crisis program. Anxiety about the political trajectory of the ADGB inspired the adamancy with which the SPD, joined by the AfA-Bund, resisted adopting a program that was surely to Social Democracy's advantage.

Down with Reparations?

Soon after the shock of the 1930 Reichstag elections, Theodor Leipart and other union chiefs began to argue privately that the drain of reparations on German capital was the source of the severity of the unfolding crisis. Leipart hinted that the ADGB should call for a revision of reparations payments. Disregarding Wels's objection that such a position would only abet the Right, the ADGB published a statement blaming the depression on reparations.[7] Through mid-1931 union leaders pressed for a revision of the Young Plan but rarely addressed the issue publicly.[8] For its part, the SPD neither retracted its support of the Young Plan nor railed against reparations.[9] Instead, *Vorwärts* vented irritation over the general turn away from Stresemann's policy of understanding and, in particular, over Brüning's alienation of France. It called for an amicable settlement of reparations, especially after the Hoover moratorium of July 1931 indicated a new sympathy on the American side.[10]

In the fall of 1931 leading Free Trade unionists began persistently and publicly to voice the opinion that reparations lay at the root of the crisis.[11] On October 13 the ADGB published a declaration to this effect. The next day in the Reichstag, in contrast, Rudolf Breitscheid pointedly denied that reparations were the sole cause of the crisis. The SPD refused to support a Nazi motion, backed by the KPD, for immediate stoppage of payment.[12] The ADGB's statement very likely influenced the timing of the NSDAP motion. Not at all taken aback, the ADGB only grew bolder, demanding in concert with the AfA-Bund and Christian and liberal trade unions, "Down with the reparations burden!" A Free Trade Union rally made the same appeal.[13] On December 16 at the gathering of Social Democratic functionaries that formed the Iron Front, Leipart cried, "End reparations!"[14] Speaking after Leipart, Breitscheid rebuked him for remarks that "land one objectionably close to National Socialism." Although SPD press reports (and an ADGB pamphlet that included Breitscheid's and Leipart's speeches) deleted this comment, it infuriated those in the Free Trade Unions who were pushing for Social Democracy to adopt an openly national stance, a group that had grown ever more intolerant of the SPD's "barely disguised tribute-apologetic."[15] Breitscheid's rebuff of Leipart spurred the determination of this circle to put reparations "in the foreground."[16] Though not of this tendency, Leipart heeded the advice of its adherents on the ADGB staff and continued to air his opposition to reparations.[17]

His campaign was not without effect, if only because many provincial and leading Social Democrats, including Otto Wels, were sympathetic to the ADGB's viewpoint.[18] In early January 1932 Grassmann and Leipart met informally with several party leaders to discuss both the reparations issue and the ADGB's crisis plan, evidence that the two incipient rebellions of the ADGB were linked in the minds of leading Social Democrats. The unionists, supported by Paul Löbe and Wilhelm Sollmann, argued for an official statement against further reparations. Breitscheid, Hilferding, and Otto Landsberg, on the other side, charged that such a demand would disrupt the toleration coalition and would bolster "nationalist currents."[19] On the Reichstag delegation executive, Wels, Sollmann, and Wilhelm Keil supported Leipart's campaign; Breitscheid and Dittmann opposed it. A majority of the full delegation nixed Keil's proposal for a rally against further payments.[20] Nonetheless, in February 1932 Breitscheid explained to the Reichstag that the SPD shared Brüning's (public) stance: "We cannot pay, rather than we do not want to pay."[21] Thus, the SPD made a concession to the ADGB point of view, while refusing to align itself with the "we won't pay" stance of the Right and, now, the Free Trade Unions.[22] The ADGB continued to peddle its line, despite the fact that its stand on reparations as the (external) cause of the crisis contradicted its allegiance to an economic program that saw domestic demand as the key to overcoming the crisis. The reparations issue per se, however, slipped off the agenda of party/union negotiations, in part because it declined in political importance in 1932 and then disappeared as an issue after the Papen regime won the end of reparations at the Lausanne conference in June.[23] Moreover, the battle over a crisis program reached its peak in early 1932 and overshadowed the reparations dispute.

Confronting the Economic Crisis

In their understanding of capitalist crises, Weimar Marxists accepted certain assumptions of classical economics: capitalism was subject to periodic disruptions of production (caused in the Marxist view by overproduction and a falling rate of profit); in the normal business cycle, production and employment recovered after a crisis liquidated inefficient producers, drove down prices and wages, and restored profitability. Without a socialist transformation, Social Democrats argued, a capitalist crisis could only be overcome from the "price side," that is, by deflation.[24] Thus, orthodox Marxists came to the same conclusion as did mainstream bourgeois economists. In the 1920s, however, Hilferding's theory of "organized capitalism" had partially modified Marxism to fit new conditions. On one hand, Hilferding assumed that a "cartelized" economy was less susceptible to crisis than was competitive capitalism. On the other hand, he suggested that the state could intervene in the economy and guide it, although he envisioned management of a socialized economy. The practical implications of Hilferding's theory depended on which of these revisions was taken to heart. Hilferding himself did not expect a severe crisis, but once a breakdown occurred, he saw it as a "classical" capitalist downturn. In Germany's noncompetitive economy, he acknowledged that the state might have to intervene, but only to expedite a "frictionless unfolding" of the crisis with a procyclical fiscal policy.[25]

Hilferding's revisionism inspired several ADGB economists to consider a different response to capitalist malaise. If the state could guide the economy, they reasoned, it could engage in "crisis management" of capitalism. The early writings of John Maynard Keynes reinforced this notion. Under this double influence, the ADGB statistician Wladimir Woytinsky called for public works to counter Germany's high structural unemployment in the mid-1920s.[26] The standard call by the ADGB and the SPD for a shorter work week to allay unemployment also received a theoretical imprimatur from Hilferding's admission that the state could intervene in the economy—in this case in a legally enforced redistribution of private employment. To muddle Social Democratic approaches to the crisis even more, in their popular propaganda the SPD and the ADGB offered an underconsumptionist explanation of capitalist crises, arguing that "mass buying power" could pull capitalism out of a slump. This demand-side theory was not only un-Marxist; it implied, in direct contradiction to Hilferding's viewpoint, that a countercyclical, "pump-priming" policy could boost an economy plagued by deflation.[27] Mass-distributed pamphlets, whose authors ignored theoretical inconsistencies, explained that crises were caused by underconsumption but must be cured from the "price side." By driving down prices faster than wages, *Massenkaufkraft* (mass-buying power) would grow and stimulate a sluggish economy.[28]

Confronted with the Great Depression, Social Democrats at both the official and the popular levels neglected to reexamine the heady brew of classical Marxist, revisionist Marxist, and semi-Keynesian elixirs that infused their understanding of capitalist crises. In 1930 the SPD called for "price slashes" on one hand and the reintroduction of the eight-hour day on the other. Socialists joined the chorus of bourgeois economists who intoned that the ailing economy required, if anything, artificial expedition of its natural curve.[29] According to Hilferding, the laws of capitalism would ultimately overcome the crisis.[30] Ideological approval of fiscal conservatism was compounded by the fear that the opposite course would rekindle the hyperinflation of 1923.[31] The SPD, then, did not dispute the principles behind Brüning's plan to accelerate deflationary tendencies with budget cuts, although it did question his tendency to balance the budget on urban workers' backs.[32] Into mid-1931 the SPD reiterated its old demands and denied that slick "recipes" could revive the economy.[33] Despite the interest in crisis management shown by union economists in the 1920s, the Free Trade Unions now lamely echoed the SPD's demands. Their press, however, tended to stress the desirability of "bolstering buying power" more than the need to lower prices.[34]

This "deflationary consensus" encompassed not only the SPD, the ADGB, and Brüning's regime but employer associations, forming the basis for informal cooperation between the ADGB and employers into early 1931.[35] The social counterpart to toleration was, however, shaky. Employers and trade union leaders grew impatient for economic results sooner than did Brüning and the SPD with their (disparate) political priorities. For Brüning, deflationary policy was, above all, a means to convince the world of Germany's inability to pay reparations.[36] As the crisis ground on but his goal remained elusive, Brüning obstinately clung to his deflationary policy, yet, relative to the businessmen who backed him, he became more willing to compromise on particular social measures within the overall package. The RDI and, especially, the very conservative employers' group called the Ruhrlade were also committed to deflation, not as a cure for crisis, but as a justification for dismantling *Sozialpolitik*, driving down wages, and discarding binding labor contracts. Their loyalty to Brüning rested on his fulfillment of these aims.[37] The unions were more adamant than SPD leaders that prices must come down first and that work hours must be reduced without shrinking the weekly paypacket.[38]

In late 1930, however, unions and employers, shaken by the Nazi surge and equally opposed to new agricultural tariffs, tried to reach the compromise that had eluded them in the spring. In meetings with Labor Minister Adam Stegerwald in November 1930, representatives of industry and labor agreed in principle on the need to lower prices but disagreed about how much to bring them down and about the relative contribution of wage decreases to such cuts.[39] Only in the vaguest terms did employer organizations concede that the work week might have to be reduced; yet they did not insist on revision of binding labor contracts, a concession that angered hard-liners in their ranks.[40] Otto Wels urged acceptance of this compromise in order to "broaden the base of support for Brüning" and "create a great block between the trade unions and employer associations" that would be "of extraordinary political importance." The ADGB national committee, less riveted by Wels's vision than by the specter of Communist competition on the shop floor, abjured the agreement as unfavorable to workers. Only Fritz Tarnow pleaded for acceptance and so emerged as toleration's most adamant supporter on the ADGB board, a position he occupied throughout 1931.[41] Rejection of the agreement meant that wage cuts were imposed by executive fiat rather than negotiated between the interested parties, a solution union leaders evidently preferred. As we have seen, however, as 1931 unfolded, they balked at the effects of wage cuts imposed from above. The contradictions in the Social Democratic crisis program dawned on them: acceptance of the principle of deflation undermined their ability to oppose wage cuts; lower wages, in turn, would cancel the benefits of a shorter work week (should employers ever concede to that demand). Shorter hours at reduced wages might lead to more jobs, but at the expense of those still working.[42]

Caught between intransigent employers and a state whose policy undercut workers' bargaining power, ADGB economists, harking back to undeveloped crisis management ideas of the 1920s, began to search for a crisis program that would rely on state intervention to stimulate the labor market. The process faltered because their bosses, the leaders of the ADGB, supported a balanced budget and feared inflation, as did so many compatriots.[43] When in March 1931 Otto Hörsing, chairman of the Reichsbanner, presented the ADGB board with a program built around public works schemes, Theodor Leipart and Fritz Tarnow rebuffed it with the very arguments Hilferding and his supporters would use against the ADGB crisis plan: it would foster the illusion that national measures could end an international crisis; it was "a watered-down Nazi program"; Hörsing's real goal was to turn the Reichsbanner into a "party." Hörsing, reasoning as would Leipart and Tarnow a year later, emphasized the political necessity of a program to counter the Communist and Nazi slur that "we allow things to drift."[44] ADGB leaders replied (correctly) that public works were already included in Social Democratic suggestions to fight the crisis. In his address to the Leipzig congress, for example, Fritz Tarnow demanded a "systematic trade cycle and work provision policy" to make up for the failure of the capitalist economy.[45] Tarnow's call, however, was one of a grab bag of measures—including lower tariffs, state control of banks, a forty-hour week, and a wage policy to bolster mass purchasing power.[46] He did not offer a plan to create jobs, much less suggest how to finance such a scheme.

In fact, debate at the SPD congress got caught on ideological snags and barely touched on ways to fight unemployment. In his speech, Tarnow illustrated the SPD's dilemma in the economic crisis with a medical metaphor: was the SPD the "cheerful heir" eager for the death of the sick patient or the physician who wanted to cure the illness? He answered that the SPD had to play both roles. Although he clearly preferred that of the doctor, or an active reformist policy, he did not offer such a plan. Leftists argued for an assault on capitalism; the party should kill off the patient, not alleviate his suffering. Wilhelm Dittmann, an old ex-radical on the SPD executive, injected an affirmation of classic abstentionism into the debate. He liked Tarnow's intimation that "there are limits to our efficacy," which worked against "the illusion that our will alone determines what we do."[47] These three positions staked out the embattled territory in the fight that soon began over a crisis program. In the early stages of the conflict, abstentionism and left-wing rhetoric were often espoused in tandem. By the spring of 1932, however, leftists, desperate for some kind of active approach, sounded more like the interventionists in the trade unions than the abstentionists in the SPD.

The catalyst of the debate was an article in *Die Arbeit* of June 1931 that offered the first argument for *Arbeitsbeschaffung* (public works) that was grounded in theory. Its author was Wladimir Woytinsky, a former Menshevik who headed the ADGB's Statistics Bureau and avidly followed Keynes's work.[48] "Aktive Wirtschaftspolitik" rested on the iconoclastic assumption that the deflationary spiral was thwarting, not promoting, the revival of the world economy. The depression would be overcome not by lowering prices but by raising them to pre-crisis levels. Prices could be stabilized through an international monetary policy that deliberately generated money, thereby strengthening demand. The creation of money would provide the means for big public works projects in Europe. The new jobs would bring new money into circulation. Implementation of his plan would help Europe rebuild its infrastructure while revitalizing its national economies.[49] Woytinsky emphasized the international nature of his program because he both believed in the need for a cross-national solution and wanted to allay fears that the dilution of national currencies would fuel inflation.[50]

At this point Woytinsky's concrete proposals were vague, but he delineated clearly the assumptions behind them. With a two-edged sword he swiped at both bourgeois economists and SPD policymakers. Modern cyclical theories, especially in Germany, were characterized by a "passive, meteorological viewpoint": trade cycles were observed and bulletins were posted. He advocated instead a "medical attitude" that diagnosed in order to intervene in the "body organism." (Medical metaphors were the rage among Social Democrats that summer.) Rather than adopt an interventionist approach, Socialist theorists lulled workers with "music of a socialist future." "It is not enough to emphasize that the capitalist system is evil," he admonished, "the time is ripe for showing . . . *how* the world economic crisis can be overcome." Toleration could only have the desired political consequences, he argued, if the economy improved rapidly. Without this improvement, the party was condemned to "live off its own substance" because the "man on the street doesn't see the bigger evil, but feels the smaller one." The workers' movement needed an active economic program, not just a list of demands.[51]

Woytinsky's public foray did not impress other union policymakers. Fritz Naphtali granted that Woytinsky put his ideas in an international framework, but, he asked, would others not insist on a national version? A national policy "lands one next to Gottfried Feder, the free-money people, or the other numerous apostles of inflation." The unions' individual demands—wage and hour adjustments, monopoly controls, and lower tariffs—made more sense than a grand program, he insisted. Naphtali took particular offense at Woytinsky's sarcastic reference to socialist music.[52] Above all, however, fear of inflation motivated his opposition to Woytinsky, as it did Hilferding's. On July 16, after the banking crisis had erupted, Naphtali defended Brüning's deflationary course: "We are for the maintenance of the currency, even if we must reckon with the shutting down of more plants. Against inflation only more expensive credit will work." To this argument, Hilferding appended the warning that an "inflationary policy" would depress real wages without addressing the underlying crisis of production.[53]

The collapse of the giant Darmstädter und Nationalbank (Danat bank) on July 13, 1931, and the rash of bankruptcies and layoffs that came in its wake did provoke a general rethinking of the nature of the current crisis. For the first time, economists of various persuasions recognized that this was not a normal downturn. Scattered businessmen, such as Paul Silverberg of the RDI; bankers, such as Max Warburg; and government bureaucrats, such as Hans Schäffer, began to discuss alternatives to Brüning's policies.[54] The shock of the banking crisis, however, did not impede Brüning's stubborn progress along his rocky path. On the contrary, his response was to cut wages and prices by 20 percent at one blow.[55] Ironically, the banking crisis briefly granted him the renewed backing of heavy industry associations that had stood poised to bolt the Brüning camp. Now they accepted the arguments of the RDI's more moderate members that the danger of losing foreign credit made continued support of the chancellor the prudent choice.[56] To publicize their growing impatience with the regime's hesitant dismantling of Sozialpolitik, however, industrialists published their own deflationary program of drastic cuts in state expenditures, taxes, pension claims, and wages.[57]

At the other end of the deflationary consensus, the bank collapse shook Hilferding's confidence in the tight money policy of the Reichsbank. To stem the panic set off by the Danat's collapse, it restricted credit to all banks. As a result, the inevitable run on the banks forced them to close and not resume full operations for several weeks. Thus, the banking crisis was not only a symptom of the severity of the general crisis but greatly exacerbated it. Hilferding chided the Reichsbank for fearing inflation when conditions demanded the free flow of customer deposits to facilitate circulation and restore public confidence.[58] He complained that it did not stick to "red-blooded capitalist methods"—an international banking policy that would have drawn in American and French credit.[59] Despite

Hilferding's dismay over the Reichsbank's action, the banking crisis only confirmed his dogged support of Brüning's fiscal policy and of toleration. Increasingly, Hilferding became the SPD's main contact with Brüning and interpreted the chancellor's political strategy for his fellow executive board members.[60] Yet Hilferding may have been the only participant in the deflationary consensus who sincerely believed in the economic underpinnings of Brüning's course. He clung to monetary orthodoxy, worried about the inflationary effects of tinkering with the monetary system in a "cartelized" economy.[61] In *Vorwärts* he lashed out against England's devaluation of the pound in September 1931, and at the AfA-Bund convention in October he predicted dire consequences from a collapse of the gold standard.[62] He also he opposed further wages reductions, however, and claimed not to understand what the phrase *deflationary policy* meant.[63] In correspondence with Kautsky, with whom he could let down his guard, he admitted his fundamental befuddlement: "The basic misfortune is that we cannot say concretely how we would get rid of the crisis. . . . The capitalist tremors surpass all expectations, but the solution of the credit crisis can only come from France and America, where we have little influence. . . . That is naturally a purely capitalist solution. A socialist solution is not there and that makes the situation terribly difficult and allows the Communists and National Socialists to grow ever larger."[64]

Unaware that their guide had lost his bearings, the SPD press and Reichstag speakers took up Hilferding's crusade against the "inflation plans" of the Right, a campaign motivated in part by a desire to frighten the middle class away from the NSDAP.[65] Aufhäuser lambasted the National Socialists for acting as if their "*Federgeld*" could attack the crisis from "the money side" without somehow intervening in the production system, adding, "We will fight all urges toward inflation." Editorials charged that industrialists in the Harzburg Front harbored yearnings for inflation.[66] The linking of capitalists with inflation was only one element in the radical rhetoric of the SPD in the fall of 1931. Letters to *Das Freie Wort* called for a campaign against capitalism.[67] Dailies, pamphlets, and speakers now emphasized socialist solutions to the crisis. After the Danat collapse, the executive committee and the party council called for an end to the "autonomy of the banks and heavy industry."[68] *Vorwärts* advocated "taking up the long struggle for a socialist economy."[69] This radicalism reflected the increasing frustration of party functionaries and members over a crisis that only got worse while their party dallied with the Hunger Chancellor;[70] yet suspicions that the depression might cause the death throes of capitalism did not extinguish wishful thinking. In December 1931 a Socialist editor tried to cheer up Anton Erkelenz with the hopeful prognosis that "next year" or in "spring 1933" conditions would surely improve. Erkelenz, unimpressed, replied that he had encountered such "economic optimism" among many party functionaries. In contrast, Erkelenz was a Cassandra who warned of the economic and political madness of deflation.[71]

Targeting Social Democrats such as Erkelenz as well as those less receptive, Woytinsky endeavored to establish the theoretical legitimacy and practicality of an active fiscal policy, in spite of the icy reception he received in the summer.[72] In popular articles and in a scholarly publication, he argued for state intervention to raise prices and create work, and against fears that these would result in inflation.[73] In opposition to Hilferding, he attacked the government's course precisely for being deflationary and praised England's devaluation of the pound.[74] His growing influence within the trade unions can be gauged by the themes that suffused their propaganda. In late September a joint ADGB–AfA-Bund rally proclaimed *Arbeitsbeschaffung* its major demand, while cautioning that there were "no magic means or miracles" to gain it. In December, when the ADGB national committee publicly criticized the fourth emergency decree, it deplored its lack of work projects and condemned *Deflationspolitik*. Most significant, in light of his unwavering support for toleration and the respect he commanded in both the ADGB and the SPD, was Fritz Tarnow's conversion to the political and economic desirability of an "action program."[75] In late December he and Woytinsky presented the ADGB executive board with their "theses on the struggle against the crisis." These proposals laid out Woytinsky's view that a grand public works program would stimulate the economy.[76] The third coauthor was Fritz Baade, the SPD's agrarian expert, who the reformers hoped would gain a friendly hearing for their ideas from the Reichstag delegation. On January 26, 1932, the Woytinsky-Tarnow-Baade team formulated their guidelines in a "public works plan" and presented it to the SPD and the ADGB for approval.[77]

WTB marked a departure from Woytinsky's proposals of 1931 that had an international basis. Rather than wait for an agreement among nations, Woytinsky wrote, he and his coauthors decided "to present a concrete program to overcome the crisis within the framework of the German economy."[78] WTB explicitly endorsed deficit spending as the best way to finance large-scale public works, aiming to put 1 million Germans to work with 2 billion marks culled from the Reich budget and a "currency loan (*Währungsanleihe*)" from the Reichsbank. Since declining tax revenues and a weak capital market ruled out raising money through normal channels, additional credit had to be created by the state. The authors assured potential critics that the limited sums involved, as well as the large excess capacity in the German economy, precluded a repetition of the great inflation of the early 1920s.[79] They promised political benefits from an active economic policy and suggested that the workers' movement begin a sustained press campaign under the slogan "the struggle against the crisis."[80] The trade union press rose to the challenge by assailing Brüning's passive stance toward unemployment.[81] In the pages of the union press, Woytinsky wielded his pen against the SPD's contradictory attitude toward Brüning's deflationary program and cited Hilferding as the main representative of a misplaced *"Angst vor der Inflation."*[82] WTB struck a chord in the provinces. From a Silesian party activist came the plea for the newly formed Iron Front to make public works its clarion call.[83] Another comrade reported that SPD functionaries, confused and crippled by indecision at the top, hoped for a "quick, clear decision" on a crisis program so they could focus all forces on one goal. After a speech by Woytinsky, an SPD chapter in Thuringia adopted a resolution in support of an "active crisis policy" to counter "the radicalization of the masses and, above all, the growth of the National Socialists."[84]

The leadership responded to the urgent prods from the ADGB and party ranks, but not as bidden. The SPD executive, the Reichstag delegation executive, and the AfA-Bund decided that the ADGB should not "officially" adopt the plan. The ADGB hesitated to proceed against SPD hostility and without the party's daily press at its disposal. Leipart told Woytinsky, Baade, and Tarnow to circulate their ideas but warned them to consider "the possible political consequences of open strife between the party and unions."[85] Paul Hertz, Hilferding, Fritz Naphtali, and several other union economists, meanwhile, drew up a "revised draft for an economic program" that called for a radical restructuring of the economy. Public works played a secondary role in its recommendations for overcoming the crisis. Indeed, its scheme to finance work provision under capitalism was extremely moderate. New jobs would be financed from current income—that is, tax revenues—or with credit raised through a high-interest national loan that would draw out hoarded money.[86]

In this fractious environment, the ADGB national committee met to decide on a program for economic revival. Against WTB, Naphtali argued vigorously that the international nature of the crisis required an "active foreign policy"—cooperation with France. He advised against awaking illusions in the working class with the promise of a million jobs. While acknowledging that the government could create credit, he maintained that the danger of an "inflation panic" shrank its maneuvering room. Tarnow and Woytinsky defended WTB as politically necessary and economically sound. Tarnow pointed out that "many theorists in the socialist and bourgeois camps" supported their plan in contrast to Hilferding's gruff rejection of it. Other union leaders spoke of "mass yearning for a way out of this chaos" and told of lower union officials who had been "waiting for months for counsel and guidance" on economic issues. They were desperate for a response to the crisis not only because unemployed members were drifting to the Communists but because the NSBO was ever more active among employed workers.[87] Worried that the tremendous enthusiasm for the Iron Front among Social Democracy's ranks would soon ebb, several leaders asserted that Social Democracy "can't wait for international cooperation" but must immediately begin a huge campaign for public works, while also calling for nationalization of the banks and the mining industry. Despite the evident sympathy of a majority for WTB, the national committee stopped short of endorsing it. Instead, it voted to call an unprecedented "special trade union congress" devoted to the problem of overcoming unemployment.[88] Leipart evidently believed such a conclave would "force change by startling the responsible authorities out of their passivity."[89] The public statement that announced the congress underscored the international nature of the crisis but, without mentioning finances, added that "in our own country large-scale public works are possible."[90] In the weeks before the congress, the union press engaged in a propaganda onslaught designed to make *Arbeitsbeschaffung* the issue of the hour.[91]

Vorwärts's response to the duel of thrust and counterthrust between economic mavericks and traditionalists suggested an official desire to bridge the gulf between the two sides.[92] On one hand, the SPD organ joined the chorus calling for jobs.[93] On the other hand, its coverage of proposals to finance public works tended to blur the line between WTB readiness and SPD disinclination to tamper with the "laws of capitalism."[94] Thus, a writer lauded a Social Democratic draft bill to create jobs through housing construction but emphasized that a tax on house rent, not government credit, should finance the initiative.[95] Clarity was not the hallmark of *Vorwärts*'s handling of the issue of creating work. Its difficulties reflected a more general ambivalence and confusion within the SPD about how to tackle the crisis. Only a narrow circle understood the differences in theory between the reformers and their opponents. Hertz and Hilferding honestly feared that inflation would negate any positive effects of state-financed job creation and for that reason did not place priority on the fight against unemployment. Wels simply followed Hilferding's judgment. Other important Social Democrats, however, did not accept Hilferding's demotion of unemployment to a secondary concern.

Paul Löbe, for one, took up the reformers' cause. Privately he "made propaganda" for WTB, and at a mass rally in Breslau he called for the adoption of a "grand plan to create jobs."[96]

There was no unified response to the plan on the party's right flank either. Wilhelm Keil argued for public works but, like the majority of the Reichstag delegation, scorned deficit spending without a fully funded government debt. In *Sozialistische Monatshefte*, Carlo Mierendorff criticized WTB as inflationary.[97] Like other writers in this Francophile journal, he emphatically seconded Naphtali's conviction that only an "active foreign policy" could stimulate the economy. Yet Mierendorff also derided Brüning's "crisis intensification" policies.[98] On the party's left, Toni Sender and Aufhäuser had long urged the SPD to adopt an active, but socialist, policy.[99] Even inside the ADGB, lack of understanding for WTB was articulated. Especially among union officials in Hamburg, where Naphtali exercised much influence, Woytinsky's *Geldpolitik* raised eyebrows.[100] The AfA-Bund, chaired by Aufhäuser, adopted a program of its own that combined elements of WTB and the Hilferding/Naphtali proposals.[101] It demanded housing construction but stressed that no matter how "urgent and important" work creation was, it would only succeed if the economy were "transformed." *Vorwärts* displayed the AfA-Bund guidelines prominently.[102]

The extraordinary congress held by the ADGB in April was, as it turned out, rather anticlimactic, in part because the ADGB was determined to present a united front with the AfA-Bund. At the congress, union leaders insisted that public works were necessary to overcome the crisis. They repeatedly criticized Brüning's regime for ignoring the plight of unemployed workers. In a barely veiled criticism of Hilferding, Tarnow charged that the "specter of inflation" was often invoked to justify passivity. He and others demanded "active intervention" to address the crisis, claiming that political radicalization must be attacked at its economic roots.[103] They reassured the SPD, however, that the ADGB neither wanted to alienate France nor supported economic autarky.[104] Moreover, speakers emphasized demands compatible with the SPD's crisis approach such as a shorter work week and, in tandem with recent party propaganda, called for "reconstructing the present system" and nationalization of mines.[105] The gathering's final resolution demanded public works but not under WTB's financial plan. Rather, it endorsed the SPD proposal for a premium loan and called for "transformation" of the economy.[106]

After the congress, the ADGB continued to push the SPD to adopt a large-scale public works program.[107] By the beginning of June, not only Tarnow but Aufhäuser was trying to persuade the Reichstag delegation of the need for an action program.[108] Increased pressure for an "active economic policy" came from voices on the party's left wing, in the Reichsbanner, and among the ranks. Some did not specify exactly what they wanted; some called for an all-out single issue effort to create work, while others demanded a broad, radical offensive for socialism.[109] Neither occurred.[110] Instead, the ADGB, in its compromise with the SPD and the AfA-Bund, took up the program of "transformation of the economy" that expounded the "buying power" theory and called for a forty-hour work week and nationalization of basic industries.[111] For its part, the SPD Reichstag delegation presented a motion for a "large-scale public works program" to be financed with a limited government loan.[112] Thus, a compromise between ADGB and SPD emerged in which neither WTB nor any specific economic program was adopted.[113]

A combination of ideological, organizational, and political factors shaped the outcome on this crucial issue. Hilferding's dismissal of WTB as "un-Marxist" was decisive.[114] In addition, party authorities were affronted by union encroachment upon the political domain. Wels pointed out to the ADGB board that the unions had never before presented a program for legislation. In the past, the party had developed the program and then cleared it with the unions. Obviously miffed, he asked if the unions now intended to reverse the arrangement.[115] This was not, however, just a battle over organizational competencies but a struggle that took on a powerful political charge because of the intensifying external pressures on the Social Democratic alliance. Initially, the desire not to come into conflict with Brüning influenced the guarded response of the SPD leadership to the ADGB project.[116] Later, new concerns came into play. WTB was not the only *Arbeitsbeschaffung* plan that appeared in early 1932, but it was the only one developed by the Left.[117] Because of its source in the ADGB, it aroused interest in right-wing circles. In particular, intellectuals around the journal *Die Tat* pricked up their ears. This circle dreamed of a front between the Free Trade Unions, the NSDAP, and the military hierarchy that in this combination would provide the popular base and elite leadership for a conservative revolution in Germany.[118]

Even more disconcerting to the SPD leadership was the blatant and public attempt by Gregor Strasser to exploit party/union differences over WTB. In a speech to the Reichstag on May 10, Strasser appealed to the "anticapitalist yearnings" of Germans. He heaped scorn on the SPD's call for a shorter work week but sympathized with the union effort to attack unemployment. Indeed, in this Reichstag speech he offered Nazi cooperation in the development of a plan to finance public works and acclaimed Woytinsky's "credit-creation" plan, reminding his audience that the NSDAP had been the first to speak out for a monetary policy that did not treat the gold standard as sacred. While the NSDAP should not "overestimate" the meaning of this development in the Social Democratic movement, neither, he warned, should the SPD underestimate it. He then presented the Nazi program to overcome the crisis, a program based on the supposition that "labor creates capital."[119] Answering for the SPD, Hilferding contrasted Strasser's "Marxist" ideas with Hitler's address to the Düsseldorf Industry Club, but he disparaged Strasser's solution to the "finance question" as the road to "pure inflation."[120] To mavericks within the ranks of Social Democracy, their own leading economist made clear once more that the SPD would brook no compromise on the issue of credit creation.

SPD distaste for the politics, as opposed to the economics, of public works intensified after Franz von Papen became chancellor in June. Stampfer reported to Leipart that the rumor was afoot that "the new regime intends to split the unions from the party. So a common front is all the more necessary."[121] In support of Stampfer, the historian Axel Schildt has suggested that the SPD's stance was perfectly reasonable since WTB would have constituted the "central block" around which a reactionary alliance between the Right and the trade unions could have been built. Schildt argues incorrectly that the nationalist group in the ADGB that sparked the rebellion against reparations was linked to the economic reformers.[122] What Schildt reads as sinister in WTB, other historians have seen as pragmatic. They have denounced, instead, SPD "dogmatism" that blinded the party to the merits of the ADGB's reform plans.[123] Schildt is correct in his assessment that the ADGB's interest in WTB reflected the organization's increasing willingness to demote political questions to economic ones. Not only Marxist ideology but also the SPD's commitment to the republic (and, hence, to Brüning) conditioned the party's hostility to a program that could be seen as a concession to the far Right. Unlike the reparations issue, however, WTB was not inherently nationalistic, unless a reformist plan to revive one nation's economy is by definition nationalistic. Economically, WTB was not "reactionary" nor even particularly autarkic (at least no more so than England's devaluation or America's New Deal). In fact, the Right was just as divided on the issue of public works as was the Left. Industrialists and bankers viewed WTB with alarm, both because of its inflationary possibilities and because it was paired with the call for the forty-hour work week.[124] The financial newspaper *Deutsche Führerbriefe*, not exactly a left-bourgeois publication, attacked Tarnow's and Woytinsky's "one-sided," "fanatic" campaign for public works and praised Naphtali and Hilferding for understanding the pitfalls of "credit expansion." Noting the "opposition" between the ADGB and the AfA-Bund crisis plans, it commended the AfA-Bund for its sensitivity to the problem of inflation.[125] Similarly, capitalists rejected Strasser's proposals as, again in the words of the *Deutsche Führerbriefe*, "autarkic" and "romantic."[126] Hilferding's charge that the NSDAP was catering to big business on this issue was simply wrong.[127]

The SPD's response to WTB and the economic reasoning that inspired it was characteristically reactive. WTB's affinity with the ideas of the SPD's archenemy was reason to shun the plan, rather than to tackle indirectly one of the sources of the NSDAP's popularity—fear of unemployment or of the unemployed. The ADGB must, however, share responsibility for the failure of Social Democracy to present a viable and politically effective crisis program. It not only accepted the compromise on public works, but its popular propaganda reflected the political shift that pushed Social Democracy to the left after Brüning's fall. Even Fritz Tarnow was affected by this new radical sensibility.[128] In June and July the two branches of the Socialist movement seemed to reconverge; yet, in fact, Leipart and Grassmann were embittered by SPD stonewalling on this vital issue. Rather than enhance the influence of the economic mavericks, their bitterness made them more open to the blandishments of those on the ADGB staff pushing for a "national" orientation.[129] This effect only manifested itself, though, after the fierce Reichstag campaign and dramatic political events of July 1932.

The Iron Front

The mood inside Social Democracy scraped bottom in the dark days of late 1931 after provincial elections produced a second Nazi wave. The party base, although intact, was demoralized and depressed. Police spies reported that only "the old stem of the party" attended meetings. Functionaries lamented the SPD's lack of resonance among the "broad masses" and its inability to break "out of its tower." Observing the "radicals" with their "soapboxes and street meetings," many Social Democrats wanted to arouse "emotion" and "feeling" to draw in the uncommitted.[1] In the Free Trade Unions, dissatisfaction was brewing over reparations and the lack of an SPD program to overcome the economic crisis. The Reichsbanner's new leader, Karl Höltermann, pressed for greater militance in street confrontations with the SA.[2] Inside the SPD executive committee, the gnawing doubts of Rudolf Breitscheid and Paul Hertz threatened to shatter its toleration consensus. Economic misery spread without relief as Germany entered another winter with millions out of work. Signs of an intense social crisis multiplied: a high suicide rate, an increasing incidence of tuberculosis, and undernourishment in children. Four hundred thousand people wandered the country in search of work, while in Berlin the long-term unemployed begged in the streets.[3] In the midst of this despair (and just before Christmas), Brüning's fourth emergency decree brought yet more cuts in wages, public employee salaries, and welfare expenditures.

In frustration, the ADGB executive board called a meeting of representatives of the SPD, the AfA-Bund, the Reichsbanner, the Free Trade Unions, and the Workers' Sports Federation to discuss Social Democracy's response to the decree. At this gathering on December 16, 1931, Theodor Leipart spoke for the ADGB; Breitscheid and Wels, for the SPD. No parliamentary plan to challenge the emergency decree emerged. Instead, Wels proclaimed the formation of an extraparliamentary "Iron Front" of these four Socialist organizations and all republicans to defend democracy against its fascist attackers and their "social reactionary" allies in the Harzburg Front.[4] With combative rhetoric, Wels aimed to infuse functionaries with hope, pep up the rank and file, bolster sagging solidarity among Social Democracy's fraternal associations, and distract attention from the fact that the SPD had accepted, albeit under protest, the fourth emergency decree.

The impetus to form some kind of "proletarian general staff" came from the Reichsbanner, Workers' Sport, and, to a lesser extent, the trade unions. Pressure also emanated from the ranks. For months, voices from below had pleaded for a nationally coordinated antifascist umbrella organization to end the dispersion of Socialist energies and wasteful duplication of propaganda, agitation, and marches.[5] The rightist gathering at Harzburg and the revelation of the Boxheim Papers made the antirepublican danger especially palpable and led to urgent calls for a "defense cartel." On December 2, a huge Reichsbanner assembly in Berlin rallied under the slogan "Take the offensive (*zupacken*)!" Reichsbanner leaders called for "republican action," a "forceful defense" of democracy, "uninhibited (*hemmungslose*) republicans at [the state's] summit," and a *Volksfront* of republican parties and organizations, "productive citizens (*schaffender Bürger*) and workers." A leader of the Berlin Reichsbanner articulated the mood of the largely Social Democratic audience: "You— the majority, unemployed, ground down and torn apart, living on meager fare—do everything for the republic that does nothing for you. . . . The state oppresses us[,] . . . treats us like the enemy, bans our parades so we can't carry the black-red-gold flag of the republic in the streets. . . . We'll fight and sacrifice for a better Germany, for the true republic, in which state power will really come from the people." Fritz Tarnow's presence on the speakers' dais signaled the ADGB's sympathy for the idea of a "common front."[6]

Pressure on the SPD leadership to adopt the Reichsbanner's proposal mounted from all sides. On December 1, Berlin functionaries first denounced toleration and then informed Breitscheid that the SPD must become "active like the Reichsbanner." On the same day, the party council heard from "representatives of its fraternal organizations" that the solid "will to struggle" in the ranks "could be more effectively set in motion in a common front of the trade unions, Reichsbanner, and sports' organizations." Over the next two weeks, local meetings took place under the name Iron Front, although Wels had not yet summoned such an entity into existence.[7]

Finally, on December 12, at the behest of the Reichsbanner's national council, leaders of Social Democratic organizations met privately and agreed to the formation of the Iron Front.[8] The project was still vague when unveiled by Wels to the public two days later, and many party leaders initially showed scant enthusiasm for it. Internal bulletins suggest that, even far into the spring, local and district functionaries remained unsure about what the concept of the Iron Front meant in practice.[9] Short on specific guidelines as they were, Wels's words were rich in meaning. Whether deliberately or not, he employed rhetoric and stressed themes that resonated deeply among Social Democrats. First, he called for heightened vigilance and disciplined militance, threatening extra-parliamentary action if violent opponents laid a hand on the republic. Second, he invoked Social Democratic unity and working-class solidarity. Third, he presented workers as the true defenders of the people's state and the upholders of bourgeois democracy against a majority of the bourgeoisie. Finally, he identified the "social rights and cultural goals of the working class" with the republic and with international peace. He called not for socialism but for a social republic, not for revolution but for defense of the majoritarian state. He fused militance and vigilance, offense and defense, and the Social Democratic association and the larger society. Wels's language and imagery set the standard for Iron Front oratory. The same themes ran like a refrain through a mass-produced pamphlet on the Iron Front with contributions by Wels, Grassmann (ADGB), Höltermann (Reichsbanner), and Fritz Wilding (Workers' Sports). Wilding explained that worker athletes wanted to step forward to defend the republic that had been good to them, ending their aloofness from politics.[10] Except for Höltermann, these men touted the working class as the heart of the Iron Front and the popular instrument of the republic's salvation.[11] In contrast with Reichsbanner leaders at the rally on December 1, no one explicitly called for a *Volksfront*.

SPD functionaries, activists, and inactive members reacted instantly and with tremendous enthusiasm to Wels's announcement, although official kickoff rallies for the Iron Front took place only five weeks later (in part because a "Christmas truce" prohibited demonstrations). *Vorwärts* broadcast that the movement would organize the popular "will to defense" of the republic.[12] Provincial dailies and the trade union press took Wels's call as the tocsin for a new, militant spirit to dominate 1932, "the year of the decision," in which elections for Germany's president and for the Prussian Landtag would occur. They proclaimed that Socialist passivity must be banished and Nazi control of the streets must be challenged.[13] The rhetoric of "force against force" suffused the public language of all sections of the Socialist movement. A Reichsbanner activist at an Iron Front rally in Berlin opined, "The Socialists deserve to end up in the madhouse if they confront the fascists with democratic means alone," while at a gathering of shop stewards in the capital, a speaker told a wildly enthusiastic crowd, "If the others threaten civil war, we can't wave the peace palm; if the others spray bullets, we can't toss candy."[14] At least initially, however, opinion makers stressed that the "offensive" meant defense of the republic, not a campaign for socialism.[15]

Friedrich Stampfer retrospectively described the Iron Front as "one of the last attempts of Social Democracy to throw itself against destiny."[16] The ranks took seriously the implication that this lunge against fate would include a resort to arms, if necessary.[17] But how did Social Democracy's leaders conceive of the Iron Front—as a movement to take back the streets, an instrument for electoral gains, or a force to be reckoned with in the event of civil war? Was it to be a militant workers' movement or a multiclass, multiparty popular front? In fact, the leadership seemed to have several, at least partially incompatible, purposes in mind. They recognized that the vacuum left by the crippling of the Reichstag had been filled by two centers of power: the nation's streets and its president.[18] In forming the Iron Front, they conceded that republicans could not leave the extraparliamentary arena to their radical opponents on left and right. Even more, though, they hoped to throw the new movement onto the electoral scales in the presidential contest in March.[19] In this sense, as the historian Rainer Schaefer has argued, the Iron Front constituted not a new strategy but a supplement to the existing one.[20] Social Democrats high in the party, in the trade unions, and in the Reichsbanner hoped to align two parties against each other—Harzburgers on one side and republicans on the other. Their invocations of the working class notwithstanding, leading Socialists were disappointed when the Iron Front emerged as a de facto Red front. While no one was terribly surprised when the Center Party formed its own *Volksfront*, Social Democrats had entertained hopes that the Christian and the Hirsch-Duncker (liberal) unions, as well as the DBB, would join them. In the end only scattered State Party chapters and sundry intellectuals aligned themselves with the new movement. When it became clear that a popular front would not cohere of itself, the idea was not pursued. The Iron Front's participants and many of its organizers clearly preferred a Red defense movement.[21]

Last but not least, Wels hoped to direct the limelight away from the toleration policy. The SPD elite wanted to continue to support Brüning but to project a new aggressive image at the same time. The Iron Front did divert attention from toleration. It also generated energy and enthusiasm in the bitterly fought election campaigns of the spring and summer. But if Wels hoped to forge harmony and unity of purpose within the SPD and the broader Socialist movement, he must have been sorely disappointed. During 1931, debate over toleration, spearheaded by the SPD's left wing, had racked the SPD. In the first half of 1932, rightist and neorevisionist Social Democrats took the lead in challenging the party leadership's centrist policies. The battle over WTB divided the SPD and the ADGB. Meanwhile, in the SPD and the Reichsbanner, younger activists focused attention on the tactics and techniques of the extraparliamentary struggle. These reformers, almost all neorevisionists, initially implemented their ideas in Hamburg and Hesse, where they had support in the party ranks and apparatus. Soon they found allies on the left in Berlin and throughout Saxony. Together, leftists and neorevisionists pressed the SPD leadership to introduce new styles of agitation and propaganda that aimed to stimulate Social Democratic crowds and the broader public with visual and acoustic imagery, rhythmic chants and marching boots, and catchy symbols and simple slogans. These were to replace the symbolically rich, but essentially discursive, language with which Social Democrats traditionally communicated their ideals to the public.[22] The reformers drew on Nazi and Communist mass-propaganda techniques that, in fact, had roots in the Socialist culture of the nineteenth century: the colors of the association, massive open-air processions, and slogans shouted in unison. The complex and, indeed, contradictory associations prompted by the "new-style" propaganda explain both the initial cool response of SPD leaders and the enthusiastic reception by the party masses. In the end, an external event cut through the ferment and renewed sense of possibility that invigorated Social Democracy in early 1932. In July, immediately before elections for the Reichstag, the Reich government forced the SPD to choose between relinquishing or fighting for the Prussian bulwark. The decision to give up power without a struggle dealt a terrible blow to the great hopes aroused by the Iron Front.

The Impact of the Iron Front

Officially launched in late January, the Iron Front touched a chord among Social Democratic workers, tens of thousands of whom signed up in the "Iron Book" to show their allegiance. SPD supporters who had drifted from active participation began to attend meetings again.[23] Everyone, from the rarely harmonious Stampfer and Leber to political enemies, testified to the front's "enlivening and heartening effect."[24] National Socialists found that suddenly "SPD speakers want to speak at every [Nazi] meeting."[25] Provincial ADGB officials described with wonder the drawing power of the new movement. Excitement gripped SPD districts of all political orientations. Neorevisionist Hamburg, centrist Hanover, and leftist Berlin numbered among its especially active centers.[26] In Berlin, the Iron Front, not the SPD, countered the "Nazi advance in the factories"; fifteen to twenty meetings were held in factories in

February. For the first time, party chapters drew on the human resources of Social Democratic cultural associations in their electoral efforts.[27]

Just as the language of the Iron Front combined class-based appeals with militant republicanism, so its style was at once paramilitary and popular Socialist. It immediately adopted the military accoutrements and pageantry of the street politics exemplified by the SA. Fife and drum corps, scores of huge banners, and Reichsbanner guards in formation accompanied all Iron Front marches. At the same time, rallies swelled with song and laughed at political skits.[28] Graphics and rhymed jingles even adorned the front page of the normally staid *Vorwärts*.[29]

Initially, the Reichsbanner had the leading role in a central defense committee to coordinate local and regional action committees of the Iron Front. These, in turn, formed the foundation of the *Kampfleitung* (combat command) established, at least on paper, in most districts in January and February. The *Reichskampfleitung* encompassed three subcommittees: finance (ADGB and SPD executive boards), technical (Reichsbanner and workers' athletes), and propaganda (SPD, Reichsbanner, and ADGB).[30] In the eyes of participants and opponents the Iron Front's general was Karl Höltermann, head of the Reichsbanner. Partly due to the Reichsbanner's reluctance to make political decisions regarding the movement and partly because the front remained purely Socialist, however, the SPD took over the directing role. Trade union and party officials constituted a majority on local committees. The *Reichskampfleitung* sat at Lindenstrasse 3, SPD headquarters, under Supreme Commander Otto Wels. It comes as no surprise that, without its own executive committee or funds, the combat command did not emerge as an independent, overarching power within Social Democracy.[31]

Wilhelm Hoegner later condemned the Iron Front as "another half-measure" on the SPD's part. In its ranks young people "drilled and marched, in uniform and with a flourish of trumpets," but their leaders did not attempt to forge their fighting spirit into a "useful" force. Two approaches would have been possible. Police officers could have trained these youth as a police reserve; alternatively, the SPD could have trained the Iron Front's troops secretly, following the SA model. The SPD leadership did not act on these possibilities because it saw the Iron Front as a political, not a military, weapon against the republic's enemies. As Stampfer later explained, "those in the know" recognized that the Iron Front would not tip the military balance in the event of civil war and that the attitude of the regular armed forces remained decisive.[32] The contrast between fighting words and peaceful deeds is not proof of intent to deceive by party leaders. They scorned the military potential of the actual

Iron Front yet idealized an abstract will to resist. Social Democratic leaders seemed to believe that if the Nazis toppled the government with unconstitutional means, the working class would put up a fight. When rumors of a Reich coup against Prussia grew persistent in June, Otto Wels told a party official, "Save me a place at a machine gun. When things explode (*wenn es los geht*), I'll be there."[33]

Despite ultimate party control, the movement had an élan closer to the Reichsbanner's fighting republicanism than to the anxious legalism of the party leadership. Nonetheless, most Reichsbanner leaders shared the SPD elite's conviction that neither the Reichsbanner nor the Iron Front could save the republic in a civil war against the state's armed forces. In the spring of 1932, the Reichsbanner national board informed district leaders that "we will never use force to carry out our goals against the Right or the constitution."[34] Unlike the Socialist *Schutzbund* in Austria, the Reichsbanner had no central committee to coordinate "defense measures." Its Reich command successfully discouraged widespread self-arming by members. Still, the Reichsbanner took seriously the notion that republican paramilitary troops could assist in a civil war. In the fall of 1930, the Reichsbanner, under Höltermann's urging, had formed the *Schufo*, defense formations that received some training from the police and drilled members in military exercises and shooting practice. After the formation of the Iron Front, Höltermann assured Reich Minister of the Interior Groener that the Reichsbanner would not engage in military preparations with the help of police groups.[35] Nonetheless, the *Schufo* conducted a course on the use of machine guns in February 1932. Moreover, individual chapters acted with gusto on the commitment to defend the republic. They not only held their own in violent melees with Nazi Stormtroopers but stockpiled caches of small weapons.[36]

The Reichsbanner's commitment to defense and its practical preparations for civil war contrasted with the antimilitarist inclinations of many party and trade union officials. The trade unions' *Hammerschaften*, organized as plant-based paramilitary groups, were, in fact, an agitational ploy to win new members and to act as a counterweight to Nazi factory cells.[37] The lack of real coordination between *Schufo* and *Hammerschaften* as well as the antidefense attitude of trade union officials frustrated Reichsbanner leaders.[38] Meanwhile, the Reichsbanner's dedication to "nonpartisan" activity occasioned conflict with party officials. Party organizers and members complained that Reichsbanner men refused to go all out for the SPD's election effort. In rebuttal, Reichsbanner activists demanded that SPD leaders hand out leaflets and wear uniforms, as did their Nazi counterparts.[39] The Iron Front also became an object of contention in the tussle between the SPD and the ADGB over *Arbeitsbeschaffung*. Impressed by the front's popularity, the ADGB board hoped to turn its soldiers into propagandists for a public works program after it fulfilled its electoral tasks. This idea ran aground on SPD opposition to an all-out effort for public works. Consequently, union leaders complained, "The trade unions only pay [for the Iron Front], while the party and Reichsbanner reap the profit."[40] The associations within the Iron Front also jealously guarded their special areas of competence. Workers' Sports protested the Iron Front's plan to hold a sports festival, which was, after all, the task of Workers' Sports, not of an organization created "to defend the working class against fascism."[41] Clearly, the Iron Front did not banish organizational rivalries or political differences among its constituent parts. The "Iron Front combat machine," according to Karl Höltermann, functioned separately as Reichsbanner, trade unions, and SPD. Its vaunted unity boiled down to "common propaganda" and a "center for exchanging views."[42]

Despite internal friction, Höltermann and other Reichsbanner leaders concurred with the SPD and trade union elites that the Iron Front was first and foremost a propaganda weapon in the battle for German streets and hearts. Indeed, their major disagreement with the party elite concerned the tactical problem of how to forge the Iron Front into a strong political instrument. Höltermann, fellow young neorevisionists, and provincial activists wanted to build the Iron Front into a psychologically modern extraparliamentary movement.[43] Kurt Schumacher, Haubach, Mierendorff, and Leber, all longtime Reichsbanner activists, threw themselves into organizing the Iron Front. They counted among the most popular orators at its rallies, traveling tirelessly around the country to lend their talents where needed.[44] Having chided republicans and Social Democrats for failing to appreciate the political significance of symbols in the fight to secure the republic, they were now eager to show that a transformed propaganda style could increase the self-confidence of the republican movement, greatly enhance its popular resonance, and so create a genuine extraparliamentary power at the service of the republic.[45]

Carlo Mierendorff, in particular, dedicated himself to building the Iron Front into a model "active" movement that could transform the SPD in its tow. By the fall of 1931, he had become a decided critic of toleration. Unlike party leftists, however, he rarely directed his fire at the SPD's parliamentary policy but instead at its extraparliamentary tactics. In early 1932, in *Marxistische Tribüne* he published a plea for the old Left to join other party radicals in a "new Left" and to work for an "anticonservative" SPD. The SPD, he agreed with the old Left, had become "reformist" and "trade unionized," overly bureaucratic and "economistic." The old Left lacked "positive" proposals, but he approved of its "attitude": militant, confrontational, risk taking, and concerned with extraparliamentary as well as parliamentary power. The "right wing," he maintained, was too preoccupied with the trappings of state power. It clung stubbornly to government administrative positions, even though backed by ever shrinking electoral strength. Mierendorff called explicitly for a "new revisionism." Classic revisionism had attacked Marxist orthodoxy; the new variety would attack reformism while eschewing an "orthodox renaissance." It would transform the SPD into an "active, radical" organization.[46]

Mierendorff deplored the transformation of the SPD into a "proletarian Economic Party" (that is, a counterpart to the *Mittelstand* interest party of that name).[47] Nevertheless, he urged the party to undertake an all-out campaign to create jobs through government action.[48] Though trade union bureaucrats were at this time trying to win the SPD to such a campaign, Mierendorff rejected their plan, bluntly telling them to stay out of political decision making.[49] Apart from his desire to confront unemployment and a long-term interest in improved Franco-German relations, Mierendorff's politics were not programmatic; yet neither was he simply concerned with technique. In his view, a focus on "street power" constituted a political orientation.[50] The KPD, ever more a party of the unemployed, had made a virtue of necessity and substituted neighborhood politics for factory organization.[51] Mierendorff wanted the SPD to do the same.

To that end, he allied himself with Sergei Chakhotin, a revolutionary socialist who shared his desire to make the Iron Front a militant movement with ever widening mass appeal. Like Woytinsky, Chakhotin was a Russian émigré with creative ideas, supported by Social Democratic reformers and resisted by party ideologues. Chakhotin, however, was a radical Marxist, although anti-Bolshevik. During the Soviet Union's early years he had directed revolutionary propaganda in southern Russia. Once an assistant to Ivan Pavlov, he now did research at the Institute for Physics in Heidelberg.[52] Inside the SPD, he argued for a system of propaganda that he claimed was based on Pavlov's theory of conditioned reflex; Pavlov's assumptions, he maintained, already guided Communist and Nazi agitation. First, propaganda must emphasize and demonstrate the power and strength of a movement. He ridiculed the psychological obtuseness of Socialist posters with "figures of misery, groaning and lamenting, and talking with anguish of the approach of the Third Reich."[53] Second, a few symbols must be exhaustively portrayed; speakers and posters should use short words that made a strong impression. The message should be simple and uniform; the media, elaborate and varied—posters, banners, graffiti, cabaret, and "stimulating dialogues" between speaker and crowd.[54] Third, feelings played an important role in the political decisions of the masses. The SPD focused exclusively on logic and reason and, to its hazard, underestimated mood and emotional impulses.[55]

Chakhotin, replete with the imposing credentials of a Russian revolutionary, provided a "scientific" theory in support of the hundreds of criticisms found in letters to *Das Freie Wort* and in party journals. He was, moreover, an imaginative man who developed symbols to accompany new-style Iron Front rallies. Walking about Heidelberg, surrounded by walls defaced with swastikas, he saw one that had been struck through with a chalk stroke and got the idea of turning the stroke into a downward-slanting arrow. He rounded up a group of young Reichsbanner members who then tramped through the city crossing out the hated "hooked crosses." One man recalled, "The effect was amazing. The Nazis were shocked, all Heidelberg abuzz with the news."[56] Next Chakhotin made the one arrow three. These *Drei Pfeile* stood for "unity, activity, discipline" as well as for party, trade unions, and Reichsbanner, the pillars of the Iron Front.[57] Thus was born an image with symbolic resonance for Social Democrats. Its political-cultural associations were old, but its purely visual appeal was new in Socialist propaganda. Its iconographic form gave it popular appeal, while its simplicity evoked the abstract modernism of Kandinsky and the constructivism of El Lissitsky.[58]

Chakhotin sent party headquarters his symbol system and a plan for propaganda during the presidential campaign in February 1932. Informed that the plan would be used "if needed," he heard nothing more. Then in mid-March Mierendorff invited him to Berlin to present his ideas to Reichsbanner district leaders. He received a mixed response. Nevertheless, Mierendorff managed to get the Russian appointed director of Reichsbanner propaganda.[59] Soon afterward provincial Reichsbanner offices directed their members to use the three arrows.[60] Chakhotin, Mierendorff, and their cohorts hoped to make a flank attack on party leaders via the Reichsbanner and so win their favor for the new methods and symbols (including a salutation, "Freedom," shouted with raised fist). The reformers also tried to convince lower-level functionaries to carry out a "palace revolution" in favor of the new propaganda. The effort was frustrating. With a few exceptions, even sympathetic officials felt that they should wait for central instructions to carry out innovations of such magnitude.[61] Though the production and orchestration of Socialist propaganda was less centralized than that of the NSDAP, it also benefited less from local creativity.[62]

Leading Social Democrats found Chakhotin's symbols and psychological theories baffling. According to Chakhotin, Wels wondered if the graffiti campaign was legal and worried about the public reaction, fearing "we
shall make ourselves ridiculous with all this nonsense."[63] The *Reichskampfleitung* rejected the *Drei Pfeile* on the grounds that the Socialist movement
had too many insignia as it was.[64] Others objected that the methods had
nothing to do with facts and policies and were superficial.[65] They had
derided the Nazis for years for just these reasons. Bureaucrats in the
recruitment and propaganda departments simply refused to believe their
own methods were inadequate or old fashioned. Chakhotin and Mierendorff closeted themselves with Vogel, Breitscheid, Hilferding, Hertz,
Heilmann, Löbe, and Stampfer. In individual interviews, they won admis-
sions that the Socialist popular style suffered from stodginess. Party pride,
however, restrained the same men from speaking out in committee. Party
authorities refused Chakhotin's request to organize a conference on his
methods prior to the Prussian election.[66]

Party leaders saw the Iron Front mainly as an electoral instrument. As
they had hoped, it played a central role in the presidential campaign in
February and March. On February 5 the party council pondered the
SPD's stance in the campaign. Gagging at the thought of working for the
reelection of the aristocratic hero of the Battle of Tannenberg, a few
members wanted to put up Otto Braun in the first round and support
Hindenburg in the second. In a tortured discussion, many stressed that
the SPD dare not split the republican vote, and in the end, all except
Mathilde Wurm (a moderate leftist) endorsed the man whom the SPD had
bitterly opposed in 1925.[67] Far from encouraging sentiment in favor of
his own candidacy, Braun was Hindenburg's strongest advocate in the
SPD.[68] As were Severing and SPD leaders, he was ever more convinced
that in Brüning lay the SPD's only hope of securing the republic, so he
wanted the authority behind Brüning to remain in office.[69] Among Hindenburg's conservative backers, however, distaste for Social Democrats
and other democratic circles ran so deep that the "Weimar parties" were
forced to stage separate rallies for the president. Hindenburg, rather than
being pleased, was humiliated by the massive Social Democratic contribution to his reelection.[70] Social Democrats had to overlook such snubs and
ingratitude because their Prussian strategy rested on the president. The
effort in favor of the old general became more palatable on February 22,
when Goebbels announced Hitler's candidacy. Under the banner of the
Iron Front, Social Democrats vigorously threw themselves into the campaign under the slogan "Smash Hitler, vote Hindenburg!", making clear
the real goal.[71] In response to Communist taunts, however, Social Demo-

crats insisted that Hindenburg had not turned out "as we feared" in 1925.[72]

The KPD ran Ernst Thälmann. The Right divided its vote also. The Stahlhelm and the DNVP backed Theodor Duesterberg, second in command of the Stahlhelm. Duesterberg received a disappointing 6.8 percent in the first round and dropped out. Thälmann's percentages, 13.2 percent and 10.2 percent, respectively, were also lower than expected. Among Hindenburg's rivals only Hitler made an impressive showing. Hindenburg garnered 49.5 percent to Hitler's 30.1 percent in the first balloting on March 13, just shy of the required absolute majority. He won with 53 percent against 36.8 percent for Hitler in the runoff on April 10. Social Democrats heard the results with pride and pleasure.[73] Their contribution to Hindenburg's count was huge. One bourgeois source estimated that the SPD contributed 8.5 million votes to the tally.[74] In fact, these voters had rallied under the banner of the Iron Front. An Iron Front memorandum reported with satisfaction that the new movement had passed its "test through fire," reminding organizers that "we can't overtake years of Nazi demagogy in two weeks." For the first round, the front had concentrated on the mobilization of urban voters; for the second, it had turned its attention to small villages where, especially in the northeast, the Nazis completely dominated the campaign despite Social Democratic efforts.[75] Socialists believed the NSDAP had suffered a significant defeat because its supporters had believed so thoroughly in victory. Mierendorff even judged Hindenburg's election an achievement for the republic because the general "symbolize[d] legality" against Nazi adventurism. Hilferding wrote to Kautsky that the election outcome "would be decisive if the economy weren't so rotten."[76]

The Prussian Landtag campaign, so crucial for the SPD, came on the heels of the Hindenburg victory and was entered with high hopes. The Iron Front's visibility remained high, but the Prussian SPD rejected Chakhotin's elaborate plan of action for the campaign.[77] Huge rallies notwithstanding, the new style did not set the tone. Otto Braun, the star of the Social Democratic effort, spoke at practically every major gathering. He found the regimen "agonizing" because "I was supposed to fill the humanity assembled in those mighty rallies with a faith in victory that I didn't possess myself." His "rational, moderate, and factual" words, dryly listing the accomplishments of the new Prussia, fell "like a cold shower" on crowds aroused by the opening music and parade of flags.[78] His mood could not but color the SPD campaign.

Stampfer recalled later how the dismal results of the Prussian balloting on April 24 destroyed the "high spirits" generated by the presidential election. The NSDAP skyrocketed from 8 to 162 seats in the Landtag, holding the 37 percent of the electorate it had cornered in the presidential runoff. The SPD lost almost 800,000 of the votes it had received in 1928, and shrank to 94 from 137 seats. It received only 21.2 percent of the vote. State elections on the same day in Bavaria, Württemberg, and Anhalt produced similar results. The NSDAP stole the SPD's place as the second largest party in Bavaria (after the BVP) and emerged as the largest in the other two states.[79] Some SPD analysts, including Hilferding, denied the magnitude of the party's defeat or the NSDAP's victory in Prussia.[80] In fact, such denials increasingly characterized SPD analysis. In the face of extravagant Nazi boasts that the NSDAP would capture a majority, Socialists could profess satisfaction at having prevented this. Besides, they had adjusted psychologically to massive Nazi returns. They insisted that the NSDAP, now *the* "bourgeois" party, had not made significant inroads into the SPD vote. The SPD organization, they claimed, stood intact.[81] The SPD's returns in Prussia, it is true, were characterized by great variations. Losses were considerable in the Rhineland and the industrial west, where they benefited the Center Party and the KPD; but analysts could point to "splendid" results in Berlin (almost 60,000 gained) and even in rural East Prussia, Pomerania, and Brandenburg, where agitation was aimed at agricultural laborers.[82] Despite these few bright spots, other analysts noted with dismay the NSDAP's conquest of rural Germany. Fritz Baade described the "catastrophic way" in which Protestant farmers in particular had succumbed to Nazi demagogy.[83] Viewed from any angle, the Prussian Weimar Coalition had been trounced, and anyone could see that the poor performance of its biggest partner had decided the rout relatively and absolutely. The liberal press surmised, moreover, that SPD gains among anti-Nazi bourgeois voters hid disproportionate losses among workers, while Communists judged that the NSDAP had made important new inroads into the ranks of working-class voters.[84]

No one tried to dress up the sorry outcomes in other states, especially Bavaria and Württemberg. The one bright spot was Hamburg. Although the NSDAP emerged as the largest party with 51 seats in the Bürgerschaft, the SPD gained 11,689 (for a total of 226,242) votes and three mandates (for 49 seats) from the election held seven months earlier, while the KPD lost almost 50,000 votes.[85] The SPD's success was modest but palpable. In Hamburg the new propaganda techniques, including the *Drei Pfeile*, had been systematically deployed.[86] Karl Meitmann, chairman of the Hamburg SPD and a leader of the Reichsbanner in Schleswig-Holstein, was responsible for Hamburg's embrace of the new methods. An Iron Front chapter had been formed there by late December 1931 and first rallied on January 14. As early as February, Chakhotin spoke to 2,000 party officials there who were eager to implement his ideas.[87] In contrast, the Iron Front in Munich staged no big rallies until late February. In early April, after the campaign for the Bavarian Landtag had already begun, the front remained in an embryonic stage, even though the SPD devoted energy to it at the expense of separate party activities.[88]

Reformers paraded the relatively better returns in districts that had adopted the new methods as proof of the significance of "technique" and "mass psychology." Chakhotin urged the SPD to accept that, in the short run, economics did not determine political life, a fact that explained Hitler's ability to win with crazy, contradictory economic promises. Not what the führer said, but how he said it, enticed millions to believe in him. His success demonstrated the importance of "Psychotechnik."[89] The neo-revisionist Theo Haubach also faced the SPD defeat head on. Hamburg and Berlin did well, he asserted, because of early and intense activity by the Iron Front. Haubach did not focus merely on technique. He faulted the Prussian campaign for neither assailing capitalism nor sprucing up the SPD's roster of candidates with Social Democrats who were young "not only in age but in outlook and daring."[90] Functionaries chimed in that the SPD must further enhance its extraparliamentary activity and "sharpen the élan of the party."[91]

The reformers decided to test their claims in the arena that mattered most to the party elite. Hesse faced a diet election on June 19. Given Mierendorff's prestige in his home state's SPD, he and Chakhotin easily prevailed on its functionaries to let them run the campaign. Their plan of action divided the campaign into four weeks of a steadily increasing tempo.[92] Assiduous use of the three arrows unleashed a veritable "symbol war" with the Nazis. Hessians bought 50,000 *Drei Pfeile* buttons.[93] Socialists saluted all citizens with "Freiheit" and a clenched fist; from homes and headquarters fluttered Iron Front flags (red with three arrows). Rallies aimed foursquare at participants' emotions. Young speakers replaced older comrades or spoke alongside them.[94] While not earth shattering, the results thrilled Hessian Socialists as well as upset Communists who found it incredible that "SPD proletarians [in Hesse] were downright enthusiastic about the Iron Front" despite the intolerable economic situation.[95] Voter participation fell from 82 to 74 percent (a drop of about 40,000 votes), but the SPD picked up more than 4,000 ballots from the previous November, garnering 172,552 votes (from 21.4 percent to 23.1) and 17 seats (up from 15). The SPD did especially well in Darmstadt. The NSDAP, in contrast, declined slightly in Darmstadt but scooped up 44 percent of the vote statewide, compared with 37.1 percent seven months earlier. The KPD lost roughly 25,000 votes. Mierendorff attributed the successes of the SPD to "intensive systematic work with the new propaganda methods."[96] He did not mention that the SPD campaign in Hesse also had a radical ideological tenor and appealed to "proletarian solidarity."[97] Although Chakhotin liked to scoff at the significance of propaganda's content as opposed to its form, the class language and militant tone of the Hessian campaign no doubt influenced the SPD's showing.

The tendency in Social Democracy toward militant, class-oriented language, noted in 1931, gained momentum in 1932, not just in Hesse, but all over. The Iron Front bolstered the SPD's proletarian image by appealing unabashedly to class solidarity, although in the republic's interest.[98] Giant posters of August Bebel at rallies recalled the proud, isolated, and feared Social Democracy of Imperial times. The Hamburg organization focused on working-class votes in its Bürgerschaft campaign in April.[99] In Prussia, a leaflet asked voters whether they wanted democracy or not—or, as it alternatively framed the question, a "Junker Prussia or Workers' Prussia?" An election pamphlet about Otto Braun began with a biographical section titled "The Proletarian."[100] The class-oriented language of the Iron Front's most dedicated promoters indicated the general tone of its propaganda. Chakhotin assumed that "class-conscious workers" were the audience of his new-style propaganda.[101] At a Hanover rally, Haubach warned, "We notice everyone—whether businessman or civil servant— who sneers at the working class and the republic."[102] The irony is, of course, that many of these promoters had long argued for broadening the social appeal of the SPD. Mierendorff's call for a "militant democracy" had been in part inspired by his desire to attract new circles, including the social revolutionary elements around Otto Strasser in the NSDAP.[103] When their version of militant republicanism finally gained support, however, it was inextricably linked with a forthright trumpeting of proletarian solidarity rather than a de-emphasis on class. This language was a concession to activists and leftists who wanted the SPD "to see itself as a workers' party."[104] Rather than swim against the current of Social Democratic political culture, the neorevisionists manipulated both its exclusive and its inclusive elements to whip up enthusiasm for the Iron Front. The popularity of the front testifies to their success and to the central place in the Social Democratic self-perception of class identification, on one hand, and republicanism, on the other.[105]

Pointing to the Harzburg Front, Social Democratic propaganda also insisted ever more vehemently that the NSDAP was the creature of the capitalist class. Hilferding told Berlin party workers that "we will only overcome fascism if we realize that the struggle against it is at the same time the struggle against capitalism, whose gold controls the National Socialists."[106] Hitler's January speech to the Düsseldorf Industry Club, *Vorwärts* trumpeted, provided "final clarity" about this "antisocialist."[107] Alongside such tirades, however, Social Democrats betrayed uncertainty about the politics of the German bourgeoisie. From mid-1931 even moderate businessmen in the RDI had become increasingly disillusioned with Brüning;[108] yet the SPD leadership recognized that political divisions still existed among industrialists.[109] The snobbery of Hindenburg's reactionary backers notwithstanding, the heterogeneous support for his reelection raised Social Democratic hopes that an alliance of republican parties and associations, including conservative groups, could be forged behind the president and, by extension, Brüning.[110] Editorials in the SPD press alluded to the "powers behind constitutional capitalism" that had so far resisted the fascists' plans. In the Reichstag, Erich Rossmann frankly stated that his party stood "lined up" with "moderate" bourgeois forces against both the proletarian KPD and the reactionary bourgeois camp.[111] Such comments, and the original, equivocal intention to build the Iron Front into an all-republican organization, suggest that SPD leaders entertained notions of a popular front policy. This idea remained just that, however. They lacked the conviction to persuade either their ranks or the middle-class public of its efficacy.

The SA Ban and Brüning's Fall

Despite Hindenburg's disgust over the SPD's support, Social Democrats had some reason to feel that their contribution to his reelection enhanced their influence on national policymaking, for on April 13, the Reich finally banned the SA and the SS. The SPD ministers in Prussia wrung this important concession from the Reich government with the cooperation of the interior ministers of other large states. The crackdown on Hitler's shock troops contradicted even the most recent Reich policy toward the NSDAP. On January 29, Defense Minister Groener had issued a decree that in effect allowed Nazis to enter the Reichswehr. Privately Groener entertained no illusions about the NSDAP's goals. Especially after Hitler refused to support Hindenburg's reelection, he wanted to distance the Reich government from the Nazis.[112] He believed, however, that Hitler would rely on legal methods to come to power and, thus, long resisted pressure from Prussia, Bavaria, Württemberg, Baden, and Hesse to outlaw the SA.[113] His January decree reflected notions current in the army that the NSDAP's nationalistic fighting spirit could be harnessed to the advantage of Germany's armed forces.[114] Even at the time, however, it was known that not Groener but General Schleicher was the main proponent of a "tame the SA" policy.[115] Indeed, soon after the decree, Groener displayed a new willingness to listen to the states' arguments for suppressing the SA.[116]

Meanwhile, Otto Braun still could not convince Brüning of the subversive nature and plans of the NSDAP. The chancellor did not even deign to acknowledge a fat memorandum documenting Nazi illegal activities that Braun sent him in March.[117] Unbeknownst to the SPD, Brüning too was pursuing the chimera of a domesticated NSDAP—one that would support a government of the traditional Right in a renascent monarchy.[118] Reluctantly, Severing made the move that finally goaded the Reich government into action. On March 17 the Prussian police raided Nazi offices and confiscated yet more incriminating material. When the Reich Interior Ministry distanced itself from this aggressive step, the interior ministers of Bavaria, Württemberg, Baden, and Hesse rose to Severing's defense by publishing some of the captured material and by putting pressure on Groener. On April 5, at a meeting with Groener, they seconded Severing's threat to act independently against the NSDAP.[119] Afterward they issued a "passionate" call for a ban of the SA and the SS. On April 11, at the SPD's opening rally for the Prussian campaign, Braun revealed sensational evidence corroborating Hitler's boast that his "fighters" would not defend republican Germany's eastern borders against attack. Reichswehr generals had previously disregarded this information, yet now even Schleicher was impressed by the fury with which the bourgeois press took up Braun's revelations.[120] Pushed into a corner, Groener feared that if he did not outlaw the SA, the Reich would lose "respect at home and abroad" and would be perceived as "weak" by "parties from the German Nationalists to the Social Democrats." In particular, he did not want to alienate the powerful states of Prussia and Bavaria. He felt, moreover, that the SPD's intense desire for a ban should not be rebuffed if only because the party "had so overburdened its left wing by [endorsing] Hindenburg's election." He pressed Brüning, immobilized by indecision, for a ban.[121] On April 12, at a meeting with Brüning and Groener, Braun and Severing threatened to act without the Reich. Their stubborn stance produced results if only because they had the backing of the conservative regimes in Bavaria and Württemberg. Brüning finally committed himself.[122]

No sooner was the ban announced than Hindenburg's camarilla persuaded him of the inequity of a decree that did not also outlaw the Reichsbanner. The Old Gentleman perused reports (planted for his eyes in rightist papers) on "dangerous" activities by the republican defense league. He wrote Groener an indignant letter that the press printed even before the minister received it.[123] Despite this flagrant attempt to force his hand, Groener stood firm because he feared pushing the SPD into opposition.[124] He denied that the evidence on the Reichsbanner proved subversion, although he did instruct a compliant Höltermann to dismantle the *Schufo* and to call off the "alarm alert" that the league had stood under during the presidential campaign.[125] Groener's obstinacy infuriated Hindenburg and his advisors but won him the respect and gratitude of the republican Left.[126] His admirers, however, could not secure his tenure in office. General Schleicher intrigued against Groener inside the Defense Ministry and with the president. On May 10, unable to parry effectively an attack on the SA ban by Hermann Göring, Groener suffered humiliation in the Reichstag. Three days later he tendered his resignation as defense minister. Although he stayed as interior minister, and the SA decree remained in effect, many Social Democrats realized that not only Groener's but Brüning's days were numbered.[127]

Hindenburg met with Brüning on May 29 and demanded a purely conservative government. The next day the chancellor and his entire cabinet resigned. Schleicher's machinations were decisive in bringing down Brüning. In addition, however, Hindenburg's Junker cronies urged him to cut loose from the chancellor. They were impressed by neither Brüning's rightist inclinations nor his closeted efforts to build a coalition extending to the Nazis.[128] They saw only his "eastern settlement plan" (that would allow farmers to settle on bankrupt estates) and his reliance on SPD support. Big business complaints about the connection with the SPD had also grown ever more clamorous.[129] On June 2 the reactionary Center Party politician Franz von Papen formed a new cabinet and immediately dissolved the Reichstag, setting new elections for July 31. The SPD vehemently opposed the new government. The NSDAP, on the other hand, initially tolerated it in return for the elections and a promise to lift the SA ban, a pledge fulfilled on June 14.[130]

Few Social Democrats wrote postmortems on the toleration policy. Oddly, its few public vindications came from party leaders who had privately expressed misgivings. Breitscheid told the Reichstag delegation, "History will confirm our policy as correct. It left no stone unturned in order to thwart a fascist regime."[131] Paul Hertz maintained that toleration had safeguarded democracy and the republic's social gains, as well as allowed the SPD to expose the capitalist character of the NSDAP and to mobilize the Iron Front.[132] The party leadership refrained from attacking the man responsible for ending this happy state of affairs, however. Breitscheid blamed not Hindenburg but his "irresponsible advisors" for the "disgusting behind-the-scenes game."[133] Other commentators doubted the positive effects of toleration or Brüning's chancellorship. Arkadij Gurland, editor of *Marxistische Tribüne*, contended that toleration had neither secured democracy, now partially dismantled, nor disposed of the Nazi threat, since the "taming" of the NSDAP had resulted in a "consolidated reactionary front." Mierendorff held Brüning responsible for 6 million unemployed, shaky foreign relations, and a Nazi party for which almost 40 percent of the population voted. A chancellor so disdainful of parliament could not complain now that the reckless forces on which he relied had discarded him.[134]

The July Reichstag Campaign

Whether distressed or relieved by Brüning's fall, Social Democrats adapted rapidly to the freedom of opposition and geared up for the Reichstag election with enthusiasm. Party authorities and union officials suddenly developed an interest in the new-style propaganda. ADGB national committee members waxed eloquent on the desirability of "uniform slogans" and "common insignia and symbols," hoping that the Iron Front would "finally shed its reserve" and adopt the new trappings. Berlin's *Kampfleitung* turned to the *Reichskampfleitung* with just this request.[135] The party council summoned Mierendorff and Chakhotin from the midst of their intense activity in Hesse to hear their ideas. On June 14, the day before the Reichstag campaign opened, the executive committee endorsed the use of the *Drei Pfeile*. The SPD was to fight the campaign under the auspices of the Iron Front. In communications to district organizations, the executive insisted that "all comrades must be involved in the symbol war." Functionaries received a campaign battle plan that bore Chakhotin's imprint. The major appeal was a powerful negative— "Iron Front against Hitler Barons." Each week propaganda was also broadcast in a secondary slogan, alternately negatively and positively framed. Thus, in the first week leaflets asked Germans if they wanted "freedom or barons? (*Freiheit oder Freiherrn?*)," while during the third week propaganda focused on capitalism's failure and Nazi compromise with a bankrupt system.[136] One pamphlet offered a dialogue between a Social Democrat and a Communist that captured well the tenor and message of the campaign. In proletarian lingo, the Social Democrat countered the Communist's arguments, concluding, "July 31 must become a day of honor for the republic. The fronts are completely clear: class against class!"[137]

Individual districts enthusiastically took up the refurbished Iron Front, urged comrades to campaign with passion, and fought an electoral campaign of "unprecedented rigor and acrimony."[138] Cologne party functionaries learned that the Iron Front's "combat command" would plot the campaign; they were to follow its direction unquestioningly. The Hanover Reichsbanner leadership exhorted its members to "touch emotion, soul, and heart so reason can conquer."[139] SPD functionaries reminded their comrades that the "contemporary spirit thinks in abstract symbols."[140] Leftist Leipzig, quiescent since the SAPD split, embraced the "new struggle methods" and experienced a surge of activity.[141] Berlin "transformed" its propaganda by emphasizing "feeling instead of insight." In addition to several huge rallies the Berlin party staged 250 smaller gatherings, many of them at factory gates. Airplanes dropped 300,000 Iron Front leaflets on the capital. Other regions, small and large, were no less fired up.[142] In particular, young Social Democrats flocked to the more militant and new-style organization. They were lured not only by youthful speakers at rallies but by the Red Pioneers, special youth formations that learned fighting techniques, carried out rural agitation, and attended opponents' meetings.[143]

The ideas of Mierendorff and Chakhotin filled, in particular, a pamphlet that provided sample scripts for "agitational speaking choruses" to perform at campaign meetings, in public squares, and at mass demonstrations. The staging and message of these performances combined the traditional language and practice of the Social Democratic association with subtle (and not so subtle) adaptations of Nazi slogans and style. The scripts were written either as a dialogue between two choirs or for a soloist who gave cues for mass response. For example, if the speaker said, "first arrow," the masses replied, "activity." Positive concepts (peace, freedom, bread) and epithets (prince, Hitler, baron) were grouped in threes, thus alluding to the three arrows.[144] The choruses chanted rhymed couplets whose rhetoric was Social Democratic (Red, worker, freedom, peace, unity, discipline, activity) and militant ("Our Iron Front will smash (schlagen) them"; "Smash Hitler!") but not socialist. The scripts contained implicit concessions to Nazi language (the ambiguous word freedom replaced the contested word republic) as well as explicit borrowings such as "Password: Germany awake!" Workers (not the working class) and the unemployed, but also Kleinbürger, were addressed. Recalling the language of both the NSDAP and prewar Social Democracy, das Volk was invoked.[145] It is, however, difficult to distinguish between originator and imitator because the Nazis too adopted slogans (freedom, work, bread) and images (the Promethean worker) from the Left's lexicon and iconography.[146] Weimar Social Democrats then (re)incorporated these into

their repertory. The mixing of language and styles from contrary traditions and with clashing symbolic meanings characterized the July 1932
campaign on both the Social Democratic and National Socialist sides.
Thus, Karl Höltermann was hailed as *der Führer* at a huge "Freedom Day
of the Iron Front" rally when he and Mierendorff addressed a massive
Nazi-style parade in Dortmund that marched under republican banners
and the *Drei Pfeile*. Meanwhile, young Nazis paraded the streets of Berlin
wearing red shirts.[147]

The SPD's activity took place under what Wels and Breitscheid described in an open letter to Hindenburg as "civil war conditions." After
the Papen government lifted the SA ban, street fights occurred daily.
Between June 14 and July 18, ninety-nine people died in political violence.[148] The Iron Front also paid a price for civic disorder in hundreds of
criminal processes against its members. Several SPD publications were
temporarily banned for violating the censorship regulations in a Papen
emergency decree.[149] Social Democrats also campaigned amidst the fren-
zied efforts of their radical opponents. In number and size of meetings,
the NSDAP campaign equaled the Socialist effort in cities and far surpassed it in the countryside, where Nazi terror made left-wing agitation
almost impossible. *Antifaschistische Aktion*, the KPD's answer to the Iron
Front, also competed fiercely with the "betrayers of the working class."[150]
Still, in comparison with its earlier self the SPD leapt forward, as both
Communists and Nazis noted. Nazi propaganda ridiculed the *Drei Pfeile*,
but internal reports anxiously remarked on the popularity of this symbol
and, especially, of the slogan "Iron Front against Hitler Barons."[151] The
SPD executive felt "the situation is favorable for us" because "for the first
time the NSDAP sees itself . . . on the defensive." Leading Social Democrats also believed the party finally had "good possibilities for an attack on
the KPD," whose "refrain 'Social Democracy is the main enemy' [is] no
longer effective."[152] Social Democrats at all levels were genuinely hopeful
about the July election, heartened by the return to parliamentary opposition and the effort to refurbish the SPD's style and image.

Brüning's fall also affected the politics of the SPD campaign. In late June
the ADGB and the AfA-Bund finally published a "program to transform
the economy." *Vorwärts* expressed great enthusiasm for this "rescue program," which called for the nationalization of key industries as well as for
other socialist measures without calling outright for socialism. Although
the *Gewerkschafts-Zeitung* maintained that the plan simply added "future"
demands to the immediate request for public works, by the time the program appeared, the short-lived focus on public works was fading.[153] Back
in opposition after the long months of restraint, the party was free to

propagate more radical policies in parliament. Even Woytinsky emphasized the need for a "future" economic program.[154] Alwin Brandes, chairman of the metalworkers, told his board that, freed from the "crippling
burden of toleration," the SPD could now carry out a consistent socialist
policy in competition with the KPD. Public works must be deemphasized
"because it might awaken doubts about the seriousness of socialism as our
goal." The fear of appearing to tolerate Papen by advocating WTB's reform measures contributed to the eagerness to stress the SPD's desire for
radical change.[155] ADGB leaders felt that Free Trade Union declarations
must criticize the Papen regime in a "very much more pointed tone" in
order to deafen workers to the siren of the "united front slogan" of the
KPD.[156]

The slogan "Iron Front against Hitler Barons" hammered home the
connection between the NSDAP and the new government of the aristocratic and capitalist rich. Social Democrats inveighed against the system
and called for socialism.[157] Election supplements laid out the SPD's plat-
form, including expropriation of coal mines and large landholdings.
Although the demand for communal housing construction was listed,
calls for jobs and public works did not stand out amidst the barrage of
propaganda.[158] With his weekly negative and positive appeals, Chakhotin
aimed to give punch and direction to the SPD campaign. The demands
provided by the party leadership, however, were general, not specific.[159]
On one hand, the party made special efforts to attract small farmers and
the *Mittelstand* with promises of economic reforms geared to their interests. On the other hand, no single positive demand, reformist or radical,
stood out as Social Democracy's goal. Ironically, while the SPD excoriated
the system and in separate leaflets aimed radical rhetoric at eleven different occupational and interest groups (civil servants, white-collar employees, farmers, smallholders, the unemployed, athletes, youth, women,
the *Mittelstand*, and industrial workers), the NSDAP made *Arbeitsbeschaffung* its major demand and targeted the SPD's working-class electorate. Its
program was inspired by WTB.[160] The SPD's failure to adopt the cry for
public works was a momentous blunder in the July campaign,[161] but
another event, too, played a part in its election defeat.

The Destruction of the Prussian Bulwark

In the halls of the Prussian government, Brüning's fall occasioned not a sense of freedom, but gloom. On June 6, four days after
Papen's appointment, Braun went on indefinite sick leave "with the firm
intention not to return." Though Braun was ill, his withdrawal from

public life was mentally more than physically conditioned. The dismal results of the Prussian election had profoundly depressed him, compound-
ing the malaise that had afflicted him since early 1932. Having lost his
majority, he stayed on as acting minister-president under a rule change
pushed through by the Weimar Coalition before the election: a new
minister-president had to be elected by a majority of the Landtag, a feat
the NSDAP could only achieve with the votes of either the Center Party or
the KPD. Braun had not supported the rule change but abided, unhap-
pily, by its provisions. Since the voters had rejected him, he believed he
should step down.[162] He now wanted to force the NSDAP to try its hand at
ruling Prussia, a viewpoint evidently shared by Severing.[163] Severing
stayed on the job, but his resigned outlook was manifest, if less dramatically so than Braun's. Severing's postponement of all important decisions
contributed to the spread of demoralization and disloyalty among non-
Socialist bureaucrats and police officers.[164] At the end of June, Grzesinski
warned Severing that the police were no longer reliable. Severing himself
noticed that his subordinates were ever more "confused and intimidated,"
but he blamed this on the insidious effects of rightist scheming.[165]

The lassitude of the Prussian ministers alarmed other Social Democrats, high and low, Left and Right. Hilferding and *Vorwärts* advocated
holding on to power in Prussia. Wels tried to dissuade Braun from his
"vacation," as did Ernest Hamburger and Ernst Heilmann.[166] Socialist
bureaucrats in the Prussian administration were disgusted by Braun's
desertion.[167] Rank and file Socialists and republicans felt abandoned by
their hero. In August, Theodor Haubach addressed a party meeting in
Weissensee near Berlin at which "Otto Braun's 'vacation' was roundly
condemned."[168] After Grzesinski publicly criticized Severing for hinting
that the SPD should relinquish Prussia, he won praise from the leftist
Zwickau district (in Saxony) for censuring Severing's "simply impossible"
stance. To no avail, the Saxons entreated the SPD executive to reprimand
Severing.[169] Weary as the Prussian ministers were of "fighting for lost
positions," probably no amount of comradely cajolery could have jolted
them out of their passivity.[170]

Their exhaustion did not go unnoticed on the other side of Wilhelmstrasse, where the Reich government sat. Rumors of plans to replace the
Braun-Severing government with a Reich commissioner surfaced soon
after Papen's appointment. *Vorwärts* brushed off such speculation with the
observation that "the constitutional prerequisites are lacking."[171] Un-
deterred by such fine points, the NSDAP and the DNVP lobbied for a
Reich commissioner. Social Democrats, including Braun, began to sus-
pect that the dissolution of the Reichstag and the lifting of the SA ban

were part of a package deal of which the third "gift" would be use of Article 48 to oust Braun's caretaker regime. After Baden, Württemberg, and Bavaria spoke out pointedly for states' rights, Grzesinski, incensed by Severing's passivity, wanted to assail the Prussian government for letting the southern German states appear more concerned about Prussia's rights than Prussia did; Heilmann dissuaded him from this attack. In late June at the Workers' Sports congress in Magdeburg, however, Grzesinski warned Hindenburg and his "evil counselors" that should the Nazis attempt to gain control of Prussia by force, the government and the Iron Front would defend the citadel.[172] Grzesinski hoped to prod Prussia into defensive measures, but instead Severing rebuked him and forbade more such outbursts. Severing also rejected the Reichsbanner's suggestion that the *Schufo* be deputized as auxiliary police units in Prussia.[173]

In the bloody wake of the relegalization of the SA and the SS, Severing asked other state interior ministers to join him in pressuring Hindenburg for a national ban on all political demonstrations.[174] Thus, he retreated to his old strategy of winning Reich support for measures aimed equally at pro- and antirepublican street activity. In a similar vein, he cautioned the other states against opposing the emergency decree of June 28, although it tied their hands by limiting state ordinances against the National Socialists. Suspicious that the Reich wanted an excuse to declare a state of emergency, Severing evidently thought that, unprovoked, it would not install a commissioner before the July 31 election.[175] Neither he nor others in his regime guessed that Reich action would take the form of a coup whose main purpose would be to set aside the SPD regime. Instead he expected a move to merge the Reichswehr and the Prussian police.[176] When Theo Haubach, in his role as press chief of the Berlin police, appeared before Severing two days before the coup with "the most precise information that the Papen regime stood before the doors," the interior minister did not believe it.[177] He did, however, feel it was time to consult with the SPD executive about what to do in case of Reich action.

Wels, Hans Vogel, and Paul Hertz met with Severing on July 18.[178] Severing inquired outright if the time had not arrived to give up in Prussia. An astonished Wels asked what inspired such a question. Severing reminded them that the previous day the Reich had summarily banned all demonstrations after a battle between Communists and Nazis in the city of Altona left seventeen people dead.[179] He sensed intrigue against Prussia behind this ultimatum and feared he would soon be without any authority. Wels called a contact in the chancellor's office to ask if something "special" was planned against Prussia. This official replied negatively. Wels then told Severing to get in touch with other states to create a broad front against Papen. With Hertz and Vogel, he reminded the interior minister that the SPD did not want to relinquish any position voluntarily. To consider the problem in more depth, they called a meeting of the leaders of the trade unions, the party, and the Reichsbanner for July 20.[180]

Also on the eighteenth, Papen arranged a meeting with Severing for the twentieth to discuss, Severing assumed, reductions in unemployment insurance. When Severing, accompanied by the Prussian welfare and finance ministers, arrived at the morning appointment, however, Papen informed them of his concern about the state of affairs on Prussia's streets—witness Altona.[181] Since Prussian ministers could not guarantee public security and order, Hindenburg, using powers invested in him by Article 48, had appointed Papen commissioner over Prussia and Franz Bracht, mayor of Essen, his deputy. Braun and Severing were relieved of their offices. Ever so politely, Papen asked Severing if he would "voluntarily" step down. Severing replied, "I will only yield to force." At that, peaceful pretense was dropped. Martial law was imposed in Berlin and Brandenburg province; the Prussian police were placed under Reich command.[182] When Grzesinski refused to relinquish control in Berlin, he was arrested. When the Prussian cabinet refused to cooperate with Papen, it was dismissed. That evening a lieutenant and two policemen entered Severing's office to remove him. To this force he yielded. Informed at home of the coup, Braun considered forcing his way into his office, but Arnold Brecht, his ministerial director, dissuaded him. Instead of resisting, Braun's cabinet decided to challenge the constitutionality of the Staatsstreich before the supreme court.[183]

The consultation of party, union, and Reichsbanner authorities was in session at ADGB headquarters on July 20 when Wels received a telephone call from Grzesinski. After Wels relayed the news, a depressing silence ensued. Not one word of disgust or outrage crossed the lips of the assembled leaders of Social Democracy. Leipart asked Wels for his opinion about how to react. The SPD chairman tried to sort out the situation: an open coup was in progress. Because the Socialist movement had always insisted it would counter a coup with any means, those present must decide which means and what forces they had at their command. He recalled the Kapp putsch of 1920, smashed by a powerful general strike: "Do we have the masses behind us now as then? No." Nevertheless, he and his colleagues must seriously consider a strike. If, however, the coup was a provocation aimed at devising an excuse to postpone the Reichstag election, perhaps Social Democracy should respond not with a strike but with the call, "Secure the election." Wels concluded that the answer turned on the trade unions' assessment of their strength.[184]

Wels's appeal to trade union opinion was not merely formal. Just as the SPD controlled parliamentary legislation, the trade unions had strict prerogative over plans for a general strike.[185] Wels deferred to Franz Scheffel, head of the railroad workers, a union crucial to a general strike. Scheffel hemmed and hawed; his members were of course prepared, but he wondered, "What would be the strike's exact aim? How long would it last?" After all, he ended lamely, the state of emergency made the situation very difficult. Otto Becker of the public workers' union spoke even more vaguely than Scheffel. The leaders of other unions sat mum. Finally, Leipart spoke for the "Secure the election" slogan. Franz Künstler, present for the Berlin SPD, and Höltermann, for the Reichsbanner, agreed with him (although later both criticized the SPD's failure to resist).[186] Wels went to meet Severing, informing the minister that he, Wels, did not think the trade unions would strike nor did he think a strike would succeed. Severing concurred, adding that the Prussian police would not fight against the Reichswehr. He, too, accepted the "Secure the election" slogan. Wels returned to ADGB headquarters to relay Severing's opinion. At that point the union leaders endorsed the decision to save the election. Although Wels had first presented this alternative, he was disheartened by the unions' stamp of approval.[187] The decision not to resist had been made.

The Social Democratic machine went to work. On the afternoon of July 20 the combined trade unions distributed a leaflet calling for "exemplary discipline" in this "difficult time"; the brochure proclaimed that "the decisive answer of the German people, especially of the working class, will be given on July 31" and that "we won't let the unions' enemy dictate the hour of action."[188] A similar appeal was signed by the "command of the Iron Front." Künstler produced a leaflet directed against the KPD's call for a general strike. Höltermann spoke to Berlin Reichsbanner leaders that evening, justifying the election alternative. The party council met the next day and approved the election call, as did Iron Front rallies on the same day. The Social Democratic press raised no dissenting voice against the leaders' decision and instead trumpeted, "Our reply: July 31!"[189]

As contradictory as it seems, one suspects that the decision not to resist rested at least partially on the hope that the authoritarian government that carried it out—and that the SPD genuinely despised—would resist Nazi claims to total power. Several days before the coup, one of its central planners, Defense Minister Schleicher, invited Stampfer and Breitscheid to a discussion in which he explained why he believed repressive measures like the SA ban could not control the Nazi threat. He promised to "deal" soon with the NSDAP. When Breitscheid wondered whether a policy to tame the Nazis might not end with them assaulting the tamers, Schleicher laughingly insisted that he was not that dumb.[190] Schleicher no doubt hoped to lull Social Democratic anxiety immediately before the move against Prussia, but at the same time he assured them of his basically anti-Nazi stance. One can only speculate that, while shocked by Schleicher's duplicity in having staged a confidential chat with his unwitting victims, Social Democratic decision makers reacted to the news of the coup with greater ambivalence than had they not spoken with him. Arnold Brecht, who advised Braun and Severing on July 20, felt it would be counterproductive to resist an attempt to strengthen a national government headed by men who opposed handing the reins of power to Hitler.[191]

Weimar Social Democrats' retrospective assessments of the failure to resist were varied. As a rule, middle-level party politicians, such as Wilhelm Hoegner, Toni Sender, Julius Leber, and Wilhelm Leuschner, condemned the decision to bend to force.[192] It is not surprising that those with power in the party or in the Prussian government defended the choice of the peaceful path.[193] Above all, Severing and Braun justified their decision to go to court instead of taking up arms or encouraging a general strike. Defenders used several arguments to vindicate the choice not to resist. First, the chances of an armed revolt were virtually nil. The police, Severing insisted, remained reliable but were too weak for even a short fight against the Reichswehr. For him the issue was moot anyway since the police stood under Reich command as of early July 20.[194] Furthermore, the Reichsbanner and the working class had no arms to speak of and could not get weapons once the army stood opposed to them. Second, defendants argued, 6 million unemployed ruled out a general strike. Added to massive unemployment was the political division of the working class. The Communist Party, they maintained, would have sabotaged a Social Democratic strike or armed resistance. In Severing's view, the Social Democratic masses also lacked enthusiasm for a resistance effort. He noted the absence of spontaneous outbreaks and cited the opinion of many functionaries that no will to fight existed at the grassroots.[195] Finally, Severing and Braun asserted that they had really lost power on April 24 when the majority of the people rejected them. What call to arms could have inspired an uprising to restore a minority regime?[196]

These justifications of Social Democratic passivity on July 20 cannot be lightly dismissed. Mass unemployment—44.4 percent of trade union members were out of work, and another 22.3 percent were on short time—explained the absence of wildcat strikes and the silence that greeted the KPD's call for a strike.[197] Hoegner was sure, however, that a strike call by the ADGB would have been "unanimously followed," given the "proletariat's feverish excitement."[198] The Free Trade Unions were simply unprepared for a strike. According to a member of the railroad workers' board, his union had discussed emergency measures in case of civil war.[199] The ADGB as a whole, however, had laid no organizational groundwork for a general strike.[200] Nonetheless, on July 17 *Vorwärts* had threatened "anyone" who tried to "suspend the republican constitution" with the Iron Front's fury, invoking the dismal fate of the Kapp putsch— an obvious reference to a general strike.[201] Surely SPD supporters, remembering such threats three days later, were bewildered by the yawning gulf between words and action.

Working-class political disunity was, as even Toni Sender conceded, a weighty objection to resistance.[202] The KPD continued to insist that SPD leaders were "capitalist agents inside the working class" and the "left wing of fascism." The only possible united front, according to the Communists, was a Red one from below with Social Democratic workers.[203] In fact, the KPD had cranked up the volume of its attacks on the SPD elite before the Prussian elections.[204] However, after the Prussian elections in which the NSDAP swept ahead and the KPD lost absolutely, faint signs of a new attitude appeared. On April 26, the KPD announced that it could work with any organization against wage reductions. In June the Communist Landtag delegation voted down its own motion to rescind the rule change that kept Braun in power, but no cooperation with his cabinet followed.[205] Divisions inside the KPD about how to act in the new situation explain its contradictory response to the Papen coup. It called for a general strike— against the coup but in effect to restore the Braun-Severing traitors; yet at several Communist rallies cheers broke out at the news of their ouster.[206]

In the preceding weeks, the SPD had made gestures toward the KPD but refused cooperation unless the KPD stopped lambasting Social Democracy's leaders.[207] In late June the ADGB felt obliged to declare its support for unity, adding that the KPD was the stumbling block. Its statement noted an intensified desire among "workers in the shops" for a united front since Brüning's fall.[208] In private meetings union leaders remarked on the "extraordinary" strength of this longing.[209] The ranks of both parties were heartily disgusted by each group's hostility to the other's leaders, although even some Communists seem to have perceived the KPD's attacks as particularly egregious.[210] Pressure from below for cooperation was quite strong in, on one hand, the largest cities and, on the other hand, small towns and villages where SA terror made collaboration imperative. The push for unity emanated from the unions as well as the SPD (and the KPD).[211] In Berlin, party members and union officials called for a "unity list" in the Reichstag elections.[212] At an Iron Front rally Franz Künstler advocated joint antifascist demonstrations. Having initiated this idea, the Berlin KPD rejected Künstler's offer because it required the cessation of mutual attacks. In Halle, "radical circles in the SPD" tried to draw the KPD into the Iron Front. In Magdeburg, the neorevisionist Grzesinski called for a truce between the KPD and the SPD so that they could fight fascism together.[213] In Stuttgart, Hamburg-Harburg, Braunschweig, Hanover, and smaller cities, joint marches and demonstrations took place.[214] Reichsbanner members and local leaders played an especially active role in such efforts.[215]

Top-level enmity between the KPD and the SPD overrode all such local flirtations with fraternity. On June 28 and again in mid-July, the SPD executive instructed district executive committees to discourage contact with the KPD. On July 14, under Comintern instructions, the KPD central committee censured unity efforts and prohibited local initiatives.[216] The very necessity of such proscriptions suggests that many Communist rank and filers, taught to hate the SPD for "collaborationism," might have rallied to a Social Democratic call to arms, just as it is likely that many Social Democrats, taught to hate the KPD for splitting the proletariat, would have responded to the Communist call for a united front if the KPD had stopped attacking SPD leaders. In fact, the prospect of too much success among Communists may have contributed to the decision not to resist on July 20. After all, in Berlin, despite a weak organization, Communists had significant support among the unemployed.[217] Fear of losing control of events perhaps influenced SPD decision makers as much as fear of Communist sabotage.

Were Social Democrats themselves eager to fight? According to Hoegner, a "will to struggle and wild determination" gripped the Reichsbanner. He found "the prospects of armed resistance . . . not at all hopeless."[218] After hearing of the coup, men and women amassed in the streets of working-class Berlin, talking among themselves in great agitation. At the rumor that Nazis and Stahlhelm men had stationed themselves in the government quarter, a large crowd moved off intent on supporting the Prussian cabinet. As the police escorted Grzesinski out of the building, this throng shouted, "Freedom!"[219] More significantly, thousands of young Berlin workers gathered at their "watch posts" in the afternoon.[220] In Magdeburg (Reichsbanner national headquarters and a Social Democratic bailiwick under Mayor Ernst Reuter) witnesses recalled intense excitement and preparation for fighting. In certain neighborhoods, men, women, and children waited half the night for a signal from Berlin. In Frankfurt, Darmstadt, Berlin, and Kassel and throughout Saxony and Hanover, small troops of Reichsbanner members and union and party functionaries stood on guard.[221] Later that summer, union and party members all over the country told ADGB investigators of their will to fight and "intense disappointment" that nothing was done. Many reported, "We believed we had to march. In our district tens of thousands waited for the orders to march."[222] In Oldenburg and Braunschweig, where Social Democrats already lived under Nazi rule, "a very aggressive fighting mood reigned inside the Iron Front." Throughout the country, "the masses in the Iron Front expect some positive decision from us, above all, they want for their activity to produce results," complained the chairman of the garment workers' union.[223]

Wilhelm Keil, however, remembered his audience in Ravensburg (in Württemberg) as unmoved by the news of the coup.[224] Even in Magdeburg, the isolated nature of preparations for combat led one participant to believe a local party bureaucrat was unaware of them.[225] In Berlin, trade union secretaries sent out to take the pulse of the capital on July 20 gained the impression that the "broad masses" lacked the will to fight.[226] That night Iron Front assemblies in the capital were packed, but the mood was quietly militant rather than aggressive; participants at one meeting passed a resolution praising their leaders and assuring them of the loyalty of "republicans and members of the Iron Front."[227]

Compelling evidence of the contradictory reactions of Social Democrats is found in the accounts of Communist "worker correspondents" who worked alongside them in factories and offices. Several days after the coup the correspondents met to discuss the mood in Berlin's largest concerns (from four hundred to four thousand employees). The Communists told of "excitement," "disgust" with the coup, and acute interest in shop-floor meetings and direct action on the actual day of the *Preussenstreich*. Communists, Social Democrats, and Reichsbanner members joined in spontaneous demonstrations outside several plants; at other workplaces, leftist workers cooperatively barred Nazis from distributing leaflets. Many correspondents reported that on July 20 the ranks expected SPD and ADGB leaders to call a general strike; indeed, several union officials confidently predicted such a summons. Yet a countercurrent ran against this militance. Some workers were focused entirely on their personal situation and seemed indifferent to the coup. Moreover, many of the workers and functionaries who expected a strike said they would only act under leadership direction. By the next day, when it became clear that no strike call was in the offing, they defended this decision and the "Secure July 31" slogan. The correspondents offered several explanations for the mixture of desire for action, passivity, and indifference that they encountered. Some workers, especially those in municipally owned shops, still idolized Severing. In contrast, others, especially white-collar workers, were so disgusted with Severing and Braun that they would have refused to rescue their government. As did their leaders, a number of Social Democrats argued that action was impossible because Nazi workers would break a strike. Others feared a civil war. Many, even of those who wanted to strike, said they refused to heed the call to resistance made by a party as inconsistent, mercurial, and adventurist as the KPD. Finally, fatalism and revulsion against all political leaders had numbed many workers. Even those who condemned SPD passivity said they felt helpless and unable to act on their own.[228] The disappointment and anger of those who *were* prepared to act, however, can be gauged in the notably larger presence of Social Democrats and Reichsbanner members at Communist rallies in the days between the coup and July 31.[229]

Like their leaders, then, many Social Democrats feared civic chaos and did not want to exchange a possible election victory for a military defeat.[230] According to Wilhelm Hoegner, only a minority in the party or the trade unions grasped the "political import" of the Prussian action. They did not think that passivity would negatively affect the election results and did not realize that the coup dealt a mortal blow to constitutional government and the foundations of the republic.[231] Simultaneously, however, a core of militants in the SPD, the Free Trade Unions, and, especially, the Reichsbanner not only cherished vague notions about resistance but were prepared to act on their conviction. Many of these people had gone through minimal military training in the Reichsbanner. How this core might have grown once resistance began is impossible to judge. The numbers of fighters aside, a huge drawback to armed resistance lay in the dearth of weapons. Even in the unlikely event that the Prussian police would have followed orders from Severing, the sides in a civil war would have been massively uneven. Resistance most likely would have failed. Even if the spirit was at hand, preparation and coordination were not.

Since that fateful day, German historians have debated the SPD's decision not to resist the coup. In the 1950s, liberal historians condemned the SPD's failure to act.[232] Reading their accounts, one is left with the feeling that, writing soon after Nazism's defeat, they wished so much for some sign of active opposition to authoritarianism that they simply declared it should have happened. More recently, German scholars have rejected this view.[233] Although historians' negative assessment of the chances of resistance seems correct, one cannot help but feel that heroic action would have provided an inspiration to resist the horror to come and, even in failure, might have changed the course of history. Of course, it is understandable that Social Democratic leaders, who could not foresee the future, did not risk it. They were not willing to lead their followers into a bloodbath.[234] However, they cannot escape the blame for failing to prepare for the eventuality of a coup—preparations which, as Karl Rohe and Hans Mommsen have suggested, very well might have caused Papen and Schleicher to think twice before acting.[235] After having sacrificed so much for the Prussian bulwark, the SPD let it slide from its hands over several months before the final yank came on July 20.

In June and July the SPD was switching horses in midstream. Forced by its opponents, the SPD had gone from a defensive parliamentary stance, sacrificing electoral strength in the interest of the state's stability, to all-out opposition aimed at rebuilding the SPD's electoral position. The dilemma about what to do in Prussia in this new situation caused surprising divisions among Social Democrats. Braun and Severing, convinced the defeat of April 24 guaranteed the death of the Prussian regime, wanted to cut SPD losses by giving up Prussia. They received support from Mierendorff, the outspoken advocate of an extraparliamentary strategy.[236] Grzesinski, on the other hand, gained allies among party leftists when he challenged Severing's passivity. Wels and Hilferding disapproved of Braun's vacation but took no steps to build other supports for the Prussian government—whether by pressuring the trade unions to prepare seriously for a strike, training the Reichsbanner for combat, cultivating contacts with the southern states, or, alternatively, making a serious approach to the KPD. On one hand, the party's national leaders did not want to give up Prussia voluntarily (just as they had refused to end toleration). On the other hand, neither to them nor to the leaders of the Free Trade Unions did Prussia seem worth fighting for, given the minority position of the Weimar Coalition and the hostility of the Reich government.[237] At an ADGB national committee meeting on July 21, several union leaders voiced support for the decision not to strike; none opposed it or, indeed, expressed the slightest outrage over the *Staatsstreich*. At the same meeting, however, they were awed by the continuing power of the Iron Front to mobilize the masses and were eager to harness this force to organize unemployed workers.[238] This curious mix of passive resignation on the political stage and active organizational plans characterized the outlook of many Social Democrats at the time of the coup against Prussia and suggests, once again, that they did not comprehend its significance.

Determined to refurbish its popular image, the SPD made an effort to take up the methods of its radical opponents in the streets. In this arena, however, Social Democrats at the grassroots felt frustrated by the prohibitions on uniforms, marches, and open air rallies approved by Social Democrats in the Prussian executive, resenting the fact that the republic's saviors had to suffer as much as those bent on destroying it.[239] In the July campaign, the cry from below was "Forward to the militant republic!" Increasingly, Social Democratic workers wanted a "second republic," one with freedom for republicans only.[240] SPD leaders did not endorse this attitude but also did not discourage it. They placed the extraparliamentary "new methods" and the passion they aroused at the service of parliamentary politics—an election campaign. Electoral politics require a program, however, and this the SPD did not possess, having dropped a tentative focus on public works in its veer to the left after Brüning's fall. Instead, in a nod to other tenets of Social Democratic culture, its campaign attacked capitalism and appealed to proletarian solidarity.

Events in these months exposed the clashing requirements of the several fronts on which Social Democracy struggled and the conflicting priorities of participants. Reformers in the Reichsbanner and the Free Trade Unions bombarded the party leadership with suggestions for change but did not ally with each other in a general assault to reform the SPD. Focused on the extraparliamentary mobilization of the SPD, Mierendorff, Chakhotin, and the militant Socialists did not appreciate the importance of program as addressed by Tarnow, Woytinsky, and other economic reformers. In the dispute over public works, the trade union elite tried to galvanize the party elite, but it is too simple to see the unionists as visionary innovators against party bureaucrats and ideologues.[241] July 20 exposed *their* conservative stripes. Mavericks in the area of economic legislation, they were risk averse when it came to direct political action. In this case Wels was ready to consider a militant tactic but not to defy the unions;[242] nor did trade union reformers join ranks with the Iron Front militants.

Even in the maelstrom of mid-1932, Social Democrats clung to an exaggerated respect for their movement's various associations and their areas of responsibility. The Iron Front existed in name only. The party leadership was also blinded by an unhappy combination of fatalism (the depression must play itself out, Prussia is lost) with optimism (we can do well in the next election, the Nazi appeal is on the wane, socialism is on the agenda). Such wishful thinking certainly influenced the choice of "a promising election campaign" over a "hopeless armed conflict."[243] Finally, leading Social Democrats demonstrated a disturbing ability to delude themselves about their intentions. On July 31, *Vorwärts* wrote that the "working class knows the election campaign is only a preparation for the great decisive struggles to come."[244] On the same day Grzesinski began a speech in Düsseldorf, "It is no longer a matter of words." But the SPD's enemies could not be fooled. The Nazis screamed gleefully that the Iron Front had been found to be made of tin.[245]

Into the Abyss

On November 10, 1932, Otto Wels told assembled members of the party council that he had driven to Berlin through a thick fog that reminded him of German politics: what lurked ahead lay shrouded in mist. As he had on the road that morning, the SPD leadership must proceed slowly so as not to endanger its fellow travelers.[1] With this metaphor, Wels confessed his perplexity about German politics in late 1932 and revealed that the executive committee's only plan of action was to avoid reckless turns; yet the SPD chief aimed to reassure, not alarm, the party's provincial leaders. The helplessness and confusion conveyed by Wels's poignant analogy characterized SPD thinking and behavior during Weimar's twilight and the months of the Nazi consolidation of power. The salient features of SPD politics in Weimar's final days were radical language and the refusal to deal with an overtly authoritarian government. In Berlin and in the provinces, Social Democrats colored their propaganda and proposals "more brightly red" or, as one functionary put it, "hoisted the red flag to the main mast."[2] Radicalization also spread through the lower levels of the Reichsbanner and the ADGB.[3] Thus in August 1932 the Reichsbanner's *Schufo* in Berlin and Berlin-Brandenburg expanded military exercises. Encouraged by the left-wing leaders of diverse Berlin unions, ADGB *Hammerschaften* in the capital encompassed forty thousand participants and continued to grow. "Small provincial towns and the countryside," meanwhile, reported scattered cooperation between the Iron Front and the KPD against the "unbraked hegemony" of the NSDAP outside the big cities.[4] At the national level, in contrast, not only did relations between Social Democracy and the KPD become, if possible, more hostile, but unity inside the Iron Front began to fray. The SPD's partners in the Iron Front did not adopt its intransigent stance to the Papen regime. The ADGB and the Reichsbanner looked upon certain programs of the government, and even some of its goals, with approbation. Differences in how the party and its fraternal associations reacted to the electoral decline and shrinking influence of Social Democracy fed tensions and mutual suspicions that further weakened the Socialist movement. At the same time, low morale inside the SPD, overcome in the euphoria generated by the Iron Front, reemerged in the fall of 1932 as a crisis of confidence in its leadership.

Pragmatism versus Principle

The SPD's turn to the left, begun in the spring, was completed under the impact of the July 31 returns. From an election approached with relatively high hopes, the SPD emerged with ten fewer seats (133) and only 21.9 percent of the vote. For the first time since 1912, the SPD did not return to the Reichstag as its largest delegation. The Center Party gained 7 seats (for a total of 75), but the State Party shrank to a measly 4. Germans massively rejected the Papen government. The parties friendly to it suffered from that attitude; the DNVP was reduced to 37 seats, and the DVP shrank to 7. Voters turned to the extremes. The NSDAP came out on top with 13,779,017 ballots, 37.4 percent of the vote, and 230 seats. The KPD gained 12 mandates (for a total of 89) by marshaling 14.6 percent of the vote. Parliament was as hamstrung as before. Despite the NSDAP's size, the National Opposition controlled less than half of the Reichstag. The only majority of any likelihood was a "Black-Brown" coalition between the Center Party and the NSDAP.[5]

As after the Prussian fiasco, Social Democrats tried to show the outcome in a positive light, although internal circulars acknowledged that the political situation was exceedingly dangerous.[6] Wels declared the results a "victory for democracy" since the NSDAP had been denied its coveted majority. "The dream of the Third Reich is dreamed out," party editorials announced; "the Nazi wave has come to a standstill" because the NSDAP vote had stagnated since the presidential election.[7] Observers, Socialist and otherwise, agreed that the NSDAP had reached the limits of its expansion. It had already raided the Protestant bourgeois parties and mobilized nonvoters, while the Center Party and the Left parties had successfully withstood its onslaught through four major elections. Without growth, it was believed, the Nazi movement would lose its allure and start to wither.[8] After the Prussian election, the Nazi vote did stagnate in many districts, such as the Ruhr. The NSDAP's increases in July were negligible in the Protestant countryside and small towns, where its vote had skyrocketed from 1930 through the presidential race. It barely compensated for losses among farmers and the urban *Mittelstand* with gains among the upper middle class and in previously neglected regions. The SPD actually picked up votes in Oldenburg, where the NSDAP had won an absolute majority in the Landtag election in early June. Thomas Schnabel has suggested that in June many Social Democratic voters stayed home, in protest against SPD policies in Oldenburg, but flocked to the polls in July after their "brief, but very bad experience" with Nazi rule.[9] The SPD also won votes in some rural districts in Upper Rhine province, Kassel, Upper Pa-

latinate, and Schleswig-Holstein.[10] Nonetheless, subsequent analysis has
shown that, over the entire country, the SPD relinquished about 14 percent of its total losses to the NSDAP. Communists believed that SPD losses
among workers were hidden by gains among petit bourgeois voters in
cities such as Mannheim. In the university town of Göttingen the SPD
gained relatively among upper-class voters while stagnating among the
lower class and losing among middle-class voters. The working-class contribution to the Nazi vote, estimated at between 25 and 33 percent across
all national elections between 1928 and 1933, increased somewhat, but
not substantially, from 1930 to July 1932.[11]

Social Democrats combined SPD and KPD tallies and spoke noncha-
lantly of a "Marxist vote," but bravado masked real concern about the
KPD's gains.[12] In the heavily industrial *Ruhrgebiet*, the KPD outpolled the
SPD by 50 percent. Submission to Papen's force on July 20, Social Democrats now recognized, drove tens of thousands of SPD voters to the KPD.[13]
Communists claimed that after the "impressive agitational impact" of the
Iron Front, July 20 had knocked the enthusiasm out of the Social Democratic campaign. Chakhotin agreed.[14] Albert Grzesinski, however, believed that only "gradually did a very critical attitude toward the politics
before July 20 develop." Others, too, noted that only after July 31 did a
widespread revulsion against their leaders' passivity wash over the SPD as
the "significance of July 20 becomes ever clearer and more ominous."[15] At
SPD gatherings in Berlin, left oppositionists argued that July 20 demonstrated the need for a united front with the KPD. In August and throughout the fall, complaints about passivity plagued SPD speakers.[16] Orators
who condemned the failure to act received standing ovations.[17] Prominent Reichsbanner men, in particular, "reproached the party for not
sounding the call to street fighting on July 31." In the autumn of 1932,
however, these same Reichsbanner critics wanted to participate in the
Papen regime's scheme to give German youth military training, an about-
face that was perhaps less "strange" than it appeared to Otto Wels.[18]
Inside the SPD, in contrast, the "morning-after blues" intensified hatred
of a regime that had forced Social Democrats to make a humiliating
decision whose consequences reverberated to the KPD's advantage.[19]

Leading Social Democrats still ranked the Nazi menace to the republic
higher than Papen's threat to revise the constitution in an authoritarian
direction. Wels met with Papen in early August and tried in vain to
convince him to change his course. Wels and others felt encouraged,
nonetheless, by signs of enmity between Papen with his "New State" and
the Nazis with their sights set on a "fascist party state."[20] Papen and
Schleicher had hoped to include Hitler in the cabinet as vice-chancellor.

When he met with Hindenburg on August 13, however, Hitler lay claim to "leadership of the regime and total state power" and got a brusque rebuff from the president. The Nazis answered with wrathful opposition to the Papen regime, simultaneously carrying out murderous attacks on opponents and posing as parliament's staunch defenders.[21]

Socialist analysts reacted ambivalently to the break between Papen and Hitler. *Vorwärts* explained that the Nazis really supported Papen, even while voting against him in the Reichstag. Düsseldorf's *Volkszeitung* asserted that "heavy industry," one of Papen's sources of support, was dissatisfied by the Nazi failure to win a majority on July 31. The writer conceded that the mine owners' newspaper had described the NSDAP as a socialist party, but he insisted that big industrialists were merely pretending to reject Nazi "socialism."[22] In *Die Gesellschaft* Alexander Schifrin detected a "sharpening of the contradictions between the feudal, military, bureaucratic and the fascist, terrorist, demagogic sides of the German counterrevolution," but he doubted that this would last. Caught between the authoritarian state and political Catholicism, Hitler would have to turn to one or the other. Schifrin perceived greater danger in a "bourgeoisification" of the Nazi movement through an agreement with Papen than in a parliamentary understanding between the Center Party and the NSDAP. In December he again warned that an understanding between the authoritarian state and the NSDAP would lead to a "radical-fascist state."[23] In general, party leaders emphasized the "contradictions" between the state and the Nazis, rather than the possibility of rapprochement. Wels took heart from Hindenburg's rebuff of Hitler. For Ernst Heilmann, the president's obduracy vindicated SPD passivity on July 20. Resistance, he wrote, would have thrown the Reichswehr and the SA together, while such an alliance was now unthinkable.[24] A primer for SPD speakers explained that Hindenburg's refusal to appoint Hitler chancellor demonstrated that he and "the reactionary powers of the nobility, armed forces, and bureaucracy" opposed handing Hitler complete power.[25] The party elite continued to see state authority, parliamentary or not, as the best protection for Weimar. Hilferding drew the logical conclusion from such a position. When the SPD Reichstag delegation debated its tactic for the new Reichstag, he argued that to allow Papen's regime to remain in power was "the lesser evil" since an immediate vote of no-confidence fit into Hitler's game.[26]

In contrast, Otto Wels and Paul Löbe advocated a parliamentary solution to the government crisis. According to Wels, after careful debate the SPD had determined that the depression was not a normal cyclical downturn but a crisis of capitalism, and the party had decided that the time had come to transform the economy through parliamentary action. Thus, Paul Löbe explained, the SPD would present a socialist transition program in the Reichstag, challenging the other radical parties to join a majority vote to implement it.[27] So, in a parliament where Nazis had the upper hand, influential Social Democrats proposed essentially the strategy advocated by the party's far left wing in September 1930. Then, not wanting to throw the NSDAP and the bourgeois parties into each other's arms, the majority had chosen toleration as the only viable alternative. Now, feeling they had little to lose and votes to gain, leading Social Democrats were willing to risk a course considered unthinkable when the SPD still formed the largest block in the Reichstag. They hoped to challenge and expose their radical opponents while relying on Hindenburg, the authority behind the despised Papen regime, to withhold power from Hitler. Following Wels and Löbe, and rejecting Hilferding, the Reichstag delegation adopted a position of no-holds-barred hostility to Papen.[28] His emergency decree of September 4, which allowed employers who hired new workers to break labor contracts and reduce wages, fueled their opposition. At the second session of the new Reichstag on September 12, Social Democrats joined in an overwhelming vote of no-confidence (512 against 42). The new Reichstag president, Hermann Göring, Weimar democracy's archenemy, orchestrated this stunning parliamentary defeat of Papen's government. When the chancellor signaled his desire to speak in order to dissolve the Reichstag before it could reject his cabinet, Göring assiduously directed his attention to the KPD as it moved the vote of no-confidence. After this drama, Papen nonetheless dissolved the Reichstag.[29] Thus ended the parliamentary crisis of September. One more election, scheduled for November 6, was added to 1932's long list. During the brief parliamentary session, the SPD proposed a "heavy bundle" of bills for the revival of economic life. Based on the program for "transformation of the economy" published in June, these draft bills, collectively called Socialist Action, included proposals for expropriation of large landowners and socialization of basic industry and the banks. The SPD also demanded the reinstatement of pensions and unemployment benefits cut by Papen's June emergency decree. The party press and agitational material backed up this initiative, declaring "economics is destiny" and advocating a "socialist planned economy."[30]

The cumulative effects of its unrelenting electoral decline, the aftershock of July 20, and the economic crisis pushed the SPD to the left. The same causes evoked a different response from the top leadership of the ADGB. By the summer of 1932, the Free Trade Unions had been decimated by unemployment. Despite the first faint signs of an economic upturn, union membership, down 28 percent since late 1930, continued to decline. Stripped of their clout, the union leaders found alarming the political isolation of the SPD.[31] Fearful that, if the SPD were outlawed, "the close tie between party and trade unions would not be entirely without danger," they began to distance themselves from the party.[32] On July 21, a statement on the coup against Prussia stressed ADGB "self-reliance," thus delicately dissociating the Free Trade Unions from the debacle of the day before.[33] More significantly, on July 30, the ADGB leaders Leipart, Wilhelm Eggert, and Grassmann met confidentially with the organizers of the coup—Chancellor von Papen, Interior Minister Wilhelm von Gayl, and Defense Minister von Schleicher—to discuss the economic and political concerns of the trade unions.[34] The union leaders used the opportunity to remind the government of the April crisis congress's plan for public works. Leipart asked the ministers to give some assurance that they would soon take some "psychologically effective" step against unemployment. Grassmann and Eggert expressed concern about the regime's friendliness to the NSDAP. Schleicher, who dominated the meeting from the government side, insisted that the "highest goal of the regime is to put the workers back to work." He reassured the union leaders about his relations with the NSDAP and averred that the regime would restore civil order.[35] Papen unveiled the political agenda behind the conference only at its end when he asked the ADGB to persuade the SPD "to allow the regime to do its work in the Reichstag."[36]

At an ADGB board meeting on August 3, Leipart and Fritz Tarnow spoke for pursuing these contacts in light of the SPD's poor showing at the polls. Confusion about how to respond to the SPD's decline motivated this approach more than an inclination to collaborate with the government. Immediately after Tarnow approved of talks with Papen, he suggested an alternative strategy: the ADGB should present a "revolutionary socialist economic program that would bring us closer to the Communists and honest elements among the National Socialists." Leipart also argued that the ADGB must appear more "independent" from the SPD in order to counter Communist growth.[37] Not only ambivalence but disagreement characterized discussion inside the Free Trade Unions about where to turn for allies. Lothar Erdmann stood on the far right of Social Democracy, from whence he pressed for a "national orientation"; yet he rebuked Leipart and Grassmann for their friendly chat with Papen and Schleicher, appalled that they "said not a word about July 20" nor "about the double standard of justice against National Socialists and Communists." Disgusted as he was with the "unforgettable and unforgotten unanimity-in-passivity of Wels-Leipart-Höltermann" on July 20, Erdmann did not shift to a left-wing course. Instead, he cultivated his contacts with a member of the *Tat* circle who hoped to separate the trade unions from the SPD. Erdmann also encouraged Leipart to put out feelers to the Gregor Strasser wing of the NSDAP.[38]

The ADGB permitted Erdmann and others on the ADGB staff to pursue this counterstrategy. In July, Franz Furtwängler, the ADGB's expert on international issues, got in touch with Otto Strasser with the full knowledge of Leipart and Grassmann.[39] At the end of August, a supporter of Gregor Strasser in the Nazi Economic Policy Section initiated a "confidential, nonbinding" conversation with Tarnow about public works. They agreed that the NSDAP and the ADGB shared certain affinities on this issue.[40] Around the same time, Reichsbanner chief Karl Höltermann met with Gregor Strasser personally, as did Tarnow in the early fall. Like many political observers, Leipart believed a split between Gregor Strasser and Hitler was imminent. He agreed to meet Strasser if Höltermann were present. At the end of August rumors flew that a Schleicher-Strasser-Leipart cabinet was likely and that the Reichsbanner would support such a regime.[41] In fact, Leipart never met with Strasser. Hitler vetoed Strasser's plan to talk with the ADGB leader, and Strasser submitted to Hitler's will precisely because he did not want to break with the führer.[42]

Edgily aware of the ADGB's sundry suitors, party leaders realized they must meet the ADGB halfway on the issue of job creation.[43] In late August, with its Socialist Action program the SPD presented a draft bill for public works worth 1 million marks. It did not relinquish its principles, however. The SPD's plan was to be financed largely with higher taxes, not credit creation, and the bill did not provide for public works on the grand scale advocated by the unions. Even this modest gesture came only after difficult negotiations inside the Reichstag delegation and between the unions and the SPD.[44] In August a closed conference of forty union functionaries and forty party representatives discussed WTB once more. Wels chaired and Hilferding spoke for the SPD. A nonunion economist, Gerhard Colm, laid out the union viewpoint, and Woytinsky rebutted Hilferding's comments. Hilferding accused Colm and Woytinsky of "questioning the very foundations of our program, Marx's labor theory of value." When Woytinsky responded that WTB had neither a negative nor a positive relationship to Marxism, Wels accused him of implying that Hilferding was a liar. According to Woytinsky, "Hell broke out, a dozen people shouting." WTB was voted down by every party delegate except Fritz Baade.[45] The SPD's worldview was bound up with Marxist economics. Suspicion of a challenge to its premises triggered deep feelings in

Social Democrats, especially in times so hostile to their whole outlook. Hilferding, advocate of a flexible political approach to Papen's regime, as an economist stood rigidly by his Marxist guns.

ADGB leaders were not satisfied with the compromise bill on public works that emerged from these negotiations. During the fall, Leipart made public and private remarks distancing the ADGB from the SPD.[46] His public avowal, "Our decisions are free from political and partisan considerations," elicited speculation in the bourgeois press about an SPD/ADGB split, praise from Otto Strasser, and private protests from Social Democrats.[47] Angered by Papen's attack on labor contracts, the ADGB was nevertheless intrigued by his plan for economic recovery, which, like WTB, involved a rapid infusion of credit. The government's plan gave subsidies directly to industry, rather than stimulating market demand through public hiring. Still, in *Die Arbeit* Woytinsky noted similarities between Papen's deficit-financing plan and WTB.[48] Tarnow deplored the antilabor parts of Papen's September 4 decree but explained that the unions supported the decision to intervene actively in the economy.[49] In general, ADGB utterances in the fall combined defenses of working-class rights and attacks on capitalism with assertions of the unions' political autonomy and coy intimations of their desire to be cooperative. The ADGB thus cracked the door to the government even while it rejected "the premises and solutions" of Papen's program.[50]

The response of the Reichsbanner to the July events was even more complex than the ADGB's. Höltermann fumed against "spiritually corrupt weaklings" who could not see beyond the parliamentary stage. He began to consider uncoupling the Reichsbanner from the SPD.[51] His anger, and that at lower levels of the Reichsbanner, prompted a double course. The Reichsbanner took new steps to provide military training to the membership. Shooting exercises were required. A technical department under two former Prussian police officers coordinated these efforts.[52] This militant activity was coupled, oddly enough, with an effort to improve the Reichsbanner's relationship with the army. Höltermann and his comrades wanted to ensure that the Reichswehr did not end up on the wrong side in a Nazi seizure of power. For this reason, he met with Schleicher several times. Moreover, the Reichsbanner decided to take part in the National Board for Youth Training (Reichskuratorium für Jugendertüchtigung) directed by Schleicher's friend, General Joachim von Stülpnagel. Initiated by presidential order in September, this program set up voluntary camps where young men received physical training from army officers. All paramilitary organizations were encouraged to take part. Höltermann believed the Reichsbanner should participate in

order to get the best possible training for young members.[53] In addition
to numerous Reichsbanner functionaries, ADGB leaders, Otto Braun,
and SPD neorevisionists such as Theo Haubach backed the decision to
participate.[54]

Party leaders looked askance at the Reichsbanner's heightened military
emphasis and plans for defense training. While they did not prevent it
from engaging in such activities under its own auspices, Wels virtually
ordered the Reichsbanner out of the Reichskuratorium.[55] Party authorities believed (correctly) that the youth training program was a step toward
the introduction of general conscription and, thence, German rearmament. As did SPD leftists and Aufhäuser of the AfA-Bund, Wels viewed the
issue from a political perspective: the SPD could not oppose Papen and
then join one of his programs, much less a militaristic one.[56] Rank and file
Reichsbanner members evidently agreed. In Munich they were eager for
military training but balked at the idea of participating in Stülpnagel's
program.[57] On the other side, Otto Braun felt the Reichsbanner *should*
participate on political grounds because "we have to grasp every hold we
have" to prevent the "forces for an authoritarian state" from gaining
complete control of the republic's infrastructure. At least some supporters
of the Reichskuratorium in the ADGB, such as Erdmann, viewed participation, instead, as an opportunity to force the SPD to rethink its antimilitarism. Höltermann shared Braun's justification of participation, not
Erdmann's.[58] He shied, however, from using a political argument of any
sort to convince skeptics in the SPD and instead assured them that participation was a technical matter.[59] From mid-October to late November
Höltermann adopted an aggressive tone against SPD resistance to participation.[60] Intervening in Höltermann's favor, the ADGB pressured the
party executive to drop its opposition, but to no avail. After several weeks
of tense negotiations, Höltermann decided against participation "for the
sake of Iron Front unity."[61]

Not only this conflict raised the old conundrum of the SPD's attitude to
the Reichswehr, military defense of the country, and, more generally,
nationalism. In August, Schleicher called for the institution of a three-
month militia to correct the military imbalance imposed on Germany
since World War I. Wilhelm Sollmann, a neorevisionist Reichstag deputy,
argued that the SPD should endorse this proposal. Backed by the rightist
Wilhelm Keil, Sollmann convinced the delegation to set up a commission
to reconsider the SPD's stand on equal German armament (as opposed to
European disarmament).[62] In the meantime, the delegation and the party
executive supported parity for Germany but rejected rearmament and a
militia. Despite impulses in the other direction, on the whole the SPD

reaffirmed its opposition to German nationalism as part of its retreat from involvement in bourgeois politics.[63]

One should not overemphasize conflict inside Social Democracy during Papen's chancellorship. When Wels saw signs of independent striving in the Reichsbanner, he demanded discipline, and Höltermann stepped into line. With the trade unions, however, Wels played the conciliatory role. He defended Leipart and Tarnow against the charge of having dealt with Gregor Strasser.[64] Moreover, the differences over economic recovery seemed to be narrowing. Many unionists demoted public works in favor of radical economic change. In August, even Fritz Tarnow told the ADGB national committee, "We have to switch from evolutionary to revolutionary socialism."[65] Not only did Communist competition plague the unions too, but personal ties among the SPD, the Free Trade Unions, and the Reichsbanner were too numerous for the fraternal associations to escape the radicalization affecting the SPD. Nonetheless, it is noteworthy that Wels stressed the unity of Social Democracy at internal gatherings as well as in public, while Leipart and even Aufhäuser told fellow unionists that the Iron Front was "only a name," not an "umbrella organization" that could "infringe on the independence" of its constituent parts.[66]

Excitement about the new-style propaganda, if not about the Iron Front, had dissipated at the lower levels of the movement. On one hand, the SPD executive found that "rally announcements and propaganda almost exclusively use the designation 'Iron Front,'" a practice that threatened to "push the name of our party from public consciousness." As a result of a decision from above, the Iron Front was not emphasized in the election campaign, except in Saxony.[67] On the other hand, Social Democrats had to be exhorted to wear the *Drei Pfeile*.[68] Mierendorff continued to argue for the new methods but admitted they were ridiculed among the ranks as copies of Nazi practices, while the three arrows were denigrated as "hollow."[69] Such cynicism was a sign of a veritable crisis of confidence that engulfed the party after the summer's traumatic events.[70] In the fall, demoralization and bitterness spread, making it difficult to summon the energy for the new election effort.[71] *Vorwärts* felt obliged to deny that Berlin's contentious district conference in October justified rumors in the bourgeois and Communist press about "internal unrest." Correspondents in *Das Freie Wort* told of rank and file "resentment," "exhaustion," and "despair."[72] Campaign costs and skyrocketing legal expenses for hundreds of comrades arrested in street fights (or just campaigning) provoked incessant internal pleas for money and forced cutbacks in local campaign efforts.[73]

Indefatigable, neorevisionists intensified their efforts to rescue the SPD from enslavement to tradition and rigid organizational thinking. At the summer's end, Kurt Schumacher in the Reichstag delegation and Karl Meitmann in the party council tried to infuse younger blood into the SPD's leading committees. With leftists Fritz Ebert and Toni Pfülf, Schumacher managed to secure a seat on the Reichstag delegation executive. Meitmann, however, failed to get Arthur Crispien (fifty-seven years old) and Wilhelm Dittmann (fifty-eight) removed from the party executive.[74] In Württemberg, Schumacher's bailiwick, sixty-two-year-old Keil decided to forgo reelection to the Reichstag in November. No one tried to dissuade him. His even older colleague, Karl Hildenbrand, a member of the national executive, was not endorsed by the *Land* executive, which instead honored Schumacher with second place on Württemberg's list.[75] Demands for the immediate rejuvenation of the national and the local leadership arose in districts as diverse as Berlin and Munich. In Leipzig the plea for "democratization of the party" was put forward with new insistence.[76]

The most controversial case of a local effort to revitalize Social Democracy's parliamentary representation occurred in Hamburg, where Karl Meitmann led the SPD. Social Democrats in Hamburg dropped ADGB cochairman Peter Grassmann from their Reichstag list, saying a younger candidate must head the November electoral effort. This affront infuriated union leaders as the most flagrant sign of a wider, and growing, "anti–trade union tendency" in the SPD. The ADGB asked the party executive to intervene to restore Grassmann to his rightful place at the top of Hamburg's list.[77] Far from put off by this request, the executive responded with alacrity, for it "decidedly did not endorse developments" in Hamburg. Pulling out the big guns, it sent two of its members to the city "to settle the matter." The Hamburg SPD rebuffed this blatant attempt to overrule the local right to select candidates.[78] The ADGB had to make do with the addition of Grassmann to the national list and with the executive's promise to convince the next party congress "to grant the national executive greater power" in the selection process. A disgruntled Leipart detected in the Hamburg affair an antiunion plot organized by party elements who preferred "radical phrases" to the unions' "realpolitik."[79] Although the Left too was pressing for internal reforms, Leipart's biases distorted his perception of this incident. Meitmann, who masterminded the rebellion, was not only a neorevisionist but district chairman of the Reichsbanner. Moreover, Hamburg members replaced Grassmann not with a radical hothead but with Hans Staudinger, an economist in Prussia's Ministry of Trade and Commerce before July 20.[80] Far from a left-wing challenge to the unions, Hamburg's attempt at rejuvenation was coupled with an effort to convince the middle class that the SPD was not captive to narrow, interest-based politics. In general, the issue of organizational reform cut across inner political groupings. Confronted with demands for *Verjüngung*, party and union elites closed ranks against provincial reformers, both leftist and neorevisionist. When it came to participation on Papen's youth training board, on the other hand, rightist ADGB leaders and the revisionist Reichsbanner leadership crossed swords with party ideologues at different organizational levels.

Wilhelm Sollmann created the intraparty sensation of the season. In an article widely picked up by the Social Democratic press in December, he charged that from top to bottom the SPD was administered by men and (a few) women so burdened with daily tasks they could not get an overview of the political landscape. The executive committee required "political-intellectual" leaders, not "organization men" wrapped up in a "thousand small matters." The SPD needed not bureaucrats but leaders with a "will to power."[81] Sollmann had expressed the same view in *Neue Blätter* two years earlier to little effect; now his analysis corresponded to that of many activists. For this reason, his article generated heated remarks in the party council. Meitmann seconded his diagnosis of the SPD's malaise, while the leftist Georg Dietrich agreed that the organization suffered from "rigidity." Others denied the need for a shakeup. The SPD's much-maligned inflexibility, they said, had actually helped the organization survive recent traumas.[82] Wels, no doubt stung by Sollmann's critique, rejected a division between organizational and political leaders such as that, he pointedly remarked, of the Nazis. "If ever an organization has passed muster, it is the SPD," he stoutly averred. "To reform it without a clear plan would insult the simple people on whose shoulders the apparatus rests." Wels also denied the need to bring in younger leaders. Rather than foolishly cast aside experienced functionaries, the party should undertake a campaign to inform youth of their accomplishments. Nonetheless, in acknowledgment of the stir Sollmann had created, if not the validity of his points, the executive committee coopted him in January.[83]

Certainly, the organization was not falling apart. In September 1932, the SPD still had 971,499 members, though it had lost 12,618 over the previous three months alone.[84] Social Democrats showed "incredible discipline" in following the leadership's commands even when, as Wels admitted, they wondered why it did not tread a straight path toward a clear goal.[85] Alongside demoralization appeared signs of dedication and even innovation. In the autumn Social Democrats in Saxony, Bavaria, the Rhineland, the Ruhr, and Hamburg began to imitate Communist methods of organizing the unemployed by having them meet and distribute propaganda separately and argue with opponents at street corners and halls where the unemployed gathered.[86] Some local districts and the national propaganda office systematically directed propaganda at non-proletarian social strata.[87] After the November elections brought more SPD gains in rural areas, the national executive finally prepared to carry out intensive rural agitation. Urban Social Democrats traveled into the countryside on "Rural Red Sundays" to spread the word. A week-long training course in rural affairs had been attended by fifteen hundred activists by January 1933. The Reichstag delegation introduced bills that promoted the economic interests of small settlers and leaseholders, while Social Democratic consumer coops began to deal directly with farmers. The first issues of several publications for farmers appeared at the end of 1932.[88] As a rule, though, energy and innovation did not emanate from the center (organizational or ideological) but from districts dominated by neorevisionists (Hamburg and, to a lesser extent, Munich) or leftists (Berlin, Chemnitz, and Leipzig). These cities held relatively more rallies in the slack November election campaign. In Munich, for example, the activity of the clubs for the unemployed helped compensate for the lethargy of other party groups.[89]

To the public the most obvious mark of Social Democracy during the fall campaign was its radicalization. As did bourgeois observers, Socialists sensed that the call to "save the republic" had gone "flat" and no longer called forth an "echo" among left-oriented workers.[90] They did not stop defending the republic and "freedom," but they now declared, "Socialism is the goal!"[91] Especially from Saxony came the determination to pull the party back to its proletarian roots. However, even the centrist Hanover *Volkswacht* described November 9 (anniversary of the declaration of the republic in 1918) as the "beginning of the proletarian revolution."[92] In campaign speeches, Aufhäuser, Wels, and Löbe emphasized the serious-ness of the SPD's "offensive for socialism."[93] Nevertheless, Socialist Action landed with a thud, not the resounding boom anticipated by Social Demo-crats.[94] Provincial activists charged that the program came too late. *Vor-wärts* had to explain why only now, instead of in 1918–19, the SPD advocated the transition to socialism: then, circumstances forced it to share power with bourgeois partners, whereas in late 1932, objective and subjective factors appeared favorable.[95]

Several other trends characterized the November campaign. Recogniz-ing that the NSDAP too was in the grips of a financial and political crisis, Social Democrats predicted that it would lose votes in November. Conse-quently, the party press devoted much less space to the Nazis. The cam-paign slogan "Freiheit" was seen as a counter to the Papen regime's authoritarian proclivities more than to the Nazi threat. For the first time, the KPD was publicly acknowledged as the main rival.[96] In order not to alienate radical workers and to show its disdain for the Communists as a real electoral threat, the SPD daily press had demonstratively ignored the KPD during campaigns. Not only KPD electoral gains but the activity of the RGO and Communist infiltration of Social Democratic cultural organizations, and even the party itself, counseled against such contemptuous disregard.[97] Several days before the November polling, the *Leipziger Volkszeitung* prominently featured a sketch of a muscle-bound worker with raised fist who admonished, "You must stick with us! You dare not vote Communist! It's a question of freedom!" In Bavaria campaign posters proclaimed, "Fascism feeds on the stupidity of the KPD!"[98] Taking the opposite tack, the committee that organized the SPD's municipal campaigns in Saxony offered to attach their candidate lists to those of the Communists (Communists rejected the offer). Only in little Binow in Pomerania did the SPD and KPD run a common list. For its part, under Comintern pressure and emboldened by its gains in July, the KPD hardened its stance against the SPD and the ADGB, proclaiming in September that there was absolutely no difference between the SPD and the NSDAP.[99]

In addition to the misfire of its socialist initiative and the tendency of diverse districts to strike out in different directions, the SPD suffered political embarrassments during the fall election campaign. In October the German supreme court ruled on Prussia's case against the *Staatsstreich*. The court decided that the Prussian ministers had not been negligent of their duties, as claimed by the Reich, and that they had the right to represent Prussia in the Reichstag and Reichsrat. While handing Papen a political slap, however, the court also bowed to the prerogatives of power and accepted the Reich's right to intervene in a situation in which public order was threatened. Thus, Commissioner Bracht retained his authority. Irritated by this moral vindication of Braun's regime, Papen sabotaged the court ruling by denying Braun's request for control of justice and the police. In response, Braun, who suddenly appeared at work after months at home, politely appealed to Hindenburg for "gentlemanly treatment," while Bavaria's conservative premier, in contrast, castigated Papen for trying to "Prussify" Germany.[100] Braun planned to reconstruct Prussian autonomy gradually, but the public took his meekness as one more sign of lethargy and resignation. His behavior seems to have hurt the SPD's turnout on November 6.[101] Wels defended Braun but admitted, "The party is not pleased." Hilferding, Breitscheid, and the leftists Künstler and Sender all argued that with nothing to lose in Prussia, Braun should have lambasted Papen rather than let a southern states-rightist steal the glory.[102] Once more, Prussian Social Democrats and the national party marched out of step.

Adding to the SPD's headaches, Berlin transportation workers walked off the job on November 2 in protest against a wage reduction. The Berlin Transportation Authority (BVG) employed 23,000 workers, which made it the third largest employer in Germany and the largest municipal enterprise in the world. The ADGB had managed to organize only one-third of its work force. With roughly 1,300 members each, the RGO and the NSBO enjoyed unusually high support among its drivers and repairmen. When 78 percent of the 18,500 workers who showed up to vote endorsed a strike, RGO members walked out, carrying most others with them. The Berlin strike was only the most spectacular of a rash of small work stoppages that swept Germany that fall, racking up impressive successes. This strike wave showed workers' increasing readiness to fight wage cuts, in contrast with their quiescence during the Brüning years.[103] These strikes often began spontaneously or under Communist urging, but as a rule Free Trade Union officials assumed leadership of them.[104] Despite this trend, the ADGB, caught off guard by rank and file militancy in Berlin, refused to bless the wildcat action at the BVG.[105] The KPD's eagerness to step into the breach surprised no one, but the active cooperation of the Nazi factory cell organization raised eyebrows. Union supporters stayed on the job while strikers, led by Communists and Nazis, attacked streetcars, sent passengers home, and snarled traffic. Four strikers were killed in fights with the police. On November 8 the dwindling strike was called off, unresolved; but it succeeded as a political maneuver: the SPD suffered at the polls on November 6.[106] Wels had to defend the ADGB against party leftists disgusted by its bungling of the strike.[107]

The strike did not improve the electoral position of one of its instigating parties. On November 6, for the first time in four years, the Nazi vote declined. Two million Germans fewer chose the NSDAP than had three months earlier. It captured only 33.6 percent compared with 37.8 percent of the electorate and lost 34 Reichstag seats. Voter weariness hurt the NSDAP: 80.6 percent went to the polls as compared with 84.1 percent in July. The Nazis' socially radical line and antigovernment stance since July had alienated conservative voters. Financially as well as emotionally drained by constant electioneering that had produced no concrete political results, Hitler's party entered several months of internal crisis. The DNVP benefited from the NSDAP's slump. From 37 seats it grew to 52. The DVP also came out with 4 more seats, raising its delegation to 11. Altogether, parties friendly to Papen had picked up a million votes since July.[108] Social Democrats read the November 6 returns with decidedly

mixed feelings. The NSDAP slide was good news undiminished by Papen's minor victory. The combined "Marxist" vote of 37.3 percent now
topped the Nazis' 33.6 percent. That was scant comfort, however, given
that a steep decline in the SPD vote was matched by an abrupt rise in the
KPD tally: the SPD dropped 708,000 votes; the KPD picked up 611,000.
Social Democracy garnered 20.7 percent of the ballots to the KPD's 17.1
percent; with 121 representatives in the Reichstag, the SPD faced 100
Communist deputies. The parliamentary crisis was still not overcome.
Even now Papen held the allegiance of only a small minority in the
Reichstag. With 196 deputies, the NSDAP formed the largest block. The
Center Party had lost 5 of its 75 seats, so even a Black-Brown coalition was
no longer possible.[109]

Several days after the election, the party council convened in Berlin to
discuss the political situation. Wels took Social Democratic losses calmly,
referring to that old favorite, the losses of May 1924. Arthur Crispien
shared Wels's belief that the masses would eventually return to an SPD
in opposition. In contrast, Breitscheid and every leftist speaker were
alarmed by Social Democratic losses. Georg Dietrich (from Thuringia)
said with despair that the SPD had no drawing power to its left or right.
The leftists' solution, surprisingly enough, was centralization of decision
making within the Iron Front in the hands of the party executive committee. They blamed the Reichsbanner and the trade unions for having
weakened the Socialist front by dallying with the Papen government.[110]
No one, on left or right, doubted the significance of the NSDAP's set-
back.[111] Expressing the general view, Wels noted, "We fought five election
battles [in 1932] under the slogan 'Smash Hitler' and in the fifth one he
was beaten." According to Ernst Heilmann, Nazi confidence in victory
had been broken. Franz Künstler credited the party's "tactics and politics"
with this feat. Strikingly, most participants simply did not mention the
NSDAP. Heilmann alone ritually intoned that the "struggle must go
on."[112] Social Democrats of all persuasions believed the acute threat from
Nazism had been overcome and the NSDAP thrown on the defensive.[113]

Yet, all agreed, new perils loomed. First of all, Papen's government
posed a grave danger to democracy. Wels, in fact, spoke of "Papen fascism." Heilmann argued that the SPD should "not distinguish the struggle against fascism from the struggle against the presidential regime."
Many speakers called for the sharpest possible opposition to Papen, but
the party elite in the Reich and Prussia—Wels, Hilferding, Breitscheid,
Severing, and Heilmann—wanted to prolong the new Reichstag's life as
long as possible, if only to give the SPD a breathing spell from elections.
Although they suggested a campaign in tandem with the Center Party to

limit the scope of Article 48, several warned against playing what was now the KPD's "game" of voting to bring down the regime before the Reichstag even met. Berlin leftist Mathilde Wurm alone wanted an immediate vote of no-confidence, although all agreed that the SPD dare not appear to tolerate Papen.[114] Not surprisingly, several days later the SPD delegation turned down an invitation from the chancellor to discuss the parliamentary situation.[115]

The other danger to the republic and the greatest one to the SPD, participants concurred, was the KPD. They feared that the KPD might obliterate the SPD if it once pulled even with it.[116] Sensitivity to Communist criticism was one reason for opposition to participation in the Reichswehr's Reichskuratorium.[117] To counter Communist influence, Hilferding said, the SPD must make clear its determination to defend working-class interests. Disagreement arose on the question of a united front. Not only party leftists but also Friedrich Stampfer and Karl Meitmann wanted to emphasize the need for unity and make a sustained appeal to Communist workers, if not to KPD leaders. Hilferding, Wels, and Arthur Crispien advocated, instead, an aggressively antagonistic line against the KPD.[118] This difference was symptomatic of a broader conflict over how to frame the party's radical opposition. Hilferding, seconded by Breitscheid, proposed a campaign stressing the SPD's absolute commitment to democracy. They wanted to dig out the Weimar constitution from under Article 48.[119] Echoing a growing sentiment among intellectuals and activists, leftists on the party council believed the SPD should distance itself from "Weimar" and emphasize the new goals of popular democracy and socialism. For them, political democracy had proven itself inadequate; social and economic democracy stood on the agenda.[120] They also disagreed with both moderates and rightists about the tactical and strategic alternatives open to the SPD for defense of democracy of any kind. Hilferding and Heilmann argued that extraparliamentary action was not a viable option, so party propaganda should shy away from threats to use it. Leftists, again voicing views that could be heard throughout the party, chided the leaders for their enthrallment with "parliamentarism." Lipinski, Sender, Lehmann, and Oskar Edel insisted that in a crisis the SPD should use (unspecified) extraparliamentary means to defend democratic rights and carry out the SPD's greater goals.[121]

Defeated a year earlier, the traditional Left had recovered its old pluck. Delegates from Saxony, Thuringia, and Berlin dominated discussion at these council meetings. Their strategic agenda—social democracy, the Iron Front, and extraparliamentary orientation—coincided with that of neorevisionists.[122] Both tendencies pressed the centrist leadership to adopt an active policy; yet the Left wanted to pull Social Democracy back to its proletarian roots, while, after the heady hiatus of the spring offensive, neorevisionists pleaded with renewed urgency that the SPD must abandon the old dualities—"class against state" or "proletariat against *Bürgertum*"—and address the nation.[123] The two flanks labored on some issues in tandem and in other cases at cross purposes in their drive to galvanize the centrist party elite. On the whole, the Left had more success because it spoke the traditional language of Social Democracy and seemed more in touch with the party ranks. The leadership was turning hesitantly to the left after a decade and a half of political responsibility. The sheer single-mindedness of the Nazi drive for power and the precipitous collapse of bourgeois liberalism affected the outlook of men such as Wels, Hilferding, and Breitscheid. Hilferding declared that when the SPD was again able to exercise power, unlike in 1918–19 it would know how to wield it. Nonetheless, the essential passivity of the leadership's political conception kept it from confronting the current situation aggressively. Wels concluded the meeting with a prophecy redolent of classic radical abstentionism, declaring, "We won't make a revolution—it's coming."[124]

The Schleicher Interlude

On November 10 Wels warned council members that the political situation could change from one day to the next.[125] He was right. Three weeks later, before the newly elected Reichstag even convened, Hindenburg reluctantly replaced the universally despised Papen with a new chancellor—General Kurt von Schleicher. The man who had hoisted the obscure Papen to the chancellorship now stepped to center stage. Since July Schleicher had been the focus of political rumor. He has been the subject of historical debate ever after. Many of his contemporaries as well as historians argued that Schleicher wanted to create a *Querbindung* (political liaison) between the Reichswehr, all the trade union federations, and the Gregor Strasser wing of the Nazi party.[126] Recently, however, several scholars have presented evidence showing that Schleicher neither actively courted the ADGB before he became chancellor nor tried to divide the NSDAP.[127] Schleicher did entertain corporatist notions, believing popular support for an authoritarian government could be forged through good relations with, and perhaps the participation of, economic organizations like the Free and the Catholic trade unions.[128] He was, above all, interested in winning the support of the nationalist NSDAP—and of the whole party, not only its moderate wing.

As chancellor, Schleicher presented himself as the man in the middle, determined to bridge opposing interests. Upon taking office, he announced that his contacts with the NSDAP would continue but that his larger aim was an "alliance with the unions and party leaders of all stripes." He retained all of Papen's ministers except one, thus assuring businessmen of the government's basic conservatism. On the other hand, the cabinet member dropped was Interior Minister Gayl, hated by the Center Party and the SPD as the architect of the coup against Prussia. He also appointed Günther Gereke, an advocate of public works schemes, commissioner of public works.[129] In his first address to the nation, Chancellor Schleicher described himself as neither a capitalist nor a socialist. As proof of his goodwill to the organized working class, he reinstated the inviolability of labor contracts rescinded by Papen's emergency decree.[130] Schleicher also renewed his contacts with the ADGB. On November 28, not yet chancellor, he met with Leipart and Eggert. This time the trade union leaders consulted with the SPD executive beforehand. Together they agreed that the SPD would not tolerate Schleicher should he ask for support, which he did not. He wanted to hear the union leaders' economic recommendations. They urged him to institute a large-scale public works program.[131] The historian Axel Schildt has argued that this amicable chat contributed to Schleicher's decision to accept the chancellorship.[132] Certainly, Schleicher's initial acts as chancellor pleased the ADGB, gratification the union press did not hide. The *Gewerkschafts-Zeitung* stressed the "political neutrality" of the trade unions toward the state and "all parties."[133] Further meetings between ADGB leaders and Schleicher took place, but no concrete form of cooperation emerged.[134] Simultaneously, contacts were renewed between the ADGB and the RDI (which also supported Schleicher's policies, in particular his rejection of Papen's autarkic tendencies).[135]

ADGB overtures to the regime and the organization's coolness to the SPD (and the Iron Front) fueled foreign and domestic speculation that the ADGB was poised to become a pillar of the presidential state and a partner in Versailles revisionism.[136] The ADGB's behavior, and the reactions it evoked, alarmed Social Democrats. The Reichstag deputation voted to condemn Leipart's flirtation with Schleicher.[137] The union ranks too expressed irritation not only with this friendliness but with signs of a more positive attitude toward prominent industrialists.[138] In his year-end address to union members Leipart felt obliged to respond to "reproaches" for negotiating with Schleicher and reaffirm the decades-long unity of the SPD and the trade unions.[139]

The party leadership itself was divided about how to behave toward the enigmatic chancellor.[140] In a meeting with Breitscheid on November 28, the soon-to-be chancellor wondered whether the SPD would "resort to the barricades" if the Reichstag were dissolved and new elections were postponed until spring with the assurance that in the meantime he would not meddle with the constitution. Breitscheid did not threaten barricades but vowed that the SPD would react against such a move "with all available legal means."[141] Responding to a breach of the constitution and bringing in a no-confidence motion against Schleicher, however, were two different matters. When the Reichstag delegation voted in early December on whether to fell Schleicher immediately, more than twenty deputies opposed such an action. Peter Grassmann, Severing, and Hilferding argued against a no-confidence vote, while Wels spoke for it. In the end the SPD held back its motion so the government could pass several bills before the Christmas recess.[142] The SPD's ambivalent reaction to Schleicher was evident in its press coverage. He fared much better than his predecessor, who, in fact, remained the favorite target of Social Democratic ire. Leading Social Democrats recognized that Schleicher did not belong to the "rabidly antidemocratic and antisocial circle around Papen."[143] But his role in the coup against Prussia, his retention of most of Papen's ministers, his relations with the NSDAP, his apparent effort to entice the ADGB away from the SPD, and his military status made Social Democrats deeply suspicious of him.[144] Given the great gulf between Schleicher and the SPD, he could not, and evidently did not, expect the kind of support the SPD had offered Brüning.[145] Still, the SPD's blindness to the severity of the underlying political crisis, and especially to the power vacuum in which Schleicher operated, hardened the inflexibility of the party's stance toward his government.[146] Party authorities believed Schleicher would be around for some time and that Hindenburg would continue to oppose Hitler's demand for power.[147]

In the first weeks of Schleicher's tenure the Social Democratic leaders grew more, not less, hopeful that the worst was over. Wels told the party council, "I'm optimistic about future developments. Though I don't see the economic crisis slackening, neither do I see catastrophe at the door." According to Stampfer, the SPD felt it could again flex its muscles, although only negatively for the moment.[148] The illusion of calm created by Schleicher's relatively good relations with the Reichstag and by a Christmas "civic truce" in the streets fooled other observers too, including many businessmen and the liberal press. Schleicher himself failed to notice that he teetered over an abyss.[149] The continuing Nazi electoral decline in state elections fed hopes that the nadir had been passed. On New Year's Day, *Vorwärts* wrote that the "Hitler business" was not yet finished, but like the Boulanger craze in France by 1889, its heyday was over.[150] One prominent Social Democrat recognized the precariousness of the situation. On January 6, Otto Braun went to Schleicher with a drastic plan to save the republic. Braun suggested Schleicher lift the Reich decree over Prussia; Braun would again take over state business. Schleicher would dissolve the Reichstag, he the Landtag, and they would postpone elections until the spring. Meanwhile they would jointly combat the NSDAP. Hitler's party, on the decline and in rough financial straits, could now be crushed, Braun reasoned. As a result, workable parliaments would return. Braun was willing to break with his party and the constitution to smash the NSDAP, but Schleicher refused. Not only had he just begun new negotiations with Gregor Strasser to make *him* minister-president of Prussia, but he also had no desire to reestablish Prussian autonomy.[151]

The new year, rung in with balmy editorials, soon brought a chill wind. On January 4, Papen and Hitler began a series of negotiations aimed at toppling Schleicher and putting themselves in power.[152] Papen and Oskar Hindenburg put sustained pressure on the elderly president to relinquish his opposition to Hitler. Hindenburg's Junker friends filled his ear with their hatred of Schleicher's agrarian settlement plan. Several powerful generals told the impressionable president of their favorable inclinations toward Hitler. The Nazis exerted themselves extraordinarily to win votes in the tiny state of Lippe on January 15, and when they succeeded, trumpeted this as a great triumph.[153] Meanwhile, the battle for Hitler's allegiance fought by Gregor Strasser, on one side, and Göring and Goebbels, on the other, finally ended with Strasser's defeat and resignation as head of the NSDAP's party organization.

At last Schleicher recognized the danger he was in. He abandoned his effort to convince the NSDAP to accept a lesser role in the government. Only now did he try to form an anti-Nazi front. On January 26, Schleicher met one last time with ADGB leaders Eggert and Grassmann, whose ardor for his regime had cooled because he had done nothing to reduce unemployment.[154] The chancellor posed essentially the same question to them that he had presented to Breitscheid two months earlier. Would they assent to dissolution of the Reichstag without new elections until October? Their answer was an adamant "no."[155] Several days earlier at a party gathering in Berlin Breitscheid had reiterated his warning against constitutional experiments.[156] The Iron Front stood united again.

It is easy to condemn the sterile legalism of the leaders of the Social Democratic movement, but Schleicher was also at fault.[157] He acted too late and too suddenly to expect Social Democratic support for a breach of the constitution. Moreover, the SPD could not have saved him at this point. On January 28, Hindenburg refused Schleicher the power to dissolve the Reichstag, and the chancellor resigned. While the anti-Schleicher political intrigue played itself out behind closed doors, the SPD executive and leaders of the Reichstag delegation and the ADGB met early on January 30 in the Reichstag building. The gathered leaders seemed at last to realize that "catastrophe was at the door." Stampfer proposed an appeal to Hindenburg that would assure SPD readiness to support any regime that would end anarchy in Germany and reinstate constitutional conditions. He left the meeting to telephone *Vorwärts's* press room with this message for the evening edition. As he stepped into the hall, he heard wild running and shouting in the hallways of the parliament building. Adolf Hitler had been appointed chancellor of Germany.[158]

In the Grip of the Enemy:
Principle versus Opportunism

During the political uncertainty of late January, Red Berlin braced itself for the worst. The SPD encouraged a defiant mood. On January 29 a huge rally proclaimed "Berlin remains Red!" and warned against a coup, Hitler's appointment, or any attempt to rob the people of their rights. The resolution of the crisis only intensified the city's nervousness. "Tremendous tension blankets the capital, excitability runs high," wrote a correspondent for *Das Reichsbanner* four days after Hitler's appointment.[159] The tumultuous victory celebrations of the Nazis fed the frustration and anger of working-class Berlin. The mood of the masses, a leader of the metalworkers recalled, was militant.[160] Many believed the SPD would summon them to topple Hitler.[161] At least some lower functionaries seemed to feel they had to give their leadership backbone, as suggested by exhortations for "union and party leaders to wear the *Drei Pfeile*" immediately after Hitler's appointment.[162]

Meanwhile the leaders deliberated. On January 30, before the news of Hitler's appointment arrived, Siegfried Aufhäuser passionately rejected yet another admonition to wait. He had opposed resistance on July 20, but he believed the time for action had come. The Iron Front must prepare for the "defensive struggle." Carl Litke, a Reichstag deputy and cochairman of the Berlin district, also wanted to call mass actions. These two fought a losing battle against overwhelming sentiment in favor of restraint. Union leader Eggert wondered what would be the goal of an extraparliamentary movement if Hitler and Papen came to power constitutionally. Otto Braun opposed a general strike because of unemployment. Hilferding, "astounded by the polemic against 'waiting,'" found a strike call precipitous before a new government was named.[163] When the leaders gathered after Hitler's appointment, however, they again concluded that the time had not arrived and officially decided against mass protests. Höltermann, present at this conclave, endorsed passivity, just as he had on July 20.[164]

On February 5, Wels called a meeting with trade union leaders to discuss the issue again. Even more than on July 20, he appeared confused about what to do. The working class was very agitated, he said, "Constant inquiries come from the shops about when they should walk out." Alluding to a one-hour strike in Lübeck that protested Julius Leber's arrest, Wels feared some similar provocation might "start the ball rolling." If an "avalanche" were imminent, he wanted to make sure the SPD, not the KPD, sat atop it. Grassmann assured Wels that this time the ADGB had made the proper preparations. Nonetheless, union leaders opposed even a day-long protest strike, Leipart claiming that the employed entertained little enthusiasm for a walkout.[165] In a speech before a large Iron Front rally, Grassmann acknowledged that a burning desire for action existed, but he claimed that the time for a general strike still had not arrived.[166] With no strong urge of his own to call a strike, Wels deferred once again to the ADGB's expertise.

Party and union leaders' understanding of the situation influenced their decision not to strike. In a lengthy address to the party council on January 31 (distributed as a pamphlet a few days later), Breitscheid presented this analysis. First, he laid great importance on the fact that the new cabinet was politically divided. In it, three Nazi ministers—Hitler, Interior Minister Wilhelm Frick, and Minister without Portfolio Göring— faced nine conservatives, including Vice-Chancellor Papen, Economics and Agriculture Minister Hugenberg, and Reichswehr Minister Werner von Blomberg. Hindenburg and these traditional reactionaries, Breitscheid said, hoped to limit the fascists' power. Germany had not a fascist regime but a dictatorship of capital.[167] "We are now in the class struggle in its purest form," Breitscheid warned. No doubt Hitler, like Mussolini before him, would maneuver to gain total power, but Breitscheid was sure that the cabinet members, like thieves dividing their spoils, would be at each others' throats before he succeeded.[168]

In the meantime, Breitscheid argued, the working class must wait for the contradictions within the new regime to ripen. If workers took to the barricades immediately, the cabinet would unite against its democratic enemies. For the moment the regime wanted to retain some semblance of parliamentary government. At Hitler's request, Hindenburg had dissolved the Reichstag and set new elections for March 5. As long as the new chancellor did not step off constitutional ground, Breitscheid maintained, the cue for extraparliamentary action had not come. If the SPD moved precipitously, the workers' movement would lose its press, its meetings, and all its rights. Instead, Social Democrats must watch for Hitler's breach of the constitution and prepare for resistance. The SPD's slogan, Breitscheid declared, must be "Preparedness is everything!"[169]

Breitscheid noted the subdued foreign reaction to Hitler's accession to power. Europe, he pointed out, had grown accustomed to authoritarian government in Germany. He failed to see that a similar malaise afflicted German Social Democrats. Hitler's cabinet did not look qualitatively different from Papen's or Schleicher's. In the summer of 1931 the party leadership had insisted that Italian-style fascism was possible in Germany. Now, with Hitler in power, *Vorwärts* declared, "Germany is not Italy!" "Berlin is not Rome, Hitler is not Mussolini."[170] An SPD journalist lamented the contrast between earlier warnings about the Italian parallel and the inability to see in 1933 "that the end was at hand." "It was," he recalled, "as if the . . . insight were forgotten and a terrible confusion gripped responsible comrades."[171] It is also peculiar that Social Democrats found reassuring the regime's alliance of capitalists, Junkers, and Nazis, the Harzburg Front so dreaded earlier. Party leaders feared "plebeian fascism" more than "monarchical reaction," yet they also thought Nazism the weak partner in the pact, calculating that the rabid fascist Hitler would be outsmarted by the vicious procapitalist Hugenberg, who, they hoped, would not suppress all legal rights.[172] They grasped at other straws too. Hindenburg, the executive prayed, would stand by his oath to secure the constitution, even if he did ignore Wels's pleas to meet with him.[173] In addition, party authorities initially hoped the Reichswehr and the southern states, especially federalist Bavaria, would resist the creation of a unitary fascist state.[174]

The second reason for not calling a general strike, it should come as no surprise, was the split in the working class. The KPD, Breitscheid said, would stab the SPD in the back and turn even a limited strike into a bloody confrontation with the Reichswehr. The two parties needed to forge a new relationship, but first the KPD leadership must change its attitude.[175] From below, nonetheless, came pressure for the SPD to initiate a united front. Indeed, various sources suggest that in the ranks the desire for unity reached a fever pitch in the weeks surrounding Hitler's *Machtergreifung*.[176] At the top, Friedrich Stampfer (supported, in fact, by Breitscheid) was the main advocate of concrete steps to end the hostility between the two leftist parties.[177] During the week preceding January 30, Stampfer had made blunt appeals to the good will of Communist workers. When the Communists marched to protest a Nazi rally held in front of their national headquarters, Stampfer praised their discipline. The KPD's ranks struck him not as "subhuman" but as a poorer version of Social Democracy's troops. "We do not struggle against these Communist masses, but for them," he concluded, "all the more as many are the children of Social Democrats."[178] This article made an impression in Berlin's workplaces and pleased left-wing members of the Reichstag delegation and party council. The gesture was not, however, appreciated by the party and ADGB elites. Hilferding in particular was disturbed by Stampfer's personal campaign. After Hitler's appointment, Stampfer proposed a jointly led, limited strike to protest the new government, leaving his colleagues aghast over his naivete regarding the wily KPD.[179] Nonetheless, they did not prevent him from privately pursuing better relations with the Communists.

Stampfer had already begun this process. Convinced that German Communists would repulse any direct approach, Stampfer had contacted the Soviet ambassador in Berlin, telling him the SPD hoped to normalize relations with the Soviet Union. At the end of 1932, Stampfer and Ambassador L. M. Khinchuk began to hold discussions that excluded the KPD and that Khinchuk broke off in mid-January. Immediately after Hitler's accession to power, the KPD central committee instructed its functionaries that the struggle against Social Democracy would continue.[180] Within a few weeks, however, KPD leaders broached the idea of high-level contacts with the SPD. On February 27, a Communist sympathizer came to the editor of *Vorwärts* with the message that the KPD had known and approved of his talks with Khinchuk. Ernst Torgler and another leading Communist wanted to speak with Stampfer. The three were to meet the next day. That night the Reichstag building burned, Torgler was charged with masterminding the deed, and the KPD was suppressed. No direct discussions between the two groups of leaders ever took place.[181] At the local and provincial levels, meanwhile, offers of "unity from below" poured from the KPD. In general, provincial party and union officials declined these offers, though with mounting consternation and urgent requests for central direction.[182] Several joint demonstrations of Communists, Social Democrats, and Free Trade unionists took place. Social Democratic leaders did not forbid such activities but warned local functionaries to beware of the KPD's "unity maneuvers" and to remember that the "reaction wants to throw us into the same pot with the Bolsheviks."[183] In Bavaria, at least, SPD Reichstag candidates adopted a cordial attitude toward the KPD, while party authorities tended to oppose cooperation.[184]

Thus Social Democracy wove its way between the Nazi threat above and the Communist menace below. It adopted a tone of acid hostility to Hitler and his cabinet. In mobilizing its masses for the election, it sought to impress the new rulers with Socialist strength without actually challenging their authority. Hitler and his henchmen cut short this course with their first wave of terror. Over the next months abrupt escalations of repression were followed by periods of milder treatment. The SPD elite adjusted its strategy to this carrot and stick policy but stuck to its plan to exploit legal opportunities rather than organize resistance. The leadership hoped to hold the party together under conditions of semilegality until the regime collapsed.[185] During the early weeks of the Hitler cabinet, the SPD behaved as would an uncompromising opposition toward a repressive, but parliamentary, regime. Its campaign for the March election combined radical economic slogans with stirring calls for freedom and democratic rights. In big cities across the country, anger and energy emanated from the Social Democratic rank and file immediately after Hitler took power.[186] Taking advantage of this mood, the party organized rallies attended by many thousands at which rang out the vibrant, militant phrases of old. The campaign was conducted with amazing vigor in view of the internal slump in the fall and current harassment from outside.[187] Censors repeatedly banned party newspapers. Arthur Crispien, Wilhelm Dittmann, and Philipp Scheidemann, excoriated as "November criminals" for their role in the 1918 revolutionary government, could not speak publicly. The police broke up rallies when an especially snide phrase crossed a speaker's lips.[188] While the SPD managed to hold its own in its urban strongholds, its presence in the countryside was negligible because the SA and the SS swarmed over small towns and villages.[189] Repression made mass propaganda difficult but also fostered solidarity and zealous word-of-mouth agitation. It provoked as well a bravado that rested on a combination of complacency and the inability to imagine how bad things could get. In late February, after watching a film on Marxism, five hundred members of the Social Democratic movement for the unemployed in Munich talked about Hitler. The discussion leader assured the audience that "he can't squash Marxism, even Bismarck couldn't do that. . . . Repression can act as a hammer to forge unity in the working-class movement."[190]

On the night of February 27, the Reichstag building went up in flames. A psychotic Dutchman, Marinus van der Lubbe, was seized at the scene of the crime. German Communists were accused of being his coconspirators in an alleged "Red uprising," signaled by the fire. Van der Lubbe also implicated Social Democrats in the plans. A police dragnet scooped up hundreds of party functionaries; others went into hiding. The SPD press in Prussia was banned for two weeks but in fact never appeared again. By early March every Socialist newspaper in the country had been shut down.[191] Rallies were prohibited, posters were ripped off walls, and printing presses were smashed. The Nazis spewed out accusations against "Marxists," culminating on election morning with headlines blaring that the "traitor" Otto Braun had abandoned the faithful and fled to Switzerland.[192] According to Wels, these "blows" not only crippled the SPD organizationally but also broke the will to fight that had coursed through Social Democracy after Hitler's appointment.[193] Nonetheless, the party did comparatively well on March 5. It fell to 18.3 percent of the total because participation rose to 88 percent; yet it relinquished only 70,000 of its November votes and retained 120 seats. In Bavaria, the SPD actually picked up over 40,000 votes, almost all in urban districts. Even the KPD— its deputies under arrest, its apparatus in ruins—emerged with 12.3 percent and almost 5 million votes. Leftists, mainly working class, had registered loyalty to their parties one last time. The NSDAP received a whopping 17,277,328 ballots; yet with 43.9 percent of the electorate, the majority it had fought for so viciously still eluded it. Adding the DNVP's 8 percent, the regime, however, controlled a majority of the new chamber.[194]

After the election, isolated acts of terror continued, but in the Reich as a whole things calmed down. However, in Bavaria, whose conservative regime was deposed by force on March 9, persecution only now began. The order went out from Nazi Interior Minister Adolf Wagner to break up the Reichsbanner, the Iron Front, and the SAJ, confiscate their assets, and arrest all Reichsbanner leaders. Though many party functionaries and Reichstag deputies were taken into custody, outright suppression of the SPD was not the immediate goal. The main thrust of Bavarian, and Reich, actions against the SPD in March and April was the rapid, but piecemeal, exclusion of Social Democrats from state parliaments, city councils, and communal committees via maneuvers, threats, and repression. Simultaneously, charges of SPD complicity in the Reichstag fire were quietly dropped, and some members were released from prison.[195] Although the pretense of normality had been permanently rent, Social Democratic illusions died hard. The leadership's new hope was that with its majority the regime would feel confident enough to rule through parliament and allow the SPD a limited, but legal, existence on the edges of a semiauthoritarian state, similar to the years under Bismarck's Anti-Socialist Law. Stampfer waxed ecstatic over the SPD's performance on March 5. "Social Democracy stands firm," he declared in the Socialist International's newsletter, *International Information*. "A party that can

weather such a storm is as unshakable as a rock." The aging Kautsky
assessed the SPD's situation more soberly, conceding that "our opponents
are firmly in the saddle"; yet he was convinced the regime would crumble
under the weight of its incompetence. The masses, accustomed to democracy, would reject dictatorship. Until they did, the SPD should not call for
resistance.[196]

Within the confines of the party council, Wels appraised the SPD's
position in mid-March. In a rambling monologue, he oscillated between
depression and optimism. Twice he said, "We have been beaten and must
start afresh." As an organization man, he saw the devastating effects of the
loss of the party press. Not only were ten thousand SPD employees
without jobs or support, the party's lifeline was cut. He believed, however,
that the party's "elasticity" would allow it to survive even if outlawed, and
he emphasized, once more, that the cabinet, and even the Nazi leadership, was not homogeneous. To get the SPD press restored to legality,
comrades were advised to write Hindenburg and Papen. The party executive, he emphasized, supported neither groveling appeals for special
treatment nor defiant gestures that would only provoke reprisals.[197] Immediately after the Reichstag fire, fearing the SPD and the ADGB would
soon be outlawed, Wels had asked Leipart if the time to strike had not
arrived.[198] Now, three weeks later, Wels warned party lieutenants not to
entertain such rebellious thoughts themselves.

Its tortured course between resistance and adaptation did not keep the
SPD from registering its moral and political rejection of the regime.
Hitler, it turned out, wanted to use his majority in the Reichstag not to
govern through parliament but to have parliament confer on him the
right to rule without it. He needed, the chancellor explained, a four-year
law that would enable the government to dispense with constitutional
forms and limitations in dealing with the country's problems. That authority, he promised, would not be used to infringe on the rights of the
Reichstag or the presidency. Such a law required a two-thirds majority.
Every bourgeois party, including the Center Party with its indispensable
73 votes, agreed to grant Hitler this Enabling Act. The SPD refused this
request, but its delegation decided to attend the session in order to motivate its negative vote. Otto Wels insisted on delivering a speech setting
forth the party's position, despite warnings from bourgeois politicians
that his life would be endangered and offers from younger deputies to
take his place.[199]

On March 23 the Reichstag met in Berlin's Kroll opera house. Outside,
Stormtroopers formed a gauntlet down which Social Democrats had to
walk, taunted and threatened. The police intercepted Severing and Leber

on their way to the sitting. Eight Social Democratic deputies were already under arrest; Sollmann lay in the hospital after having been beaten by SA "auxiliary police," and others had gone into exile. Ninety-four Social Democrats faced a phalanx of 448 deputies ready to give Hitler full powers.[200] Stormtroopers stalked the aisles, screaming "We demand an Enabling Act—or there'll be a price to pay (*sonst gibt's Zunder*)."[201] Under this extraordinary pressure, Wels delivered his intrepid message on behalf of the SPD. He affirmed his party's desire to see Germany justly treated by other nations, but, he said, a national community could not be imposed by force. The people must have their rights. The government could now rule constitutionally; instead it sought to deprive the Reichstag of its powers. Social Democracy would gladly support economic measures in favor of the people. The NSDAP claimed to be carrying out a national revolution. However, positive achievements, not the destruction of the Reichstag, were the hallmarks of a genuine revolution. Social Democracy, in contrast, had accomplished much for Germans by opening public office to working people and, thus, to the new chancellor himself. National Socialism could not turn back the wheel of history, nor could the Enabling Act destroy the ideas of justice and equality, and freedom and socialism, which Social Democracy stood for. He ended with a salutation to the "persecuted and oppressed." Observers, Social Democratic and not, were moved by Wels's simple words.[202] The party scored a moral victory recognized by posterity; yet at the time Carlo Mierendorff, and presumably other neorevisionists and leftists, saw the speech as not defiant enough and as more evidence of the leadership's inability to mount an effective challenge.[203]

As if to confirm such views, a week later Wels took a step that showed readiness to bow to certain kinds of government pressure in order to protect the party organization. On March 25 Göring announced that the SPD press would not appear again until the international socialist press stopped publishing "false" reports about the persecution and mishandling of political prisoners in Germany. In response, Wels pleaded with Fritz Adler, the secretary of the Socialist International, to pull "exaggerated" stories. When the International bureau declared its intention to publicize any and all atrocities, Wels resigned in protest from the governing body of the Socialist International.[204]

The ADGB was not impressed by the party leadership's tightrope act. Far from disputing the plan to act as a legal opposition, it hoped to convince Hitler that the Free Trade Unions were not incompatible with his national revolution. Though initially hostile to the regime, they broadcast immediately that the unions would pay attention to "deeds" rather than be guided by "emotional viewpoints."[205] By mid-February Leipart decided that pragmatic considerations required the ADGB to adopt the vocabulary of the "new state." At a talk at the Hochschule für Politik in Berlin, he warned the government not to shut out the working class, saying that attacks on the workers' movement "wounded his national feeling" and "filled his German heart with sadness." In a letter to his friend Wilhelm Keil he noted with some irony that his speech had not lacked "national warmth." His gesture was not merely rhetorical, however. He felt that for the good of the trade unions he must distance himself from the SPD. Wels watched with dismay as Leipart fell prey to "divide and rule" tactics.[206]

In its call to vote on March 5, the ADGB told members, "You know which front leads the freedom struggle," but it did not name Social Democracy. On March 21 it declared that the ADGB represented workers' social and economic interests independently of employers *and* political parties. In *Die Arbeit* Lothar Erdmann separated the union movement from the intellectual heritage of political Social Democracy. Rejecting socialist internationalism, he wrote, "We are socialists, because we are Germans." This socialism, he added, was "practical," not Marxist. After faulting the SPD for not heeding the national feelings of Germans, he denied its claim to "spiritual leadership" over the trade unions. Erdmann ended, "The trade unions have declared their readiness to cooperate with the new state. They do not need . . . to change their slogan, 'To the nation through socialism,' if the National Revolution's *will* to socialism is followed with *socialist deeds*."[207]

In factory council elections at about three hundred enterprises in March, the Free Trade Unions fared well, winning an average 81.5 percent of the vote among blue-collar workers compared with the NSBO's 4.9 percent, the RGO's 9.2. percent, and the Christian unions' 3.9 percent.[208] No doubt because of these results, and despite ADGB efforts to convince the regime of its loyalty, in late March local unions felt the boot of repression. By April 6 the SA, the SS, or the police had occupied Free Trade Union halls in forty-one cities, destroying files and furniture and terrorizing officials and employees. These acts prompted the ADGB to assure the regime that the unions were "ready to place the autonomous organizations of the German working class, developed over decades by the trade unions, at the service of the new state."[209] Siegfried Aufhäuser resigned as chairman of the AfA-Bund in protest against this course, but the ADGB remained convinced that it could prove that "the trade unions have a right to state protection" and that "the government should recog-

nize their historic contribution" to the nation.[210] Its leaders even considered merging with the NSBO, although this was not their preferred
solution. On April 5, Leipart, Grassmann, Eggert, and Wilhelm Leuschner met with representatives of the NSBO about a possible "understanding." Leipart reminded the Nazis, "We are Social Democrats. . . . We stand
by our time-honored views," although he also stressed, "I speak as a
German." After sparring for some hours, the two sets of leaders reached
no agreement.[211]

This parley as well as the tortured diary entries of Theodor Thomas,
chairman of the roofers' union, reveal the ADGB's "ambivalence and the
equilibrium between accommodation and resistance" that it tried to maintain;[212] yet it soon gave up any pretense of opposition and succumbed
to collaboration. On April 13 the ADGB decided to participate in the
May Day celebration planned by Hitler's regime. *Gewerkschafts-Zeitung*
explained that in the "new epoch" even those who had harked to "symbols" other than those of the "national revolution" did not want to "stand
aside in resigned inactivity."[213] On May 1 the Free Trade Unions marched
under the banners of the victorious National Socialists in "celebration of
national labor" while thousands of Social Democrats celebrated defiantly,
albeit quietly, in Berlin's zoological garden.[214] On May 2, their usefulness
past, Leipart, Grassmann, Eggert, and hundreds of lesser union officials
were arrested. The Free Trade Unions were suppressed, their buildings
and records confiscated.[215] The Nazis proceeded to "coordinate" German
labor with the fascist state.

With the *Gleichschaltung* of the trade unions, the SPD executive realized
that "the blow against the party would follow" and that any "public
effectiveness" it still possessed would end. On May 4 the executive decided
unanimously that Wels, Stampfer, and Siegmund Crummenerl, the party
treasurer, should leave Berlin.[216] This decision was confirmed on May 10,
when the Nazis confiscated all SPD assets and occupied the party's offices.
They did not outlaw the party, however, believing this would alienate rank
and file Socialists. Instead the regime hastened the SPD's demise by
severing the ties between leadership and base in a variety of ways. The
silence of its press, in particular, crippled the SPD. The weekly news
sheets that appeared in its stead offered a poor replacement.[217] They
could not answer the mountain of lies and allegations in Nazi and conservative newspapers. Stories in proregime publications about the flight
abroad of prominent Social Democrats had the desired effect of angering
members and functionaries who could not escape.[218] The banning of the
Workers' Sports Federation and other Social Democratic cultural organi-

zations on March 30 was another crushing blow. Arrests and beatings terrorized lower functionaries and their families and disorganized the SPD at the grassroots level.[219]

The famed SPD organization disintegrated with dismaying speed, a process exacerbated by leadership passivity.[220] In mid-March Wels admitted that "from below comes the cry 'What is the party doing?' "[221] Not only current but past policies rankled. In Bavaria, members contrasted SPD compromises and waffling in 1918 with Nazi decisiveness in 1933 and regretted bitterly that the SPD had not handled its enemies with ruthless dispatch.[222] Many (volunteer) local functionaries dropped out, although others tried to save the organization by forming personal communication networks. Several branches experimented with having women, less closely watched than male Socialists, relay vital information.[223] Most small chapters simply dissolved.[224] Those still in existence received ever more letters of resignation, above all from professionals and public officials.[225] Chapters gained few new members to replace dropouts because after the suppression of the KPD, to keep out Communists the SPD closed membership (except in cases with "sufficient guarantees").[226] Especially after May 10, more and more district officials resigned their posts, to the disgust of militants.[227] Participants recalled that by the end of May the organization had virtually ceased to function. The process of dissolution was, however, uneven. A few urban districts remained cohesive into the summer. Fritz Naphtali did not think the organization could be rebuilt under the old leadership. Comrades, he wrote Paul Hertz, were especially upset with Wels because of how he had chosen party personnel.[228]

A small number of Social Democrats responded to leadership passivity by building illegal groups to replace the old structure. Mierendorff, for example, began to carry out illegal work as early as March.[229] In Hanover and in a few other localities, Social Democrats were attracted to Communist attempts to build an (illegal) united front. Such secret negotiations were, however, rare.[230] In Berlin, Erich Schmidt, the popular leader of the local SAJ, joined the underground group Neu Beginnen, which, with members in both the SPD and the KPD, had prepared itself for illegal activity even before Hitler took power. Following its model, Schmidt created a network of five-person cells. After January 30 he began to set aside funds for future illegal work. When Berlin party leaders discovered what he was up to, a conflict erupted. The adults rejected Schmidt's notions about illegal activity, especially insofar as this involved party funds. He was kicked out of the SPD on April 5.[231] Other branches in Leipzig, Hamburg, Magdeburg, Hanover, and towns in Thuringia also organized "groups of five."[232] With their small numbers and "authoritarian leadership" they broke with the organizational principles of Social Democracy; yet not only were all their members Social Democrats, but most of their organizers belonged to the party's left wing.[233] Several Reichsbanner chapters responded differently to the SPD's passivity. In the vain hope that the Stahlhelm might resist the Nazi regime, they infiltrated it, only to be exposed by zealous National Socialists.[234]

Aware of the party's desperate condition, Wels called a national conference of a few delegates from each district. This rump of a congress met in late April in the ruins of the Reichstag building. Surviving fragments of its proceedings suggest a wide-ranging and self-critical debate about policies (such as coalitionism and toleration of Brüning) and Social Democratic organizations (such as the Reichsbanner and the Iron Front). In his address Wels again confirmed his commitment to principle as well as his refusal to blame SPD policy for Germany's catastrophe. Not individual error, he said, but the immaturity of the working class and its divided condition lay at the root of the present situation. He reaffirmed the SPD's espousal of a state founded on justice, civil liberties, and equal rights for all. In an implicit rebuke of the ADGB, he avowed that the party would never jettison its ideas to save itself, for that would invalidate the very organization it hoped to preserve. He reassured his comrades that "no system of government has endured forever." The SPD, he promised, would carry its great ideals "safely across the raging flood to the opposite bank of a brighter future."[235]

Wels and other executive members at long last accepted the need for organizational changes. In a gesture of goodwill they waived their voting rights and encouraged the election of new executive members. Paul Hertz, Erich Rinner, and Erich Ollenhauer were chosen to represent the younger generation; Karl Böchel, Georg Dietrich, Franz Künstler, and Siegfried Aufhäuser would represent the left wing. Paul Löbe was also elected. Dropped were all executive members in exile as well as several very old men. Despite its critical spirit, a sense of comradeship suffused this final SPD conference.[236] The new executive, however, met only once, and good relations rapidly turned sour. In early May, Wels, Stampfer, and Crummenerl crossed the border into the Saarland and set up a branch of the executive safe from the Nazi grasp.[237] Now a curious thing happened—the émigrés instantly realized the futility of their course of legal opposition.[238] Those still in Germany, however, led by Paul Löbe, looked at the situation from the old vantage point and hoped to salvage what they could by making further adjustments to Nazi demands. Moreover, functionaries and Reichstag deputies resented being given instructions from people out of danger.[239] A conflict between at-home and exiled executive members became inevitable.

As in the case of every shift in Social Democratic behavior during these months, a move by Hitler provoked the fight. On May 17, the chancellor announced, he would speak to the Reichstag to assure Europe of the German people's commitment to peace. The majority of the SPD delegation decided that it would attend the session but make a statement, similar to Wels's on March 23, distancing itself from the regime. The émigrés disagreed. They wanted the delegation to boycott the session to protest the incarceration of hundreds of Social Democrats. Stampfer and Vogel returned to Berlin hoping to change the delegation's mind. In stormy meetings on May 16 and 17 a majority rejected what was seen as a dictate by the émigrés, especially after Wels rang up with a formal order against attendance.[240] A minority, led by Kurt Schumacher, passionately backed Stampfer. The neorevisionists Schumacher, Mierendorff, and Hans Staudinger and the leftists Agnes, Buchwitz, Dietrich, August Fröhlich, Graf, Künstler, Litke, Franz Petrich, Pfülf, and Hugo Saupe made up the bulk of the seventeen deputies who opposed attendance.[241] The majority had just decided to attend *and* to deliver a protest against Nazi persecution when Paul Löbe returned from a meeting of the Reichstag senior council. The bourgeois parties had composed a statement expressing their support for Hitler's peace aims and for the equality of rights of the German people. Only this resolution, Göring had ruled, would be allowed. Interior Minister Frick had said ominously, "We don't care if the Social Democrats agree to the resolution or not. They should know that for us the life of the nation comes before that of individuals."[242]

A long silence followed Löbe's report. Löbe himself finally spoke for endorsing the statement since it contained no more than Social Democracy's traditional call for peace with equal rights. Toni Pfülf, a moderate leftist from Bavaria, interjected that such an act would betray pacifist principles, but Löbe's reasoning convinced most of her comrades. Of the sixty-five deputies present, forty-eight voted to support the peace declaration.[243] Under discipline, almost every delegate attended the Reichstag session. Only Pfülf, Mierendorff, and Schumacher refused to go. When the Social Democratic deputies rose as a body to vote with the bourgeois parties, the chamber, including Hitler, broke into a storm of applause. The German Nationalists burst into *Deutschland, Deutschland über Alles*, and many Social Democrats joined in. Hoegner later reflected, "It was as if we Social Democrats, ever cursed as the prodigal sons of the fatherland, for one eternal moment clasped Mother Germany to our hearts."[244]

Three weeks later, unable to bear the collapse of her party, Toni Pfülf committed suicide.[245] A schoolteacher active in educational reform and Social Democratic cultural organizations, Pfülf epitomized the idealistic, reforming Socialist who often identified with the Left but whose dedication to Social Democracy was rooted less in ideology than in moral commitment to social change. Her suicide testified both to the intense loyalty evoked by Social Democracy and to the sense of betrayal that its post-January course provoked among such activists.

Over the next days the conflict between émigré executive members and those in Germany heated up. The outsiders decided to publish a weekly, *Neuer Vorwärts*, that would call for resistance against Hitler. They also set up permanent residence in Prague. Having forsworn the "adaptation without capitulation" strategy embodied by Wels's March 23 speech, Wels, Stampfer, and Vogel now wanted to reorganize the party on an illegal basis.[246] Abhorrence of the Nazi regime in democratic and leftist circles in Western Europe, Czechoslovakia, and Austria influenced their change of heart. Moreover, with consternation they watched as Communist propaganda in Paris earned the KPD the favor of international public opinion, and they feared that nascent Communist resistance in Germany would attract Social Democratic workers.[247] Most party officials inside Germany opposed the "Prague" course. The fault line in this conflict did not follow any traditional ideological divides. It was, first and foremost, a revolt of the party apparatus (such as it was) and backbench deputies against the old leadership.[248] After May 17, however, leftists joined the rebels. At a Reichstag delegation meeting on June 10, left-wing speakers denounced the émigrés for having abandoned the masses and called for total reform of the party leadership.[249] Executive members Löbe and Max Westphal led the rebellion. They felt that legal work remained possible, feared endangering those in the concentration camps, and simply did not think "emigration politics" could destroy a fascist regime.[250] Löbe believed he could continue to use his position as former Reichstag president to get the ear of Göring and perhaps obtain the freedom of some prisoners. In the final analysis, those inside the Third Reich simply balked at being led by people free of its oppression.[251]

At the delegation meeting on June 10, only Kurt Schumacher argued both for the importance of having a decision-making center outside Germany and for illegal work.[252] He and Mierendorff alone voted against a resolution proclaiming Germany as the executive's seat and demanding the émigrés' return.[253] With Haubach, Mierendorff had decided not to emigrate. Like Schumacher, they planned to work illegally should the SPD be banned.[254] During the spring Mierendorff and Schumacher coauthored a pamphlet, "Revolution against Hitler," which was to call for a liberation movement against the Third Reich that was national, not class based. The pamphlet was unfinished upon Mierendorff's arrest on June 13 and Schumacher's on July 6.[255]

In the face of Löbe's refusal to go to Prague and discuss the disagreements, the émigrés tried to win lower functionaries to their side. They agreed to allow several executive members to return to Germany but remained adamant that the executive have a seat outside Germany. They also insisted that it, or at least individual executive members, call for resistance to Hitler.[256] On June 18 *Neuer Vorwärts* appeared. Under the headline "Break the Chains!" the Prague executive called on compatriots "to join the struggle which shall restore to the German people its honor and liberty."[257] In reaction, Löbe advocated breaking, instead, with Prague. He convened a "national conference" in Berlin the day after *Neuer Vorwärts* appeared. The rightist Ernst Heilmann and the leftist Lipinski both endorsed a complete split. Johannes Stelling spoke for organizing resistance, evidently under a unified leadership in Berlin. The delegates elected a new executive, consisting of Stelling, Löbe, Westphal, and Paul Szillat, who had replaced the Jewish Heilmann as leader of the Prussian delegation. They hoped to save the party by disavowing the Prague course. Hoegner, who supported the rebels at the time, wrote later that the Berliners had become "captives" of Wels's March 23 policy.[258] As he had done with earlier efforts, Hitler ended this last attempt to work out a modus vivendi under the Third Reich. On June 22 the government prohibited all activity by the SPD, in essence outlawing it. More than three thousand Social Democrats were arrested, including Löbe, Stelling, and Heilmann. Stelling was murdered a few days later.[259] His fate foreshadowed that of millions of Europeans over the next twelve years. For German Social Democracy the debacle of 1933 marked the end of a momentous era in its history.

Conclusion

Assessing SPD strategy and tactics in the struggle against Nazism, Hilferding exonerated the party for its inability to stem the NSDAP's rise to power. He acknowledged that "serious mistakes" were made in the "plastic" conditions between 1914 and 1922, but he insisted that SPD "policies after 1923 were by and large dictated by the situation and could not have been much different. During these years other policies would have had much the same result."[1] Of course, Hilferding may have been right, but it is hard to accept Weimar Social Democracy as a mere victim of circumstance. A complicated process culminated in its immobilization at the end of the republic. Certainly the SPD struggled under exceedingly adverse conditions. Moreover, Social Democrats, desperate to rescue Weimar democracy and to protect workers from social injustice, self-consciously made significant sacrifices. Nonetheless, certain characteristics of Social Democracy's ideology, structure, and political culture also hindered the SPD's effort to save itself and the republic.

Social Democratic ideology was a rich composite of nineteenth-century republican, socialist, democratic, and liberal thought. Weimar Social Democrats upheld a complex legacy of ideals that impinged on their behavior from several directions. Democratic principles did not allow them to implement socialism by decree; Marxism deterred them from tinkering with capitalism, as opposed to getting rid of it. From republicanism came the imperative not only to protect but to participate in and celebrate the new state; from class solidarity emanated powerful distrust of a state that sanctioned social injustice and economic oppression. As Hans Muhle (a Social Democrat in Braun's administration) wrote after the defeat on July 20, the SPD was caught between the "formalistic dualities" of "class consciousness and state consciousness," "proletarian struggle and bourgeois reconciliation," and "internationalism and nationalism."[2] The formalism of German Social Democratic thought compounded the effect of its several allegiances. Social Democrats were less ideological than Bolsheviks, for example, yet they were also less willing to experiment and improvise for fear of compromising their ideals. In particular, Social Democratic commitment to democratic representation (based on the principle of one person, one vote) conflicted with the belief in the class foundations of political interest. If the proletariat was not the emergent ority, how was the SPD to effect a democratic transition to socialism? ....e reigning "two-class" analysis hindered the implementation of an all-out effort to attract social groups other than the organized working class. Social Democrats were uncomfortable in coalitions with bourgeois parties, but the SPD's leaders at least, if not the party's ranks, could also not justify armed resistance to maintain a government that had lost at the polls or against one that had not openly breached the constitution.

German Social Democrats tended to believe that the "forces of history" would determine the course of events. They did not by any means sit back and let things take their course and, indeed, were committed social and political reformers; yet a peculiar fatalism-optimism fostered passivity at decisive moments. Wels continued to insist that a ruler such as Hitler could not last long, even after the Nazis smashed the trade unions, the SPD, and the KPD and banned other political parties.[3] Social Democrats saw themselves as objects of bourgeois society rather than as subjects who could fundamentally shape events. Again, Wels gave a striking formulation of this attitude in his address to the Socialist International congress in August 1933. "We were," he averred, "driven by the compulsion of events more than the parties in any other country. We were indeed at the mercy of events."[4] In a letter to Stampfer in 1936, Erich Kuttner, like Hans Muhle a Social Democrat in Braun's administration, criticized such reasoning as applied to the economic crisis: the party leadership claimed, " 'That's something we can't do anything about,' " forgetting that "people prefer an active rescue effort that could fail to being comforted with a mere 'Wait, children!' by someone watching the disaster with folded arms."[5]

Ideological blinders hampered the ability of Social Democrats to comprehend National Socialism. Thinking in class categories, most Social Democrats tied Nazism to capitalists and wiped their hands of one along with the other. As a result, they failed to exploit their political leverage in the fluid situation immediately following the Reichstag elections of September 14, 1930, and preferred Hindenburg and even the despised Reichswehr to dealing directly with the social forces that allegedly backed fascism. Social Democrats initially underestimated and later misinterpreted the political consequences of the crises that engulfed Germany after 1928. As Detlef Lehnert and Klaus Megerle have written, "The ominous . . . fragmentation [of German society] into a multitude of political subcultures that barely interacted and could make no claim to [political] hegemony . . . facilitated the rise of the National Socialists with their 'one people, one Reich, one leader' ideology."[6] Rooted in a political culture that was profoundly ambivalent about its relationship to bour-

geois society and the nation, most Social Democrats could not fathom the
intense yearning for national unity that fed the phenomenal popularity
and political dynamism of Germany's first successful people's party. Even
Hilferding, who had grown distant from his party's cultural traditions and
who saw the Weimar crisis as political, misread the significance of the
popular response to the NSDAP. He attributed Weimar's crisis to the
contempt of the Nazis, Communists, and bourgeois parties for the principles of parliamentary democracy.[7]

As a rule, Social Democrats denied the importance of non-economic
issues in political life and only reluctantly catered to nonrational sen-
sibilities. They downplayed the role in modern mass politics of "subclass"
factors such as personality and "supraclass" components such as nationalism. Fear of inflation as well as Marxist ideas about the nature of capitalist
crisis nevertheless prevented the SPD from accepting an economic program that might have had political repercussions. Even though Socialists
believed that economic interest dictated political allegiance, their propaganda emphasized democratic rights and republican loyalties. It did so
with a social twist, however, insisting that proletarians were the only real
defenders of the republic and democracy. Only in late 1932 did the SPD
produce an economic program, and that plan propagated an abstract
socialism. National Socialism turned this irony on its head. For it, personality, the nation, and politics determined all; economic interest, nothing.
Yet the NSDAP, not the SPD, made public works its clarion call in the
critical Reichstag campaign of July 1932.

Individual Social Democrats—neorevisionists, Alexander Schifrin in
Die Gesellschaft, and myriad lower functionaries—formulated cogent analyses of Nazism and of the dilemmas facing Social Democracy. Left oppositionists, neorevisionists, functionaries, and rank and file activists wanted
to abjure the determinism that underlay SPD passivity and legalism and
fight the "inevitable." Neorevisionists and some party bureaucrats entreated their comrades to break with the class viewpoint that limited the
party's options. An innovative solution to the economic crisis originated
within the Free Trade Unions. In fact, the sympathetic historian becomes
exasperated precisely because so many of the pieces of the puzzle were
there, yet the puzzle could not be solved.

Clearly the SPD's structure contributed to its immobility. Bureaucratic
"deformations" bred inertia. Functionaries and party leaders resisted reforms that would have enhanced their party's popular appeal, yet the SPD
was far from a bureaucratic behemoth. Indeed, the political and organizational fissures that ran through Social Democracy contributed to the
SPD's paralysis. Social Democratic politics were neither the product of a

monolithic ideology nor the preserve of a small elite. They emerged from the interplay of the different, even contradictory, priorities of a variety of decision-making bodies, oppositional circles, and vocal individuals in the Socialist movement. The years between 1928 and 1933 saw a series of shifting alliances among political tendencies and organizational centers of power. In the Panzerkreuzer affair, a decision by SPD ministers provoked an intense reaction from below. Party leftists and neorevisionists took advantage of this outcry to press for a dialogue about the SPD's political strategy and for internal democratization. In March 1930, leftists and trade union reformists, again representing a broad current in the rank and file of the SPD and the trade unions, formed a de facto alliance to defeat the few leading centrists and Prussian *Staatspolitiker* who wanted to compromise on the issue of how to fund unemployment insurance in order to keep Müller in power.

In September 1930, the centrist leadership's toleration policy prevailed against critics on its right and left who were angered by the "inconsistency" and passivity of SPD politics. Defeated on the parliamentary stage, critics turned their energies to the extraparliamentary mobilization of the SPD. They became frustrated, however, when this mobilization began to ebb. In mid-1931 dissatisfaction with toleration and criticism of the message, media, audience, and coordination of SPD propaganda and agitation burst from the ranks, lower functionaries, the Left, and neorevisionists. Brewing discontent also infected the Free Trade Unions. A leftist rebellion against toleration erupted, only to be defeated by the centrist executive committee. After ejecting the organized Left Opposition, however, the party leadership had to concede to pressure from the grassroots, neorevisionists, and Reichsbanner to form a militant extraparliamentary organization, the Iron Front. In early 1932, separate struggles over Social Democratic parliamentary and extraparliamentary politics occurred simultaneously. After prolonged foot dragging, the party elite demonstrated some willingness to compromise with the reformers in both areas, but the tentative focus on public works in April and May was sacrificed in the turn to the left after Brüning's fall. The new-style propaganda of June and July disappeared at the national level after the defeats of July 20 and July 31. In late 1932 and early 1933, neorevisionists and leftists argued for organizational reforms, an extraparliamentary reorientation, and resistance against Hitler. The ADGB and SPD executives closed ranks against such suggestions, but they diverged in their attitude toward the Papen regime. The relationship between the SPD and the Reichsbanner was strained in the tussle over military training in the fall of 1932.

More definitive and certainly more ominous was the split between the SPD and the ADGB over the extent to which the Socialist movement should accommodate the "national revolution" after Hitler came to power. The same dilemma divided the émigré leadership and the neo-revisionists from the Berlin executive and its supporters. At the republic's end and after the *Machtergreifung*, one sees the nebulous contours of an alliance among revisionists, leftists, and some centrists in rebellion against the passivity, accommodationism, and organizational fetishism that immured the party. Until this last conflict the party executive's hegemony had not been decisively challenged. It had maintained its authority, in part by acting as a mediator in disputes among divergent currents and organizational interests. Its power, prestige, and politics of the middle had meant that the executive committee generally prevailed, but not always and frequently only by modifying its original scheme.

The decisions of the centrist leaders were also affected by the concerns and passions of the membership or, at certain turning points, by their interpretation of the inclinations of the rank and file. Party authorities tried to read the ranks' views from their behavior. Activists and functionaries, however, had learned to rely on guidance from above. As early as 1909, describing the Imperial SPD that he had so fundamentally influenced, Karl Kautsky wrote, "Responsible party leaders could not call mass actions for which the masses did not press, yet the German masses were drilled to wait for a command from above."[8] Almost twenty-five years later, on July 20, 1932, and January 30, 1933, "responsible party leaders" awaited a powerful signal such as the massive strike that the Kapp putsch had spontaneously ignited. Confronted with no act that revealed the extent of the will to resist, they did not think it existed and did not want to take the risk of trying to generate it. Simultaneously, they took pride in rank and file discipline and saw it as a sign of Social Democracy's invincibility.

Indeed, the ties between leaders and followers held the Socialist movement together through extremely trying times. These ties rested on the class sociability that stamped Social Democratic associationism and gave Social Democracy its resilience, solidarity, and vitality. Yet the *Solidarge-meinschaft* was the movement's weakness as well as its strength. The cohesiveness of the association under external pressure belied the need for the SPD to adjust its self-conception to fit changes in its social composition that were already taking place, much less to transform itself into a majority party. Loyalty to the organization did not preclude internal dissent and even encouraged it. One is, indeed, struck by the dissonance inside Social Democracy during these years. Demands for purification of the association and a return to its original democratic and social precepts became louder after 1928, although they were rarely expressed openly after 1931. Simultaneously (and sometimes from the same people), calls to open the association to the wider society also became more widespread and insistent. Seen retrospectively, the urge for reform that made its internal life so contentious appears as a distinctive and attractive feature of Social Democracy, especially in contrast to its radical rivals. This tendency also turned the association inward, however, even in the midst of a battle for its own and the republic's survival. When the Nazi victors first frayed and then cut the ties between top and bottom, Social Democracy fell apart. The vast majority of the ranks and functionaries did not understand the ways and means of an illegal, cadre organization. The leaders, stripped of their mass base, fell out with each other.

Among the political tendencies inside the SPD, the neorevisionist or "militant republican" current has received particular attention, in part because, more than any other political tendency, it was a child of the republic. Neorevisionists combined acceptance of national feeling and the desire for a charismatic leader of Social Democracy with militant street politics and popular democracy. In the turbulence of the struggle against Nazism, this loose circle branched in two directions. One arm, represented by Wilhelm Sollmann, Walther Pahl, and the "national" tendency in the ADGB, pressed, above all, for a national reorientation of Social Democratic politics. The other arm, represented by Mierendorff, Haubach, Schumacher, and Leber, could be characterized as left populist or neo-Jacobin. This group aimed, first and foremost, to democratize the republic and give it a solid popular foundation. They perceptively analyzed the dilemmas of their party, but they succumbed to the inexorable pressures of Social Democratic political culture in their effort to forge a powerful extraparliamentary movement from the Iron Front. In the battles of 1932 they couched their appeals in the language of working-class exclusivism. On one hand, in these months the SPD addressed many leaflets and pamphlets specifically to civil servants, employees, farmers, and even the old *Mittelstand*; yet, on the other hand, its general propaganda presented the working class as the only true defender of the republic. Thus neorevisionists gained the enthusiastic support of leftists and the ranks for the Iron Front but did not help the SPD break out of its tower. Only after the SPD had ceased to function as a mass organization and its leadership had fallen into disarray did Mierendorff and Schumacher act on the idea of a national, rather than a class based, movement for freedom.[9] Earlier they found it easier to challenge party traditions in propaganda technique and style than to change the message and audience of the propaganda.

The SPD's struggle against Nazism did not produce heroes or heroines in the grand sense. No charismatic leader of vision and decisiveness came forth who could have broken the bonds of tradition and led the party out of its predicament. Wels, at the beginning an opaque figure who seemed to be the ultimate bureaucrat, emerged in 1932–33 as a leader dedicated as much to the political ideals as to the organizational apparatus of his beloved association. He lacked, however, the qualities of an outstanding political leader. The brilliant Hilferding, on the other hand, possessed political insight but put too much faith in Brüning's desire and ability to save parliamentary democracy. He proved a disaster as a practical politician because his understanding of Marxist economics led to a virtual obsession with the importance of a balanced budget and so to unyielding opposition to deficit spending projects. Otto Braun, in contrast to both Wels and Hilferding, was an able, pragmatic politician. Despite his position on the SPD's right flank, his ability to stand up to his bourgeois partners made him a hero among the party ranks; yet he too, in the words of the antirepublican *Deutsche Führerbriefe*, was "not a reforming republican, but a conservative protector of the state."[10] Like Hilferding, he naively relied on Brüning and Hindenburg to safeguard democracy and the republic. After discounting the importance of the popular resonance of his government in 1931, he wrapped himself in the mantle of democratic legalism in 1932.

No party leftist had the stature of these men. Toni Sender, Franz Künstler, Siegfried Aufhäuser, and others enjoyed regional popularity. In part because leftists were especially subject to their culture's suspicion of the cult of personality, however, they did not project themselves as national leaders of the SPD. Several neorevisionists, such as Höltermann, Mierendorff, Haubach, Leber, and Schumacher, had begun to attain national recognition, but their youth prevented them from becoming candidates for top posts in a party that expected its leaders to serve a long apprenticeship. It is noteworthy that Kurt Schumacher, the only prominent militant republican who survived the Third Reich, became the national leader of a renascent SPD after Nazism's collapse.[11]

The failure to produce a charismatic leader is seen as one of Weimar Social Democracy's drawbacks when it is compared with the NSDAP. Most Social Democrats, however, did not see the need for such a heroic leader. They believed they had a heroine in the SPD. Their dedication is understandable. Social Democracy embodied more than any other Weimar milieu the Other Germany so often forgotten in that country's twentieth-century history. It stood for the ideals of humanity, not narrow German interest, and it encompassed the largest mass of anti-Nazi Germans.

Through it ran many currents of democratic thought—from radical socialist to Jacobin to parliamentarian. The movement thus represented the diversity of a democratic society. The SPD, the political hub of Social Democracy, was a democratic party in both senses of that much-abused word. It preached, as well as practiced, political rights, justice, and freedom of expression. It also advocated and contributed to social equality and the economic welfare of the poorest Germans so that the whole people might participate in political life. The SPD was a great, but flawed, party that both saw and was blind to the roots and significance of the German crisis. Like the protagonist in a tragedy, the SPD struggled within itself to change but could not. Rather than taking control of its destiny, Weimar Social Democracy allowed the "compulsion of events" to dictate its history. The tragic consequence was its inability to save itself, Germany, and Europe from disaster.

Notes

Abbreviations

AsD	Archiv der sozialen Demokratie at the Friedrich-Ebert-Stiftung (Bonn–Bad Godesberg)
BA	Bundesarchiv (Koblenz)
BVW	*Volkswacht* (Breslau)
DA	*Die Arbeit*
DF	*Deutsche Führerbriefe*
DG	*Die Gesellschaft*
DGB Archiv	Archiv des Deutschen Gewerkschaftsbundes (Düsseldorf)
DR	*Deutsche Republik*
DVZ	*Düsseldorf Volkszeitung*
EVW	*Volkswacht* (Essen)
FVS	*Frankfurter Volksstimme*
FW	*Das Freie Wort*
GStAPK	Geheimes Staatsarchiv, Preussischer Kulturbesitz (Berlin)
GZ	*Gewerkschafts-Zeitung*
HE	*Hamburger Echo*
HVF	*Hessischer Volksfreund* (Darmstadt)
HVW	*Volkswacht* (Hanover)
II	*International Information*
IISH	International Institute of Social History (Amsterdam)
JB	*Jungsozialistische Blätter*
JCH	*Journal of Contemporary History*
JMH	*Journal of Modern History*
KK	*Der Klassenkampf*
LVZ	*Leipziger Volkszeitung*
NHStAH	Niedersächsisches Hauptstaatsarchiv Hannover
NSDAP HA	NSDAP Hauptarchiv
NWStAM	Nordrhein-Westfälisches Staatsarchiv Münster
MT	*Marxistische Tribüne für Politik und Wirtschaft*
NB	*Neue Blätter für den Sozialismus*
RB	*Das Reichsbanner*
RF	*Rote Fahne*
RZ	*Rheinische Zeitung* (Cologne)
SM	*Sozialistische Monatshefte*
SPW	*Sozialistische Politik und Wirtschaft*
ST	*Schwäbische Tagwacht* (Stuttgart)
StAFr	Stadtarchiv Frankfurt
UW	*Unser Weg*

VB   *Völkischer Beobachter*
VW   *Vorwärts*

Introduction

1. SPD, Vorstand, *Jahrbuch der deutschen Sozialdemokratie 1929* (hereafter cited as *SPD Jahrbuch* . . .), 240, 178.

2. I use the term *Social Democracy* to refer to the Social Democratic movement, including the SPD, the Free Trade Unions, the Socialist cultural organizations and cooperatives, and the Reichsbanner.

3. *SPD Jahrbuch 1928*, 385, 378; Heinrich A. Winkler, *Schein*, 158–59; Lösche and Walter, "Organisationskultur," 513.

4. Lösche and Walter, "Organisationskultur," 513–15; Guttsman, *Workers' Culture*, 6–7, 137; Hagemann, *Frauenalltag*, 650.

5. See Lehnert, "Klassenintegration." On Austrian Social Democracy in the 1920s, see Rabinbach, *Austrian Socialist Experiment*.

6. See Schulze, *Weimar*, 73–75, 398–99; Erdmann and Schulze, *Weimar*; Bracher, *Auflösung*, 460, 700; Bracher, "20. Juli 1932." For a version of this thesis that is more sympathetic to the SPD's ideology, if not its practice, see Hans Mommsen, "Sozialdemokratie in der Defensive," esp. 108–10. For this point made within a leftist critique, see Klönne, *Deutsche Arbeiterbewegung*, 243.

7. Quoted in Jasper, *Gescheiterte Zähmung*, 13.

8. Grebing, "Thesen zur Niederlage," 101. Grebing argues against "neoconservative circles" who blame the SPD for Weimar's demise. Hagen Schulze does not agree that the SPD's good intentions let it off the hook (Schulze, *Weimar*, 424).

9. See, e.g., praise for the work of Carlo Mierendorff by Schnabel, " 'Wer wählte Hitler?,' " 117; Broszat, "Struktur der NS-Massenbewegung," 54. For appreciations of the insights of Social Democrats in general, see Sturm, "Faschismusauffassungen"; Grebing, "Faschismus, Mittelschichten."

10. *Traditionalism* is the term used by Schönhoven in his *Reformismus und Radikalismus* (132). Wolfram Pyta considers both party politics and organization in his well-documented *Gegen Hitler und für die Republik*. For an older (and classic) synthetic analysis of the SPD's struggle against Nazism between 1930 and 1933, see Matthias, "Sozialdemokratische Partei." Also see G. A. Ritter, *Staat, Arbeiterschaft und Arbeiterbewegung*, esp. 91–92. Although it focused on the prewar SPD, Guenther Roth's study is an example of an early synthetic analysis of Social Democracy (Roth, *Social Democrats in Imperial Germany*). In his monumental three-volume study, *Arbeiter und Arbeiterbewegung in der Weimarer Republik*, Heinrich A. Winkler thoroughly covers both the ideology and structure of the SPD, but his interpretation concentrates on its ideology.

11. See, e.g., Richard Hunt, *German Social Democracy*; Hans Mommsen, "Sozialdemokratie in der Defensive"; Pirker, "Verhalten der Organisationen." For a contemporary structural critique, see Fritz Bieligk, "Organisation wie sie

ist," in *Organisation im Klassenkampf*, by Bieligk et al. The framework of the structural analysis was first provided in Michels, *Political Parties* (originally published in 1915).

12. Lösche and Walter, "Organisationskultur"; Reck, *Arbeiter nach der Arbeit*; Rebentisch, "Die treuesten Söhne"; Scholing and Walter, "Der 'Neue Mensch.'"

13. For a powerful presentation of this viewpoint, see Heinrich A. Winkler, *Arbeiter und Arbeiterbewegung in der Weimarer Republik*. Numerous scholars share this interpretation: Pyta, *Gegen Hitler*; Breitman, *German Social Democracy*; Schulze, *Otto Braun*; Bracher, *Auflösung*; Hodge, "Three Ways to Lose a Republic"; Gates, "German Socialism and the Crisis of 1929–1933"; Sturmthal, *Tragedy of European Labor*.

14. This critical tradition can be traced back to Rosenberg, *Geschichte der Weimarer Republik*. For recent studies from a left-wing perspective, see Franz Ritter, *Theorie und Praxis des demokratischen Sozialismus*; Heupel, *Reformismus und Krise*; Klönne, *Deutsche Arbeiterbewegung*; Saage, "Gleichgewicht der Klassen-Kräfte"; Peukert, *Ruhrarbeiter gegen den Faschismus*, esp. 15–21; Hebel-Kunze, *SPD und Faschismus*; Saggau, *Faschismustheorien*.

15. On the roots of and challenges to SPD passivity, see Nettl, "German Social Democratic Party"; Potthoff, "Sozialdemokratie," 137.

16. See Nettl, "German Social Democratic Party"; Roth, *Social Democrats in Imperial Germany*; Matthias, "Kautsky"; Gay, *Dilemma of Democratic Socialism*; Steinberg, *Sozialismus*; Groh, *Negative Integration*.

17. Lidtke, *Outlawed Party*; Grebing, *Revisionismus*, esp. 21–24; G. A. Ritter, "Sozialdemokratische Arbeiterbewegung"; Na'aman, "Lassalle."

18. Reinhard Rürup has argued that this misunderstanding shaped the SPD leaders' reaction to the *Rätebewegung*. They did not appreciate the democratic political impulse behind the council movement and instead saw it as Bolshevik (Rürup, "Problems of the German Revolution").

19. Lidtke, *Outlawed Party*, 229–39, 324.

20. For a similar analysis, see Lehnert, "'Staatspartei der Republik' oder 'revolutionäre Reformisten'?," esp. 95. For a contemporary appraisal of this attachment, see Ernst Fraenkel, "Abschied von Weimar?," *DG*, Aug. 1932, 120–22.

21. Dieter Rebentisch makes this point for the Frankfurt SPD ("Die treuesten Söhne," 352).

22. Nolan, *Social Democracy and Society*, 291–92. On the differences within the radicalism of Ruhr workers, see Lucas, *Arbeiterradikalismus*.

23. Walter, "Jugend," 312–13.

24. Fülberth, *Beziehungen zwischen SPD und KPD*, 128; Rebentisch, "Die treuesten Söhne," 351.

25. Grebing, *Revisionismus*, 37; also see Moring, *Sozialdemokratische Partei in Bremen*, 59–67.

26. Grebing, *Revisionismus*, 23–24.

27. Fülberth, *Beziehungen zwischen SPD und KPD*, 138; Wickham, "Working-Class Movement in Frankfurt," 168; NSDAP HA R.93/F.1898: Ortsversammlung (Munich), 19.8.26. Files on the Munich SPD in the NSDAP Hauptarchiv consist of police informers' accounts of membership meetings, functionary meetings, and Reichsbanner meetings between 1922 and 1933; scattered clippings from the SPD's *Münchner Post* and the bourgeois press; and periodic summary reports by the police on the campaigns and "state" of the SPD in Munich and elsewhere in Bavaria. I identify files according to Ortsversammlung, Bezirkversammlung, Generalversammlung, Jahresversammlung, Reichsbannerversammlung, etc. or as a PND Bericht or Lagebericht if they are police reports on the SPD in general.

28. Geary, *European Labour Protest*, 119.

29. The term *associationism* was suggested in part by Eduard Bernstein's *Evolutionary Socialism* (originally published in 1899), where he writes that the "most exact characterization" of socialism "starts from the concept of association" and that socialism is "a movement towards—or the state of—an order of society based on the principle of association" (95–96).

30. On club life among Social Democrats before World War I, see Lidtke, *Alternative Culture*, esp. chap. 3. On class-based sociability among non–Social Democratic workers before 1914, see Abrams, *Workers' Culture in Imperial Germany*, 121–28, 134.

31. The latter interpretation has been offered by Saldern, *Auf dem Wege zum Arbeiterreformismus*, 45–46; Hickey, *Workers in Imperial Germany*, 294.

32. On the origins of the cultural organizations, see Langewiesche, "Impact of the German Labor Movement," 515.

33. On the skilled worker social basis of SPD, see Lösche and Walter, "Auf dem Weg?"; Nolan, *Social Democracy and Society*, 100–112; Mehringer, "Bayerische Sozialdemokratie," 301–2; Geary, "German Labour Movement," 310; Geary, *European Labour Protest*, 95; Fricke, *Zur Organisation und Tätigkeit der deutschen Arbeiterbewegung*, 73, 210; Schadt, *Sozialdemokratische Partei in Baden*, 150. On the pre-SPD roots of skilled worker activism, see Birker, *Die Deutschen Arbeiterbildungsvereine*, 139.

34. Gotthardt, *Industrialisierung, bürgerliche Politik und proletarische Autonome*, 400–405; Schieder, *Anfänge der deutschen Arbeiterbewegung*, 174–79, 310; Tenfelde, "Anmerkungen zur Arbeiterkultur," 119–20; Birker, *Die Deutschen Arbeiterbildungsvereine*, 56–57, 183, 189; Reichard, *Crippled from Birth*. For an interpretation that stresses the lack of a popular tradition on which Lassalleanism could draw, see Eisenberg, "Chartismus und Allgemeiner Deutscher Arbeiterverein."

35. Conze and Groh, *Arbeiterbewegung in der nationalen Bewegung*, 123–25; Tenfelde, "Anmerkungen zur Arbeiterkultur," 119–20; Offermann, "Das liberale Vereinsmodell," 39–40; Trautmann, "Scheitern liberaler Vereinspolitik," 167; Saldern, "Wilhelminische Gesellschaft und Arbeiterklasse," 503; Birker, *Die Deutschen Arbeiterbildungsvereine*, 74–77.

36. See Lidtke, *Alternative Culture*; Saldern, "Wilhelminische Gesellschaft und Arbeiterklasse," 484; Saldern, "Arbeiterkulturbewegung"; Potthoff, "Sozialdemokratie," 25–39.

37. Offermann, "Das liberale Vereinsmodell," 45–46; Tenfelde, "Anmerkungen zur Arbeiterkultur," 119–20; Geary, *European Labour Protest*, 120. See Lidtke, *Alternative Culture* (89) on Jacobin symbols and claims to the mantle of the French Revolution at Social Democratic festivals before 1900. On bourgeois associations in nineteenth-century Germany, see Nipperdey, "Verein als soziale Struktur"; Koshar, *Social Life, Local Politics, and Nazism*, 92–95. My thesis has been influenced by two works on nineteenth-century France: Sewell, *Work and Revolution in France*; Agulhon, *Republic in the Village*.

38. A moderately left-wing Social Democrat, Ernst Fraenkel, noted in 1932 that "the republic initially encouraged the rise of the working class [and] later was neutral toward the progress of the workers' movement" ("Abschied von Weimar?," *DG*, Aug. 1932, 122).

39. Further testimony to the republicanism of workers exists in police reports about the angry furor in Berlin factories over Walter Rathenau's murder, news of which was accompanied by Communist rumors about a second Kapp putsch. Independent and majority Socialist messengers frantically reassured workers that the republic was secure. Huge demonstrations took place in working-class neighborhoods over the next several days (NSDAP HA R.92/F.1893: Lagebericht, 27.6.22).

40. Detlef Lehnert argues along the same lines ("Sozialdemokratie," esp. 95 and 108–11). Hagen Schulze has suggested that the republic not only lacked bourgeois, but working-class and "even" Social Democratic republicans (*Weimar*, 421). I disagree. Especially Social Democrats, but also a broad section of industrial workers, supported the republic, at least in its early years. Among unemployed and younger workers, it is true, republicanism eroded noticeably between 1929 and 1932. Schulze confuses dissatisfaction with Weimar with a lack of commitment to the republic as a state form.

41. Studies of local and regional working-class organization and politics have investigated the social and historical roots of reformism and radicalism among Social Democrats and German workers in general. See Nolan, *Social Democracy and Society*; Saldern, *Auf dem Wege zum Arbeiterreformismus*; Lucas, *Arbeiterradikalismus*; Boll, *Massenbewegungen in Niedersachsen*; Wickham, "Working-Class Movement in Frankfurt." For a stimulating discussion of the complex and often contradictory conditions that produced either radical or reformist SPD clubs, see Saldern, "Arbeiterradikalismus-Arbeiterreformismus."

42. Lösche and Scholing, "Solidargemeinschaft"; Lösche and Walter, "Auf dem Weg?," 126.

43. Lösche and Walter, "Organisationskultur," 521–23. Lösche and Walter delineate the geographical distribution of this core (524–27, 535).

44. Lösche and Walter estimate the "carriers" of this consciousness at 200,000 ("Organisationskultur," 535). Lehnert proposes a "typology" of the

Social Democratic "subculture (*Teilkultur*)": in total it encompassed the SPD's electorate (5–9 million); its "political camp" included members of the Reichsbanner and the party and active trade unionists (about 3 million); its *Solidargemeinschaft* was about 100,000 strong (mainly left-wing activists); and the functionary corps numbered 20–30,000 (Lehnert, "Sozialdemokratie," 84). Hartmut Wunderer questions the notion that the 1920s saw a blossoming of the *Solidargemeinschaft* (Wunderer, "Noch einmal").

45. Among others, Klaus Schönhoven has used the term *Lagermentalität* to describe Social Democratic consciousness ("Der demokratische Sozialismus," 75).

46. See, e.g., Schönhoven, "Der demokratische Sozialismus," 74–77; Kolb, "Zwischen Parteiräson und staatspolitischer Verantwortung," 115–16; Feldman, "Von Krise zu Krise," 637–38.

47. Lösche and Walter, "Auf dem Weg?," 103–19.

48. Lehnert, "Klassenintegration," 230.

49. Schönhoven, "Der demokratische Sozialismus"; Jasper, *Gescheiterte Zähmung*, 15–16.

50. See Hermann Weber, "KPD im Kampf," 85–91; Schönhoven, *Reformismus und Radikalismus*, 173–74.

51. Schildt, "Militärische Ratio," 349–57.

52. Grebing, "Auseinandersetzung"; Sturm, "Faschismusauffassungen"; Lehnert, "Klassenintegration," 242–43; Breitman, "Nazism in the Eyes of German Social Democracy"; Pyta, *Gegen Hitler*, 98–102, 194, 505; Schaefer, *SPD in der Ära Brüning*, 433; Saggau, *Faschismustheorien*, 30–36, 45.

53. Critics of the bureaucratization thesis include Landauer, Review of R. Hunt, *German Social Democracy*; Lösche, "Über den Zusammenhang," 22; Wickham, "Working-Class Movement in Frankfurt," 331, 342. For the argument that party leaders wanted a *Volkspartei*, see Lösche and Walter, "Auf dem Weg?," 77–83, 135.

54. See, e.g, Larry Eugene Jones, *German Liberalism*, 1–12; Neebe, "Konflikt und Kooperation," 237; Peukert, *Weimarer Republik*, esp. 271. For an overview of scholarly interpretations of the Weimar republic, see Kolb, *Weimarer Republik*, 140–52.

55. I have borrowed the term *hindsight bias* from Fischoff, "Heuristics and Biases in Hindsight."

56. The most important historians of what is also called the Bielefeld school are Hans-Ulrich Wehler, Jürgen Kocka, Hans-Jürgen Puhle, and Heinrich August Winkler. On the history of the *Sonderweg* thesis and controversies surrounding it, see George Iggers, "Introduction," in Iggers, *Social History of Politics*; Moeller, "The *Kaiserreich* Recast?"; Fletcher, "Recent Developments in West German Historiography." One of its original proponents was the sociologist Ralf Dahrendorf in his famous *Society and Democracy in Germany*. The thesis has even older roots and, indeed, a version was put forward in 1922

by Rudolf Hilferding—or such is my interpretation of his views as presented by Euchner, "Sozialdemokratie und Demokratie," 150.

57. Important critiques of the Bielefeld interpretation of Imperial history are Eley and Blackbourn, *Peculiarities of German History*; Nipperdey, "1933."

58. See, e.g., Larry Eugene Jones, *German Liberalism*; Moeller, *German Peasants*; Fritzsche, *Rehearsals for Fascism*.

59. Nipperdey, "1933," 231.

60. For a similar viewpoint, see Neebe, "Verantwortung der Grossindustrie"; Turner, *German Big Business*. Structural analyses of the Weimar republic have been offered not only by Marxist historians. The pathbreaking work of political scientist K. D. Bracher, *Die Auflösung der Weimarer Republik*, focused on cracks in the republic's structure and inspired younger historians in the 1960s to examine the origins of the republic's foundations in 1918–19. See Kolb, *Weimarer Republik*, esp. 148.

61. Wolfgang J. Mommsen, "German Revolution," 48.

62. Maier, *Unmasterable Past*, 112–15.

63. Peukert, *Weimarer Republik*, 9–31, 266.

64. Historians who posit continuities within the modernity of the Weimar years include Jasper, *Gescheiterte Zähmung*, esp. 14; Hans Mommsen, *Verspielte Freiheit*; Geiss, "Weimar Republic." On the concept of political culture and how historians can use it, see Rohe, "Politische Kultur"; Rohe, *Vom Revier zum Ruhrgebiet*, esp. 61–65; Schirmer, "Politisch-kulturelle Deutungsmuster," esp. 32.

65. Gerald Feldman has approached these issues through a reassessment of the applicability of modernization theory (Feldman, "Weimar Republic").

66. For a succinct summary of the issues, see Maier, *Unmasterable Past*, 100–121.

67. Childers, "Social Language of Politics," quote from p. 357. For important works characterized by a focus on language, see Furet, *Interpreting the French Revolution*; Lynn Hunt, *Politics, Culture, and Class in the French Revolution*; Sewell, *Work and Revolution in France*; Stedman Jones, *Languages of Class*. Important discussions of the methodological issues involved in the "linguistic turn" are offered by Lynn Hunt, "Introduction"; Scott, *Gender and the Politics of History*; Toews, "Intellectual History after the Linguistic Turn."

68. Childers, "Social Language of Politics," 355. Also see Fritzsche, *Rehearsals for Fascism*, 11–15. Others have made a similar point about the political consciousness of German workers: Moore, *Injustice*, 220–23; Geary, "Identifying Militancy," 225.

69. Nipperdey, "1933," 231–39; Fritzsche, *Rehearsals for Fascism*, 219–29.

70. Blackbourn, "Politics of Demagogy in Imperial Germany," in Blackbourn, *Populists and Patricians*; Eley, "The German Right, 1880–1945," in Eley, *From Unification to Nazism*; Farr, "Populism in the Countryside"; Sheehan, *German Liberalism in the Nineteenth Century*, 221–38.

71. Weimar Social Democrats noted such contradictions in National Socialism—that is, its "authoritarian democratic" tendencies and its attempt to combine "fascist practice with democratic ideology" (Kurt Wilk, "Die Krise des Parlamentarismus und sozialdemokratische Politik," *DG*, Dec. 1931, 505).

72. On Germany's *Teilkulturen*, see Lehnert and Megerle, "Politische Identität"; Schirmer, "Politisch-kulturelle Deutungsmuster." For discussions of other working-class traditions and cultures in Germany, see Crew, *Town in the Ruhr*; Hickey, *Workers in Imperial Germany*; Tenfelde, *Sozialgeschichte der Bergarbeiterschaft*; Eley, "Labor History"; Brose, *Christian Labor*; Patch, *Christian Trade Unions*.

73. Nipperdey, "1933," 231.

74. Lösche and Walter, "Auf dem Weg?," 125.

75. Peukert, *Weimarer Republik*, 269–70; Jasper, *Gescheiterte Zähmung*, 15–16. For analyses that see economic structure and social interest as determinant, see (from sophisticated Marxist perspectives) Abraham, *Collapse of the Weimar Republic*; Eley, "What Produces Fascism?," in Eley, *From Unification to Nazism*; (from a conservative perspective) Borchardt, *Wachstum*.

76. Jasper, *Gescheiterte Zähmung*, 17–32; Peukert, *Weimarer Republik*, 252–65; Hans Mommsen, "Failure of the Weimar Republic"; Neebe, "Konflikt und Kooperation," 237; Potthoff, *Freie Gewerkschaften 1918–1933*, 297–300. Charles Maier has placed such an analysis of Weimar Germany within a broader European framework (*Recasting Bourgeois Europe*, esp. 586–87).

77. Neebe, "Verantwortung der Grossindustrie," 362; Neebe, "Konflikt und Kooperation," 237.

Chapter One

1. For a recent presentation of this viewpoint, see Boll, "Vergleichende Aspekte," 101–2. Guenther Roth first developed the "negative integration" thesis in *Social Democrats in Imperial Germany*. Some scholars who accept the subculture thesis point out, however, that provincial Social Democrats socialized with Germans of similar background but different worldviews (Mehringer, "Bayerische Sozialdemokratie," 336).

2. Lidtke, *Alternative Culture*; G. A. Ritter, *Arbeiterkultur*. Also see Nolan, *Social Democracy and Society*, 134; Tenfelde, "Anmerkungen zur Arbeiterkultur," 124–25.

3. Saldern, "Wilhelminische Gesellschaft und Arbeiterklasse," 484.

4. See, e.g., Moore, *Injustice*, 220–23; Conze and Groh, *Arbeiterbewegung in der nationalen Bewegung*, 126.

5. Heinrich Brüning described his surprise upon realizing that Socialist state ministers "were ready to put their own and their party's future on the line when it was a question of the general interest" (*Memoiren*, 218).

6. See the vivid descriptions of the terrible living conditions of cottage

toymakers in the Erzgebirge and Thuringia by Stenbock-Fermor, *Deutschland von unten*, 81–83, 93–95.

7. On the relative wages of the skilled and the unskilled, see Heinrich A. Winkler, *Schein*, 50; Kukuck and Schiffmann, "Einleitung," in *Gewerkschaften 1924–1930*, vol. 3, pt. 1. For the "revisionist" view that Weimar wages were too high compared to profits, see Borchardt, "Zwangslagen und Handlungsspielräume in der grossen Wirtschaftskrise der früheren dreissiger Jahre: Zur Revision des überlieferten Geschichtsbildes," in Borchardt, *Wachstum*. Harold James agrees that wages rose substantially (James, "Economic Reasons"). Several recent critiques of this view include Köhler, "Borchardts 'Revision' "; Holtfrerich, "Zu hohe Löhne in der Weimarer Republik?"; Potthoff, *Freie Gewerkschaften 1918–1933*, 133–50; Heinrich A. Winkler, *Schein*, 46–57; Maier, "Die Nicht-Determiniertheit ökonomischer Modelle." Gerald Feldman argues that labor made significant gains, perhaps not in relation to capital, but certainly relative to the old middle class (Feldman, "Weimar Republic," 23).

8. See, e.g., SPD-Kassel, *Zehn Jahre Revolution*, 38–52.

9. See the comments to this effect by ADGB officials at a private meeting in mid-1929 (ADGB Bundesausschusssitzung [hereafter cited as Bundesausschuss], 26/27.5.29, Dok. 210, in *Gewerkschaften 1924–1930*, 3[2]:1234, 1237, 1243). Also see Dok. 247, n. 7, in ibid., 1386.

10. James, *German Slump*, 88–89; Wickham, "Working-Class Movement in Frankfurt," 163–68; Hipp, "Wohnungen für Arbeiter." Despite public building, Germany suffered from a deficit of about 800,000 housing units in 1927 (James, *German Slump*, 206).

11. Langewiesche, "Politik-Gesellschaft-Kultur," 402; Guttsman, *Workers' Culture*, 263.

12. Wunderer, *Arbeitervereine und Arbeiterparteien*, 74–77; G. A. Ritter, *Arbeiterkultur*. Also see Wunderer's critique of the concept of *Solidargemeinschaft* in which he argues that the cultural movement became ever less political in the Weimar years ("Noch einmal," 89–90).

13. Langewiesche, "Politik-Gesellschaft-Kultur," 373–74, 381, 392–93, 402.

14. Geary, "Unemployment and Working-Class Solidarity," 266–69.

15. Lösche and Walter, "Organisationskultur," 520.

16. Ibid., esp. 511–15, 517, 520; Scholing and Walter, "Der 'Neue Mensch' "; Reck, *Arbeiter nach der Arbeit*, 167–69; Van der Will and Burns, *Arbeiterkulturbewegung*, 104. Heinrich A. Winkler adopts a middle position in this debate (*Schein*, 120, 144).

17. Saldern, "Arbeiterkulturbewegung," 40.

18. NSDAP HA R.92/F.1898: Ortsversammlung, 21.10.22; R.94/F.1905: Waldfest der Sicherheitsabteilung München Sud-Ost, 22.7.23; Guttsman, *Workers' Culture*, 236.

19. NSDAP HA R.94/F.1905: Nürnberg Funktionärsversammlung, 10.11.22.

20. See, e.g., NSDAP HA R.93/F.1903: Lagebericht, 18.7.24; R.93/F.1902: Lagebericht, 14.4.30. On working-class participation in bourgeois sport leagues, see Überhorst, "Bildungsgedanke und Solidaritätsbewusstsein," 280.

21. Langewiesche, "Politik-Gesellschaft-Kultur," 375; Braunthal, *Socialist Labor*, 87; Potthoff, *Freie Gewerkschaften 1918–1933*, 248–49.

22. Quoted in Schorske, *German Social Democracy*, 49.

23. See, e.g., the argument used by Theodor Leipart, chairman of the ADGB, in a letter to Hermann Müller, chancellor and Social Democrat, in favor of ADGB inclusion in the Young Plan negotiations (26.6.29, Dok. 217, in *Gewerkschaften 1924–1930*, 3[2]:1262–63).

24. Kukuck and Schiffmann, "Einleitung," in *Gewerkschaften 1924–1930*, 3(1):21, 14.

25. See, e.g., the decision to contribute 1 million marks to the Reichstag campaign of 1930 (Wilhelm Eggert to Gertrud Hanna: 2.8.30, Dok. 6, in *Gewerkschaften 1930–1933*, 4:116).

26. Potthoff, *Freie Gewerkschaften 1918–1933*, 225; Jahn, "Einleitung," in *Gewerkschaften 1930–33*, 4:55–56.

27. Langewiesche, "Politik-Gesellschaft-Kultur," 384–85. Also see the comments of Clemens Nörpel, an employee of the ADGB executive board, at a meeting of the ADGB Bundesausschuss (26/27.3.29, Dok. 210, in *Gewerkschaften 1924–1930*, 3[2]:1233).

28. Kukuck and Schiffmann, "Einleitung," in *Gewerkschaften 1924–1930*, 3(2):21, 49–50; Potthoff, *Freie Gewerkschaften 1918–1933*, 223–25, 313.

29. Petersen, "Labor and the End of Weimar," 91–92; Potthoff, *Freie Gewerkschaften 1918–1933*, 297–300, 288.

30. Reiche, *SA in Nürnberg*, 24, 34; NSDAP HA R.94/F.1905: Lagebericht, 1.2.23; R.92/F.1895: Lagebericht, 21.2.23; R.92/F.1897: Lagebericht, 9.3.23; R.94/F.1905: Lagebericht, 25.5.23.

31. Rohe, *Reichsbanner*, 97–98, 105, 314, 318.

32. NSDAP HA R.94/F.1907: Lagebericht, [1929?], 19–23; Chickering, "Reichsbanner and the Weimar Republic," 524–34; Rohe, *Reichsbanner*, 266–67, 93.

33. Saage, "Gefährdete Republik"; Gotschlich, *Zwischen Kampf und Kapitulation*. An excerpt from the anthem of the Reichsbanner in Stuttgart: "We'll break the princes' power . . . then we'll give the final blow to the miserable black-white-red rabble" (printed in Deutschnationale Schriftenvertriebstelle, *Das Reichsbanner Schwarz-Rot-Gold*, 4).

34. Herbert Scherer, *Literaten und sozialdemokratische Arbeiterbewegung*, 8–17, 182–88; Wunderer, *Arbeitervereine und Arbeiterparteien*, 39–47, 76; Überhorst, "Bildungsgedanke und Solidaritätsbewusstsein," 280–83; Lidtke, "Die kulturelle Bedeutung der Arbeitervereine." These authors see bourgeois influence as one ingredient in a Social Democratic brew. Brigitte Emig argues that bourgeois culture *was* the content of Social Democracy's cultural life (*Veredelung des Arbeiters*).

35. Scholing and Walter, "Der 'Neue Mensch,'" 254–55; Heinrich A. Winkler, *Schein*, 360–65; Saldern, "Arbeiterkulturbewegung," 40; Guttsman, *Workers' Culture*, 297; Walter, *Nationale Romantik*, 18, 21–22.

36. SPD-Kassel, *Zehn Jahre Revolution*, 2–8. Works by Toller and Tucholsky also appeared on SPD and SAJ programs in Bottrop (NWStAM Bestand SPD und Reichsbanner, Bd. 1, Nr. 1: "Programm für die 1848 Gedenkfeier [n.d.]"; Nr. 5: "Proletarische Feierstunde" [SAJ, Bottrop], 2.4.32).

37. Wickham, "Working-Class Movement in Frankfurt," 177.

38. Allen, *Nazi Seizure of Power*, 17.

39. *Frankfurter Zeitung*, #612, 18.10.30.

40. See Allen, *Nazi Seizure of Power*, 16–18; Koshar, *Social Life, Local Politics, and Nazism*, 96–99, 106–12; Fritzsche, *Rehearsals for Fascism*, 75–83, 169–77.

41. Überhorst, "Bildungsgedanke und Solidaritätsbewusstsein," 280; Guttsman, *Workers' Culture*, 148.

42. The German Kinderfreunde movement was inspired by the Austrian one (Heinrich A. Winkler, *Schein*, 257–60). Also see Hagemann, *Frauenalltag*, 318–19. On Workers' Welfare, see Hagemann, *Frauenalltag*, 600–601, 606–9; Heinrich A. Winkler, *Schein*, 352–57; Lösche and Walter, "Organisationskultur," 526.

43. Reck, *Arbeiter nach der Arbeit*, 172–73.

44. NSDAP HA R.93/F.1898: Sektionsversammlung, 21.10.26; R.92/F.1894: Lagebericht, 22.2.26; R.92/F.1897: Funktionärsversammlung, 11.10.26; R.93/F.1901: Bezirkversammlung, 24.3.30; R.92/F.1898: Sektionsversammlung, 20.5.30; R.93/F.1898: Sektionsversammlung, 7.10.30.

45. Guttsman, *Workers' Culture*, 141.

46. ADGB Restakten, Film Nr. 23/1, #001, 003–5, 008–015, 017–21, 023–25, 029, 031, 033–34, 040, 042–44 (1926–27), DGB Archiv; NSDAP HA R.92/F.1897: Munich district meeting, 27.2.27, 5.3.27.

47. NSDAP HA R.93/F.1989: Ortsversammlung Schwabing, 17.6.24, 20.6.24. This issue was part of an old debate among Social Democrats—see Saldern, "Wilhelminische Gesellschaft und Arbeiterklasse," 476.

48. Lösche and Walter, "Auf dem Weg?," 121; NSDAP HA R.92/F.1897: Sektionsversammlung, 29.3.27; R.93/F.1898: Sektionsversammlung, 11.11.30.

49. On Hilferding's influence in the SPD and his political theory, see Breitman, *German Social Democracy*, 114–31, and Gottschalch, *Strukturveränderungen*, 189–90, 204–10. Hilferding was an Austrian.

50. Arkadij Gurland and Fritz Bieligk recalled Levi's unease with the Seydewitz group (Drechsler, *Sozialistische Arbeiterpartei Deutschlands* [hereafter cited as *SAPD*], 23 n. 17).

51. Günter Arns has estimated the number at 55 of 178 deputies in 1923 ("Die Linke in der SPD Reichstagsfraktion," 201).

52. Richard Hunt includes Baden and the Lower Rhine (*German Social Democracy*, 81). Düsseldorf had a moderately leftist Reichstag representative

(Lore Agnes) as did Hamburg (Paul Bergmann), although the latter city was a center of neorevisionism. Both these cities lost their left wings to the KPD. See Nolan, *Social Democracy and Society*; Witt, *Hamburger Sozialdemokratie*; Comfort, *Revolutionary Hamburg*.

53. Potthoff, *Freie Gewerkschaften 1918–1933*, 253.

54. Rathmann, *Ein Arbeiterleben*, 117; Heinrich A. Winkler, *Schein*, 369–74; Albrecht, *Der militante Sozialdemokrat*, 72. On de Man, see Sternhell, *Ni droite ni gauche*, 147, 151–58; Sternhell, "Anti-Materialist Revision of Marxism," 379–400.

55. Langewiesche, "Politik-Gesellschaft-Kultur," 382–86; Scholing and Walter, "Der 'Neue Mensch,'" 251; Walter, *Nationale Romantik*, 2–3.

56. See Carlo Mierendorff, "Republik oder Monarchie?," *SM*, July 1926, 435–39; Mierendorff, *Zehn Jahre nach dem Kapp-Putsch*; Leber, "Todesursachen," 221–22; Theodor Haubach, "Republik und Universität," *Die Glocke* [1922], 540–43.

57. Leber, "Todesursachen," 187, 192, 210; Hermann Heller, "Nationalsozialismus," *NB*, Apr. 1931, 155; Meyer, "Hermann Heller," 297; Edinger, *Kurt Schumacher*, 46–47; Walther G. Oschilewski's contribution in Hammer, *Theodor Haubach zum Gedächtnis*, 41.

58. Martiny, "Entstehung," 373–419; Osterroth, "Hofgeismarkreis," 535–44; Rathmann, *Ein Arbeiterleben*, esp. 161; Borinski, "'Neue Blätter für den Sozialismus'"; Heinrich A. Winkler, *Schein*, 658; Walter, *Nationale Romantik*, 6, 40–45, 82–83, 85, 203. The Hofgeismar circle had supporters in Hamburg, Cologne, Frankfurt, Dessau, Kiel, Berlin, and the Ruhr valley (Osterroth, "Hofgeismarkreis," 545).

59. Osterroth, "Hofgeismarkreis," 559–64. Woodruff D. Smith thinks they crowded into the Reichsbanner in part because the party leadership did not control it ("Mierendorff Group").

60. On Schumacher's politics, see Waldemar Ritter, *Kurt Schumacher*, esp. 32–52. On the militant socialists in general, see Dorothea Beck, "Theodor Haubach, Julius Leber, Carlo Mierendorff, Kurt Schumacher"; Moraw, *Parole der "Einheit,"* 13–15.

61. Walther Pahl, "Die ökonomischen und politisch-moralischen Lehren der Sklarekaffäre," *SM*, Nov. 1929, 914; Theodor Haubach, "Die Generationsfrage und der Sozialismus," in Luthardt, *Sozialdemokratische Arbeiterbewegung*, 2:91.

62. Heinrich A. Winkler, *Schein*, 658; Oschilewski in Hammer, *Theo Haubach zum Gedächtnis*, 38.

63. Richard Hunt, *German Social Democracy*, 43, 50, 99–101; Heinrich A. Winkler, *Schein*, 319; Fritz Bieligk, "Organisation wie sie ist," in Bieligk et al., *Organisation im Klassenkampf*, 58–59; *SPD Jahrbuch 1929*, 178.

64. Richard Hunt, *German Social Democracy*, 46–48; Pirker, "Verhalten der Organisationen," 335.

65. Richard Hunt, *German Social Democracy*, 66–73; Heinrich A. Winkler, *Schein*, 647.

66. Bieligk, "Organisation wie sie ist," 75–76.

67. Alexander Schifrin, "Parteiapparat und Parteidemokratie," *DG*, June 1930, 513; Schmidt, "Memoiren," 14. I would like to thank Erich Schmidt for allowing me to cite his memoirs and Albert O. Hirschman for providing me with an introduction to Mr. Schmidt.

68. Kurt Laumann, "Organisation und Apparat," in Bieligk et al., *Organisation im Klassenkampf*, 134–35, 137; Bieligk, "Organisation wie sie ist," 65.

69. Nettl, "German Social Democratic Party," 80.

70. Laumann, "Organisation und Apparat," 138; Richard Hunt, *German Social Democracy*, 78.

71. Quoted in Hans Mommsen, "Sozialdemokratie in der Defensive," 114.

72. Richard Hunt, *German Social Democracy*, 85–88.

73. Walther Pahl, "Der Run zum Nationalsozialismus," *SM*, 26.9.30, 871.

74. Möller, *Parlamentarismus*, 267.

75. Richard Hunt, *German Social Democracy*, 64–65.

76. Koszyk, *Zwischen Kaiserreich und Diktatur*, 188, 170. For leftist criticism, see Laumann, "Organisation und Apparat," 147–49.

77. Laumann, "Organisation und Apparat," 138.

78. See Lösche, "Über den Zusammenhang," 22; Klenke, *SPD Linke*, 23–25, 591–92; Schaefer, *SPD in der Ära Brüning*, 291 n. 25.

79. Breitman, *German Social Democracy*, 49. Even Richard Hunt (*German Social Democracy*, 249) admitted that the deputation was more independent of the party leadership in the Weimar period than earlier.

80. Schulze, *Otto Braun*, 605, 646.

81. Potthoff, "Sozialdemokratie," 115; Richard Hunt, *German Social Democracy*, 103–5; Lösche and Walter, "Auf dem Weg?," 86.

82. Sühl, *SPD und öffentlicher Dienst*, 226–27; Potthoff, "Freie Gewerkschaften und sozialistische Parteien," 55.

83. Staudinger, *Wirtschaftspolitik im Weimarer Staat*, 111–12. The percentage of employees in Hamburg's party had grown from just 1.4 in 1914 to 11.4 in 1931. This increase seems less striking when set against the percentage of employees in the Hamburg NSDAP: 38 (Prinz, "Wandel durch Beharrung," 60).

84. Mehringer, "Bayerische Sozialdemokratie," 328, 336. This sample is culled from Gestapo records on Lower Franconians who were Social Democrats between 1925 and 1933. Mehringer points out that Lower Franconia's work force was disproportionately artisanal. On the KPD's pull on the unskilled, see Petersen, "Labor and the End of Weimar," 91–93; Rosenhaft, *Beating the Fascists?*, 15, 175.

85. *SPD Jahrbuch 1930*, 195; Richard Hunt, *German Social Democracy*, 107–9.

86. Heinrich A. Winkler, *Schein*, 360–61, 365; Lösche and Walter, "Auf dem

Weg?," 87–88; Prinz, "Wandel durch Beharrung," 61; Walter, "Jugend," 348–51.

87. See, e.g., Lösche and Walter, "Auf dem Weg?," 136.

88. Heinrich A. Winkler, *Schein*, 346–48.

89. In 1907, 54.9 percent of all employed were "workers"; in 1925, 50.1 percent (Petzina, Abelshauser, and Faust, *Materialien*, 56, 35).

90. Hans Staudinger remembered evenings when Hilferding spoke with friends about the SPD's need to "break out of the working class" (Staudinger, *Wirtschaftspolitik im Weimarer Staat*, 85). On his Heidelberg speech, see Breitman, *German Social Democracy*, 122.

91. Heinrich A. Winkler, *Schein*, 322.

92. Prinz, "Gespräch mit Hans Speier," 555. The AfA-Bund was notably successful among technicians (Lenger, "Mittelstand und Nationalsozialismus?," 185).

93. See, e.g., Alexander Schifrin, "Der Kampf um die kommunistischen Arbeiter," *DG*, Aug. 1930, 127–28.

94. Lösche and Walter, "Auf dem Weg?," 99–100.

95. Prinz, "Gespräch mit Hans Speier," 558; Potthoff, "Freie Gewerkschaften und sozialistische Parteien," 54. The AfA-Bund had 689,806 members at its peak in 1920 and only 450,741 in 1929 (Petzina, Abelshauser, and Faust, *Materialien*, 112). On employees in the SPD's electorate in the early years of the republic, see Jürgen Winkler, "Soziale Basis," 169–70).

96. Lösche and Walter, "Auf dem Weg?," 100. On Hilferding's opposition to such arguments, see Staudinger, *Wirtschaftspolitik im Weimarer Staat*, 85. Also see the remarks by Fritz Tarnow, chairman of the woodworkers' union, to the ADGB Bundesausschuss on the outmodedness of the immiseration theory (4/5.6.28, Dok. 192, in *Gewerkschaften 1928–30*, 3[2]:1133). On workers' dislike of white-collar employees, see Hans Speier's comments in Prinz, "Gespräch mit Hans Speier," 556–58.

97. Lösche and Walter, "Auf dem Weg?," 102. On the political evolution of Weimar professionals, both "free" and state employed (such as high school teachers), see Jarausch, "Crisis of the German Professions," 379–98. On the ADGB's position, see Larry Eugene Jones, *German Liberalism*, 251.

98. Sühl, *SPD und öffentlicher Dienst*, 168–69. This charge grew out of a general suspicion of Socialist intellectuals—academics, lawyers, or physicians—on the part of SPD functionaries. See, e.g., Landauer, "Erinnerungen," 311–18.

99. NSDAP HA R.92/F.1897: Bezirkversammlung, 11.4.27. At this meeting, over leadership disapproval, the ranks passed a resolution requiring eligible party members to join the ADB or a free trade union. The issue arose again in 1930 (Bezirkversammlung, 28.3.30; "Die Kluft in der Münchner SPD," *Die Neue Zeit* [KPD], 28.3.30). See the leftist attack on members of the DBB at the Kiel congress and Wels's defense of the DBB (Sozialdemokratische Partei Deutschlands, *Sozialdemokratischer Parteitag 1927* [hereafter cited as

SPD Parteitag 1927], 37–38, 76, 80–82. Also see Potthoff, "Freie Gewerkschaften und sozialistische Parteien," 54; Lösche and Walter, "Auf dem Weg?," 105. Lösche and Walter discuss similar efforts by SPD teachers (106).

100. Heinrich A. Winkler, *Schein*, 339–41, 384–85. On the economic straits of the self-employed in the mid-1920s, see Larry Eugene Jones, *German Liberalism*, 252.

101. Lösche and Walter, "Auf dem Weg?," 116–17; Leuschen-Seppel, "Budget-Agrarpolitik der SPD," 91–92; Pyta, *Gegen Hitler*, 399.

102. Hodge, "Three Ways to Lose a Republic," 181–82. On the unrest, see Larry Eugene Jones, *German Liberalism*, 285–89. For a gripping fictional portrayal of farmer militancy in Schleswig-Holstein, see Hans Fallada, *Bauern, Bomben, und Bonzen*.

103. Lösche and Walter, "Auf dem Weg?," 116.

104. NSDAP HA R.92/F.1897: Öffentliche Versammlung, 21.9.23; #75, Lagebericht, 18–31.10.24. Also see Lösche and Walter, "Auf dem Weg?," 114.

105. For the SPD, the gap was uneven. In cities such as Berlin, Leipzig, and Magdeburg, it did not exist (Frevert, *Women in German History*, 172).

106. But only 5 percent of city councilors and 8 percent of community representatives for the SPD were women (Hagemann, *Frauenalltag*, 630, 632). On the local level, Social Democrats urged husbands to recruit wives and daughters and organized special meetings for women. See the efforts of the Munich district during its 1924 Women's Recruitment Week (NSDAP HA R.92/F.1855: Öffentliche Frauenversammlung, 16.10.24). On the uneven record of the SPD on women's issues and, especially, in promoting women within the party hierarchy, see Bridenthal and Koonz, "Beyond Kinder, Küche, Kirche," 37–40; Hagemann, *Frauenalltag*, 637–38, 552–53.

107. Max Schneider, "Frauen an der Wahlurne," *DG*, Jan. 1933, 74.

108. See Lösche and Walter, "Auf dem Weg?"

109. For the revisionist position, see Pahl, "Der Run zum Nationalsozialismus." For the leftist position, see *LVZ*, 22.5.28, and Arkadij Gurland, "Proletarische Politik," *LVZ*, 12.6.28.

110. Heinrich A. Winkler, *Schein*, 385–88; Prinz, "Gespräch mit Hans Speier," 558. Hans Mommsen argues that the unions more than the SPD's program stamped the organization as working class ("Sozialdemokratie in der Defensive," 121). Detlef Lehnert also discounts the influence of the SPD's program on its electoral results ("Klassenintegration," 230.) On ADGB talk about a labor party, see Potthoff, *Freie Gewerkschaften 1918–1933*, 228.

111. Wels quoted in Guttsman, *German Social Democratic Party*, 124; Prinz, "Wandel durch Beharrung," 63.

112. SPD, Vorstand des Unterbezirks Hamburg, *Tätigkeitsbericht*, 93. For examples of festive language, see NSDAP HA R.94/F.1905: Waldfest der Sicherheitsabteilung München Sud-Ost, 22.7.23; Rebentisch, "Die treuesten Söhne," 352–53.

113. Symbolic coherence, however, did not always concern even the most

hard-line Social Democrats. After a raging debate, this meeting ended on a harmonious note with speaker and audience singing the *Internationale*—after wishing each other Merry Christmas (NSDAP HA R.92/F.1897: Bezirkversammlung, 16.12.23).

114. Gottschalch, *Strukturveränderungen*, 207–8; Breitman, *German Social Democracy*, 124; Heinrich A. Winkler, *Organisierter Kapitalismus*, 10–12, 14.

115. Heinrich A. Winkler, *Schein*, 338–39.

116. Potthoff, "Freien Gewerkschaften: Perspektiven," 25; Potthoff, *Freie Gewerkschaften 1918–1933*, 178–83.

117. In 1913, public expenditure as a portion of the entire social product was 15 percent; by 1929, it had climbed to 31 percent (Petzina, "Merkmale der Weltwirtschaftskrise," 129).

118. Heinrich A. Winkler, *Schein*, 607–10. See also Naphtali's presentation to the ADGB Bundesausschuss (30.7.28, Dok. 195, in *Gewerkschaften 1924–1930*, 3[2]:1130–32. According to Gerald Feldman, despite its gradualism Naphtali's program greatly alarmed industrialists (Feldman, "Weimar Republic," 18). On the SPD's acceptance of gradualism, see Euchner, "Sozialdemokratie und Demokratie," 144.

119. Zuckmayer, *Carlo Mierendorff*, 29; Julius Leber, "Zehn Jahre Reichswehr," *HE*, 2.1.31; Julius Leber, "Republikanisches Denken gehört in die Reichswehr!," *HE*, 20.3.31; Theodor Haubach, "Reichswehr und Macht," *DR*, April–Sept. 1927, 6–9; Osterroth, "Hofgeismarkreis," 555–57.

120. Caspar, *Sozialdemokratische Partei*, 91–92.

121. See, e.g., Max Seydewitz, "Warum die Reichswehr?," *KK* 7.1.28, 391–93.

122. For Braun's position, see Schulze, *Otto Braun*, 608, 611–13; Ehni, *Bollwerk Preussen?*, 64–66. For Müller's and Stampfer's, see Heinrich A. Winkler, *Schein*, 647; Rohe, *Reichsbanner*, 254; Stampfer, *Vierzehn Jahre*, 478–79.

123. Breitman, *German Social Democracy*, 49.

124. *SPD Parteitag 1927*, Aufhäuser, 199–200. Also see Saage, "Gleichgewicht der Klassen-Kräfte," 157.

125. Heinrich A. Winkler, "Klassenbewegung oder Volkspartei?," 12–23, 41–45. Friedrich Stampfer, editor of *Vorwärts*, felt the Heidelberg program expressed a "class struggle ideology" (*Vierzehn Jahre*, 477).

126. "Die Aufgaben der Sozialdemokratie in der Republik," in *SPD Parteitag 1927*, 173.

127. Lehnert, "Sozialdemokratie," esp. 98–100, 105. For Levi's position, see Levi, "Rechnungslegung," *KK*, 1.12.29, 709–10; Gransow and Krätke, "'Koalitionspopo,'" 140. On his politics in general, see Beradt, *Ein demokratischer Sozialist*.

128. See, e.g., the polemics at *SPD Parteitag 1927*: Löbe, 197; Severing, 201–2; Breitscheid, 206.

129. Ernst Fraenkel, "Kollektive Demokratie," *DG*, 1929, reprinted in Fraenkel, *Reformismus und Pluralismus*, esp. 82; Euchner, "Sozialdemokratie

und Demokratie," 161–62; Krumbein, "Vorläufer eines 'Dritten Weges zum Sozialismus'?," 171–72.

130. Euchner, "Sozialdemokratie und Demokratie," 164–65.

131. Ibid., 144; NSDAP HA R.92/F.1897: Bezirkversammlung, 11.4.27; Lösche and Walter, "Auf dem Weg?," 79, 81–82.

132. Rebentisch, "Frankfurter SPD," 1, StAFr; Euchner, "Sozialdemokratie und Demokratie," 144.

133. Hilferding described coalition with bourgeois parties as a tactical question (*SPD Parteitag 1927*, 181–82). For the leftist position, see *SPD Parteitag 1927*, Toni Sender, 184–86. Also see the analysis of the Left Opposition by Georg Decker, "Opposition," *DG*, Mar. 1930, 196–204.

134. Breitman, *German Social Democracy*, 142. See Ernst Eckstein's denial that he thought the SPD should leave the Prussian coalition (*SPD Parteitag 1927*, 189–90).

135. Hans Mommsen, "Sozialdemokratie in der Defensive," 110.

136. *SPD Parteitag 1927*, 174–75; Breitman, *German Social Democracy*, 127, 130.

137. According to Detlef Lehnert, before the war the SPD was a de facto *Volkspartei* with its call for an equal franchise (Lehnert, "Sozialcharakter, politisches Selbstverständnis und Klassen-Strategien," 248–49).

Chapter Two

1. Larry Eugene Jones, *German Liberalism*, 247–48; Heinrich A. Winkler, *Schein*, 261–62, 301.

2. Stampfer, *Vierzehn Jahre*, 377; Heinrich A. Winkler, *Schein*, 265, 250, 302.

3. Nachlass Paul Levi, Box 58A/2, AsD; Georg Decker, "Opposition," *DG*, Mar. 1930, 202.

4. Stürmer, *Koalition und Opposition*, 210–13. On the origins of the unemployment compensation system, see Faust, "Von der Fürsorge zur Arbeitsmarktpolitik."

5. Carlo Mierendorff, "Republik oder Monarchie?," *SM*, July 1926, 435–36; Hoegner, *Flucht*, 27; Stampfer, *Vierzehn Jahre*, 443–47.

6. See, e.g., *VW*, #226, 14.5.28.

7. Roloff, *Braunschweig und der Staat von Weimar*, 138, 140; *Statistisches Jahrbuch des Deutschen Reiches* 47 (1928), 582.

8. On Braun, see Schulze, *Otto Braun*, 537–38, 541; Stampfer, *Vierzehn Jahre*, 469; Breitman, *German Social Democracy*, 134. On Grzesinski, see Glees, "Grzesinski," 823; Schulze, *Otto Braun*, 620.

9. *HE*, 27.4.28; "Die Berliner Parteiorganisation im Wahlkampf," *UW*, June 1928, 26–28.

10. Stampfer, *Vierzehn Jahre*, 481.

11. *RZ*, 21.4.28; *HE*, 19.5.28; *LVZ*, 21.4.28, 3.5.28; *VW*, #227, 15.5.28; *HVW*, 28.4.28.

12. "Banaler Wahlkampf," *SPW*, 18.5.28.

13. *LVZ*, 12.4.28. Also see Paul Bergmann, a leftist deputy, in *HE*, 18.4.28.

14. *Flugblattsammlung 1928* (SPD), AsD; *HE*, 22.4.28, 13.5.28; *FVS*, 19.5.28.

15. For evidence of the popularity and prominence of the Panzerkreuzer slogan, see Felix Fechenbach, "Kinderelend und Panzerkreuzer", in *VW*, #208, 3.5.28; *RZ*, 13.5.28; *FVS*, 14.5.28; *VW*, #228, 15.5.28 (cartoon); *HE*, 18.4.28; "Brauchen wir ein Panzerschiff?," *Flugblattsammlung 1928* (SPD), AsD; Stampfer, *Vierzehn Jahre*, 481; Caspar, *Sozialdemokratische Partei*, 84; Walter, *Jungsozialisten*, 111–12.

16. NWStAM Bestand SPD und Reichsbanner, Nr. 14: (SPD) Rundschreiben, Bezirk Westliches Westfalen, Dortmund, 27.3.28, 10.4.28, 8.5.28; Rundschreiben, Recklingshausen, 5.4.28.

17. Stoltenberg, *Die politischen Strömungen im schleswig-holsteinischen Landvolk*, 116. On the plight of small farmers across the country, see Childers, *Nazi Voter*, 145–47.

18. Larry Eugene Jones, *German Liberalism*, 285–89; Childers, *Nazi Voter*, 147–48. Also see Larry Eugene Jones, "Crisis and Realignment."

19. See, e.g., "Klassenkampf in der Reichstagswahl," *HE*, 19.5.28; "Klassenkampf," *HVW*, 1.5.28.

20. See the assessment of the results in NWStAM Bestand SPD und Reichsbanner, Nr. 14: (SPD) Rundschreiben, Recklingshausen, 31.5.28.

21. On Munich's problems, see NSDAP HA R.93: Lagebericht, 9.5.24. On demoralization in Württemberg, especially Stuttgart, see Edinger, *Kurt Schumacher*, 26. On the split in Saxony, see Richard Hunt, *German Social Democracy*, 211–21. For election statistics, see Falter, Lindenberger, and Schumann, *Wahlen und Abstimmungen*, 41, 44, 89, 91, 100, 101, 113.

22. On gains from bourgeois parties, see Hans Vogel's remarks from the Sozialdemokratische Partei Deutschlands, *Sozialdemokratischer Parteitag 1929* (hereafter cited as *SPD Parteitag 1929*), 34. On Catholic voters, see *RZ*, 21.5.28; Georg Decker, "Die Reichstagswahlen," *DG*, June 1928, 484. On rural votes, see *HVW*, 22.5.28.

23. Heinrich A. Winkler, *Schein*, 522, 527; Lösche and Walter, "Auf dem Weg?," 89.

24. Georg Decker, "Zur Soziologie der Reichstagswahlen," *DG*, July 1928, 1–12. Decker, alias Denicke, had an outlook similar to that of fellow Menshevik Alexander Schifrin, who also contributed many articles to Hilferding's journal. They offered more basic criticisms of SPD policies than did many contributors.

25. Larry Eugene Jones, *German Liberalism*, 480, 297–98. Also see Childers, *Nazi Voter*, 125–27.

26. In later elections, the SPD in Leipzig and Dresden proved relatively immune to KPD competition. See Anna Siemsen, *LVZ*, 11.9.28; SPD, Vorstand des Unterbezirks Gross-Leipzig, *Gross-Leipzig Jahresbericht*, 243–45.

27. Georg Decker, "Wahlergebnisse in Gross-Berlin," *UW*, July 1928, 146;

Karl Birnbaum, "Grossstadtpropaganda für die Partei," *UW*, Aug. 1928, 187; *VW*, #257, 2.6.28. Election results are in Falter, Lindenberger, and Schumann, *Wahlen und Abstimmungen*, 70–71.

28. For procoalition editorials, see *HE*, 22.5.28, 29.5.28; *HVF*, 1.6.28; *HVW*, 7.6.28. *RZ* (26.5.28) published a selection of opinions from the regional SPD press which indicated that most non-Saxon districts did not reject a coalition.

29. *FVS*, 30.5.28, 4.6.28; *LVZ*, 22.5.28, 7.6.28. *Der Klassenkampf* dedicated an entire issue to "coalition or not" (*KK*, 1.6.28).

30. *BVW*, 30.5.28, 24.5.28; *FVS*, 4.6.28; *LVZ*, 22.5.28.

31. See, e.g., *KK*, 1.6.28 and 1.7.28, and Paul Levi, "Verantwortung und Regierung," *SPW*, 25.5.28. For discussion at party meetings, see *BVW*, 24.5.28; *LVZ*, 5.6.28; Osterroth and Schuster, *Chronik der deutschen Sozialdemokratie*, 190.

32. Stampfer to Kautsky, 25.5.28, NL Karl Kautsky, D/XXI/304, IISH; NSDAP HA R.92/F.1898: Sektionsversammlung, 19.6.28.

33. *HVW*, 7.6.28.

34. *HVF*, 1.6.28.

35. Heinrich A. Winkler, *Schein*, 531.

36. Schulze, *Otto Braun*, 540–41; Braun, *Weimar*, 245–46; Heinrich A. Winkler, *Schein*, 531–32.

37. XYZ, "Schaut auf Preussen!," *KK*, 1.4.30, 207; Staudinger, *Wirtschaftspolitik im Weimarer Staat*, 81.

38. Braun, *Weimar*, 246.

39. Schulze, *Otto Braun*, 540, 543, 563. On the links between republicanization and patronage in Prussia, see Glees, "Grzesinski," 823; Schulze, *Otto Braun*, 620; Orlow, *Weimar Prussia*, 115–35, 219–30.

40. *SPD Parteitag 1929*, Hilferding, 194–95. Council and delegation declarations are in *LVZ*, 7.6.28.

41. Eyck, *Geschichte der Weimarer Republik*, 2:206.

42. Paul Levi, "Wege und Irrwege," *KK*, 1.7.28, 390–91.

43. Hoegner, *Flucht*, 27.

44. Leber, "Todesursachen," 211–13, 220–21.

45. Cabinet meeting, 8.10.28, in *Akten: Müller II*, 2:63.

46. Schulze, *Otto Braun*, 545–46. Also see Julius Leber, "Zur Klärung des Wehrproblems," *DG*, Feb. 1929, 125–26.

47. *LVZ*, 11.8.28; Wacker, *Bau des Panzerschiffs "A,"* 120.

48. Kurt Rosenfeld, "Panzerkreuzer und Regierungskoalition," *KK*, 15.8.28, 481–85; *HE*, 11.8.28; Kurt Schumacher, *ST*, 16.8.28; Heine, *Kurt Schumacher*, 37.

49. Braun, *Weimar*, 252; Brecht, *Mit der Kraft*, 52–53.

50. On the reactions of the ranks and lower functionaries, see NHStAH Hann. 310, II/A, Nr. 12: Protokoll der gemeinsamen Sitzung des Hann. Bezirkvorstandes und Beirates, 23.8.28; BA R45IV/41: (KPD) An die Exeku-

tive der Komintern, 18.10.28. For a sample of centrist and right-wing opinion and commentary on its roots, see *HVF*, 15.8.28, 16.8.28; *HE*, 17.8.28; *ST*, 20.8.28; *BVW*, 15.8.28; *RZ*, 15.8.28. For the editorial response, see, e.g., *HE*, 11.8.28, 13.8.28; *RZ*, 14.8.28.

51. *ST*, 25.8.28, 28.8.28.

52. On Saxony, see *RZ*, 17.8.28, and Walter, *Jungsozialisten*, 123; on Aachen, see *RZ*, 12.9.28; on Braunschweig and Berlin, see Koszyk, *Zwischen Kaiserreich und Diktatur*, 182. The following districts condemned the decision, although not all called for leaving the cabinet: Hamburg (*HE*, 18.8.28), Altona (*ST*, 25.8.28), Lübeck (*RB*, 16.9.28), Hesse-Darmstadt (*HVF*, 18.8.28), Cologne (*RZ*, 21/22.8.28), Magdeburg (*ST*, 25.8.28), Anhalt (*ST*, 25.8.28), Munich (NSDAP HA R.92/F.1897: Lagebericht, 24.8.28), Bielefeld (*RZ*, 21.8.28), Upper Rhine (*RZ*, 22.8.28).

53. NSDAP HA R.92/F.1897: Lagebericht, 8.24.28. Severing was the only Social Democratic minister who went out to justify his vote before rank and file audiences. Besides Munich, he spoke in Bielefeld (*RZ*, 21.8.28), his hometown.

54. *VW*, #403, 26.8.28.

55. On the successful channeling of discontent, see BA R45IV/41: (KPD) An die Exekutive der Komintern, 18.10.28. For evidence of it, see *HVW*, 19.8.28; *EVW*, 17.8.28, 18.8.28.

56. Paul Levi, "Der Panzerkreuzer," *SPW*, 17.8.28; Leber, "Zur Klärung des Wehrproblems," 126. Kurt Schumacher described the Panzerkreuzer as a symbol of "imperial nationalism" that the masses opposed (*ST*, 16.8.28).

57. NHStAH Hann. 310, II/A, Nr. 12 (Lehmann at joint meeting of Hanover's district executive and council); Toni Sender, "Kritik an den Richtlinien zur Wehrpolitik," *DG*, Feb. 1929, 113–14; *BVW*, 14.8.28; Levi, "Der Panzerkreuzer"; *HE* 16.8.28; Stampfer, *Vierzehn Jahre*, 481–82; Braun, *Weimar*, 253.

58. Leber, "Todesursachen," 217. On opinion at the base, see a (pre-Panzerkreuzer) discussion in Munich of the relationship between the party and its deputies (NSDAP HA R.92/F.1898: Sektionsversammlung, 19.6.28).

59. Braun, *Weimar*, 252. On August 16, Braun wrote Müller that as finance minister, Hilferding could have insisted that the money for the appropriations was not at hand (NL Müller, Mappe I, #6, AsD). Müller replied, "Political reasons were the decisive ones" (Müller to Braun, 20.8.28, NL Müller, Mappe IV, #60, AsD).

60. Sollmann speech to Cologne membership, *RZ*, 21.8.28. For Grzesinski's view, see Breitman, *German Social Democracy*, 149–50.

61. Kurt Schumacher, *ST*, 16.8.28, 20.8.28, 28.8.28. Schumacher's critical articles reversed the line set by *Tagwacht* editor Wilhelm Keil, who defended the ministers' decision (*ST*, 14.8.28). His apology published, Keil went on vacation, leaving Schumacher in charge of the paper (Keil, *Erlebnisse*, 2:342–43). Schumacher proceeded to attack the decision, reporting on every Social

Democratic community meeting that denounced the ministers, most of which he personally addressed. According to his protégé, Erwin Schoettle, the popularity Schumacher won in August 1928 forced Keil and other old-timers to put him in an electable slot on the Reichstag list in Württemberg in 1930 (Schoettle, "Der Parteiführer in Stuttgart," in Scholz and Oschilewski, *Turmwächter der Demokratie*, 470).

62. Hugo Sinzheimer, "Koalitionspolitik," *NB*, Mar. 1930, 122. Also see Sinzheimer's speech to a Frankfurt membership meeting (*FVS*, 7.2.30). Leftists too used the phrase "will to power" when they talked about Social Democratic failures in the government. See, e.g., Toni Sender's assessment of Müller's first six months in office (*BVW*, 31.12.28).

63. *VW*, #390, 18.8.28.

64. Braun to Müller, 16.8.28, NL Müller, Mappe I/6, AsD.

65. Quoted in Schulze, *Otto Braun*, 548. Müller let Braun know how trying he found the meeting by describing the absent Rudolf Wissell as "the lucky one" (Müller to Braun, 24.8.28, NL Müller, Mappe IV/555, AsD).

66. This motion was the idea of Paul Löbe, president of the Reichstag (Müller to Braun, 24.8.28, NL Müller, Mappe IV/555, AsD).

67. *Reichstag: Sten. Berichte*, Bd. 423, 15.11.28, 324–332; cabinet meetings, 14.11.28 and 15.11.28 (11 A.M. and 6 P.M.), in *Akten: Müller II*, 1:224–30. In the cabinet, Müller and Severing tried to explain their Reichstag votes to their bourgeois colleagues. Also see Adolph, *Wels*, 164–65, 169.

68. Brecht, *Mit der Kraft*, 54. Leber agreed ("Todesursachen," 225).

69. NWStAM Bestand SPD und Reichsbanner, Bd. 1, Nr. 1: Rundschreiben, Bezirk Westliches Westfalen, 23.8.28; meeting of Hamburg organization, *HE*, 18.8.28; *SPD Parteitag 1929*, Breitscheid, 160–61. Leftists held to a strict interpretation of the ties between delegation and ministers. Sender and Aufhäuser wrote Breitscheid, "It is self-understood that socialist ministers see themselves as deputies of the party and delegation" (Sender and Aufhäuser to Breitscheid, 13.8.28, NL Felix Fechenbach, AsD).

70. *VW*, #391, 19.8.28.

71. Julius Leber cited Stresemann, Severing, and Hilferding as critics of delegation power ("Todesursachen," 217).

72. *SPD Parteitag 1929*, Breitscheid, 160–61.

73. Noske, *Erlebtes*, 309.

74. This sentiment was voiced by people from all political tendencies. See, e.g., *HE*, 15.8.28; *LVZ*, 5.9.28; *FVS*, 20.8.28.

75. *HVF*, 12.9.28; Karl [Carlo] Mierendorff, "Warnung vor Illusionen," *HVF*, 15.9.28.

76. Breitman, *German Social Democracy*, 150–51. Hilferding suggested this response.

77. *LVZ*, 18.9.28; Mierendorff, "Warnung vor Illusionen." The left-wing Breslau *Volkswacht* reprinted this article (*BVW*, 18.9.28).

78. *SPD Parteitag 1929*, Schumacher, 151; Haubach, 149. Karl Hölter-

mann, second in command of the Reichsbanner, made Haubach's point earlier (*RB*, 16.9.28).

79. Hugo Sinzheimer pointed out in *Neue Blätter* (Mar. 1930, 121–23) that Müller had opposed a Great Coalition in 1922–23 while Sinzheimer had even then advocated partnership with the DVP. Now he had grave doubts about how coalition was being practiced.

80. Some critics: Adolph, *Wels*, 172 n. 242; Eyck, *Geschichte der Weimarer Republik*, 2:310–12; Bracher, *Auflösung*, 298, 302; Turner, *German Big Business*, 103. Some defenders: Abendroth, *Aufstieg und Krise*, 66; Heupel, *Reformismus und Krise*, 109; Schönhoven, *Reformismus und Radikalismus*, 147; Maurer, *Reichsfinanzen*, 125–28, 131, 135–36.

81. Others who take this position include Timm, *Deutsche Sozialpolitik*, 202–3, 185; Heinrich A. Winkler, *Schein*, 815–23.

82. This judgment is shared by Potthoff, "Freie Gewerkschaften und sozialistische Parteien," 78–79.

83. *LVZ*, 27.12.28, 28.12.28, 4.1.29, 7.1.29, 10.1.29.

84. *HVF*, 25.5.29.

85. Drechsler, *SAPD*, 48–49; Richard Hunt, *German Social Democracy*, 79–80; *SPD Parteitag 1929*, 269–72. On Frankfurt's mood, see Wickham, "Working-Class Movement in Frankfurt," 196.

86. *SPD Parteitag 1929*: Vogel, 37–39; Breitscheid, 160–61; Stampfer, 173–74; Sollmann, 75; Müller, 80–85. Speaking for the Left, see Maeder, 64–65; Wendt, 67; Seydewitz, 68–69; Eckstein, 71–72; Fleissner, 77–78; Rosenfeld, 88–89.

87. *SPD Parteitag 1929*, 267–68.

88. Preller, *Sozialpolitik*, 428–29.

89. Noske, *Erlebtes*, 309.

90. *SPD Parteitag 1929*: Müller, 80; Wels, 13; Breitscheid, 165; Stampfer, 173–74.

91. Bundesausschuss, 30/31.7.29, Dok. 219, in *Gewerkschaften 1924–1930*, 3(2):1279–83. Only Fritz Tarnow of the woodworkers' union argued that some kind of reform must be accepted because the issue would not make a "good election slogan" (1284).

92. Hermann Müller (Lichtenberg) to Theodor Leipart, 24.5.28, Dok. 191, 1091; Leipart at Bundesausschuss meeting, 4/5.6.28, Dok. 192, 1093–94; Kukuck and Schiffmann, "Einleitung," 18; all in *Gewerkschaften 1924–1930*, vol. 3, no. 2.

93. Schreiben des ADGB-Bundesvorstandes an die sozialdemokratische Reichstagsfraktion, 8.4.29, Dok. 211, 1251; Kukuck and Schiffmann, "Einleitung," 19; both in *Gewerkschaften 1924–1930*, vol. 3, no. 2. The ADGB was also upset that it was left out of negotiations over the Young Plan (Leipart to Chancellor Müller, 26.6.29, Dok. 217, in ibid.).

94. *LVZ*, 1.8.29, 21.8.29, 22.8.29, 6.9.29, 14.9.29, 23.9.29. Thomas to Grassmann, 18.8.29, Dok 221, 1294–95; Besprechung der Vorstände der

SPD, der Reichstagsfraktion und des ADGB, 23.8.29, Dok. 222, 1296–98; both in *Gewerkschaften 1924–1930*, vol. 3, no. 2.

95. Thomas to Wels, 11.9.29, Dok. 224, in *Gewerkschaften 1924–1930*, 3(2): 1301–2.

96. Adolph, *Wels*, 171.

97. Müller to Stampfer, 2.9.29, Dok. 223, in *Gewerkschaften 1924–1930*, 3(2):1299–1300.

98. Heinrich A. Winkler, *Schein*, 599–603.

99. Thomas to Wels, in *Gewerkschaften 1924–1930*, 3(2):1303.

100. Wilhelm Keil, "Die Schwachen des Reichsetats" *LVZ*, 8.7.29.

101. Timm, *Deutsche Sozialpolitik*, 159.

102. Breitman, *German Social Democracy*, 154; James, "Rudolf Hilferding," 859–61.

103. Maurer, *Reichsfinanzen*, 41.

104. Timm, *Deutsche Sozialpolitik*, 151; Keil, *Erlebnisse*, 2:359–61. Despite their different tax plan, Social Democrats accepted the assumption that profitability must be strengthened and capital formation encouraged in order to stimulate the German economy (Maurer, *Reichsfinanzen*, 91, 100).

105. Staatssekretär Hans Schäffer to Max Warburg, 2.8.30, #126, in *Politik und Wirtschaft*, 1:353.

106. Maurer, *Reichsfinanzen*, 98–99; Timm, *Deutsche Sozialpolitik*, 152–53.

107. Cabinet meetings, 9.12.29 and 11.12.29, in *Akten: Müller II*, 2:1238–44, 1247–48; delegation leaders' meetings, 11.12.29 and 13.12.29, ibid., 1246–47, 1256.

108. Max Seydewitz, "Macht Schluss mit der Regierung," *KK*, 1.1.30, 3–4; Keil, *Erlebnisse*, 2:361–62; *VW*, #589, 17.12.29.

109. Delegation leaders' meeting, 14.12.29, in *Akten: Müller II*, 2:1262 n. 6.

110. Seydewitz, "Macht Schluss mit der Regierung," 4, 8; Timm, *Deutsche Sozialpolitik*, 156.

111. James, "Rudolf Hilferding," 864.

112. Maurer, *Reichsfinanzen*, 90–91, 105; Heinrich A. Winkler, *Schein*, 747–49. Winkler (753) notes similarities between Schacht's attacks and the SPD's critique of Hilferding's program.

113. Quoted in Timm, *Deutsche Sozialpolitik*, 159. Also see Paul Levi, "Zeitgenosse Schacht," *KK*, 15.12.29, 741–43. He stressed the lack of leadership within the government. After Schacht's first attack, the SPD in Hamburg demanded that the party develop a finance program (Büttner, *Hamburg*, 445).

114. Karl Böchel, "Die Sachsenwahlen," *KK*, 1.7.30, 393.

115. Seydewitz, "Macht Schluss mit der Regierung," 3–4.

116. Georg Decker, "Koalitionskrämpfe," *DG*, Jan. 1930, 3. On Aufhäuser's views, see Heinrich A. Winkler, *Schein*, 765.

117. *HE*, 2.3.30, 3.3.30, 28.2.30; Witt, *Hamburger Sozialdemokratie*, 69; *FVS*, 7.2.30; *RZ*, 11.2.30; *DVZ*, 24.3.30.

118. See the comments of Theodor Thomas at a Bundesausschuss meeting.

His remarks provoked angry interruptions from Otto Wels and Paul Hertz (present for the SPD) (17.2.30, Dok. 250b, in *Gewerkschaften 1924–1930*, 3[2]:1423–24).

119. Breitman, *German Social Democracy*, 156–58; Maurer, *Reichsfinanzen*, 117–18.

120. Cabinet meeting, 3.3.30, in *Akten: Müller II*, 2:1519, 1521.

121. Notes on a telephone conversation with Brüning, 1.3.30, in *Politik und Wirtschaft*, 1:63. Hindenburg was not just a passive object in these intrigues. Already in 1929 he had made "soundings" about the possible formation of a conservative cabinet (Jasper, *Gescheiterte Zähmung*, 22).

122. Heinrich A. Winkler, *Schein*, 786–96, 801–2; Maurer, *Reichsfinanzen*, 125–28, 134–35, 139.

123. Delegation leaders' meetings, 26.3.30 and 27.3.30, in *Akten: Müller II*, 2:1600, 1603. Present for the SPD: Breitscheid, Wels (26.3.30 only), Hertz, Keil, and Aufhäuser.

124. Leber, "Todesursachen," 228; Timm, *Deutsche Sozialpolitik*, 183–84; Stampfer, *Vierzehn Jahre*, 516.

125. *VW*, #147, 28.3.30; Adolph, *Wels*, 171.

126. Leber, "Todesursachen," 228.

127. Keil, *Erlebnisse*, 2:371–72; Breitman, "Socialism and the Parliamentary System in Germany," 363–64.

128. Leber, "Todesursachen," 228–29; Max Seydewitz, "Der Himmel ist nicht eingestürzt," *KK*, 1.4.30, 193. August Rathmann, not a deputy, also reported that political implications were not discussed ("Neuer Anfang sozialdemokratischer Politik?," *NB*, Sept. 1930, 388–89).

129. *HE*, 23.4.30.

130. Timm, *Deutsche Sozialpolitik*, 187.

131. Jasper, *Gescheiterte Zähmung*, 19.

132. *LVZ*, 28.3.30, 4.4.30, 5.4.30; *DVZ*, 29.3.30; *BVW*, 28.3.30; *HVF*, 29.3.30; *FVS*, 1.4.30; *VW*, #176, 14.4.30; *FW*, 4.5.30, 17, 21–2. *Das Freie Wort* consisted of letters from functionaries and was intended for functionaries. Ernst Heilmann edited it and introduced each issue.

133. Schulze, *Otto Braun*, 625. See the editorial by "Illo" (*FW*, 6.4.30, 1–2), a pseudonym Heinrich A. Winkler attributes to Heilmann, head of the Prussian delegation (*Schein*, 811 n. 291).

134. Hoegner, *Verratene Republik*, 208–9; Witt, *Hamburger Sozialdemokratie*, 70–71; Leber, "Todesursachen," 213–14. Also see Rathmann, "Neuer Anfang sozialdemokratischer Politik?," 388–89; Dr. Süssheim, *FW*, 4.5.30, 19–21.

135. Braun, *Weimar*, 292; Schulze, *Otto Braun*, 624–25.

136. Hilferding, "Der Austritt aus der Regierung," *DG*, May 1930, 388–89. Also see the critique of the vote by Severing, *Lebensweg*, 2:239.

137. *HE*, 3.4.30; Büttner, *Hamburg*, 445; Witt, *Hamburger Sozialdemokratie*, 70–71.

138. Paul Bergmann spoke of the countrywide lack of enthusiasm in comments made before a Hamburg audience (*HE*, 23.4.30).

139. *FW*, 4.5.30, 18–19, 21. Also see Rathmann, "Neuer Anfang sozialdemokratischer Politik?," 389.

140. Stampfer, *Vierzehn Jahre*, 522; *VW*, #157, 2.4.30; #170, 10.4.30; #171, 11.4.30; #173, 12.4.30. Braun objected to the no-confidence motion because it did not "give Brüning a chance" and strained relations with the Center Party in Prussia (*Weimar*, 295).

141. Pistorius, "Rudolf Breitscheid," 289; *VW*, #151, 30.3.30.

142. Braun, *Weimar*, 297–98; *RB*, 10.4.30.

143. The words in quotes are in a letter from Hans Staudinger to Otto Braun that explains the background to the RDI/ADGB talks (14.6.30, #87a, in *Politik und Wirtschaft*, 1:233).

144. Wengst, "Unternehmerverbände und Gewerkschaften," 102–3; Neebe, "Unternehmerverbände und Gewerkschaften," 310–11; Neebe, "Konflikt und Kooperation," 229–30. Whatever the RDI's motivation, the SPD leadership clearly supported these negotiations—see *VW*, #256, 4.6.30; #261, 6.6.30.

145. Neebe, "Konflikt und Kooperation," 227–29. This deflationary consensus between capital and labor, which is discussed in chapter 6, came on the heels of a "rationalization consensus" of the late 1920s (Feldman, "Weimar Republic") and an "inflationary and revaluation consensus" of the early 1920s (Maier, *Recasting Bourgeois Europe*, 510).

146. *VW*, #289, 24.6.30.

147. Stampfer, *Vierzehn Jahre*, 525.

148. Keil, *Erlebnisse*, 2:388.

149. Ibid., 391–92; Eyck, *History of the Weimar Republic*, 2:269; Stampfer, *Vierzehn Jahre*, 526. Paul Hertz had also made a conciliatory speech (*Reichstag: Sten. Berichte*, Bd. 428, 7.7.30, 6199).

150. *Reichstag: Sten. Berichte*, Bd. 428, 16.7.30, 6400–6401. Also see *VW*, #328, 16.7.30, with its banner headline: "The Poll Tax must fall! Social Democracy ready to negotiate—but without the Negro tax."

151. Breitscheid believed Hindenburg's opposition to SPD participation in a regime lay at the root of Brüning's refusal to compromise (A. Erkelenz to K. Rothenbücher, 10.8.30, NL Erkelenz, 72/133/51, BA).

152. *Reichstag: Sten. Berichte*, Bd. 428, 18.7.30, 6501–5; Eyck, *History of the Weimar Republic*, 2:273. Braun voted for the Social Democratic motion only because he opposed the anticonstitutional path he feared Brüning was embarking upon (*Weimar*, 305). In his memoirs, Severing distanced himself from Landberg's position, without mentioning his own earlier suggestion that Müller use Article 48 (*Lebensweg*, 2:246–47).

153. Stampfer, *Vierzehn Jahre*, 478; Leber, "Todesursachen," 211–12.

Chapter Three

1. *Reichstag: Sten. Berichte*, Bd. 423, 16.11.28, 373D; Bd. 425, 7.6.29, 2167B; 8.6.29, 2210D.

2. G. Decker, "Der Kampf um die Demokratie," *DG*, Apr. 1929, 312–13.

3. *VW*, #162, 7.4.29; NSDAP HA R.92/F.1897: Lagebericht, 17.5.29.

4. Leber, "Todesursachen," 229.

5. *SPD Parteitag 1929*: Vogel, 37; Breitscheid, 170.

6. *HVF*, 25.5.29.

7. *SPD Parteitag 1929*: Sender, 178.

8. NSDAP HA R.93/F.1902, Ortsversammlung, 7.9.29.

9. SPD, Landesarbeitsausschuss der SPD Sachsens, *Material II zur Land-tagswahl*. Meanwhile, police reports, at least in the Ruhr, noted that the KPD and the NSDAP were "especially active" and "exceptionally inflammatory" (NWStAM Reg. Münster VII, Nr. 2, Bd. 6: Lageberichte 1.1–31.3.29 [Reck-lingshausen, 18.4.29]).

10. *LVZ*, 7.5.29, 13.5.29, 15.5.29, 16.5.29.

11. Krall, *Landespolitik der SPD in Bayern*, 105–6; Böhnke, *NSDAP im Ruhr-gebiet*, 122, 133. Also see Childers, *Nazi Voter*, 128–29.

12. Grill, *Nazi Movement in Baden*, 171–76.

13. *HE*, 30.10.29.

14. *FW*, 17.11.29, 1–2; 15.12.29, 1–2.

15. *LVZ*, 17.11.29, 18.11.29, 19.11.29, 10.12.29.

16. NSDAP HA R.92/F.1895: Lagebericht, 14.9.29.

17. Childers, *Nazi Voter*, 129–30. According to Waldemar Besson, the National Opposition succeeded in making the Young Plan the central issue of *Württemberg* politics in the second half of 1929 (Besson, *Württemberg und die deutsche Staatskrise*, 74). Thomas Schnabel questions the assumption that the anti–Young Plan campaign was decisive for the Nazi breakthrough into respectable circles, which, he argues, had already occurred (Schnabel, "'Wer wählte Hitler?,'" 128). Ottmar Jung maintains that the NSDAP concentrated on its own electoral efforts, not the Young Plan, and accrued neither publicity nor money from participation in the national committee for the referendum (Jung, "Plebiszitärer Durchbruch 1929?").

18. Krall, *Landespolitik der SPD in Bayern*, 109. On the campaign's contribution to rising antirepublicanism, see Eyck, *History of the Weimar Republic*, 2:211. Also see Berghahn, "Volksbegehren gegen den Young Plan," esp. 438–42.

19. Three-fourths of the signatures and many of the 5.8 million yes votes came from DNVP strongholds in Mecklenburg, Pomerania, East Prussia (Milatz, *Wähler und Wahlen*, 124–25). Also see Falter, Lindenberger, and Schumann, *Wahlen und Abstimmungen*, 80. This explains in part why the results did not frighten Social Democrats—these areas were not SPD *Hoch-burgen*. Yet they were exactly the districts where the Nazis did well in September 1930 (Nicholls, *Weimar and the Rise of Hitler*, 108).

20. ADGB-Bundesvorstand an die Spitzenverbände der Gewerkschaften, 10.10.29, Dok. 229, 1316; Mitteilung des ADGB Bundesvorstandes an den ADB, AfA-Bund und DBB, 22.10.29, Dok. 236, 1327; Kukuck and Schiffmann, "Einleitung," 48; all in *Gewerkschaften 1924–1930*, vol. 3, no. 2.

21. Hoegner, *Verratene Republik*, 202.

22. Schulze, *Otto Braun*, 570–71; dairy entry of 7.10.29, Pünder, *Politik*, 16.

23. Stampfer, *Vierzehn Jahre*, 478–79; Keil, *Erlebnisse*, 2:350–51.

24. Grill, *Nazi Movement in Baden*, 200; Hennig, "Anmerkungen zur Propaganda der NSDAP."

25. See the battles over this issue in Munich's local sections in late 1930 and early 1931: NSDAP HA R.93/F.1898: Sektionsversammlung, 7.10.30; F.1901: Jahresversammlung des Bezirkes, 23.2.31; R.92/F.1895: Lagebericht über Oppositionsgruppe, 7.3.31; R.93/F.1898: Sektionsversammlung, 27.3.31; Sektionsversammlung, 9.4.31; Sektionsversammlung, 19.5.31.

26. *VB*, 28.9.29, 1.10.29, 3.10.29, 6/7.10.29, 13.11.29; *RF*, #190, 27.9.29; #197, 5.10.29; #203, 12.10.28; #204, 13.10.29.

27. *Berliner Tageblatt*, #462, 1.10.29; #463, 1.10.29; #466, 3.10.29; #477, 9.10.29; #488, 16.10.29.

28. "Umgang mit Menschen: Lehren des Falles Sklareks," *VW*, #483, 15.10.29.

29. *RF*, #204, 13.10.29.

30. See the early analysis of the Sklarek affair's consequences by Rosenberg, *History of the Weimar Republic*, 304–5, as well as the recent evaluation by Fülberth, *Beziehungen zwischen SPD und KPD*, 311. The SPD slipped from 73 to 64 seats in the city council; the KPD rose from 43 to 56; and the NSDAP leaped from 0 to 13 (*Berliner Tageblatt*, #545, 18.11.29). In contrast, the SPD gained seats in other Prussian and in Saxon cities.

31. Adolf Lau, *KK*, 1.12.29, 716. Also see letters to *FW*, 1.12.29, 1–3; 15.12.29, 13; and Ernst Heilmann's defense of the official response, *FW*, 1.12.29. In a clear attempt to make up for *Vorwärts*'s handling of the affair, the Berlin SPD published as a pamphlet the speech of an SPD city councilor who defended the SPD by going on the offensive against the KPD and other parties. The pamphlet included a Berlin SPD resolution that attacked the KPD but also promised to clean out all implicated Socialists (Erich Flatau, *Zum "Sklarek Skandal,"* 8–15).

32. Leber, "Todesursachen," 226–27.

33. Niewyk, *Socialist, Anti-Semite, and Jew*, 184, 190, 194–99.

34. *RF*, #198, 6.10.29. This article "exposed" an obscure Social Democrat as a secretly rich capitalist and Sklarek crony. It was adorned by a grotesque anti-Semitic caricature of the "culprit," who was described as whining and weak. This piece, admittedly the only one of its kind in the *Rote Fahne*, trumped any single story on the case in the *Völkischer Beobachter*.

35. On the SPD's defense of Jewish rights and denunciations of anti-

Semitism, see Niewyk, *Socialist, Anti-Semite, and Jew*, esp. 95–103, 150–62. On the tendency to discount Nazi sincerity, see ibid., 200–205.

36. The quote is from *VB*, 8.10.29.

37. Walther Pahl, "Die ökonomischen und politisch-moralischen Lehren der Sklarek-Affäre," *SM*, Nov. 1929, 912.

38. *VW*, #483, 15.10.29. Twenty-five percent were employees in public service; 13 percent were civil servants (Lösche and Walter, "Auf dem Weg?," 86).

39. Paul Levi, "Rechnungslegung," *KK*, 1.12.29, 709–10.

40. *LVZ*, 24.1.30.

41. *LVZ*, 31.1.30. On Graf's personality and popularity, see Walter, *Nationale Romantik*, 74–75.

42. Breitman, *German Social Democracy*, 89–91.

43. Kurt Rosenfeld, "Das neue Republikschutzgesetz," *KK*, 15.10.29, 625–27.

44. "Denkschrift des Reichsinnenministers Severing, Dec. 1929," printed in Jasper, "Zur innenpolitischen Lage"; *Reichstag: Sten. Berichte*, Bd. 427, 13.3.30, 4415A–B, 4416.

45. Meeting of Hamburg SPD, *HE*, 28.2.30.

46. Pyta, *Gegen Hitler*, 282–83. Ehni argues that even Prussia tended to act more decisively against Communists than against right-wing extremists, its maneuvering room narrowed by the lack of cooperation from the Reich (*Bollwerk Preussen?*, 177–78).

47. Kurt Rosenfeld, for example, did not oppose laws to protect the republic but believed existing ones sufficient (*KK*, 15.10.29, 625).

48. *FW*, 15.12.29, 2; 2.2.30, 24–28.

49. *FW*, 9.2.30, 24–28; 6.4.30, 17–23; 20.4.30, 16–17. Heilmann also felt that the Nazi policy of excluding Jews made it improper for Social Democrats to frequent their rallies.

50. Arthur Schweriner, "Nazisturm auf Berlin," *UW*, Apr. 1930: 76–80.

51. *HVW*, 1.4.30.

52. NSDAP HA R.93/F.1902: Versammlung des Reichsbanners und Jungbanners, 27.3.30; Jungbannerversammlung, 29.3.30.

53. Rundschreiben des ADGB zur Tätigkeit des Stahlhelms und der NSDAP, 24.1.30, Dok. 246, in *Gewerkschaften 1924–1930*, 3(2):1382–83; Bundesausschuss, 4/5.5.30, Dok. 1, in *Gewerkschaften 1930–1933*, 4:84–89.

54. Mierendorff, *Zehn Jahre nach dem Kapp-Putsch*, 5, 8.

55. Georg Decker, "Der erste Schritt," *DG*, Feb. 1930, 97–103.

56. *FVS*, 1.4.30.

57. "Denkschrift an den Geldquellen der NSDAP" (n.d.), 2–6, NL Grzesinski B/X/1558, IISH.

58. "Die NSDAP: Referentendenkschrift" (May 1930), 32–48, NL Grzesinski B/X/1559, IISH.

59. Stampfer, *Vierzehn Jahre*, 522.

60. The recruitment department, set up in January 1929, printed the *Partei-Korrespondenz*, put together material on other parties, and evaluated 190 newspapers (Rupieper, "'Kampf gegen die nationalsozialistische Seuche,'" 1–2).

61. "Stürzt den Bürgerblock! Gegen den Panzerkreuzerbau! Besteurt die Besitzenden!," *Flugblattsammlung 1930* (NSDAP), AsD.

62. *LVZ*, 5.6.30, 7.6.30, 14.6.30.

63. *VW*, #288, 23.6.30.

64. Karl Böchel, *KK*, 1.7.30, 393–96; *LVZ*, 23.6.30, 24.6.30; *VW*, #288, 23.6.30.

65. *FW*, 6.7.30, 1–6, 8–11, 13–15; 17.8.30, 1–2.

66. See, e.g., Walter Mannzen, "Die sozialen Grundlagen des National-sozialismus," *NB*, Aug. 1930, 371–72. Recognition of working-class support of the NSDAP existed as early as 1923, though its significance was down-played. See the replies of local ADGB officials to inquiries about Nazi support-ers from national headquarters, printed in Ruck, *Bollwerk gegen Hitler?*, 191, 193, 198.

67. Oskar Edel, "Die Gemeindewahlen," *KK*, 1.12.29, 711–12.

68. Ernst Heilmann, *FW*, 17.11.29, 1–2.

69. See, e.g., NSDAP HA R.93/F.1902: Reichsbannerversammlung, 20.6.30.

70. *FW*, 12.1.30, 17–19; 27.7.30, 19–20, 13–18.

71. Engelbert Graf, *Die Faschistische Gefahr*, 17, 22. This pamphlet was an expanded version of Graf's talk on fascism in Leipzig earlier in the year.

72. *DVZ*, 29.2.29.

73. *SPD Parteitag 1929*, 35–36.

74. *FW*, 20.7.30, 14–33; 10.8.30, 26–28.

75. Carlo Mierendorff, "Gesicht und Charakter der Nationalsozialistischen Bewegung," *DG*, June 1930, 489–504.

76. Mierendorff discounted the view of Nazism as a replay of earlier anti-Semitic parties not to deny that it was anti-Semitic but to stress that it was new and highly dangerous. However, his later writings, as well as most SPD analyses, did tend to underestimate the significance of racial anti-Semitism as a central element of Hitler's ideology. In Mierendorff's case, this is noteworthy not only because his understanding of National Socialism was impressive but because in the summer of 1930 several of his anti-Nazi speeches were secretly underwritten by the Central Association of German Citizens of the Jewish Faith (E. Jacobi to Berthold Sender, 30.6.30, printed in Paucker, *Der jüdische Abwehrkampf*, 174; Albrecht, *Der militante Sozialdemokrat*, 109).

77. Mierendorff, "Gesicht und Charakter der Nationalsozialistischen Be-wegung," 494–97, 503–4.

78. Larry Eugene Jones, *German Liberalism*, 386.

79. Noakes, *Nazi Party in Lower Saxony*, 152, 151 n. 5. Also see Pridham, *Hitler's Rise to Power*, 135–37; Grill, *Nazi Movement in Baden*, 187. Quote from Childers, *Nazi Voter*, 138–39.

80. Larry Eugene Jones, *German Liberalism*, 385–86.

81. Police reports noted that Nazis and Communists inundated each other's and SPD meetings, while Social Democrats did not return the gesture (NWStAM Reg. Münster VII, Nr. 2, Bd. 6: Lageberichte 10.9.30 and 4.10.30 [from Bremen]).

82. *FW*, 10.8.30, 4–6, 26–28; 17.8.30, 20–22, 25; 24.8.30, 14–15.

83. This article appeared, e.g., in *RZ*, 22.8.30, and *FVS*, 19.8.30.

84. The substance of SPD propaganda is analyzed below.

85. SPD, Vorstand, *Reichstagswahl 1930*, 44–55, SPD Broschüre; *Flugblatt-sammlung 1930*, AsD; *VW*, #337,,22.7.30; #356, 1.8.30; #357, 2.8.30; #368, 8.8.30, #370, 14.8.30; #388, 20.8.30; #394, 23.8.30; #400, 27.8.30; #410, 2.9.30.

86. *DVZ*, 19.8.30; *FVS*, 20.8.30; *RZ*, 21.8.30, 9.9.30; *HVW*, 2.9.30; NHStAH Hann. 310, II, Nr. 93: An die Unterbezirks-und Kreisvereinsvor-stände, SPD Bezirk Hannover, 19.8.30. Crispien addressed Düsseldorf's opening electoral rally (*DVZ*, 27.8.30); Prussian Interior Minister Heinrich Waentig spoke at the second big rally (*DVZ*, 3.9.30); *RZ*, 20.8.30 (Severing in Cologne); *FVS*, 8.9.30 (Scheidemann in Frankfurt).

87. Keil, *Erlebnisse*, 2:395.

88. *FVS*, 14.8.30; *DVZ*, 26.8.30; *HE*, 18.8.30; *HVF*, 22.8.30, 26.8.30; *ST*, 26.8.30.

89. *HE*, 18.8.30; *HVF*, 18.8.30, 29.8.30. Mierendorff was second on a list of fourteen candidates in Hesse-Darmstadt. Darmstadt was his hometown.

90. *VW*, #388, 20.8.30.

91. Rudolf Breitscheid, "Worum es ging und geht," *DG*, Aug. 1930, 98.

92. See, e.g., *VW*, #337, 22.7.30; #378, 14.8.30.

93. See, e.g., *VW*, #386, 19.8.30; #387, 20.8.30.

94. Brecht, *Mit der Kraft*, 141; Büttner, *Hamburg*, 453.

95. *VW*, #388, 20.8.30. For commentary on the dissolution of the tradi-tional bourgeois parties, see, e.g., the cartoon in *VW*, #349, 28.7.30; *VW*, #353, 31.7.30; Fritz Bieligk, "Die Umgruppierung der Bourgeois Parteien," *KK*, 15.8.30, 495.

96. Childers, *Nazi Voter*, 154.

97. *RZ*, 17.8.30, 2.9.30; *ST*, 30.8.30; Carlo Mierendorff, "Die Nazis," *HE*, 18.8.30.

98. Wilhelm Sollmann, "Die grosse Trommel um 'dritten Reich'" *RZ*, 19.8.30; Otto Grotewohl at meeting on 3.9.30 (quoted in Roloff, *Braunschweig und der Staat von Weimar*, 158).

99. *VW*, #339, 23.7.30.

100. Bezirkssekretär des ADGB für den Freistaat Hessen und die Provinz

Hessen-Nassau an die Ortsausschüsse und Gau- und Bezirksleitungen im IV. Bezirk: Reichstagswahl, 4.8.30, Dok. 7, in *Gewerkschaften 1930–1933*, 4:118.

101. Siegfried Aufhäuser, "Platz für die Arbeit—Der Sinn des Wahlkampfes von 1930," *VW*, #343, 25.7.30; *VW*, #373, 12.8.30.

102. *VW*, #359, 3.8.30.

103. Larry Eugene Jones, *German Liberalism*, 386.

104. *FVS*, 18.8.30; *DVZ*, 8.8.30.

105. *HVW*, 27.8.30.

106. *ST*, 27.8.30, 5.9.30, 6.9.30, 12.9.30.

107. Schneider, "Tolerierung-Opposition-Auflösung," 1:152.

108. The quotes are from a bulletin that the ADGB district secretary for Hesse and Hesse-Nassau sent to local and district committees (4.8.30, Dok. 7, in *Gewerkschaften 1930–1933*, 4:118). On financial support, see Eggert to Hanna, 2.8.30, Dok. 6, ibid., 117. For similar assessments of the seriousness of the situation, see Georg Decker, "Noch einmal: Kampf um die Demokratie," *DG*, Sept. 1930, 194; *FVS*, 18.8.30, 6.9.30.

109. Aufzeichnung des ADGB-Vorsitzenden Leipart für den Journalisten Graudenz über die politische Lage, 6.8.30, Dok. 8, in *Gewerkschaften 1930–1933*, 4:119.

110. *LVZ*, 13.9.30; *FVS*, 30.8.30; *HVW*, 14.9.30; *RZ*, 18.8.30.

111. Franz Künstler, "Auf dem Kampf gegen die Diktatur!," *UW*, Aug. 1930, 169–70.

112. *DVZ*, 26.8.30.

113. Schneider, "Tolerierung-Opposition-Auflösung," 1:152.

114. Quoted by Decker, "Noch einmal," 193.

115. Heinrich A. Winkler, *Katastrophe*, 64, 68.

116. James, *German Slump*, 98; Treue, *Deutschland in der Weltwirtschaftskrise*, 125, 129–30, 133.

117. SPD, Vorstand, *Reichstagswahl 1930*, 1, 56–57.

118. *VW*, #395, 24.8.30.

119. *FVS*, 30.8.30.

120. See, e.g., "Auch Deutschlands Jugend muss Sozialdemokratisch wählen!," *RZ*, 9.9.30; "Bauern, wählt Liste 1!," *HVW*, 12.9.30, 13.9.30; "Die Klasse ist alles—Der Stand ist nichts! Angestellte und Beamte—Kämpft unter roten Fahnen!," *VW*, #419, 7.9.30. Also see the list of campaign leaflets in *SPD Jahrbuch 1930*, 219; of twenty-nine, four were directed at women of different social groups and one each to civil servants, employees, farmers, agricultural laborers, elementary school teachers, and railroad workers, employees, and officials.

121. *HVW*, 7.9.30.

122. See, e.g., Breitscheid's speech to Cologne functionaries in *VW*, #359, 3.8.30.

123. *VW*, #420, 8.9.30.

124. *VW*, #421, 9.9.30.

Chapter Four

1. Leber, "Todesursachen," 229; R. Kleineibst, "Gegen den Brüning-plan! Positive Politik!," *LVZ*, 10.10.30. Kleineibst edited the *Volkszeitung für den Oberlausitz* in Löbau, Saxony.

2. *DVZ*, 7.11.30.

3. Falter, Lindenberger, and Schumann, *Wahlen und Abstimmungen*, 41, 44.

4. See, e.g., *HE*, 16.9.30, and *ST*, 16.9.30, which described the vote as an anticapitalist protest directed at the Weimar state instead of the economic system.

5. *VW*, #439, 19.9.30; #465, 4.10.30.

6. Neebe, "Unternehmerverbände und Gewerkschaften," 312.

7. See *RZ*, 15.9.30; "Das Ergebnis der Reichstagswahl," *GZ*, 20.9.30, 593; Ernst Heilmann, *FW*, 21.9.30, 4.

8. On the psychological reaction of hypervigilance, see Janis and Mann, *Decision-Making*, 81, 245–46, 364.

9. Interview in the *New York Herald Tribune*, 16.9.30.

10. Weichmann, "Kritische Bemerkungen," 459.

11. Matthias, "Sozialdemokratische Partei," 113; Schulze, *Otto Braun*, 638.

12. Neebe, "Unternehmerverbände und Gewerkschaften," 312–14; Grübler, *Spitzenverbände*, 209–10.

13. Weichmann, "Kritische Bemerkungen," 459.

14. Brüning, *Memoiren*, 187, 191. Individuals who pushed for a Great Coalition included the state secretaries Pünder, Meissner, and Weismann (diary entry, 17.9.30, Pünder, *Politik*, 61). Also see H. Schäffer's diary entry of 15.9.30 on his talks with Weismann about bringing the SPD into the cabinet (Nr. 135, in *Politik und Wirtschaft*, 1:381–82). The liberal *Frankfurter Zeitung* also called for a Great Coalition (#612, 18.10.30).

15. Bracher, *Auflösung*, 371 n. 20. Wolfram Pyta agrees that Müller supported SPD participation in a regime (*Gegen Hitler*, 207).

16. Schulze, *Otto Braun*, 638–39. Also see Feder, *Heute sprach ich mit*, 270.

17. *VW*, #432, 15.9.30.

18. On this meeting, see Pünder, *Politik*, 61; Müller to Braun, undated (sometime between Sept. 23 and 30), printed in Braun, *Weimar*, 309. Brüning and Hilferding were friends (Brüning, *Memoiren*, 116). Almost a decade later, Hilferding claimed to be the "spiritual father" of toleration (Adolph, *Wels*, 235 n. 509).

19. Diary entry, 9.30.30, Pünder, *Politik*, 62.

20. Heupel, *Reformismus und Krise*, 145–46.

21. Schulze, *Otto Braun*, 639; Matthias, "Sozialdemokratie und die Macht im Staate," 82. Many have judged toleration harshly: Rosenberg, *History of the Weimar Republic*, 305–6; Matthias, "Sozialdemokratie und die Macht im Staate," 80; Bracher, *Auflösung*, 380; Klönne, *Deutsche Arbeiterbewegung*, 243. But it has also found defenders, especially in the more recent literature:

Skrzypczak, "Führungsprobleme," 141–42; Rovan, *Geschichte der deutschen Sozialdemokratie*, 154–55; Kolb, "Sozialdemokratische Strategie," 165, 171; Heinrich A. Winkler, *Katastrophe*, 304–5; Schaefer, *SPD in der Ära Brüning*, 442–43; Pyta, *Gegen Hitler*, 209.

22. Hamburger, "Betrachtungen über Heinrich Brünings Memoiren," 35–36.

23. Heinrich A. Winkler, *Katastrophe*, 276.

24. "Denkschrift aus den Akten der Reichskanzlei," printed in Matthias, "Sozialdemokratische Partei," 203–5.

25. *VW*, #433, 9.16.30. Alexander Schifrin ("Parteiprobleme nach den Wahlen," *DG*, Nov. 1930, 406) argued that the KPD organization was in bad shape, its separatist trade union tactic a failure.

26. *HVW*, 18.9.30; *FVS*, 16.9.30; *BVW*, 15.9.30; *VW*, #433, 16.9.30. Both before and after the elections, Alexander Schifrin urged the SPD to try harder to recruit its "political reserve" among KPD voters ("Der Kampf um die Kommunistischen Arbeiter," *DG*, Aug. 1930, 127–28; "Parteiprobleme nach den Wahlen," 407).

27. Matthias, "Sozialdemokratische Partei," 109; Neebe, *Grossindustrie, Staat und NSDAP*, 78.

28. Braun, *Weimar*, 308. Braun himself (309–10) expressed this very opinion to Brüning in a conversation in October, saying either the Reich must join with Prussia and come down hard on the Nazis in the streets or allow them into the government. Braun worried, though, that they might gain more prestige than they would lose due to "exposure." In *Inside Germany* (114), Albert Grzesinski recalled Braun's early viewpoint and, in hindsight, judged it correct.

29. Braun, *Weimar*, 309.

30. Feder, diary entry, 29.9.30, *Heute sprach ich mit*, 270.

31. See, e.g., *Mannheimer Volksstimme*, reprinted in *RZ*, 16.9.30.

32. See, e.g., election assessments in the *BVW*, 15.9.30; *FVS*, 16.9.30; August Rathmann, "Antikapitalistische Politik?," *NB*, Oct. 1930, 439. Activists in Berlin hotly disputed Hilferding's assertion that the election results did not constitute a defeat for the SPD. However, Max Seydewitz too emphasized that the party had emerged unshaken from the elections ("Der Sieg der Verzweiflung," *KK*, 15.9.30, 545).

33. Besides Hilferding, see *VW* Sonderausgabe, 15.9.30; *RZ*, 16.9.30; *HVW*, 15.9.30.

34. *HE*, 15.9.30; F. D. H. Schulz, *DVZ*, 16.9.30; J. Altmeier, "Klarheit tut Not," *FVS*, 16.9.30; A. Kranold, *BVW*, 15.9.30; "Was die sozialdemokratische Presse sagt," *RZ*, 16.9.30. Also see "Die Gewerkschaftspresse über die Reichstagswahl," *GZ*, 4.10.30, 635–36.

35. R. Lipinski, "Nach der Sturmflut: Was brachte der 14. September?," *LVZ*, 16.9.30.

36. *ST*, 17.9.30. Schumacher was now coeditor of the *Schwäbische Tagwacht* and chairman of the Stuttgart district (Dorothea Beck, *Julius Leber*, 112).

37. *HE*, 26.9.30. The headlines underlined the Hamburg viewpoint: "Active Struggle for Democracy" and "Hamburg Social Democracy Demands Active Policy."

38. *VW*, #460, 1.10.30. Max Seydewitz also referred obliquely and disapprovingly to "Braun-talk" ("Der Sieg der Verzweiflung," 546).

39. *VW*, #460, 1.10.30. On the SPD's defeat and the KPD's victory, see "Trotz alledem, es lebe die Sozialdemokratie!," *UW*, Oct. 1930, 2171–78; Falter, Lindenberger, and Schumann, *Wahlen und Abstimmungen*, 71–72. The Nazis were relatively weak in Berlin with 12.8 percent (Reich: 18.3 percent).

40. *VW*, #467, 5.10.30.

41. *LVZ*, 2.10.30; NSDAP HA R.93/F.1898: Ortsversammlung, 14.10.30; R.92/F.1898: Ortsversammlung, 18.11.30.

42. *LVZ*, 11.10.30.

43. *BVW*, 8.10.30.

44. Toni Sender, "Chaos der Konterrevolution," *BVW*, 7.10.30.

45. See, e.g., Ernst Eckstein, "Was nun?," *BVW*, 24.10.30.

46. Gerlach at Düsseldorf membership meeting, *DVZ*, 7.11.30. Düsseldorf's other Reichstag deputy, Lore Agnes, represented the leftist point of view at this meeting.

47. Gerlach, *DVZ*, 7.11.30; Karl Meitmann, "Der Staat soll unser sein," *HE*, 15.9.30.

48. Max Seydewitz, *KK*, 15.12.30, 737. Georg Decker, who supported toleration, agreed ("Tolerierung," *DG*, Dec. 1930, 484).

49. Hilferding's speech in Breslau, *BVW*, 8.10.30.

50. *VW*, #479, 12.10.30.

51. See, e.g., Heilmann, *FW*, 21.9.30, 1–2; Rathmann, *NB*, Sept. 1930, 388–89.

52. The *Gewerkschafts-Zeitung* explained that the SPD had to support Brüning's "silent dictatorship" to protect the workers' general economic and political rights (*GZ*, 3.1.31, 3).

53. Severing, *Lebensweg*, 2:258.

54. Bundesausschuss, 19.9.30, Dok. 13, in *Gewerkschaften 1930–1933*, 4:135–36.

55. See, e.g., SPD, Vorstand, *Diktatur!*, 12–15; Otto Landsberg, *Die politische Krise der Gegenwart* (published version of a talk held in the Freie Sozialistische Hochschule in Berlin, 17.1.31), 2–15.

56. *VW*, #489, 18.10.30; *HE*, 20.10.30.

57. *BVW*, 8.10.30. Also see *VW*, #433, 16.9.30.

58. According to Richard Kleineibst, complacency flipped into exaggerated alarm, while early Cassandras coolly appraised the NSDAP, aware of its weaknesses and its strengths ("Die Chance der Sozialdemokratie," *KK*, 1.12.30, 710).

59. *VW* (#433, 16.9.30) nervously discussed the possibility of a coup; in his diary, Ernst Feder mentioned general putsch rumors (diary entry, 20.9.30, *Heute sprach ich mit*, 268). Leber described sarcastically how the party's "biggest pacifists" dashed around asking if the Reichswehr could be relied on if the Nazis tried to seize power ("Todesursachen," 229).

60. F. D. H. Schulz, "Die Kampfbasis," *DVZ*, 4.10.30.

61. Feder, diary entry, 2.10.30, *Heute sprach ich mit*, 270–71.

62. Crispien in Berlin, *VW*, #467, 5.10.30; Stampfer, *Vierzehn Jahre*, 531. Also see Rudolf Hilferding, "In der Gefahrenzone," *DG*, Oct. 1930, 294–95.

63. "Denkschrift," in Matthias, "Sozialdemokratische Partei," 204–5.

64. Sitzung des ADGB-Bundesvorstandes (hereafter cited as Bundesvorstand), 14.1.31, Dok. 24, in *Gewerkschaften 1930–1933*, 4:229. Paul Löbe ("Warum so bescheiden?," *VW*, #437, 18.9.30) and F. D. H. Schulz ("Erkenntnis—Konsequenz," *DVZ*, 11.10.30) also thought big business hostility to the SPD had paled.

65. *ST*, 16.9.30; *HE*, 15.9.30. Also see Hoegner's speech to the Reichstag, *Reichstag: Sten. Berichte*, Bd. 444, 18/19.10.30, 137; SPD, Vorstand, *Diktatur!*, 16.

66. See Turner, *German Big Business*, esp. 124–41, on the alarm of big industrialists over the sudden emergence of the NSDAP as a potential power broker. See Jasper on the financial situation that made a coalition with the extreme Right "unthinkable" (*Gescheiterte Zähmung*, 56).

67. Paul Löbe, "Wo steht die Mehrheit? Der Sinn der Wahlen," *VW*, #457, 30.9.30. Also see Siegfried Aufhäuser ("Was nun?," *RZ*, 23.9.30): "Before September 14 [the bourgeois parties] wanted to save Germany from the rising Red flood but, having conjured up spirits they can't exorcise, now the SPD is supposed to save the Bürgerblock."

68. Hilferding, "In der Gefahrenzone," 294–95.

69. Hamburger, "Betrachtungen über Heinrich Brünings Memoiren," 36. For the high estimation of Brüning at the time, see, e.g., Julius Kaliski, "Überwindung der Krise?," *SM*, 22.12.30, 1197.

70. Hoegner, *Verratene Republik*, 236. Hoegner was a neorevisionist Bavarian Social Democrat, first elected to the Reichstag in 1930.

71. According to Stampfer, the SPD never placed much confidence in the Old Gentleman's reliability (*Vierzehn Jahre*, 531–32).

72. Leber, "Todesursachen," 229–30. In his 1933 bitterness, Leber exaggerated. Social Democrats did worry about Nazi efforts to infiltrate the Reichswehr. Severing, though, believed the top brass more reliable than the lower officer corps (Breitman, *German Social Democracy*, 168). The reassessment went both ways. Brüning referred disapprovingly to generals who suggested "cooperation" with Social Democracy (*Memoiren*, 188, 189). He felt the Reichswehr's change of heart was a reaction to Goebbels's announcement that the NSDAP was going to overthrow the system and to revelations during the Ulm trial of three lieutenants who handed out Nazi literature.

73. On the tendency toward executive independence, see Neebe, "Konflikt und Kooperation," 231.

74. *VW*, #481, 14.10.30; Theodor Geiger, "Panik im Mittelstand," *DA*, Oct. 1930, 653.

75. *EVW*, 16.9.30; *FVS*, 16.9.30; *VW* Sonderausgabe, 15.9.30. In *BVW*, 15.9.30, Arnold Kranold lampooned *Vorwärts* for its "rose-colored view" of the political situation. Even Georg Decker made the analogy to 1924, while acknowledging that a warm December might not follow a cold May (*VW*, #434, 16.9.30). *HVW* (18.9.30) tallied the DNVP and NSDAP votes from both elections and showed that this "anti-Semitic" block had risen by fewer than a million votes from May 1924 to 1930. It summed the "Marxist" (SPD and KPD) vote to show it too had increased. On the passive support of Marx's regime in 1924, see Breitman, *German Social Democracy*, 121.

76. Seydewitz ("Der Sieg der Verzweiflung," 548) drew the opposite conclusion from the same comparison with 1924, pointing out that the DNVP eventually joined the cabinet and was, thereby, defused.

77. See, e.g., Heilmann, *FW*, 21.9.30, 5–6; Hilferding, "In der Gefahrenzone," 289–90.

78. Fritz Naphtali, as quoted in Brauckmüller and Hartmann, "Organisierter Kapitalismus und Krise," 1:357.

79. Hilferding speech in Breslau, *BVW*, 8.10.30. See also "Denkschrift," in Matthias, "Sozialdemokratische Partei," 203.

80. Hoegner, *Verratene Republik*, 236.

81. Forty years later Ernest Hamburger still felt that in this sense the toleration policy succeeded since the SPD survived the Brüning period relatively unscathed organizationally and even electorally (Hamburger, "Betrachtungen über Heinrich Brünings Memoiren," 35–36).

82. See Hilferding's speech at Berlin district conference, *VW*, #467, 5.10.30; Gates, "Economic Policies," 160–61, 99–100.

83. *VW*, #519, 5.11.30; #525, 8.11.30; #529, 11.11.30; #531, 12.11.30; #569, 5.12.30.

84. The positions of the SPD elite and its critics are discussed in chapter 6.

85. See Müller to Braun, printed in Braun, *Weimar*, 308.

86. Schulze, *Otto Braun*, 637.

87. *BVW*, 8.10.30. Pünder wrote in his diary in late November that the SPD leadership was currently very understanding: "They know, of course, that with the fall of Brüning the guillotine would immediately fall on the Prussian coalition" (23.11.30, *Politik*, 76).

88. Breitman, *German Social Democracy*, 167 n. 43.

89. Sender, *Autobiography*, 279–80; Aufhäuser in Hamburg, *HE*, 17.12.30. According to Hans Schäffer, he convinced Sender to support toleration (diary entry, 17.9.30, in *Politik und Wirtschaft*, 1:382 n.2).

90. *VW*, #481, 14.10.30.

91. *HE*, 5.10.30; NSDAP HA R.93/F.1898: Ortsversammlung, 14.10.30.

92. *DVZ*, 7.11.30. The editor of the *Düsseldorf Volkszeitung* came out forcefully for toleration (*DVZ*, 4.10.30, 11.10.30, 25.10.30).

93. *BVW*, 1.11.30.

94. "Die Partei ist kampfbereit," *VW*, #492, 20.10.30. Richard Lipinski, district chairman, did not defend the new policy, but his *Leipziger Volkszeitung* also did not attack it (see, e.g., *LVZ*, 8.12.30, 10.12.30).

95. Max Seydewitz, "Der falsche Weg," *KK*, 1.11.30, 644–45; Max Seydewitz, "Aktivität und Politik," *KK*, 15.11.30, 673–74; Kurt Rosenfeld, "Gewissenszwang und Partei," *KK*, 1.1.31.

96. In November, Müller was bothered by reliance on Article 48 (Heinrich A. Winkler, *Katastrophe*, 262–63). In December, he initially resisted pressure to postpone reconvening the Reichstag until early February 1931 (8.12.30, Pünder, *Politik*, 80).

97. Stampfer, *Vierzehn Jahre*, 533–34; Bracher, *Auflösung*, 380.

98. *VW*, #540, 17.11.30; *FVS*, 18.11.30; Kurt Alt, "Die Gemeindewahlen," *KK*, 1.12.30, 722–23.

99. *VW*, #563, 3.12.30; #583, 13.12.30. Others also stressed these gains: *FVS*, 7.12.30; even Seydewitz (*KK*, 15.12.30, 738) conceded that improvements had been won.

100. The KPD walked out too but quickly returned. The NSDAP and the DNVP absented themselves until October, when the Reichstag reconvened after a six-month recess.

101. *VW*, #67, 10.2.31; #68, 10.2.31; #69, 11.2.31.

102. "Eine Niederlage des Antiparlamentarismus," *GZ*, 21.2.31, 113–5. *Der Klassenkampf* criticized widespread talk in the party about parliamentary victories ("Parlamentarische Zwischenspiele," *KK*, 15.2.31, 97). Also see "Brüning-Front," *KK*, 15.2.31, 122.

103. *BVW*, 8.10.30.

104. Martiny, "Entstehung," 387; "Protokoll eines Treffens des Kreises der 'Neuen Blätter für den Sozialismus', November 1930," printed in ibid., 408–11; Borinski, "'Neue Blätter für den Sozialismus,'" 178–79. Among those present: August Rathmann, Hans Müller, Franz Osterroth, Theo Haubach, and Carlo Mierendorff. Karl Meitmann and Gustav Dahrendorf were invited to the second meeting. On their criticisms of the SPD, see Skrzypczak, "Führungsprobleme," 132–33.

105. Seydewitz, "Aktivität und Politik," 673. Helga Grebing agrees that "young rightists" emphasized the need for militant struggle, while leftists focused on a structural analysis of capitalism and demanded "active politics" (Grebing, "Auseinandersetzung," 267–68).

106. Privately Mierendorff questioned the toleration policy from the beginning, according to Paul Hertz ("Carlo Mierendorff zum Gedenken" [written 1944] printed in *Sozialistische Tribüne*, 1 Jg., Nr. 2/3 [1946?], NL Hertz, XXVII/37/I/d, AsD).

107. Borinski, "'Neue Blätter für den Sozialismus,'" 180–81.

108. Theodor Haubach, "Parole: Angriff," *HE*, 19.9.30.

109. Carlo Mierendorff, "Lehren der Niederlage," *NB*, Nov. 1930, 481–84.

110. Kurt Schumacher too was very concerned that the SPD take the offensive (Waldemar Ritter, *Kurt Schumacher*, 48–50). Also see [Georg Decker], "Der Riss durch das Proletariat," *VW*, #462, 2.10.30.

111. Quote from Ernst Heilmann, *FW*, 5.10.30, 1–2. For examples of the tenor of these letters, see *FW*, 12.10.30, 21, 23.

112. *FW*, 28.9.30, 15; 12.10.30, 20–21; 19.10.30, 16–19. Also see NSDAP HA R.93/F.1903: Reichsbannerversammlung, 22.11.30, and R.92/F.1895: Besprechung des SPD-Vorstandes München, 31.10.30.

113. *FW*, 28.9.30, 16–17; 25.1.31, 12–22; 15.3.31, 17–18; 26.10.30, 22–23; 16.11.30, 23–25.

114. *FW*, 12.10.30, 22–32; 14.12.30, 19–20.

115. *FVS*, 15.11.30; Witt, *Hamburger Sozialdemokratie*, 94 n. 34; Wickham, "Working-Class Movement in Frankfurt," 228.

116. *VW*, #508, 29.10.30; Anton Erkelenz, "Aktivität!," *VW*, #557, 28.11.30; #1, 1.1.31. The trade union leadership also began to stress the need to activate the socialist movement (*GZ*, 3.1.31, 3). *Wo bleibt der zweite Mann?* means, roughly, "Where is your comrade?"

117. *LVZ*, 18.11.30.

118. NSDAP HA R.92/F.1894: Lagebericht, 23.1.31; Munich formed a local alert service consisting of unemployed comrades who rode the streets on bicycles night and day (R.92/F.1894: Lagebericht, 12.3.31). The police in Bremen noted the "extraordinarily lively political activity . . . of all organizations" (NWStAM Reg. Münster VII, Nr. 2, Bd. 7: Lageberichte [Bremen]).

119. *Vorwärts* (#75, 12.2.31) reported with pride that the *Deutsche Allgemeine Zeitung* had noted the "Social Democratic offensive." On rallies in Berlin, see *VW*, #543, 19.11.30; #547, 22.11.30; #575, 9.12.30; #587, 16.12.30; #598, 22.12.30. The following figures, provided by the SPD press service, are culled from the *BVW* (23.2.31) and the *HVW* (1.3.31): Upper Rhine, 23 meetings and rallies in a week; Rhineland-Westphalia, 68 in a week in February (with 9,000 attending); Hesse-Nassau, 44; Hesse-Kassel, 39 (with 10,000) and 26 films; the Palatinate, 107 (also see NSDAP HA R.92/F.1894: Lagebericht, 12.3.31); Baden, 18 SPD, 22 Reichsbanner; Württemberg, 35; Franken, 30; Upper Palatinate–Lower Bavaria, 30; Magdeburg-Anhalt, 57; Thuringia, 60 in two weeks; Halle, 236 in a month; Chemnitz-Zwickau, 58 (23,000 attending); Leipzig, 18 in a week; Eastern Saxony, 32 (40,000); Lower Silesia, 19; Middle Silesia, 50 (17,000); Berlin, 13 general and 4 women's meetings (80,000); Brandenburg, 74; Pomerania, 31; Mecklenburg-Lübeck, 44; Schleswig-Holstein, 36. At a rally in Hanover, Erik Nölting (*HVW*, 8.2.31) announced the formation of 15 new party clubs. On 16.3.31, the *Hannover Volkswacht* reported 471 meetings in the district in recent months. Also see

Allen, *Nazi Seizure of Power*, 48–52; Witt, *Hamburger Sozialdemokratie*, 93–98; Klotzbach, *Gegen den Nationalsozialismus*, 41.

120. Hermann Weber, "KPD im Kampf," 85–88; Fischer, *German Communists*, 1103–7. Also see Weitz, "State Power, Class Fragmentation."

121. Bramke, "Faschismusbild in der KPD," 615; Kurz, "Arbeitermörder und Putschisten"; Bowlby, "Blutmai 1929."

122. Rank and file Communists in Württemberg expressed contempt for Social Democrats (Simms, "Worker Correspondents' Movement," 502–3), but in interviews with a *Vorwärts* reporter, a variety of Berlin workers spoke wistfully about working-class unity (#474, 9.10.30). As a rule, *Vorwärts* ignored the KPD rather than attacking it. This silence expressed contempt for the KPD as a rival but also tacitly acknowledged the strong sentiment for unity among workers.

123. On Altona, see *HE*, 1.12.30. On Augsburg, see NSDAP HA R.92/ F.1894: Polizeidirektion Augsburg an das Staatsministerium des Innern, München, 1.10.30. On Munich, see NSDAP HA R.93/F.1901: Öffentliche Versammlung (SPD), 28.1.31. At this rally, a Social Democrat who was a former Bavarian minister ascribed the Nazis' strength to the "ugly struggle between the Socialists and Communists." At a party meeting in Munich, a speaker advocated "closing ranks" with the KPD (R.92/F.1898: 18.11.30).

124. In Lambrecht, an anti-Nazi leaflet was signed by the local KPD, the SPD, the ADGB, the Reichsbanner, and Workers' Sport (NSDAP HA R.92/ F.1895: Lagebericht, Ludwigshafen a.Rh., 18.12.30).

125. Gotschlich, *Zwischen Kampf und Kapitulation*, 91.

126. In *Vorwärts* (#103, 3.3.31), Otto Grotewohl reported that the election (in which the SPD lost five of its nineteen seats) produced "no transformation in the relationship of power" because a "red majority" still existed.

127. Fülberth, "Übereinkunft zwischen SPD und KPD," 132–56; Kücklich, "Einheitsfrontinitiativen."

128. In Hanover *Gau*, the Reichsbanner was "stagnant" from 1928 through mid-1930, fluctuating between 200 and 220 local chapters. It began to grow again after September 1930 and averaged 245 chapters in 1931 (NHStAH Hann. 310, II/A, Nr. 21: Berichte des Gausekretärs über seine Tätigkeit und die Agitation und Organisationsarbeit im Gau [Hannover]). Also see Rohe, *Reichsbanner*, 364–65; Gotschlich, *Zwischen Kampf und Kapitulation*, 84–85; Loewenstein-Scharffeneck, *Tragedy of a Nation*, 85; Allen, *Nazi Seizure of Power* (1984 ed.), 48; Klotzbach, *Gegen den Nationalsozialismus*, 41.

129. See the discussion by Reichsbanner leaders in Hanover of a conference held by the national executive on 21.9.30 (NHStAH Hann. 310, II/A, Nr. 16: Sitzung der Ortsleitung, 24.9.30). For public calls to join the Reichsbanner, see *HE*, 13.10.30; *RZ*, 12.10.30; *HVW*, 30.1.31; NSDAP HA R.93/ F.1898: Ortsversammlung, 22.10.30.

130. NSDAP HA R.93/F.1903: Sektionsversammlung, 8.3.31; NHStAH

Hann. 310, II/C, Nr. 2: Gauvorstandes in Hannover an alle Abteilungs-und Kameradschaftsführer, 26.11.30; An die Kreisführer und Führer der Schutz-formationen, 22.1.31. Also see Rohe, *Reichsbanner*, 365–66; Matthias, "Sozial-demokratische Partei," 122–23;

131. Bundesausschuss, 14/15.12.30, Dok. 19, in *Gewerkschaften 1930–1933*, 4:181–86. The ADGB's sudden generosity did not last. In May it rejected a Reichsbanner request for more financial support (Bundesvorstand, 29.5.31, Dok. 42, in ibid., 311).

132. Rohe, *Reichsbanner*, 325; Klenke, *SPD Linke*, 347–48; Ziegs, "Die Haltung der Leipziger Parteiorganisation der SPD," 71, 76.

133. *LVZ*, 18.11.30, 1.12.30.

134. *LVZ*, 14.10.30, 23.2.31.

135. *BVW*, 2.10.30, 6.1.31 (article by Hörsing), 8.1.31, 22.1.31, 23.2.31.

136. "Kampforganisationen überall," *KK*, 1.11.30, 652–53.

137. Martiny, "Sozialdemokratie und junge Generation," 2:59–60. Also see *FW*, 14.12.30, 25–26. Signs of this group exist for Frankfurt (*FVS*, 15.11.30). In Munich, the police reported increased tension between young and old in the Reichsbanner (NSDAP HA R.95/F.1910: Lagebericht, 23.1.31). On the brawl, see Schmidt, "Memoiren," 152–53.

138. NSDAP HA R.93/F.1898: Sektionsversammlung, 10.12.30; R.92/F.1895: SPD Besprechung der Sektionsleitungen, 15.12.30; R.92/F.1894: 21.1.31; R.92/F.1894: Lagebericht, 23.1.31.

139. Some examples: NHStAH Hann. 310, II/A, Nr. 21: Sitzung der Ortsleitung, 9.10.30, 4.11.30, 29.1.31; *HVW*, 24.2.31 (Hanover); *VW*, #464, 3.10.30 (Brandenburg); #468, 6.10.30 (Berlin); *RZ*, 23.2.30 (Cologne); *Münchner Post*, 17.11.30, in NSDAP HA R.93/F.1902 (Munich). Georg Fül-berth ("Übereinkunft zwischen SPD und KPD," 153) describes the Reichs-banner's intense activity in the March 1931 Braunschweig municipal election.

140. NSDAP HA R.93/F.1903: Lagebericht, 10.11.30; R.95/F.1910: Lage-bericht, 23.1.31; R.92/F.1894: Lagebericht, 12.3.31. Haubach ("Nicht ein-schlaffen! Der Faschismus in Umgruppierung—neue Methoden, alte Ziele," *RB*, 23.5.31) also noted "astounding successes" in recruitment.

141. *HVW*, 8.2.31; Fritz Tarnow, "Niederlage des Antiparlamentarismus," *GZ*, 21.2.31, 113–15.

142. Georg Decker, "Deutschland erwacht," *DG*, Mar. 1931, 197–98. Also see *HVW*, 16.3.31.

143. For overviews of the historical debate on the Nazi electorate, see Falter and Hänisch, "Anfälligkeit von Arbeitern"; Hamilton, *Who Voted for Hitler?*, 9–18; Childers, *Nazi Voter*, 3–14.

144. Falter and Hänisch, "Anfälligkeit von Arbeitern," 213; Falter, "Wähler der NSDAP," 91–94; Childers, *Nazi Voter*, 157–59, 168–71, 240–43. Also see Lenger, "Mittelstand und Nationalsozialismus?"; Prinz, "Gespräch mit Hans Speier," 553.

145. Falter and Hänisch, "Anfälligkeit von Arbeitern," 207–8, 214–15; Childers, *Nazi Voter*, 265.

146. Hamilton, *Who Voted for Hitler?*, 34–35, 90–91. Also see Childers, *Nazi Voter*, 175–77.

147. Falter and Hänisch, "Anfälligkeit von Arbeitern," 193–94, 200, 204, 207, 215; Childers, *Nazi Voter*, 265.

148. Childers, *Nazi Voter*, 180, 185–87; Falter and Hänisch, "Anfälligkeit von Arbeitern," 196, 206, 214. Also see Geary, "Nazis and Workers." For the raw data on how neighborhoods voted and on their social composition in Göttingen, see the maps in Hasselhorn, *Wie wählte Göttingen?*, tables 1–3, 5, 9, 11, 14, 16, 20. Thanks to Eric Gropp for running regression analyses on these data.

149. Schnabel, "'Wer wählte Hitler?,'" 121.

150. Falter and Hänisch, "Anfälligkeit von Arbeitern," 211–12, 215; Fischer, "Class Enemies or Class Brothers?," 265.

151. Hamilton, *Who Voted for Hitler?*, 18, 47–48.

152. Geiger, "Panik im Mittelstand," 647, 637–39.

153. Georg Decker, "Wo hatten die Nazis am meisten Erfolg?," *VW*, #456, 29.9.30; Hans Neisser, "Sozialistische Analyze des Wahlergebnisses," *DA*, Oct. 1930, 657–59. Also see Ernst Fraenkel, "Antifaschistische Aufklärungsarbeit," (1930) in Fraenkel, *Reformismus und Pluralismus*, 185–87; Rathmann, "Antikapitalistische Politik?," 437; Ph. Künkele, "Wahllehren des 14. September 1930," *JB*, Jan. 1931, 16.

154. Neisser, "Sozialistische Analyse des Wahlergebnisses," 657–59; Geiger, "Panik im Mittelstand," 647.

155. Decker, "Wo hatten die Nazis am meisten Erfolg?"; Fraenkel, "Antifaschistische Aufklärungsarbeit," 186; Geiger, "Panik im Mittelstand," 647.

156. Hilferding, "In der Gefahrenzone," 293.

157. See, e.g., SPD, Vorstand, *Referentenmaterial: Nr. 3.*, 32–33.

158. Rathmann, "Antikapitalistische Politik?," 433–35.

159. Geiger, "Panik im Mittelstand," 643–46, 648–49. Also see Max Klesse, "Warum es so kommen musste, und wie es nun gehen soll," *SM*, 27.10.30, 969. For similar explanations, see Georg Decker, "Das unbekannte Volk," *DG*, Oct. 1930, 299; "Das Ergebnis der Reichstagswahl," *GZ*, 20.9.30, 594; *HVW*, 16.9.30; *LVZ*, 16.9.30.

160. Geiger, "Panik im Mittelstand," 648–49, 651; Hilferding at Berlin district conference, *VW*, #467, 5.10.30; "Wie wählten die Berlinerinnen? Jedenfalls besser als die Männer!," *VW*, #470, 7.10.30; Falter, "Wähler der NSDAP," 84–87.

161. Schifrin, "Parteiprobleme nach den Wahlen," 396–97. Several neo-revisionists came very close to Schifrin's position. See Carlo Mierendorff, "Was ist der Nationalsozialismus?" *NB*, Apr. 1931, 153; Walther Pahl, "Verjüngung, Aktivierung, Konstruktive Politik," *NB*, May 1931, 205–6; Theodor Haubach, "Nun erst recht-es lebe die Republik!," *RB*, 8.8.31.

162. Geiger, "Panik im Mittelstand," 652.

163. Alexander Schifrin, "Gegenrevolution in Europa," *DG*, Jan. 1931, 18–19.

164. They were especially common in the daily press (e.g., *ST*, 16.9.30; *HE*, 15.9.30), but the quote here is from Decker, "Das unbekannte Volk," (*DG*, Oct. 1930, 299). Decker later suggested it was "not clarifying" to focus on fascism as the "weapon of capitalism" since that emphasis hid its petit bourgeois, farmer, and civil servant social basis ("Deutschland erwacht," *DG*, Mar. 1931, 200). He probably aimed this criticism at the Left Opposition, which did not reassess Nazism after the Reichstag elections. The pages of *Vorwärts*, however, also peddled the old view; for example, according to "Die Revision des Nationalsozialismus" (#101, 1.3.31), Hans Reupke's new book on the Nazi economic program proved conclusively that the NSDAP was "the protection squad of the industrial barons."

165. Schifrin, "Parteiprobleme nach den Wahlen," 399.

166. Neisser, "Sozialistische Analyse des Wahlergebnisses," 657–58; Decker, "Wo hatten die Nazis am meisten Erfolg?" Also see *HE*, 20.11.30, on gains in rural environs around Hamburg. Recent research has confirmed that after 1918 the SPD did well among white-collar employees and lower civil servants who lived in urban areas. See Hamilton, *Who Voted for Hitler?*, 47–51; Lösche and Walter, "Auf dem Weg?," 89.

167. See, among many such comments, Georg Decker, "Die Sozialdemokratie in den Wahlkreisen," *VW*, #448, 24.9.30; Schifrin, "Parteiprobleme nach den Wahlen," 406; Neisser, "Sozialistische Analyze des Wahlergebnisses," 657. Modern researchers do not dispute that the SPD lost industrial workers' votes to the KPD but stress that it also lost employees and small-town workers to the NSDAP. See Falter and Hänisch, "Anfälligkeit von Arbeitern," 2131–35; Lösche and Walter, "Auf dem Weg?," 90.

168. Neisser, "Sozialistische Analyse des Wahlergebnisses," 659; Julius Kaliski, "Was sollen wir also tun?," *SM*, 26.9.30, 863.

169. Examples of those calling for a rural campaign: *FW*, 28.9.30, 16–17; 2.11.30, 17; 25.1.31, 12–22; 15.3.31, 15–16.

170. *HE*, 20.11.30; SPD, Vorstand des Unterbezirks Hamburg, *Tätigkeitsbericht 1929–30*, 89–91.

171. See, e.g., *FW*, 12.10.30, 21–22; 7.12.30, 18–20; 4.1.31, 3–5, 9–12, 12–15; 1.3.31, 15–16; 15.3.31, 17–19. Even an analyst in the left-wing Young Socialist journal called for attracting "the new proletariat"—i.e., the *Mittelstand* (Künkele, "Wahllehren des 14. September 1930," 19). Calls to orient toward the working class were fewer: *FW*, 4.1.31, 1–3; 1.3.31, 13–15.

172. Geiger, "Panik im Mittelstand," 653–54; Fraenkel, "Aufklärungsarbeit," 188–90.

173. Georg Decker, "Politische Wandlung," *DG*, Nov. 1930, 385–87, 392; Walther Pahl, "Der Run zum Nationalsozialismus," *SM* 26.9.30, 867–68.

Chapter Five

1. *Statistik des Deutschen Reichs*, 51 (1932): 290–91; 52 (1933): 290–91; Falter, Lindenberger, and Schumann, *Wahlen und Abstimmungen*, 38; Stachura, *Weimar Republic and the Younger Proletariat*, 60.

2. Hans Mommsen, *Verspielte Freiheit*, 369; Bundesvorstand, 10.2.32, Dok. 75, *Gewerkschaften 1930–1933*, 4:485.

3. Diary entry, 17.10.30, NL Grzesinski B/X/2017, IISH. Braun's dissatisfaction with Heinrich Waentig as Prussian minister of the interior had been growing for some time.

4. Ehni, *Bollwerk Preussen?*, 194; Schulze, *Otto Braun*, 641–43; Brecht, *Mit der Kraft*, 119; Braun, *Weimar*, 309. Also see Breitman's excellent discussion of the Prussian strategy and its problems (*German Social Democracy*, 131–43).

5. *VW*, #578, 10.12.30.

6. Braun, *Weimar*, 314–16; *VW*, #597, 21.12.30.

7. M. W. Kempner, "Einführung," in Kempner, *Der verpasste Nazi-Stopp*, 7–11. After summarizing the putschist history of the NSDAP, the memorandum (published for the first time by Kempner) described its centralized organizational structure, criminal standing under the Law for Protection of the Republic, illegal intentions, "high-treasonous" nature, and preparation for overthrowing the government by undermining the republic's civic peace and stability.

8. Diary entry, 17.10.30, NL Grzesinski B/X/2017, IISH.

9. On past differences, see Ehni, *Bollwerk Preussen?*, 50–52; Glees, "Grzesinski," 832. On new ones, see Kohler, "Crisis in the Prussian Schutzpolizei," 138–40.

10. Pyta, *Gegen Hitler*, 310, 313, 316–19, 321, 330–38, 362, 350, 341–43, 356.

11. Brecht, *Mit der Kraft*, 140; Breitman, *German Social Democracy*, 168.

12. *VW* (#350, 29.7.31) reprinted an article by the KPD's East Prussian chairman that attacked the referendum as a diversion maneuver of the big bourgeoisie. The next day he had to reverse his view. Ernst Thälmann, chairman of the KPD, only joined the campaign under pressure from Stalin and the Comintern (Schulze, *Otto Braun*, 666). An internal circular took pains to explain why the KPD was supporting a "reactionary plan" (NWStAM Reg. Münster VII, Nr. 1, Bd. 2: An alle Funktionäre der RGO und der roten Verbände!).

13. Schulze, *Otto Braun*, 661–64.

14. See, e.g., the warning in an SPD pamphlet of February 1931: "Whoever violently assaults the foundations of democracy has no right to appeal to democracy's freedoms" (SPD, Vorstand, *Diktatur!*, 16). Also see J. Leber, *Lübecker Volksbote*, 10.10.29. Luthardt discusses this issue in "Sozialdemokratie und Legalstrategie," esp. 142–44, 163.

15. Pyta, *Gegen Hitler*, 345–48, 271–74, 318, 510.

16. An example of a failed attempt to discriminate against the NSDAP was the complicated affair over whether to ban the sport festivals of both the NSDAP and the KPD in the summer of 1931; despite Severing's best efforts to spare the KPD's Spartakiade, in the end, he prohibited it too. See Schulze, *Otto Braun*, 665–66; Severing, *Lebensweg*, 2:288–90; Pyta, *Gegen Hitler*, 366–69.

17. Pyta, *Gegen Hitler*, 336, 341. To placate party opinion, Severing wrote an apology for a press law that permitted censorship (*VW*, #335, 21.7.31). *Vorwärts* was also defensive (#332, 18.7.31).

18. Grzesinski to Braun, 26.5.31, NL Grzesinski A/II/204, IISH.

19. *VW*, #365, 7.8.31. A State Party Landtag deputy had the idea for the proclamation, but Social Democratic ministerial advisor Hans Goslar composed it (Schulze, *Otto Braun*, 667–68).

20. *VW*, #370, 10.8.31. Sixteen million eligible voters did not vote or voted "no." *Vorwärts* believed that Communist workers stayed away in droves.

21. Schulze, *Otto Braun*, 668–69.

22. Brüning, *Memoiren*, 259.

23. See, e.g., Wilhelm Dittmann, *VW*, #95, 26.2.31; *RZ*, 28.2./1.3.31.

24. *VW*, #113, 8.3.31; #119, 12.3.31; F. D. H. Schulz, "Was die Stunde fordert," *DVZ*, 7.3.31. Also see Ehni, *Bollwerk Preussen?*, 192. Several newspapers (*RZ*, 5.3.31; *FVS*, 6.3.31) printed a piece by the pacifist Gerhart Segert in favor of abstention.

25. Brüning, *Memoiren*, 259–60.

26. Schulze believes Braun decided the issue (*Otto Braun*, 652–53). Brüning credited Müller, however (*Memoiren*, 260).

27. Kurt Rosenfeld, "Das Nein der Neun," *KK*, 1.4.31.

28. In Bremen, Seydewitz explained that he would have abstained if Brüning's budget had included significant concessions in the "social-political area" (H. Kranold, "Der Panzerkreuzerstreit," *SM*, 11.5.31, 444 n. 4).

29. For districts that endorsed the Nine, see *FVS*, 1.4.31; *RZ*, 24.3.31; *VW*, #204, 3.5.31. On opinion in Leipzig, see *LVZ*, 21.3.31, 10.4.31, 27.4.31.

30. *RZ*, 19.3.31.

31. Noakes, *Nazi Party in Lower Saxony*, 202.

32. Falter, Lindenberger, and Schumann, *Wahlen und Abstimmungen*, 100; *VW*, #227, 18.5.31; Z, "Die Landtagswahlen in Oldenburg," *KK*, 1.6.31, 347–48. Social Democrats across the political spectrum had hoped that the Nazi movement was losing steam in the spring of 1931. See, e.g., Curt Geyer, *VW*, #204, 3.5.31. The Oldenburg results dashed these hopes.

33. See, e.g., Portune at a meeting in Frankfurt (*FVS*, 1.4.31); Mathilde Wurm quoted in *FVS*, 12.3.31; Fritz Bieligk, "Das missbrauchte Beispiel Italien," *KK*, 15.4.31, 227–31.

34. M. Seydewitz, "Die Zersetzung der Nazibewegung," *KK*, 15.4.31, 225.

35. Kurt Rosenfeld, Max Seydewitz, and Heinrich Ströbel, "Für Einberu-

fung des Reichstages!," *KK*, 15.5.31; Max Seydewitz, "Der Parteitag hat das Wort," *KK*, 1.6.31, 321–23.

36. Hamburg: *HE*, 24.4.31; Berlin: *VW*, #195, 27.4.31; Darmstadt: *HVF*, 29.5.31.

37. *VW*, #204, 3.5.31.

38. Georg Decker, "Umstellung des Faschismus," *DG*, May 1931, 389, 393; Carlo Mierendorff, "Tolerieren—und was dann?," *SM*, 13.4.31, 315–16. Also see Alexander Schifrin, "Wandlungen des Abwehrkampfes," *DG*, May 1931, 414–15.

39. Even before Hermann Müller died on March 20, these four men became the SPD's negotiating team.

40. "8.April.1931: Besprechung des Reichskanzlers Brüning mit Vertretern der sozialdemokratischen Reichstagsfraktion am 17. März," printed in Matthias, "Sozialdemokratische Partei," 205–9.

41. Heinrich A. Winkler, *Katastrophe*, 323. Despite Severing's admonitions, *Vorwärts* asked that the SPD be told the content of the decree before the party congress (#245, 29.5.31).

42. Schaefer, *SPD in der Ära Brüning*, 118–21.

43. Wickham, "Working-Class Movement in Frankfurt," 214–15. For an evocative portrayal of popular misery, see Treue, *Deutschland in der Weltwirtschaftskrise*, 207–12.

44. Parteiführungbesprechung in der Reichskanzlei, 15.6.1931, printed in Matthias, "Sozialdemokratische Partei," 211–13. On the mood in the Reichstag delegation and Braun and Severing's resistance to it, see Brüning, *Memoiren*, 289, 276, 286. On Brüning's threat, see *Memoiren*, 289; Hans Mommsen, *Verspielte Freiheit*, 393–94.

45. Bundesvorstand, 17.6.31, Dok. 46, in *Gewerkschaften 1930–1933*, 4:327; *VW*, #277, 17.6.31.

46. Heupel, *Reformismus und Krise*, 147–48. SPD negotiators did succeed in getting unemployed youth included again in the insurance plan (*VW*, #290, 24.6.31).

47. Sozialdemokratische Partei Deutschlands, *Sozialdemokratischer Parteitag 1931* (hereafter cited as *SPD Parteitag 1931*). For the majority: Breitscheid, 175, 102; Sollmann, 121–22, 114, 179; Rossmann, 148; Sender, 129; Hertz, 155. For the opposition: Jenssen, 149.

48. *SPD Parteitag 1931*. For the opposition: Jenssen, 149; Kirchmann, 145. For the majority: Dittmann, 140, Sollmann, 114. The leftist Ernst Eckstein (152) lamented the loss of local rights under Prussian and Reich decrees.

49. Dittmann charged that Seydewitz was as irrational as Hitler (ibid., 141). Eckstein (152) was severely reprimanded by congressional chairman Lipinski (traditionally an oppositionist himself) for accusing the Prussian Interior Ministry—i.e. Severing—of doing heavy industry's bidding. According to Drechsler, the minutes leave out the most insulting interruptions (mainly

Red-baiting) of minority speakers (*SAPD*, 77). Also see Max Seydewitz, "Die liebe Kameradschaft," *KK*, 15.6.31, 359.

50. *HE*, 3.6.31; *HVW*, 4.6.31; *LVZ*, 3.6.31; Karl Böchel, "Der Eintagssieg der Mehrheit," *KK*, 15.6.31, 356.

51. Martiny, "Sozialdemokratie und junge Generation," 2:60–62. On the politics of the SAJ, see Brücher and Hartmann, "Sozialistische Arbeiterjugend."

52. *SPD Parteitag 1931*, 287–88. Stampfer noted that Berliners took the lead on the most important issue facing the SPD ("Der gute Parteitag," *VW*, #259, 6.6.31).

53. A. Kranold, "Die Bekämpfung des Faschismus und die Taktik der Partei," *BVW*, 4.6.31; "Unfruchtbare Opposition," *HVF*, 6.6.31; Carlo Mierendorff, "Das Fazit von Leipzig," *NB*, July 1931, 324–27.

54. Aufhäuser in Berlin, *VW*, #277, 17.6.31.

55. On Berlin: SPD, Vorstand des Bezirks Berlin, *Berlin Jahresbericht*, 58–60. On Munich: NSDAP HA R.92/F.1894: Lagebericht, 12.7.31; R.93/F.1898: Tagung der Sektionsleitungen München, 8.6.31.

56. Büttner, *Hamburg*, 455–56; *HE*, 11.6.31.

57. Potthoff, *Freie Gewerkschaften 1918–1933*, 279.

58. "Vor der neuen Notverordnung," *GZ*, 6.6.31, 353; *HE*, 31.5.31; *VW*, #267, 11.6.31; #269, 12.6.31; #285, 21.6.31; h.a. (Hans Aron), "Notverordnung, Finanzen und Wirtschaft," *GZ*, 20.6.31, 385–97. Also see Schneider, "Tolerierung-Opposition-Auflösung," 1:156.

59. Bundesvorstand, 10.6.31, Dok. 44, in *Gewerkschaften 1930–1933*, 4:313–20. Also see Leipart's and Fritz Tarnow's comments at a later meeting of the ADGB executive without party leaders: Bundesvorstand, 17.6.31, Dok. 46, in ibid., 327, 329.

60. Bundesausschuss, 20.6.31, Dok. 47, in *Gewerkschaften 1930–1933*, 4:338–39, 342–43.

61. *VW*, #277, 17.6.31. These marchers were members of the Gesamtverband der Arbeitnehmer der öffentlichen Betriebe.

62. *RZ*, 15.7.31.

63. "Anträge zum Gewerkschaftskongress," *GZ*, 18.7.31, 449–52; Allgemeiner Deutscher Gewerkschaftsbund, *Protokoll der Verhandlungen des 14. Kongresses*, 26–27, 122, 125–27, 130–31.

64. "Entschliessung zu Punkt 2 der Tagesordnung: Bericht des Bundesvorstandes," printed in Schneider, "Tolerierung-Opposition-Auflösung," 1:185.

65. SPD, Vorstand, *Die neue Notverordnung*, 2.

66. *VW*, #281, 19.6.31.

67. Rudolf Hilferding, "In Krisennot," *DG*, July 1931. The editorial "Innerpolitischer Befund" (*VW*, #333, 19.7.31) was unsigned but was probably written by Stampfer.

68. *SPD Parteitag 1931*, Breitscheid, 87–88; F. D. H. Schulz, "Leipzig 1931," *DVZ*, 30.5.31.

69. *SPD Parteitag 1931*, Breitscheid, 104; SPD, Vorstand, *Die neue Not-verordnung*, 2.

70. *SPD Parteitag 1931*, Breitscheid, 97, 99. Sollmann agreed with Breitscheid that the new, legal National Socialism was more dangerous than the "laughable putschism of 1923" (114).

71. Ibid., 102. Also see Georg Decker, "Faschistische Gefahr und Sozialdemokratie," *DG*, June 1931, 486–89.

72. Quote from Düwell, *Gewerkschaften und Nationalsozialismus*, 14. See also Seydewitz, "Teil III," in Seydewitz et al., *Krise des Kapitalismus*, 113–14; "Die Überwindung des Faschismus," in *Ergebnis des Leipziger Parteitages*, 29.

73. *SPD Parteitag 1931*, Jenssen, 149; Kurt Stechert, "'Schiff' Katastrophe vom 'Freien Wort,'" *KK*, 15.5.31, 311.

74. "Überwindung," in *Ergebnis des Leipziger Parteitages*, 29; Stechert, "'Schiff' Katastrophe vom 'Freien Wort,'" 310.

75. Stechert, "'Schiff' Katastrophe vom 'Freien Wort,'" 312. The Left found an ally in Ferdinand Tönnies, the eminent sociologist, who joined the SPD in his, and the republic's, last years. He believed it would take too long to attract the *Mittelstand* ("Parteipolitische Prognosen," *DA*, Oct. 1931, 774–84).

76. E. W. Eschmann, "Zur Krise des Bürgertums," *DA*, May 1931, 362–70; Walter Dirks, "Katholizismus und Nationalsozialismus," *DA*, Mar. 1931, 205–8. In a pamphlet advocating trade union unity aimed at members of the non-Socialist unions, Anton Erkelenz claimed the "trade unions opposed the immiseration theory" (Erkelenz, *Um die Einheit der deutschen Gewerkschaftsbewegung*, 26–27).

77. Theodor Geiger, "Braunschweig—die Mittelschichten und die Sozialdemokratie," *DA*, Aug. 1931, 619–21, 634–35.

78. This was part of a rare, full-page appeal to the *Mittelstand* in *Vorwärts* that began, "The system inevitably ruins," and then listed every old *Mittelstand* profession from the "finishing industry" to the "chicken farmer" ("Wirtschaft und Bürgertum," *VW*, #523, 7.11.31).

79. See, e.g., *FW*, 15.3.31, 9–18; 12.7.31, 5–9; 11.10.31, 26–28; 8.11.31, 25–26; 29.11.31, 10–11.

80. Keiser saw the Nazi movement as neither pro- nor anticapitalist, but acapitalist; its animus was purely reactionary. He too rejected the "immiseration" theory ("Der Nationalsozialismus, eine reaktionäre Revolution," *NB*, June 1931, 271–77).

81. Erik Nölting, *VW* #393, 23.8.31. See Hermann Heller's similar analysis in *Europa und der Faschismus*, 155.

82. *SPD Parteitag 1931*, Hertz, 155. Wilhelm Hoegner's plea at the congress that the party give up the idea of the "pure Klassenpartei" stands out as unique (133).

83. Aufhäuser, *Ideologie und Taktik der Angestellten-Bewegung*, 7, 22.

84. Prinz, "Wandel durch Beharrung," 69; Aufhäuser, *Ideologie und Taktik der Angestellten-Bewegung*, 19–20.

85. Remmele, *Die Fritterkrippe*, 28; Pyta, *Gegen Hitler*, 117, 436.

86. Prinz, "Gespräch mit Hans Speier," 558.

87. Falter, "Aufstieg der NSDAP in Franken," 327, 330.

88. See, e.g., *FW*, 2.11.30, 19–20; 5.10.30, 26; *SPD Parteitag 1931*, 297–98.

89. SPD, Vorstand, *Köpfe in den Sand?*, 16.

90. SPD, Vorstand, *Wichtiges Material für die Landagitation*.

91. Rupieper, "'Kampf gegen die nationalsozialistische Seuche,'" 14–16; Pyta, *Gegen Hitler*, 275–76.

92. Leber, "Todesursachen," 230; *SPD Parteitag 1931*, Hoegner, 133; Heller, "Nationaler Sozialismus," *NB*, Apr., 1931, 154–56. Also see Paul Gerlach at general membership meeting in Düsseldorf, *DVZ*, 7.11.30.

93. Carl Severing, "Zurück zur Politik!," *SM*, 19.1.31, 5; Carlo Mierendorff, "Überwindung des Nationalsozialismus," *SM*, 16.3.31: 227–28; "Was ist der Nationalsozialismus?," *NB*, Apr. 1931, 153.

94. Geiger, "Braunschweig—die Mittelschichten und die Sozialdemokratie," 627–28. For the official line, see "Vorschläge der Gewerkschaften zur Überwindung der gegenwärtigen Krise," *GZ*, 1.8.31, 481.

95. An activist in Magdeburg wrote that "we aren't breaking out of our circles" (*FW*, 19.7.31, 20–21). See Bracher's figures on meetings and rallies in Hesse-Nassau between April 1 and August 8, 1931: NSDAP, 1,910; KPD, 1,129; Stahlhelm, 467; SPD, 447; DNVP, 73; Center, 50; DVP, 30 (*Auflösung*, 386 n. 87).

96. Theodor Haubach, "Die militante Partei," *NB*, May 1931, 209–10. Also see Walter Glenlow (Haubach), "Politik und Agitation," *NB*, Dec. 1931, 607; Walther Pahl, "Raum für den sozialistischen Vortrupp," *SM*, 16.2.31, 142.

97. See *FW*, 26.10.30, 22–23; 9.11.30, 23; 13.12.31, 5–11; 29.12.31, 14–19. At meetings speakers argued for combining Socialist content with Nazi style (*HE*, 20.11.30). A correspondent urged Socialists to adopt the Nazis' "modern advertising" methods (*FW*, 12.10.30, 30). For praise of emotion-evoking propaganda from intellectuals on both the right and the left, see Theodor Haubach, *RB*, 4.10.31; Geiger, "Braunschweig—die Mittelschichten und die Sozialdemokratie," 634–35; Alexander Schifrin, "Einstellung auf die Expansion," *DG*, June 1931, esp. 514.

98. See, e.g., *FW*, 11.2.30, 8–10. The Mannheim *Volksstimme* stressed "organization and enlightenment," addressing "workers who still think normally" (Matthias and Weber, *Widerstand gegen den Nationalsozialismus in Mannheim*, 113).

99. Ernst Heilmann, *FW*, 11.1.31, 5; 13.12.31, 1–5. For leftist critiques of the cry for more feeling, see letters by Siegfried Marck and E. Chossudowsky, *FW*, 27.12.31, 18–20. But the moderately leftist Schifrin ridiculed the "exaggerated rationalism" of the moderately leftist Kurt Laumann, who saw "consciousness raising" as the SPD's main task ("Der Streit um die Parteidemokratie," *DG*, Nov. 1931, 476).

100. Alexander Schifrin, "Kritik an der Organisation," *DG*, Aug. 1931, 169; Z, "Die Landtagswahlen in Oldenburg," 347. Also see Herbert Duwald, "Ausserparlamentarische Abwehr dem Faschismus," *UW*, June 1931, 125.

101. In Bavaria, for example, individual districts plotted campaigns (Krall, *Landespolitik der SPD in Bayern*, 277–78).

102. Johannes Han, *FW*, 27.9.31, 24–25.

103. Pahl commented on their touchiness at being called *Bonzen* ("Verjüngung, Aktivierung, Konstruktive Politik," *NB*, May 1931, 200).

104. See, e.g., *FW*, 26.10.30, 31.5.31, 23.8.31, in which entire sections of letters were devoted to this problem. The daily press also addressed the issue. See, e.g., Arno Scholz, "Jugend und Partei," *HVW*, 28.5.31. On the situation of youth in the Great Depression and their political response, see Stachura, *Weimar Republic and the Younger Proletariat*, 158–59.

105. See, e.g., *FW*, 31.5.31, 58–59. At a Hamburg meeting (*HE*, 24.4.31) Heilmann insisted the party was young enough.

106. *HE*, 13.3.31; Witt, *Hamburger Sozialdemokratie*, 103.

107. Leber, "Todesursachen," 231, 235; Kurt Laumann, "Organisation und Apparat," in Bieligk et al., *Organisation im Klassenkampf*, 133.

108. Seydewitz wrote of widespread bitterness against high salaries and pensions (*KK*, 15.9.30, 549) as did Ph. Künkele in *Jungsozialistische Blätter* (Jan. 1931, 16–17). In *Unser Weg*, Eugen Siklos commented on the indisputable impact of Nazi and Communist charges of corruption and high salaries ("Einige wichtige Aufgaben der nächsten Zukunft," *UW*, Dec. 1930, 275). Also see *FW*, 12.10.30, 27–28, 30.

109. *FW*, 5.10.30, 11–12; *VW*, #204, 3.5.31.

110. *VW*, #460, 1.10.30.

111. On the evolution of this conflict, see NSDAP HA R.93/F.1903: Sektionsversammlung, 10.5.30; R.93/F.1898: Besprechung des Sektionsausschusses, 7.10.30; Sektionsversammlung, 14.10.30; R.93/F.1898: 11.11.30; R.93/F.1898: Ortsversammlung, 2.12.30; R.93/F.1901: 23.2.31; R.93/F.1895: Lagebericht, 7.3.31; R.93/F.1901: Besprechung der Führer der SPD und Gewerkschaften München, 8.3.31; R.93/F.1898: Ortsversammlung, 19.5.31, Sektionsversammlung, 14.4.31; R.93/F.1901: Besprechung der Bezirksleitung München, 11.6.31.

112. *HVF*, 19.9.31.

113. Writers to *Das Freie Wort* were more likely to complain that bureaucrats were not doing their share of work than to demand the bureaucracy be dismantled. See, e.g., *FW*, 11.1.31, 23–24; 15.3.31, 17–18. I found only one letter calling for the election of all party officials and congressional delegates (*FW*, 31.5.31, 56). Of course, editor Heilmann may have tended to suppress such calls.

114. Bieligk, "Organisation wie sie ist," in Bieligk et al., *Organisation im Klassenkampf*, 76; Laumann, "Organisation und Apparat," 145–47.

115. The Left also believed the SPD needed new leaders but insisted that

policies, not personalities, lay at the root of its malaise (Seydewitz, *KK*, 15.9.30, 546–49; Riel, *KK*, 15.1.31, 50–53).

116. August Rathmann, "Positiver Radikalismus," *NB*, Jan. 1931, 5; Wilhelm Sollmann, "Mehr Führung!," *HE*, 28.12.30; Hans Müller, "Kritik an der Führung," *NB*, Jan. 1931, 9; Walther Pahl, "Der Run zum Nationalsozialismus," *SM*, 26.9.30, 871; Karl Meitmann, "Führer und Masse im deutschen Sozialismus," *HE*, 4.10.30. See similar comments by the nonrevisionist Alexander Schifrin, "Parteiprobleme nach den Wahlen," *DG*, Nov. 1930, 409–12.

117. *VW*, #525, 8.11.31. Also see SPD, Vorstand, *Die neue Notverordnung*, esp. 9. Other examples abound: "[The SPD] uses all its power, in this gigantic struggle of the working class" (*HE*, 21.6.31); at Leipzig, Arthur Crispien explained that the SPD had to show it was fighting for the proletariat (*SPD Parteitag 1931*, 137); in an article on the banking crisis, *Vorwärts* emphasized the "interests of the proletariat" (*VW*, #322, 13.7.31).

118. Grebing, "Sozialdemokratische Arbeiterbewegung," 484.

119. Van der Will and Burns, *Arbeiterkulturbewegung*, 103, 110–11; Guttsman, *Workers' Culture*, 134–35. Helmut Gruber noted the same trend toward social isolation in Austrian Social Democracy after 1930 (*Red Vienna*, 86).

120. *SPD Parteitag 1931*, Breitscheid, 102–3; *LVZ*, 12.10.31.

121. Stampfer, *Vierzehn Jahre*, 551; *SPD Jahrbuch 1931*, 109. Communists, who had no reason to exaggerate, acknowledged that "on the whole the SPD is still organizationally and politically thoroughly solid" (BA R45IV/25: An das Zentralkomitee [KPD], Braunschweig, 29.4.32).

122. See, e.g., NHStAH Hann. 310, II/B, Nr. 9I: Schönleiter to Hass, 9.1.32.

123. Besson, *Württemberg*, 31. After the June emergency decree, Schumacher made public his opposition to toleration (Keil, *Erlebnisse*, 2:403).

124. Klotzbach, *Gegen den Nationalsozialismus*, 49; NSDAP HA R.92/F.1894: Lagebericht, 28.9.31; R.93/F.1903: Lagebericht, 12.7.31; Allen, *Nazi Seizure of Power*, 80.

125. *HVF*, 21.9.31, 22.9.31.

126. Witt, *Hamburger Sozialdemokratie*, 125. The Hamburg SPD had roughly 75,000 members. In September 1930 its share of the vote stood well above the national average (31.79 percent : 24.53 percent) (*SPD Jahrbuch 1930*, 210). For the 1931 results, see Falter, Lindenberger, and Schumann, *Wahlen und Abstimmungen*, 94. The old senate coalition no longer had a majority after 1931, although the SPD and KPD did. The SPD refused even to support a Communist as vice-president of the Bürgerschaft, allowing a Nazi to be elected (Witt, *Hamburger Sozialdemokratie*, 12, n. 43).

127. *HE*, 28.9.31.

128. Ernst Heilmann, *FW*, 8.11.31, 21–22. He printed some of these (1.11.31, 13–15; 8.11.31, 13–15, 19–20, 20–21) and rebutted them, but his editorial on the election hinted that he too was beginning to wonder if the sacrifices were worth it (*FW*, 4.10.31, 1).

NOTES TO PAGES 146-48

129. Witt, *Hamburger Sozialdemokratie*, 121–23.

130. After the rally, tensions resulted in fights, in which five people were badly hurt and twenty were mildly injured (*Münchner Zeitung*, 15.9.31).

131. *VW*, #431, 15.9.31; Tosstorff, "'Einheitsfront,'" 2:209. On the strike, see Rosenhaft, *Beating the Fascists?*, 209.

132. Drechsler, *SAPD*, 87–98; *VW*, #445, 23.9.31; #457 30.9.31. The Reichstag deputies were August Siemsen, Andreas Portune, Hans Ziegler, and Heinrich Ströbel. Siemsen soon returned to the fold.

133. Drechsler, *SAPD*, 166; Dorothea Beck, *Julius Leber*, 124; Brandt, *Links und frei*, 54–56, 36–39. Only in Berlin did a left-wing SAJ chapter remain intact. Its chairman, Erich Schmidt, was involved with a secret group that was organizing an underground opposition of dissident Communists and Socialists (Schmidt, "Memoiren," 167–69). Its adult contact convinced him to remain in the SPD. He in turn persuaded the majority of Berlin SAJers. The party leadership was pleasantly surprised by Schmidt's stand (*VW*, #476, 11.10.31). The Org, as Schmidt called it, became Neu Beginnen in 1933.

134. Heinrich A. Winkler, *Katastrophe*, 404–6. In Zwickau, Seydewitz's home, the majority voted to suspend him (*VW*, #450, 25.9.31). Zwickau lost 29 percent of its members. According to Breslau's yearly report, that city lost 20 percent (*BVW*, 25.1.32). In Frankfurt, after a 5½-hour meeting, at which Heilmann spoke for the leadership, a majority condemned the expulsions but stayed in the SPD (*HVF*, 1.10.31). On other chapters, see *VW*, #451, 26.9.31; #457, 30.9.31. In Berlin (*VW*, #463, 3.10.31) and Leipzig (*LVZ*, 12.10.31) speakers assailed the tactics of the "splitters" while endorsing their politics.

135. Arkadij Gurland, "Kampf gegen die Spaltung!," *HE*, 13.10.31; A. Kranold, "Die Tragödie der Opposition," *BVW*, 3.10.31. Besides Kranold and Gurland, others who stayed were Engelbert Graf, Paul Bergmann, Otto Jenssen, and Kurt Laumann. Moderate leftists such as Aufhäuser and Sender also remained in the SPD.

136. The AfA-Bund, chaired by Aufhäuser, helped finance *MT*. It survived until June 1932 (Drechsler, *SAPD*, 124, 123 n. 22).

137. Arkadij Gurland told Drechsler that former USPDers, silent for years, began to speak critically at party meetings in 1931–32 (ibid., 128 n. 37).

138. Rudolf Breitscheid, "Brünings Plötzlichkeiten," *RZ*, 7.10.31; Georg Decker, "Nach der Entscheidung," *DG*, Nov. 1931, 385.

139. Witt, *Hamburger Sozialdemokratie*, 128; Adolph, *Wels*, 237; Grebing, "Auseinandersetzung," 266–67; Breitman, *German Social Democracy*, 170; Schaefer, *SPD in der Ära Brüning*, 175.

140. *VW*, #473, 9.10.31; Turner, *German Big Business*, 165–66; Brüning, *Memoiren*, 426–28.

141. *VW*, #475, 10.10.31.

142. See Henry Turner's discussion of the historical judgment and his convincing revision of it (*German Big Business*, 167–70).

143. *VW*, #477, 11.10.31; #478, 12.10.31; #479, 13.10.31; #481, 14.10.31.

144. Besides *Vorwärts*'s articles cited above, see "Class unity of all workers!" (*HE*, 20.10.31). In Hamburg, Aufhäuser warned that the National Opposition was preparing an all-out attack on the working class (*HE*, 16.10.31). *Vorwärts* defended toleration after Harzburg by explaining that "not individual votes, but the preservation of the workers' movement is its goal" (#489, 18.10.31).

145. *Reichstag: Sten. Berichte*, Bd. 446, 14.10.31, 2085. On October 13, when the delegation voted on whether to topple Brüning, two voted "yes" and twenty abstained (Keil, *Erlebnisse*, 2:406).

146. Both Severing and the Reichstag delegation executive clashed with Brüning and Groener on this issue (Heinrich A. Winkler, *Katastrophe*, 446–47). Evidence of increased Nazi violence in Berlin and in the countryside (e.g., *VW*, #536, 14.11.31; #437, 15.11.31; *FW*, 11.10.31, 30–31; 29.11.31, 10–12) as well as pressure for government action appeared in the Social Democratic press. In the Hamburg Bürgerschaft, Gustav Dahrendorf called for "active defense" by the Reich (*HE*, 17.12.31), as did the ADGB national committee (*GZ*, 19.12.31, 806).

147. Ehni, *Bollwerk Preussen?*, 232; *VW*, #537, 15.11.31. At Clou, too, Breitscheid pointed out that a condition of toleration was government action against rightist and leftist rowdyism (*VW*, #547, 22.11.31).

148. *VW*, #539, 17.11.31; Pistorius, "Rudolf Breitscheid," 297.

149. *RF*, #210, 18.11.31, reprinted by Tosstorff, "'Einheitsfront,'" 2:227–28; *VW*, #541, 18.11.31. According to Stampfer, *Vorwärts* did not attack the KPD except in cases like this and during the Stahlhelm referendum (*Vierzehn Jahre*, 557).

150. According to Mierendorff's friends, a Nazi deputy actually gave the documents to Mierendorff ("Carlo Mierendorff—Zur Erinnerung an seinen Todestag am 4.12.1943," Artur E. Bratu [written in 1978], 7; "Carlo Mierendorff [1897–1943]—Stationen seines Lebens und Wirkens," Jakob Rietz [n.d.], 25; both in NL Mierendorff, Hessisches Staatsarchiv [Darmstadt]).

151. Stampfer, *Vierzehn Jahre*, 555.

152. Kempner, "Einführung," 11.

153. Brüning, *Memoiren*, 463–64; Eyck, *History of the Weimar Republic*, 2:338; Ehni, *Bollwerk Preussen?*, 233. Though Groener later emerged as the strongest advocate of an SA ban, at this point he rejected pressure from the state governments to use police measures against the Nazis. See Gerhard Schulz, "Einleitung," in *Staat und NSDAP 1930–1932*, 45–47, 50–52. Also see the following documents printed in *Staat und NSDAP*: #41b, 17.11.31 (notes on a conference of state interior ministers), 220–26; #42, 18.11.31 (instructions from Groener for State Secretary Zweigert) 277–78; #43, 26.11.31 (note by ministerial counselor Wienstein re Boxheim Papers) 229–30.

154. Brüning, *Memoiren*, 465–66. The Nazis had leaped from one to twenty-seven mandates in Hesse.

155. *VW*, #554, 26.11.31; #555, 27.11.31; #556, 27.11.31; statement of SPD executive committee, #557, 28.11.31; #560, 30.11.31.

156. Ehni, *Bollwerk Preussen?*, 232–34; Schulz, "Einleitung," 54. Schulze, *Otto Braun*, 720.

157. Diary entry, 11.12.31, NL Grzesinski B/X/1555, IISH; Severing, *Lebensweg*, 2:316–17. In this instance, Brüning did not want to disturb his negotiations with the Nazis for their support of Hindenburg in the presidential election (Schulze, *Otto Braun*, 720; Brüning, *Memoiren*, 461, 473). Severing reported that he did not know of these negotiations. He told Feder that he was reluctant to arrest Hitler because Hindenburg had just received Hitler, and Schleicher had breakfasted with him (Feder, diary entry, 8.12.31, *Heute sprach ich mit*, 307).

158. *VW*, #502, 26.10.31; #514, 2.11.31; #538, 16.11.31. Most major national figures appeared in Hesse: Hitler, Gregor Strasser, Goebbels, Hugenberg, Eduard Dingeldey, and Brüning (Carlo Mierendorff, *HE*, 13.11.31).

159. Georg Decker, "Eine zweite faschistische Welle?," *DG*, Dec. 1931, 486. For evidence of the defensive tone, see Scheidemann's speech before a crowd of five thousand in Hamburg (*HE*, 18.12.31).

160. This was the title of an editorial in the pro-toleration *Frankfurter Volksstimme* (14.12.31). The *Echo* asked, "Hat die Tolerationspolitik noch einen Sinn?," its writer concluding that no better alternative existed (*HE*, 14.12.31).

161. Erkelenz an Redaktion (Genosse Schulz) der *Düsseldorf Volkszeitung*, f. 30, 14.12.31, NL Erkelenz, NL 72/138, BA.

162. See, e.g., *FW*, 22.11.31, 11–14.

163. Schulz to Erkelenz, f.31, 21.12.31; f.35, 28.12.31, NL Erkelenz, NL 72/138, BA.

164. Grebing, "Auseinandersetzung," 267; Stampfer to Luise Kautsky, 3.12.31, NL Kautsky D/XXI/311, IISH.

165. Hilferding to Karl Kautsky, 21.12.31, NL Kautsky, D/XII/655, IISH. See the similar language in Hilferding's letter to Erkelenz on 30.11.31 (NL Erkelenz, NL 72/138: f.26, BA). For Gurland's claim, see Drechsler, *SAPD*, 83 n. 112.

166. Hilferding to Karl Kautsky, 2.10.31, NL Kautsky D/XII/653, IISH.

167. Bundesausschuss, 15.12.31, Dok. 67, in *Gewerkschaften 1930–1933*, 4:446, 455–56. Otto Wels attended this meeting. Public airing of ADGB disgruntlement over Brüning's fourth emergency decree appeared in *HE* (16.12.31) and the *Gewerkschafts-Zeitung* ("Gewerkschaften und Notverordnung," 19.12.31, 801; "Sinn und Widersinn der vierten Notverordnung," 803; "Der Bundesausschuss des ADGB über die Notverordnung," 804–5).

168. See the comments at Bundesausschuss, 25.11.31, Dok. 63, in *Gewerkschaften 1930–1933*, 4:427–33. Paul Hertz attended for the SPD. Press reports on this meeting allowed a glimpse of its discontented mood, explaining

that union leaders wondered if their members' "unshaken trust" had not reached the breaking point ("Tagung des Bundesausschusses des ADGB," *GZ*, 5.12.31, 777).

Chapter Six

1. Petzina, Abelshauser, and Faust, *Materialien*, 119, 121, 111; Stachura, *Weimar Republic and the Younger Proletariat*, 59–60; Petzina, "Arbeitslosigkeit," 240, 244–45; NSDAP HA R.92/F.1894: police report, 12.7.31.

2. Peter Scherer, "Ausbruch der Weltwirtschaftskrise, 46. Proportionately, the construction workers' union was even harder hit (ADGB, Vorstand, *Jahrbuch des Allgemeinen Deutschen Gewerkschaftsbundes für das Jahr 1930* [hereafter cited as *ADGB Jahrbuch . . .*], 184).

3. In 1931 there were more strikes (458) than in 1930 (342), but they were on average much smaller and shorter than those in 1930 and had a very low success rate (Petzina, Abelshauser, and Faust, *Materialien*, 114).

4. NSDAP HA R.92/F.1894: police report, 12.7.31.

5. Stenbock-Fermor, *Deutschland von unten*, 11.

6. Recent scholarship has shown that unemployed workers voted heavily KPD but that unemployment was negatively correlated with the Nazi vote. See Childers, *Nazi Voter*, 185; Falter, "Politische Konsequenzen von Massenarbeitslosigkeit"; McKibbon, "Myth of the Unemployed."

7. Bundesausschuss, 12/13.9.30, Dok. 14, in *Gewerkschaften 1930–1933*, 4:149–50, 157–58. Also see Schulz, "Reparationen und Krisenprobleme," 201–2; Schildt, "Sozialdemokratische Arbeiterbewegung und Reichswehr," 119.

8. The exception was a joint statement of the ADGB, the AfA-Bund, and Christian and liberal trade unions in May 1931 that called for the cancellation of international war debts and a "revision of reparations treaties" (30.5.31, Dok. 43, in *Gewerkschaften 1930–1933*, 4:312).

9. Occasionally a public speaker proclaimed SPD opposition to the Young Plan (e.g., Erik Nölting at an SPD rally in Hanover, *HVW*, 8.2.31).

10. See *VW*, #321, 12.7.31; #325, 15.7.31; #453, 27.9.31.

11. See, e.g., Leipart to Margreve (U.S. General Consulate, Berlin), 31.7.31, Dok. 51, in *Gewerkschaften 1930–1933*, 4:365. Peter Grassmann denounced reparations at the ADGB congress in September (ADGB, Vorstand, *Gewerkschaften, Friedensvertrag, Reparationen*, 20).

12. *Reichstag: Sten. Berichte*, Bd. 446, 14.10.31, 2080; Schildt, "Sozialdemokratische Arbeiterbewegung und Reichswehr," 119. Other Social Democrats did not deny that reparations were in part responsible for the crisis. See, e.g., Lederer, *Die Umwälzung in der Wirtschaft*, 14.

13. *VW*, #570, 5.12.31; "Kundgebung der Gewerkschaften," *GZ*, 12.12.31, 785. It is instructive to compare the *Jahrbuch* of the ADGB from 1930 to that of 1931 on the reparations issue. In 1930, "Economics and Politics" did not

mention reparations as a cause of the crisis (*ADGB Jahrbuch 1930*, 20–23), while in 1931 this section, subtitled "Position on the Reparations Issue," outlined the ADGB's view that reparations greatly worsened the crisis (*ADGB Jahrbuch 1931*, 43–47). Nonetheless, in a 1932 pamphlet, the ADGB insisted that its current position on reparations had been the same since 1918 (ADGB, Vorstand, *Gewerkschaften, Friedensvertrag, Reparationen*, 2, 5–8).

14. ADGB, Vorstand, *Leipart und Breitscheid über die Notverordnung*, 9.

15. Furtwängler to Leipart, 22.12.31, NL Furtwängler, #0062; Leipart to Furtwängler, 28.12.31, NL Furtwängler, #0055; Leipart to Wilhelm Keil, 8.1.32, ADGB Restakten (17), Film Nr. 22/2, #390, DGB Archiv. Also see Schildt, "Sozialdemokratische Arbeiterbewegung und Reichswehr," 119. Furtwängler was on the staff of the ADGB executive board.

16. Notes by Aron (ADGB) on reparations, 19.12.31, Dok. 68, in *Gewerkschaften 1930–1933*, 4:462–64.

17. Potthoff, "Freie Gewerkschaften und sozialistische Parteien," 83–84. For the campaign against reparations, see "Gemeinsame Abwehr," *GZ*, 26.12.31, 817–18; Theodor Leipart, "Aufklärung tut not!," *VW*, #610, 31.12.31; Theodor Leipart, "Stellung der Deutschen Gewerkschaften zur Reparationsfrage," *GZ*, 16.1.32, 33–35; Theodor Leipart, "Entschiedene Aussenpolitik—Tatkräftige Wirtschaftspolitik," *GZ*, 6.2.32, 81–83. Also see "Besprechung der Spitzenverbände der Gewerkschaften über die Reparationsfrage," 8.1.32, Dok. 72, in *Gewerkschaften 1930–1933*, 4:475–76. Peter Grassmann conducted the campaign in the Reichstag executive.

18. During Breitscheid's remarks, for example, Wels whispered to Leipart, "Well, should we be the last ones who support reparations!" (Leipart to Wilhelm Keil, 8.1.32, ADGB Restakten (17), Film Nr. 22/2, #390, DGB Archiv). At the party base, however, there was support for Breitscheid's point of view (Pyta, *Gegen Hitler*, 458 n. 19).

19. Leipart to Wilhelm Keil, 8.1.32, ADGB Restakten (17), Film Nr. 22/2, #390, DGB Archiv; Keil, *Erlebnisse*, 2:428–29; Hilferding to Kautsky, 27.2.32, NL Kautsky D/XII/656, IISH; Leipart report to the ADGB board, 6.1.32, Dok. 70, in *Gewerkschaften 1930–1933*, 4:465, 470–71.

20. Keil, *Erlebnisse*, 2:429–31.

21. *Reichstag: Sten. Berichte*, Bd. 446, 24.2.32, 2276. This speech was published as a pamphlet: August Weber, "Zwei mütige Reden," and Rudolf Breitscheid, "Eine Reichstagsrede," in *Wider den Nationalsozialismus*, Republikanische Bibliothek, Bd. II, esp. 126–27.

22. Material for provincial speakers for state election in spring 1932 stressed that it was "wrong" to place full blame for the crisis on reparations (SPD, Vorstand, *Um die Macht!*, 7).

23. Heinrich A. Winkler, *Katastrophe*, 634–35; Kolb, *Weimarer Republik*, 130.

24. For a concise rendition of the classical Social Democratic position, see Lederer, *Wege aus der Krise*, 4, 17, 29–30.

25. Held, *Sozialdemokratie und Keynesianismus*, 108–9, 113–14, 124.

26. Potthoff, *Freie Gewerkschaften 1918–1933*, 227–28; Scholing, "Wirtschaftstheorie," 384–85; Held, *Sozialdemokratie und Keynesianismus*, 94, 103–5.

27. Held, *Sozialdemokratie und Keynesianismus*, 103, 110–11; Schneider, *Arbeitsbeschaffungs-Programm*, 53–54.

28. See, e.g., Leipart's list of ADGB demands presented to Brüning in June 1931 (Bundesausschuss, 20.6.31, Dok. 47, in *Gewerkschaften 1930–1933*, 4:337–38. For the same program as it appeared in SPD propaganda, see SPD, Vorstand, *Gespenst der Arbeitslosigkeit*.

29. Held, *Sozialdemokratie und Keynesianismus*, 110–11. The Bavarian SPD pressed for budget cuts as late as the fall of 1931 (Krall, *Landespolitik der SPD in Bayern*, 205–9). On the widespread tendency to see the crisis as normal, see Borchardt, *Wachstum*, 167; Petzina, "Elemente der Wirtschaftspolitik," 128; Woytinsky, *Internationale Hebung der Preise*, 20; Holtfrerich, "Alternativen," 619; Köhler, "Borchardts 'Revision,'" 174. K. D. Krohn, on the other hand, has pointed out that some economists did recognize unusual features and causes of the crisis early ("Ökonomische 'Zwangslagen,'" 423).

30. Hilferding in Berlin, *VW*, #467, 5.10.30. Also see Gates, "German Socialism and the Crisis of 1929–1933," 347–48. For a thorough discussion of Hilferding's economic ideas, see Gates, "Free Trade Unions," esp. chaps. 2, 4, 5; Heinrich A. Winkler, *Organisierter Kapitalismus*, 12; Gottschalch, *Strukturveränderungen*, 196; George Garvy, "Introduction," in Schneider, *Arbeitsbeschaffungs-Programm*.

31. James, "Rudolf Hilferding," 865; Scholing, "Wirtschaftstheorie," 385.

32. According to Brüning, *his* economic thinking was influenced by Hilferding (Brüning, *Memoiren*, 116, 315). On this, also see Gates, "German Socialism and the Crisis of 1929–1933," 342–43.

33. See SPD, Vorstand, *Gespenst der Arbeitslosigkeit*, and SPD, Vorstand, *Referentenmaterial: Nr. 3*, 26.

34. See, e.g., ADGB and AfA-Bund to Brüning, 23.4.31, Dok. 39, in *Gewerkschaften 1930–1933*, 4:298. See also Gates, "Free Trade Unions," 171; Schneider, *Arbeitsbeschaffungs-Programm*, 47–53.

35. Neebe, "Konflikt und Kooperation," 234.

36. Holtfrerich, "Alternativen," 628; Weisbrod, "Befreiung," 318.

37. Weisbrod, "Befreiung," 320–21; Hans Mommsen, *Verspielte Freiheit*, 379. On the economic disagreements among industrialists, see James, *German Slump*, 233–35, 244–45.

38. For the ADGB's public position in early 1931, see Tarnow's speech in the Reichstag (*Reichstag: Sten. Berichte*, Bd. 444, 12.2.31, 956).

39. Schneider, *Kleine Geschichte der Gewerkschaften*, 200.

40. On negotiations between the RDI and the ADGB to work out an industrial compromise in late 1930, see Neebe, "Unternehmerverbände und Gewerkschaften," 316–18; Wengst, "Unternehmerverbände und Gewerkschaften," 109–118; Weisbrod, "Befreiung," 295–325: 305; Heinrich A. Winkler, *Katastrophe*, 278–82.

41. Bundesausschuss 14/15.12.30, Dok. 19, 192–97, 199; Bundesvorstand, 14.1.31, Dok. 24, 229; both in *Gewerkschaften 1930–1933*, vol. 4. For Tarnow's similar plea to accept the second emergency decree six months later, see Bundesausschuss, 20.6.31, Dok. 47, ibid., 342. On the fears of Communist expansion, see Neebe, "Konflikt und Kooperation," 232.

42. Tarnow noted this problem in October 1930 (Bundesausschuss, 12/13.10.30, Dok. 16. in *Gewerkschaften 1930–1933*, 4:155–56). It occupied numerous sessions of the ADGB board and national committee in spring, 1931. See, e.g., Bundesausschuss, 10.3.31, Dok. 35, ibid., 279–81.

43. As late as October, Leipart pointed out that the ADGB shared with industry "an interest in cutting unnecessary public expenditures" (Bundesausschuss, 2.10.31, Dok. 36, in *Gewerkschaften 1930–1933*, 4:407). Also see Weisbrod, "Befreiung," 321.

44. Bundesvorstand, 9.3.31, Dok. 34, in *Gewerkschaften 1930–1933*, 4:262– 63, 266–68. At an ADGB national committee meeting, Wels said the party executive's objections were the same as the board's (Bundesauschuss, 10.3.31, Dok. 35, ibid., 278). Despite the hostility of the SPD and the ADGB, Hörsing took his program to the public, supported by Karl Höltermann and other writers in *Das Reichsbanner*. See Curius, *Otto Hörsings Kriegsplan zur Nieder- ringung der Arbeitslosigkeit*; Otto Hörsing, "Nur so Geht's!," *DR*, Apr. 1931, 841–44; Karl Mayr, "Dank des Vaterlandes," *RB*, 9.5.31; Karl Höltermann, "Arbeit statt Unterstützung!," *RB*, 30.5.31. These efforts fueled suspicions about his political ambitions.

45. *SPD Parteitag 1931*, 49. Also see *VW*, #214, 9.5.31; Gates, "Free Trade Unions," 158, 186; Allen, *Nazi Seizure of Power*, 110.

46. Schneider points out that a confusing proliferation of remedies charac- terized the early trade union discussion of the crisis (*Arbeitsbeschaffungs- Programm*, 60).

47. *SPD Parteitag 1931*: Tarnow, 45; Ziegler, 67; Kirstein, 73; Dittmann, 65–66. Also see Schneider, *Arbeitsbeschaffungs-Programm*, 69–70.

48. Woytinsky initially presented his ideas to the ADGB board in the spring of 1931. The ADGB received his views with less skepticism than Hörsing's and let him submit them for public discussion. See Schneider, *Arbeitsbeschaffungs- Programm*, 61, 63, 69–71.

49. Wladimir Woytinsky, "Aktive Wirtschaftspolitik," *DA*, June 1931, 438– 39. Also see Woytinsky's presentation to the ADGB-Bundesvorstand, 17.6.31, Dok. 46, in *Gewerkschaften 1930–1933*, 4:330.

50. Schneider, *Arbeitsbeschaffungs-Programm*, 62.

51. Woytinsky, "Aktive Wirtschaftspolitik," 415, 438–39, 413–14.

52. Fritz Naphtali, "Neuer Angelpunkt der aktiven Konjunkturpolitik oder Fehlleitung von Energien?," *DA*, July 1931, 488–97. Woytinsky answered in the same issue (498–506). Decker also reacted against Woytinsky's proposals (*VW*, #303, 2.7.31).

53. Gates, "Free Trade Unions," 205–6; Rudolf Hilferding, "Ein Irrweg,"

VW, #465, 4.10.31. See Breitman on Hilferding's policy as finance minister in 1923 (*German Social Democracy*, 120).

54. Holtfrerich, "Alternativen," 619–22; Köhler, "Borchardts 'Revision,'" 174; Plumpe, "Wirtschaftspolitik," 346; Büttner, "Politische Alternativen," 225–33, 242–47. Executives at I. G. Farben considered reinflation schemes (James, "Rudolf Hilferding," 865). Schäffer, a Social Democratic state secretary in the Finance Ministry, presented Brüning with a memorandum on the futility of further deflation ("Gedanken zum Krisenbekämpfung: Niederschrift Schäffers vom 2.9.31," printed in Wandel, *Hans Schäffer*, 308). Brüning ignored Schäffer's ideas (Plumpe, "Wirtschaftspolitik," 352). Büttner makes the interesting point that many of the liberals and leftist liberals who began to consider reinflation plans were Jewish or from Jewish families and, therefore, particularly sensitive to the political fallout of deflation (Büttner, "Politische Alternativen," 251).

55. Plumpe, "Wirtschaftspolitik," 345.

56. Weisbrod, "Befreiung," 314; Hans Mommsen, *Verspielte Freiheit*, 380.

57. James, "Rudolf Hilferding," 865.

58. Rudolf Hilferding, "Unheimliche Tage," *DG*, Aug. 1931, 101–4. On government and Reichsbank policy before and after the collapse, and on the economic impact of the crash, see James, *German Slump*, 309–17, 283.

59. Held, *Sozialdemokratie und Keynesianismus*, 125.

60. On Hilferding's ties to Brüning, see James, "Rudolf Hilferding," 865.

61. So he explained his position to Han Staudinger and Emil Lederer (Staudinger, *Wirtschaftspolitik im Weimarer Staat*, 89).

62. Hilferding, "Ein Irrweg"; Gates, "Free Trade Unions," 241–42. According to Brüning, he and Hilferding had long talks about these issues (*Memoiren*, 227).

63. Hilferding to Erkelenz, 30.11.31, NL Erkelenz, NL 72/138: f. 26, BA.

64. Hilferding to Kautsky, 10.2.31, NL Kautsky D/XII/653, IISH.

65. Heinrich A. Winkler, *Katastrophe*, 434–35.

66. Aufhäuser's speech to Reichstag, *Reichstag: Sten. Berichte*, Bd. 446, 15.10.31, 2161; *VW*, #484, 15.10.31; *HE*, 20.10.31; Kurt Heinig, *VW*, #493, 21.10.31. In Berlin, mass meetings assembled under the slogans "Against Harzburg! Against Braunschweig reaction! Against inflation and civil war!" (*VW*, #516, 3.11.31).

67. *FW*, 11.10.31, 11; 18.10.31, 23–25; 8.11.31, 13–15. Also see NHStAH Hann. 310, II/A, Nr. 6I: Wm. Hildebrandt to Lau, 7.10.31.

68. "An das deutsche Volk!" *VW*, #324, 14.7.31.

69. *VW*, #417, 6.9.31. In early October an executive committee appeal exclaimed, "Against capitalism! For socialism! . . . To overcome the capitalist system give the SPD power!" (*VW*, #463, 3.10.31).

70. See, e.g., the letter from a Thuringian Social Democrat to SPD national authorities (Hans Schumann an die Partei-Instanzen, 4.2.32, Restakten ADGB, Film Nr. 25/4, #263, DGB Archiv).

71. Erkelenz to Schulz, 14.12.31, NL Erkelenz, NL 72/138, BA. On his opposition to deflation, see Erkelenz to Hilferding, 5.10.31, NL Erkelenz, NL 72/138, BA. Also see Büttner, "Politische Alternativen," 235–38.

72. Woytinsky reprimanded an SPD admirer for his plan to call for a "referendum on monetary policies," saying that supporters of an active policy must avoid the charge of "demagogy" (Woytinsky to Schumann, 25.8.31, ADGB Restakten 25/4, #260, DGB Archiv).

73. "Ein neues Programm zur Bekämpfung der Krise in England," GZ, 5.9.31, 563–66; "Internationale Arbeitsbeschaffung," GZ, 14.11.31, 721–23. According to Gates, Woytinsky's Internationale Hebung der Preise established him as the leading spokesman for an activist government policy ("Free Trade Unions," 210). Schneider (Arbeitsbeschaffungs-Programm, 39–40) and James (German Slump, 325–26, 339–40) discuss "bourgeois" reformers, such as Ernst Wagemann and Wilhelm Lautenbach, who propagated similar ideas.

74. Schneider, Arbeitsbeschaffungs-Programm, 79. Woytinsky praised Keynes's remark that price stabilization alone would not overcome the crisis (Internationale Hebung der Preise, 128).

75. VW, #450, 25.9.31; "Der Bundesausschuss des ADGB über die Notverordnung," GZ, 19.12.31, 804–6; "Sinn und Widersinn der vierten Notverordnung," 801–3; Bundesausschuss, 25.11.31, Dok. 63, in Gewerkschaften 1930–1933, 4:429 (Tarnow).

76. "Thesen zum Kampf gegen die Wirtschaftskrise," printed in Schneider, Arbeitsbeschaffungs-Programm, 225–30.

77. Schneider, Arbeitsbeschaffungs-Programm, 81–82. Baade, director of the National Research Institute for the Rural Market, did not contribute substantially to the proposal. Leipart presented Hilferding and others with a draft of the WTB plan at the meeting in early January 1932 where reparations were also discussed (Bundesvorstand, 6.1.32, Dok. 70, in Gewerkschaften 1930–1933, 4:470–71).

78. Wladimir Woytinsky, "Wann kommt die aktive Wirtschaftspolitik?," DA, Jan. 1932, 22–23.

79. "Der Arbeitsbeschaffungsplan (Baade-Tarnow-Woytinsky)," printed in Schneider, Arbeitsbeschaffungs-Programm, 231–34; also see Gates, "Free Trade Unions," 217.

80. "Thesen zum Kampf gegen die Wirtschaftskrise," 230.

81. See, e.g., "Das Jahr der Notverordnungen," GZ, 2.1.32, 2; "Sechseinhalb Millionen Arbeitslose!," GZ, 30.1.32, 67. For a discussion of varying levels of concern about unemployment among different unions, see Zollitsch, "Einzelgewerkschaften."

82. Woytinsky, "Wann kommt die aktive Wirtschaftspolitik?," 21.

83. G. Portulka an die Redaktion der Eiserne Front in Berlin, 23.2.32, NL Furtwängler, Kasten 1, DGB Archiv.

84. Schumann an die Parteiinstanzen, 4.2.32, #263; excerpt from Ost-

thüringen Volkszeitung (n.d.), #265, both in ADGB Restakten, Film Nr. 25/4, DGB Archiv.

85. Bundesvorstand, 3.2.32, Dok. 74, in *Gewerkschaften 1930–1933*, vol. 4.

86. Gates, "Free Trade Unions," 221; Schneider, *Arbeitsbeschaffungs-Programm*, 130.

87. Concern about the NSBO had steadily mounted throughout 1931. See Bundesausschuss, 7.1.31, Dok. 21, in *Gewerkschaften 1930–1933*, vol. 4; Redaktion von *Die Bergbau Industrie* an den ADGB-Bundesvorstand, 26.11.31, Dok. 64, ibid., 437; Bundesausschuss, 15/16.2.32, Dok. 76, ibid. (Alwin Brandes [chairman of the DMV]), 493. On the activity of the NSBO, see Mai, "Nationalsozialistische Betriebszellen-Organisation." On the mounting concern in the ADGB about how to keep unemployed workers inside the Free Trade Unions or possibly in friendly organizations for the unemployed, see Bundesvorstand, 2.3.32, Dok. 78, 518–22, and Bundesausschuss, 22.3.32, Dok. 83, 535–36, both in *Gewerkschaften 1930–1933*, vol. 4.

88. Bundesausschuss, 15/16.2.32, Dok. 76, in *Gewerkschaften 1930–1933*, 4:506–13. On the Iron Front, see chapter 7 below.

89. Leipart quoted in *VW*, #79, 17.2.32.

90. Ibid.

91. The ADGB put out a pamphlet before the congress, ADGB, Vorstand, *Arbeitsbeschaffung: Die Forderung der Gewerkschaften*. The following are only a selection of the many articles on the subject in *GZ*: "Arbeitsbeschaffung, die zentrale Aufgabe deutscher Wirtschaftspolitik," 20.2.32, 114–19; "Unsere Lösung: Arbeitsbeschaffung!," 20.2.32, 113; Fritz Tarnow, "Arbeit schaffen!," 27.2.32, 129; "Für und wider Arbeitsbeschaffung," 5.3.32, 148–50; Wladimir Woytinsky, "Wieder und wieder: Schafft Arbeit!," 12.3.32, 162–64. Also see Wladimir Woytinsky "Arbeitsbeschaffung und keine Inflationsgefahr!," *DA*, Mar. 1932, 142–54. Anton Erkelenz propagandized for WTB in *Die Hilfe* and *Der Beamtenbund* (NL Erkelenz, NL 72/102, fol. 1–312, #35, #77, #80, BA).

92. So Schneider sees it too (*Arbeitsbeschaffungs-Programm*, 129).

93. See, for example, "The most important task of 1932: jobs!" *VW*, #1, 1.1.32; "Offensive! Das Wirtschaftsprogramm der Arbeiterbewegung," *VW*, #81, 18.2.32.

94. Gates, "Free Trade Unions," 224.

95. *VW*, #79, 17.2.32.

96. Hilferding continued to insist that only "a world policy" could overcome the crisis (Hilferding to Kautsky, 27.2.32, NL Kautsky D/XII/656, IISH; *VW*, #10, 7.1.32). On Hertz, Wels, and Löbe, see Adolph, *Wels*, 238 n. 521. For Löbe's speech, see *BVW*, 20.1.32.

97. Keil, *Erlebnisse*, 2:427; Carlo Mierendorff, "Bedrohtes Deutschland," *SM*, 7.3.32, 220–21. Also see Walther Pahl (who worked for the ADGB), "Die deutsche Situation nach den Landtagswahlen," *SM*, 9.5.32, 229; Carlo Mierendorff, "Primat der Innenpolitik?," *SM*, 8.2.32, 111.

98. Carlo Mierendorff, "Die volle Wahrheit," *SM*, 9.5.32, 397.

99. Sender, *Autobiography*, 284. Also see "Sozialistische Wirtschaftspolitik oder aktive Währungspolitik?," in *LVZ* (20.2.32), which concluded that Woytinsky's proposal would not provide what workers needed—a "socialist economic policy."

100. Büttner, "Politische Haltung der Hamburger Freien Gewerkschaften," 524.

101. Gates, "Free Trade Unions," 225. The AfA-Bund and the ADGB engaged in long but unsuccessful negotiations to work out a common program. See Bundesvorstand, 9.3.32, Dok. 80, 525–26; Bundesvorstand, 11.3.32, Dok. 81, 527–28, both in *Gewerkschaften 1930–1933*, vol. 4.

102. *VW*, #139, 23.3.32; *HE*, 23.3.32.

103. Allgemeiner Deutscher Gewerkschaftsbund, *Protokoll der Verhandlungen des Ausserordentlichen (15.) Kongresses*, 29, 88–92, 103, 74–76, 84, 69, 27. Also see *VW*, #173, 13.4.32.

104. Allgemeiner Deutscher Gewerkschaftsbund, *Protokoll der Verhandlungen des Ausserordentlichen (15.) Kongresses*, 27, 85; *VW*, #174, 14.4.32.

105. Allgemeiner Deutscher Gewerkschaftsbund, *Protokoll der Verhandlungen des Ausserordentlichen (15.) Kongresses*, 67–68; "Der ausserordentliche Gewerkschaftskongress," *GZ*, 23.4.32, 266.

106. "Arbeitsbeschaffung—die Forderung der Zeit. Beschluss des ausserordentlichen Gewerkschaftskongresses vom 13. April zu Berlin," *GZ*, 23.4.32, 257.

107. See, e.g., "Für und wider Arbeitsbeschaffung," *GZ*, 30.4.32, 274–78; "Arbeitsbeschaffung durch Hausreparaturen," *GZ*, 21.5.32, 321–22; Keil, *Erlebnisse*, 2:440. At an ADGB national committee meeting in June, Leipart explained that the trade unions would still call for public works under Papen's regime ("Notverordnungen gegen Sozialpolitik," *GZ*, 18.6.32, 387).

108. Keil, *Erlebnisse*, 2:448.

109. See, e.g, Arkadij Gurland, "Entscheidung?," *MT*, 1.5.32: 259; *LVZ*, 6.6.32; NSDAP HA R.93/F.1898: Sektionsversammlung, 24.5.32; "Bedeutsamer Beschluss des Berliner Bezirksvorstandes," *UW*, June 1932; Hans Cohn, "Die Aufgaben nach der Schlacht," *UW*, May 1932, 133; Karl Höltermann, "Heraus aus der Krise! Schafft Arbeit!," *RB*, 4.6.32.

110. SPD guidelines for speakers in the state campaigns of spring 1932 offered a typical laundry list: nationalization of mining, a law on monopolies, and public works (SPD, Vorstand, *Um die Macht!*, 11). Also see the popular pamphlet by Georg Decker, *So kommen wir zum Sozialismus*, which provided an orthodox Marxist explanation of the crisis and called for a planned economy.

111. ADGB, Vorstand, *Umbau der Wirtschaft*.

112. Schneider, *Arbeitsbeschaffungs-Programm*, 131; *VW*, #247, 28.5.32. In 1932, SPD propaganda continued to insist that no economic *Wunderrezepte* existed (Prager, *Wer hat uns verraten?*, 5) and that the SPD had already done much in favor of *Arbeitsbeschaffung* (NWStAM Bestand SPD und Reichsbanner, Nr. 8: An die Ortsvereine!, Parteivorstand, 9.5.32).

113. On this compromise, see Potthoff, "Freie Gewerkschaften und sozialistische Parteien," 82.

114. Zollitsch, "Einzelgewerkschaften," 104.

115. Woytinsky, *Stormy Passage*, 468–69.

116. Schneider, *Arbeitsbeschaffungs-Programm*, 123. However, right before Brüning's fall, his regime had begun to consider its own public works plans. See James, "Gab es eine Alternative zur Wirtschaftspolitik Brünings?," 179.

117. Barkai, *Wirtschaftssystem*, 44–45; Köhler, "Borchardts 'Revision,'" 177–78; Holtfrerich, "Alternativen," 623–26.

118. Schildt, *Militärdiktatur?*, 139–41; Schildt, "Militärische Ratio," 353. Avraham Barkai has also noted that *Die Tat* praised WTB and made much of points of agreement between the Free Trade Unions and the NSDAP (*Wirtschaftssystem*, 46).

119. *Reichstag: Sten. Berichte*, Bd. 446, 10.5.32, 2511–14. The background to Strasser's speech is discussed by Avraham Barkai, *Wirtschaftssystem*, 37–39. According to Axel Schildt, a member of the *Tat* circle encouraged Strasser to deliver this talk ("Militärische Ratio," 354).

120. *Reichstag: Sten. Berichte*, Bd. 446, 11.5.32, 2636–37. This speech was published as a pamphlet: Hilferding, *Nationalsozialismus und Marxismus*.

121. Leipart relayed this to the Bundesvorstand, 8.6.32, Dok. 96, in *Gewerkschaften 1930–1933*, 4:584.

122. Schildt, *Militärdiktatur?*, 139–41. In fact, different tendencies inside the ADGB spearheaded these efforts. Schildt counts the ADGB staff member Walther Pahl as part of the nationalist tendency led by Furtwängler and Lothar Erdmann ("Militärische Ratio," 353); yet Pahl criticized WTB because it might undermine an active foreign policy (Pahl, "Die deutsche Situation nach den Landtagswahlen," *SM*, 9.5.32, 229).

123. See, e.g., Gates, "Free Trade Unions"; Moses, "German Free Trade Unions."

124. Weisbrod, "Befreiung," 320–22.

125. Franz Reuter, "Der Ruf nach Arbeitsbeschaffung," *DF*, #18, 3.4.32; "Gegen das Arbeitsbeschaffungsprogramm," *DF*, #19, 3.8.32. On Reuter's politics, see Turner, *German Big Business*, 299. Oddly enough, Reuter found an ally on this issue in the KPD, which pilloried Tarnow as an inflation monger. See KPD, *Krisenkongress des ADGB*, 19. Earlier the KPD, like the SPD, had excoriated the inflationary plans of the Harzburg Front. See KPD, *Inflation und Massenelend*.

126. Barkai, *Wirtschaftssystem*, 40–41.

127. Hilferding, *Nationalsozialismus und Marxismus*, 14.

128. See his comments to the ADGB board on his negotiations with Aufhäuser and Sender over the content of an "action program": "Large-scale public works are much easier to carry out if they don't have to be introduced

in the framework of a private economic system" (1.6.32, Dok. 95, in *Gewerkschaften 1930–1933*, 4:579).

129. Potthoff, "Freie Gewerkschaften und sozialistische Parteien," 83.

Chapter Seven

1. NSDAP HA R.92/F.1894: Lagebericht, 29.1.32; *FW*, 29.11.31, 12–15; 13.12.31, 5–11, 14–18.

2. Rohe, *Reichsbanner*, 392–93.

3. Treue, *Deutschland in der Weltwirtschaftskrise*, 143–44, 245–49, 251–53, 338.

4. Wels's speech, printed in ADGB, Vorstand, *Leipart und Breitscheid über die Notverordnung*, 29–31.

5. Johannes Han, *FW*, 27.9.31, 24–25; Gustav Ferl, *FW*, 29.11.31; "Eiserne Front aller Republikaner," *HE*, 25.11.31; Herbert Duwald, "Ausserparlamentarische Abwehr dem Faschismus," *UW*, June 1931, 125. On the Reichsbanner's role, see Walther Pahl, "Was bedeutet die Eiserne Front?," *SM*, 7.3.32, 230–31; Schaefer, *SPD in der Ära Brüning*, 305–8.

6. *VW*, #565, 3.12.31.

7. Ibid.; #563, 2.12.31; Schaefer, *SPD in der Ära Brüning*, 311, 313.

8. Höltermann communicated this news to district leaders, who informed local functionaries (NWStAM Bestand SPD und Reichsbanner, Nr. 9: Rundschreiben des Gauvorstandes, Westliches Westfalen, Dortmund 13.12.31).

9. See ibid., 12.1.32; (SPD) Rundschreiben, Westliches Westfalen, Dortmund, 5.2.32, 10.2.32, 21.5.32; Nr. 14: (SPD) Rundschreiben, Recklingshausen, 27.5.32. Also see Rohe, *Reichsbanner*, 392–93; Leber, "Todesursachen," 240.

10. Wels et al., *Eiserne Front*: Wels, 1–4; Höltermann, 5; Grassmann, 10–11; Wilding, 14–15. See Guttsman on the politicization of Social Democratic cultural organizations at the end of the republic (*Workers' Culture*, 135).

11. This language was not only for public consumption. In internal correspondence, the ADGB board maintained that the Iron Front aimed to unify "all male and female workers, young and old in a common effort" (ADGB-Bundesvorstand an G. Portulka, 28.2.32, NL Furtwängler, Kasten 1, DGB Archiv).

12. *VW*, #589, 17.12.31.

13. "1932: Jahr der Entscheidung" was a frequent headline in the local press (e.g., *LVZ*, 31.12.31; *RZ*, 31.12.31). See also Werner Zorn, "Angreifen—die Parole für 1932," *UW*, Jan. 1932, 5–7; "Gemeinsame Abwehr," *GZ*, 26.12.31, 817; "Eiserne Front für Volksrechte—Gegen Diktatur," *GZ*, 30.1.32, 65.

14. *Schulthess' Europäischer Geschichtskalender 1932*, 8.1.32, 5; *VW*, #88, 22.2.32.

15. See, for example, Haubach in Hanover (*HVW*, 23.2.32) and Grzesinski in Leipzig (*LVZ*, 8.2.32).

16. Stampfer, *Vierzehn Jahre*, 556–57.

17. Leber, "Todesursachen," 235–36.

18. For contemporary recognition of the "shift in the center of gravity of political decision making," see "Das Jahr der Notverordnungen," *GZ*, 2.1.32, 1.

19. See the remarks of union leader Schlimme after the Hindenburg election (Aufzeichnung Schlimmes [ADGB]: Betreuung der Arbeitslosen durch die Eiserne Front, 25.4.32, Dok. 85, in *Gewerkschaften 1930–1933*, 4:550). Leipart commented on "the electoral significance of the Iron Front" at an ADGB board meeting (28.4.32, Dok. 86, ibid., 552).

20. Schaefer, *SPD in der Ära Brüning*, 311.

21. Rohe, *Reichsbanner*, 394–95, 400, 398. A few bourgeois papers reported on Iron Front activities with enthusiasm, such as the *General Anzeiger* in Dortmund (Klotzbach, *Gegen den Nationalsozialismus*, 53).

22. On the NSDAP's *Symbolkult* that excited the senses rather than appealing to "sense," and on Social Democratic innovators' desire to emulate it, see Paul, *Aufstand der Bilder*, 165–79.

23. *VW*, #37, 23.1.32; #41, 26.1.32; #49, 30.1.32; #52, 1.2.32; #53, 2.2.32; Witt, *Hamburger Sozialdemokratie*, 136; Wickham, "Working-Class Movement in Frankfurt," 238. Berliners claimed that 250,000 had signed the Iron Book there by late February (*VW*, #88, 22.2.32). Iron Front meetings also attracted an "unusual influx" of people earlier "bitten by the Third Reich bug" (*FW*, 28.2.32, 7–8).

24. The quote is from Stampfer, *Vierzehn Jahre*, 556–57; Leber, "Todesursachen," 235–36. The right-wing *Deutsche Führerbriefe* admitted that the Iron Front "took off with a spirited offensive" ("SPD Spiegel," *DF*, #83, 25.10.32). The bourgeois press, liberal and conservative, was very impressed by the crowds mobilized by the Iron Front (Schaefer, *SPD in der Ära Brüning*, 325–26).

25. NHStAH Hann. 310, I/B13: (NSDAP local monthly report to Gau headquarters) 9.2.32.

26. See the comments of union leaders at an ADGB board meeting, 28.4.32, Dok. 86, in *Gewerkschaften 1930–1933*, 4:552. Hamburg is discussed below. Hanover had dozens of meetings in January, February, and March (NHStAH Hann. 310, II/C, Nr. 25: Rundschreiben des Gauvorstandes [Hanover] 4.2.32; *HVW*, 20.1.32, 22.1.32, 24.1.32, 2.2.32, 5.2.32, 6.2.32, 7.2.32, 12.2.32, 13.2.32, 25.2.32, 3.3.32, 8.3.32). Smaller Northeim, also in Lower Saxony, saw a great increase in activity by the SPD and the Reichsbanner (Allen, *Nazi Seizure of Power*, 80–81, 87, 114–15). Other cities, of course, joined the fray. See Wickham, "Working-Class Movement in Frankfurt," 238, 297; Klotzbach, *Gegen den Nationalsozialismus*, 53; *DVZ*, 22.1.32; Matthias and

Weber, *Widerstand gegen den Nationalsozialismus in Mannheim*, 109; NWStAM Bestand SPD und Reichsbanner, Nr. 9: Rundschreiben des Gauvorstandes, Westliches Westfalen, Dortmund, 5.2.32. On activities in Augsburg, Nuremberg, and Munich, see Krall, *Landespolitik der SPD in Bayern*, 218.

27. On the Iron Front in Berlin's factories, see Karl Dressel, "Der Nazisturm auf die Betriebe," *UW*, Feb. 1932, 34–35. For evidence that cultural associations were drawn in, see NSDAP HA R.92/F.1894: Lagebericht, 4.4.32.

28. See, e.g., Allen, *Nazi Seizure of Power*, 87, 114, on Northeim. Peter Friedemann points out that as early as the 1890s, the Socialist sport movement used military metaphors ("Krise der Arbeitersportbewegung," 231–32), but the militarization of Social Democratic pageantry was new.

29. See, e.g., *VW*, #87, 21.2.32: "Iron the front, iron the hand, republican all the land."

30. Bundesausschuss, 15/16.2.32, Dok. 76, in *Gewerkschaften 1930–1933*, 4:491.

31. Rohe, *Reichsbanner*, 396–99. The ADGB provided the bulk of financial support (100,000 marks), while the SPD put in 34,000 marks and the AfA-Bund 7,000 (Bundesvorstand, 18.5.32, Dok. 92, in *Gewerkschaften 1930–1933*, 4:571). Trade union and party employees were required to make "emergency contributions" to the Iron Front (NWStAM Bestand SPD und Reichsbanner, Nr. 7: [SPD] Rundschreiben #1, Dortmund, 5.2.32).

32. Hoegner, *Flucht*, 29; Stampfer, *Vierzehn Jahre*, 556.

33. Adolph, *Wels*, 240 n. 525.

34. "Bundesvorstand des Reichsbanners an die Gauvorstände," 14.4.32, in Matthias, "Sozialdemokratische Partei," 219.

35. Rohe, *Reichsbanner*, 375, 369, 366, 371–72; Groener speech to the Reichstag, 24.2.32, printed in *Staat und NSDAP 1930–1932*, 280.

36. BA R58/557: #77, 20.9.32; Allen, *Nazi Seizure of Power*, 92, 96. The Augsburg police confiscated infantry bayonets from a Reichsbanner member (NSDAP HA R.94/F.1908: Lagebericht (Augsburg), 1.5.32). The Munich police noted an increase in "small caliber shooting exercises" in late 1931 (NSDAP HA R.95/F.1910: Lagebericht (Munich), 26.11.31). According to Heinrich A. Winkler, Hesse, Magdeburg, Berlin, and Hamburg were particularly involved in self-defense and target practice (*Katastrophe*, 593–94).

37. The *Hammerschaften* were formed in early 1932; each unit had one hundred men (Rohe, *Reichsbanner*, 412–13). On the ever growing concern of ADGB leaders about the NSBO, see Bundesausschuss, 15/16.2.32, Dok. 76, in *Gewerkschaften 1930–1933*, 4:493. Also see ADGB, Vorstand, *Geheim! Geheim!*, which warns of Nazi strike-breaking plans and calls on unionists to "build the *Hammerschaften* of the Iron Front in all shops."

38. On tensions in Munich, see NSDAP HA R.93/F.1902: Reichsbannerversammlung, 13.2.32; R.93/F.1903: Besprechung der Führer des Reichsbanners und der SPD München, 8.8.32.

39. NSDAP HA R.93/F.1901: Besprechung der Bezirksleitung, 23.3.32; R.93, F.1898, Sektionsversammlung, 12.4.32; NSDAP HA R.93/F.1903: Reichsbannerversammlung, 4.6.32.

40. (Schlimme's note) 25.4.32, Dok. 85, 550–51; Bundesvorstand, 28.4.32, Dok. 86, 552; Bundesvorstand, 18.5.32, Dok. 92, 571; Bundesausschuss, 21.7.32, Dok. 113, 629; all in *Gewerkschaften 1930–1933*, vol. 4.

41. NHStAH Hann. 310, II/C, Nr. 23: Arbeiter Turn-und Sportbund an die Kampfleitung der Eiserne Front, 17.6.32.

42. Rohe, *Reichsbanner*, 414, 398–99. The Social Democratic propagandist Sergei Chakhotin denied that propaganda was centrally coordinated in any way (*Rape of the Masses*, 195–96). For evidence of lack of coordination at the local level, see NWStAM Bestand SPD und Reichsbanner, Nr. 5: Mutsch [Dortmund SPD secretary] to Baran [in Bottropp], 21.5.32.

43. See the urgent plea of an activist from Silesia: An die Redaktion der *Eiserne Front*, 23.2.32, NL Furtwängler, Kasten 1, DGB Archiv.

44. Matthias, "Sozialdemokratische Partei," 125 n. 22; Dorothea Beck, *Julius Leber*, 115–16; Edinger, *Kurt Schumacher*, 49; Heine, *Kurt Schumacher*, 38, 41; Witt, *Hamburger Sozialdemokratie*, 138 n. 74; Zuckmayer, *Carlo Mierendorff*, 31–32. Rohe credits Höltermann with the introduction of the new methods (*Reichsbanner*, 404).

45. See, e.g., Carlo Mierendorff, "Republik oder Monarchie?," *SM*, July 1926, 437–38. Also see "Protokoll eines Treffens des Kreises der 'Neuen Blätter für den Sozialismus', November 1930," in Martiny, "Entstehung," 409.

46. "Aufbau der neuen Linken," *MT*, Feb. 1932, reprinted by Heinemann, "Linksopposition," 2:179–85.

47. "Aufbau," in Luthardt, *Sozialdemokratische Arbeiterbewegung*, 2:181. Ernst Fraenkel first used the epithet "proletarian Economic Party" ("Die politische Bedeutung des Arbeitsrechts," *DG*, Jan. 1932, 46).

48. Darmstadt annual meeting, *HVF*, 17.2.32.

49. "Bedrohtes Deutschland," *SM*, 7.3.32, 220–21. His vehemence against union politicking largely arose from his disgust with the ADGB position on reparations (222).

50. "Germany's future," he wrote, "will be decided by the extraparliamentary situation: public opinion" ("Die volle Wahrheit," *SM*, 9.5.32, 399).

51. On the street politics of the KPD, see Rosenhaft, *Beating the Fascists?*, 3–9, 25, 53–55; McElligott, "Street Politics in Hamburg."

52. Sergei Tschachotin [Chakhotin], "Aktivierung der Arbeiterschaft," *NB*, Mar. 1932, 149. A biographical note appended to his first article in *Neue Blätter* does not always agree with the information provided by Albrecht, "Symbolkampf." According to Albrecht, Chakhotin worked on propaganda for the White General Kornilov in 1918. In exile, however, he became less hostile to Bolshevism and was, in fact, quite favorable to the USSR by the mid-1920s ("Symbolkampf," 509–13).

53. Chakhotin, *Rape of the Masses*, 99–101, 191; Sergei Tschachotin, "Die positive Seite unserer Niederlage," *DR*, 24.5.32, 1093; Rohe, *Reichsbanner*, 404–5. Chakhotin noted the powerful effect of the Nazis' total belief in their victory (Sergei Tschachotin, "Die Technik der politischen Propaganda," *SM*, 9.5.32, 425).

54. Chakhotin, *Rape of the Masses*, 121; Sergei Tschachotin, "Lehren der Wahlkämpfe," *DR*, 31.5.32, 1135.

55. Chakhotin, *Rape of the Masses*, 94–95; Tschachotin, "Die Technik der politischen Propaganda," 425–31. Prince Loewenstein-Scharffeneck too was irked by the republicans' lack of understanding "for all things psychological" (*Tragedy of a Nation*, 100–101).

56. Albrecht, "Symbolkampf," 523.

57. Chakhotin, *Rape of the Masses*, 103–6.

58. Albrecht, "Symbolkampf," 525. Chakhotin abhorred the "kitsch" that, in his eyes, marred Social Democratic propaganda. It assumed "falsely" that the masses were "crude and artistically inferior," unable to appreciate the "truly beautiful" (Tschachotin, "Lehren der Wahlkämpfe," 1136).

59. Chakhotin, *Rape of the Masses*, 191; Rohe, *Reichsbanner*, 406–7.

60. NHStAH Hann. 310, II: Rundschreiben #9/1932, Gauvorstandes Hannover, 3.23.32; Rundschreiben #12/1932, 31.3.32; NSDAP HA R.93/ F.1902: Lagebericht, 6.4.32.

61. Chakhotin, *Rape of the Masses*, 192. "Palace revolution" is from Rohe (*Reichsbanner*, 410).

62. A report on Iron Front propaganda after the presidential campaign noted continuing poor application of talent and money, urging centralization and homogenization of propaganda and a nationally planned agitation effort ("Die 'Eiserne Front' im Kampf," NSDAP HA R.40/F.799). In contrast to the SPD effort, in the Nazi presidential campaign even the distribution of leaflets was nationally coordinated (Böhnke, *NSDAP im Ruhrgebiet*, 181); yet local Nazis were also encouraged to report on their "field" experiences and to try out new techniques (Noakes, *Nazi Party in Lower Saxony*, 219).

63. Chakhotin, *Rape of the Masses*, 201–2.

64. Bundesausschuss, 14.6.32, Dok. 97, in *Gewerkschaften 1930–1933*, 4:594–95 (Schlimme).

65. Rohe, *Reichsbanner*, 409.

66. Chakhotin, *Rape of the Masses*, 201–3, 196.

67. Keil, *Erlebnisse*, 2:435; Braun, *Weimar*, 372. On the vote, see Sitzung des Parteiausschusses am 10.11.32 (hereafter cited as Parteiausschuss, November), in Schulze, *Anpassung oder Widerstand?*, 45. Several union leaders, such as Brandes of the DMV and Thiemig of the factory workers' union, also argued for a separate candidate before resigning themselves to Hindenburg (Bundesausschuss, 15/16.2.32, Dok. 76, in *Gewerkschaften 1930–1933*, 4:493–94).

68. Otto Braun, *VW*, #117, 10.3.32; Braun, *Weimar*, 372; Schulze, *Otto Braun*, 719.

69. Braun wrote Severing and Kautsky in this vein in January 1932 (Schulze, *Otto Braun*, 716; Braun to Kautsky, 2.19.32, in Matthias, "Hindenburg zwischen den Fronten," 84). Earlier Severing sounded out Hugo Eckener, a popular zeppelin commander, as a possible candidate even though he had ties to the Stahlhelm. This idea was dropped when Hindenburg's candidacy was announced (Dorpalen, *Hindenburg*, 258). Severing, then, pushed the "hesitant" Reich Interior Minister Groener to get out material on the candidate that would draw "democratic circles" (Severing, *Lebensweg*, 2:321–22).

70. Bracher, *Auflösung*, 479–80; Dorpalen, *Hindenburg*, 268–69, 275, 283–84, 298–99.

71. See, e.g., *LVZ*, 29.2.32; *FVS*, 7.3.32; Breitscheid in Spandau (*VW*, #100, 29.2.32) and in the Reichstag (*Reichstag: Sten. Berichte*, Bd. 446, 24.2.32, 2277–78). Allen describes the anti-Hitler emphasis of the SPD campaign in Northeim (Allen, *Nazi Seizure of Power*, 87). Also see "Um den Reichspräsidenten," *GZ*, 5.3.32, 146–48. For evidence of the vigor of the campaign, see NSDAP HA R.93/F.1901: Funtionärsbesprechung, 23.3.32.

72. *VW*, #92, 24.2.32. Also see the published version of Breitscheid's Reichstag speech on SPD support (Breitscheid, "Reichstagsrede," in *Wider den Nationalsozialismus*, 102-3).

73. Hilferding informed Kautsky, "The elections turned out well and the party fought famously" (Hilferding to Kautsky, 16.3.32, NL Kautsky, D/XII/657, IISH). Election statistics in Falter, Lindenberger, and Schumann, *Wahlen und Abstimmungen*, 46.

74. Carlo Mierendorff, "Der Hindenburgsieg 1932," *SM*, 4.4.32, 297.

75. NSDAP HA R.40/F.799: "Eiserne Front im Kampf"; NHStAH Hann. 310, II/C, Nr. 25, Rundschreiben des Gauvorstandes (Dortmund) #6/1932, 5.3.32, Rundschreiben #7/1932, 8.3.32, Rundschreiben #8/1932, 17.3.32; Schaefer, *SPD in der Ära Brüning*, 336; BA R45 IV/26: An das Sekretariat des Zentralkomitees [KPD], Bericht über die Versammlungstournee im Unterbezirk Neu-Stettin, Bezirk Pommern, 11.4.32.

76. Georg Decker, "Die Entscheidung vom 13. März," *DG*, Apr. 1932, 281–84; *FW*, 27.3.32, 16–19; Mierendorff, "Bedrohtes Deutschland," 217; Hilferding to Kautsky, 16.3.32, NL Kautsky D/XII/657, IISH.

77. *VW*, #166, 9.4.32; Chakhotin, *Rape of the Masses*, 196–200, 203; Pyta, *Gegen Hitler*, 341.

78. Braun, *Weimar*, 374. Arnold Brecht remembered the difficulty of turning rallies into "successes" when Braun spoke (Schulze, *Otto Braun*, 723). Stampfer recalled Braun's visible dejection (*Vierzehn Jahre*, 565).

79. Falter, Lindenberger, and Schumann, *Wahlen und Abstimmungen*, 101, 89, 91, 113.

80. Hilferding, *Nach den Wahlen*, 2. According to Heilmann, the SPD had fared relatively better than in 1930. The vote was, thus, a victory for the working class, although also for National Socialism (*FW*, 1.5.32, 1–3). After a week of reflection, he came up with the beloved 1924 comparison (April 1932

was relatively better than May 1924) and concluded, "We are back on the way up" (*FW*, 8.5.32, 1).

81. "Das Ergebnis des 24. April," *GZ*, 30.4.32, 273; F. D. H. Schulz, *DVZ*, 25.4.32.

82. For Social Democratic commentary on the mixed results in Prussia, see *RZ*, 25.4.32. Rural laborers were the only social group targeted by a "special leaflet" (NWStAM Bestand SPD und Reichsbanner, Nr. 7: [SPD] Rundschreiben, Westliches Westfalen, Dortmund, 12.4.32).

83. Kurt Schumacher, "Die Landtagswahlen in Württemberg," *MT*, 8.4.32, 245; "Die Lehren des 10.April," *MT*, 15.4.32, 225–26; *BVW*, 9.1.32; Fritz Baade, "Agrarpolitik und Preussenwahl," *DG*, Apr. 1932, 299–302.

84. In East Prussia (including Königsberg), the SPD won 30,000 new votes. The Center Party tally actually increased from 2.7 to 3.3 million votes. The State Party retained only 2 of 21 seats (Falter, Lindenberger, and Schumann, *Wahlen und Abstimmungen*, 101). For the views of bourgeois analysts, see Schaefer, *SPD in der Ära Brüning*, 343. For the opinion of Communists that Nazis had made gains among workers, see BA R45 IV/25: Protokoll der Sekretariatssitzung der Bezirksleitung Pommern [KPD], 26.4.32.

85. *HE* Sonderausgabe, 25.4.32. The State Party did even better than the SPD with 17,000 new votes (of 84,146). See Falter, Lindenberger, and Schumann, *Wahlen und Abstimmungen*, 94.

86. Chakhotin, *Rape of the Masses*, 203; Witt, *Hamburger Sozialdemokratie*, 138, 143.

87. Witt, *Hamburger Sozialdemokratie*, 131; *HE*, 15.1.32; Chakhotin, *Rape of the Masses*, 203.

88. NSDAP HA R.93/F.1901: Geschäftsbericht der SPD München, 1.1.31–31.12.32; R.92/F.1894: Lagebericht, 4.4.32; R.93/F.1901: 23.3.32, Besprechung der Partei-und Reichsbannerführer (Munich).

89. Tschachotin, "Die positive Seite unserer Niederlage," 1093–96. He provided examples of the new methods as instituted in Heidelberg ("Lehren der Wahlkämpfe," 1132–36). Chakhotin was especially adamant about the use of rhymed chants such as "Hitler will not come to power, the Iron Front watches by the hour (*Hitler kommt nicht an die Macht, die Eiserne Front steht auf der Wacht*)"; "If a putsch you just dare, the Iron Front its fists will bare (*Wollt das Putschen Ihr nur wagen, die Eiserne Front holt aus zum Schlagen*)." The Reichsbanner made sure that their chapters used these rhymes (see, e.g., NHStAH Hann. 310, II/A, Nr. 2: [Reichsbanner] An alle Ortsgruppen im Gau Hannover, 6.4.32).

90. Walter Glenlow [Haubach], "Geist und Technik des Preussenwahlkampfes," *NB*, May 1932, 233–39.

91. "Die Aufgaben der Partei in der Zukunft," *Münchner Post*, 20.5.32. This article reported on a functionary meeting.

92. Chakhotin, *Rape of the Masses*, 206. Mierendorff was close to Wilhelm Leuschner, Hesse's SPD interior minister. See Hans Mommsen, "Deutschen

Gewerkschaften," 275–76. For an explicit acknowledgment that Hesse was seen as a "model," see NHStAH Hann. 310, II/C, Nr. 25: Reichsbanner-Mitteilungen der Bundes-Pressestelle #7, 10.6.32.

93. K. Wiegner, "Mit Höltermann im Hessenwahlkampf," *RB*, 18.6.32. The SPD financed the campaign with the proceeds from these sales (Chakhotin, *Rape of the Masses*, 125). Not only Socialists fought under the sign of the *Drei Pfeile:* at Chakhotin's urging, Büro Wilhelmstrasse, the Jewish defense bureau, helped spread the *Drei Pfeile* in the Hessian and Reichstag campaigns (Paucker, "Der jüdische Abwehrkampf," 471).

94. Chakhotin, *Rape of the Masses*, 207, 209; FW, 3.7.32, 24–25; *HVF*, 11.6.32, 18.6.32. It was hard, however, to outdo the Nazis. According to Chakhotin, Hitler spoke in every district.

95. Chakhotin described the wild excitement inside the Hessian SPD (*Rape of the Masses*, 217). The Communist view is expressed in BA R45 IV/21: Remscheid, 29.6.32 (report of a Communist who campaigned in Hesse).

96. Carlo Mierendorff, "Die Freiheitspfeile siegen in Hessen," *NB*, July 1932, 386–87; Carlo Mierendorff, VW, #287, 21.6.32. Also see Sergei Tschachotin, "Das Hessische Experiment," *DR*, 19.7.32, 1355–58; Ph. Künkele, "Lehren der Hessenwahl," *FW*, 3.7.32, 24–26. For voting statistics, see Falter, Lindenberger, and Schumann, *Wahlen und Abstimmungen*, 95. Communists compared their campaign's organization and coordination unfavorably with those of the SPD and the NSDAP, both of which "for two weeks daily brought in forces from neighboring regions" (BA R45 IV/21: [KPD] Bericht über Wahlversammlungen in Hessen, Mannheim, 19.6.32).

97. Chakhotin, *Rape of the Masses*, 206; *HVF*, 28.5.32.

98. A pamphlet on the virtues of the democratic republic by Wilhelm Keil was clearly aimed at workers: Keil, *Wisst Ihr das?: Was mit der demokratischen Republik erreicht wurde.*

99. Rohe, *Reichsbanner*, 402 n. 4; Witt, *Hamburger Sozialdemokratie*, 143.

100. "Junker-Preussen oder Arbeiter-Preussen?," *Flugblattsammlung 1932* (SPD), AsD; Kuttner, *Otto Braun*, 7.

101. Tschachotin, "Aktivierung der Arbeiterschaft," 149. Yet all Chakhotin's articles appeared in revisionist Social Democratic journals—*Sozialistische Monatshefte*, *Neue Blätter*, *Deutsche Republik.*

102. *HVW*, 23.2.32. Still, Haubach chided party speakers who focused on the working class before small-town audiences of employees, civil servants, artisans, and shopkeepers ("Geist und Technik," *NB*, May 1932, 235).

103. Borinski, "'Neue Blätter für den Sozialismus,'" 75–78.

104. NSDAP HA R.93/F.1898: Sektionsversammlung, 10.5.32.

105. Letters to *Das Freie Wort* expounded on this double identity. According to a member from Dortmund, the SPD must mobilize the "masses of the working-class" to defend "freedom, democracy, republic" (*FW*, 3.7.32, 10–12). Another wanted to win Communist workers to fight for the republic (*FW*, 3.7.32, 12–13).

106. See, e.g., Wels et al., *Eiserne Front*, 1; Breitscheid, "Reichstagsrede," in *Wider den Nationalsozialismus*, 131; Prager, *Wer hat uns verraten?*, 13; Deutscher Metallverein, *Der Nationalsozialismus in Theorie und Praxis*, 15; SPD, Vorstand, *Nationalsozialismus und Frauenfragen*, 20; Hilferding at Berlin rally, *VW*, #10, 7.1.32. *Das Echo der Woche*, a new weekly inside the *Hamburger Echo*, asked the now rhetorical question, *Wer finanziert Hitler?* (*HE*, 20.3.32); on July 15, its banner headline was "Die Goldquelle der Hitler-Partei."

107. "Der Antisozialist!," *VW*, #191, 23.4.32. Also see *VW*, #107, 4.3.32. Nazis countered with the charge not that capitalists financed the SPD but that Social Democratic leaders were capitalists (NHStAH Hann. 310, I/Bll/II: "Signale" [NSDAP local dispatch]).

108. Grübler, *Spitzenverbände*, 434–46.

109. *Vorwärts* (#297, 26.6.32) acknowledged these differences when it asked, after Brüning's fall, if the RDI now supported "constitutional change in a fascist direction" rather than the "political reason" it earlier espoused.

110. Severing considered it his "duty" to establish cooperation among all republican parties (*Lebensweg*, 2:318). The SPD's hopes were not without some foundation; according to Keil, "democratic capitalists" helped finance the SPD effort in the Hindenburg campaign (*Erlebnisse*, 2:439).

111. *FVS*, 27.2.32; Erich Rossmann, quoted in *VW*, #95, 26.2.32.

112. #55 (Decree of the Reich Defense Ministry), 29.1.32, 276–78, and Schulz, "Einleitung," 56, 58, both in *Staat und NSDAP 1930–1932*.

113. #42 (instructions from Groener to State Secretary Zweigert), 18.11.31, 227–28; #54 (Groener to Generalmajor a.D. von Gleich), 26.1.32, 275; both in *Staat und NSDAP 1930–1932*. Also see Bracher, *Auflösung*, 466 n. 91. On Groener's public justification of the policy, see *VW*, #93, 25.2.32.

114. Vogelsang, *Reichswehr*, 160; Hayes, "'Question Mark with Epaulettes'?," 43–44; Stampfer, *Vierzehn Jahre*, 570. Brüning supported the decree, hoping to convince Hitler to support extension of Hindenburg's term (*Memoiren*, 504–5).

115. See, e.g., *VW*, #72, 12.2.32.

116. #60 (Groener to Severing), 8.3.32, 299; #61 (Groener to Schleicher), 23.3.32, 300; #63 (minutes of conference of interior ministers with Reich interior minister), 5.4.32, 304–5; all in *Staat und NSDAP 1930–1932*.

117. #59a (Braun to Brüning), 4.3.32; #59b (excepts from a memorandum on the NSDAP from the Prussian Interior Ministry), 290–98, both in *Staat und NSDAP 1930–1932*. Also see Schulze, *Otto Braun*, 721. According to Kempner, Brüning had part of this memo destroyed ("Einführung," in Kempner, *Der verpasste Nazi-Stopp*, 13). The SPD executive committee sent Groener the same material even earlier (*VW*, #54, 2.2.32).

118. Vogelsang, *Reichswehr*, 160.

119. Severing, *Lebensweg*, 2:328–29; Vogelsang, *Reichswehr*, 164, 166; #62a (Bavarian Interior Ministry to Reich minister of the interior), 30.3.32, 301–2, and #63 (conference of the interior ministers and Reich interior minister),

5.4.32, 307, in *Staat und NSDAP 1930–1932*. Severing also released some of the information (*VW*, #160, 6.4.32). Baden had an SPD-Center Party government until November 1932 (Matthias, "Mannheimer Sozialdemokraten"). Hesse was ruled by a coalition whose interior minister was the Social Democrat (and ADGB leader) Wilhelm Leuschner (Leithäuser, *Wilhelm Leuschner*). Württemberg had a Center-DNVP government. Bavaria too had a conservative government under Heinrich Held of the BVP.

120. Brüning, *Memoiren*, 538; *VW*, #170, 12.4.32; Braun, *Weimar*, 380–81; Schulze, *Otto Braun*, 722.

121. Quotes from Groener to Brüning, 10.4.32, #65, in *Staat und NSDAP 1930–1932*, 312–15. On the pressure he put on the chancellor, see Vogelsang, *Reichswehr*, 169; Brüning, *Memoiren*, 542–43.

122. Schulz, "Einleitung," 60–61; Bracher, *Auflösung*, 488–89; Ehni, *Bollwerk Preussen?*, 241.

123. Brüning, *Memoiren*, 544–45; *Schulthess' Europäischer Geschichtskalender 1932*, 68; Eyck, *History of the Weimar Republic*, 2:369–71.

124. Bracher, *Auflösung*, 493.

125. *VW*, #180, 17.4.32; Vogelsang, *Reichswehr*, 177, 175; Bracher, *Auflösung*, 492. The *Schufo* was re-formed after the SA ban was lifted (Rohe, *Reichsbanner*, 424–25). That the promise to dissolve the *Schufo* was carried out is evident from NHStAH Hann. 310, II/C, Nr. 25: Rundschreiben des Reichsbannergaues Hannover, 18.4.32 and 21.4.32.

126. Rohe, *Reichsbanner*, 424.

127. Eyck, *History of the Weimar Republic*, 2:373–77; Breitman, *German Social Democracy*, 180.

128. Kolb, *Weimarer Republik*, 132; Brüning, *Memoiren*, 597–600; Eyck, *History of the Weimar Republic*, 2:379–86. Brüning conducted negotiations with the Gregor Strasser wing of the NSDAP in the spring of 1932 (*Memoiren*, 568).

129. Morsey, *Entstehung*, 41; Kolb, *Weimarer Republik*, 132. Turner discusses the complaints of business (*German Big Business*, 227).

130. Stampfer, *Vierzehn Jahre*, 574; Bracher, *Auflösung*, 522, 530–31; "Aktennotiz über die Besprechungen des Herrn Reichspräsidenten betr. Regierungsbildung am 30. und 31. Mai 1932," in Hubatsch, *Hindenburg*, 321.

131. Keil, *Erlebnisse*, 2:448.

132. *LVZ*, 6.6.32.

133. These comments were made to skeptical Berlin functionaries (*VW*, #263, 7.6.32).

134. Arkadij Gurland, "Tolerierungsscherben—und was weiter?," *MT*, 15.6.32, 355–56; Carlo Mierendorff, "Die Rettung Deutschlands," *SM*, 1.7.32, 578–79.

135. Bundesausschuss, 14.6.32, Dok. 97, in *Gewerkschaften 1930–1933*, 4:593–95.

136. The second week's slogan was "Yes, we want a welfare state!" See NWStAM Bestand SPD und Reichsbanner, Nr. 8: Mobilmachung für den

Wahlkampf, Parteivorstand, 14.6.32; NHStAH Hann. 310, II/C, Nr. 25: Rundschreiben des Reichsbannergaues Hannover #16/1932, 17.6.32; Hann. 310, II/A, Nr. 38: Material für die Reichstagswahl 1932. Also see Chakhotin, *Rape of the Masses*, 215–19.

137. SPD, Vorstand, *An der Stempelstelle*, quote from p. 7.

138. See NWStAM Bestand SPD und Reichsbanner, Nr. 8: (SPD) Rundschreiben, Westliches Westfalen, Dortmund, 13.6.32 and 18.7.32; (SPD) Rundschreiben, Recklingshausen, 13.7.32. The quote is from Frey, *Deutschland, wohin?*, 12–13. Lothar Frey was the pseudonym for the neorevisionist Walther Pahl.

139. *RZ*, 15.6.32; NHStAH Hann. 310, II/C, Nr. 25: Rundschreiben des Gauvorstandes Hannover des Reichsbanners, 7.5.32 (also in Matthias, "Sozialdemokratische Partei," 222–23).

140. *FW*, 10.7.32, 13. Also see the same issue, p. 21.

141. *LVZ*, 6.6.32, 4.7.32, 2.8.32. Leftist intellectuals endorsed the new methods. In the Chemnitz paper, the only one still outspokenly left wing, Gurland argued the importance of mass psychology (Klenke, *SPD Linke*, 360). According to Eugen Chossudowsky of Berlin, the *Drei Pfeile* symbolized "socialist logic and ethics" (*FW*, 3.7.32, 22–23).

142. G. W., "Die Berliner Partei im Wahlkampf," *UW*, Sept. 1932, 257–60. *Vorwärts* covered all this and Iron Front activities in other locales diligently (e.g., #323, 12.7.32; #346, 25.7.32). Also see NSDAP HA R.93/F.1901: Besprechung der Sektionsleitungen, 28.6.32; Allen, *Nazi Seizure of Power*, 114–15; Keil, *Erlebnisse*, 2:451–52; *FW*, 10.7.32, 13–14, 21; *HVW*, 1.8.32; *FVS*, 1.8.32; *DVZ*, 18.7.32.

143. On youthful involvement, see the comments of Brennecke, secretary of the tailors' union in Hanover-Braunschweig, and Karl, chairman of the factory workers, to the ADGB national committee, 21.7.32, Dok. 112, in *Gewerkschaften 1930–1933*, 4:628–29; Pyta, *Gegen Hitler*, 441–42. On the Red Pioneers, first formed in Hamburg and later adopted by the SPD executive to tighten the "bonds between the generations" and integrate youth into the party, see NWStAM Bestand SPD und Reichsbanner, Nr. 8: Richtlinien zur Erweiterung der Parteipropaganda (Parteivorstand); Witt, *Hamburger Sozialdemokratie*, 134.

144. A KPD pamphlet from the Papen era propagated "work, bread, peace." Both slogans echoed the famous Bolshevik cry of 1917—"peace, land, bread." See KPD, *Wer regiert?*, 15.

145. SPD, Vorstand, *Agitations Sprechchöre*. Activists were urged to use youth in the *Sprechchören* to "enliven" demonstrations (NWStAM Bestand SPD und Reichsbanner, Nr. 8: [SPD] Rundschreiben, Dortmund, 15.7.32). On choral works as a long-standing feature of Social Democratic *Festkultur*, see Lidtke, *Alternative Culture*, 76–78, 93; Guttsman, *Workers' Culture*, 144, 234.

146. See the SPD, KPD, and NSDAP campaign posters between chapters 4 and 5.

147. "Freiheitstag der Eiserne Front," *RB*, 16.7.32; Georg Decker, "Nach der Preussenwahl," *DG*, June 1932, 473.

148. Wels and Breitscheid in *VW*, #328, 14.7.32. *Vorwärts* charted the bloody course: "Blutiger Sonntag in Reich," "Aufruhr in München," #286, 20.6.32; "Es brennt überall!," #288, 21.6.32; "Terror über Breslau," "SA tobt durch die Nacht!," #292, 23.6.32; "Bürgerkrieg in Permanenz," #322, 11.7.32. Also see Möller, *Parlamentarismus*, 564; Braun, *Weimar*, 404. Most victims were Nazis or Communists. Eight Reichsbanner men were killed and seventy-two were wounded between June 14 and July 18 (Rohe, *Reichsbanner*, 425 n. 2).

149. According to Otto Wels, between January 1 and August 1, 1932, there were 1,132 court proceedings against Iron Front members and 900 more were pending. A total of about 500 years of prison terms was imposed. Twenty-nine Reichsbanner men died in fights (Sitzung der Reichskampfleitung der Eiserne Front, 26.8.32, Dok. 121, in *Gewerkschaften 1930–1933*, 4:655–56). On press censorship, see Koszyk, *Presse der deutschen Sozialdemokratie*, 47.

150. NHStAH Hann. 310, II/A/13: Kreisverein Peine an den Bezirkssekretariat Hannover, 15.6.32; Hann. 310, I/B11/I: Leibenau, 4.8.32 (NSDAP report on SPD campaign in Nienburg); Keil, *Erlebnisse*, 2:452; Allen, *Nazi Seizure of Power*, 113–14; Skrzypczak, "Kanzlerwechsel," 496–97.

151. BA R45 IV/28: [KPD] Bericht über die Durchführung der Reichstagswahl im Juli 1932 and Bericht über die Wahlkampagne Reichstagswahl 1932, Unterbezirk II (Dresden); NHStAH Hann. 310, I/B11/I: Bezirksleitung Goslar (NSDAP) [n.d.]; Ortsgruppe NSDAP Alfeld, 8.8.32; Blankenburg/Harz, 10.8.32; Kreisleitung Göttingen, 4.8.32; Hann. 310, I/B13: Südhannover Gau (all the above are monthly reports sent to NSDAP headquarters); "NSDAP Rundschreiben, 12.7.32," in SPD, Vorstand, *An die Bezirksleitungen!*, 11–13. Also see Noakes, *Nazi Party in Lower Saxony*, 217. A Nazi leaflet attacking the SPD was titled "Freiheit!" and showed the *Drei Pfeile* with the caption "going down (*abwärts*)" (*Flugblattsammlung 1932*, AsD).

152. SPD, Vorstand, *An die Bezirksleitungen!*, 1–2; Hilferding to ADGB-Bundesvorstand, 21.6.32, Dok. 100, in *Gewerkschaften 1930–1933*, 4:610.

153. *VW*, #291, 23.6.32; "Der Umbau der Wirtschaft," *GZ*, 2.7.32, 418.

154. Schneider, *Arbeitsbeschaffungs-Programm*, 97.

155. Zollitsch, "Einzelgewerkschaften," 109.

156. Bundesausschuss, 14.6.32, Dok. 97, in *Gewerkschaften 1930–1933*, 4:592–93.

157. "Her zum roten Banner des Sozialismus!," *VW*, #267, 9.6.32; "Das System muss verschwinden!," *Flugblattsammlung 1932* (SPD), AsD.

158. *Betriebswacht*, May 1932 and July 1932, *Flugblattsammlung 1932* (SPD), AsD.

159. See, e.g., SPD, Vorstand, *Reichstagswahl 31. Juli 1932*, 30–36.

160. For evidence that rural voters were targeted, see NWStAM Bestand

SPD und Reichsbanner, Nr. 8: (SPD) Rundschreiben, Recklingshausen, 8.7.32; Pyta, *Gegen Hitler*, 415–17, 433, 397. The SPD's occupational leaflets are listed in NHStAH Hann. 310, II/A, Nr. 38: Material für die Reichstagswahl 1932, Sonderflugblätter. Also see SPD leaflet directed at farmers in NSDAP HA R.40/F.798. On the NSDAP's campaign, see Noakes, *Nazi Party in Lower Saxony*, 217–18; Barkai, *Wirtschaftssystem*, 39; Paul, *Aufstand der Bilder*, 100; Gates, "Free Trade Unions," 288–89.

161. Heinrich Winkler and Robert Gates see the public works issue as the main reason the SPD did badly on July 31 (Winkler, "Dilemma der Weimarer SPD," 1183–84; Gates, "Free Trade Unions," 301–4).

162. Braun, *Weimar*, 395–96, 379; Breitman, *German Social Democracy*, 181; Schulze, *Otto Braun*, 733, 723, 726.

163. Stampfer, *Vierzehn Jahre*, 576; Breitman, *German Social Democracy*, 179.

164. Fritz Tejassy (a Social Democrat in the Interior Ministry) wrote to Stampfer about demoralization, 30.1.35, NL Stampfer, Mappe 15/826, AsD. On Grzesinski's warning to Severing, see Schulze, *Otto Braun*, 739–42.

165. Bracher, *Auflösung*, 594 n. 174; Severing, *Lebensweg*, 2:347.

166. Breitman, *German Social Democracy*, 179–81; Stampfer, *Vierzehn Jahre*, 576. Wels reported on his effort in "Aufzeichung von Otto Wels zum 20. Juli 1932," in Schulze, *Anpassung oder Widerstand?*, 4. On Hamburger and Heilmann, see Breitman, *German Social Democracy*, 181. In *Die Gesellschaft* (June 1932, 468), Decker warned against the "defeatist" politics of bringing the NSDAP into the regime.

167. In exile Fritz Tejassy wrote Stampfer that "[Braun] made it easy for Papen to prove to the Old Gentleman that Prussia drifted leaderless" (30.1.35, NL Stampfer, Mappe 15/826, AsD).

168. Diary entry, 31.8.32, NL Grzesinski, B/XII/2045, IISH. Hermann Zucker, editor of Berlin's "8 Uhr-Abendblatt," wrote Braun that "your vacation has unleashed downright catastrophic dismay in all republican circles" (8.6.32, NL Braun, Teil 2/B/I/49, GStAPK I.HA Rep. 92).

169. B. Düwell, editor of the *Sächsisches Volksblatt*, to the SPD executive, 28.4.32, NL Severing Mappe 52/22, AsD. Zwickau's executive stood behind this epistle. Saxon disapproval of Braun's vacation was vented by Lipinski in the fall (Parteiausschuss, November, in Schulze, *Anpassung oder Widerstand?*, 37).

170. Braun, *Weimar*, 396.

171. *VW*, #259, 4.6.32. But the talk persisted. See *VW*, #264, 7.6.32; #265, 8.6.32; Earl Beck, *Death of the Prussian Republic*, 95–96.

172. Matthias, "Sozialdemokratische Partei," 128–29, 136; Schulze, *Otto Braun*, 731; Breitman, *German Social Democracy*, 182–83.

173. Grzesinski, *Inside Germany*, 155; Hans Mommsen, *Verspielte Freiheit*, 450.

174. Breitman, *German Social Democracy*, 183. This conference did not take place.

175. Schulze, *Otto Braun*, 738–39.

176. Brecht, *Mit der Kraft*, 216; Heinrich A. Winkler, *Katastrophe*, 631. Hans Mommsen diverges from this assessment. He thinks Severing not only expected the *Staatsstreich* but looked forward to it (*Verspielte Freiheit*, 451).

177. Tejassy to Stampfer, 30.1.35, NL Stampfer, Mappe 15/826, AsD. On July 12 the cabinet set July 20 as the date for the action against Prussia (Höner, *Zugriff auf Preussen*, 317). On the planning of July 20, see Heinrich A. Winkler, *Katastrophe*, 646–52.

178. In early 1933 Wels wrote down his rendition of this and the July 20 meeting of party, trade union, and Reichsbanner representatives (Hagen Schulze, "Einleitung," to Wels, "Aufzeichung von Otto Wels zum 20. Juli," 16). In his autobiography and in correspondence, Severing described a similar meeting as having occurred "on July 16" (*Lebensweg*, 2:347), "the week before" (Severing to Braun, 17.2.48, NL Braun, Teil 2/C/I/276, GStAPK I.HA Rep. 92), and "long before July 20" (Severing to Brecht, 8.2.50, in Brecht, *Mit der Kraft*, 435–36). He evidently meant Wels's July 18 meeting (Breitman, *German Social Democracy*, 184 n. 69; Adolph, *Wels*, 240–42). Severing maintained that he and the others decided not to step outside constitutional bounds. Wels's account seems more reliable because he wrote it down less than a year after the event. Adolph discusses the discrepancies (*Wels*, 240–42).

179. On events in Altona, see Severing, *Lebensweg*, 2:345; Höner, *Zugriff auf Preussen*, 319–26; Heinrich A. Winkler, *Katastrophe*, 654–55; Kopitzsch, " 'Altonaer Blutsonntag.' "

180. Wels, "Aufzeichung von Otto Wels zum 20. Juli," 5–7.

181. Altona, besides being in Prussia, had a Social Democratic police commissioner. In his radio speech justifying the Reich action, Papen made much of the Communist menace (*Schulthess' Europäischer Geschichtskalender 1932*, 122). This justification was aimed at the southern German states as well as the bourgeois public. In planning the *Staatsstreich*, the cabinet had considered the legal and political problems involved and had settled on anti-Communism as the best political justification (Höner, *Zugriff auf Preussen*, 314–16).

182. Severing, *Lebensweg*, 2:348–50, 354; Höner, *Zugriff auf Preussen*, 334–35. On this and the Prussian *Staatsstreich* in general, see Schulze, *Otto Braun*, 743–48; Heinrich A. Winkler, *Katastrophe*, 656–60; Bracher, *Auflösung*, 585.

183. Grzesinski, *Inside Germany*, 157–60; Brecht, *Mit der Kraft*, 211; Severing, *Lebensweg*, 2:352.

184. Wels, "Aufzeichung von Otto Wels zum 20. Juli," 7–9.

185. Schulze, *Otto Braun*, 750.

186. Editor's note, Schulze, *Anpassung oder Widerstand?*, 9 n. 23. Karl Rohe accepts Höltermann's assertion that he pleaded for action at a meeting of the Iron Front command (which could have been this one) (*Reichsbanner*, 430). See the similar judgment of Matthias, "Sozialdemokratische Partei," 139; Gotschlich, *Zwischen Kampf und Kapitulation*, 137.

187. Wels, "Aufzeichung von Otto Wels zum 20. Juli," 10–11.

188. "Aufruf der Gewerkschaften," *Flugblattsammlung 1932*, AsD. This was signed not only by all branches of the Free Trade Unions but also by the Gesamtverband der christlichen Gewerkschaften, the Gesamtverband deutscher Verkehrs und Staatsbediensteter, the DBB, and the Gewerkschaftsring deutscher Arbeiter und Angestellten.

189. "Republikaner! Volksgenossen!," *Flugblattsammlung 1932* (SPD), AsD; Rohe, *Reichsbanner*, 427; Wels, "Aufzeichung von Otto Wels zum 20. Juli," 11–12. Examples of press acquiescence include *VW*, #338, 20.7.32; "Am 31. Juli Abrechnung!," *HE*, 21.7.32; "Sturmtag: 31. Juli," *RZ*, 22.7.32; "Wir sind bereit!," *HVW*, 22.7.32.

190. Stampfer, *Erfahrungen*, 254–55. On Schleicher's central role in planning the coup, see Schildt, *Militärdiktatur?*, 55.

191. Brecht, *Mit der Kraft*, 212–13.

192. Sender, *Autobiography*, 291; Hoegner, *Verratene Republik*, 315; Leber, "Todesursachen," 236–37; Leithäuser, *Wilhelm Leuschner*, 82. Leuschner was a high-level union bureaucrat, although he was not involved in policymaking while he was interior minister in Hesse. He returned to the ADGB board in December 1932.

193. Stampfer, *Vierzehn Jahre*, 578; Dittmann, "Wie alles kam: Deutschlands-Weg seit 1914," 304, NL Dittmann, Mappe XIV, AsD; Grzesinski, *Inside Germany*, 161–62.

194. Severing, *Lebensweg*, 2:353–54. According to Hsi-Huey Liang, rank and file policemen preferred to watch the crisis from the sidelines since "few . . . felt strongly enough to fight for their political leaders" (*Berlin Police Force*, 155). Eric Kohler gives figures on the low number of police officers and patrolmen purged by Papen or even the Nazis. He believes Severing's sense of police unreliability "influenced" his passivity ("Crisis in the Prussian Schutzpolizei," 147–50). Yet Severing himself insisted that the police would have followed him if he had been in control and had time to prepare them (*Lebensweg*, 2:354; postwar interview with Paul Bourdan, NL Severing, Mappe 59/125, AsD).

195. Braun, *Weimar*, 405–10; Severing, *Lebensweg*, 2:355–57. Functionaries answered questions about July 20 in a survey sent out by Wels shortly thereafter.

196. Braun, *Weimar*, 410; Severing, *Lebensweg*, 2:358–59. Leipart used the minority regime argument when explaining the decision against a general strike to the ADGB national committee on July 21 (Dok. 112, in *Gewerkschaften 1930–1933*, 4:628).

197. Wels, "Aufzeichung von Otto Wels zum 20. Juli," 12; Grzesinski, *Inside Germany*, 162; Bahne, *KPD*, 26; Möller, *Parlamentarismus*, 570. Wels predicted that a KPD call would fall flat ("Aufzeichung von Otto Wels zum 20. Juli," 9–10).

198. Hoegner, *Verratene Republik*, 315.

199. Matthias, "Sozialdemokratische Partei," 124. This was Hans Jahn, who later was influenced by the radical politics of Neu Beginnen (Löwenthal, *Der Widerstandsgruppe "Neu Beginnen,"* 7).

200. See the admission of neglect by Martin Plettl, chairman of the clothing workers, at an ADGB national committee meeting on July 21 (Dok. 112, in *Gewerkschaften 1930–1933*, 4:630). Also see Rohe, *Reichsbanner*, 414.

201. "Seid gewarnt!," *VW*, #333, 17.7.32.

202. Sender, *Autobiography*, 291.

203. First quote from KPD, *SPD Arbeiter fragt*, 24; second quote from KPD, *Was ist die "Eiserne Front"?*, 7. Also see KPD, *Hindenburg oder Thälmann*, 1.

204. Bahne, *KPD*, 23. Berlin's chairman, Walter Ulbricht, was especially zealous about anti-SPD propaganda.

205. Hermann Weber, "Politik der KPD," 138–39; Bahne, *KPD*, 23; Ehni, *Bollwerk Preussen?*, 259–60; Skrzypczak, "Kanzlerwechsel," 495–97.

206. Bahne, *KPD*, 23, 26; Bahne, "Kommunistische Partei," 670–71; Grzesinski, *Inside Germany*, 162. Moscow's state radio quoted from *Vorwärts* in its report on the coup and, unlike *Rote Fahne*, did not attack Grzesinski and Severing (*HE*, 22.7.32). The Comintern criticized both the SPD and the KPD for their behavior on July 20 (Bahne, *KPD*, 28).

207. *VW*, #195, 26.4.32; #283, 18.6.32.

208. "Der Weg zur Einheitsfront: Eine Erklärung der Bundesvorstandes des ADGB, 22.6.32," printed in Tosstorff, "'Einheitsfront,'" 2:235–36. This statement was a response to a letter signed by Albert Einstein, Käthe Kollwitz, Heinrich Mann, and Anton Erkelenz, among others. It called for a united front and was sent to Leipart, Wels, and Thälmann. See Einstein, Kollwitz, H. Mann to Leipart, 17.6.32, Dok. 98, 607; Leipart to the Bundesvorstand, 21.6.32, Dok. 100; both in *Gewerkschaften 1930–1933*, 4:608–9; "Dringender Appel!" and Erkelenz to P. Löbe, 29.6.32, both in NL Erkelenz NL 72/138, f. 96, BA. At the meeting that produced the ADGB declaration, Tarnow, backed by Leipart and other union leaders, wanted to ask the KPD for a "cease fire" and offered to mediate a meeting between Wels and Thälmann. Hilferding argued for a vague statement on the ADGB's wish for unity, and Leipart gave up his support of Tarnow's suggestion (Bundesvorstand, 21.6.32, Dok. 100, in *Gewerkschaften 1930–1933*, 4:608–11). Also see Skrzypczak, "Kanzlerwechsel," 492–95.

209. Bundesausschuss, 14.6.32, Dok. 97, 591–93; Bundesvorstand, 21.6.32, Dok. 100, 609–10; both in *Gewerkschaften 1930–1933*, vol. 4. Also see Deppe and Rossmann, "Hätte der Faschismus verhindert werden können?," 28.

210. In early July, a group of friendly SPD members met with Ernst Thälmann. Several of them predicted that the KPD would not win the SPD masses as along as it attacked their leaders (BA R45IV/42: 8.7.32 [transcript of discussion between Thälmann et al. and SPD delegates], esp. 123–26). In other cases, Communists themselves expressed this view. See BA R45IV/16:

Berichte der Arbeiterkorrespondenten über die Lage in den Grossbetrieben unter der Militärdiktatur u. dem Ausnahmestand, 22.–26.7.32, esp. 10, 15–16, 21.

211. For evidence of the SPD ranks acting on their own to effect cooperation, see BA R45 IV/21: (KPD) Bericht von der Versammlungstournee Hessen-Frankfurt vom 14.6. bis zum 18.6.32, Berlin, 22.6.32; BA R45 IV/25: An das Zentralkomitee, Braunschweig, 2.5.32. Communists noted the greater tendency toward united action in villages and towns tyrannized by the SA (BA R45 IV/21: Versammlungen in Württemberg, Baden u. der Pfalz vom 19. bis zum 30.7.32; BA R45 IV/26: Versammlungen in Hessen-Kassel, Berlin, 23.7.32). For evidence of pressure from functionaries, see the plea for unity by the printers' union in Kassel (Federation of German Printers, Kassel district, to the ADGB, Dok. 105, in *Gewerkschaften 1930–1933*, 4:616–17). Also see letters in the section "Rote Einheitsfront in Theorie und Praxis," in *FW*, 3.7.32, 9–14, 24. For evidence of "reformist deviations" in the KPD, see BA R45 IV/25: Protokoll der Sekretariatssitzung (Schlesien), 24.6.32; BA R45 IV/21: Bericht über die Versammlungen am 8. und 9.7.32 in Bezirk Baden-Pfalz.

212. A Social Democrat proposed a unity list at a factory meeting; 700 voted for it against 30 to 40 Communists (*VW*, #296, 25.6.32). On July 7, functionaries in Berlin's electric works published such an appeal (Skrzypczak, "Kanzlerwechsel," 491). Already in early 1932 the SPD and Reichsbanner and the KPD engaged in joint activities in East Berlin (BA R58/458: #99 [police report] Berlin, 29.12.32).

213. Bahne, "Kommunistische Partei," 675; BA R58/458: #81–82, An Herrn Oberpräsidenten der Provinz Sachsen, Halle, 15.7.32. On Groener's overture, see Höner, *Zugriff auf Preussen*, 336.

214. Hermann Weber, "Politik der KPD," 139–40. Also see NSDAP HA R.92/F.1894: (Württemberg Criminal Police Division to Munich Police Headquarters) [n.d.]. This report noted the "recently observed demonstrative cooperation of Communists and Social Democrats in different localities." In Stuttgart, the KPD joined in an Iron Front march. In Tübingen, where the Nazis were very strong, the Iron Front and the KPD each told followers to attend the other's meetings in the week before July 31. On Hanover, see NHStAH Hann. 310, II/C, Nr. 25: Rundschreiben des Gauvorstandes Hannover, 24.6.32. The SPD *Kasseler Volksblatt* reported on Communist participation in an Iron Front rally there (Fischer-Defoy, "20.000 gemeinsam gegen die Nazis," 54–60).

215. Peukert, *Ruhrarbeiter gegen den Faschismus*, 17, 19. Communists praised "Reichsbanner comrades" for their anti-Nazi work even after the July 20 coup and July 31 elections. See BA R58/458: #84–87, Bericht über die Einheitsfrontversammlung in Berlin am 4.8.32 (Berlin, 8.8.32). KPDers and SPDers from municipal and private firms attended this meeting.

216. SPD, Vorstand, *An die Bezirksleitungen!*, 1–2. Inside this circular the

SPD executive printed "KPD Rundschreiben, 14.7.32" to show SPD functionaries that the KPD was running scared. Also see Skrzypczak, "Kanzlerwechsel," 496–98; Heinrich A. Winkler, *Katastrophe*, 623–24; *VW*, #334,
18.7.32; #336, 19.7.32.

217. According to Klaus Schönhoven, the KPD experienced a membership
turnover of 54 percent in 1932. In April 1932, 85 percent of its members were
unemployed (Schönhoven, *Reformismus und Radikalismus*, 137).

218. Hoegner, *Verratene Republik*, 315.

219. *VW*, #339, 21.7.32. Matthias quoted a report that "the entire city" put
on both Social Democratic and Communist insignia and greeted each other
with the clenched fist salute ("Sozialdemokratische Partei," 140).

220. Skrzypczak interview with Dr. Hans Hirschfeld, a Reichsbanner activist, on 17.1.69 ("From Carl Legien to Theodor Leipart," 37 n. 45). Another
Reichsbanner man gave the same information to Matthias ("Sozialdemokratische Partei," 140 n. 66).

221. Matthias, "Sozialdemokratische Partei," 142 n. 74; BA R45IV/22: An
die Bezirksleitung Sachsen [KPD], Leipzig, 6.8.32. Philipp Scheidemann
wrote Dittmann from exile that he had heard that 200,000 Reichsbanner men
in Saxony awaited the signal from Berlin during the night of July 20 (15.3.33,
NL Dittmann, Kassette VI/Teil I/135, AsD). Since KPD reports never mention this, it seems unlikely that it occurred, at least not with such a large
number of men. Still, for some time, Social Democrats in Halle, Leipzig, and
smaller cities in Saxony had worked to attract railroad workers and lower-level
officials to the Iron Front because they were crucial to shutting down the
economy (BA R58/458: An Herrn Oberpräsidenten der Provinz Sachsen,
Halle, 15.7.32).

222. Franz J. Furtwängler, "Die deutschen Gewerkschaften und ihr Ende
durch Hitler," 202, NL Furtwängler, Kasten 5, DGB Archiv.

223. Bundesausschuss, 21.7.32, Dok. 112, in *Gewerkschaften 1930–1933*,
4:630 (Plettl). See the similar comments of Brennecke of the tailors' union
(628).

224. Keil, *Erlebnisse*, 2:451.

225. Matthias, "Sozialdemokratische Partei," 141 n. 72.

226. Told to Skrzypczak by Erich Wöllner on 12.9.63, "From Carl Legien to
Theodor Leipart," 37 n. 45.

227. Heinrich A. Winkler, *Katastrophe*, 668.

228. BA R45IV/16: Berichte der Arbeiterkorrespondenten über die Lage
in den Grossbetrieben unter der Militärdiktatur und dem Ausnahmestand
(this meeting took place on July 25, 1932); Sektionsleitungsitzung des EVMB,
Berlin 26.7.32 (held on July 24, 1932). The firms canvassed included Sie-
mens, General Electric Company (AEG), Dresdner Bank, and other private
firms as well as the municipal docks and the Berlin Transportation Authority.
For evidence of Saxon reluctance to fight without their leaders, despite dis-

gust with them, see BA R45IV/28: An das Sekretariat der KPD und die Bezirksleitung Sachsen, Thalheim, 6.8.32.

229. BA R45IV/21: Bericht über die Versammlungstournee in den Bezirken Ruhrgebiet, Mittelrhein, Saargebiet u. Niederrhein vom 30.6. bis zum 30.7.32; Versammlungen in Württemberg, Baden u. der Pfalz vom 19. bis zum 30.7.32; Versammlungstournee in Thüringen vom 11. bis zum 22.7.32.

230. See, e.g, Mierendorff's optimism about the elections in a piece published after July 21 ("Sommer der Entscheidungen," *SM*, 29.7.32, 656).

231. Hoegner, *Verratene Republik*, 315.

232. In 1952, Erich Matthias maintained that resistance might have succeeded because, faced with imminent civil war, Papen and Hindenburg might have retreated (Matthias, "Sozialdemokratische Partei," 143). In 1955, Karl Dietrich Bracher deplored the failure to resist; even if the republicans had been defeated, their resistance would have shown determination to fight and thus perhaps would have prevented Hitler's seizure of power. If nothing else, German democrats would have inherited a legacy of honorable defeat rather than ignominious submission to force (Bracher, *Auflösung*, 596–99). Also see Bracher, "20. Juli 1932," 243–49, where he answered Arnold Brecht's response to his earlier critique. In 1956, Erich Eyck, a Weimar Democrat become historian, also argued that Social Democracy should not have surrendered without a fight (Eyck, *History of the Weimar Republic*, 2:417).

233. Arnold Brecht, participant turned scholar, eloquently defended Braun and Severing (*Mit der Kraft*, 215–17). Heinrich Winkler ("Dilemma der Weimarer SPD," 1183) and Hagen Schulze (*Otto Braun*, 246–54) do not think resistance would have succeeded. Hans Mommsen ("Deutschen Gewerkschaften," 276) endorsed the view that it would have played into Hitler's hands. Helga Grebing defended the trade union decision not to strike ("Gewerkschaftliches Verhalten," 29–33). Henryk Skrzypczak agreed ("From Carl Legien to Theodor Leipart," 37–38). Writing in 1966, Karl Rohe stood between in time and viewpoint: given the failure to prepare the Reichsbanner and the Prussian police, resistance would have been hopeless (*Reichsbanner*, 436–37). Ehni, however, in 1975 believed resistance would have scared Schleicher and Hindenburg (*Bollwerk Preussen?*, 268). Leftist historians in East Germany and outside continued to condemn the SPD and the trade unions for not resisting. For example, see Heer, *Burgfrieden*, 60–67, and Klönne, *Deutsche Arbeiterbewegung*, 243–44. For the DDR view, see Walter Ulbricht et al., *Geschichte der deutschen Arbeiterbewegung*, 4:355–56.

234. Stampfer, *Vierzehn Jahre*, 579; Grzesinski, *Inside Germany*, 162; Matthias, "Sozialdemokratische Partei," 137.

235. Rohe, *Reichsbanner*, 437; Hans Mommsen, *Verspielte Freiheit*, 452. According to Höner, the Reich cabinet did consider the possibility of resistance and a general strike in planning the action—it would have proclaimed martial law in Berlin and Brandenburg, just as leading Social Democrats predicted (Höner, *Zugriff auf Preussen*, 317).

236. Mierendorff, "Sommer der Entscheidungen," 656.

237. See the justification of nonresistance in an SPD pamphlet for the November 6 election. The reasons given included Braun's electoral defeat, Brüning's fall, and the fact that the civil service had been infiltrated by Nazis (SPD, Vorstand, *Reichstagswahl 6. November 1932*, 43–44).

238. Bundesausschuss, 21.7.32, Dok. 112, in *Gewerkschaften 1930–1933*, 4:628–30. Only Plettl criticized the ADGB for not scrutinizing the possibilities for a general strike earlier (630).

239. Chakhotin, *Rape of the Masses*, 222–23; Rohe, *Reichsbanner*, 417.

240. Frey, *Deutschland, wohin?*, 12–13. At a meeting in early July 1932 between SPDers and Communist leaders, a Social Democratic worker asked Ernst Thälmann about the KPD's view of the "SPD solution of the second republic and restoration of the Weimar system" (BA R45IV/42: 8.7.32 [transcript of discussion between Thälmann et al. and SPD delegates], 142).

241. Gates ("Free Trade Unions," 278, 302–3) leans in this direction. But one author, Hanno Heer, cannot be accused of a bias in the unions' favor. His book is in places a slanderous attack on their leaders. Thus, he wonders if they were privately informed by Schleicher of the coup (*Burgfrieden*, 67).

242. Privately Wels described the trade union decision as the "collapse of a world (*Zusammenbruch einer Welt*)" (Adolph, *Wels*, 246). He seems to have repressed the fact that he was party to this decision.

243. See, e.g., "Auf dem Weg zur Entscheidung! Die Zeit ist mit uns! Wir sind die aufsteigende Klasse!," *VW*, #349, 27.7.32. The quotes are from Stampfer (*Vierzehn Jahre*, 578), who made clear that post-coup optimism was not just bravado.

244. *VW*, #357, 31.7.32. The article only hints at resistance. It is an attempt to prepare supporters for a high Nazi vote and to assure them that that will not mean the end of the struggle.

245. Grzesinski in Düsseldorf, *DVZ*, 1.8.32. To be fair, one must mention that in private, too, Grzesinski advocated "extraparliamentary strength" (Grzesinski to Braun, 8.2.32, in Matthias, "Sozialdemokratische Partei," 226). Hoegner recalled Nazi contempt after July 20 (*Verratene Republik*, 316).

Chapter Eight

1. Parteiausschuss, November: Wels, 18–19, in Schulze, *Anpassung oder Widerstand?*

2. The first quote is from an SPD editor who told Erkelenz how to make his brochure, "Frau, Freiheit, und Politik," acceptable for publication (NL Erkelenz, NL 72/102, fol. 1–289, #5, 2.8.32, BA). The second quote is from *FW*, 21.8.32, 18–19.

3. In August, Leipart told Hans Schäffer about "radicals in the trade unions [who] lean in part toward a shift from evolutionary to revolutionary socialism"

(Hans Schäffer diary entry, 10.8.32, Dok. 115a, in *Gewerkschaften 1930–1933*, 4:643).

4. BA R58/557: Betr[effend]: Reichsbanner Schwarz-Rot-Gold, Hammerschaften, Aug. 1932. Unions in Berlin active in building *Hammerschaften* were the DMV, the railroad workers, the municipal workers, and the construction workers.

5. Bracher, *Auflösung*, 608–10. Statistics in Falter, Lindenberger, and Schumann, *Wahlen und Abstimmungen*, 41, 44.

6. NWStAM Bestand SPD und Reichsbanner, Nr. 8: (SPD) Rundschreiben, Bezirk Westliches Westfalen, Dortmund, 4.8.32.

7. Adolph, *Wels*, 248; Keil, *Erlebnisse*, 2:454; *RZ*, 1.8.32; *HVW*, 1.8.32.

8. "Die Reichstagswahl," *GZ*, 6.8.32, 497; *DVZ*, 1.8.32; *HVW*, 1.8.32; Georg Decker, "Klarlegung der Fronten," *VW*, #377, 12.8.32.

9. Peukert, *Ruhrarbeiter gegen den Faschismus*, 26; Hans Mommsen, *Verspielte Freiheit*, 359; Schnabel, "'Wer wählte Hitler?,'" 128.

10. Pyta, *Gegen Hitler*, 426–27.

11. Analysis of the vote by Communists can be found in BA R45IV/21: Bericht über die Wahlergebnisse, Baden. To estimate the composition of the SPD vote in Göttingen, regression analyses were run on data in Hasselhorn, *Wie wählte Göttingen?*, tables 1–3, 5, 6, 11, 22. On the NSDAP's working-class vote, see Falter, "Wähler der NSDAP," 54, 57–58.

12. See, e.g., *HVW*, 1.8.32, and SPD, Vorstand, *Materialien zur politischen Situation*, 3. For expression of underlying concern, see, e.g., Decker, *VW* "Klarlegung der Fronten." In his diary, Harry Graf Kessler noted Social Democratic shock at the KPD's rise (Skrzypczak, "Kanzlerwechsel," 499 n. 93).

13. Peukert, *Ruhrarbeiter gegen den Faschismus*, 26; Ernst Heilmann, "Hindenburg gegen die Nazidiktatur," *FW*, 21.8.32, 1–2; Franz Künstler at a meeting of the Berlin SPD, *VW*, #373, 10.8.32; Lothar Erdmann diary entry, 31.7.32, printed in Deppe and Rossmann, *Wirtschaftskrise*, 190–91. Not only Social Democrats blamed July 20; see "SPD Spiegel," *DF*, #83, 25.10.32, and opinion of foreign press as reported by *Vorwärts* (#361, 3.8.32).

14. BA R45IV/21: (KPD) Bericht über die Wahlergebnisse, Bezirk Magdeburg-Anhalt, 25; Chakhotin, *Rape of the Masses*, 227–28. So too argued Frey [Pahl], *Deutschland, wohin?*, 16. Chakhotin (*Rape of the Masses*, 232) dropped out of political life at the end of July.

15. First quote from Grzesinski, diary entry, 29.8.32, NL Grzesinski B/XII/2045, IISH; second quote from Lothar Erdmann, diary entry, 10.8.32, printed in Deppe and Rossmann, *Wirtschaftskrise*, 191. Also see letters to *FW*, 4.9.32, 19–21; Rohe, *Reichsbanner*, 438.

16. BA R58/458: #99, 29.12.32; Erwin Schoettle, "Der Parteiführer in Stuttgart," in Scholz and Oschilewski, *Turmwächter der Demokratie*, 471. In Berlin in October, Severing was asked why he and his police did not intervene

(Dittmann, "Wie Alles kam: Deutschlands-Weg seit 1914," 345, NL Dittmann, Mappe XIV, AsD). Breitscheid had to justify July 20 in Berlin in November (*VW*, #559, 27.11.32). On July 31, Bielefeld, Severing's hometown, gave him (as head of the SPD list) three thousand *more* votes than in September 1930, but by the fall critical discussion of his role on July 20 was widespread (BA R45IV/26: [KPD] Bericht über die öffentliche Versammlung in Bielefeld, 1.10.32).

17. Diary entry, 29.8.32, NL Grzesinski B/XII/2045, IISH; NSDAP HA R.93/F.1898, Sektionsversammlung, 10.8.32. A writer to *Das Freie Wort* complained about the constant "fruitless discussion about our stance on July 20" (*FW*, 4.9.32, 19).

18. See Otto Wels, Notizen über einen Artikel von Otto Bauer, 2, Emigration SOPADE, Mappe 161, AsD. See Loewenstein-Scharffeneck (*Tragedy of a Nation*, 201) and Leber ("Todesursachen," 237) on disgust in the Reichsbanner. After July 20, Reichsbanner activist Heinz Kühn buried his pistol in his parents' garden (Kühn, *Widerstand und Emigration*, 49).

19. The quote is from Grzesinski (diary entry, 29.8.32, NL Grzesinski B/XII/2045, IISH).

20. Breitman, "German Social Democracy and General Schleicher," 359. Schifrin outlined the differences between "the fascist party state" and Papen's "authoritarian state" ("Neue Kampfepoche," *DG*, Oct. 1932, 282).

21. *Schulthess' Europäischer Geschichtskalender 1932*, 140; Bracher, *Auflösung*, 618–20.

22. *VW*, #431, 13.9.32; E. Gr., "Die Schwerindustrie ist 'unzufrieden,'" *DVZ*, 10.8.32.

23. Schifrin, "Neue Kampfepoche," 281–83; Alexander Schifrin, "Krisenfazit und Kampfperspektiven," *DG*, Dec. 1932, 476–77. Also see Alexander Schifrin, "Die Krise der deutschen Gegenrevolution," *DG*, Nov. 1932, 395–402.

24. Adolph, *Wels*, 248; *FW*, 21.8.32, 2.

25. SPD, Vorstand, *Materialien zur politischen Situation*, 6.

26. Keil, *Erlebnisse*, 2:456–57.

27. Otto Wels, "Sozialistische Aktion," *VW*, #403, 27.8.32; Paul Löbe, "Das neue Gesicht," *VW*, #359, 2.8.32; #381, 14.8.32; also see Wels, "Sozialistische Aktion."

28. Keil, *Erlebnisse*, 2:457.

29. Eyck, *History of the Weimar Republic*, 2:429–32.

30. *DVZ*, 22.8.32; *VW*, #381, 14.8.32; #369, 7.8.32; Siegfried Aufhäuser, *HVF*, 8.8.32; SPD, Vorstand, *Materialien zur politischen Situation*, 10.

31. On the state of the unions, see "Der ADGB im Jahre 1931," *GZ*, 30.7.32, 481; editor's note, Schulze, *Anpassung oder Widerstand?*, 63 n. 128. At this point, the SPD was still represented in the governments of seven of sixteen states. Outside Hesse and Baden, they were small (Lippe and Schaumburg-Lippe) or city-states (Hamburg, Bremen, and Lübeck). In November the SPD

lost its role in the Baden and Hesse governments. On Baden, see Matthias, "Mannheimer Sozialdemokraten."

32. So spoke the chairman of the hatmakers at a national committee meeting, 21.7.32, Dok. 112, in *Gewerkschaften 1930–1933*, 4:630.

33. Schneider, *Arbeitsbeschaffungs-Programm*, 132.

34. This conclave has provoked much controversy. In late 1932 a far left magazine published a forged protocol of it, according to which the union leaders guaranteed Papen "unconditional quiet" following the elections. See appendix 1b in Skrzypczak, "Fälscher machen Zeitgeschichte," 468. Only in the 1970s did historians prove this document fake. Besides Skrzypczak, see Emig and Zimmermann, "Ende einer Legende," and Muth, "Schleicher."

35. Protokoll einer Besprechung, 30.7.32 (Leipart, Eggert, and Grassmann report on their talk with Papen, Schleicher, and Gayl), in Emig and Zimmermann, "Ende einer Legende," 34–37 (also printed in *Gewerkschaften 1930–1933*, 4:635–37).

36. Leipart did not include this in his notes on the meeting. He told it privately to Hans Schäffer (a former Prussian state secretary). See Hans Schäffer dairy entry, 10.8.32, Dok. 115, in *Gewerkschaften 1930–1933*, 4:641.

37. Bundesvorstand, 3.8.32, Dok. 116, in *Gewerkschaften 1930–1933*, 4:644.

38. Diary entries, L. Erdmann, 31.7.32 and 10.8.32; 8.10.32; 4.8.32, printed in Deppe and Rossmann, *Wirtschaftskrise*, 190–91. Erdmann met with Dr. Carl Rothe, who, according to Schildt, was well disposed toward WTB. Other contacts with the *Tat* circle took place around this time. Kurt Schumacher and Carlo Mierendorff visited Hans Zehrer, editor of *Die Tat*, as did Furtwängler and Otto Strasser. Zehrer opposed the Papen regime and saw himself as a conduit between "left" Nazis and "right" Social Democrats (Schildt, *Militärdiktatur?*, 112–13, 140).

39. Henryk Skrzypczak to Furtwängler, 28.6.65, NL Furtwängler, DGB Archiv. On the ADGB's awareness of these contacts, see Skrzypczak, "From Carl Legien to Theodor Leipart," 39–40 n. 55. The ADGB, though, denied the contacts when *Vorwärts* reported them (#341, 22.7.32; Bundesvorstand, 27.7.32, Dok. 113, in *Gewerkschaften 1930–1933*, 4:632, [Leipart]).

40. Tarnow sent Leipart and Wels confidential summaries of this discussion (Tarnow to Leipart, 27.8.32, Dok. 122, in *Gewerkschaften 1930–1933*, 4:657–60). Erdmann also met with a Strasser supporter at the end of August (Akten-Notiz: Erdmann über ein Gespräch mit Dr. Lübhert, 29.8.32, NL Furtwängler, Kasten 1, #100, DGB Archiv).

41. See, e.g., NHStAH Hann. 310, II/C, Nr. 25: Politischer Pressedienst, #97, 2 Jg., 20.8.32, Berlin.

42. Muth, "Schleicher," 205–6. Minutes of a purported meeting in September of Schleicher, Gayl, Strasser, Grassmann, and Eggert have been exposed as fabricated. See Emig and Zimmermann, "Ende einer Legende," 28; Muth, "Schleicher," 203, 207; Heinrich A. Winkler, *Katastrophe*, 716. The Free Trade Unions defended themselves against the forgeries in a pamphlet published in

January 1933 that denounced the false protocol while admitting that Leipart et al. had met with Papen in July (ADGB, Vorstand, *Klassenverrat?*, 2, 5, 7). The ADGB also took the Lenin Bund to court (Emig and Zimmermann, "Ende einer Legende," 31). This sect published the "documents" but did not produce them—Skrzypczak believes the guilty party was in either the KPD, the NSDAP, or the Reichswehr ("Fälscher machen Zeitgeschichte," 452–53, 464–65).

43. Wels mentioned press reports about ADGB/Papen contacts at an Iron Front *Reichskampfleitung* meeting but said such rumors emanated from the Defense Ministry, which aimed to split the Iron Front (26.8.32, Dok. 121, in *Gewerkschaften 1930–1933*, 4:655). In August, however, Paul Hertz told Hans Schäffer that "subterranean efforts toward an understanding between the Nazis and trade unions are in earnest" (Muth, "Schleicher," 205).

44. Schneider, *Arbeitsbeschaffungs-Programm*, 132. In 1936 Leipart wrote another board member that the gesture in favor of public works was made to avoid a break between the unions and the party.

45. Woytinsky, *Stormy Passage*, 470–72.

46. Tarnow voted against the proposed bill at the Reichstag delegation meeting (Schneider, *Arbeitsbeschaffungs-Programm*, 133). For evidence of Leipart's distancing efforts, see Bundesvorstand, 16.9.32, Dok. 128, in *Gewerkschaften 1930–1933*, 4:701. Also see Schneider, *Arbeitsbeschaffungs-Programm*, 159; Skrzypczak, "From Carl Legien to Theodor Leipart," 40; Neebe, "Unternehmerverbände und Gewerkschaften," 321.

47. "Gegen die Lohntribüte-Für die Erhaltung des Kollektiven Arbeitsrechts," *GZ*, 22.10.32, 675. The *Deutsche Führerbriefe* wrote that Leipart's talk "showed that he understood the logic of development and was ready to accept its consequences" (*DF*, #94, 2.12.32). On press and Social Democratic reactions, see Leipart's comments, Bundesvorstand, 26.10.32, Dok. 137, in *Gewerkschaften 1930–1933*, 4:738. On Otto Strasser's response, see Schildt, "Militärische Ratio," 356.

48. Gates, "Free Trade Unions," 283–86. Employer organizations applauded Papen's plan, although few businesses took advantage of its credit provisions (Schildt, *Militärdiktatur?*, 90–91).

49. Fritz Tarnow, "Ankurbelung der Wirtschaft?," *GZ*, 3.9.32, 561–63; "Der Wirtschaftsplan der Reichsregierung und die Gewerkschaften," *GZ*, 18.10.32, 675–79.

50. See, e.g., the contributions of Leipart and Tarnow in Leipart et al., *Gegen den Wirtschaftsplan der Papen-Regierung*, 9, 11–13. Only Aufhäuser's speech was resolutely anti-Papen (43, 46). Also see the comments on Papen's program by Eggert, Bundesausschuss, 9/10.9.32, Dok. 126, in *Gewerkschaften 1930–1933*, 4:672–73.

51. Gotschlich, *Zwischen Kampf und Kapitulation*, 137.

52. Rohe, *Reichsbanner*, 441. The Prussian interior minister noted weapons stockpiling by numerous members in northern Germany, Hesse, and Franken

(Niemann, *Geschichte der deutschen Sozialdemokratie*, 296–97). Weapons were smuggled from Holland and Belgium, although the official word was "no weapons" (Kühn, *Widerstand und Emigration*, 45).

53. Parteiausschuss, November: Höltermann, 81; Ferl, 89, in Schulze, *Anpassung oder Widerstan?* Höltermann entertained a grand scheme of building a German Freedom Army from activists in the Iron Front. See police notes on a secret meeting of Munich Reichsbanner leaders in December 1932 (NSDAP HA R.95/F.1910: Lagebericht, 15.12.32).

54. NSDAP HA R.93/F.1903: Ortsversammlung des Reichsbanners, 26.11.32; Haubach, "Wehrsport und Arbeiterbewegung," *NB*, Dec. 1932, 658–60; Karl Wiegener, in Hammer, *Theodor Haubach zum Gedächtnis*, 32–33; Loewenstein-Scharffeneck, *Tragedy of a Nation*, 103; Parteiausschuss, November: Grassmann, 77–78, in Schulze, *Anpassung oder Widerstand?*; Bundesvorstand, 26.10.32, Dok. 137, in *Gewerkschaften 1930–1933*, 4:739; Braun to Höltermann, 31.12.32, printed in Matthias, "Sozialdemokratische Partei," 230–31. ·

55. Rohe, *Reichsbanner*, 450–51; Loewenstein-Scharffeneck, *Tragedy of a Nation*, 102–3; Gotschlich, *Zwischen Kampf und Kapitulation*, 137. For Wels's order, see his comments at the meeting of the party council with the Control Commission, 16.12.32, in Schulze, *Anpassung oder Widerstand?*, 117.

56. Parteiausschuss, November: Wels, 73, 91; Lipinski, 81; Künstler, 85; Erich Ollenhauer (chair of the SAJ), 86; Litke, 87; Marie Juchacz, 88, in Schulze, *Anpassung oder Widerstand?* For Aufhäuser's opposition to the Reichskuratorium, see Schlimme's report on a closed meeting between Reichsbanner and SPD representatives about the Reichskuratorium für Jugendertüchtigung, 13.12.32, Dok. 156, in *Gewerkschaften 1930–1933*, 4:789–90. On Reichswehr plans to build a militia, see Rohe, *Reichsbanner*, 449, and Vogelsang, *Reichswehr*, 285–87, 348.

57. NSDAP HA R.93/F.1903: Lagebericht, 10.12.32. See Rohe on rank and file sentiment against Schleicher (*Reichsbanner*, 446 n. 1).

58. Braun to Höltermann, 31.12.32, in Matthias, "Sozialdemokratische Partei," 230–31; L. Erdmann to Leipart, 9.11.32, Dok. 143, in *Gewerkschaften 1930–1933*, 4:751–2; Höltermann to Braun, 3.1.33, NL Otto Braun, Teil 2/B/I/16, GStAPK I.HA Rep. 92.

59. Parteiausschuss, November: Höltermann, 81–82, in Schulze, *Anpassung oder Widerstand?* Höltermann supported the reintroduction of conscription. *Vorwärts* (#613, 29.12.32) gave a straightforward account of the debate in the party council, conceding the validity of Höltermann's claim that military training was needed in the Reichsbanner.

60. Höltermann's memorandum to Reichsbanner district offices implied that he would buck the SPD executive (Rundschreiben #24, 19.10.32, Emigration SOPADE, Mappe 1, AsD). Also compare the calm discussion of the issue at the November party council meeting (Schulze, *Anpassung oder Widerstand?*, 72–94) with the angry exchange at the December meeting, after the

Reichsbanner had made a declaration of independence at its "leadership congress" in Bremen on November 12 and 13. In November the council just registered disapproval of participation in the Reichskuratorium. Now it was ready to order the Reichsbanner to bend to its will (Sitzung des Parteiausschusses mit der Kontrolkommission am 16.12.32 [hereafter cited as Parteiausschuss, Dezember], 112–30).

61. On the ADGB's efforts to sway the SPD, see Bundesvorstand, 26.10.32, Dok. 137, 739; Leipart's comments at Bundesvorstand meeting, 9.11.32, Dok. 142, 750; Schlimme's report on a closed meeting, 13.12.32, Dok. 156, 789–90; all in *Gewerkschaften 1930–1933*, vol. 4. For Höltermann's decision, see Parteiausschuss, Dezember: Höltermann, 120–21, in Schulze, *Anpassung oder Widerstand?*; also, Höltermann to Braun, 3.1.33, NL Braun, Teil B/2/I/16, GStAPK I.HA Rep. 92. For an example of how his decision was presented to the public, see "Iron Front remains unified!," *FVS*, 31.12.32. The Reichsbanner continued with its own defense training. Also, it took part, as before, in border patrols (Vogelsang, *Reichswehr*, 348 n. 1662).

62. Schildt, "Sozialdemokratische Arbeiterbewegung und Reichswehr," 121–22; Keil, *Erlebnisse*, 2:457–60, 463.

63. *VW*, #409/415, 3.9.32; #435, 15.9.32. On national impulses, see Keil, *Erlebnisse*, 2:459–60. Such impulses provoked Alexander Schifrin to attack *Neue Blätter* for its "synthesis of radical socialist views with active nationalist policies" that recalled Jacobinism but that, he wrote, was a political oxymoron in Germany ("Nationaler Linkssozialismus," *DR*, 22.11.32, 266). Haubach replied with a defense of *NB* and the belief that the NSDAP encompassed some revolutionary elements ("Nationaler Linkssozialismus? Eine Erwiderung," *DR*, 13.12.32, 364–67). In his answer, Schifrin exempted Haubach and other "healthy elements" around *NB* from its nefarious tendencies but insisted that these still permeated the journal (Schifrin, *DR*, 13.12.32, 368–73).

64. Parteiausschuss, November: Wels, 24–25, in Schulze, *Anpassung oder Widerstand?*

65. Heinrich A. Winkler, *Katastrophe*, 714; James, *German Slump*, 241; Zollitsch, "Einzelgewerkschaften," 107.

66. During the negotiations over the Reichskuratorium, Wels said, "We are all together and will stay together" (see Schlimme's report on closed meeting, 13.12.32, Dok. 156, in *Gewerkschaften 1930–1933*, 4:791). For the very different outlooks of Aufhäuser and Leipart, see AfA-Bund Vorstand to ADGB (signed by Aufhäuser), 28.10.32, Dok. 138, 740–44; Leipart's comments at Bundesvorstand meeting, 2.11.32, Dok. 141, 746–47, both in ibid.

67. NHStAH Hann. 310, II/A, Nr. 38: Parteivorstand an die Bezirksleitungen, 7.10.32; *LVZ*, 10.9.32, 12.9.32, 17.9.32, 1.11.32.

68. NHStAH Hann. 310, II/C, Nr. 25: Rundschreiben des Gauvorstandes Hannover des Reichsbanners, 9.9.32 (also printed in Matthias, "Sozialdemokratische Partei," 227). Berlin district passed a motion calling for obligatory wearing of the three arrows (*VW*, #560, 28.11.32).

69. Carlo Mierendorff, "Die Bedeutung der neuen Propaganda," *NB*, Oct. 1932, 517. ADGB board member Peter Grassmann, for example, derided the "new struggle methods" (Parteiausschuss, November, 63, in Schulze, *Anpassung oder Widerstand?*). But Schifrin too pleaded for continued reliance on the "new methods and use of mass psychology" ("Neue Kampfepoche," *DG*, Oct. 1932, 296). Decker attributed demoralization to the hopes awakened by the Iron Front and dashed by July 20, July 31, and November 6 ("Nach den Wahlen," *DG*, Dec. 1932, 469).

70. Florian Geyer [Hans Muhle], "Die SPD am Scheideweg," *NB*, Sept. 1932, 458. Muhle was a privy councilor in the Prussian Ministry of Trade who joined the SPD in 1931 and became very active in the Reichsbanner. See Heinrich A. Winkler, *Katastrophe*, 672, 674 n. 41.

71. Sollmann, "Positive Parteikritik—Erneuerung und Machtwille," *NB*, Jan. 1933, 25–32; *FW*, 13.11.32, 17–18; 20.11.32, 24. Also see "SPD Spiegel," *DF*, #83, 25.10.32, and complaints about sluggishness at a Munich branch meeting (NSDAP R.93/F.1898: 1.9.32); a report on party dropouts in Munich (party committee meeting, 6.10.32); and the report by a Nazi observer of an SPD meeting near Leipzig (NSDAP HA R.40/F.798: Oct. 1932).

72. *VW*, #477, 9.10.32; #478, 10.10.32; *FW*, 13.11.32, 17–18; 20.11.32, 24. In Berlin, the mood was no better at an extraordinary district conference after the November elections (*VW*, #559, 27.11.32).

73. See, e.g., NHStAH Hann. 310, II/A, Nr. 13: Kreisverein Peine an die SPD Bezirksleitung [n.d.]; NWStAM Bestand SPD und Reichsbanner, Nr. 7: Parteivorstand an die Bezirksleitungen, 23.9.32; (SPD) Rundschreiben #19, Bezirk Westliches Westfalen, Dortmund, 30.9.32; Rundschreiben #24, Bezirk Westliches Westfalen, Dortmund, 9.12.32; NSDAP HA R.93/F.1898: Sitzung des Parteiausschusses München, 6.10.32. One money-making idea showed that the *Drei Pfeile* still had appeal. Several firms agreed to produce packs of cigarettes stamped with the *Drei Pfeile* and stuffed with pictures of famous Social Democrats. "Aktivität" cost 2½ pfennig per pack; "Freiheit," 3½; "Discipline," 5. Party members were urged to sell these; the SPD evidently got a percentage of the profits. See NWStAM Bestand SPD und Reichsbanner, Nr. 7: (SPD) Rundschreiben #22, Bezirk Westliches Westfalen, Dortmund, 3.12.32.

74. *VW*, #409/415, 3.9.32; Keil, *Erlebnisse*, 2:456; Matthias, "Sozialdemokratische Partei," 147 n. 10; Adolph, *Wels*, 247–48. Also see Heinrich A. Winkler, *Katastrophe*, 742.

75. Keil, *Erlebnisse*, 2:464.

76. "Berliner Bezirksparteitag," *VW*, #559, 27.11.32. Haubach (in last place) and Arthur Neihardt, the popular leader of the Berlin Reichsbanner, were added to the November candidate lists in Berlin and Potsdam. Crispien still topped the roster (*VW*, #477, 9.10.32). On Munich, see NSDAP HA R.93/F.1898: Sektionsversammlung, 1.9.32. Section Nord elected a "younger, more left-oriented" leader as its annual assembly demanded; the new man was

born in 1902; the ex-candidate, in 1886 (R.93/F.1898: 24.1.33). See calls for rejuvenation in *FW*, 11.12.32, 13—14, 16—17, and for democratization in *FW*, 13.11.32, 16—20. On Leipzig, see "Generalversammlung des Unterbezirks Gross-Leipzig," *LVZ*, 10.10.32.

77. Leipart and Schlimme at Bundesvorstand meeting, 28.9.32, Dok. 129, 703—4; Scheibel (chairman of construction workers) at Bundesausschuss meeting and Leipart at Bundesausschuss meeting, 7.10.32, Dok. 132, 727, 728, both in *Gewerkschaften 1930—1933*, vol. 4. Also see Heer, *Burgfrieden*, 98.

78. Crummenerl (SPD executive committee) at Bundesausschuss meeting, 7.10.32, Dok. 132, 727; Bundesvorstand, 28.9.32, Dok. 129, 704; Bundesvorstand, 5.10.32, Dok. 131, 713, all in *Gewerkschaften 1930—1933*, vol. 4.

79. Wels to Leipart, 11.10.32, and Wels to A. Erkelenz, 11.10.32, ADGB Restakten, Film Nr. 21/1, #97, #98, DGB Archiv; Bundesausschuss, 7.10.32, Dok. 132, in *Gewerkschaften 1930—1933*, 4:727, 729.

80. Bundesvorstand, 28.9.32, Dok. 129, in *Gewerkschaften 1930—1933*, 4:703—4. Asked by Meitmann to run, Staudinger quickly had to get a feel for the Social Democratic electorate in Hamburg. He mastered the ways of the hustings with evident aplomb and won. See Staudinger, *Wirtschaftspolitik im Weimarer Staat*, 111—12. For a biographical sketch of Staudinger, see Peter M. Rutkoff and William B. Scott, "Biographical Afterword," in Staudinger, *Inner Nazi*.

81. "Positive Parteikritik," *NB*, Jan. 1932, 25—29. Letters to *Das Freie Wort* endorsed Sollmann's critique (*FW*, 25.12.32, 27; 22.1.33, 21—22).

82. Parteiausschuss, Dezember: Dietrich, 106; Meitmann, 111; Klupsch (Dortmund), 109; Junke (Braunschweig), 110, in Schulze, *Anpassung oder Widerstand?* Meitmann invited Sollmann to address Hamburg's annual delegates' meeting (*HE*, 13.1.33).

83. Parteiausschuss, November: Wels, 103, 68; also see Grassmann (63); Parteiausschuss, Dezember: Junke, 110, in Schulze, *Anpassung oder Widerstand?* Wilhelm Dittmann answered Sollmann in the press (*FVS*, 7.1.33). Members of the SPD executive committee are listed in appendix 1, Schulze, *Anpassung oder Widerstand?*, 199.

84. NHStAH Hann. 310, II/A, Nr. 38: Parteivorstand, Dec. 1932 (#2) (communication to district organizations).

85. Parteiausschuss, November: Wels, 18, in Schulze, *Anpassung oder Widerstand?* The quote is from Geyer [Muhle], "SPD am Scheideweg," 458.

86. See the report at Cologne's year-end membership meeting (*RZ*, 19.12.32) and an article on a special meeting for the unemployed in Düsseldorf (*DVZ*, 27.9.32). A committee in Chemnitz urged the national executive to set up an organization for the unemployed (NSDAP HA R.40/F.798: "Über den Gegner, October 1932"). Munich's group began to function during the July campaign (NSDAP HA R.92/F.1894: #16); by September 14 it had two sections (R.92/F.1894: 14.9.32, #1). On the clubs' activities, see R.92/F.1894: 26.10.32, #7. On Hamburg, the Ruhr, and Münster, see NWStAM Bestand

SPD und Reichsbanner, Nr. 8: "Hauptaufgabe" (no further designation, n.d.); Erwerbslosengemeinschaften in Hamburg (n.d.); Reg. Münster VII, Nr. 1, Bd. 1: An Herrn Regierungspräsidenten (Münster), Lüdinghausen, 20.12.32. On the KPD's methods, see Rosenhaft, *Beating the Fascists?*, 43–45, 49–50.

87. See, e.g., "Pächter, Kleinbauer, Siedler aufgepasst!"; "Einzelhandel und Kleingewerbetreibende!"; "Was hat das 'November-System' gebracht?"; "Arbeitsbauer, warum geht's dir so schlecht?"; all in *Flugblattsammlung 1932* (SPD), AsD. Also see Löbe, *Sozialismus! Ja oder Nein?*, where he denied that the SPD supported "senseless equality"—instead it defended equal opportunity for all (12).

88. NHStAH Hann. 310, II/A, Nr. 38: Rundschreiben des Parteivorstandes, 13.12.32 (also printed in Matthias, "Sozialdemokratische Partei," 228–29); Zeitschriften für Bauern (e.g., *Roter Bauer*), 23.1.33; Pyta, *Gegen Hitler*, 400–3, 411–12, 516. Electoral gains were made in the environs of Oppeln, Koblenz-Trier, Cologne-Aachen, Görlitz, and Düsseldorf. The SPD also experienced a resurgence in Günzburg, a small town in Bavaria (Zofka, *Ausbreitung des Nationalsozialismus auf dem Lande*, 179).

89. NSDAP HA R.92/F.1894: (police report on SPD unemployed movement), 10.12.32. By the end of October, of 1,700 unemployed Social Democrats in Munich, 500 were organized into groups for the unemployed. Their citywide meetings attracted between 300 and 500 into February 1933 (NSDAP HA R.92/F.1894: 29.9.32 [#4], 24.10.32 [#6], 21.2.33 [#19]).

90. "SPD Spiegel," *DF*, #83, 25.10.32.

91. See, e.g., *HE*, 8.10.32, 19.10.32.

92. See, e.g, "Generalversammlung," *LVZ*, 10.10.32; *HVW*, 9.11.32.

93. *VW*, #445, 21.9.32; #477, 9.10.32.

94. Stampfer, *Vierzehn Jahre*, 585. At the party council meeting after the election, participants admitted that Socialist Action had failed.

95. "Generalversammlung—Leipzig," *LVZ*, 10.10.32; *VW*, #423, 8.9.32; #459, 29.9.32.

96. See, e.g., the report of a Nazi observer regarding disparaging comments on his party made at an SPD meeting near Leipzig (NSDAP HA R.40/F.798: Oct. 1932); A. Schifrin, "Die Krise der deutschen Gegenrevolution," 403–4; "Es lebe die SPD," *VW*, #525, 6.11.32. At the national level, the Communist challenge was still only obliquely acknowledged. See, e.g., Max Westphal, "Einheitsfront," *VW*, #495, 20.10.32.

97. On the ADGB's determination to use the *Hammerschaften* as "a defense against the RGO and NSBO on the shop floor," see Grassmann to the DMV Vorstand, 12.11.32, Dok. 145, in *Gewerkschaften 1930–1933*, 4:767. On Social Democratic concern about KPD activity in cultural organizations, especially Workers' Sports, see NSDAP HA R.93/F.1900: Lagebericht, 11.1.33. Because of Communist infiltration, the Berlin SPD suspended acceptance of new members at the end of 1932 (Sitzung des Parteiausschusses mit Vertretern der

Reichstagsfraktion und der Eiseren Front am 31.1.33 [hereafter cited as Parteiausschuss et al., 31.1.33]: Vogel, 152, in Schulze, *Anpassung oder Widerstand?*).

98. *LVZ*, 3.11.32; "Volk regiere dich selbst!" in NSDAP HA R.40/F.799.

99. BA R58/458: 29.10.32; Fülberth, *Beziehungen zwischen SPD und KPD*, 358–59; Hermann Weber, "Politik der KPD," 141–43.

100. Schulze, *Otto Braun*, 763–65; Heinrich A. Winkler, *Katastrophe*, 761–62; Möller, *Parlamentarismus*, 573; editor's note, Schulze, *Anpassung oder Widerstand?*, 19 n. 11.

101. Schulze, *Otto Braun*, 769, 767.

102. Parteiausschuss, November: Wels, 19–20; Breitscheid, 46; Hilferding, 39; Künstler, 51–52; Sender, 56, in Schulze, *Anpassung oder Widerstand?*

103. For a legal strike, 75 percent of *all* employees was required. Skrzypczak, "'Revolutionäre' Gewerkschaftspolitik," 265, 267–69. Altogether 800 to 1,000 strikes occurred in protest against wage cuts imposed by Papen (Deppe and Rossmann, "Hätte der Faschismus verhindert werden können?," 29; Schneider, *Kleine Geschichte der Gewerkschaften*, 210). In the Ruhr, of 159 strikes with 33,242 participants, workers won 123 (Peukert, *Ruhrarbeiter gegen den Faschismus*, 31).

104. K. L. Gerstorff, "Die Streikwelle-Ein Gesamtüberblick," *Die Weltbühne*, 8.11.32: 678–82. Gerstorff agreed with the right-wing *Deutsche Führerbriefe* (*DF*, #94, 2.12.32) that only the KPD's incompetence and its separatist folly, the RGO, prevented it from winning support on the shop floor comparable to its electoral gains.

105. Frey, *Deutschland, wohin?*, 19; Parteiausschuss, November: Lipinski, 38; Sender, 56; Dietrich, 41–42, in Schulze, *Anpassung oder Widerstand?*

106. *VW*, #520, 3.11.32; Stampfer, *Vierzehn Jahre*, 594; Schulze, *Anpassung oder Widerstand?*, 16 n. 5. In Berlin, the SPD still had a following greater than the national average but lost relatively more between July and November 1932—Berlin SPD: 27 percent to 23.8 percent; national SPD: 21.6 percent to 20.4 percent (Schulze, *Anpassung oder Widerstand?*, 16 n. 4; Gates, "Free Trade Unions," 280).

107. Parteiausschuss, November: Wels, 70; Lipinski, 38; Dietrich, 41–42; Edel, 49; Böchel, 54; Sender, 56; Litke, 67–68, in Schulze, *Anpassung oder Widerstand?* A union leader had rough going at a meeting of union and party officials in Berlin (*VW*, #544, 18.11.32). In the party council, Stampfer was put on the hot seat. *Vorwärts*, relying on ADGB information, reported the strike on the evening of November 3 (#520). Every other Berlin paper had covered it that morning (Schulze, *Anpassung oder Widerstand?*, 54 n. 113). Stampfer admitted that *Vorwärts*'s coverage was a "catastrophe" (Parteiausschuss, November: 64, ibid.).

108. Orlow, *History of the Nazi Party*, 1:285–98; Heinrich A. Winkler, *Katastrophe*, 774–75; Turner, *German Big Business*, 292–93. For election statistics, see Falter, Lindenberger, and Schumann, *Wahlen und Abstimmungen*, 41, 44.

109. As usual, the press emphasized the positive: *HVF*, 8.11.32; *DVZ*, 7.11.32; *HE*, 7.11.32; *FVS*, 8.11.32; *RZ*, 7.11.32. SPD losses of 708,000 over three months should be compared with 598,000 votes lost between September 1930 and July 1932. The KPD impressively outpolled the SPD in the Ruhr, emerging as the largest party in cities such as Dortmund, Duisburg, and Gelsenkirchen (Peukert, *Ruhrarbeiter gegen den Faschismus*, 33). For statistics, see Falter, Lindenberger, and Schumann, *Wahlen und Abstimmungen*, 41, 44.

110. Parteiausschuss, November: Wels, 69; Crispien, 65; Breitscheid, 45–46; Lipinski, 37; Sender, 55; Dietrich, 41; Lehmann, 58, in Schulze, *Anpassung oder Widerstand?*

111. This held true outside the party council as well. See "Das zerbrochene Hakenkreuz," *RZ*, 7.11.32, and *FVS*, 8.11.32; *FW*, 25.12.32, 17; 1.1.33, 21; NWStAM Bestand SPD und Reichsbanner, Nr. 7: An die Leitungen der Ortsgruppen, Bielefeld, 20.12.32.

112. Parteiausschuss, November: Wels, 71; Heilmann, 31–32; Künstler, 51, in Schulze, *Anpassung oder Widerstand?* Also see *FW*, 25.12.32, 27. Kautsky wrote Paul Hertz that without toleration Germany would have become a dictatorship. Social Democrats could hope now that the NSDAP and the KPD would "eat each other up" (NL Paul Hertz, Film II/I/4, AsD). Hilferding, on the other hand, wrote Kautsky that the "fascist danger still threatens" (12.1.32, NL Kautsky D/XII/658, IISH).

113. See, e.g., the judgment of the centrist Dittmann, "Wie alles kam," 319, NL Dittmann, Mappe XIV, AsD. Similarly, the revisionist Sollmann told an audience in Hamburg, "[National Socialism's] power is broken" (*HE*, 13.1.33).

114. Parteiausschuss, November: Wels, 22–24; Heilmann, 31; Severing, 33; Hilferding, 40–41; Breitscheid, 46–47; Wurm, 43, in Schulze, *Anpassung oder Widerstand?* According to Keil, after November 6, "anti-Papen sentiment was stronger than hatred of Hitler" (*Erlebnisse*, 2:468). Georg Decker also advised all-out hostility to Papen ("Nach den Wahlen," 469–70).

115. *VW*, #541, 16.11.32. Keil criticized the decision not to meet with Papen because it cut the SPD off from Hindenburg (*Erlebnisse*, 2:469).

116. Parteiausschuss, November: Böchel, 53; Breitscheid, 45, in Schulze, *Anpassung oder Widerstand?* Also see Hilferding to Kautsky, 1.12.32, NL Kautsky, D/XII/658, IISH. Kautsky wrote Hertz, "The situation would not be so bad if the KPD possessed a shimmer of reason and responsibility" (13.11.32, NL Hertz, Film II/I/4, AsD).

117. Parteiausschuss, November: Wels, 74, 91, in Schulze, *Anpassung oder Widerstand?* To Höltermann, Braun lamented the "recent" tendency to allow the KPD to "dictate [SPD] actions" (31.12.32) (in Matthias, "Sozialdemokratische Partei," 231); Höltermann shared Braun's concern (Höltermann to Braun, 3.1.33, NL Braun, Teil 2/B/I/16, GStAPK I.HA Rep. 92).

118. Parteiausschuss, November: Wels, 44, 69; Hilferding, 39–41; Wurm, 44; Stampfer, 64–65; Crispien, 67; Parteiausschuss, Dezember: Junke, 110;

Meitmann, 111; Dietrich, 105, in Schulze, *Anpassung oder Widerstand? Vorwärts* directed hostile articles toward the KPD through early January (#576, 7.12.32; #13, 8.1.33; #16, 10.1.33), but the *Hessischer Volksfreund* called for a friendlier attitude (8.11.32).

119. Parteiausschuss, November: Hilferding, 39; Breitscheid, 45, 47; Severing, 33–34, in Schulze, *Anpassung oder Widerstand?* At a speech in Düsseldorf, his electoral district, Hilferding passionately defended democracy (*DVZ*, 2.12.32).

120. Parteiausschuss, November: Dietrich, 43; Edel, 49–50; Böchel, 53–54; Sender, 56, in Schulze, *Anpassung oder Widerstand?* For provincial expressions of the same view, see Liebmann at Leipzig general assembly, *LVZ*, 10.10.32; Bienstock, *Kampf um die Macht*; Eugen Chossudowsky, *FW*, 13.11.32, 16–17. Also see the debate on the Weimar constitution in *Die Gesellschaft* and *Sozialistische Monatshefte*. Otto Kirchheimer argued that the SPD must move beyond Weimar democracy's failed attempt to balance class power ("Legalität und Legitimität," *DG*, July 1933; "Verfassungsreform und Sozialdemokratie," *DG*, Jan. 1933). (Ellen Kennedy has recently argued that Kirchheimer's analysis and conclusion showed the influence of the conservative legal theorist Carl Schmitt. See Kennedy, "Carl Schmitt," 393–97). Ernst Fraenkel agreed with Kirchheimer that the SPD should not be wedded to the Weimar constitution, but he wanted to save its democratic core after stripping it of undemocratic deformities ("Abschied von Weimar?," *DG*, Aug. 1932; "Verfassungsreform und Sozialdemokratie," *DG*, Dec. 1932). Mierendorff leaned toward Fraenkel's position, arguing that the SPD must fight for social, not liberal, democracy but also must "win back the republic" ("Der sozialistische Weg," *SM*, 8.12.32, 989–93).

121. Parteiausschuss, November: Lipinski, 39; Edel, 50; Sender, 57; Lehmann (Breslau), 57, in Schulze, *Anpassung oder Widerstand?* For other calls for a focus on "extraparliamentary struggle," see the report on a party meeting in Berlin (*VW*, #544, 18.11.32); *FW*, 20.11.32, 22–23; Carlo Mierendorff, "Was ist ausserparlamentarischer Kampf?" *DR*, 10.1.33, 486–89; Mierendorff, *FW*, 22.1.33, 123–24. Mierendorff was not the only neorevisionist who shared the Left's extraparliamentary focus. For explicit statements in favor of "revolutionary means" to defend constitutional rights, see Geyer [Muhle], "SPD am Scheideweg," 456; [Hans Simon] "Die Sieger von Übermorgen," *NB*, Oct. 1932, 514).

122. The *Hamburger Echo* published an editorial by Toni Sender that argued for social democracy, extraparliamentary means to defend the republic, and a strong Iron Front ("Rüsten!," 28.11.32).

123. The quotes are from Geyer [Muhle], "SPD am Scheideweg," 453–54. Also see [Simon], "Sieger," 512–13; Mierendorff, "Der sozialistische Weg," 990.

124. Parteiausschuss, November: Hilferding, 41; Wels, 70, in Schulze, *Anpassung oder Widerstand?* Wels alluded to Kautsky's famous 1893 statement:

"The SPD is a revolutionary, but not a revolution-making party" (editor's note, ibid., 70 n. 141). Wels (28) also made more explicitly optimistic remarks: "We are not at the end of democracy. The five elections this year show we are at its beginning."

125. Parteiausschuss, November: Wels, 27, ibid.

126. Bracher, "20. Juli 1932," 245. On the historical consensus of the 1950s and 1960s, see Muth, "Schleicher," 207. Schildt has recently revived this thesis in a slightly different form. He does not believe that Schleicher wanted to split Strasser from Hitler, and he emphasizes the affinities between Schleicher and the *Tat* circle (a point made earlier by Klemens von Klemperer, *Germany's New Conservatism*, 131). *Tat* writers did promote a *Querfront* that would replace party politics and parliamentarism with a "national movement" (Schildt, *Militärdiktatur?*, 164, 98–101; Schildt, "Militärische Ratio," 348–49. Also see Sontheimer, "Der Tatkreis," 234–36). I am unconvinced, however, by Schildt's insistence on a strong political tie between Schleicher and Hans Zehrer, editor of *Die Tat*, despite the apparent influence of Zehrer's ideas on Schleicher. Before becoming chancellor, Schleicher distanced himself from *Die Tat*, yet Zehrer was pleased by Schleicher's appointment as chancellor. Such indirect evidence leads Schildt to conclude that Schleicher shared Zehrer's "conception" (*Militärdiktatur?*, 113–15). Having made this assumption, he then infers that Zehrer's blueprint guided Schleicher's behavior, an unproven deduction.

127. Muth, "Schleicher," 210–11; Hayes, "'Question Mark with Epaulettes'?," 51.

128. Keil, *Erlebnisse*, 2:470–71. On this point I agree with Schildt ("Militärische Ratio," 348).

129. Hayes, "'Question Mark with Epaulettes'?," 57–58; Turner, *German Big Business*, 307–11; Schildt, *Militärdiktatur?*, 91, 96.

130. *Schulthess' Europäischer Geschichtskalender 1932*, 225; "Die Aufhebung der Notverordnung vom 5. September," *GZ*, 24.12.32, 817.

131. Protokoll einer Besprechung am 28.11.32 (Leipart and Eggert report on their talk with Schleicher), printed in Emig and Zimmermann, "Ende einer Legende," 38–40; Bundesvorstand, 29.11.32, Dok. 150, in *Gewerkschaften 1930–1933*, 4:774.

132. Schildt, *Militärdiktatur?*, 166–67.

133. See, e.g., H. A. (Hans Aron), "Wirtschaftspolitische Aufgaben der Gegenwart," *GZ*, 10.12.32, 785–87; "Die Aufhebung der Notverordnung vom 5. September," *GZ*, 24.12.32, 817; Clemens Nörpel, "Selbstständige Gewerkschaften oder parteipolitische Agitationsausschüsse," *GZ*, 24.12.32, 819–22.

134. Breitman, "German Social Democracy and General Schleicher," 365.

135. Neebe, "Konflikt und Kooperation," 235.

136. For evidence of French concern, see an "ADGB communique" that corrected the impression given by an interview with Leipart about Schleicher

conducted by the Paris *Excelsior* (14.12.32, #318, ADGB Restakten, Film Nr. 21/1, DGB Archiv). For a pleased domestic reaction, see *DF*, #94, 2.12.32. On the ADGB's loosening of its ties to the Iron Front, see Potthoff, *Freie Gewerkschaften 1918–1933*, 302.

137. Leber, "Todesursachen," 242. Wels, however, assured Leipart that the party did not mistrust the unions (Leipart speaking at Bundesvorstand meeting, 8.12.32, Dok. 153, in *Gewerkschaften 1930–1933*, 4:781).

138. Heinrich A. Winkler, *Katastrophe*, 840–41. In a letter to the ADGB, its local organization in Garmisch-Partenkirchen "sharply" protested Leipart's laudatory obituary for Ernst von Borsig (23.1.32, Dok. 161, in *Gewerkschaften 1930–1933*, 4:797).

139. "Theodor Leipart an die deutsche Arbeiterschaft," *GZ*, 31.12.32, 833. Grassmann expressed concern about public misunderstanding of the ADGB's high political profile during the Schleicher interlude (Grassmann comments at Bundesausschuss meeting, 21.1.33, Dok. 159, in *Gewerkschaften 1930–1933*, vol. 4).

140. An internal bulletin admitted that it was "not clear what [Schleicher's chancellorship] means" (NWStAM Bestand SPD und Reichsbanner, Nr. 7: Rundschreiben #22, Bezirk Westliches Westfalen, Dortmund, 3.12.32).

141. "Warnung an Schleicher," *VW*, #33, 20.1.33; Heinrich A. Winkler, *Katastrophe*, 795. On May 14, 1948, Severing jotted down his recollection of a party council session at which Breitscheid reported on this meeting with Schleicher. From Severing's description it seems that Schleicher made (or perhaps repeated) the proposal after the election in Lippe on January 15, 1933 (NL Severing, Mappe 52/32, AsD). Breitman accepts Severing's version as proof that the proposal came at a later date ("German Social Democracy and General Schleicher," 367–68, 372–73). Heinrich Winkler thinks that it was made in November only (*Katastrophe*, 838 n. 149). I accept Winkler's version because on January 19, 1933, Breitscheid referred to the November conversation in a new warning to Schleicher not to touch the constitution (*VW*, #33, 20.1.33).

142. Adolph, *Wels*, 250; Breitman, "German Social Democracy and General Schleicher," 370. Hoegner was also critical of the refusal to deal with Schleicher (*Verratene Republik*, 330).

143. Stampfer, *Vierzehn Jahre*, 596. For ambivalence toward Schleicher, see, e.g., F. D. H. Schulz, *DVZ*, 3.12.32; *VW*, #571, 4.12.32. For attacks on ex-chancellor Papen, see *VW*, #565, 1.12.32; #567, 2.12.32; #573, 6.12.32.

144. Stampfer, *Erfahrungen*, 255–56; Hoegner, *Verratene Republik*, 329–30; Emig and Zimmermann, "Ende einer Legende," 26.

145. Hayes, "'Question Mark with Epaulettes'?," 61–62. Bracher, writing before new evidence appeared, was too ready to see Schleicher as a principled opponent of Hitler (*Auflösung*, 684, 710 n. 102, and "20. Juli 1932," 245–46).

146. Here I agree with Bracher (*Auflösung*, 684).

147. Stampfer, *Vierzehn Jahre*, 599.

148. Parteiausschuss, Dezember, 98, in Schulze, *Anpassung oder Widerstand?*; Stampfer, *Vierzehn Jahre*, 599. Even Mierendorff now believed "Social Democracy enters the new year under a good sign" ("Die Sozialdemokratie im Kampf mit Schleicher," *DR*, 20.12.32, 392).

149. Turner, *German Big Business*, 311–12; Hayes, "'Question Mark with Epaulettes'?," 62.

150. Siegfried Aufhäuser, "Positive Erfolge," *FVS*, 28.12.32; *VW*, #1, 1.1.33.

151. Braun, *Weimar*, 436–38; Furtwängler, "Die deutschen Gewerkschaften und ihr Ende durch Hitler," 225, 127, NL Furtwängler, Kasten 5, DGB Archiv; Schulze, *Otto Braun*, 774–75.

152. *VW*, #8, 5.1.32. Because their meeting was brokered by a Cologne banker, *Vorwärts* found new evidence that big business supported Hitler (#10, 6.1.33; #11, 7.1.33). But confusion about who was lined up behind whom was evident. On January 10 (#16), a headline announced that "heavy industry and agrarians" wanted Papen back. On January 12 (#20), though, "agrarians" led by German Nationalists and National Socialists were found to be "wild" against Schleicher and industry.

153. Bracher, *Auflösung*, 701–3, 707–14, 717–18; Stampfer, *Vierzehn Jahre*, 610. The Nazis did not regain their July 31 peak, however. The SPD gained votes as well (*VW*, #26, 16.1.33).

154. Hayes, "'Question Mark with Epaulettes'?," 63; "Aufgabe: Arbeitsbeschaffung. Zensur: Unbefriedigend," *GZ*, 21.1.33, 33. SPD pressure may have played a role in the ADGB's lack of enthusiasm for Schleicher's plans.

155. Report by Eggert and Grassmann on a discussion with Schleicher, 26.1.33, in Emig and Zimmermann, "Ende einer Legende," 41–43. According to Ernst Lemmer, Leipart did consider agreeing to an attempt to stop Hitler with a Reichswehr/union front. Lemmer thought Schleicher's insistence on the inclusion of Strasser changed Leipart's mind (Lemmer, *Manches war doch anders*, 166–67).

156. "Warnung an Schleicher," *VW*, #33, 20.1.33.

157. Bracher judged the SPD too harshly for its negative attitude toward Schleicher (*Auflösung*, 700). Brecht (*Mit der Kraft*, 256) believed the SPD was wrong not to negotiate with Schleicher but defended the party against Bracher's shrill attack. Heinrich A. Winkler criticizes SPD "legalism" in its relations with Schleicher (*Katastrophe*, 863).

158. Stampfer, *Erfahrungen*, 260; Sitzung des Parteivorstandes mit Vertretern der Reichstagsfraktion und des ADGB am 30.1.33 (hereafter cited as Parteivorstand et al., 30.1.33), in Schulze, *Anpassung oder Widerstand?*, 134–36. The content of the call is given by Stampfer (*Erfahrungen*, 260). Due to high blood pressure, Wels was "at the cure" in Ascona on January 30 and thus not present (Adolph, *Wels*, 250).

159. *VW*, #47, 28.1.32; #50, 30.1.33; *RB*, 4.2.33.

160. Heer, *Burgfrieden*, 196–97.

161. Klinger [Curt Geyer], *Volk in Ketten*, 19.

162. See, e.g., NSDAP HA R.93/F.1901: Funktionärssitzung, 3.2.32.

163. Parteivorstand et al., 30.1.33: Aufhäuser, 133; Litke, 134; Eggert, 134; Braun, 135; Hilferding, 135, in Schulze, *Anpassung oder Widerstand?* Toni Sender also argued for a general strike (*Autobiography*, 301–2).

164. Parteiausschuss et al., 31.1.33: Höltermann, 152, in Schulze, *Anpassung oder Widerstand?*

165. Sitzung des Parteivorstandes mit Vertretern des ADGB am 5.2.33 (hereafter cited as Parteivorstand et al., 5.2.33): Wels, 161, Grassmann, 162, Leipart, 162, Schlimme, 164; Parteiausschuss et al., 31.1.33, Grassmann, 149, both in Schulze, *Anpassung oder Widerstand?* Sender recalled that stewards from Dresden, her district, were ready to strike. They went to Berlin where their offer was turned down (*Autobiography*, 310). On the strike in Lübeck, see Dorothea Beck, *Julius Leber*, 129–32. According to Breitscheid, Grassmann bragged that if he "press[ed] a button," all work would stop (Hoegner, *Der schwierige Aussenseiter*, 154).

166. BA R58/557: #2, Eiserne Front Versammlung [in Clou], 12.2.33.

167. This is how the SPD press immediately described the regime. See "Regierung der kapitalistischen Diktatur!," *FVS*, 31.1.33.

168. Parteiausschuss et al., 31.1.33: Breitscheid, 141–44, in Schulze, *Anpassung oder Widerstand?* (The pamphlet, "Bereit sein ist alles!," contained a few modifications.) Philipp Scheidemann offered the same optimistic analysis in a letter to Wilhelm Dittmann, 15.3.33, NL Dittmann VI/I/135, AsD.

169. Parteiausschuss et al., 31.1.33: Breitscheid, 142, 146–47, in Schulze, *Anpassung oder Widerstand?* A street flyer warned that any anticonstitutional act would encounter the "most extreme resistance from workers and all freedom-loving circles" (30.1.33, *Flugblattsammlung 1933*, AsD). The rhetoric was not totally hollow. Armed *Hundertschaften* guarded trade union and party buildings; short-wave radios connected SPD headquarters to all thirty-three districts in case of alarm; an illegal relay station awaited the signal to act (Niemann, *Geschichte der deutschen Sozialdemokratie*, 319).

170. Parteiausschuss et al., 31.1.33: Breitscheid, 144–45, 139, in Schulze, *Anpassung oder Widerstand?*; *VW*, #59/63, 7.2.33; #65, 8.2.33.

171. Werner Blumenberg, "Erfahrungen in der illegalen Arbeit," printed in Matthias, "Sozialdemokratische Partei," 271.

172. Paul Hertz to Luise Kautsky, 8.3.33, NL Kautsky, Familiearchief 11.5, IISH; Stampfer, "On the Eve," *International Information*, #13, 11.3.33, 107. *International Information* was the English-language internal information organ of the Socialist International.

173. Keil, *Erlebnisse*, 2:472–73.

174. Sitzung des Parteiausschusses am 14.3.33 (hereafter cited as Parteiausschuss, 14.3.33): Wels, 168, in Schulze, *Anpassung oder Widerstand?* In fact, the SPD executive planned to move to Munich. Thus, Wels, Hilferding, Crispien, and Dittmann were in Munich on March 9 when Hitler did in

Bavaria what Papen had done in Prussia and with similar ease (Hoegner, *Flucht*, 98–104). Crispien and Dittmann went into exile; the others returned to Berlin.

175. Parteiausschuss et al., 31.1.33: Breitscheid, 146–47, in Schulze, *Anpassung oder Widerstand?*

176. See Parteivorstand et al. . . . 5.2.33: Wels, 161; Vogel, 162, in Schulze, *Anpassung oder Widerstand?*; BA R58/561, KPD Versammlung, Königsberg, 17.2.33; NHStAH Hann. 310, II/6II: SPD Kreis Gandersheim Jahresbericht (Anträge zur Reichskonferenz), 22.1.33; Pyta, *Gegen Hitler*, 260. A post-*Machtergreifung* pamphlet warned people away from a united front (SPD Vorstand, *SPD oder KPD? Die Wege zur Einheitsfront*) as did internal circulars (NWStAM Bestand SPD und Reichsbanner, Nr. 8: Rundschreiben, Bezirk Westliches Westfalen, 2.2.33).

177. Stampfer, *Erfahrungen*, 263–64.

178. *VW*, #43, 26.1.33.

179. Parteivorstand et al. . . . 5.2.33: Künstler, 164; Aufhäuser, 165; Hilferding, 164; Stampfer, 163; Vogel, 163; Grassmann, 164; Dittmann, 164; Sitzung des Parteivorstandes mit Vertretern der preussischen Landtagsfraktion am 2.2.33: Carl Litke, 158; Löbe, 158; Hilferding, 159; both in Schulze, *Anpassung oder Widerstand?* ADGB-Bundesvorstand (Schlimme) to Stampfer, 6.2.33, Dok. 172, in *Gewerkschaften 1930–1933*, 4:838–40.

180. Andersen, "KPD und die nationalsozialistische Machtübernahme," 368–69.

181. Stampfer, *Erfahrungen*, 263–65.

182. ADGB-Vorstand (Schlimme) an Bergarbeiter (Bochum), 15.2.33, Dok. 176, in *Gewerkschaften 1930–1933*, 4:842–43; Wickham, "Working-Class Movement in Frankfurt," 246.

183. This warning came from the ADGB (ADGB-Vorstand [Schlimme] an Ortsausschuss Halle, 14.2.33, Dok. 174, in *Gewerkschaften 1930–1933*, 4:841). Communists joined SPD rallies in Frankfurt and Cologne (*FVS*, 4.2.33; *Freie Presse*, 6.2.33); Socialists attended private Communist meetings in Münster only to hear their leaders maligned (BA R58/561: #9, KPD Stubenversammlungen, Münster, 9.3.33).

184. Krall, *Landespolitik der SPD in Bayern*, 281. At Düsseldorf's party conference, members were warned to watch out for agents provocateurs *and* Communists in their ranks (*DVZ*, 6.2.33).

185. Karl Kautsky, "What Now?," *II*, #15, 18.3.33, 116.

186. Matthias, "Sozialdemokratische Partei," 163. Hilferding suggested this approach at the executive meeting on February 2 (Parteivorstand mit Vertretern der preussischen Landtagsfraktion . . . 2.2.33, 159, in Schulze, *Anpassung oder Widerstand?*). Werner Blumenberg remarked on the masses' militant spirit ("Erfahrungen," in Matthias, "Sozialdemokratische Partei," 269–70).

187. Löbe spoke to ten thousand in Cologne ("Für sozialistische Staatsge-

walt," *RZ*, 30.1.33); "Das rote Berlin antwortet Hitler!," *VW*, #51, 31.1.33, announced a rally in Berlin's Lustgarten that was prohibited (#56, 2.2.33) but then triumphantly held (#65, 8.2.33); tens of thousands marched in Düsseldorf ("Nieder mit dem Faschismus!," *DVZ*, 6.2.33); in Hamburg ("Jetzt Einheit, oder die Freiheit ist tot!," *HE*, 18.2.33); and in Altona ("Zehntausend marschierten für die Freiheit!," *HE*, 20.2.33). Munich planned six rallies and a leaflet for every week of the campaign (NSDAP HA R.93/F.1901: Sitzung des Parteiausschusses München, 3.2.33); Hoegner recalled that "halls were filled" (*Flucht*, 63). Also see Mehringer, "Bayerische Sozialdemokratie," 339. On Frankfurt's imposing rallies in February, see Wickham, "Working-Class Movement in Frankfurt," 247. But not everywhere was the mood good— Hoegner contrasted depression and resignation in Magdeburg on February 27 with a huge, excited audience in Hamburg the next day (*Flucht*, 82, 84). The intervening Reichstag fire certainly helps explain the contrast.

188. Schulze, *Anpassung oder Widerstand?*, 177 n. 36; Stampfer, *Erfahrungen*, 261–62. *Vorwärts* was banned on February 5 and 6 and again between February 16 and 22 (#79, 16.2.33).

189. Beier, *Arbeiterbewegung in Hessen*, 296; Mehringer, "Bayerische Sozialdemokratie," 341.

190. NSDAP HA R.92/F.1894: 21.2.33. See a description of the campaign in Düsseldorf, where enthusiasm ran high for campaign work and for preparation for extraparliamentary actions (*DVZ*, 6.2.33).

191. Edinger, *German Exile Politics*, 12–13; Koszyk, *Zwischen Kaiserreich und Diktatur*, 213–15. See Hans Mommsen, "Political Effects of the Reichstag Fire."

192. Edinger, *German Exile Politics*, 13–14. Warned of imminent arrest, Braun left on March 4 (Schulze, *Otto Braun*, 785), although Wels begged him to stay through the election (Hertz to L. Kautsky, 8.3.33, NL Kautsky, Familiearchief 11.5, IISH). Grzesinski went into exile on March 5 (Hoegner, *Flucht*, 92).

193. Wels, Notizen über einen Artikel von Otto Bauer, 3, Emigration SOPADE, Mappe 161, AsD.

194. Mehringer, "Bayerische Sozialdemokratie," 324. For statistics, see Falter, Lindenberger, and Schumann, *Wahlen und Abstimmungen*, 41, 44.

195. Mehringer, "Bayerische Sozialdemokratie," 340–44; Edinger, *German Exile Politics*, 13.

196. Adolph, *Wels*, 266; Stampfer, "A Red Letter Day for the Party," *II*, #14, 11.3.33, 111; Kautsky, "What Now?," 115–16. Social Democrats were pleased in the provinces as well. On Bavaria, see Krall, *Landespolitik der SPD in Bayern*, 284.

197. Parteiausschuss, 14.3.33: Wels, 169–70, 173–74, in Schulze, *Anpassung oder Widerstand?*

198. Adolph, *Wels*, 252. Hoegner (Adolph, *Wels*, 252 n. 565) and Sender (*Autobiography*, 303–4) believed Wels wanted to fight and was held back by the unions.

199. Adolph, *Wels*, 257–58; *II*, #18, 31.3.33, 141. Kurt Schumacher was eager to give the speech.

200. Adolph, *Wels*, 259; Severing, *Lebensweg*, 2:385; Hoegner, *Flucht*, 125. Severing managed to get free before the session started. Pleading illness, Breitscheid and Hilferding did not attend and immediately afterward went into exile (Matthias, "Sozialdemokratische Partei," 256 n. 13). Breitscheid was ill, but Hilferding was not. He had particular reasons to fear for his safety: he had twice been finance minister and was Jewish. All eighty-one Communist deputies were in custody. On Sollmann, see "Communications on the Conditions of Political Prisoners," a publication of the Labor and Socialist International (inside *II*, but dated and numbered separately), #6, 22.4.33, 20–22.

201. Craig, *Germany*, 577.

202. *Reichstag: Sten. Berichte*, Bd. 457, 23.3.33, 32–34. The speech was written by Wels, Stampfer, Schumacher, and Heilmann (Adolph, *Wels*, 258). The Reichstag delegation as a group decided not to refer to the suppression of the KPD, although the executive suggested doing so (Hoegner, *Flucht*, 125). Hoegner wrote of the "formidable impression" the speech made on the SPD delegation (*Flucht*, 135). Ernst Lemmer, though he voted for the Enabling Act, found Wels's talk "powerful" and recalled that it "shook up all of us" (*Manches war doch anders*, 172).

203. Albrecht, *Der militante Sozialdemokrat*, 134. After the Reichstag session, Mierendorff, Schumacher, Meitmann, Gustav Dahrendorf, and August Rathmann discussed the political situation with a fellow neorevisionist, Curt Geyer, who was now second-in-command at *Vorwärts* (Rathmann, *Ein Arbeiterleben*, 216, 112). One can only speculate that this group shared Mierendorff's disappointment in Wels's speech (although Schumacher helped compose it).

204. *II*, #17, 27.3.33, 140; #19, 1.4.33, 146–48. Pressure on the SPD from the International to form an illegal united front with the KPD also contributed to Wels's decision.

205. "Die Gewerkschaften und der Regierungswechsel. 13. Bundesausschusssitzung des ADGB am 31. Jan. 1933," *GZ*, 4.2.33, 67. For the full transcript of this meeting, see Dok. 170 in *Gewerkschaften 1930–1933*, 4:830–32.

206. Leipart to Keil, 3.3.33, ADGB Restakten (17), Film Nr. 22/2, #391–391a, DGB Archiv; Parteiausschuss, 14.3.33: Wels, 172, in Schulze, *Anpassung oder Widerstand?*

207. "An die Mitglieder der Gewerkschaften," *GZ*, 25.2.33; "Erklärung des ADGB," *GZ*, 25.3.33, 177; Lothar Erdmann, "Nation, Gewerkschaften und Sozialismus," *DA*, Mar.–Apr. 1933, 131, 149–50, 161 (emphasis in original).

208. SPD, "Was wird werden?," Sonderdienst 1, ADGB Restakten, Film Nr. 26/1, #116, DGB Archiv. The ADGB did much less well at certain Berlin shops, such as the gasworks, where the RGO won 34 percent. Among Ruhr miners it fell from 37 percent in 1930 to 30.5 percent, but the RGO's vote

collapsed (from 29.4 percent to 9.2 percent). These were the only workers among whom the NSBO did notably well (30.7 percent, up from 4.2 percent). The NSBO fared much better among employees, winning 17.3 percent even in Berlin (at the electricity works) compared with the AfA-Bund's 75.4 percent. See Furtwängler, "Die deutschen Gewerkschaften und ihr Ende durch Hitler," 247–51, NL Furtwängler, Kasten 5, DGB Archiv. Also see Gotschlich, "Zur Organisationsstruktur der SPD."

209. An *Oberregierungsrat* (senior civil servant) Dr. Diele, Polizeipräsidium, 4.6.33, NL Furtwängler, DGB Archiv; ADGB-Bundesausschuss an die Reichsregierung, 9.4.33, Dok. 197, in *Gewerkschaften 1930–1933*, 4:881–82.

210. "Der Bundesausschuss des ADGB. zur Lage am 5. April 1933," *GZ*, 15.4.33, 229–30.

211. Protokolle, 5.4.33 (meeting between ADGB and NSBO), NL Erkelenz, NL 72/139, f.50–51, BA.

212. Quote is from Beier, "Entstehung des Führerkreises," 367–68; Theodor Thomas, diary entries, 8.4.–29.4.33, Dok. 213, in *Gewerkschaften 1930–1933*, vol. 4.

213. Theodor Thomas, diary entry, 13.4.33, Dok. 213, in *Gewerkschaften 1930–1933*, vol. 4; "An die Mitglieder der Gewerkschaften!," *GZ*, 22.4.33, 241; "Der 1. Mai 1933," *GZ*, 29.4.33, 257–58. The neorevisionist Pahl wrote that if National Socialism's victory led to socialism, workers would celebrate it ("Der Feiertag der Arbeit und die sozialistische Arbeiterschaft," *GZ*, 29.4.33, 259–60).

214. *GZ*, 22.4.33, 241. On the separate demonstration of the SPD, see Stampfer, *Erfahrungen*, 269. In Stuttgart, at least, some rank and file Socialists did join the official celebration (as remembered by Helene Schoettle in Fichter, "'Es ist nicht so gekommen,'" 237–38).

215. "Communications . . . Political Prisoners," *II*, #7, 17.5.33, 29. Fritz Tarnow was arrested on May 5 (Kayser to Keil, 13.5.33, Dok. 212, in *Gewerkschaften 1930–1933*, vol. 4).

216. BA R58/484: #6–10 Parteivorstand an "Sehr geehrte Genossen!," 5.6.33.

217. Hamburg produced such a newsletter (Hebel-Kunze, *SPD und Faschismus*, 118 n. 112); also Leipzig (meeting of the Reichstag delegation, 10.6.33: Lipinski, 262, in Matthias, "Sozialdemokratische Partei"). On the National Socialist strategy, see Bracher, Sauer, and Schulz, *Nationalsozialistische Machtergreifung*, 195.

218. From Karlsbad, Scheidemann wrote Dittmann (also in exile) that "I hear the mood against emigrated comrades is very angry" (15.3.33, NL Dittmann VI/I/135, AsD).

219. Matthias and Weber, *Widerstand gegen den Nationalsozialismus in Mannheim*, 121; Blumenberg, "Erfahrungen," in Matthias, "Sozialdemokratische Partei," 271. Virtually every functionary's family was affected.

220. At the end of May, "A" (Aufhäuser?) in Berlin wrote Paul Hertz in

exile, "Certainly the masses are depressed. But the depression is more the result of dissatisfaction with the passivity of the top, than the effect of a panicked desire to flee that one sees in the functionary corps" (30.5.33, NL Paul Hertz, Film XXXIII/33/I, AsD).

221. Parteiausschuss, 14.3.33: Wels, 177, in Schulze, *Anpassung oder Widerstand?*

222. NSDAP HA R.92/F.1895: An die Ortsvorsitzenden der SPD "Sehr geehrte Genossen!" (from Bavarian SPD leadership), n.d.

223. Parteiausschuss, 14.3.33: Lange, 176; Juchacz, 177, in Schulze, *Anpassung oder Widerstand?*

224. See "Niederschrift über die Auflösung der SPD-Ortsgruppe Seltmanns-Kleinweilershofen," 26.3.33, in Matthias, "Sozialdemokratische Partei," 238. Also see Hebel-Kunze, *SPD und Faschismus,* 119 n. 115; Hoegner, *Flucht,* 215.

225. NHStAH Hann. 310, II/A, Nr. 11: "Februar/März 1933: Austrittserklärungen, Ortsverein Hannover" (a selection of these letters is printed in Matthias, "Sozialdemokratische Partei," 239–41). Mehringer, "Bayerische Sozialdemokratie," 345–46. In Munich the district leadership distributed a questionnaire to local functionaries that asked who and how many had left (NSDAP HA R.92/F.1895, #10, n.d.). Also see Schnabel, *Württemberg,* 206.

226. "Rundschreiben des Parteivorstandes," 8.3.33, printed in Matthias, "Sozialdemokratische Partei," 235; "Was wird werden?," Sonderdienst 1 (n.d.), ADGB Restakten, Film Nr. 26/1, #116, DGB Archiv.

227. NSDAP HA R.92/F.1895: "An die Ortsvorsitzenden . . ." (from Bavarian leadership), n.d. Also see Edinger, *German Exile Politics,* 27. In Württemberg, state executive members, led by Keil and Erich Rossmann, laid down all party offices. Kurt Schumacher reported that this "outrageous behavior" was assailed at illegal gatherings in Karlsruhe and the Black Forest (Schnabel, *Württemberg,* 207–8).

228. Erich Schmidt, "Der Berliner Jugendkonflikt vom April 1933," 242, and Blumenberg, "Erfahrungen," 271, in Matthias, "Sozialdemokratische Partei"; "The National Conference in Berlin" (4.26.33), *II,* #24, 6.5.33, 190; Naphtali to Hertz, 14.7.32, in Riemer, "Nach dem Zusammenbruch," 335–36. Hanover remained cohesive. Munich held together but engaged only in collecting money for the families of those imprisoned (Hoegner, *Flucht,* 142, 215).

229. Albrecht, *Der militante Sozialdemokrat,* 134.

230. BA R58/561: #156a, Hannover, 30.4.33.

231. Schmidt, "Berliner Jugendkonflikt," in Matthias, "Sozialdemokratische Partei," 243–50. In May, SAJ functionaries met with members of the Bolshevik-Leninists, a Communist opposition group, to plan a "Marxist reorganization to fight fascism" (BA R58/484: #3, 19.5.33). On Neu Beginnen, see Löwenthal, *Der Widerstandsgruppe "Neu Beginnen,"* and Moraw, *Parole der "Einheit,"* 16.

232. Kühn, *Widerstand und Emigration*, 76. Also see "Die Anfänge der illegalen Arbeit in Sachsen und Thüringen," 252, and Blumenberg, "Erfahrungen," 270–71, both in Matthias, "Sozialdemokratische Partei."

233. BA R58/484: #11–12, An das Auswärtiges Amt und das Ministerium des Inneren, Rotterdam, 7.6.33.

234. NHStAH Hann. 310, II/C, Nr. 25: "Stützpunktleiters der NSDAP in Hilwartshausen (Kreis Einbeck) an die Gauleitung der NSDAP, 22.5.33"; Hoegner, *Flucht*, 237. On the Reichsbanner's continuing efforts to train troops after January 30, see Rohe, *Reichsbanner*, 459. Reichsbanner headquarters were occupied by the SA on March 10. The Reichsbanner wanted to fight in Bavaria and was bitter that it could not (Hoegner, *Flucht*, 104–7).

235. SPD Reichskonferenz, 26.4.33 (fragments), Emigration SOPADE, Mappe 2, AsD; "Proceedings of the National Conference of the German Social Democratic Party," *II*, #24, 6.5.33, 189–93. A selection of delegates elected earlier for a never-held party congress attended. Only Hesse-Kassel, where arrests had decimated the apparatus, was not represented.

236. So claimed the anonymous report in *International Information* (#24, 6.5.33, 189–90). The reporter was, presumably, Curt Geyer, who covered the SPD during 1933 for *International Information* (Schulze, *Anpassung oder Widerstand?*, 191 n. 2). The dropped exiles: Crispien, Dittmann, Hilferding, Breitscheid; the old men: Hildenbrand, Julius Moses, Otto Frank (*II*, #24, 6.5.33, 190).

237. Memorandum des Prager Parteivorstandes für die Gruppenvertrauensleute am 3.6.33 (hereafter cited as Memorandum, 3.6.33), in Schulze, *Anpassung oder Widerstand?*, 181–83; Stampfer, *Erfahrungen*, 270. Soon Aufhäuser, Vogel, Hertz, and Ollenhauer joined the first three in exile.

238. Foreign air seemed to produce this effect: as early as mid-March the exiled Scheidemann complained to Dittmann that he found the "passivity at home" inexplicable (Scheidemann to Dittmann, 15.3.33, NL Dittmann VI/I/135, AsD).

239. Hoegner, *Flucht*, 193, 195. It is interesting that Löbe repudiated "useless self-criticism" at the conference on April 26 and argued that the main tasks were to hold the organization together and find support among youth (SPD Reichskonferenz, 26.4.33 [fragments], Emigration SOPADE, Mappe 2, AsD).

240. Compare Stampfer's account of these meetings (*Erfahrungen*, 270–71) with Hoegner's (*Flucht*, 194–200; *Aussenseiter*, 108) where Stampfer appears highhanded and arrogant.

241. Delegation (and voting) list from 16.5.33 meeting, NL Paul Hertz, Film XXIII/33/I/m, AsD.

242. Hoegner, *Flucht*, 198.

243. Twenty-two deputies were in exile (including by now Karl Höltermann, elected in March), seventeen were in jail, one had been killed, and one had gone over to the NSDAP (delegation list from 16.5.33 meeting, NL Paul Hertz XXIII/33/I/m, AsD; Hoegner, *Flucht*, 200). According to Fritz Naph-

tali, in a prison cell on May 17, the many Social Democrats with him were angered by the delegation's decision, but that "disgust . . . does not equal support for [the émigrés]" (Naphtali to Hertz, 14.7.33, in Riemer, "Nach dem Zusammenbruch," 334–35).

244. Hoegner, *Flucht*, 203–4. On Mierendorff and Schumacher, see Albrecht, *Der militante Sozialdemokrat*, 137.

245. Hoegner, *Flucht*, 207–9; Rudolf Breitscheid, "In Memory of Toni Pfülf," *II*, #33, 17.6.33, 280. For a short biography of Pfülf, see Dertinger, "Toni Pfülf."

246. Memorandum, 3.6.33, 183–85, in Schulze, *Anpassung oder Widerstand?*

247. Westphal, explaining the émigré position in Berlin, "Reichstag delegation meeting, 10.6.33," in Matthias, "Sozialdemokratische Partei," 258. Also see Hilferding (in Zurich) to Paul Hertz, 14.6.33, NL Hertz Film XLII/54/xvii/b, AsD; Aufhäuser (in Paris) to Hertz, 19.6.33, NL Hertz Film XXX/A/c, AsD.

248. The Dutch Socialist paper, *Voorwaarts*, wrote that the opposition included "a number of people whose only incomes are their salaries as Reichstag and Landtag deputies" (BA R58/484: #11–12, An das Auswärtiges Amt und das Ministerium des Inneren, Rotterdam, 7.6.33).

249. Sitzung der Reichstagsfraktion am 10.6.33: Lipinski, 262; Dietrich, 264; Künstler, 264; Saupe, 264, in Matthias, "Sozialdemokratische Partei."

250. See the comments of Jesse and Wellhausen, two lower functionaries who met with Wels et al. in Prague: Besprechung des Prager Parteivorstandes mit Vertretern des Berliner Parteivorstand und der Gruppenvertrauensleute, 9.6.33, in Schulze, *Anpassung oder Widerstand?*, 189; Sitzung der Reichstagsfraktion am 10.6.33: Löbe, 261, in Matthias, "Sozialdemokratische Partei."

251. See Löbe to Otto Braun, 5.6.33, NL Braun, Teil 1/A/12, GStAPK I.HA Rep. 92, and Löbe to Wilhelm Sollmann, 13.6.33, NL Hertz, Film XXIII/33/I/n, AsD. Löbe showed his trust in Göring in March, expressing surprise that the press prohibition had not been lifted after Göring had assured him it would be (Parteiausschuss, 14.3.33: Löbe, 180, in Schulze, *Anpassung oder Widerstand?*). On resentment against the exiles, see Sitzung der Reichstagsfraktion am 10.6.33: Heinig, 265, in Matthias, "Sozialdemokratische Partei."

252. Sitzung der Reichstagsfraktion am 10.6.33: Schumacher, 263, in Matthias, "Sozialdemokratische Partei." Disappointed as he was by the emigration of the executive, Leber nonetheless opposed Löbe's course, but he was in prison through all this (Dorothea Beck, *Julius Leber*, 119).

253. Sopade to Sollmann, 11.6.33, NL Hertz, Film XXIII/33/I/n, AsD. The Prussian Landtag delegation passed a similar resolution the day before.

254. On Schumacher, see Heine, *Kurt Schumacher*, 43. Hans Hirschfeld and others met Haubach and Mierendorff in Zurich in March. After a debate about whether to remain in exile or to return, only Haubach and Mierendorff went back (Hammer, *Theodor Haubach zum Gedächtnis*, 40).

255. Edinger, *Kurt Schumacher*, 51 n. 83, 52; Leithäuser, *Wilhelm Leuschner*, 122. Frey [Pahl], *Deutschland, wohin?* (148–49), also called for a national liberation movement.

256. Besprechung des Prager Parteivorstandes mit Vertretern des Berliner Parteivorstandes und der Gruppenvertrauensleute, 9.6.33, 13.6.33: 188–90, 191–93; Memorandum, 3.6.33, 184–85; all in Schulze, *Anpassung oder Widerstand?*

257. *II*, #35, 24.6.33, 309–10. In its call for resistance, the executive did try to protect Social Democrats inside Germany: "We declare that we alone bear the responsibility for actions, and that no organization or body in Germany can be made to share our responsibility."

258. Notes on the all-national conference held on 19.6.33, n.d., 195–97, in Schulze, *Anpassung oder Widerstand?*; Hoegner, *Flucht*, 229–32.

259. Hoegner, *Flucht*, 232, 281, 293. Ernst Heilmann was murdered in Buchenwald in 1940. For a short biography, see Lösche, "Ernst Heilmann."

Conclusion

1. Hilferding to Kautsky, 9.23.33, NL Kautsky D/XII/661, IISH.

2. Florian Geyer [Hans Muhle], "SPD am Scheideweg," *NB*, Sept. 1932, 454–56.

3. *II*, #36, 1.7.33, 328.

4. *II*, #44, 22.8.33, 433.

5. Kuttner to Stampfer, 2.9.36, NL Stampfer Mappe 8/377, AsD.

6. Lehnert and Megerle, "Politische Identität," 15.

7. Euchner, "Zum sozialdemokratischen Staatsverständnis," 114.

8. Kautsky in a letter to Victor Adler, as quoted by Steinberg, *Sozialismus*, 82. Helga Grebing echoed Kautsky's view: "While the members waited on a 'signal from above,' the leadership hoped for a 'signal from below' . . . in order to share responsibility in a difficult situation" ("Ökonomische Krise und politische Moral," 117).

9. Mierendorff continued to work illegally for a "democratic people's movement" after his release from Buchenwald in 1938. See Richard Albrecht's discussion of the Socialist Action program he drafted for the Kreisauer circle in 1943 (Albrecht, "Carl Mierendorff").

10. von **, "Ist Otto Braun am Ende?," *DF*, #9, 2.2.32.

11. Mierendorff, Haubach, and Leber all died the year before the war ended after having been active in the Kreisauer circle that planned the July 20, 1944, attempt to assassinate Hitler. Mierendorff was killed in an Allied bombing attack on Leipzig in 1944. Haubach and Leber were both arrested after July 20 and executed in early 1945. On the involvement of "militant republicans" in the anti-Nazi resistance, see Moraw, *Parole der "Einheit*," 13–15.

Bibliography

Archival Sources

Archiv der sozialen Demokratie at the Friedrich-Ebert-Stiftung (AsD)
  (Bonn–Bad Godesberg)
  NL Otto Braun (*Teilnachlass*)
  NL Wilhelm Dittmann
  NL Felix Fechenbach
  NL Paul Hertz
  NL Paul Levi
  NL Hermann Müller-Franken (*Teilnachlass*)
  NL Carl Severing
  NL Friedrich Stampfer
  Emigration SOPADE
  Flugblattsammlung, 1928–33
  SPD Broschüre
Archiv des Deutschen Gewerkschaftsbundes (DGB Archiv) (Düsseldorf)
  ADGB Restakten
  NL Franz-Josef Furtwängler
Bundesarchiv (BA) (Koblenz)
  NL Anton Erkelenz
  R45IV (Zentralkomitee der Kommunistischen Partei Deutschlands)
  R58 (Reichssicherheitsamt)
  Plakatsammlung
Geheimes Staatsarchiv, Preussischer Kulturbesitz (GStAPK) (Berlin)
  NL Otto Braun
Hessisches Staatsarchiv (Darmstadt)
  NL Carlo Mierendorff
International Institute of Social History (IISH) (Amsterdam)
  NL Otto Braun (*Teilnachlass*)
  NL Albert Grzesinski
  NL Karl Kautsky
Niedersächsisches Hauptstaatsarchiv Hannover (NHStAH) (Hanover)
  Hann. 310 I, NSDAP Gau Südhannover-Braunschweig und Gau Ost-
    Hannover, 1919–45
  Hann. 310 II, SPD-Bezirk Hannover
Nordrhein-Westfälisches Staatsarchiv Münster (NWStAM) (Münster)
  Reg. Arnsberg
  Reg. Münster
  SPD und Reichsbanner Schwarz-Rot-Gold

NSDAP Hauptarchiv (NSDAP HA) (Hoover Institution Microfilm Collection)
Stadtsarchiv Frankfurt (StAFr) (Frankfurt a.M.)
   Rebentisch, Dieter. "Die Frankfurter SPD in der Weimarer Epoche" (S6a/238 Manuskripte).

Unpublished Memoir

Schmidt, Erich. "Memoiren." Private collection.

Published Documents, Statistics, Government Reports, and Party Proceedings

Akten der Reichskanzlei Weimarer Republik: Das Kabinett Müller II, 3. Juli 1928 bis 27. März 1930. Edited by Martin Vogt. Historische Kommission bei der Bayerischen Akademie der Wissenschaften und das Bundesarchiv. 2 vols. Boppard am Rhein, 1971.
Allgemeiner Deutscher Gewerkschaftsbund. *Protokoll der Verhandlungen des 14. Kongresses der Gewerkschaften Deutschlands. (4. Bundestag des ADGBes), Frankfurt 31.8 bis 4.9.1931.* Berlin, 1931.
————. *Protokoll der Verhandlungen des Ausserordentlichen (15.) Kongresses der Gewerkschaften Deutschlands 13.4.32.* Berlin, 1932.
Falter, J.; Lindenberger, T.; and Schumann, S. *Wahlen und Abstimmungen in der Weimarer Republik.* Munich, 1986.
Die Gewerkschaften in der Endphase der Republik 1930–1933. Compiled, annotated, and introduced by Peter Jahn. Vol. 4, *Quellen zu Geschichte der deutschen Gewerkschaftsbewegung im 20. Jahrhundert.* Edited by Hermann Weber, Klaus Schönhoven, and Klaus Tenfelde. Cologne, 1987.
Die Gewerkschaften von der Stabilisierung bis zur Wirtschaftskrise 1924–1930. Compiled, annotated, and introduced by Horst A. Kukuck and Dieter Schiffmann. Vol. 3, pts. 1 and 2, *Quellen zu Geschichte der deutschen Gewerkschaftsbewegung im 20. Jahrhundert.* Edited by Hermann Weber, Klaus Schönhoven, and Klaus Tenfelde. Cologne, 1986.
Hubatsch, Walther. *Hindenburg und der Staat: Aus den Papieren des Generalfeldmarschalls und Reichspräsidenten von 1878–1934.* Berlin, 1966.
Kempner, M. W. *Der verpasste Nazi-Stopp. Die NSDAP als Staats-und republikfeindliche, hochverräterische Verbindung: Preussischer Denkschrift von 1930.* Frankfurt a.M., 1983.
Petzina, D.; Abelshauser, W.; and Faust, A. *Materialien zur Statistik des deutschen Reichs 1914–1945.* Munich, 1978.
Politik und Wirtschaft in der Krise 1930–1932: Quellen zur Ära Brüning. 2 vols. Introduced by Gerhard Schulz. Edited by Ilse Maurer and Udo Wengst with assistance from Jürgen Heideking. Düsseldorf, 1980.
Reichstag: Stenographische Berichte und Anlagen. 1928–32.

Schulthess' Europäischer Geschichtskalendar. 1931–32.

Schulze, Hagen, ed. *Anpassung oder Widerstand?: Aus den Akten des Parteivor-standes der deutschen Sozialdemokratie 1932/33.* Archiv fur Sozialgeschichte, Supplement 4. Bonn–Bad Godesberg, 1975.

Sozialdemokratische Partei Deutschlands. *Sozialdemokratischer Parteitag 1927 in Kiel: Protokoll mit dem Bericht der Frauenkonferenz.* Bonn–Bad Godes-berg, 1927. Reprint. 1974.

———. *Sozialdemokratischer Parteitag 1929 in Magdeburg: Protokoll. . . .* Bonn–Bad Godesberg, 1929. Reprint. 1974.

———. *Sozialdemokratischer Parteitag 1931 in Leipzig. Protokoll. . . .* Bonn–Bad Godesberg, 1931. Reprint. 1974.

Staat und NSDAP 1930–1932. Quellen zur Ara Brüning. Introduction by Gerhard Schulz. Edited by Ilse Maurer and Udo Wengst. Düsseldorf, 1977.

Statistik des Deutschen Reichs. 1931, 1932.

Newspapers and Periodicals

Die Arbeit
Berliner Tageblatt
Deutsche Führerbriefe
Deutsche Republik
Düsseldorf Volkszeitung
Frankfurter Volksstimme
Das Freie Wort
Die Gesellschaft
Gewerkschafts-Zeitung
Hamburger Echo
Hessischer Volksfreund (Darmstadt)
International Information
Jungsozialistische Blätter
Der Klassenkampf
Leipziger Volkszeitung
Marxistische Tribüne für Politik und Wirtschaft
Neue Blätter für den Sozialismus
Das Reichsbanner
Rheinische Zeitung (Cologne)
Rote Fahne
Schwäbische Tagwacht (Stuttgart)
Sozialistische Monatshefte
Sozialistische Politik und Wirtschaft
Unser Weg
Völkischer Beobachter
Volkswacht (Breslau)

Volkswacht (Essen)
Volkswacht (Hanover)
Vorwärts

Contemporary Books, Pamphlets, and Memoirs

ADGB, Vorstand. *Arbeitsbeschaffung: Die Forderung der Gewerkschaften*. Berlin,
  1932.
————. *Geheim! Geheim! Neueste Nazibefehle gegen Gewerkschaften, gegen Ham-*
  merschaften. Berlin, 1932.
————. *Gewerkschaften, Friedensvertrag, Reparationen*. Berlin, 1931.
————. *Jahrbuch des Allgemeinen Deutschen Gewerkschaftsbundes für das Jahr*
  1930. Berlin, 1931.
————. *Jahrbuch des Allgemeinen Deutschen Gewerkschaftsbundes für das Jahr*
  1931. Berlin, 1932.
————. *Klassenverrat?* Berlin, 1933.
————. *Leipart und Breitscheid über die Notverordnung*. Berlin, 1931.
————. *Material aus dem Bericht des Bezirksausschusses an die 4.ordentliche*
  Bezirkskonferenz in Düsseldorf am 18. November 1931. Berlin, 1931.
————. *Umbau der Wirtschaft: Die Forderungen der Gewerkschaften*. Berlin, 1932.
Aufhäuser, Siegfried. *Ideologie und Taktik der Angestellten-Bewegung: Referat*
  gehalten auf dem 4. AfA-Gewerkschaftskongress, 1931 in Leipzig. Berlin, 1931.
Bernstein, Eduard. *Evolutionary Socialism*. New York, 1961.
Bieligk, Fritz, et al. *Die Organisation im Klassenkampf*. Berlin, 1931.
Bienstock, Gregor. *Kampf um die Macht: Zur neuen Politik der Sozialdemokratie*.
  N.p., 1932.
Borinski, Fritz. "Die 'Neue Blätter für den Sozialismus': Ein Organ der
  jungen Generation von 1930 bis 1933." In *Ein Arbeiterleben: Erinnerungen*
  an Weimar und danach, by August Rathmann. Wuppertal, 1983.
Brandt, Willy. *Links und frei: Mein Weg 1930–1950*. Hamburg, 1982.
Braun, Otto. *Von Weimar zu Hitler*. New York, 1940.
Brecht, Arnold. *Mit der Kraft des Geistes: Lebenserinnerungen 1927–1967*, vol.
  2. Stuttgart, 1967.
Brüning, Heinrich. *Memoiren 1918–1934*. Stuttgart, 1970.
Chakhotin, Sergei. *The Rape of the Masses: The Psychology of Totalitarian Politi-*
  cal Propaganda. London, 1940.
Curius, D. *Otto Hörsings Kriegsplan zur Niederringung der Arbeitslosigkeit*.
  Berlin, 1931.
Decker, Georg. *So kommen wir zum Sozialismus*. N.p., 1932.
Deutscher Metallverein, ed. *Der Nationalsozialismus in Theorie und Praxis*.
  Berlin, n.d.
Deutschnationale Schriftenvertriebstelle, ed. *Das Reichsbanner Schwarz-Rot-*
  Gold. N.p., 1928.
Düwell, Bernhard. *Gewerkschaften und Nationalsozialismus*. Berlin, 1931.

Das Ergebnis des Leipziger Parteitages—Der Standpunkt der Opposition. KK Sonderheft #3. Berlin, 1931.

Erkelenz, Anton. *Um die Einheit der deutschen Gewerkschaftsbewegung.* Cologne, 1932.

Feder, Ernst. *Heute sprach ich mit . . . Tagebücher eines Berliner Publizisten 1926–1932.* Stuttgart, 1971.

Flatau, Erich. *Zum "Sklarek Skandal."* Berlin, 1929.

Fraenkel, Ernst. *Reformismus und Pluralismus: Materialien zu einer ungeschriebenen politischen Autobiographie.* Edited by F. Esche and F. Grube. Hamburg, 1973.

Frey, Lothar. *Deutschland, wohin?* Zurich, 1934.

Fromm, Erich. *The Working Class in Weimar Germany: A Psychological and Sociological Study.* Introduction by W. Bonss. Cambridge, Mass., 1984.

Graf, Engelbert. *Die Faschistische Gefahr.* Leipzig, 1930.

Grzesinski, Albert. *Inside Germany.* New York, 1939.

Hammer, Walter, ed. *Theodor Haubach zum Gedächtnis.* Frankfurt, 1955.

Heller, Hermann. *Europa and der Faschismus.* Berlin/Leipzig, 1931.

Hilferding, Rudolf. *Nach den Wahlen: Referat des Genossen Dr. Hilferding vor dem Parteiausschuss am 4. Mai 1932.* Berlin, 1932.

———. *Nationalsozialismus und Marxismus.* Berlin, 1932.

Hoegner, Wilhelm. *Flucht vor Hitler. Erinnerungen an die Kapitulation der ersten deutschen Republik.* Munich, 1978.

———. *Der schwierige Aussenseiter: Erinnerungen eines Abgeordneten, Emigranten und Ministerpräsidenten.* Munich, 1959.

———. *Die Verratene Republik: Geschichte der deutschen Gegenrevolution.* Munich, 1958.

Keil, Wilhelm. *Erlebnisse eines Sozialdemokraten.* 2 vols. Stuttgart, 1948.

———. *Wisst Ihr das?: Was mit der demokratischen Republik erreicht wurde.* Berlin, 1932.

Klinger, Max [Curt Geyer]. *Volk in Ketten.* Karlsbad, 1934.

Knickerbocker, H. R. *Deutschland so oder so?* Berlin, 1932.

KPD, ed. *Hindenburg oder Thälmann.* Berlin, 1932.

———. *Inflation und Massenelend.* Berlin, 1931.

———. *Krisenkongress des ADGB: Material für Referenten und Diskussionsredner in Betriebs-und Gewerkschaftsversammlungen.* Berlin, 1932.

———. *SPD Arbeiter fragt: Wir antworten.* N.p., 1931.

———. *Was ist die "Eiserne Front"?* Berlin, 1932.

———. *Wer regiert? Wer kommandiert? Wer toleriert?* Berlin, 1932.

———. *Wo bleibt der zweite Mann?* Berlin, 1931.

Kühn, Heinz. *Widerstand und Emigration: Die Jahren 1928–1945.* Hamburg, 1980.

Kuttner, Erich. *Otto Braun.* Berlin, [1932].

Landauer, Carl. "Erinnerungen an die Münchner Sozialdemokratie." In *Von Juden in München,* edited by Hans Lamm. Munich, 1958.

Landsberg, Otto. *Die politische Krise der Gegenwart*. Berlin, 1931.

Leber, Julius. *Ein Mann geht seinen Weg*. Berlin, 1952.

————. "Die Todesursachen der deutschen Sozialdemokratie." In *Julius Leber: Schriften, Reden, und Briefen*, edited by Dorothea Beck and Wilfried F. Schoeller. Munich, 1976.

Lederer, Emil. *Kapitalismus, Klassenstruktur und Probleme der Demokratie in Deutschland, 1910–1940*. Edited by Jürgen Kocka. Afterword, "Emil Lederer: Leben und Werk," by Hans Speier. Göttingen, 1979.

————. *Die Umwälzung in der Wirtschaft und die 40 Stunde Woche: Vortrag, gehalten auf dem 14. Kongress der Gewerkschaften Deutschlands in Frankfurt a.M. 1931*. Berlin, 1931.

————. *Wege aus der Krise*. Tübingen, 1931.

Leipart, Theodor, et al. *Gegen den Wirtschaftsplan der Papen-Regierung: Gegen die Misswirtschaft des Kapitalismus*. Öffentliche Kundgebung des ADGB und AfA-Bundes. N.p., [1931].

Lemmer, Ernst. *Manches war doch anders*. Frankfurt, 1966.

Löbe, Paul. *Sozialismus! Ja oder Nein?* Berlin, 1932.

Loewenstein-Scharffeneck, Prince Hubertus. *The Tragedy of a Nation*. New York, 1934.

Marck, Siegfried. "Sozialdemokratie." In *Die geistige Struktur der Parteien Europas: Deutsches Reich*, edited by Kurt Metzner. Berlin, [1931].

Michels, Robert. *Political Parties: A Sociological Study of the Oligarchical Tendencies of Modern Democracy*. Glencoe, Ill., 1949.

Mierendorff, Carlo. *Zehn Jahre nach dem Kapp-Putsch*. Berlin, 1930.

Neumann, Sigmund. *Die Parteien der Weimarer Republik*. Stuttgart, 1970.

Noske, Gustav. *Erlebtes aus Aufstieg und Niedergang einer Demokratie*. Offenbach/Main, 1947.

Prager, Eugen. *Wer hat uns verraten?* N.p., 1932.

Pünder, Hermann. *Politik in der Reichskanzlei: Aufzeichnungen aus den Jahren 1929–1932*. Edited by Thilo Vogelsang. Stuttgart, 1967.

Rathmann, August. *Ein Arbeiterleben: Erinnerungen an Weimar und danach*. Wuppertal, 1983.

Remmele, Adam. *Die Fritterkrippe: Eine Auseinandersetzung mit den Nationalsozialisten*. Berlin, 1931.

Sender, Toni. *Autobiography of a German Rebel*. New York, 1939.

Severing, Carl. *Mein Lebensweg*. 2 vols. Cologne, 1950.

Seydewitz, Max, et al. *Krise des Kapitalismus und die Aufgabe der Arbeiterklasse*. Berlin, 1931.

SPD-Kassel. *Zehn Jahre Revolution: Gedenkfeier*. Kassel, [1928].

SPD, Landesarbeitsausschuss der SPD Sachsens. *Material II zur Landtagswahl: Die Gegner in Sachsen*. Dresden, 1929.

SPD, Vorstand. *Agitations Sprechchöre: Reichstagswahl 1932*. N.p., [1932].

————. *An der Stempelstelle: Ein Wahlgespräch*. Berlin, [1932].

————. *An die Bezirksleitungen!* N.p., [1932].

————. *Diktatur!* Berlin, 1931.

————. *Das Gespenst der Arbeitslosigkeit und die Vorschläge der SPD zu ihrer Überwindung.* [Berlin], 1931.

————. *Jahrbuch der deutschen Sozialdemokratie für das Jahr 1928.* Berlin, 1929.

————. *Jahrbuch der deutschen Sozialdemokratie für das Jahr 1929.* Berlin, 1930.

————. *Jahrbuch der deutschen Sozialdemokratie für das Jahr 1930.* Berlin, 1931.

————. *Jahrbuch der deutschen Sozialdemokratie für das Jahr 1931.* Berlin, 1932.

————. *Köpfe in den Sand?: Die wirklichen Novemberverbrecher.* Berlin, [1930].

————. *Materialien zur politischen Situation bei Beginn des Reichstages August 1932 und zu Anträgen der Sozialdemokratie auf Umbau der Wirtschaft und Sicherstellung der Existenz der notleidenden Schichten.* Berlin, 1932.

————. *Material-Sammlung gegen die Nationalsozialisten: Für Redner und Funktionäre.* Berlin, 1930.

————. *Nationalsozialismus und Frauenfragen.* Berlin, 1932.

————. *Die neue Notverordnung: Material für die Referenten der Sozialdemokratischen Partei.* Berlin, 1931.

————. *Referentenmaterial: Nr. 3. 1931.* Berlin, 1931.

————. *Reichstagswahl 1930: Referentenmaterial.* Berlin, 1930.

————. *Reichstagswahl 31. Juli 1932: Rededisposition und Referentenmaterial.* Berlin, 1932.

————. *Reichstagswahl 6. November 1932: Redevorschlag und Rednermaterial.* Berlin, 1932.

————. *Sozialdemokratische-Partei-Korrespondenz (Ergänzungsband 1923–1928).* Berlin, 1930.

————. *Um die Macht! Nach der Präsidentenwahl, Neuwahlen in Preussen, Bayern, Württemberg, Anhalt und Hamburg. Rededisposition.* Berlin, 1932.

————. *Wichtiges Material für die Landagitation.* N.p., 1931.

SPD, Vorstand des Bezirks Berlin. *Berlin Jahresbericht 1931.* Berlin, [1932].

SPD, Vorstand des Unterbezirks Gross-Leipzig. *Gross-Leipzig Jahresbericht.* Leipzig, 1928.

SPD, Vorstand des Unterbezirks Hamburg. *Tätigkeitsbericht 1929–30.* N.p., [1931].

Stampfer, Friedrich. *Erfahrungen und Erkenntnisse: Aufzeichnungen aus meinem Leben.* Cologne, 1957.

————. *Die Vierzehn Jahre der ersten deutschen Republik.* Karlsbad, 1936.

Staudinger, Hans. *The Inner Nazi: A Critical Analysis of "Mein Kampf."* Edited with an introduction and a biographical afterword by Peter M. Rutkoff and William B. Scott. Baton Rouge, 1981.

————. *Wirtschaftspolitik im Weimarer Staat: Lebenserinnerungen eines politischen Beamten im Reich und in Preussen 1889 bis 1934.* Bonn, 1982.

Stenbock-Fermor, Graf Alexander. *Deutschland von unten: Reise durch die proletarische Provinz.* Stuttgart, 1931.

Weber, August. "Zwei mütige Reden." Breitscheid, Rudolf. "Eine
    Reichstagsrede." In *Wider den Nationalsozialismus*, Republikanische Biblio-
    thek, Bd. II. Berlin, [1932].
Wels, Otto, et al. *Eiserne Front: Vier Aufrüfe*. Berlin, 1932.
Woytinsky, Wladimir. *Internationale Hebung der Preise als Ausweg aus der Krise*.
    Leipzig, 1931.
————. *Stormy Passage*. New York, 1961.
Zuckmayer, Carl. *Carlo Mierendorff*. N.p., 1944.

Secondary Literature

Abendroth, Wolfgang. *Aufstieg und Krise der deutschen Sozialdemokratie: Das
    Problem der Zweckentfremdung einer politischen Partei durch die Anpassungsten-
    denz von Institutionen an vorgegebene Machtverhältnissse*. Cologne, 1978.
Abraham, David. *The Collapse of the Weimar Republic*. Princeton, 1981.
Abrams, Lynn. *Workers' Culture in Imperial Germany: Leisure and Recreation in
    the Rhineland and Westphalia*. London and New York, 1992.
Adolph, Hans J. *Otto Wels und die Politik der deutschen Sozialdemokratie 1894–
    1939*. Berlin, 1971.
Agulhon, Maurice. *The Republic in the Village: The People of the Var from the
    French Revolution to the Second Republic*. Cambridge, 1982.
Albrecht, Richard. "Carl Mierendorff und das Konzept einer demokrati-
    schen Volksbewegung." In *Der Widerstand gegen den Nationalsozialismus:
    Die deutsche Gesellschaft und der Widerstand gegen Hitler*, edited by
    J. Schmädeke and P. Steinbach. Munich, 1985.
————. *Der militante Sozialdemokrat: Carlo Mierendorff 1897–1943. Eine Bio-
    graphie*. Berlin/Bonn, 1987.
————. "Symbolkampf in Deutschland 1932: Sergej Tschachotin und der
    'Symbolkrieg' der drei Pfeile gegen den Nationalsozialismus als Episode
    im Abwehrkampf der Arbeiterbewegung gegen Faschismus in Deutsch-
    land." *Internationale Wissenschaftliche Korrespondenz zur Geschichte der
    deutschen Arbeiterbewegung* 22 (1986): 498–533.
Allen, William Sheridan. *The Nazi Seizure of Power: The Experience of a Single
    German Town, 1922–1945*. Rev. ed. New York, 1984.
Andersen, Arno. "Die KPD und die nationalsozialistische Marchtüber-
    nahme. Ein Rundschreiben der KPD vom 2. Februar 1933." *Internationale
    Wissenschaftliche Korrespondenz zur Geschichte der deutschen Arbeiterbewegung*
    22 (1986): 368–69.
Arns, Günter. "Die Linke in der SPD Reichstagsfraktion im Herbst 1923."
    Vierteljahrshefte für Zeitgeschichte 22 (1974): 191–203.
Aviv, Aviva. "The SPD and the KPD at the End of the Weimar Republic:
    Similarity within Contrast." *Internationale Wissenschaftliche Korrespondenz
    zur Geschichte der deutschen Arbeiterbewegung* 14 (1978): 171–86.
Bahne, Siegfried. "Die Kommunistische Partei Deutschlands." In *Das Ende*

der Parteien 1933, edited by Erich Matthias and Rudolf Morsey. Düsseldorf, 1960.

———. *The KPD und das Ende von Weimar: Das Scheitern einer Politik 1932–1935*. Frankfurt, 1976.

Barkai, Avraham. *Das Wirtschaftssystem des Nationalsozialismus: Der historische und ideologische Hintergrund 1933–1936*. Cologne, 1977.

Beck, Dorothea. *Julius Leber: Sozialdemokrat zwischen Reform und Widerstand.* Berlin, 1983.

———. "Theodor Haubach, Julius Leber, Carlo Mierendorff, Kurt Schumacher: Zum Selbstverständnis der 'militanten Sozialisten' in der Weimarer Republik," *Archiv für Sozialgeschichte* 26 (1986): 87–133.

Beck, Earl. *The Death of the Prussian Republic.* Tallahassee, 1959.

Beier, Gerhard. *Arbeiterbewegung in Hessen.* Frankfurt a.M., 1985.

———. "Zur Entstehung des Führerkreises der vereinigten Gewerkschaften Ende April 1933." *Archiv für Sozialgeschichte* 25 (1975): 365–92.

Beradt, Charlotte. *Ein demokratischer Sozialist in der Weimarer Republik.* Frankfurt a.M., 1969.

Berghahn, Volker R. "Das Volksbegehren gegen den Young Plan und die Ursprünge des Präsidialregimes, 1928–1930." In *Industrielle Gesellschaft und politisches System: Beiträge zur politischen Sozialgeschichte*, edited by Dirk Stegmann and Peter-Christian Witt. Bonn, 1978.

Besson, Waldemar. *Württemberg und die deutsche Staatskrise 1928–1933: eine Studie der Auflösung der Weimarer Republik.* Stuttgart, 1959.

Birker, Karl. *Die deutschen Arbeiterbildungsvereine.* Berlin, 1973.

Blackbourn, David. *Populists and Patricians.* London, 1987.

Böhnke, Wilfried. *Die NSDAP im Ruhrgebiet 1920–1933.* Bonn–Bad Godesberg, 1974.

Boll, Friedhelm. *Massenbewegungen in Niedersachsen 1906 bis 1920: Eine sozialgeschichtliche Untersuchung zu den unterschiedlichen Entwicklungstypen Braunschweig und Hannover.* Bonn, 1981.

———. "Vergleichende Aspekte europäische Arbeiterkulturbewegung." In *Arbeiterkulturen zwischen Alltag und Politik: Beiträge zum europäischen Vergleich in der Zwischenkriegszeit*, edited by Friedhelm Boll. Zurich, 1986.

Borchardt, Knut. *Wachstum, Krise, Handlungsspielräume der Wirtschaftspolitik.* Göttingen, 1982.

Bowlby, Chris. "Blutmai 1929: Police, Parties and Proletarians in a Berlin Confrontation." *Historical Journal* 29 (1986): 137–58.

Bracher, Karl Dietrich. "Der 20. Juli 1932." *Zeitschrift für Politik* 3 (1956): 243–49.

———. *Die Auflösung der Weimarer Republik.* Stuttgart, 1957.

Bracher, Karl Dietrich; Sauer, Wolfgang; and Schulz, Gerhard. *Die nationalsozialistische Machtergreifung: Studien zur Errichtung des totalitären Herrschaftssystems in Deutschlands 1933/34.* Cologne, 1962.

Bramke, Werner. "Das Faschismusbild in der KPD Mitte 1929 bis Anfang 1933." *Beiträge zur Geschichte der Arbeiterbewegung* 28 (1986): 612–21.

Brauckmüller, Bernd, and Hartmann, Reinhard. "Organisierter Kapitalismus und Krise." In *Sozialdemokratische Arbeiterbewegung und Weimarer Republik: Materialien zur gesellschaftlichen Entwicklung 1927–1933*, edited by Wolfgang Luthardt, vol. 1. Frankfurt a.M., 1978.

Braunthal, Gerard. *Socialist Labor and Politics in Weimar Germany*. Hamden, Conn., 1978.

Breitman, Richard. *German Social Democracy and the Weimar Republic*. Chapel Hill, 1981.

———. "Nazism in the Eyes of German Social Democracy." In *Towards the Holocaust: The Social and Economic Collapse of the Weimar Republic*, edited by Michael N. Dubkowski and Isidor Wallimann. Westport, Conn., 1983.

———. "Negative Integration and Parliamentary Politics: Literature on German Social Democracy, 1890–1933." *Central European History* 13 (1980): 175–97.

———. "On German Social Democracy and General Schleicher, 1932–1933." *Central European History* 9 (1976): 352–78.

———. "Socialism and the Parliamentary System in Germany, 1918–1933: The Political Strategy of the German Social Democratic Party Leaders." Ph.D. dissertation, Harvard University, 1975.

Bridenthal, Renate, and Koonz, Claudia. "Beyond Kinder, Küche, Kirche: Weimar Women in Politics and Work." In *When Biology Became Destiny: Women in Weimar and Nazi Germany*, edited by Renate Bridenthal, Atina Grossmann, and Marion Kaplan. New York, 1984.

Brose, Eric Dorn. *Christian Labor and the Politics of Frustration in Imperial Germany*. Washington, D.C., 1985.

Broszat, Martin. "Zur Struktur der NS-Massenbewegung." *Vierteljahrshefte für Zeitgeschichte* 31 (1983): 52–76.

Brücher, Bodo, and Hartmann, Günter. "Die Sozialistische Arbeiterjugend in der Weimarer Republik: Ihr Verhältnis zur SPD und ihr Eintreten für die Republik." *Jahrbuch des Archivs der deutschen Jugendbewegung* 13 (1981): 35–50.

Büttner, Ursula. *Hamburg in der Staats-und Wirtschaftskrise 1928–1931*. Hamburg, 1982.

———. "Die Politik der Hamburger SPD in der Endphase der Weimarer Republik." In *Arbeiter in Hamburg: Unterschichten, Arbeiter und Arbeiterbewegung seit dem ausgehenden 18. Jahrhundert*, edited by Arno Herzig, Dieter Langewiesche, and Arnold Sywottek. Hamburg, 1983.

———. "Politische Alternativen zum Brüningschen Deflationskurs." *Vierteljahrshefte für Zeitgeschichte* 37 (1989): 209–51.

———. "Die politische Haltung der Hamburger Freien Gewerkwschaften in der Weltwirtschaftskrise." In *Arbeiter in Hamburg: Unterschichten, Arbeiter und Arbeiterbewegung seit dem ausgehenden 18. Jahrhundert*, edited by Arno Herzig, Dieter Langewiesche, and Arnold Sywottek. Hamburg, 1983.

Caspar, Gustav Adolf. *Die sozialdemokratische Partei und das deutsche Wehrproblem in den Jahren der Weimarer Republik*. Frankfurt, 1959.

Chickering, Roger. "The Reichsbanner and the Weimar Republic, 1924–1926." *Journal of Modern History* 40 (1968): 524–34.

Childers, Thomas. *The Nazi Voter: the Social Foundations of Fascism, 1919–1933*. Chapel Hill, 1983.

———. "The Social Language of Politics in Germany: The Sociology of Political Discourse in the Weimar Republic." *American Historical Review* 95 (Apr. 1990): 331–58.

Comfort, Richard. *Revolutionary Hamburg*. Stanford, 1966.

Conze, Werner. "Die politische Entscheidungen in Deutschland 1929–1933." In *Die Staats- und Wirtschaftskrise des deutschen Reiches 1920/33*, edited by Werner Conze and Hans Raupach. Stuttgart, 1967.

Conze, Werner, and Groh, Dieter. *Die Arbeiterbewegung in der nationalen Bewegung*. Stuttgart, 1966.

Craig, Gordon. *Germany, 1866–1945*. New York, 1978.

Crew, David. *Town in the Ruhr: A Social History of Bochum, 1860–1914*. New York, 1979.

Dahrendorf, Ralf. *Society and Democracy in Germany*. Garden City, N.J., 1967.

Deppe, Frank, and Rossmann, Witich. "Hätte der Faschismus verhindert werden können?: Gewerkschaften, SPD und KPD 1929–33." *Blätter für deutsche und internationale Politik* 28 (1989): 18–29.

———. *Wirtschaftskrise, Faschismus, Gewerkschaften*. Cologne, 1983.

Dertinger, Antje. "Toni Pfülf." In *Vor dem Vergessen bewahren: Lebenswege Weimarer Sozialdemokraten*, edited by Peter Lösche, Michael Scholing, and Franz Walter. Berlin, 1988.

Dorpalen, Andreas. *Hindenburg and the Weimar Republic*. Princeton, 1964.

———. "SPD und KPD in der Endphase der Weimarer Republik." *Vierteljahrshefte für Zeitgeschichte* 31 (1983): 77–107.

Drechsler, Hanno. *Die Sozialistische Arbeiterpartei Deutschlands: Ein Beitrag zur Geschichte der deutschen Arbeiterbewegung am Ende der Weimarer Republik*. Meisenheim am Glan, 1965.

Edinger, Lewis. *German Exile Politics*. Berkeley, 1956.

———. *Kurt Schumacher: A Study in Personality and Political Behavior*. Stanford, 1965.

Ehni, Hans-Peter. *Bollwerk Preussen?: Preussen-Regierung, Reich-Länder Problem und Sozialdemokratie*. Bonn–Bad Godesberg, 1975.

Eisenberg, Christine. "Chartismus und Allgemeiner Deutscher Arbeiterverein: Die Entstehung der politischen Arbeiterbewegung in England und Deutschland." In *"Der kühnen Bahn nur folgen wir . . .": Ursprünge, Erfolge und Grenze der Arbeiterbewegung in Deutschland*. Bd. 1, *Entstehung und*

Wandel der deutschen Arbeiterbewegung, edited by Arno Herzig and Günter Trautmann. Hamburg, 1989.

Eley, Geoff. *From Unification to Nazism*. Boston, 1986.

———. "Labor History, Social History, *Alltagsgeschichte*: Experience, Culture, and the Politics of the Everyday—a New Direction for German Social History." *Journal of Modern History* 61 (June 1989): 297–343.

Eley, Geoff, and Blackbourn, David. *The Peculiarities of German History: Bourgeois Society and Politics in Nineteenth Century Germany*. Oxford, 1984.

Emig, Brigitte. *Die Veredelung des Arbeiters: Sozialdemokratie als Kulturbewegung*. Frankfurt a.M., 1980.

Emig, Dieter, and Zimmermann, Rüdiger. "Das Ende einer Legende: Gewerkschaften, Papen und Schleicher. Gefälschte und echte Protokolle." *Internationale Wissenschaftliche Korrespondenz zur Geschichte der deutschen Arbeiterbewegung* 12 (1976): 19–43.

Erdmann, Karl Dietrich, and Schulze, Hagen. *Weimar: Selbstpreisgabe einer Demokratie. Eine Bilanz Heute*. Düsseldorf, 1980.

Euchner, Walter. "Sozialdemokratie und Demokratie: Zum Demokratieverständnis der SPD in der Weimarer Republik." *Archiv für Sozialgeschichte* 26 (1986): 125–78.

———. "Zum sozialdemokratischen Staatsverständnis zwischen den Weltkriegen: Einige Beobachtungen." In *Reformsozialismus und Sozialdemokratie*, edited by Horst Heimann and Thomas Meyer. Berlin, 1982.

Eyck, Erich. *Geschichte der Weimarer Republik*. 2 vols. Zurich, 1965.

———. *A History of the Weimar Republic*. 2 vols. New York, 1963.

Falter, Jürgen. "Der Aufstieg der NSDAP in Franken bei den Reichstagswahlen 1924–1933." *German Studies Review* 9 (May 1986): 319–59.

———. "Politische Konsequenzen von Massenarbeitslosigkeit: Neue Daten zu Kontroversen Thesen über die Radikalisierung der Wählerschaft am Ende der Weimarer Republik." *Politische Vierteljahresschrift* 25 (1984): 277–95.

———. "Die Wähler der NSDAP 1928–1933: Sozialstruktur und parteipolitische Herkunft." In *Die nationalsozialistische Machtergreifung*, edited by Wolfgang Michalka. Munich, 1984.

Falter, Jürgen W., and Hänisch, Dirk. "Die Anfälligkeit von Arbeitern gegenüber der NSDAP 1928–1933." *Archiv für Sozialgeschichte* 26 (1986): 179–216.

Farr, Ian. "Populism in the Countryside: The Peasant Leagues in Bavaria in the 1890's." In *Society and Politics in Imperial Germany*, edited by Richard J. Evans. New York, 1978.

Faust, Anselm. "Von der Fürsorge zur Arbeitsmarktpolitik: Die Errichtung der Arbeitslosenversicherung." In *Die Weimarer Republik als Wohlfahrtsstaat: Zum Verhältnis von Wirtschafts-und Sozialpolitik in der Industriegesellschaft*, edited by Werner Abelshauser. *Vierteljahrsschrift für Sozial-und Wirtschaftsgeschichte*, Beiheft 81. Stuttgart, 1987.

Feldman, Gerald. "Von Krise zu Krise: Zu Heinrich August Winklers Ersten Beiden Bänden über die Geschichte der 'Arbeiter und Arbeiterbewegung in der Weimarer Republik.'" *Historische Zeitschrift* 242 (June 1986): 629–38.

———. "The Weimar Republic: A Problem of Modernization?" *Archiv für Sozialgeschichte* 26 (1986): 1–26.

Fichter, Michael. "'Es ist nicht so gekommen, wie man gehofft hat': Erinnerungen Sozialdemokratischer Funktionäre in Stuttgart." In *"Wir kriegen jetzt andere Zeiten": Auf der Suche nach der Erfahrung des Volkes in nachfaschistischen Ländern*, edited by Lutz Niethammer and Alexander von Plato. Vol. 3 of *Lebensgeschichte und Sozialkultur im Ruhrgebiet 1930 bis 1960.* Bonn, 1985.

Fischer, Conan. "Class Enemies or Class Brothers?: Communist-Nazi Relations in Germany, 1929–32." *European History Quarterly* 15 (1985): 259–79.

———. *The German Communists and the Rise of Nazism.* New York, 1991.

Fischer-Defoy, Christine. "20.000 gemeinsam gegen die Nazis." In *Hessen vor 50 Jahren-1933: Nazi Terror und antifaschistischer Widerstand zwischen Kassel und Bergstrasse 1932–1933*, edited by Ulrich Schneider. Frankfurt a.M., 1983.

Fischoff, Baruch. "For Those Condemned to Study the Past: Heuristics and Biases in Hindsight." In *Judgment under Uncertainty: Heuristics and Biases*, edited by D. Kahneman, P. Slovic, and A. Tversky. New York, 1982.

Fletcher, Roger. "Recent Developments in West German Historiography: The Bielefeld School and Its Critics." *German Studies Review* 7 (1984): 451–80.

Frevert, Ute. *Women in German History.* Oxford/Hamburg/New York, 1989.

Fricke, Dieter. *Zur Organisation und Tätigkeit der deutschen Arbeiterbewegung (1890–1914).* Berlin [East], 1962.

Friedemann, Peter. "Die Krise der Arbeitersportbewegung am Ende der Weimarer Republik." In *Arbeiterkulturen zwischen Alltag und Politik: Beiträge zum europäischen Vergleich in der Zwischenkriegszeit*, edited by Friedhelm Boll. Zurich, 1986.

Fritzsche, Peter. *Rehearsals for Fascism: Populism and Political Mobilization in Weimar Germany.* New York and Oxford, 1990.

Fülberth, Georg. *Die Beziehungen zwischen SPD und KPD in der Kommunalpolitik der Weimarer Periode 1918/19 bis 1933.* Cologne, 1985.

———. "Die Übereinkunft zwischen SPD and KPD in Braunschweig nach den Kommunalwahlen vom 1. März 1931." In *Deutsche Arbeiterbewegung vor dem Faschismus*, edited by Heike Haumann and Axel Schildt. Berlin, 1981.

Furet, Francois. *Interpreting the French Revolution.* Cambridge, 1981.

Gates, Robert A. "The Economic Policies of the German Free Trade Unions and the German Social Democratic Party, 1930–1933." Ph.D. dissertation. University of Oregon, 1970.

――――. "German Socialism and the Crisis of 1929–1933." *Central European History* 7 (1974): 332–59.

――――. "Von der Sozialpolitik zur Wirtschaftspolitik?: Das Dilemma der deutschen Sozialdemokratie in der Krise 1929–1933." In *Industrielles System und politische Entwicklung in der Weimarer Republik*, edited by Hans Mommsen, Dietmar Petzina, and Bernd Weisbrod, vol. 1. Düsseldorf, 1977.

Gay, Peter. *The Dilemma of Democratic Socialism: Eduard Bernstein's Challenge to Marx*. New York, 1962.

Geary, Dick. *European Labour Protest*. London, 1981.

――――. "The German Labour Movement, 1848–1919." *English Studies Review* 6 (1976): 297–330.

――――. "Identifying Militancy: The Assessment of Working-Class Attitudes toward State and Society." In *The German Working Class, 1888–1933*, edited by Richard J. Evans. London, 1982.

――――. "Nazis and Workers: A Response to Conan Fischer's 'Class Enemies or Class Brothers?'" *European History Quarterly* 15 (1985): 453–64.

――――. "Unemployment and Working-Class Solidarity: The German Experience, 1929–33." In *The German Unemployed*, edited by Richard J. Evans and Dick Geary. New York, 1987.

Geiss, Imanuel. "The Weimar Republic between the Second and the Third Reich: Continuity and Discontinuity in the German Question, 1919–1933." In *The Burden of German History, 1919–1925*, edited by Michael Laffan. London, 1988.

Glees, Anthony. "Albert Grzesinski and the Politics of Prussia, 1926–1930." *English Historical Review* 89 (1974): 814–34.

Gotschlich, Helga. "Zur Organisationsstruktur der SPD in Januar 1933." *Jahrbuch für Geschichte* 27 (1983): 35–39.

――――. *Zwischen Kampf und Kapitulation: Zur Geschichte des Reichsbanners Schwarz-Rot-Gold*. Berlin [East], 1987.

Gotthardt, Christian. *Industrialisierung, bürgerliche Politik und proletarische Autonome: Voraussetzungen und Varianten sozialistischer Klassenorganisationen in Nordwestdeutschland 1863 bis 1875*. Bonn, 1992.

Gottschalch, Wilhelm. *Strukturveränderungen der Gesellschaft und politisches Handeln in der Lehre von Rudolf Hilferding*. Berlin, 1962.

Gransow, Volker, and Krätke, Michael. "Vom 'Koalitionspopo', von unsozialistischen Praktikern und unpraktischen Sozialisten: Paul Levi oder Dilemmata von Linkssozialismus in der Sozialdemokratie." In *Solidargemeinschaft und Klassenkampf*, edited by Richard Saage. Frankfurt a.M., 1986.

Grebing, Helga. "Auseinandersetzung mit dem National-Sozialismus." In *Sozialdemokratische Arbeiterbewegung und Weimarer Republik: Materialien zur gesellschaftlichen Entwicklung 1927–1933*, edited by Wolfgang Luthardt, vol. 2. Frankfurt a.M., 1978.

————. "Faschismus, Mittelschichten und Arbeiterklasse. Probleme der Faschismus-Interpretation in den sozialistischen Linken während der Weltwirtschaftskrise." *Internationale Wissenschaftliche Korrespondenz zur Geschichte der deutschen Arbeiterbewegung* 12 (1976): 443–60.

————. "Gewerkschaftliches Verhalten in der politischen Krise der Jahre 1930–1933." Sonderdruck aus *Gewerkschafts-Zeitung*. Reprints zur Sozialgeschichte. Bonn, 1982.

————. "Ökonomische Krise und politische Moral: Thesen zur Niederlage der organisierten Arbeiterschaft im Kampf gegen den deutschen Faschismus." Offprint from *Idee und Pragmatik in der politischen Entscheidung*, edited by Bernd Rebe, Klaus Lompe, and Rudolf von Thadden. Bonn–Bad Godesberg, n.d.

————. *Der Revisionismus: von Bernstein bis zum "Prager Frühling."* Munich, 1977.

————. "Sozialdemokratische Arbeiterbewegung am Ende der Weimarer Republik: Der Fall Emden." *Beiträge zur niedersächsischen Landesgeschichte*, Sonderband (1984): 475–500.

————. "Thesen zur Niederlage der organisierten Arbeiterschaft im Kampf gegen den deutschen Faschismus." In *Aufstieg des Nationalsozialismus, Untergang der Republik, Zerschlagung der Gewerkschaften: Beiträge zur Geschichte der Arbeiterbewegung zwischen Demokratie und Diktatur*, edited by Ernst Breit. Cologne, 1984.

Grill, Johnpeter. *The Nazi Movement in Baden, 1920–1945.* Chapel Hill, 1983.

Groh, Dieter. *Negative Integration und Revolutionärer Attentismus: Die deutsche Sozialdemokratie am Vorabend des Ersten Weltkrieges.* Frankfurt a.M., 1973.

Gruber, Helmut. *Red Vienna: Experiment in Working-Class Culture.* Oxford, 1991.

Grübler, Michael. *Die Spitzenverbände der Wirtschaft und das erste Kabinett Brüning.* Düsseldorf, 1982.

Guttsman, W. L. *The German Social Democratic Party, 1875–1933.* London, 1981.

————. *Workers' Culture in Weimar Germany.* New York, 1990.

Hagemann, Karen. *Frauenalltag und Männerpolitik: Alltagsleben und gesellschaftliches Handeln von Arbeiterfrauen in der Weimarer Republik.* Bonn, 1990.

Hall, Alex. *Scandal, Sensation and Social Democracy: The SPD Press and Wilhelmine Germany, 1890–1914.* Cambridge, 1977.

Hamburger, Ernest. "Betrachtungen über Heinrich Brünings Memoiren." *Internationale Wissenschaftliche Korrespondenz zur Geschichte der deutschen Arbeiterbewegung* 15 (1972): 18–39.

Hamilton, Richard. *Who Voted for Hitler?* Princeton, 1982.

Hasselhorn, Fritz. *Wie wählte Göttingen?: Wahlverhalten und die soziale Basis der Parteien in Göttingen 1924–1933.* Göttingen, n.d.

Hayes, Peter. "A 'Question Mark with Epaulettes'?: Kurt von Schleicher and Weimar Politics." *Journal of Modern History* 52 (1980): 35–65.

Hebel-Kunze, Bärbel. *SPD und Faschismus: Zur politischen und organisatorischen Entwicklung der SPD 1932–1935.* Frankfurt a.M., 1977.

Heer, Hannes. *Burgfrieden oder Klassenkampf.* Berlin, 1971.

Heine, Friedrich. *Dr. Kurt Schumacher: Ein demokratischer Sozialist europäischer Prägung.* Göttingen, 1969.

Heinemann, Ulrich. "Linksopposition und Spaltungstendenzen in der sozialdemokratischen Arbeiterbewegung." In *Sozialdemokratische Arbeiterbewegung und Weimarer Republik: Materialien zur gesellschaftlichen Entwicklung 1927–1933,* edited by Wolfgang Luthardt, vol. 2. Frankfurt a.M., 1978.

Held, Michael. *Sozialdemokratie und Keynesianismus.* Frankfurt a.M./New York, 1982.

Hennig, Eike. "Anmerkungen zur Propaganda der NSDAP gegenüber SPD und KPD in der Endphase der Weimarer Republik." *Tel Aviver Jahrbuch für deutsche Geschichte* 17 (1988): 209–33.

Heupel, Eberhard. *Reformismus und Krise: Zur Theorie und Praxis von SPD, ADGB und AfA-Bund in der Weltwirtschaftskrise 1929–1932/3.* Frankfurt a.M./New York, 1981.

Hickey, S. H. F. *Workers in Imperial Germany: The Miners of the Ruhr.* Oxford, 1985.

Hipp, Hermann. "Wohnungen für Arbeiter." In *Arbeiter in Hamburg: Unterschichten, Arbeiter und Arbeiterbewegung seit dem ausgehenden 18. Jahrhundert,* edited by Arno Herzig, Dieter Langewiesche, and Arnold Sywottek. Hamburg, 1983.

Hodge, Carl. "Three Ways to Lose a Republic: The Electoral Politics of the Weimar SPD." *European History Quarterly* 17 (1987): 165–93.

Holtfrerich, Carl-Ludwig. "Alternativen zu Brünings Wirtschaftspolitik in der Weltwirtschaftskrise." *Historische Zeitschrift* 235 (1982): 605–31.

———. "Zu hohe Löhne in der Weimarer Republik?: Bemerkungen zur Borchardt-These." *Geschichte und Gesellschaft* 10 (1984): 122–41.

Holzer, Jerzy. *Parteien und Massen: Die politische Krise in Deutschland 1928–1930.* Wiesbaden, 1975.

Höner, Sabine. *Der nationalsozialistische Zugriff auf Preussen: Preussischer Staat und nationalsozialistische Machterorberungsstrategie 1928–1934.* Bochum, 1984.

Hunt, Lynn. "Introduction: History, Culture, and Text." In *The New Cultural History,* edited by Lynn Hunt. Berkeley, 1989.

———. *Politics, Culture, and Class in the French Revolution.* Berkeley, 1981.

Hunt, Richard. *German Social Democracy, 1918–1933.* Chicago, 1970.

Iggers, George, ed. *The Social History of Politics: Critical Perspectives in West German Historical Writing since 1945.* Heidelberg, 1985.

James, Harold. "Economic Reasons for the Collapse of the Weimar Republic." In *Why Did German Democracy Fail?,* edited by Ian Kershaw. New York, 1990.

————."Gab es eine Alternative zur Wirtschaftspolitik Brünings?" *Viertel-jahrsschrift für Sozial-und Wirtschaftsgeschichte* 70 (1983): 523–42.

————. *The German Slump: Politics and Economics, 1924–1936.* Oxford, 1986.

————. "Municipal Finance in the Weimar Republic." In *The State and Social Change in Germany, 1880–1980,* edited by W. R. Lee and Eve Rosenaft. New York/Oxford/Munich, 1990.

————. "Rudolf Hilferding and the Application of the Political Economy of the Second International." *Historical Journal* 24 (1981): 847–69.

Janis, Irving, and Mann, Leon. *Decision-Making.* New York, 1977.

Jarausch, Konrad H. "The Crisis of the German Professions, 1918–1933." *Journal of Contemporary History* 20 (1985): 379–98.

Jasper, Gotthard. *Die gescheiterte Zähmung: Wege zur Machtergreifung Hitlers 1930–1934.* Frankfurt a.M., 1986.

————. *Der Schutz der Republik: Studien zur staatlichen Sicherung der Demokratie in der Weimarer Republik.* Tübingen, 1963.

————. "Zur innenpolitischen Lage in Deutschland im Herbst 1929." *Vierteljahrshefte für Zeitgeschichte* 8 (1960): 288–99.

Jones, Arneta Ament. "The Left Opposition in the German Democratic Republic—1922–1933." Ph.D. dissertation, Emory University, 1968.

Jones, Larry Eugene. "Crisis and Realignment: Agrarian Splinter Parties in the Late Weimar Republic, 1928–1933." In *Peasants and Lords in Modern Germany,* edited by Robert G. Moeller. Boston, 1986.

————. *German Liberalism and the Dissolution of the Weimar Party System, 1918–1933.* Chapel Hill, 1988.

Jung, Ottmar. "Plebiszitärer Durchbruch 1929?: Zur Bedeutung von Volksbegehren und Volksentscheid gegen den Youngplan für die NSDAP." *Geschichte und Gesellschaft* 15 (1989): 489–510.

Kennedy, Ellen. "Carl Schmitt und die Frankfurter Schule." *Geschichte und Gesellschaft* 12 (1986): 380–419.

Klemperer, Klemens von. *Germany's New Conservatism.* Princeton, 1968.

Klenke, Dietmar. *Die SPD Linke in der Weimarer Republik.* Münster, 1983.

Klönne, Arno. *Die deutsche Arbeiterbewegung.* Düsseldorf, 1980.

————. "Fragwürdige Leitbilder der politischen und gewerkschaftlichen Arbeiterbewegung in der Weimarer Republik." In *Aufstieg des Nationalsozialismus, Untergang der Republik, Zerschlagung der Gewerkschaften: Beiträge zur Geschichte der Arbeiterbewegung zwischen Demokratie und Diktatur,* edited by Ernst Breit. Cologne, 1984.

Klotzbach, Kurt. *Gegen den Nationalsozialismus: Widerstand und Verfolgung in Dortmund 1930–1945.* Hanover, 1969.

Kohler, Erich D. "The Crisis in the Prussian Schutzpolizei 1930–1932." In *Police Forces in History,* edited by George Mosse. London, 1975.

Köhler, Henning. "Knut Borchardts 'Revision des überlieferten Geschichtsbildes' der Wirtschaftspolitik in der grossen Krise—Eine Zwangsvorstellung?" *Internationale Wissenschaftliche Korrespondenz zur Geschichte der deutschen Arbeiterbewegung* 19 (1983): 164–80.

Kolb, Eberhard. "Die sozialdemokratische Strategie in der Ära des Präsidialkabinetts Brüning—Strategie ohne Alternative?" In *Das Unrechtsregime*, 2 vols., edited by Ursula Büttner. Hamburg, 1986.

———. *Die Weimarer Republik*. 2d ed. Munich, 1988.

———. "Zwischen Parteiräson und staatspolitischer Verantwortung—Die Sozialdemokratie in der Weimarer Republik" (review of H. A. Winkler, *Von der Revolution zur Stabilisierung* and *Der Schein der Normalität*). *Geschichte und Gesellschaft* 13 (1987): 101–16.

Kopitzsch, Wolfgang. "Der 'Altonaer Blutsonntag.'" In *Arbeiter in Hamburg: Unterschichten, Arbeiter und Arbeiterbewegung seit dem ausgehenden 18. Jahrhundert*, edited by Arno Herzig, Dieter Langewiesche, and Arnold Sywottek. Hamburg, 1983.

Koshar, Rudy. *Social Life, Local Politics, and Nazism: Marburg, 1880–1935*. Chapel Hill, 1986.

Koszyk, Kurt. *Presse der deutschen Sozialdemokratie: Eine Bibliographie*. Hanover, 1966.

———. *Zwischen Kaiserreich und Diktatur: Die sozialdemokratische Presse von 1914 bis 1933*. Heidelberg, 1958.

Krall, Herbert. *Die Landespolitik der SPD in Bayern von 1924 bis 1933*. Munich, 1985.

Kratzenberg, Volker. *Arbeiter auf dem Weg zu Hitler?: Die Nationalsozialistische Betriebszellenorganisation: Ihre Entstehung, ihre Programmatik, ihr Scheitern 1927–34*. Frankfurt a.M., 1987.

Kriegenherdt, Fritz. "Die Opposition der Sozialdemokratie in Sachsen gegen die Politik des Parteivorstandes der Sozialdemokratischen Partei Deutschlands vom Ausbruch des sächsischen Parteikonflikts in der SPD um die Jahreswende 1923/24 bis zur Gründung der Sozialistischen Arbeiterpartei Deutschlands Anfang Oktober 1931." Dissertation, Potsdam, 1971.

Kritzer, Peter. *Wilhelm Hoegner: Politische Biographie eines bayerischen Sozialdemokraten*. Munich, 1979.

Krohn, K. D. "Ökonomische 'Zwangslagen' und das Scheitern der Weimarer Republik: Zu Knut Borchardts Analyse der deutschen Wirtschaft in den 20er Jahren." *Geschichte und Gesellschaft* 8 (1982): 415–26.

Krumbeim, Wolfgang. "Vorläufer eines 'Dritten Weges zum Sozialismus'?: Bemerkungen zu einigen theoretischen Konzepten der Weimarer Sozialdemokratie." In *Solidargemeinschaft und Klassenkampf*, edited by Richard Saage. Frankfurt a.M., 1986.

Kücklich, Erika. "Einheitsfrontinitiativen der KPD unter Leitung Johnschers in Braunschweig 1931." *Beiträge zur Geschichte der Arbeiterbewegung* 28, no. 1 (1986): 97–107.

Kurz, Thomas. "Arbeitermörder und Putschisten: Der Berliner 'Blutmai' von 1929 als Kristallisationspunkt des Verhältnisses von KPD und SPD vor der Katastrophe." *Internationale Wissenschaftliche Korrespondenz zur Geschichte der deutschen Arbeiterbewegung* 22 (1986): 297–317.

Landauer, Carl. *European Socialism*. Berkeley, 1960.

———. Review of R. Hunt, *German Social Democracy 1918–1933. Journal of Modern History* 57 (1965): 113–14.

Langewiesche, Dieter. "The Impact of the German Labor Movement on Workers' Culture." *Journal of Modern History* 59 (1987): 506–23.

———. "Politik-Gesellschaft-Kultur: Zur Problematik von Arbeiterkultur und kulturellen Arbeiter-Organisationen in Deutschland nach dem Ersten Weltkrieg." *Archiv für Sozialgeschichte* 22 (1982): 359–402.

Leaman, Jeremy. "The *Gemeinden* as Agents of Fiscal and Social Policy in the Twentieth Century: Local Government and State-form Crises in Germany." In *The State and Social Change in Germany, 1880–1990*, edited by W. R. Lee and Eve Rosenhaft. New York/Oxford/Munich, 1990.

Lehnert, Detlef. "Klassenintegration und Hegemonie-Fähigkeit: Organisationscharakter und Wahlattraktivität der deutschen und österreichischen Sozialdemokratie in der Zwischenskriegszeit." In *Solidargemeinschaft und Klassenkampf*, edited by Richard Saage. Frankfurt a.M., 1986.

———. "Sozialcharakter, politisches Selbstverständnis und Klassen-Strategien der Weimarer Sozialdemokratie: Thesen zum Verhältnis von Parteihabitus und sozialistischem Transformationspotential." In *Reformsozialismus und Sozialdemokratie*, edited by Horst Heimann and Thomas Meyer. Berlin, 1982.

———. " 'Staatspartei der Republik' oder 'revolutionäre Reformisten'?: Die Sozialdemokratie." In *Politische Identität und Nationale Gedenktage*, edited by Detlef Lehnert and Klaus Megerle. Opladen, 1989.

Lehnert, Detlef, and Megerle, Klaus. "Politische Identität und Nationale Gedenktage." In *Politische Identität und Nationale Gedenktage*, edited by Detlef Lehnert and Klaus Megerle. Opladen, 1989.

Leithäuser, Joachim. *Wilhelm Leuschner: Ein Leben für die Republik*. Cologne, 1962.

Lenger, Friedrich. "Mittelstand und Nationalsozialismus?: Zur politischen Orientierung von Handwerkern und Angestellten in der Endphase der Weimarer Republik." *Archiv für Sozialgeschichte* 29 (1989): 173–98.

Leuschen-Seppel, Rosemarie. "Budget-Agrarpolitik der SPD." In *Sozialdemokratische Arbeiterbewegung und Weimarer Republik: Materialien zur gesellschaftlichen Entwicklung 1927–1933*, edited by Wolfgang Luthardt, vol. 2. Frankfurt a.M., 1978.

Liang, Hsi-Huey. *The Berlin Police Force in the Weimar Republic*. Berkeley, 1970.

Lidtke, Vernon L. *The Alternative Culture: Socialist Labor Movement in Imperial Germany*. New York, 1985.

―――. "Die kulturelle Bedeutung der Arbeitervereine." In *Kultureller Wander im 19. Jahrhundert*, edited by Günter Wiegelmann. Göttingen, 1973.

―――. *The Outlawed Party: Social Democracy in Germany, 1878–1890*. Princeton, 1966.

Lönne, Karl-Egon. *Faschismus als Herausforderung: Die Auseinandersetzung der "Roten Fahne" und des "Vorwärts" mit dem italienischen Faschismus 1920–1933*. Cologne, 1983.

Lösche, Peter. "Ernst Heilmann." In *Vor dem Vergessen bewahren: Lebenswege Weimarer Sozialdemokraten*, edited by Peter Lösche, Michael Scholing, and Franz Walter. Berlin, 1988.

―――. "Über den Zusammenhang von reformistischen Sozialismus-theorien und sozialdemokratischer Organisationspraxis in der Weimarer Republik: Robert F. Wheeler zum Gedächtnis." In *Reformsozialismus und Sozialdemokratie*, edited by Horst Heimann and Thomas Meyer. Berlin, 1982.

Lösche, Peter, and Scholing, Michael. "Solidargemeinschaft im Widerstand: Eine Fallstudie über 'Blick in die Zeit.'" *Internationale Wissenschaftliche Korrespondenz zur Geschichte der deutschen Arbeiterbewegung* 19 (1983): 517–60.

Lösche, Peter, and Walter, Franz. "Auf dem Weg zur Volkspartei?: Die Weimarer Sozialdemokratie." *Archiv für Sozialgeschichte* 29 (1989): 75–135.

―――. "Zur Organisationskultur der sozialdemokratischen Arbeiterbewegung in der Weimarer Republik." *Geschichte und Gesellschaft* 15 (1989): 511–36.

Löwenthal, Richard. *Der Widerstandsgruppe "Neu Beginnen": Beiträge zum Thema Widerstand*. Berlin, 1982.

Lucas, Erhard. *Arbeiterradikalismus: Zwei Formen von Radikalismus in der deutschen Arbeiterbewegung*. Frankfurt a.M., 1976.

Luthardt, Wolfgang, ed. *Sozialdemokratische Arbeiterbewegung und Weimarer Republik: Materialien zur gesellschaftlichen Entwicklung 1927–1933*. 2 vols. Frankfurt a.M., 1978.

―――. "Sozialdemokratie und Legalstrategie: Überlegungen zu ihrem Verhältnis in der Weimarer Republik." In *Geschichte als politische Wissenschaft*, edited by Jürgen Bergmann, Klaus Megerle, and Peter Steinbach. Stuttgart, 1979.

McElligott, Anthony. "Street Politics in Hamburg, 1932–33." *History Workshop Journal* 16 (1983): 83–90.

McKibbon, R. I. "The Myth of the Unemployed: Who Did Vote for the Nazis?" *Australian Journal of Politics and History* 15, no. 2 (1969): 25–40.

Maehl, William Harvey. *The German Socialist Party: Champion of the First Republic, 1918–1933*. Philadelphia, 1986.

Mai, Gunther. "Nationalsozialistische Betriebszellen-Organisation: Zum Verhältnis von Arbeiterschaft und Nationalsozialismus." *Vierteljahrshefte für Zeitgeschichte* 31 (1983): 573–613.

Maier, Charles. "Die Nicht-Determiniertheit ökonomischer Modelle: Überlegungen zu Knut Borchardts These von der 'kranken Wirtschaft' der Weimarer Republik." *Geschichte und Gesellschaft* 11 (1985): 275–94.

———. *Recasting Bourgeois Europe*. Cambridge, Mass., 1975.

———. *The Unmasterable Past: History, Holocaust, and German National Identity*. Cambridge, Mass., 1988.

Martiny, Martin. "Die Entstehung und politische Bedeutung der 'Neue Blätter für den Sozialismus' und ihres Freundkreises." *Vierteljahrshefte für Zeitgeschichte* 25 (1977): 373–419.

———. "Sozialdemokratie und junge Generation am Ende der Weimarer Republik." In *Sozialdemokratische Arbeiterbewegung und Weimarer Republik: Materialien zur gesellschaftlichen Entwicklung 1927–1933*, edited by Wolfgang Luthardt, vol. 2. Frankfurt a.M., 1978.

Matthias, Erich. "German Social Democracy in the Weimar Republic." In *German Democracy and the Triumph of Hitler*, edited by Erich Matthias and Anthony Nicholls. London, 1971.

———. "Hindenburg zwischen den Fronten 1932." *Vierteljahrshefte für Zeitgeschichte* 14 (1966): 75–84.

———. "Kautsky und der Kautskyanismus." In *Marxismus-Studien*. Tübingen, 1957.

———. "Die Mannheimer Sozialdemokraten und der Bruch der badischen Koalition am 30. November 1932." *Internationale Wissenschaftliche Korrespondenz zur Geschichte der deutschen Arbeiterbewegung* 15 (1979): 437–42.

———. "Die Sozialdemokratie und die Macht im Staate." In *Der Weg in die Diktatur 1918–1933*. Munich, 1962.

———. "Die Sozialdemokratische Partei Deutschlands." In *Das Ende der Parteien 1933*, edited by E. Matthias and Rudolf Morsey. Düsseldorf, 1960.

Matthias, Erich, and Weber, Hermann, eds., *Widerstand gegen den Nationalsozialismus in Mannheim*. Mannheim, 1984.

Maurer, Ilse. *Reichsfinanzen und grosse Koalition: Zur Geschichte des Reichskabinetts Müller (1928–1930)*. Bonn, 1973.

May, Ernst. *"Lessons" of the Past: The Use and Abuse of History in American Foreign Policy*. New York, 1973.

Mehringer, Hartmut. "Die bayerische Sozialdemokratie bis zum Ende des NS-Regimes." In *Die Parteien KPD, SPD, BVP in Verfolgung und Widerstand: Bayern in der NS-Zeit*, edited by Martin Broszat and H. Mehringer, vol. 5. Munich, 1983.

Meyer, Klaus. "Hermann Heller—Eine biographische Skizze." *Politische Vierteljahresschrift* 8 (1967): 293–313.

Milatz, Alfred. *Wähler und Wahlen in der Weimarer Republik*. Bonn, 1968.

Moeller, Robert G. *German Peasants and Conservative Agrarian Politics, 1914–1924*. Chapel Hill, 1986.

———. "The *Kaiserreich* Recast? Continuity and Change in Modern German Historiography." *Journal of Social History* 17 (1984): 442–50.

Möller, Horst. "Ernst Heilmann: Ein Sozialdemokrat der Weimarer Republik." *Jahrbuch des Instituts für deutsche Geschichte* (Tel Aviv) 11 (1982): 261–94.

———. *Parlamentarismus in Preussen 1919–1932*. Düsseldorf, 1985.

Mommsen, Hans. "Die deutschen Gewerkschaften zwischen Anpassung und Widerstand 1930–1944." In *Von Sozialistengesetz zur Mitbestimmung*, edited by H. O. Vetter. Cologne, 1975.

———. "The Failure of the Weimar Republic and the Rise of Hitler." In *The Burden of German History, 1919–1925*, edited by Michael Laffan. London, 1988.

———. "The Political Effects of the Reichstag Fire." In *Nazism and the Third Reich*, edited by H. A. Turner. New York, 1972.

———. "Die Sozialdemokratie in der Defensive: Der Immobilismus der SPD und der Aufstieg des Nationalsozialismus." In *Sozialdemokratie zwischen Klassen-Bewegung und Volkspartei*, edited by Hans Mommsen. Frankfurt, 1974.

———. *Die verspielte Freiheit: Der Weg der Republik von Weimar in den Untergang 1918 bis 1933*. Berlin, 1989.

Mommsen, Wolfgang J. "The German Revolution, 1918–1920: Political Revolution and Protest Movement." In *Social Change and Political Development*, edited by Richard Bessel and E. J. Feuchtwanger. London, 1981.

Moore, Barrington. *Injustice: The Social Bases of Obedience and Revolt*. New York, 1978.

Moraw, Frank. *Die Parole der "Einheit" und die Sozialdemokratie*. 2d ed. Bonn, 1990.

Morgan, David. *The Socialist Left and the German Revolution: A History of the German Independent Social Democratic Party, 1917–1922*. Ithaca, 1975.

Moring, Karl-Ernst. *Die sozialdemokratische Partei in Bremen 1890–1914*. Hanover, 1968.

Morsey, Rudolf. *Zur Entstehung, Authentizität und Kritik von Brünings "Memoiren 1918–1934."* Opladen, 1975.

Moses, John A. "The German Free Trade Unions and the Problem of Mass Unemployment." In *Unemployment and the Great Depression in Germany, 1929–1933*, edited by Peter D. Stachura. New York, 1986.

Muth, Heinrich. "Schleicher und die Gewerkschaften 1932: Ein Quellenproblem." *Vierteljahrshefte für Zeitgeschichte* 29 (1981): 189–215.

Na'aman, Schlomo. "Lassalle—Demokratie und Sozialdemokratie." *Archiv für Sozialgeschichte* 3 (1963): 21–80.

Neebe, Reinhard. *Grossindustrie, Staat und NSDAP 1930–1933*. Göttingen, 1981.

———. "Konflikt und Kooperation 1930–1933: Anmerkungen zum Verhältnis von Kapital und Arbeit in der Weltwirtschaftskrise." In *Die Weimarer Republik als Wohlfahrtsstaat: Zum Verhältnis von Wirtschafts-und Sozialpolitik in der Industriegesellschaft*, edited by Werner Abelshauser. *Vierteljahrsschrift für Sozial-und Wirtschaftsgeschichte*, Beiheft 81. Stuttgart, 1987.

————. "Unternehmerverbände und Gewerkschaften in den Jahren der Grossen Krise 1929–33." *Geschichte und Gesellschaft* 9 (1983): 302–33.

————. "Die Verantwortung der Grossindustrie für das Dritte Reich: Anmerkungen zu H. A. Turners Buch 'Die Grossunternehmer und der Aufstieg Hitlers.'" *Historische Zeitschrift* 244 (1987): 353–63.

Nettl, Peter. "The German Social Democratic Party 1890–1914 as a Political Model." *Past and Present* 30 (1965): 64–95.

Nicholls, A. J. *Weimar and the Rise of Hitler*. New York, 1986.

Niemann, Heinz. *Geschichte der deutschen Sozialdemokratie 1917–1945*. Frankfurt a.M., 1982.

Niewyk, Donald L. *Socialist, Anti-Semite, and Jew: German Social Democracy Confronts the Problem of Anti-Semitism, 1918–1933*. Baton Rouge, 1971.

Nipperdey, Thomas. "1933 und die Kontinuität der deutschen Geschichte." In *Nachdenken über die deutsche Geschichte*, by Thomas Nipperdey. Munich, 1986.

————. "Verein als soziale Struktur in Deutschland im späten 18. und frühen 19. Jahrhundert." In *Gesellschaft, Kultur, Theorie*, by Thomas Nipperdey. Göttingen, 1976.

Noakes, Jeremy. *The Nazi Party in Lower Saxony, 1921–1933*. London, 1971.

Nolan, Mary. *Social Democracy and Society: Working-class Radicalism in Düsseldorf, 1890–1920*. New York, 1981.

Offermann, Toni. "Das liberale Vereinsmodell als Organisationsform der frühen Arbeiterbewegung der 1860er Jahre." In *"Der kühnen Bahn nur folgen wir . . .": Ursprünge, Erfolge und Grenze der Arbeiterbewegung in Deutschland*. Bd. 1, *Entstehung und Wandel der deutschen Arbeiterbewegung*, edited by Arno Herzig and Günter Trautmann. Hamburg, 1989.

Orlow, Dietrich. *History of the Nazi Party, 1919–1933*. 2 vols. Pittsburgh, 1969.

————. *Weimar Prussia, 1918–1925: The Unlikely Rock of Democracy*. Pittsburgh, 1986.

Osterroth, Franz. "Der Hofgeismarkreis der Jung-Sozialisten." *Archiv für Sozialgeschichte* 4 (1964): 535–44.

Osterroth, Franz, and Schuster, Dieter. *Chronik der deutschen Sozialdemokratie*. Hanover, 1963.

Patch, William L. *Christian Trade Unions in the Weimar Republic, 1918–1933*. New Haven, 1985.

Paucker, Arnold. "Der jüdische Abwehrkampf." In *Entscheidungsjahr 1932: Zur Judenfrage in der Endphase der Weimarer Republik*, edited by Werner E. Mosse. Tübingen, 1965.

————. *Der jüdische Abwehrkampf gegen Antisemitismus und Nationalsozialismus in den letzten Jahren der Weimarer Republik*. Hamburg, 1968.

Paul, Gerhard. *Aufstand der Bilder: Die NS-Propaganda vor 1933*. Bonn, 1990.

Petersen, Larry. "Labor and the End of Weimar: The Case of the KPD in the November 1928 Lockout in the Rhenish-Westphalian Iron and Steel Industry." *Central European History* 15 (1982): 57–95.

Petzina, Dietmar. "Arbeitslosigkeit in der Weimarer Republik." In *Die Weimarer Republik als Wohlfahrtsstaat: Zum Verhältnis von Wirtschafts-und Sozialpolitik in der Industriegesellschaft*, edited by Werner Abelshauser. *Vierteljahrsschrift für Sozial-und Wirtschaftsgeschichte*, Beiheft 81. Stuttgart, 1987.

———. "Elemente der Wirtschaftpolitik in der Spätphase der Weimarer Republik." *Vierteljahrshefte für Zeitgeschichte* 21 (1973): 127–33.

———. "Merkmale der Weltwirtschaftskrise in Deutschland." In *Aufstieg des Nationalsozialismus, Untergang der Republik, Zerschlagung der Gewerkschaften: Beiträge zur Geschichte der Arbeiterbewegung zwischen Demokratie und Diktatur*, edited by Ernst Breit. Cologne, 1984.

Peukert, Detlef. *Ruhrarbeiter gegen den Faschismus: Dokumentation über den Widerstand im Ruhrgebiet 1933–1945*. Frankfurt a.M., 1976.

———. *Die Weimarer Republik: Krisenjahre der klassischen Moderne*. Frankfurt a.M., 1987.

Pirker, Theo. "Zum Verhalten der Organisationen der deutschen Arbeiter-Bewegung in der Endphase der Weimarer Republik." In *Weimar: Selbstpreisgabe einer Demokratie: Eine Bilanz heute*, edited by K. D. Erdmann and Hagen Schulze. Düsseldorf, 1980.

Pistorius, Peter. "Rudolf Breitscheid, 1874–1944: Ein biographischer Beitrag zur deutschen Parteiengeschichte." Ph.D. dissertation. Cologne, 1970.

Plumpe, Gottfried. "Wirtschaftspolitik in der Weltwirtschaftskrise: Realität und Alternativen." *Geschichte und Gesellschaft* 11 (1985): 326–57.

Potthoff, Heinrich. *Freie Gewerkschaften 1918–1933: Der Allgemeine Deutsche Gewerkschaftsbund in der Weimarer Republik*. Düsseldorf, 1987.

———. "Freie Gewerkschaften und sozialistische Parteien in Deutschland." *Archiv für Sozialgeschichte* 26 (1986): 49–85.

———. "Die Freien Gewerkschaften: Perspektiven, Programme und Praxis." In *Solidargemeinschaft und Klassenkampf*, edited by Richard Saage. Frankfurt a.M., 1986.

———. "Die Sozialdemokratie von den Anfängen bis 1945." In *Kleine Geschichte der SPD*, by Susanne Miller and Heinrich Potthoff. Bonn, 1988.

Preller, Ludwig. *Sozialpolitik in der Weimarer Republik*. Stuttgart, 1949.

Pridham, Geoffrey. *Hitler's Rise to Power: The Nazi Movement in Bavaria, 1923–1933*. New York, 1973.

Prinz, Michael. "Angestellte und Nationalsozialismus: Ein Gespräch mit Hans Speier." *Geschichte und Gesellschaft* 15 (1989): 552–62.

———. "Wandel durch Beharrung: Sozialdemokratie und der 'neue Mittelstand' in historischer Perspektive." *Archiv für Sozialgeschichte* 29 (1989): 35–76.

Pyta, Wolfram. *Gegen Hitler und für die Republik: Die Auseinandersetzung der deutschen Sozialdemokratie mit der NSDAP in Weimarer Republik*. Düsseldorf, 1989.

Rabinbach, Anson, ed. *The Austrian Socialist Experiment: Social Democracy and Austro-Marxism, 1918–1934.* Boulder, 1988.

Rebentisch, Dieter. "Die treuesten Söhne der deutschen Sozialdemokratie: Linksopposition und kommunale Reformpolitik in der Frankfurter Sozialdemokratie in der Weimarer Republik." *Archiv für Frankfurts Geschichte und Kunst* 61 (1987): 299–354.

Reck, Siegfried. *Arbeiter nach der Arbeit: Sozialhistorische Studies zu den Wandlungen des Arbeiteralltags.* Lahn-Giessen, 1977.

Reichard, Richard W. *Crippled from Birth: German Social Democracy, 1844–1870.* Ames, Iowa, 1969.

Reiche, Eric G. *The Development of the SA in Nürnberg, 1922–1939.* Cambridge, 1986.

Riemer, Jehuda. "Nach dem Zusammenbruch: Fritz Naphtali im Briefwechsel 1933–1934." *International Review of Social History* 27 (1982): 324–56.

Ritter, Franz. *Theorie und Praxis des demokratischen Sozialismus in der Weimarer Republik.* Frankfurt a.M., 1981.

Ritter, G. A. *Arbeiterkultur.* Königstein, 1979.

———. "Die sozialdemokratische Arbeiterbewegung Deutschlands bis zum Ersten Weltkrieg." In *Arbeiterbewegung, Parteien und Parlamentarismus*, by G. A. Ritter. Göttingen, 1976.

———. *Staat, Arbeiterschaft und Arbeiterbewegung in Deutschland.* Bonn, 1980.

Ritter, Waldemar. *Kurt Schumacher: Eine Untersuchung seiner politischen Konzeption und seine Gesellschafts- und Staatsfassung.* Hanover, 1964.

Rohe, Karl. "Politische Kultur und ihre Analyse: Probleme und Perspektiven der politischen Kulturforschung." *Historische Zeitschrift* 250 (Apr. 1990): 321–46.

———. *Das Reichsbanner Schwarz Rot Gold: Ein Beitrag zur Geschichte und Struktur der politischen Kampfverbände zur Zeit der Weimarer Republik.* Düsseldorf, 1966.

———. *Vom Revier zum Ruhrgebiet: Wahlen, Parteien, Politische Kultur.* Essen, 1986.

Roloff, E. A. *Braunschweig und der Staat von Weimar: Politik, Wirtschaft und Gesellschaft 1918–1933.* Braunschweig, 1964.

Rosenberg, Arthur. *Geschichte der Weimarer Republik.* Frankfurt a.M., 1961.

———. *History of the Weimar Republic.* London, 1936.

Rosenhaft, Eve. *Beating the Fascists?: The German Communists and Political Violence, 1929–1933.* Cambridge, 1983.

Roth, Guenther. *The Social Democrats in Imperial Germany: A Study of Working-Class Isolation and Negative Integration.* New Jersey, 1963.

Rovan, Joseph. *Geschichte der deutschen Sozialdemokratie.* Frankfurt, 1980.

Ruck, Michael. *Bollwerk gegen Hitler?: Arbeiterschaft, Arbeiterbewegung und die Anfänge des Nationalsozialismus.* Cologne, 1988.

Rupieper, Hans-Josef. " 'Der Kampf gegen die nationalsozialistische Seuche': Die Werbeabteilung der SPD und die Auseinandersetzung mit der NSDAP 1929–1932." *Internationale Wissenschaftliche Korrespondenz zur Geschichte der deutschen Arbeiterbewegung* 19 (1983): 1–22.

Rürup, Reinhard. "Problems of the German Revolution, 1918–1919." *Journal of Contemporary History* 3 (1968): 109–35.

Saage, Richard. "Die gefährdete Republik: Porträt der Zeitung des 'Reichsbanners Schwarz-Rot-Gold.'" In *Solidargemeinschaft und Klassenkampf*, edited by Richard Saage. Frankfurt a.M., 1986.

———. "Gleichgewicht der Klassen-Kräfte und Koalitionsfrage als Problem sozialdemokratischer Politik in Deutschland und Österreich zwischen den Weltkriegen." In *Reformsozialismus und Sozialdemokratie*, edited by Horst Heimann and Thomas Meyer. Berlin, 1982.

Saggau, Wolfgang. *Faschismustheorien und antifaschistische Strategien in der SPD*. Cologne, 1981.

Saldern, Adalheid von. "Arbeiterkulturbewegung in Deutschland in der Zwischenkriegs-Zeit." In *Arbeiterkulturen zwischen Alltag und Politik: Beiträge zum europäischen Vergleich in der Zwischenkriegszeit*, edited by Friedhelm Boll. Zurich, 1986.

———. "Arbeiterradikalismus-Arbeiterreformismus: Zum politischen Profil der sozialdemokratischen Parteibasis im deutschen Kaiserreich. Methodisch-inhaltliche Bemerkungen zu Vergleichsstudien." *Internationale Wissenschaftliche Korrespondenz zur Geschichte der deutschen Arbeiterbewegung* 20 (1984): 483–98.

———. *Auf dem Wege zum Arbeiterreformismus: Parteialltag in sozialdemokratischer Göttingen (1870–1920)*. Frankfurt a.M., 1984.

———. "Wilhelminische Gesellschaft und Arbeiterklasse: Emanzipations- und Integrations-Prozesse im kulturellen und sozialen Bereich." *Internationale Wissenschaftliche Korrespondenz zur Geschichte der deutschen Arbeiterbewegung* 13 (Dec. 1977): 469–508.

Schadt, Jörg. *Die Sozialdemokratische Partei in Baden: Von den Anfängen bis zur Jahrhundertwende (1868–1900)*. Hanover, 1971.

Schaefer, Rainer. *Die SPD in der Ära Brüning: Tolerierung oder Mobilisation? Handlungsspielräume und Strategien sozialdemokratischer Politik 1930-1932*. Frankfurt/New York, 1990.

Scherer, Herbert. *Bürgerlich-oppositionelle Literaten und sozialdemokratische Arbeiterbewegung nach 1890*. Stuttgart, 1968.

Scherer, Peter. "Ausbruch der Weltwirtschaftskrise 1929/30 und der deutsche Metallarbeiter-Verband." In *Recht, Justiz, Kritik: Festschrift für Richard Schmid zum 85. Geburtstag*, edited by H. E. Böttcher. Baden-Baden, 1985.

Schieder, Wolfgang. *Die Anfänge der deutschen Arbeiterbewegung*. Stuttgart, 1963.

Schildt, Axel. *Militärdiktatur auf Massenbasis?: Die Querfrontkonzeption der Reichswehrführung um General von Schleicher am Ende der Weimarer Republik*. Frankfurt a.M., 1981.

———. "Militärische Ratio und Integration der Gewerkschaften: Zur Querfrontkonzeptionen der Reichswehrführung am Ende der Weimarer Republik." In *Solidargemeinschaft und Klassenkampf*, edited by Richard Saage. Frankfurt a.M., 1986.

———. "Sozialdemokratische Arbeiterbewegung und Reichswehr—Zur Militärpolitik der SPD in den letzten Jahren der Weimarer Republik." In *Deutsche Arbeiterbewegung vor dem Faschismus*, edited by Heike Haumann and Axel Schildt. Berlin, 1981.

Schirmer, Dietmar. "Politisch-kulturelle Deutungsmuster: Vorstellungen von der Welt der Politik in der Weimarer Republik." In *Politische Identität und Nationale Gedenktage*, edited by Detlef Lehnert and Klaus Megerle. Opladen, 1989.

Schnabel, Thomas. " 'Wer wählte Hitler?': Bemerkungen zu einigen Neuererscheinungen über die Endphase der Weimarer Republik." *Geschichte und Gesellschaft* 8 (1982): 116–33.

———. *Württemberg zwischen Weimar und Bonn 1928–1945/6*. Stuttgart, 1986.

Schneider, Michael. "Arbeitsbeschaffung: Die Vorstellungen von Freien Gewerkschaften und SPD zur Bekämpfung der Wirtschaftskrise." In *Sozialdemokratische Arbeiterbewegung und Weimarer Republik: Materialien zur gesellschaftlichen Entwicklung 1927–1933*, edited by Wolfgang Luthardt, vol. 2. Frankfurt a.M., 1978.

———. *Das Arbeitsbeschaffungs-Programm des ADGB: Zur gewerkschaftlichen Politik in der Endphase der Weimarer Republik*. Bonn–Bad Godesberg, 1975.

———. *Kleine Geschichte der Gewerkschaften: Ihre Entwicklung in Deutschland von den Anfängen bis heute*. Bonn, 1989.

———. "Konjunkturpolitische Vorstellungen der Gewerkschaften in den letzten Jahren der Weimarer Republik: Zur Entwicklung des Arbeitsbeschaffungsplans des ADGB." In *Industrielles System und politische Entwicklung in der Weimarer Republik*, edited by Hans Mommsen, Dietmar Petzina, and Bernd Weisbrod, vol. 1. Düsseldorf, 1977.

———. "Tolerierung-Opposition-Auflösung: Die Stellung des Allgemeinen Deutschen Gewerkschaftsbundes zu den Regierungen Brünings bis Hitler." In *Sozialdemokratische Arbeiterbewegung und Weimarer Republik: Materialien zur gesellschaftlichen Entwicklung 1927–1933*, edited by Wolfgang Luthardt, vol. 1. Frankfurt a.M., 1978.

Scholing, Michael. "Wirtschaftstheorie und Politik in der Weimarer Republik." *Internationale Wissenschaftliche Korrespondenz zur Geschichte der deutschen Arbeiterbewegung* 20 (Sept. 1984): 382–93.

Scholing, Michael, and Walter, Franz. "Der 'Neue Mensch': Sozialistische Lebensreform und Erziehung in der sozialdemokratischen Arbeiterbewegung Deutschlands und Österreichs." In *Solidargemeinschaft und Klassenkampf*, edited by Richard Saage. Frankfurt a.M., 1986.

Scholz, Arno, and Oschilewski, Walter G., eds. *Turmwächter der Demokratie:*

Ein Lebensbild von Kurt Schumacher. Bd. 1, *Sein Weg durch die Zeit.* Berlin, 1954.

Schönhoven, Klaus. "Der demokratische Sozialismus im Dilemma: Die Sozialdemokratie und der Untergang der Weimarer Republik." In *Die nationalsozialistische Machtergreifung,* edited by Wolfgang Michalka. Munich, 1984.

———. *Reformismus und Radikalismus: Gespaltene Arbeiterbewegung im Weimarer Sozialstaat.* Munich, 1989.

Schorske, Carl. *German Social Democracy, 1905–1917: The Development of the Great Schism.* New York, 1955.

Schulz, Gerhard. "Reparationen und Krisenprobleme nach dem Wahlsieg der NSDAP 1930." *Vierteljahrsschrift für Sozial-und Wirtschaftsgeschichte* 67 (1980): 200–222.

Schulze, Hagen. *Otto Braun oder Preussens demokratische Sendung.* Frankfurt a.M., 1977.

———. *Weimar: Deutschland 1917–1933.* Berlin, 1982.

Scott, Joan W. *Gender and the Politics of History.* New York, 1981.

Sewell, William H. *Work and Revolution in France: The Language of Labor from the Old Regime to 1848.* Cambridge, 1980.

Sheehan, James J. *German Liberalism in the Nineteenth Century.* Chicago, 1978.

Simms, Brendan. "The Worker Correspondents' Movement in Württemberg during the Weimar Republic: 1928–1933." *European History Quarterly* 21 (1991): 481–514.

Skrzypczak, Henryk. "Fälscher machen Zeitgeschichte: Ein quellenkritischer Beitrag zur Gewerkschaftspolitik in der Ära Papen und Schleicher." *Internationale Wissenschaftliche Korrespondenz zur Geschichte der deutschen Arbeiterbewegung* 11 (1975): 452–69.

———. "From Carl Legien to Theodor Leipart, from Theodor Leipart to Robert Ley: Notes on Some Strategic and Tactical Problems during the Weimar Republic." *Internationale Wissenschaftliche Korrespondenz zur Geschichte der deutschen Arbeiterbewegung* 13 (1971): 26–47.

———. "Führungsprobleme der sozialistischen Arbeiterbewegung in der Endphase der Weimarer Republik." In *Herkunft und Mandat: Beiträge zur Führungsproblematik in Arbeiterbewegung.* Cologne, 1976.

———. "Kanzlerwechsel und Einheitsfront: Abwehrreaktionen der Arbeiterbewegung auf die Machtübergaben an Franz von Papen." *Internationale Wissenschaftliche Korrespondenz zur Geschichte der deutschen Arbeiterbewegung* 18 (1982): 482–99.

———. "'Revolutionäre' Gewerkschaftspolitik in der Weltwirtschaftskrise: Der Berliner Verkehrsarbeiterstreik 1932." *Gewerkschaftliche Monatshefte* 34 (Apr.–May 1983): 264–77.

Smith, Woodruff D. "The Mierendorff Group and the Modernization of German Social Democratic Politics, 1928–33." *Politics and Society* 5 (1975): 109–29.

Sontheimer, Kurt. "Der Tatkreis." *Vierteljahrshefte für Zeitgeschichte* 7 (1959): 221–60.

Stachura, Peter D. *The Weimar Republic and the Younger Proletariat.* New York, 1989.

Stedman Jones, Gareth. *Languages of Class: Studies in English Working Class History, 1832–1982.* Cambridge, 1983.

Steinbach, Peter. "'Aus dem Reichsfeind von früher ist der Verteidiger der Republik geworden': Sozialdemokratisches Verfassungsverständnis im Spiegel der Weimarer Verfassungsfeiern." In *Solidargemeinschaft und Klassenkampf*, edited by Richard Saage. Frankfurt a.M., 1986.

Steinberg, Hans-Josef. *Sozialismus und Sozialdemokratie: Zur Ideologie der Partei vor dem 1. Weltkrieg.* Hanover, 1967.

Sternhell, Zeev. "The Anti-Materialist Revision of Marxism as an Aspect of the Rise of Fascist Ideology." *Journal of Contemporary History* 22 (1987): 379–400.

———. *Ni droite ni gauche: L'idèologie fasciste en France.* Paris, 1983.

Stoltenberg, Gerhard. *Die politischen Strömungen im schleswig-holsteinischen Landvolk vom 1918–1933: Ein Beitrag zur politischen Meinungsbildung in der Weimarer Republik.* Düsseldorf, 1962.

Sturm, Reinhard. "Faschismusauffassungen der Sozialdemokratie in der Weimarer Republik." In *Solidargemeinschaft und Klassenkampf*, edited by Richard Saage. Frankfurt a.M., 1986.

Stürmer, Michael. *Koalition und Opposition in der Weimarer Republik 1924–1928.* Düsseldorf, 1967.

Sturmthal, Adolf. *The Tragedy of European Labor.* New York, [1943].

Sühl, Klaus. *SPD und öffentlicher Dienst in der Weimarer Republik.* Opladen, 1988.

Tenfelde, Klaus. "Anmerkungen zur Arbeiterkultur." In *Erinnerungsarbeit: Geschichte und demokratische Identität in Deutschland*, edited by Wolfgang Ruppert. Opladen, 1982.

———. *Sozialgeschichte der Bergarbeiterschaft an der Ruhr im 19. Jahrhundert.* Bonn, 1977.

Timm, Helga. *Die deutsche Sozialpolitik und der Bruch der Grossen Koalition im März 1930.* Düsseldorf, 1952.

Toews, John E. "Intellectual History after the Linguistic Turn: The Autonomy of Meaning and the Irreducibility of Experience." *American Historical Review* 92 (1987): 879–907.

Tosstorff, Reiner. "'Einheitsfront' und/oder 'Nichtsangriffpakt' mit der KPD." In *Sozialdemokratische Arbeiterbewegung und Weimarer Republik: Materialien zur gesellschaftlichen Entwicklung 1927–1933*, edited by Wolfgang Luthardt, vol. 2. Frankfurt a.M., 1978.

Trautmann, Günter. "Das Scheitern liberaler Vereinspolitik und die Entstehung der sozialistischen Arbeiter-Bewegung in Hamburg zwischen 1862 and 1871." In *Arbeiter in Hamburg: Unterschichten, Arbeiter und Arbeiter-*

bewegung seit dem ausgehenden 18. Jahrhundert, edited by Arno Herzig, Dieter Langewiesche, and Arnold Sywottek. Hamburg, 1983.

Treue, Wilhelm, ed. *Deutschland in der Weltwirtschaftskrise in Augenzeugenberichten*. Düsseldorf, 1967.

Turner, Henry A., Jr. *German Big Business and the Rise of Hitler*. Oxford, 1985.

Überhorst, Horst. "Bildungsgedanke und Solidaritätsbewusstsein in der deutschen Arbeitersportbewegung z.Z. der Weimarer Republik." *Archiv für Sozialgeschichte* 14 (1974): 275–92.

Ulbricht, Walter, et al. *Geschichte der deutschen Arbeiterbewegung*. 8 vols. Berlin [East], 1966.

Van der Will, Wilfried, and Burns, Robert. *Arbeiterkulturbewegung in der Weimarer Republik: Eine historische-theoretische Analyse der kulturellen Bestrebungen der deutschen Arbeiterschaft*. Frankfurt a.M., 1982.

Vogelsang, Thilo. *Reichswehr, Staat und NSDAP*. Stuttgart, 1962.

Wacker, Wolfgang. *Der Bau des Panzerschiffs "A" und der Reichstag*. Tübingen, 1959.

Walter, Franz. "Jugend in der sozialdemokratischen Solidargemeinschaft: Eineoganisationssoziologische Studie über die Sozialistische Arbeiterjugend Deutschlands (SAJ)." *Internationale Wissenschaftliche Korrespondenz zur Geschichte der deutschen Arbeiterbewegung* 23 (1987): 311–76.

———. *Jungsozialisten in der Weimarer Republik: Zwischen sozialistischer Lebensreform und revolutionärer Kaderpolitik*. Göttingen, 1983.

———. *Nationale Romantik und Revolutionärer Mythos: Politik und Lebensweisen im frühen Weimarer Jungsozialismus*. Berlin, 1986.

Wandel, Eckhard. *Hans Schäffer*. Stuttgart, 1974.

Weber, Hermann. "Die KPD im Kampf gegen SPD und NSDAP." In *Die nationalsozialistische Machtergreifung*, edited by Wolfgang Michalka. Munich, 1984.

———. "Zur Politik der KPD 1929–1933." In *Kampflose Kapitulation: Arbeiterbewegung 1933*, edited by Manfred Scharrer. Reinbek, 1984.

Weichmann, Herbert. "Kritische Bemerkungen Herbert Weichmanns zu den Briefen Brünings an Sollmann." *Vierteljahrshefte für Zeitgeschichte* 22 (1974): 458–60.

Weisbrod, Bernd. "Die Befreiung von den Tarifsesseln: Deflationspolitik als Krisenstrategie der Unternehmer in der Ära Brüning." *Geschichte und Gesellschaft* 11 (1985): 295–325.

Weitz, Eric D. "State Power, Class Fragmentation, and the Shaping of German Communist Policy, 1890–1933." *Journal of Modern History* 62 (1990): 253–97.

Wengst, Udo. "Unternehmerverbände und Gewerkschaften in Deutschland im Jahre 1930." *Vierteljahrshefte für Zeitgeschichte* 25 (1977): 99–119.

Wette, Wolfgang. "Mit dem Stimmzettel gegen den Faschismus?: Das Dilemma des sozialdemokratischen Antifaschismus in der Endphase der

Weimarer Republik." In *Frieden, Gewalt, Sozialismus: Studien zur Geschichte der sozialistischen Arbeiterbewegung*, edited by Hubert Wolfgang and Johannes Scheidtgeger. Stuttgart, 1976.

Wickham, James. "Working-Class Movement and Working-Class Life: Frankfurt am Main in the Weimar Republic." *Social History* 8 (Oct. 1983): 315–43.

———. "The Working-Class Movement in Frankfurt am Main during the Weimar Republic." Dissertation, University of Sussex, 1979.

Winkler, Heinrich A. "Die Arbeiterpartei und die Republik von Weimar." In *Weimarer Republik: Eine Nation im Umbruch*, edited by Gerhard Schulz. Würzburg, [1987].

———. "Choosing the Lesser Evil: The German Social Democrats and the Fall of the Weimar Republic." *Journal of Contemporary History* 25 (1990): 205–25.

———. "Das Dilemma der Weimarer SPD." *Merkur*, Dec. 1982.

———. "Klassenbewegung oder Volkspartei?: Zur Programmdiskussion in der Weimarer Sozialdemokratie 1920–1925." *Geschichte und Gesellschaft* 8 (1982): 9–54.

———. "Klassenkampf versus Koalition: Die französischen Sozialisten und die Politik der deutschen Sozialdemokraten 1928–1933." *Geschichte und Gesellschaft* 17 (1991): 182–219.

———. *Organisierter Kapitalismus*. Göttingen, 1974.

———. *Der Schein der Normalität*. Bd. 2, *Arbeiter und Arbeiterbewegung in der Weimarer Republik*. Bonn/Berlin, 1985.

———. *Der Weg in die Katastrophe*. Bd. 3, *Arbeiter und Arbeiterbewegung in der Weimarer Republik*. Bonn/Berlin, 1987.

Winkler, Jürgen. "Die soziale Basis der sozialistischen Parteien in Deutschland vom Ende des Kaiserreichs bis zur Mitte der Weimarer Republik 1912–1924." *Archiv für Sozialgeschichte* 29 (1989): 137–71.

Wippermann, Wolfgang. "SPD und Faschismus in Bremerhaven-Wesermünde 1922–1933: Weder Hitler-Knechte noch Stalin-Sklaven." *Jahrbuch der Männer von Morgenstern* 61 (1982): 389–412.

Witt, Friedrich-Wilhelm. *Die Hamburger Sozialdemokratie in der Weimarer Republik*. Hanover, 1971.

Wunderer, Hartmut. *Arbeitervereine und Arbeiterparteien: Kultur und Massenorganisationen in der Arbeiterbewegung (1890–1933)*. Frankfurt, 1980.

———. "Noch einmal: Niedergang der Klassenkultur oder solidargemeinschaftlicher Höhepunkt? Anmerkungen zu einem Beitrag von Peter Lösche und Franz Walter in *Geschichte und Gesellschaft* 15 (1989)." *Geschichte und Gesellschaft* 18 (1992): 88–93.

Ziegs, Detlef. "Die Haltung der Leipziger Parteiorganisation der SPD zur wachsenden faschistischen Gefahr, 1929–1933." *Jahrbuch für Regionalgeschichte* 8 (1981): 63–83.

Zofka, Zdenak. *Ausbreitung des Nationalsozialismus auf dem Lande: Eine region-*

ale Fallstudie zur politischen Einstellung der Landbevölkerung in der Zeit des Aufstiegs und der Machtergreifung der NSDAP 1928–1936. Munich, 1979.

Zollitsch, W. "Einzelgewerkschaften und Arbeitsbeschaffung: Zum Handlungsspielraum der Arbeiterbewegung in der Spätphase der Weimarer Republik." *Geschichte und Gesellschaft* 8 (1982): 87–115.

Index

ADB, 30, 68, 260 (n. 99)

ADGB (Free Trade Unions), 2, 11, 15, 17, 31, 39, 68, 83, 94, 166; membership, 1, 2, 19, 20, 84, 152, 195, 207–8, 306 (n. 87); relations with SPD, 5, 20, 27, 31, 53–54, 56, 94, 154, 169, 201, 207–14, 221, 232, 235; and AfA-Bund, 30, 139–40, 153, 166, 168, 189, 232, 307 (n. 101); economic policy, 33, 153, 156, 158, 189–90, 212, 262 (n. 118); and unemployment insurance system, 39, 51–52, 53–56, 57; and NSDAP, 73, 83, 209, 275 (n. 66), 308 (n. 118); and toleration policy, 94, 127, 137–38, 151, 152–53, 157, 169, 299 (n. 168); and Reichsbanner, 104, 175, 211; and nationalism, 141, 208, 244, 308 (n. 122); and reparations, 153–55, 300 (nn. 8, 13); and KPD, 157, 196, 208, 216, 227, 324 (n. 208), 337 (n. 97); and Iron Front, 169–71, 173, 174, 176, 187, 212, 221, 309 (n. 11), 310 (n. 19), 311 (n. 31), 335 (n. 69); response to Prussian coup, 193–94, 196, 199, 200, 208; and Papen regime, 203, 208, 210, 242, 331 (nn. 34, 39, 42), 332 (n. 43); and *Tat* circle, 209, 333 (n. 38); and Schleicher regime, 220–21, 223, 341 (n. 136), 342 (n. 139), 343 (n. 155); response to Hitler's appointment as chancellor, 224–25; under Hitler regime, 231–33, 243. *See also* DMV; Factory councils; Grassmann, Peter; Hammerschaften; Leipart, Theodor; NSBO; RDI; RGO; Strikes; Unemployment; Workers, unemployed; WTB

Adler, Fritz, 231

AfA-Bund, 20, 24, 68, 211, 297 (n. 136), 300 (n. 8), 348 (n. 208); membership, 30, 109, 260 (n. 95); congress in 1931, 139–40, 161; economic policy, 153, 161, 162, 168, 169; and Iron Front, 169, 311 (n. 31), 334 (n. 66). *See also* ADGB; Aufhäuser, Siegfried; WTB

Agnes, Lore, 86, 98, 236

Altona, 103, 192, 193, 266 (n. 52), 322 (n. 181), 346 (n. 187)

Auer, Erhard, 22, 29, 143

Aufhäuser, Siegfried, 24, 47, 82, 215, 235, 245, 298 (n. 144), 332 (n. 50); as head of AfA-Bund, 30, 99, 139, 212, 232; criticizes SPD, 33, 52, 56, 93, 165, 224, 267 (n. 69); and toleration policy, 91–92, 98, 99, 135, 136, 148, 150, 270 (n. 123), 281 (n. 67); economic views, 161, 165; differences with ADGB, 211, 232, 308 (n. 128)

Baade, Fritz, 162, 163, 181, 209, 305 (n. 77)

Baden, 38, 184, 185, 192, 318 (n. 119), 331 (n. 31); SPD in, 52, 102, 257 (n. 52), 284 (n. 119); election results, 67, 79, 99; efforts of regime to curb NSDAP and KPD, 72, 129, 130

Bavaria, 41, 184, 185, 192, 226, 229, 345 (n. 174); Reichsbanner in, 21, 350 (n. 234); SPD in, 28, 32, 136, 214–15, 216, 227, 234, 284 (n. 119), 295 (n. 101): election results, 181, 229, 337 (n. 88)

Becker, Otto, 194
Bergmann, Paul, 58, 258 (n. 52), 271
    (n. 138), 297 (n. 135)
Berlin, 128; election results, 42–43,
    92, 107, 108, 181, 261 (n. 105),
    273 (n. 30), 338 (n. 106); KPD in,
    43, 103, 146, 197, 198, 217, 324
    (n. 204); workers in, 66, 198–99,
    224, 251 (n. 39); NSDAP in, 69–71,
    73, 75, 107, 128, 189, 280 (n. 39),
    298 (n. 146); police, 103, 127, 192;
    economy, 152, 169; BVG strike,
    217, 338 (nn. 103, 107)
—SPD in, 28, 82–83, 183, 215, 223,
    284 (n. 119), 304 (n. 66), 335
    (n. 76); as left-wing center, 8, 23,
    24, 47, 52, 58, 191, 212, 213, 273
    (n. 31), 279 (n. 32), 297 (n. 133);
    and NSDAP, 73, 90, 91–92, 284
    (n. 119); and toleration policy,
    90–92, 136; and Reichsbanner,
    170, 171, 203; and Iron Front, 171,
    173, 182, 187, 188, 319 (n. 141);
    response to Prussian coup, 194,
    198–99, 330 (n. 16); under Hitler
    regime, 233, 234, 346 (n. 187).
    See also Künstler, Franz; Sklarek
    scandal
Bernstein, Eduard, 8, 24, 250 (n. 29)
Bieligk, Fritz, 144
Blomberg, Werner von, 225
Böchel, Karl, 235
Boxheim documents, 149, 170, 298
    (n. 150)
Bracher, Karl Dietrich, 3, 88, 253
    (n. 60), 278 (n. 21), 327 (n. 232),
    343 (n. 157)
Bracht, Franz, 193, 216
Brandes, Alwin, 190, 306 (n. 87), 313
    (n. 67)
Brandt, Willy, 147
Braun, Otto, 25, 44, 95, 149, 180,
    183, 211, 245, 314 (n. 78); and
    SPD leaders, 28, 44, 98, 132, 134,

200, 216, 271 (n. 140), 290 (n. 26),
    291 (n. 44), 339 (n. 117); and
    Reichswehr, 34, 46; popularity of,
    39, 196, 199, 321 (n. 168); as seen
    by Social Democrats, 44, 90, 92,
    94, 179, 191, 216, 321 (n. 169);
    and Müller regime, 46, 48, 58, 266
    (n. 59); and first Brüning regime,
    60, 85, 271 (nn. 140, 152); efforts
    to curb NSDAP and KPD, 72, 98,
    127–30, 185; and toleration policy,
    87–88, 90, 94, 95, 98, 132, 134,
    179, 185, 279 (n. 28); and referen-
    dum to recall Prussian Landtag,
    129–30; response to Prussian coup,
    190–91, 193, 195, 200, 216; and
    Schleicher regime, 223; under
    Hitler regime, 224, 229, 346
    (n. 192)
Braunschweig, 38, 39, 47, 82, 103,
    197, 198
Brecht, Arnold, 49, 129, 193, 195,
    314 (n. 78), 327 (n. 233), 343
    (n. 157)
Breitscheid, Rudolf, 169, 170, 179,
    330 (n. 16), 347 (n. 200), 350
    (n. 236); and Müller regime, 48,
    49, 52, 53, 54; and first Brüning
    regime, 59, 60, 61, 82, 83, 271
    (n. 151); political views, 64, 65, 82,
    150, 189, 219; analyzes NSDAP, 80,
    89, 138–39, 225–26; and KPD, 89,
    149; and toleration policy, 131,
    133–34, 145, 148, 149, 150, 154,
    169, 186, 298 (n. 147); and repara-
    tions, 154, 301 (n. 18); and Papen
    regime, 194–95, 216, 218; and
    Schleicher regime, 222, 223, 342
    (n. 141)
Breslau, 24, 52, 58, 77, 93, 104, 132,
    147, 297 (n. 134)
Brüning, Heinrich, 60–61, 96, 186,
    278 (n. 18), 299 (n. 158); and
    reform of unemployment compen-

sation, 57–58; and SPD, 59–60, 61–62, 82, 83, 85, 91–93, 127, 131, 133–35, 138, 151, 154, 160–61, 166, 179, 186–87, 245, 254 (n. 5), 271 (nn. 151, 152), 281 (n. 72); and origins of toleration policy, 88–89; economic policies, 97, 127, 133, 134, 136–37, 144, 147–48; attitude toward efforts to curb NSDAP, 128, 130–31, 149, 185–86, 299 (n. 157), 317 (n. 114), 318 (n. 128); and Prussian coalition, 131; and reparations, 154–55, 157; relations with businessmen, 156–57, 160

BVP, 38, 45, 79, 88, 181, 318 (n. 119)

Center Party, 38, 65, 186; electorate of, 31, 79, 86, 108, 172, 181, 204, 218, 315 (n. 84); and Prussian coalition, 44, 98, 128, 191, 271 (n. 140); and Müller regime, 45, 48, 55–56, 57; and SPD, 61, 82, 218, 318 (n. 119); and Weimar republic, 63, 64, 66, 88, 151; and Papen regime, 221; and Hitler regime, 230

Chakhotin, Sergei, 177–80, 182, 183, 187–88, 190, 201, 205, 312 (nn. 42, 52), 313 (n. 58), 315 (n. 89), 316 (n. 93), 329 (n. 14)

Chemnitz: election results, 42, 67, 77, 107; SPD in, 93, 104, 132, 215, 284 (n. 119), 319 (n. 141), 336 (n. 86)

Childers, Thomas, 13, 106

Cologne, 137; SPD in, 40, 47, 56, 188, 258 (n. 58), 266 (n. 56), 286 (n. 139); election results, 41, 42, 337 (n. 88)

Communists. See KPD

Crispien, Arthur, 23, 80, 95, 213, 218, 219, 228, 296 (n. 117), 335 (n. 76), 344 (n. 174), 350 (n. 236)

Crummenerl, Siegmund, 233, 235

Dahrendorf, Gustav, 25, 136, 283 (n. 104), 298 (n. 146), 347 (n. 203)

Darmstadt, 52, 58, 80, 133, 148, 150, 182, 198, 266 (n. 52), 276 (n. 89)

Darmstädter und Nationalbank (Danat bank), 160, 161

Dawes Plan, 51

DBB, 30, 68, 172, 260 (n. 99), 323 (n. 188)

DDP, 22, 25, 38, 45, 55, 56, 65, 67, 80, 132, 146. See also State Party

Decker, Georg, 65, 264 (n. 24), 303 (n. 52), 307 (n. 110), 339 (n. 114); analyzes elections, 42, 109, 110, 282 (n. 75), 335 (n. 69); and Müller regime, 56; analyzes NSDAP, 66, 74, 107, 133, 150, 288 (n. 164), 321 (n. 166); and toleration policy, 148

De Man, Hendrik, 24

Deutsche Führerbriefe, 167, 168, 245, 310 (n. 24), 332 (n. 47), 338 (n. 104)

Dittmann, Wilhelm, 23, 135, 146, 154, 158, 213, 228

DMV (Metalworkers), 104, 137, 152, 190, 224, 313 (n. 67), 329 (n. 4)

DNVP, 38, 61, 148, 180, 191, 283 (n. 100), 318 (n. 119); electorate of, 42, 43, 80, 106, 108, 204, 217, 229; and NSDAP, 68, 272 (n. 19); SPD view of, 71, 83, 97, 282 (nn. 75, 76)

Dortmund, 49, 145, 189, 310 (n. 21), 316 (n. 105), 319 (n. 145), 339 (n. 109)

Drei Pfeile, 178, 179, 181, 182, 187, 189, 212, 224, 316 (n. 93), 319 (n. 141), 320 (n. 151), 335 (n. 73)

Dresden, 24, 42, 47, 104, 147, 264 (n. 26), 344 (n. 165)

Duesterberg, Theodor, 180

Düsseldorf, 93; workers in, 7; KPD in, 42; Industry Club, 167, 184

—SPD in, 83, 86, 93, 206, 257
(n. 52), 336 (n. 86), 340 (n. 119),
345 (n. 184), 346 (nn. 187, 190);
electorate of, 41, 337 (n. 88); and
Müller regime, 52, 56, 58; and
NSDAP, 80, 83; and toleration policy, 98, 132, 150
DVP: and SPD, 43–45, 59, 63, 65, 67,
81, 83, 95, 146; plan to reform
unemployment compensation,
51, 53, 54, 57–58, 60; opposes
Hilferding's budget, 55–56; electorate of, 80, 204, 217

Ebert, Fritz, 213
Eckstein, Ernst, 93, 99, 147, 263
(n. 134), 291 (n. 48)
Edel, Oskar, 219
Eggert, Wilhelm, 208, 223, 224, 233
Elections, results of: in 1928, 1, 2, 42;
in 1929, 67, 69; in 1930, 76, 86, 296
(n. 126); in 1931, 132, 146, 150; in
1932, 180, 181–83, 204–5, 217, 315
(nn. 84, 85), 338 (n. 106); in 1933,
229
Emergency decrees, 99, 136–37, 169
Enabling Act, 230–31
Erdmann, Lothar, 83, 208, 209, 211,
232, 308 (n. 122), 331 (n. 38)
Erkelenz, Anton, 150, 161, 162, 293
(n. 76), 306 (n. 91), 324 (n. 208),
328 (n. 2)

Factory councils, 18, 19, 152, 232,
347 (n. 208)
Fallada, Hans, 17, 261 (n. 102)
Falter, Jürgen, 106, 108, 140
Farmers, 41, 55, 98, 186, 261
(n. 102); SPD and, 11, 29–31, 41,
84, 110, 140–41, 190, 215, 244, 277
(n. 120), 293 (n. 78); NSDAP and,
78, 107, 108, 111, 132–33, 181, 204,
288 (n. 164)
Fascism: Social Democratic definition

of, 66, 83, 138, 205, 206, 218,
225–26, 317 (n. 109)
Fischer, Conan, 106
Fraenkel, Ernst, 35, 107, 109, 110,
249 (n. 20), 251 (n. 38), 312
(n. 47), 340 (n. 120)
Frankfurt, 149
—SPD in, 21, 74, 267 (n. 67), 278
(n. 14), 286 (n. 137), 345 (n. 183),
346 (n. 187); as left-wing center, 8,
24, 52, 56, 58, 297 (n. 134); and
NSDAP, 80, 102; and toleration
policy, 132; response to Prussian
coup, 198
Free Trade Unions. See ADGB
Frick, Wilhelm, 71, 143, 225, 236
Fröhlich, August, 236
Furtwängler, Franz, 209, 308 (n. 122)

Gayl, Wilhelm von, 208, 221
Geary, Dick, 8
Geiger, Theodor, 106–10, 139–41
Gessler, Otto, 148
Göring, Hermann, 149, 186, 207,
223, 225, 231, 236, 237, 351
(n. 251)
Göttingen, 106, 205
Graf, Engelbert, 71, 93, 132, 236, 297
(n. 135)
Grassmann, Peter, 96, 171, 209, 225;
and SPD, 20, 94, 154, 165, 213–
14; and Papen regime, 208; and
Schleicher regime, 222, 223; and
NSBO, 233
Grebing, Helga, 3
Groener, Wilhelm, 46, 148, 149, 175,
184–86, 298 (n. 153)
Grzesinski, Albert, 25, 39, 197, 346
(n. 192); and Müller regime, 48;
advocates legal curbs on NSDAP
and KPD, 72, 103, 128, 130; views
on NSDAP, 74, 202, 279 (n. 28),
327 (n. 245); as Berlin police commissioner, 128–29, 149, 191, 192;

conflict with Severing, 149, 191,
192, 200; and Prussian coup, 193,
197, 202
Gurland, Arkadij, 151, 187, 257
(n. 50), 297 (n. 131)

Hamburg, 42, 81, 129, 130, 136, 152,
165, 288 (n. 166)
—SPD in, 38, 40, 80, 109, 311
(n. 36); social composition, 28,
259 (n. 83); neorevisionists in, 32,
215, 258 (nn. 52, 58); election
results of, 39, 146, 296 (n. 126);
and Müller regime, 49, 52, 56, 58,
59, 269 (n. 113); and toleration
policy, 91, 98, 136, 146; efforts to
reform party, 146, 213; and Iron
Front, 173, 181, 183; and KPD,
197; under Hitler regime, 234, 346
(n. 187), 348 (n. 217). See also Red
Pioneers
Hamburger, Ernest, 89, 97, 191, 282
(n. 81)
Hammerschaften, 175, 203, 311
(n. 37), 329 (n. 4), 337 (n. 97)
Hänisch, Dirk, 106
Hanover, 72; SPD in, 40, 43, 73, 80,
83, 84, 105, 173, 183, 197, 198,
215, 234, 286 (n. 139), 310 (n. 26);
NSDAP in, 79; Reichsbanner in,
188, 285 (nn. 128, 129)
Harzburg Front, 148, 161, 169, 170,
183, 226, 298 (n. 144)
Haubach, Theodor, 192, 211, 335
(n. 76); as neorevisionist, 25, 100,
244, 245, 283 (n. 104); criticizes
SPD, 26, 50, 101, 141, 182, 316
(n. 102); analyzes NSDAP, 67, 334
(n. 63); and Iron Front, 176, 183;
under Hitler regime, 237, 351
(n. 254)
Heilmann, Ernst, 142, 179, 270
(nn. 132, 133), 273 (n. 31), 295
(n. 113), 352 (n. 259); political

views, 25, 295 (n. 105); and NSDAP,
67, 68, 73, 218, 219, 274 (n. 49),
314 (n. 80); and toleration policy,
297 (n. 134); and Prussian coup,
191, 192, 206; under Hitler regime,
238, 347 (n. 202)
Heimann, Eduard, 25, 70
Heller, Hermann, 35, 141
Hertz, Paul, 179, 192, 193, 234, 235,
271 (n. 149), 350 (n. 237); and
toleration policy, 133, 148, 150,
169, 186; and WTB, 163, 164; and
ADGB, 270 (n. 118), 299 (n. 168),
332 (n. 43)
Hesse (Darmstadt), 318 (n. 119);
SPD in, 52, 143, 146, 147, 173,
182–83, 187, 276 (n. 89), 299
(n. 158), 311 (n. 36), 332 (n. 52);
efforts of regime to curb NSDAP
and KPD, 72, 129, 130, 149, 185;
election results, 150, 182–83, 298
(n. 154)
Hildenbrand, Karl, 213, 350 (n. 236)
Hilferding, Rudolf, 179, 350 (n. 236);
political theory of, 23, 29, 30,
34–36, 44, 219–20, 239, 241, 260
(n. 90), 263 (n. 133), 340 (n. 119);
economic theory of, 32–33, 153,
155–56, 161, 167, 306 (n. 96); as
Reich Finance Minister, 46, 49, 50,
54–56; relations with SPD, 53, 266
(n. 59), 267 (n. 71); and fall of
Müller regime, 58; and toleration
policy, 89–90, 92, 93, 94, 98, 99,
133–34, 137, 138, 151, 161, 245;
and NSDAP, 95, 96, 107, 151,
167–68, 183, 241, 339 (n. 112);
analyzes elections, 108, 180, 181,
279 (n. 32), 314 (n. 73); and reparations, 154; opposes WTB, 158,
160, 163–64, 166, 209–10; relations
with Brüning, 161, 278 (n. 18),
302 (n. 32), 304 (n. 62); criticizes
Braun, 191, 216; and Papen

regime, 206, 207, 218–19; and KPD, 219, 224, 324 (n. 208); and Schleicher regime, 222; under Hitler regime, 224, 344 (n. 174), 345 (n. 186), 347 (n. 200)

Hindenburg, Paul von: and SPD, 44, 51, 60, 88, 179, 184, 271 (n. 151); as Reich president, 57, 61, 96, 220, 222, 225; SPD view of, 96, 179–80, 186, 192, 207, 225–26, 230, 240, 245, 270 (n. 121), 313 (n. 67), 339 (n. 115); and Prussian government, 128, 130, 131, 193, 216; in presidential election, 179–80; and SA ban, 185–86; and Hitler, 206, 222–23, 299 (n. 157)

Hitler, Adolf: and SPD, 131; as presidential candidate, 179–80; and Papen regime, 205–6; ADGB view of, 209, 243; and Schleicher regime, 223; as chancellor, 225, 230–31, 236, 238

—Social Democratic views of, 67, 95; Reichswehr and, 80, 150; Papen regime and, 188, 190, 206; as chancellor, 225–26, 237–38, 240. See also NSDAP

Hoegner, Wilhelm, 141, 281 (n. 70); criticizes SPD, 45, 58, 68, 96, 174, 238, 293 (n. 82), 342 (n. 142), 350 (n. 240); response to Prussian coup, 195, 196, 197, 199, 328 (n. 245); under Hitler regime, 236, 346 (n. 187)

Hofgeismar circle, 25, 258 (n. 58)

Höltermann, Karl, 25, 60, 245, 303 (n. 44), 309 (n. 8), 339 (n. 117), 350 (n. 243); and NSDAP, 169, 209; and Iron Front, 171, 174, 176, 189, 312 (n. 44), 333 (n. 53); and Schutzformationen, 175, 186; response to Prussian coup, 194, 208, 210, 322 (n. 186); and SPD, 210–12, 333 (n. 60); response to

Hitler's appointment as chancellor, 225

Hörsing, Otto, 104, 158, 303 (n. 44)

Hugenberg, Alfred, 61, 67, 131, 143, 225, 226, 299 (n. 158)

I. G. Farben, 148, 304 (n. 54)

Independent Socialists. See USPD

Jensen, Toni, 48

Juchacz, Marie, 22, 83

Kaas, Ludwig, 89

Kapp putsch, 9, 74, 193, 196, 243, 251 (n. 39)

Kassel, 21, 198, 204, 284 (n. 119), 350 (n. 235)

Kastl, Ludwig, 88

Kautsky, Karl, 30, 151, 161, 180, 230, 243, 340 (n. 124)

Kautsky, Luise, 150

Keil, Wilhelm, 61, 80, 198, 213, 266 (n. 115); and Müller regime, 56; attitude toward Versailles treaty, 68, 154, 211; and toleration policy, 145; and WTB, 165; and Papen regime, 339 (n. 115); under Hitler regime, 349 (n. 227)

Kempner, Robert, 128, 289 (n. 7)

Keynes, John Maynard, 155, 159, 305 (n. 74)

Kiel congress (SPD), 34, 36, 52, 260 (n. 99)

Kirchheimer, Otto, 340 (n. 120)

Kirdorf, Emil, 75

Klassenkampf group. See Left Opposition

KPD, 47, 154; attacks SPD, 11, 64, 69–70, 103, 143, 149, 189, 196, 197; joint actions with Social Democrats, 21, 101, 146, 149, 196–97, 203, 227, 234, 285 (n. 124), 325 (nn. 212, 214); social composition of members/electorate, 28, 29, 31,

143, 177, 300 (n. 6), 326 (n. 217); election results of, 41, 42–43, 74, 76, 86, 92, 109, 132, 146, 181, 183, 204, 205, 218, 229, 273 (n. 30), 300 (n. 6), 339 (n. 109); Social Democratic views of, 42–43, 64, 66–68, 72, 74, 80, 81, 89–90, 95, 101, 131, 146, 205, 216, 219, 225, 227, 234, 339 (nn. 112, 116); and Brüning regimes, 61, 132, 283 (n. 100); as object of state repression, 72, 103, 290 (n. 16); and referendum to recall Prussian Landtag, 129, 289 (n. 12); propaganda/agitation of, 180, 189, 272 (n. 9), 294 (n. 95); and Prussian coup, 194, 196, 324 (n. 206); under Hitler regime, 227; and WTB, 308 (n. 125). *See also* RGO; Roter Frontkämpfer-Bund; Thälmann, Ernst

Kranold, Arnold, 98

Künstler, Franz, 132, 135, 146, 194, 197, 216, 218, 235, 236, 245

Kuttner, Erich, 240

Landsberg, Otto, 61, 154

Law for Protection of the Republic, 72, 289 (n. 7)

Leber, Julius, 147, 352 (n. 11); politics of, 25, 244; and Müller regime, 45, 47, 50, 58; criticizes SPD, 62, 65, 69, 86, 96, 141, 143, 281 (n. 59); and Iron Front, 173, 176; response to Prussian coup, 195; under Hitler regime, 225, 230, 351 (n. 252)

Left Opposition, 34, 242; and Social Democratic political culture, 6, 7–8, 11, 22–23; composition of, 24; criticizes SPD organization, 27, 142, 144; attitude toward coalitions, 35, 50, 52, 65; and Müller regime, 56, 58–59; and NSDAP, 64, 66, 138, 288 (n. 164); and KPD,

72; and toleration policy, 99–100, 127, 132, 133, 135, 137, 146, 283 (n. 102); splits to form SAPD, 147; presses for extraparliamentary action, 219–20, 340 (n. 122); under Hitler regime, 235, 237. *See also* Aufhäuser, Siegfried; Levi, Paul; Sender, Toni; Seydewitz, Max

Lehnert, Detlev, 240

Leipart, Theodor, 20, 53, 83, 310 (n. 19); and toleration policy, 136, 169; and reparations, 153–54; economic views, 158, 303 (n. 43); and WTB, 163–64, 305 (n. 77), 307 (n. 107); relations with SPD, 168, 210, 212, 213, 222, 332 (nn. 44, 47); response to Prussian coup, 193–94, 323 (n. 196); meets with Papen, 208; and Schleicher regime, 222, 343 (n. 155); under Hitler regime, 225, 232, 233; and KPD, 324 (n. 208)

Leipzig: SPD congress in, 133, 135, 136, 138–40, 142, 143, 145, 158, 296 (n. 117); SAPD in, 147, 297 (n. 134)

—SPD in, 8, 40, 102, 104, 188, 213, 215, 326 (n. 221); election results of, 42, 261 (n. 105); propaganda, 67, 76; and NSDAP, 68, 71, 76, 80, 337 (n. 96); and toleration policy, 91, 93, 99, 132; and KPD, 216, 264 (n. 26); under Hitler regime, 234, 348 (n. 217)

Leuschner, Wilhelm, 149, 195, 233, 315 (n. 92), 318 (n. 119)

Levi, Paul, 24, 34, 35, 45, 47, 50, 71, 257 (n. 50)

Liebmann, Hermann, 71, 340 (n. 120)

Lipinski, Richard, 219, 238, 283 (n. 94), 291 (n. 49), 321 (n. 169)

Litke, Carl, 224, 236

Löbe, Paul, 82, 96, 154, 165, 179,

206, 207, 215, 235–38, 267 (n. 66),
    345 (n. 187), 350 (n. 239), 351
    (n. 251)
Lösche, Peter, 11, 14, 251 (n. 44)
Löwenstein, Kurt, 22
Lübeck, 25, 147, 225, 266 (n. 52),
    284 (n. 119), 330 (n. 31)

Magdeburg, 261 (n. 105); SPD con-
    gress in, 50, 52–54, 65, 66; SPD in,
    77, 140, 197, 198, 234, 266 (n. 52),
    284 (n. 119), 294 (n. 95), 311
    (n. 36), 346 (n. 187)
Mannheim, 205, 294 (n. 98)
Mannheim Agreement, 20
Mecklenburg, 81, 99, 150
Megerle, Klaus, 240
Meitmann, Karl, 143, 181; and
    Müller regime, 56, 58; and NSDAP,
    72; and toleration policy, 91, 93–
    94, 98; as neorevisionist, 144, 219,
    283 (n. 104), 347 (n. 203); efforts
    to reform SPD, 146, 213–14, 336
    (nn. 80, 82)
Mierendorff, Carlo, 276 (n. 89). 298
    (n. 150); as neorevisionist, 25, 50,
    100, 101, 141, 165, 176–77, 180,
    201, 237–38, 244, 283 (n. 104),
    340 (n. 120); analyzes NSDAP, 74,
    77–78, 80, 81, 275 (n. 76), 343
    (n. 148); and toleration policy,
    133, 136, 146, 165, 187, 283
    (n. 106); and Iron Front, 178–79,
    182–83, 187, 188–89, 200, 212;
    response to Prussian coup, 200,
    327 (n. 230); under Hitler regime,
    231, 234, 236, 237, 347 (n. 203),
    351 (n. 254), 352 (nn. 9, 11);
    meets Hans Zehrer, 331 (n. 38)
Mittelstand, 42, 177; SPD and, 11, 30,
    84, 103, 110–11, 139–40, 190, 244,
    288 (n. 171), 293 (n. 75); NSDAP
    and, 75, 77, 78, 107–9, 138, 204
Moldenhauer, Paul, 57

Mommsen, Hans, 36, 200, 261
    (n. 110), 327 (n. 233)
Mommsen, Theodor, 13
Muhle, Hans, 239, 240, 335 (n. 70)
Müller, Hermann, 26, 291 (n. 39);
    and Versailles treaty, 34, 69; repu-
    tation in SPD, 44, 45, 59, 66, 93,
    94, 268 (n. 79); as chancellor, 45,
    46, 48–50, 54–59, 68, 266 (n. 59),
    267 (n. 67); as cochairman of the
    SPD, 52–53, 56, 267 (n. 65); and
    toleration policy, 88–90, 98, 132,
    278 (n. 15), 283 (n. 96), 290
    (n. 26)
Müller-Lichtenberg, Hermann, 57,
    58
Munich, 152, 344 (n. 174); Reichs-
    banner in, 66, 73, 211, 286
    (n. 137), 333 (n. 53)
—SPD in, 41, 45, 213, 261 (n. 106),
    285 (n. 123), 335 (n. 71); political
    culture of, 8, 19, 22, 31, 143; and
    Panzerkreuzer affair, 47, 266
    (n. 58); and self-defense, 105; and
    Iron Front, 182; organizes unem-
    ployed, 214, 228, 284 (n. 118), 337
    (n. 89); under Hitler regime, 346
    (n. 187), 349 (nn. 225, 228)

Naphtali, Fritz, 33, 84, 159, 160, 163,
    165, 167, 234, 262 (n. 118), 350
    (n. 243)
Neebe, Reinhard, 14, 60
Neisser, Hans, 107, 109
Neorevisionists, 8, 56, 100–101, 143,
    182, 197, 211, 214, 281 (n. 70), 287
    (n. 161), 347 (n. 203); and Left
    Opposition, 8, 283 (n. 105); poli-
    tics of, 24, 26, 27; and Müller
    regime, 45, 48, 50; and NSDAP,
    101, 111; and Reichsbanner, 105;
    and Iron Front, 172, 173; and SPD
    political culture, 183, 244; efforts
    to reform SPD, 213–14; press for

extraparliamentary action, 219–20, 340 (n. 121)

Nettl, Peter, 26

Neu Beginnen, 234, 297 (n. 133)

Neumann, Heinz, 146

Nolan, Mary, 7

Nölting, Erik, 105, 139

Nörpel, Clemens, 140

Noske, Gustav, 49, 53, 72

NSBO, 232, 348 (n. 208); ADGB and, 164, 217, 233, 306 (n. 87), 311 (n. 37), 337 (n. 97)

NSDAP: propaganda/agitation of, 67, 69, 79, 189, 190, 317 (n. 107), 320 (n. 151); social composition of members/electorate, 71–72, 74–78, 79, 80, 105–8, 132, 138, 181, 204, 275 (n. 66)

—Social Democratic views on, 11, 63–64, 66, 109, 254 (n. 71); affinity with KPD, 64, 66, 80; anti-Semitism and, 64, 67, 70, 77, 78, 108, 275 (n. 76), 282 (n. 75); similarity to Italian Fascism, 66, 74, 108, 138, 226; relations with capitalists, 72, 75, 81–82, 83, 96, 109, 138, 139, 148, 167, 183–84, 190, 240, 293 (n. 80), 343 (n. 152); financial sources of, 74–75. *See also* Hitler, Adolf; NSBO; SA; Strasser, Gregor; Strasser, Otto

Nuremberg Resolution, 20

Oldenburg, 41, 132, 133, 142, 198, 204

Ollenhauer, Erich, 235

Osterroth, Franz, 25

Pahl, Walther, 110, 144, 244, 308 (n. 122), 348 (n. 213)

Panzerkreuzer affair, 16, 40, 46–53, 56, 59, 76, 90, 91, 242

Panzerkreuzer B, 131, 132

Papen, Franz von, 204, 217–18, 223; as chancellor, 155, 186, 189, 205, 207, 210, 332 (n. 48); SPD views of, 167, 190, 205–6, 215, 220, 222, 230, 242, 343 (n. 152); and ADGB, 208, 210

Petrich, Franz, 236

Peukert, Detlev, 13

Pfülf, Toni, 32, 213, 236–37

Pomerania, 52, 181, 216, 272 (n. 19), 284 (n. 119)

Popitz, Johannes, 56

Prussia, 25, 27, 28, 39, 44, 46, 74, 85, 88, 271 (n. 140), 291 (n. 48); election results, 41, 67, 180–81, 315 (n. 84); efforts of regime to curb NSDAP and KPD, 64, 72, 81, 103, 127–30, 149, 184–85, 274 (n. 46), 279 (n. 28); and referendum against Young Plan, 68; *Schutzpolizei*, 104, 191, 192, 194, 195, 199, 323 (n. 194); SPD in, 105, 179, 180, 183, 217, 229; relations with Reich, 127–31, 149, 184–85, 190–96, 216, 223, 321 (n. 167)

Prussian Landtag, 191; SPD delegation in, 27, 36, 41, 48, 58, 60, 238, 351 (n. 253); referendum to recall, 129–31; SPD campaign for, 180; election results, 181; KPD delegation in, 196

Pünder, Hermann, 68, 88, 89, 282 (n. 87)

Pyta, Wolfram, 72, 248 (n. 10)

Rathenau, Walter, 72, 251 (n. 39)

Rathmann, August, 25, 107, 110, 144, 270 (n. 128), 283 (n. 104), 347 (n. 203)

RDI, 55, 88, 160, 184, 222, 317 (n. 109); and ADGB, 60, 156–57

Red Pioneers, 188, 319 (n. 143)

Referendum to expropriate royal houses, 39, 45

Reichsbanner, 1, 2, 11, 31, 39, 66, 82,

83, 104–5, 185, 203, 224; rank and file attitudes, 4, 19; relations with SPD, 5, 6, 21, 142, 173, 175–76, 201, 203, 205, 211–12, 218, 333 (n. 60); and Weimar republic, 9, 21, 256 (n. 33); origins of, 20–21; membership, 21, 285 (n. 128); as neorevisionist center, 25, 176, 213, 258 (n. 59); and Brüning regimes, 60, 136; and NSDAP, 67, 73, 77, 100, 102, 104–5, 110, 146, 169, 209, 320 (nn. 148, 149); and KPD, 103, 197–99, 285 (n. 124), 325 (nn. 212, 215); *Schutzformationen*, 104, 175, 186, 192, 203, 318 (n. 125); economic ideas of, 158, 166; response to Prussian coup, 193, 194, 195, 197, 199; and Papen regime, 205, 210–11, 214. *See also* ADGB; Höltermann, Karl; Hörsing, Otto; names of individual cities and states

Reichskuratorium für Jugendertüchtigung, 210–11, 219, 333 (n. 56), 334 (n. 60)

Reichstag fire, 228–29

Reichswehr, 39, 192, 220, 225, 332 (n. 42), 343 (n. 155); SPD views of, 33–34, 37, 50, 95, 96–97, 150, 194, 195, 206, 210, 211, 219, 226, 240, 281 (n. 59); and NSDAP, 128, 184, 185, 281 (n. 72)

Reuter, Ernst, 197

Reuter, Franz, 308 (n. 125)

RGO, 152, 216, 232, 338 (n. 104), 347 (n. 208); ADGB and, 217, 337 (n. 97)

Rhineland, 181, 214, 284 (n. 119)

Rinner, Erich, 235

Rohe, Karl, 200

Rosenfeld, Kurt, 99, 147

Rossmann, Erich, 184, 349 (n. 56)

Roter Frontkämpfer-Bund, 67, 103

SA (Stormtroopers), 21, 67, 98, 148, 149, 192, 228, 230–31, 232, 350 (n. 234); SPD and, 80, 146, 169, 174, 175, 196, 206, 231, 325 (n. 211); ban of, 129, 184–86, 191, 195, 298 (n. 153)

SAJ, 29, 104, 136, 143, 147, 229, 234, 257 (n. 36), 297 (n. 133), 333 (n. 56), 349 (n. 231)

Saldern, Adalheid von, 18

SAPD, 147, 188, 297 (n. 132)

Saupe, Hugo, 236

Saxony, 152; election results, 42, 63, 67, 76

—SPD in, 41, 132, 216, 284 (n. 119); as left-wing center, 8, 24, 215, 219; and proletarian defense, 21, 105; and coalition issue, 47, 52, 58; and NSDAP, 67, 71, 77; and Iron Front, 173, 212; criticizes Braun, 191, 321 (n. 169); response to Prussian coup, 198, 326 (nn. 221, 228); organizes unemployed, 214

Schacht, Hjalmar, 55, 56, 148, 269 (n. 112)

Schaefer, Rainer, 172

Schäffer, Hans, 160, 278 (n. 14), 282 (n. 89), 304 (n. 54), 328 (n. 3), 331 (n. 36), 332 (n. 43)

Scheffel, Franz, 194

Scheidemann, Philipp, 39, 80, 228, 299 (n. 159), 326 (n. 221), 344 (n. 168), 348 (n. 218), 350 (n. 238)

Schiele, Otto, 59, 60

Schifrin, Alexander, 108–10, 142, 206, 241, 264 (n. 24), 279 (n. 26), 294 (n. 99), 296 (n. 116), 330 (n. 20), 334 (n. 63), 335 (n. 69)

Schildt, Axel, 167, 222, 308 (n. 122), 341 (n. 126)

Schleicher, Kurt von, 186, 211; and Müller regime, 57; and NSDAP, 128, 149, 185, 205, 223, 299

(n. 157), 342 (n. 145), 343
(n. 155); and SPD, 222, 342
(n. 141), 343 (nn. 152, 157); role
in Prussian coup, 194–95, 200, 327
(n. 233); and ADGB, 208, 209,
220–21, 223; and Reichsbanner,
210; and *Tat* circle, 341 (n. 126)
Schleswig-Holstein, 41, 75, 181, 284
(n. 119)
Schmidt, Erich, 234, 259 (n. 67), 297
(n. 133)
Schnabel, Thomas, 106, 204
Scholing, Michael, 11, 14
Schulze, Hagen, 88, 251 (n. 40), 327
(n. 233)
Schumacher, Kurt, 83, 280 (n. 36),
284 (n. 110), 347 (nn. 199, 203); as
neorevisionist, 25, 176, 244, 245,
347 (n. 202); and Panzerkreuzer
affair, 47–48, 50, 266 (nn. 56, 61);
and toleration policy, 91, 145, 296
(n. 123); efforts to reform SPD,
213, 236–38, 349 (n. 227); meets
Hans Zehrer, 331 (n. 38)
Seldte, Franz, 129
Sender, Toni, 24, 297 (n. 135); criticizes SPD, 52, 66, 165, 195–96,
216, 219, 245, 267 (n. 69), 340
(n. 122); and toleration policy, 93,
98, 135, 282 (n. 89); response to
Hitler's appointment as chancellor,
344 (n. 163), 346 (n. 198)
Severing, Carl, 25, 64, 76, 141, 150,
271 (n. 152), 291 (n. 49); as Reich
Interior Minister, 46–49, 52, 56,
57, 266 (n. 53), 267 (n. 67); efforts
to curb NSDAP and KPD, 72, 130,
149, 185, 290 (n. 16); and toleration policy, 94, 134, 179; as Prussian Interior Minister, 128–29,
191, 290 (n. 17), 299 (n. 157),
318 (n. 119); and Prussian coup,
191–200, 322 (nn. 176, 178), 323
(n. 194), 329 (n. 16); and Papen

regime, 218; and Schleicher regime, 222; under Hitler regime,
230, 347 (n. 200); view of Nazi
influence in Reichswehr, 281
(n. 72); and Hindenburg election,
314 (n. 69), 317 (n. 110)
Seydewitz, Max, 24, 58, 93, 99, 147,
279 (n. 32), 280 (n. 38), 282
(n. 76), 283 (n. 99), 290 (n. 28),
291 (n. 49), 295 (n. 108), 297
(n. 134)
Silesia, 75, 152, 284 (n. 119), 312
(n. 43)
Silverberg, Paul, 160
Sinzheimer, Hugo, 48, 268 (n. 79)
Sklarek scandal, 69–71, 273 (nn. 31,
34)
Social Democrats: cultural organizations of, 1–2, 5, 21–23, 141, 174,
216
—political culture, 4, 7, 8, 10, 18,
21–23, 71, 147, 189, 220, 243, 260
(n. 99), 262 (n. 113); republicanism of, 9, 11, 171, 183; as *Solidargemeinschaft*, 11, 132, 243, 252
(n. 44), 255 (n. 12); anticlericalism
of, 23; working-class language
of, 32, 70–71, 144–45, 171, 183,
188, 296 (n. 117), 316 (n. 105);
and direct democracy, 35–36, 48,
49; egalitarianism of, 143, 295
(n. 108); and Iron Front, 171, 173,
244
—rank and file, 17, 21, 163; and
bourgeois associations, 19, 22;
view of republic, 19, 66, 201, 251
(n. 40), 328 (n. 240); hostility to
Mittelstand, 30; view of Müller
regime, 47, 56, 58–59; and NSDAP,
68, 72–73, 77, 80; on SPD propa-
ganda/agitation, 79, 101–2, 105;
relations with KPD, 103, 140, 196–
97, 203, 227, 324 (n. 210), 325
(nn. 212, 214); and self-defense,

105; and Iron Front, 170, 171, 173,
175, 178, 188; response to Prussian
coup, 197–99, 205, 326 (nn. 219,
228), 329 (n. 16); in autumn
1932, 212, 214, 328 (n. 3); under
Hitler regime, 228, 233, 234, 345
(nn. 186, 187), 348 (n. 214), 349
(nn. 220, 227, 228), 351 (n. 242).
See also SPD
Socialist International, 46, 231, 347
(n. 204)
Sollmann, Wilhelm, 25, 27, 64, 135,
231; and Müller regime, 47, 48, 52;
and NSDAP, 82, 293 (n. 70), 339
(n. 113); as neorevisionist, 144,
154, 211, 214, 244, 336 (n. 82)
Sozialpolitik, 20, 31, 33, 51, 53, 59, 83,
94, 135, 157, 160
SPD: and German nationalism, 17,
22, 68, 141, 211–12, 232, 239, 241,
266 (n. 56), 334 (n. 63); membership, 25, 145, 214; social composition of members/electorate, 29–
32, 40–42, 84, 109–10, 139–41,
215, 288 (n. 166); economic program of, 32–33, 61, 84, 97, 155–56,
158, 164–68, 189, 207, 209, 215,
240, 269 (n. 104), 307 (nn. 110,
112); and Versailles treaty, 34, 39,
68–69, 141, 154–55, 222; propa-
ganda/agitation of, 40–41, 72–73,
77, 84–85, 100–102, 109, 140–41,
174, 176–78, 180, 181–83, 187,
188–90, 212, 215, 277 (n. 120), 293
(n. 78), 294 (nn. 97, 98, 99), 313
(n. 62), 319 (n. 141), 335 (n. 69);
and Prussian strategy, 93, 98, 132,
134, 179, 282 (n. 87)
—executive committee, 23, 25–28,
34, 86, 102, 110, 137, 138, 147,
161, 192, 242, 243, 304 (n. 69),
317 (n. 117); and ADGB, 20, 163,
169, 211, 213–14, 222, 303 (n. 44);
and Reichsbanner, 21; and Müller

regime, 43, 44, 49, 50, 52; and
Brüning regimes, 85, 89, 94, 95,
127, 132, 135, 152; efforts to
reform, 143, 213, 214, 235; and
Iron Front, 174, 187, 189, 212, 218,
319 (n. 143); and KPD, 197, 326
(n. 216); response to Hitler's
appointment as chancellor, 224;
under Hitler regime, 230, 233, 235,
237, 344 (n. 174), 351 (n. 252),
352 (n. 257)
—organization, 5, 25, 230, 233–35;
criticism of, 27–28, 50, 142–44,
214, 241–42, 295 (n. 113); efforts
to reform, 213, 335 (n. 76)
—party council, 26, 45, 86, 103, 147,
161, 203, 213, 222, 225, 227; in
Panzerkreuzer affair, 47–49; and
toleration policy, 90; and Iron
Front, 170, 179, 187; response to
Prussian coup, 194; discusses
reform of SPD, 214; assesses political situation, 218–19, 230, 337
(n. 94), 338 (n. 107)
—Reichstag delegation, 33, 86; and
ADGB, 20, 222; composition of,
26–27, 31; relations with SPD
executive, 28, 259 (n. 79); relations with SPD ranks, 35–36, 266
(n. 58); and Müller regime, 49, 55;
opposes reform of unemployment
compensation, 53, 57–58, 59; and
Brüning regimes, 75, 90, 98, 99,
132, 134; Left Opposition in, 144,
147, 257 (n. 51), 267 (n. 69), 297
(n. 132); under Hitler regime,
229–31, 236–37, 350 (n. 243), 351
(n. 248). *See also* Social Democrats
Stahlhelm, 21, 68, 73, 129–31, 146,
148, 180, 197, 235, 294 (n. 95), 314
(n. 69)
Stampfer, Friedrich, 34, 52, 53, 54,
62, 68, 145, 151, 167, 194, 222,
224, 338 (n. 107); and reform of

unemployment compensation, 54, 57; and toleration policy, 89, 95, 137, 281 (n. 71), 292 (n. 52); and NSDAP, 137, 150; and Iron Front, 172, 173, 174, 179, 180; and KPD, 219, 226–27, 298 (n. 149); under Hitler regime, 229, 233, 235, 236–37, 347 (n. 202), 350 (n. 240)

State Party, 83, 132, 172, 204, 290 (n. 19), 315 (nn. 84, 85). *See also* DDP

Staudinger, Hans, 213, 236, 260 (n. 90), 271 (n. 143), 336 (n. 80)

Stegerwald, Adam, 157

Stelling, Johannes, 238

Strasser, Gregor, 75, 166–68, 209, 212, 223, 299 (n. 158), 308 (n. 119), 318 (n. 128), 331 (n. 40), 341 (n. 126), 343 (n. 155)

Strasser, Otto, 75, 101, 183, 209, 210, 331 (n. 38)

Stresemann, Gustav, 38, 45, 54, 153, 267 (n. 71)

Strikes, 146, 152, 217, 225, 300 (n. 3); discussion of general, 9, 74, 93, 136, 193, 194, 195–96, 198, 224, 225–26, 327 (nn. 235, 238), 344 (n. 163)

Stülpnagel, Joachim von, 210, 211

Stuttgart: SPD in, 25, 41, 47, 52, 80, 197, 256 (n. 33), 280 (n. 36), 325 (n. 214), 347 (n. 214)

Szillat, Paul, 238

Tarnow, Fritz, 170, 260 (n. 96), 268 (n. 91), 348 (n. 215); and NSDAP, 99, 105; and toleration policy, 99, 151, 157, 162, 303 (n. 41); and WTB, 162–65, 167, 168, 308 (n. 125), 332 (n. 46); and Iron Front, 170; and Papen regime, 208, 210; and KPD, 208, 324 (n. 208); contacts with Gregor Strasser, 209, 212, 331 (n. 40)

Die Tat, 166, 209, 308 (nn. 118, 119), 331 (n. 38), 341 (n. 126)

Thälmann, Ernst, 180, 289 (n. 12), 324 (nn. 208, 210), 328 (n. 240)

Thuringia, 24, 41, 52, 67, 71, 81, 147, 163, 218, 219, 234, 255 (n. 6), 284 (n. 119)

Tillich, Paul, 25

Toennies, Ferdinand, 11, 293 (n. 75)

Torgler, Ernst, 227

Treviranus, Gottfried, 82, 85

Unemployment, 18, 38, 60, 61, 62, 84, 88, 97, 111, 127, 137, 152–53, 156, 158, 163–64, 166, 177, 195, 207–8, 223; compensation, 18, 33, 39, 51–56, 58, 60, 62, 89, 99, 102, 134, 143, 148, 193, 207, 242, 291 (n. 46)

USPD, 19, 23, 34, 72, 147, 297 (n. 137)

Vogel, Hans, 52, 65, 137, 179, 192, 193, 236, 237, 350 (n. 237)

Vögler, Albert, 148

Walter, Franz, 11, 251 (n. 44)

Warmbold, Hermann, 148

Weimar republic: Social Democrats and, 5, 17, 34–37, 63, 64–65, 245, 251 (nn. 38, 39), 340 (n. 120). *See also* Reichsbanner; Social Democrats:—political culture; Social Democrats:—rank and file

Weismann, Robert, 95, 278 (n. 14)

Wels, Otto, 26, 32, 82, 148, 189, 203, 245, 260 (n. 99), 343 (n. 158); relations with ADGB, 20, 153–54, 157, 164, 166, 209, 212, 217, 225, 230, 232, 270 (n. 118), 299 (n. 167), 303 (n. 44), 332 (n. 43), 342 (n. 137), 346 (n. 198); and Müller regime, 44, 48, 50, 53–54, 57; and toleration policy, 89, 133–34,

148, 157; and Iron Front, 169–72,
174, 175, 179, 205, 334 (n. 66);
response to Prussian coup, 191,
192–94, 200–201, 208, 322
(n. 178), 323 (nn. 195, 197), 328
(n. 242); assesses political situation, 203, 214–16, 220, 229, 235,
340 (n. 124); and NSDAP, 204, 218,
222, 240, 347 (n. 202); and Reichsbanner, 205, 211–12; and Papen
regime, 205–7; under Hitler
regime, 226, 229, 230–31, 233,
234–37, 344 (n. 174), 346
(nn. 192, 198), 347 (n. 204)
Wengst, Udo, 60
Werfel, Franz, 21
Werner, Karl, 128, 149
Westphal, Max, 81, 237, 238
Wilding, Fritz, 171
Winkler, Heinrich August, 30, 248
(n. 10), 252 (n. 56), 255 (n. 16),
269 (n. 112), 321 (n. 161), 327
(n. 233), 342 (n. 141), 343
(n. 157)
Wirth, Josef, 64, 82
Wissell, Rudolf, 46, 49, 57
Women, 18, 31, 109, 197; SPD and, 2,
21, 22, 24, 31, 40, 84, 108, 190,
214, 234, 261 (nn. 105, 106), 277
(n. 120), 284 (n. 119), 309 (n. 11)
Workers, unemployed, 165, 251
(n. 40); NSDAP and, 80, 107, 168;
KPD and, 90, 164, 177, 197, 300

(n. 6), 326 (n. 217); SPD and, 110,
170, 188, 190, 214–15, 228, 284
(n. 118), 336 (n. 86), 337 (n. 89);
ADGB and, 200, 306 (n. 87)
Workers' Sports Federation, 1, 22,
142, 144, 169, 171, 176, 192, 233,
337 (n. 97)
Woytinsky, Wladimir, 156, 159, 160,
162, 163, 165–67, 177, 190, 201,
209, 210, 303 (nn. 48, 52), 305
(nn. 72, 73, 74)
WTB, 162–68, 173, 190, 209, 210, 305
(n. 77), 306 (n. 91), 308 (nn. 118,
122), 331 (n. 38)
Wurm, Mathilde, 179, 219
Württemberg, 181, 184, 185, 192, 272
(n. 17), 285 (n. 122), 318 (n. 119);
SPD in, 41, 47, 83, 145, 198, 213,
267 (n. 61), 284 (n. 119), 349
(n. 227)

Young Plan, 55, 58, 141, 153, 256
(n. 23), 268 (n. 93), 300 (n. 9);
referendum against, 67–68, 272
(nn. 17, 18, 19)
Youth, 134, 190, 210, 211, 214, 291
(n. 46); SPD and, 24, 29, 73, 77,
84, 105, 106, 136, 142–43, 147,
174, 188, 190, 245, 319 (nn. 143,
145); NSDAP and, 71, 72, 75, 77,
80, 81, 82, 128

Zehrer, Hans. See *Die Tat*